Pro SQL Server 2005 Integration Services

James Wightman

Apress®

Pro SQL Server 2005 Integration Services

ISBN-13 (pbk): 978-1-59059-897-9

ISBN-10 (pbk): 1-59059-897-0

ISBN-13 (electronic): 978-1-4302-0447-3

ISBN-10 (electronic): 1-4302-0447-8

Lead Editor: Ewan Buckingham
Technical Reviewer: Fabio Claudio Ferracchiati
Editorial Board: Steve Anglin, Ewan Buckingham, Tony Campbell, Gary Cornell, Jonathan Gennick, Jason Gilmore, Kevin Goff, Jonathan Hassell, Matthew Moodie, Joseph Ottinger, Jeffrey Pepper, Ben Renow-Clarke, Dominic Shakeshaft, Matt Wade, Tom Welsh
Senior Project Manager: Tracy Brown Collins
Copy Editor: Eileen Cohen
Assistant Production Director: Kari Brooks-Copony
Production Editor: Liz Berry
Compositor: Diana Van Winkle
Proofreader: Linda Seifert
Indexer: John Collin
Artist: Diana Van Winkle
Cover Designer: Kurt Krames
Manufacturing Director: Tom Debolski

Distributed to the book trade worldwide by Springer-Verlag New York, Inc., 233 Spring Street, 6th Floor, New York, NY 10013. Phone 1-800-SPRINGER, fax 201-348-4505, e-mail `orders-ny@springer-sbm.com`, or visit `http://www.springeronline.com`.

For information on translations, please contact Apress directly at 2855 Telegraph Avenue, Suite 600, Berkeley, CA 94705. Phone 510-549-5930, fax 510-549-5939, e-mail `info@apress.com`, or visit `http://www.apress.com`.

The source code for this book is available to readers at `http://www.apress.com`.

Dedicated to my family: my wife Ellie and children Zakk and Layne.
To Mollie, who is sadly no longer with us, and her brother Bill, for whom life has never been the same. Finally, to William Henry Gates III, for the opportunities.

Contents at a Glance

Contents

Foreword

Working on SQL Server Integration Services was, for me, a joy. We had a team of smart people, cool technology that solved real problems, and great customers who often had those very problems by the dozen, and were keen for Microsoft to solve them. And then there were our users: the developers and consultants and database administrators and architects who stretched Integration Services to its limits—and beyond—in many beta tests and production situations.

These users often took the product into areas that were not only technically demanding, but frankly fascinating in their own right. These advanced users learned a great deal, and it has been a real pleasure to see them passing on their knowledge to others. The social network of Integration Services users is one of the product's greatest strengths.

When I look over these challenging and compelling scenarios, Jim Wightman's name has got to come to mind. Is there anyone else out there using SSIS to work on the aerodynamics of sports cars, or the sources of terrorist finance, or cell-phone fraud? But glamorous as it sounds, I think Jim's work is similar to the daily tasks you face with your data warehouses and line-of-business systems. He describes himself as chief architect and bottle washer, and I'm sure in this book you'll find much good advice on the high architectural and lowly bottle-washing aspects of working with SQL Server Integration Services.

Thanks Jim, for sharing so much of what you have learned by writing this book. Much success in integration to all your readers!

Donald Farmer
Principal Program Manager,
SQL Server Analysis Services, Microsoft Corporation

About the Author

JAMES WIGHTMAN is an average guy. A programmer, problem solver, artist, and artisan, he loves his work and his family, and he's looking for that one chance to change the world.

Born in 1975, James spent his formative years reading Marvel comics and books by Tolkien before discovering computers in 1980. Teaching himself to program computers at the age of six, he wrote himself a teaching aid to learn pure mathematics and then translated the program into Z80 machine language. From there he learned C and then became adept with 68000 assembly language and eventually C++, writing two games—one released commercially—for the Commodore Amiga.

James is an innovator in many ways and in many areas. At age eleven he invented a way for aircraft to land with increased safety, and at age twelve he invented a VCR that could record four simultaneous broadcast streams onto a standard VHS tape. That you don't own a VCR that records four channels at once, and that aircraft still make a squealing sound when their wheels touch tarmac, indicate how well the designs of a preteen are received by companies such as Sony and Boeing.

His next invention will rock the world to its very foundations. Or at least cause a ripple. Maybe. So he hopes.

Having worked on the largest of Microsoft technology–led projects for some of the biggest companies worldwide for the past 14 years, James is honored to have worked on this, his first book, and hopes that writing will remain a part of his ongoing commitment to programming and the programming community.

Currently his time is taken up learning the Mandarin, Japanese, and Russian languages as well as telling everyone who will listen just how good F# is. In his spare time he is working on his next books for Apress, which will be released in 2008.

About the Technical Reviewer

FABIO CLAUDIO FERRACCHIATI is a senior consultant and a senior analyst/developer. He works for Brain Force (`http://www.brainforce.com`) in its Italian branch (`http://www.brainforce.it`). He is a Microsoft Certified Solution Developer for .NET, a Microsoft Certified Application Developer for .NET, and a Microsoft Certified Professional, and he is a prolific author and technical reviewer. Over the past ten years he's written articles for Italian and international magazines and coauthored more than ten books on a variety of computer topics. You can read his LINQ blog at `http://www.ferracchiati.com`.

Acknowledgments

It's a humbling experience, being judged good enough by your peers to write a professional piece of work like this book. One has much to live up to, not only because of books that have gone before but also because of the technology about which the book is written. To do justice to the men and women involved in producing SQL Server 2005—or rather, to have the belief that one will do justice to them—is probably the biggest challenge. The original editor of this book, James Huddleston, gave me this belief. Sadly, he passed away suddenly in January 2007.

At the very top of my thank-you list must be everyone on the book's Apress team, especially Tracy Brown Collins, Ewan Buckingham, Eileen Cohen, Liz Berry, Linda Seifert, Fabio Claudio Ferracchiati, and everyone else I never got to meet but who have made this book into something I am truly proud to put my name to. Without their hard work—long hours and weekends included—you would not be reading this book today.

There are other people I want to thank, all on a professional level. From Microsoft this includes Donald Farmer, David Pritchard, Geoff Hughes (and his team at Microsoft UK), and Don Syme (and his team at Microsoft Research). Donald's invaluable input was really one of the biggest drivers behind this book. I'm sure our ancestors fought side-by-side on some foggy Scottish battlefield in the distant past, which might explain the rapport. David has been invaluable for his support and tireless patience with me over the past few years. Geoff needs thanks for his time in formally introducing me to Visual Studio 2005 and SQL Server 2005. And Don's F# work is the most impressive new .NET language I've seen since C#.

Thanks to Matt Bamberger, with whom I interviewed for a job at Valve Software, for making me realize that I am capable of more . . . and that hiding a flight simulator in a popular spreadsheet package can be good for your career.

Without wishing to seem biased toward it, I would like to thank the Microsoft organization as a whole. Through the endeavors of countless individuals working tirelessly at Microsoft, led by my personal hero Bill Gates, I have been empowered to further my humble skills and still keep the excitement in every day of my working life.

On a personal level, a massive and unreserved thank-you must go to my Mom and Dad—Diane and Robert—who have supported their wayward son through good times, bad times, and lean times, and who have given everything and asked for nothing. For their patience and friendship, thanks go to the rest of my family: my brother Alan (and wife Cathy), sister Nicola, nieces Hannah and Alex, and nephew George. I am very proud of them all.

My life would be incomplete without the musical talents of the iconic musical gods who are Trent Reznor, Maynard James Keenan, Rob Zombie, Ihsahn, and Layne Staley.

And finally, I am nothing without the great loves in my life—my wife, children, and dogs.

Introduction

First there was data. We were given the tools and the technology to hold and manipulate it. Then someone said, "Data is great, but what does it really tell me?"

After much muttering and stroking of beards, the idea of taking data and pushing it through various transformations and processing pipelines was born. Suddenly the data could explain forensically where fraud was taking place, show where and when to invest to increase profits, and describe trends across the most demanding of datasets. SQL Server Integration Services is a tool that can do this with your data, and more. It is the Rosetta Stone for having your data make sense and provide business insight and value. It isn't the only tool on the market that performs these tasks, but, based purely on my experiences using it and most of its competitors, I feel it is the best around.

Here are some of the reasons why I feel SSIS will knock your socks off:

- **It's user friendly**: No matter what level you come in at, SSIS is there to help you out. It uses a familiar IDE and familiar terminology to describe its capabilities. All you want to do is copy some data from one server to another? Three clicks and you're almost there. You want to do a simple transform? Choose your source and destination and apply a transform and you're done, again in just a few clicks.

- **It's easy to learn**: The most advanced tasks that can be performed in SSIS are presented and implemented in precisely the same way as the more straightforward ones. Drop the component onto the design view, connect it to the Data Flow, configure it, and you're done. Added to some of the more wizard-type behavior, such as the ability for SSIS to make reasonable assumptions about imported data types, this means that the average Joe need not worry about `DBTypes`, for example.

- **It performs with incredible speed**: Someone at Microsoft has really thought about SSIS and how to crank the best performance out of it. Features such as the ability to avoid staging data—instead, data remains resident in memory—is just one of the innovations.

- **It's natively integrated with an enterprise-level "best in class" database technology**: SQL Server has proven itself as a true enterprise-level database server since its inception. In terms of performance and capability, it far exceeds competitive products at a fraction of the cost. SSIS is not stand-alone; it ships as part of the SQL Server 2005 package and is fully integrated with the SQL Server engine.

- **You get unparalleled support**: As every DBA, SQL Server developer, or application developer knows, Microsoft Books Online (BOL) is a great starting point for support and queries. If you need help beyond BOL, then take a look around the Internet at the countless newsgroups frequented by Microsoft specialists and MVPs. If all else fails, use a support incident and contact Microsoft directly. You *will* find a solution to your problem.

- **It has a (relatively) low purchase cost and cost of ownership**: Technically, SSIS is free. It comes as a fully integrated part of the SQL Server 2005 package, out of the box.
- **SSIS is part of a readily available product**: You can buy SQL Server 2005 on Amazon and learn all about SSIS from this book! Rather than being held hostage to a data-integration vendor who builds solutions for you, you can gain insight into your company's business by doing the architecting and analysis for your own solutions, enhancing your skill set in the bargain.

If you'll allow me to digress for a moment, I'll tell you a story.

Saudi Arabia has only a few telecommunications providers. I consulted for the largest, which offers land-line, mobile, and broadband services to more than 20 million residents. This company did not use SQL Server (or any other Microsoft tools) at the time and was highly doubtful about its capabilities. My clients at this company told me they had 14 "giga" of data, spread across many disks, in Informix. (It was actually 40 TB of data.)

I leased a mighty server and purchased some huge SATA disks that I RAID-installed into the server. After installing Windows Server 2003 and SQL Server 2005 CTP, I made some guesses at the kind of structure and the kind of data I'd be seeing once I got to Riyadh. Plans changed, however, and I was left in the UK while my boss (at the time) flew to Riyadh with the server. Once he'd got the server up and running, he called me from the client's office, and I talked him through using SSIS to get 40 TB of data into my database. My boss was almost completely nontechnical; he didn't understand SQL at all, and he had never used SQL Server Management Studio or Business Intelligence Studio.

Over an echoing, scratchy voice line I was able to design and build a suitable extraction and transformation package that was thoroughly tested and set running while I was on hold. All SSIS packages completed successfully without me ever seeing the IDE, and in record time. The bill for the call was less than $40. I cannot think of more extreme and difficult conditions under which this task could have been performed—or a more glowing appraisal of SQL Server 2005 and SSIS. This telecom giant recently signed a massive deal with Microsoft in the presence of Bill Gates himself to use Microsoft tools, including SQL Server 2005.

This book is about my experiences, and those of fellow professionals, in squeezing the most out of SSIS both as it comes and by enhancing it with custom processing. I'll talk about the areas to concentrate on to increase performance or to increase flexibility. You will read where to avoid bottlenecks and when to introduce asynchronous processing, when to design and when to implement.

I think the most important aspect of the book is the origin of its content. The techniques and usage I describe are all from actual implementations performed for blue-chip clients against datasets in excess of 25 billion items—in real-world, live environments that I architected, developed, and maintained. It would be easy to write about these topics from tinkering in a sandbox environment, or even from a simple implementation of the tenets contained within, but at this level knowledge drives your reputation and ability to perform effectively. Sure, you need theory, but it needs to be backed up by practice. You need to run where others walk.

The difference I've tried my best to introduce between this book and other books on this topic is like the difference between jumping out of a plane with and without a parachute. Both ways you'll learn what it's like to fly, but one way you might make a big old mess when you land.

I don't claim to address every single facet and feature of SSIS in this book. To do so would have created a much larger volume, and still I'd have left out a feature that someone, somewhere considers "the best thing ever." Instead I've tried to concentrate on the features I've used and the parts I feel haven't been particularly well documented by Microsoft. This perspective offers a unique opportunity to experience SSIS from both sides of the fence—by exploring its features and how they are implemented while keeping a tight grip on real-world development practice and issues.

A change is coming for the database developer, and it's a big one. The emphasis is moving away from a narrowly defined and relatively sedentary set of skills to a broader, object-oriented future in .NET. SQL Server 2005 is the first step in the evolutionary journey toward fully integrating Microsoft's database strategy and .NET. Katmai (SQL Server 2008) is the next, and it includes Language-Integrated Query (LINQ) and the Entity Framework.

Take the opportunity to change and evolve along with SQL Server. Learn the new skills required to stay at the forefront of new developments, and become comfortable with object-oriented programming, test-driven development, Microsoft Team Server, Agile development, and MSBuild. This is the way SQL Server is heading, and you owe it to yourself to keep up.

CHAPTER 1

Introducing SQL Server 2005 Integration Services

SQL Server 2005 is built on solid foundations. Microsoft has repositioned the product many times over its life cycle, adding new parts and facets over the years and removing others. Young technologies have matured and become a staple of the SQL Server experience. The database engine alone has evolved beyond recognition since the original release and provides a robust, incredibly scalable database platform.

One of the major additions to the product has been an increase in business-intelligence (BI) capabilities. Data Transformation Services (DTS)—Microsoft's introduction of native Extract, Transform, Load (ETL) functionality into SQL Server—formed a major part of SQL Server BI. ETL is the practice of taking data from a source (extract), manipulating it in any of a variety of ways (transform), and finally channeling the manipulated data to a destination (load)—possibly for BI purposes. Perhaps because DTS had so many capabilities outside of the BI space, though, many SQL Server customers tended to overlook DTS in favor of third-party ETL tools such as Essbase, Datastage, and Cognos Transformer.

Once DTS launched, I stopped using third-party ETL tools, because DTS worked well and was simple to use. At the most basic level it provided an IDE as a part of SQL Server Enterprise Manager in which to use extraction, transformation, and destination components. DTS could be employed to manifest an ETL scenario such as populating an Online Analytical Processing (OLAP) database, based on calculations performed against an Online Transactional Processing (OLTP) source. DTS could also use components for modifying SQL Server settings and tables, and it had scripting components that took the basic idea of ETL far beyond comparable third-party software.

SQL Server 2005 Integration Services (SSIS) is essentially the latest iteration of DTS, enhanced and evolved into a highly versatile platform in the BI space and beyond. Leveraging new features of SQL Server 2005 such as .NET Common Language Runtime (CLR) scripting and built on a brand new processing engine, SSIS is at the pinnacle of ETL evolution. SSIS is DTS pulled apart and put back together in a more logical and mature way with new and improved features that overshadow DTS in many respects.

This chapter gives you a snapshot of the whole of SSIS to prepare you for diving into much greater detail in the following chapters. You'll find that SSIS offers a tremendous amount to work with, including its visible features, the features under the hood, and its capabilities for integrating with and extending .NET technology.

A Little History

My relationship with SQL Server began in 1995 with version 6.0 (SQL95). I remember being extremely impressed with how much potential it had and yet how easy it was to use. Now even my smallest projects could use a robust relational database management system (RDBMS), instead of Microsoft Access 2.0, at low cost. As a developer, I felt completely at home with SQL Server, in stark contrast to products like Oracle Database. I could install, configure, and implement database designs without having to turn to a database administrator (DBA) just to add a new table to my schema. SQL Server demystified the black art of RDBMS management: for many professionals it highlighted the possibility that Oracle Database was too obfuscated and abstracted power away from all but a few. SQL Server gave instantaneous and transparent power to the developer, and at a much lower cost.

I didn't hear much about ETL tools in 1995. I'm sure they existed but were considered much too expensive for my small company. We performed all data manipulation through either SQL scripting or Visual Basic 3 components based on the Windows 3.11 platform. These VB3 tools didn't have a user interface (UI), of course—certainly nothing approaching SSIS or even DTS—but they were fairly powerful and a great demonstration of the possibilities that lay ahead.

ETL capabilities became an intrinsic part of the SQL Server family in version 7.0, a release that saw a surge forward in features, capabilities, and possibilities in the OLAP space. I was working on a remote-data–capture project that involved processing and transforming a staggering amount of data—coin usage in video-game machines. Although the company concerned ran SQL Server 6.5 and 7.0 concurrently, the business value I could offer by implementing DTS in a fairly standard way earned me DBA status. I felt this title was inaccurate; I would say I was becoming a data artisan!

The effectiveness of DTS and SQL Server Analysis Services (SSAS) helped me induce an investigative group to repeal the company's decision to use Business Objects. I demonstrated that the benefits offered as part of the SQL Server package could equal or even surpass facilities within Business Objects. In pure business terms, it made sense to use a tool that had already been paid for and yet was more than powerful and capable of doing the job right, vs. a tool that cost many hundreds of thousands of dollars and required specialist consultants offered at $1,500 per day.

I expect that this is a similar scenario to one that many developers around the globe are seeing today with SSIS. The difference is that back then I wasn't 100% sure that I could back up my claims with a solution built entirely with DTS. If I'd had SSIS at the time, I probably wouldn't have allowed Business Objects to set foot in the door!

Looking back on all this reminds me how far Microsoft's ETL strategy has come since its first tentative steps with DTS. Even with DTS straight out of the box, however, I was able to match and surpass existing products' functionality. As you might imagine, I was like a kid at Christmas the day I got hold of SSIS. Any concerns about whether I could use existing DTS packages were forgotten for the moment. If DTS was great—if a little shaky at times—what would SSIS bring to the table? As I unwrapped SSIS I realized it was a gift that just kept on giving. SSIS has it all: high performance, scalable ETL, a brand new architecture, and custom capabilities.

What Can SSIS Do?

If there is *anything* you want to do with your data—or even the database itself—SSIS is the tool for you. You'll start developing SSIS packages in either Business Intelligence Development Studio (BIDS) or the full version of Visual Studio 2005, as shown in Figure 1-1. If a feature you want isn't available by default, you can either write it yourself or download it. In fact, with a little thought and a variable degree of effort on your part, there isn't anything SSIS *can't* do.

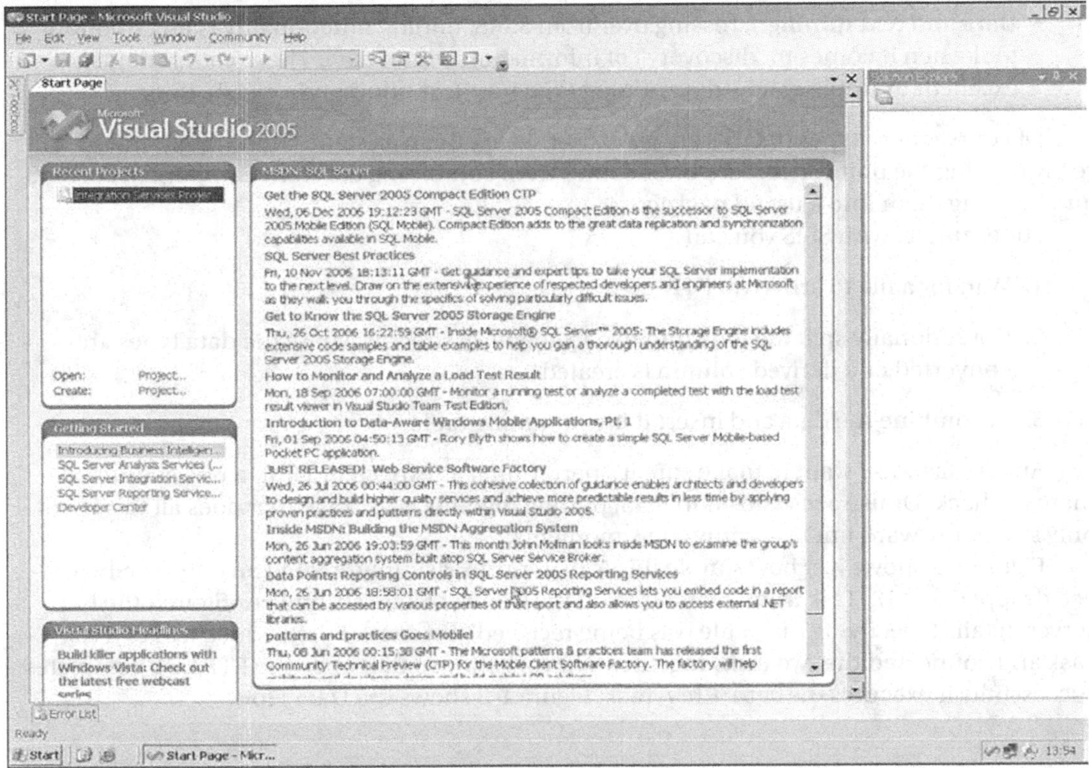

Figure 1-1. *Does this look familiar? It's where you'll be developing SSIS packages.*

Here's a brief look at some things SSIS can do straight out of the box:

- **Import/export/transfer**: By specifying the data source and destination, you can import and export content in whichever format is required without even using a transformation. Any defined imports or exports are probably the simplest elements of a package.

  Also, *Control Flow* items provide a range of capabilities for transferring database objects such as table structure and contents, or programmability items, between servers.

- **Web services**: Your SSIS package can access an XML web service as part of your Service Oriented Architecture.

- **Maintenance tasks**: You can choose from all kinds of maintenance tasks, from backups to rebuilding indexes to shrinking the database.
- **Fuzzy matching and grouping**: Microsoft Research Labs has supplied a commercial-quality implementation of fuzzy matching and grouping that is fully integrated into SSIS. Fuzzy matching is the practice of discovering inexact matches between textual values based on the algorithmic processing of input. The implementation in SSIS is fully configurable and allows many options for tweaking how the matches are made.
- **Data and text mining**: Crossing over from SSAS, mining functionality is an important tool when it comes to "discovery" of information within data. These components are an excellent example of how data mining (and now text mining) should be done.

Of course these types of tasks are great, but seeing them as stand-alone components is really missing the point. The real power comes from combining different components of SSIS and building them into a useful package.

For example, with SSIS you can

1. Wait for a file to arrive via FTP
2. Conditionally split the data into two in-memory streams where the data types are converted or a derived column is created
3. Recombine the data and insert it into a waiting table

And it's fast. You want to make sure it's performing as expected? Drop a row counter in there to check. Or use a visualizer. In SSIS, putting together a package that does all this is not only straightforward but takes only a few moments.

Figure 1-2 shows just how simple this is to perform. I simply created an empty SSIS project, dropped an `FTP Task` from the toolbar on the Control Flow tab, and configured the FTP server details (specifying that a file was being received, not sent). I then added a `Data Flow Task` and connected the two tasks together to form a flow so that once the FTP task completes successfully it executes the `Data Flow task`. Figure 1-3 shows the Data Flow.

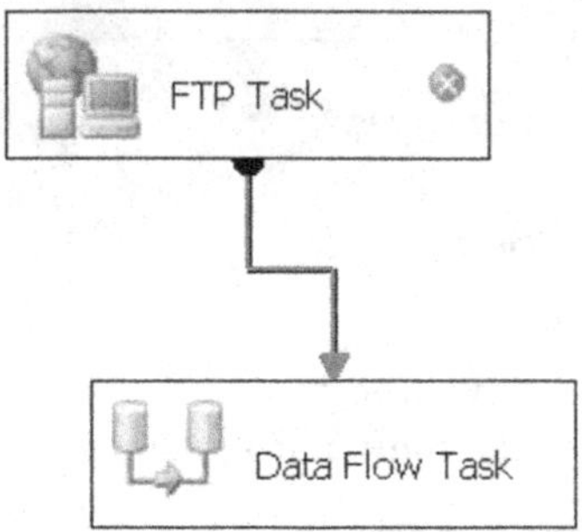

Figure 1-2. *A simple Control Flow*

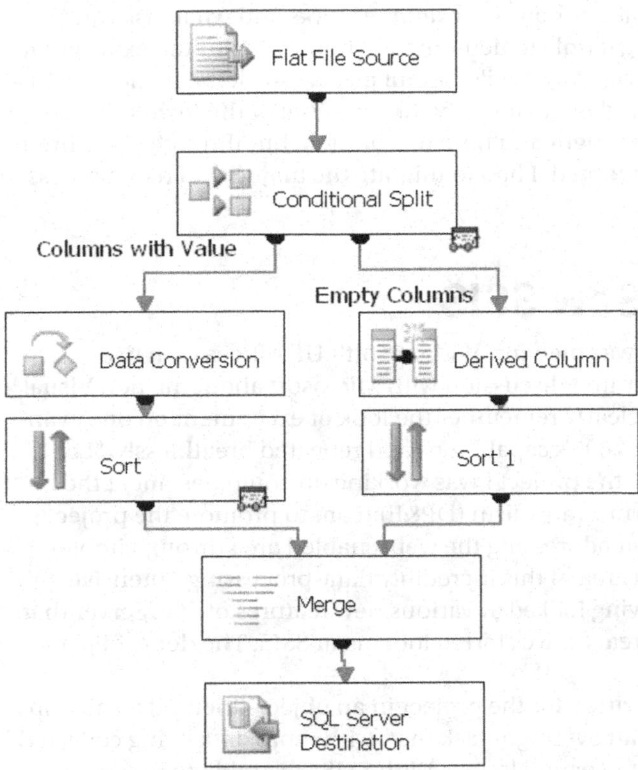

Figure 1-3. *Inside the Data Flow*

Adding the `Flat File Source` pointing to the file that will be delivered via FTP lets me easily define the necessary tasks:

`Conditional Split`: I configured this component to split the data based on whether or not the first column holds data. This gives two outputs from the component.

`Data Conversion`: This component was configured to convert the data from the `Columns with value` output to a `CHAR(2)` type.

`Derived Column`: I used this component to derive a `CHAR(2)` value from subsequent columns in the source file.

`Merge`: This merges the two datasets back together ready for output.

`SQL Server Destination`: This writes the dataset into a waiting table.

In all, this took only a few moments to put together. I was able to add two visualizers to the flow to ensure that the correct columns are being derived and that the conversion takes place as expected. This allows me to see a grid (or graph) of the data contained in memory at that point of the flow.

Don't worry too much at this point about how this example works and what tasks are actually being performed. I am including it only to demonstrate how even limited exposure to SSIS can yield enough insight to produce a worthwhile, useful package quickly. In fact, my initial experience with SSIS in the UK allowed me to identify the potential of the technology for use within a current project. Budgets were tight and time was limited, but through just a brief introduction to SSIS I could see that to succeed, I had to migrate the majority of data processing to this new platform.

The First Time Ever I Saw SSIS

It was the height of summer 2005, and I was meeting at Microsoft's UK offices with two Microsoft architecture evangelists for my first discussion with Microsoft about the new Visual Studio and SQL Server 2005 products. I clearly remember the look of excitement on one evangelist's face as he showed me SQL Server 2005's capabilities and repeated breathlessly, "Look how fast it is!" I was there to discuss how the project I was working on could best meet the criteria for the Development and Platform Evangelism (DP&E) team to promote the project through Microsoft. We'd already looked at addressing the web-enabled area through implementing ASP.NET 2.0, so the next logical area of this incredibly data-processing–intensive project to address was the database. Having looked at various new features of SQL Server that, while interesting and useful, weren't a great fit, we started looking at SSIS. The doors of perception were flung open to the wall!

Transformation processes that I'd written for the project in an object-oriented fashion in C# meant that data transformation was an overnight task that, with more data being collected on a daily basis, was only going to take longer and longer. With SSIS I was able to reengineer the solution using, initially, only the standard components. Not only was I able to implement asynchronous processing easily, but I could use the data viewer and row counter in SSIS for rapid tracing of problems in complex transformations that had taken hours to debug in C#. Processing time dropped exponentially, and development time was cut in half.

As a side note, something incredibly interesting happened during this project when I invited Google to tender a bid for the use of its Search Appliance. We didn't get as far as discussing costing; the European sales director took a long, considered look at how much data was being handled and the terabytes of output from SSIS . . . and stopped returning my calls! This speaks volumes about the capabilities of SSIS in handling massive sets of data.

The redevelopment of the ETL process was a rapid and pleasantly coherent one. The Microsoft SSIS team has worked hard on including features most used and most useful to those interested in getting unequalled value from their data.

I Have Such Delights to Show You

I have had a fantastic time learning the intricacies of SSIS. This book presents everything I've learned about SSIS, ready for assimilation. I will begin by taking a peek under the hood of SSIS and then open up the IDE to impart knowledge on

- **The architecture of SSIS**: How data is handled behind the scenes in SSIS and how the architecture can be leveraged to provide support for the most demanding of applications.

- **Migrating from DTS to SSIS**: The how, when, and why of moving from DTS to its big daddy, SSIS, observing potential pitfalls and ways to keep legacy DTS packages running as normal.
- **Visual Studio**: Information for readers unfamiliar with Visual Studio, such as DBAs and non-.NET developers, on Visual Studio as a mature and complete IDE for all kinds of CLR languages and SSIS projects.
- **Package hierarchy**: The king is dead, long live the king! Packages as you know them have changed dramatically and are now made up of a number of different components and logical concepts. Containers, Control, and Data Flow—oh my!
- **Control Flow and Data Flow components**: Content on Control Flow and Data Flow presented as both a tutorial and a source of reference on every one of the components you can use within a package.
- **Optimization**: Information not only on optimization of SSIS components but also championing the idea that forethought in database design can yield dramatic performance benefits.
- **.NET languages and object-oriented programming (OOP)**: Again aimed at those less familiar with the concepts of OOP and .NET in general, a detailed and concise body of work containing everything you need to know about leveraging the integration between SSIS and .NET.
- **Custom components**: Almost everything in SSIS is customizable. You'll learn how to create custom components that can be used in a variety of ways within a package.

By the end of this book you will be able to take advantage of the best features of SSIS, avoid potential problems, and create the most complex packages imaginable as if you had been using SSIS for years. This is SSIS from the front lines.

Where would SSIS be, however, if it weren't for the people involved in the project at Microsoft? Their gifts of creativity and insight in understanding the needs of database developers have propelled the possibilities of SSIS beyond the stars. They give us the tools and we make things happen.

An Interview with Donald Farmer

In late 2006 I was lucky enough to secure an interview with a veritable SSIS VIP, Donald Farmer, Microsoft Group Manager for SQL Server Business Intelligence. Here are some important excerpts from that interview.

> **James Wightman (JW)**: *I'd be interested to know about the perspective from which you approached the implementation and feature set of SSIS. In terms of function, did you start by examining DTS with a look to reimagining it? Or did you (as I suspect) take a clean slate and work from there?*
>
> **Donald Farmer (DF)**: The team approached the implementation of SSIS from two perspectives: what capabilities were needed to enable SQL Server to succeed in the data warehousing market, and what architecture best enabled those capabilities. There was a balancing act required as to what extent we would take dependencies on SQL Server features, and to what extent we would build a fully stand-alone product.

JW: *Was the feature set (both internal and external) provided by the new SQL Server engine tailored in particular ways so as to better integrate (and give a more rich feature set to) SSIS? I ask this because SSIS certainly feels like a more integrated and natural product than DTS, which by comparison (using it now) almost feels like a third-party add-on.*

DF: This required us to work closely with the relational engine team—on bulk-load interfaces for example. However, there is also deep integration with the Analysis Services and Data Mining engines, and with the management toolset, all of which provides a more organic data-management experience for SQL Server users.

JW: *One big advantage over existing ETL tools is how SSIS enables developers to create their own custom components. I can imagine this presented a particular set of challenges and obstacles during both design and implementation. Was including this feature a major part of the SSIS project?*

DF: It is worth pointing out that the supported interfaces for extending SSIS with custom components are managed code, while most of the components we wrote ourselves are in native code. There are a number of reasons for this, perhaps the most important being the ease with which we can support managed-code APIs, samples, etc., and the growing popularity of managed-code languages. As for problems, the most interesting have been simply explaining to third parties just how radical the capability is.

JW: *In terms of function SSIS surpasses commercially available ETL tools such as SAS and Datastage. In terms of flexibility SSIS goes way beyond these products. Would you say that SSIS is also aimed at a different type of user than these other tools? Perhaps both a more technically savvy but not necessarily BI-focused developer as well as the more traditional BI/Management Information (MI) specialist?*

DF: I tend to agree with you on our flexibility—which is partly a result of a great architecture and partly a requirement that drives, as our user base is so broad. DTS in its day was a handy utility for DBAs, a low-end ETL tool for the data-warehouse architect, and an interesting environment for developers to extend. SSIS still needs to be a utility, is still a favorite with developers, and covers a much wider range of data-integration scenarios. I often talk about a particular kind of SSIS (and SQL Server) user that I call the "data artisan." They are database-centric developers who use tools when they can, write code when they need to, and also have a responsibility for architecture and administration. They do about four jobs—and SSIS is a major component in their toolkit. So yes, SSIS has created or extended a new role.

JW: *Is SQL Server used in the back end of Xbox Live to support the service?*

DF: At Microsoft, we're famous for eating our own dog food and yes SQL Server is used throughout the business for its high-end operations, including Live services, Xbox, and AdCenter. In some cases, these teams extend the application themselves with custom components into areas where there is not yet enough commercial demand for us to put those features into the retail product. Without giving away too many secrets of the internal teams, some things they have done to squeeze extra from the engines include writing highly specialized schedulers tuned for their precise needs, or data-source components that can parse their specific file types at near-optimal speeds.

JW: *Could you please sum up what you think SSIS offers over other tools meant for the same purpose?*

DF: Value for money for one thing! If that is not a critical factor, I love the interactivity of the visual debugger. I was recently visiting with a customer who uses another very capable data-integration tool. As I helped them with some warehousing problems, I wanted to tweak their ETL processes. In SSIS I could have dived in there, made some changes, run through the debugger with visualizers and breakpoints, and validated what I was doing using a row counter as a dummy destination. Instead I had to create temporary tables, reconfigure the server and the metadata repository, run the modified jobs, and then trawl through logs and reports. Coming back to SSIS I hugely appreciated the ability to roll up my sleeves and get on with the work. I guess I'm a "data artisan" at heart myself!

In speaking with Farmer at length I found my own feelings about SSIS and the genuine potential it holds to be justified and consolidated. Such conversations often make me question the wisdom of not using a data-integration tool such as SSIS with current "large" IT projects around the world, such as the proposed plan to connect all UK physicians' surgeries together and hold a central database of patient records. At last count this was estimated as a GBP £19 billion project that would take many, many years to develop. Depending on the desired implementation, there could be a clear case here for the use of SSIS and, by extension, web services.

Here's perhaps a smaller-scale example of a similar kind of system. During the latter half of 2006, I was involved in discussions around the data-integration policy for a large American vehicle manufacturer that has a parent company and many subsidiary brands. The discussions centered around the vast global "approved dealership network," in particular how best to implement interfaces between the many different systems that had been built for each brand.

Some of these systems were accessible only via MQ Series, some of them were Oracle-based, some used SQL Server, and some used a number of legacy databases that were available for only a few minutes each day because of firewall restrictions. Some of the systems accepted only comma-separated value (CSV) files that had to be parachuted in via FTP.

Historically, data integration was performed via individual—completely stand-alone—applications that connected on a system-by-system basis to a target system and transformed the source data to fit requirements before transmitting the data. Each interface was built from the ground up with no capacity for reuse of any kind. Seemingly, cost was the driving issue, in that project funding was available for only one interface at a time. This meant that by the time another interface was paid for, the original development team had moved on, and it was left to someone else to come in completely cold. When one of the integration interfaces stopped working . . . well, no one could remember who wrote it or where the source code was, so maybe it would have to be written all over again . . .?

My idea was simple and courted considerable derision. What if a single data-artisan–type developer could replace all of these singular interfaces with an all-encompassing solution that could be modified where necessary at any time, reused and added to when needed, and all within the time and cost of creating a one-off, one-shot integration application?

Once the incredulity had subsided I invited the senior decision makers to watch on a projector screen while from my workstation I created a prototype SSIS package that connected to each of the target systems via the protocol required, and performed some basic transformations to demonstrate how the data could be restructured for the intended target to accept.

"And look," I said. "Look how clean and efficient it is! No staging of data! No temporary tables! And look how quick it is!"

I had, in a few short moments, demonstrated the power of SSIS to an audience of senior and incredibly IT-literate individuals, including BI professionals, and left them agog. "What else can it do?" they asked. "And what are the limits? Could SSIS be the answer to consolidating and transforming all of our disparate data?" I tentatively suggested a concept I had been working on for a while: creating a *knowledge brokerage* within the company.

Become a Knowledge Broker

It has been a long-held dream of mine to create a company offering the service of what I call a knowledge brokerage. It's a relatively simple concept: harvest data from as many discrete and diverse sources as possible, whatever the format; reduce the data to its component parts; and then reengineer it so it offers knowledge rather than simply data and allows the asking of "questions" that reveal accurate and insightful "answers."

In some ways I suppose the idea is similar to what credit-reference agencies such as Experian and Equifax do, but on a much larger (and less structured) scale.

I can envisage a time when knowledge brokers compete with one another to offer the most complete and reliable (i.e., accurate and comprehensive) knowledge. It might sound a little Cyberpunk or even outright Orwellian, but central repositories held in secure data silos accessible only to authorized parties would be not only more efficient, but also more accountable and manageable by the subject of the information.

On a technical level, how difficult would they be to create? Before SSIS, before the .NET Framework, and before web services, I would probably have answered in terms of decades and many billions of dollars.

A breakdown of what would be needed to make a knowledge brokerage possible consists of

- **Multi/any format data-source connections**: I would be amazed if the majority of the data being harvested weren't held in one of the MS Office products—probably Excel—but Access is also a possibility, as are legacy systems and more-modern databases such as Oracle Database and SQL Server.

- **Rapid processing turnaround**: This would be required under the many data-protection laws around the world to ensure the information supplied is accurate, valid, and pertinent to the individual concerned.

- **Knowledge-consumption services**: Using web services over Secure Sockets Layers (SSL) to provide entry to authentication and to provide for the consumption of new knowledge by other authorized parties.

Would it look, perhaps, something like Figure 1-4?

I believe today, with SSIS as the technology at the heart of such a system, development costs and ultimately total costs would be reduced by at least two orders of magnitude.

One final note: on July 7, 2005, a small group of extremists detonated explosive devices onboard public transport in London, England. Shortly afterward I had an opportunity to be involved with some of the more data-intensive investigations into the possible leaders of the group and other potentially dangerous individuals. I spoke to an incredibly hard-working but overstretched department within the Security Services that was performing investigations by printing out reams of information and checking it by hand. The data sources included XML documents, Excel, Access, SQL Server, and legacy databases spread throughout the IT infrastructure. These diverse and multiformat data feeds, and the fact they couldn't be integrated together without spending, potentially, millions of dollars, was the reason given for not using the very minimum of software-based assistance to analyze the data.

My first and only recommendation was SQL Server Integration Services.

SSIS leaves you no reason or excuse to hold your data purely relationally. In essence, a database's "data"-bearing capabilities are there out of necessity, almost as if in a legacy system. Only by performing intelligent operations on that data can you mold it into knowledge, conferring meaning and context.

Knowledge is available to us all through SQL Server Integration Services. Take control, make your data work for you, and create your own knowledge brokerage, providing the rock-solid backbone to your business.

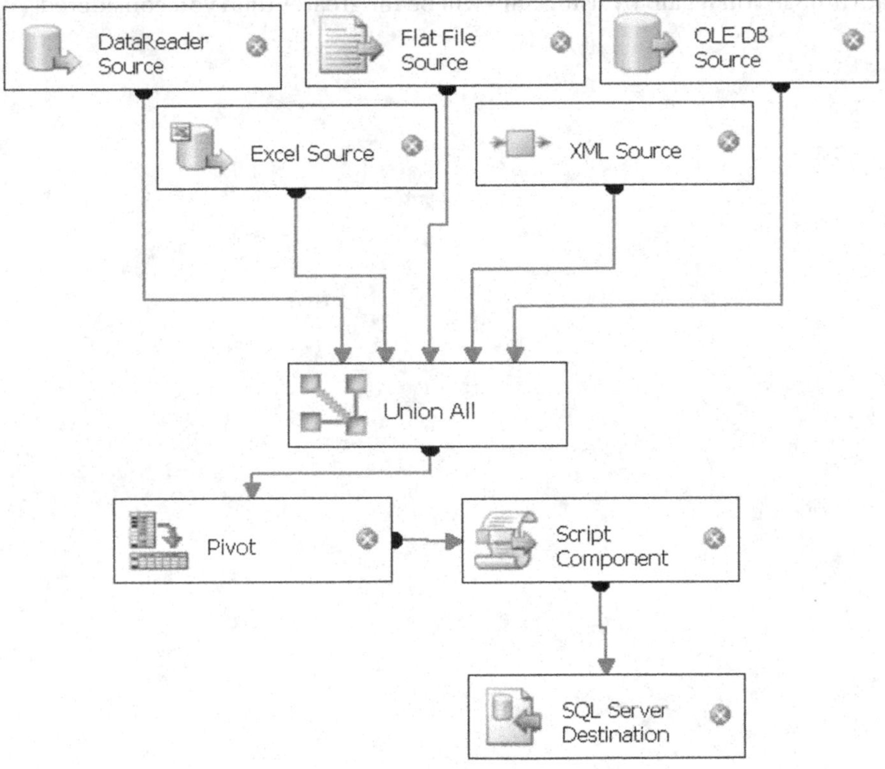

Figure 1-4. *Problem solved*

Summary

I've tried to provide a gentle introduction to SSIS in this chapter by discussing a few of its features, looking at possible applications, and talking about times I've implemented it myself.

During the time I've been developing solutions involving SSIS I have had nothing but the most amazing and complete support from Microsoft, either officially by direct contact or unofficially by reading support articles or SQL Server 2005 Books Online (`http://msdn.microsoft.com/en-us/library/ms130214.aspx`). For those of you who won't have the same level of developer support as I've had, this book should provide a viable alternative in conjunction with other readily available information. I sincerely hope your team environment is developer friendly and you feel able to ask for help, because talking your issues through with someone else, whether SSIS literate or not, gives a different perspective that might prove helpful.

SSIS is simply a great tool. Naturally it has the odd minor flaw and, in places, an occasional bug—but then I've never seen a piece of software that is completely problem free. I know you haven't either.

The business advantage you can give your company by using this technology makes SSIS much more than the sum of its parts. Because you can write your own fully integrated custom components, the advantage you'll gain by using SSIS will be far greater than you considered possible.

CHAPTER 2

The Architecture of SSIS

One of the most exciting aspects of any technology is not only what it does but how it does it. SSIS is all the more interesting because of the underlying parts it leverages to provide its services. Consider how it seamlessly integrates with the SQL Server 2005 engine, .NET, and the operating system (OS)—all in a unified way previous SQL Server versions did not manage. Yet this new version maintains support for running legacy DTS packages (known as DTS 2000 packages).

As with anything new, it's great to play around with SSIS without needing to think too much about the how and the why. It's like buying a new performance automobile: for the first 1,000 miles your foot is a little heavier on the gas and, even in winter, you've got the top down and your sunglasses on. Not until you've had your initial fun does your mind probably turn to that shiny V8 behemoth nestled tightly under the hood (or, if you're particularly lucky, where the trunk should be). As your eyes adjust to the gloom beneath the elevated carbon fiber, you start to get an idea why your new four-wheeled beau is so much fun to drive. Digging deeper, following each cable and pipe, tracing the inlet manifold to its destination, examining each of the sixty-four valves feeding the eight greedy V-mounted cylinders…it gives you a real appreciation of how these component parts have come together to create the whole: this elemental source of understated yet effective road transport.

Fortunately, at least for those of a more technical persuasion, understanding the architecture and principles behind SSIS is a much more achievable and rewarding endeavor. SSIS is nonetheless a neat and clever piece of technology that—especially when compared with DTS—creates a seamlessly integrated experience for all user levels.

Hold on to your hats for this chapter. Things get a little hairy when I discuss the dark secrets of the Data Flow and its myriad transformation implementations.

I'm exaggerating. The SQL Server teams have made Data Flow logical and consistent, like all other areas of SSIS.

A Brief SQL Server Architecture Overview

It wouldn't be proper to launch into SSIS's architecture without a refresher on how SQL Server fits together. As you can see in Figure 2-1, SSIS sits in a position of tight integration with the other parts of SQL Server 2005.

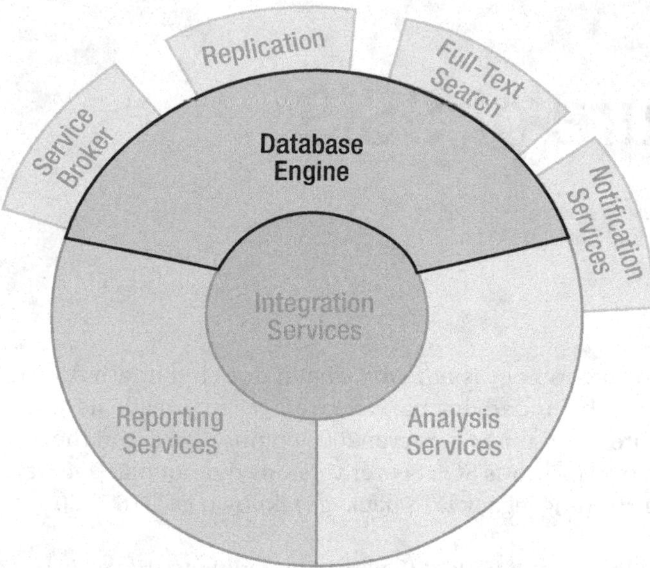

Figure 2-1. *An overview of how everything slots together in SQL Server 2005*

The SSIS team worked closely with the relational-engine team at Microsoft to ensure this integration is possible and gives the most possible benefit to both components. A suitable balance was struck within SSIS between reliance on SQL Server and SSIS-specific code.

SSIS has a neatly symbiotic relationship with the SQL Server engine and Management Studio. SSIS facilitates certain SQL Server features, such as data import and export, while leveraging the rock-solid performance of the SQL Server engine in the supply and support of data services.

SSIS and SQL Server Analysis Services

The level of integration between SQL Server Analysis Services (SSAS) and SSIS is relatively limited but offers a few important Data Flow components to assist OLAP developers.

Three Control Flow tasks have their basis in SSAS:

- `Analysis Services Execute DDL`
- `Analysis Services Processing`
- `Data Mining Query`

I'll discuss these three features in detail in Chapters 8, 9, and 15—especially data mining, including Data Mining Expression (DMX) queries and other SSAS-specific subjects.

SSIS also offers an Analysis Services connection manager, which can connect not only to a SSAS instance, but also to a SSAS project being hosted within Business Intelligence Development Studio.

Finally, four Data Flow components are specifically for the support of SSAS:

- `Dimension Processing`
- `Partition Processing`
- `Data Mining Model Training`
- `Slowly Changing Dimension`

This isn't to say that the majority of SSIS components can't or won't be used for preparing data for use in a SSAS environment. SSIS offers an incredibly powerful data-manipulation toolset for transforming and cleansing data in readiness for building into an OLAP environment. However, the discussion of these components isn't really an architectural one; they are components that can be used in any situation.

You can read more about these SSAS-centric connection managers, Control Flow tasks, and Data Flow components and destinations in Chapters 9, 10, and 11.

Common Language Runtime Integration

Version 2.0 of the .NET Framework has an efficient and rich application programming interface (API) for Common Language Runtime (CLR) hosting. This means that CLR-compliant code can be executed within a host process. Through this API, SQL Server 2005 can leverage features of.NET. You get all the advantages of using .NET, such as memory management, while the code itself is being executed from within a SQL Server process (and shares security and performance benefits as a consequence). This area of the SQL Server product is called the SQLCLR.

In a similar way, SSIS leverages the CLR-hosting API to offer hosted, managed code execution while negotiating and using the SSIS object model, and also to perform external processing. Read more about this in Chapter 13.

SSIS Architecture Overview

Let's take an overview of the SSIS architecture before diving into the detail.

Figure 2-2 is a reproduction of a diagram in the Microsoft Developer Network (MSDN) documentation. It is useful because it shows all of the component parts of SSIS in one place and makes clear how they fit together.

SSIS Designer

SSIS Designer is the familiar graphical user interface (GUI) that, among other capabilities, visually encapsulates the functionality offered by the two core namespaces: `Microsoft.SqlServer.Dts.Runtime` and `Microsoft.SqlServer.Dts.Pipeline`. It would be entirely possible to write a completely new and custom SSIS Designer that offers a more limited (or expanded) function set by interfacing with these SSIS namespaces.

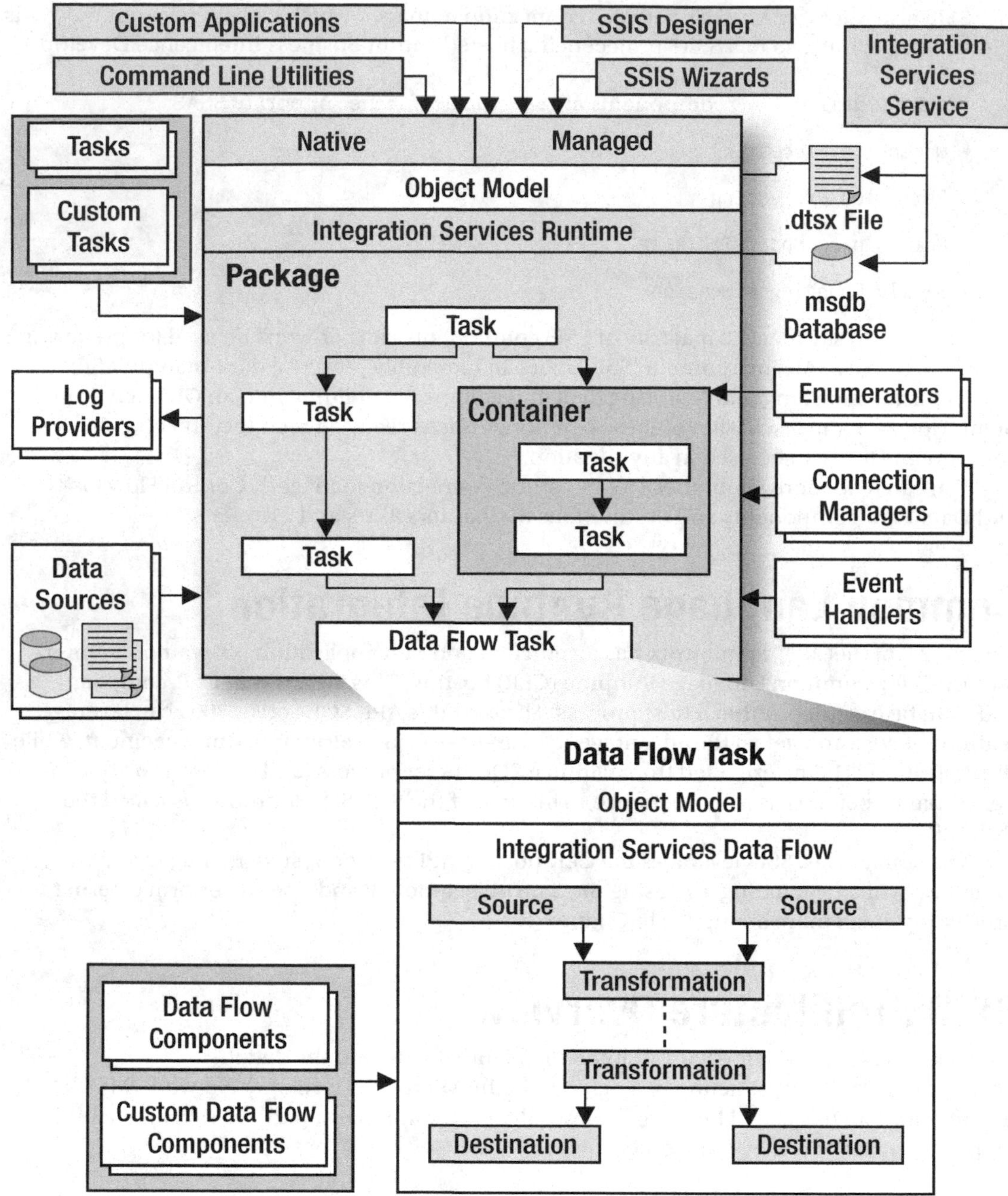

Figure 2-2. *MSDN's representation of the overall SSIS architecture*

As a precursor to discussing how these components interoperate, I'll highlight the important features and discuss some of the intricacies of each of them.

SSIS Wizards

In SQL Server 2000, the Import and Export wizard was provided through a simple DTS package. It comes as no surprise, then, that SSIS provides a similar wizard for performing the same task. SSIS also offers Package Installation and Configuration wizards, and—most pertinent to DTS users—the Package Migration Wizard. I'll discuss the Package Migration Wizard further in Chapter 3.

Custom Applications

Custom applications are included in Figure 2-2 to show that by leveraging the relevant SSIS namespaces, you can create code that builds on the SSIS architecture. Custom applications and components are discussed in Chapter 16.

Command-Line Utilities

As with SQL Server, and historically with DTS, you can use shell commands to perform operations, and combine them in a batch file or for some kind of remote operation. The commands are

`Dtexec`: Lets you execute a package. Parameters can be built and discovered using the companion `Dtexecui` command.

`DtUtil`: Lets you manage packages, wherever they are stored.

Use of these utilities is fairly straightforward and, like any good command-line utility, they have syntax helpers available. A full discussion and reference for these command-line utilities is in Appendix C.

Object Model

Every enterprise-level technology needs a great object model. The SSIS model is implemented through the interoperability of the following classes, which make up the Data Flow engine:

```
Microsoft.SqlServer.ManagedDTS.dll
Microsoft.SqlServer.RuntimeWrapper.dll
Microsoft.SqlServer.PipelineHost.dll
Microsoft.SqlServer.PipelineWrapper.dll
```

The object model is an extensive and complex construction that I'll address comprehensively in Chapters 13 and 16. Suffice it to say here that access to the object model offers incredible flexibility and programmability of the same engines that are used within all of SSIS. By leveraging this object model, you can easily extend SSIS to perform far beyond specification and answer all requirements expected of such a powerful data-integration tool.

SSIS Runtime

The SSIS runtime is handled by the `Microsoft.SqlServer.Dts.Runtime` namespace, which I'll discuss in Chapters 14 and 15. The component encapsulates packages, containers, event handlers, tasks, task connections, and more, and it provides methods for the saving and execution of packages. This is one of two core parts of SSIS (the other being the `Microsoft.SqlServer.Dts.Pipeline` namespace), and I'll pay particular attention to it later in this chapter. It's useful to remember, however, that these base classes can be leveraged within any CLR-compliant language.

Integration Services Service

As you may have guessed, the Integration Services service (see Figure 2-3) is a Windows service. When accessed through SQL Server Management Studio, it provides management of SSIS packages held in the SSIS Package Store. The SSIS Package Store is either the `msdb` database in a SQL Server instance or a folder on disk (containing `.dtsx` files). It isn't part of Business Intelligence Design Studio. The management of packages is a Management Studio–only task, so you don't need to consider this service unless you want, for example, to start or stop the running of a package or perform any other of the usual management tasks available from within Management Studio.

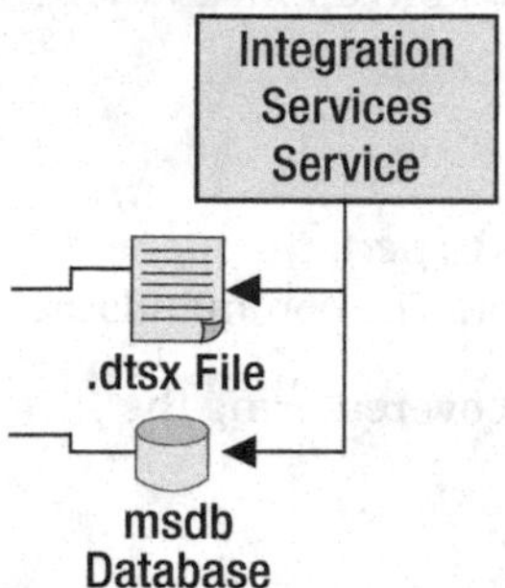

Figure 2-3. *Integration Services service*

Tasks

Tasks are Control Flow elements based upon the `Microsoft.SqlServer.Dts.Runtime.Task` namespace that exist as part of a package. A package can include multiple Control Flow tasks that, as DTS users might recognize, are connected together in proper sequence with *precedence constraints* (see Figure 2-4). I discuss tasks and precedence constraints, among other topics, in full in Chapter 8.

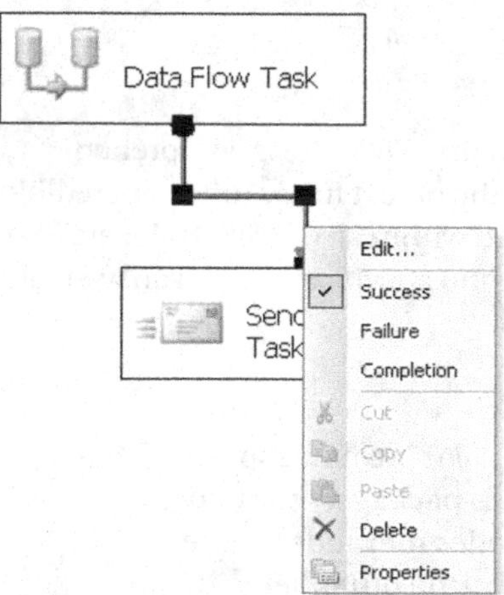

Figure 2-4. *A new task with precedence constraints shown*

Custom Tasks

Custom tasks can be developed in the same way you might create any other custom component. Essentially, your new class must inherit from `Task`, which is part of the `Microsoft.SqlServer.Dts.Runtime` namespace. The steps needed to produce custom components are described in complete detail in Chapter 15.

Log Providers

As the name suggests, log providers supply a logging framework for your SSIS package, container, or task. You can specify a provider to pipe the information to a destination such as the Windows Event Log or to the `sysdtslog90` table of the `msdb` database. Further discussion of logging facilities can be found in Chapter 4.

Enumerators

Enumerators are a useful—and necessary—inclusion for use with the `Foreach Loop` container. Naturally, as with everything else in SSIS, you can programmatically create an enumerator if the default enumerators in Table 2-1 do not meet your needs.

Table 2-1. *Stock Enumerator Types*

Enumeration Type	Usage
`ADO`	Enumerates each row in a row collection such as `Dataset`, `Data Table`, or `Recordset`.
`ADO.NET`	Enumerates schema information about a data source.
`File`	Enumerates a list of files based upon configured criteria.
`Variable`	Enumerates over the enumerable contents of a variable. The variable could contain, for example, an array or a `Dataset` table, or any other kind of collection.
`Item`	Enumerates over a list of items specified in the Enumerator Configuration.
`Nodelist`	Enumerates the result set from an XPath expression.
`SMO`	Enumerates SQL Server Management Objects (SMO) objects.

The enumerators in Table 2-1 implement the `IDTSForEachEnumerator` interface, which is a derived type that implements the `IEnumerable interface` further down the construct.

Unsurprisingly, there is much more to discuss around the topic of enumerators. I'll do so in Chapter 6.

Connection Managers

A connection manager handles the physical connection to some data source defined using the `ConnectionString` property. SSIS provides a variety of connection managers, shown in Table 2-2.

Table 2-2. *Stock Connection Managers*

Connection Manager	Used For Connecting To
`ADO`	ActiveX Data Objects (ADO) objects
`ADO.NET`	Data source with a .NET provider
`Excel`	An Excel workbook file
`File`	A file or folder
`FlatFile`	A single flat file, such as a CSV file
`FTP`	An FTP server
`HTTP`	A web server
`MSMQ`	An MSMQ message queue
`MSOLAP90`	An SSAS instance or project
`MultiFile`	Multiple files or folders
`MultiFlatFile`	Multiple data files, such as CSV files
`OLEDB`	A data source by using an OLE DB provider
`ODBC`	A data source by using ODBC
`SMOServer`	A SQL Server Management Objects (SMO) server
`SMTP`	A SMTP mail server
`SQLMobile`	A SQL Server Mobile database
`WMI`	A server while specifying the scope of Windows Management Instrumentation (WMI) management

Some of these connection managers have idiosyncrasies that I will address in Chapter 5. You can also create additional connection managers using Visual Studio, or use one supplied by your data vendor should specific extended connection features be required (beyond using an OLE DB, ODBC or ADO/ADO.NET connection). However, those offered as part of a default installation are quite comprehensive.

Data Sources

SSIS provides a fairly standard list of data sources to choose from—the usual suspects that offer connectivity to most, if not all, data-storage frameworks (see Table 2-3). The data source that stands out in particular, however, is the `DataReader`, which I'll discuss in full in Chapter 8.

Table 2-3. *Stock Data Sources*

Data Source	Usage
`DataReader`	Uses an ADO.NET connection manager to read data from a `DataReader` and channel it into the Data Flow.
`Excel`	Connects to an Excel file using the Excel connection manager.
`Flat File`	Connects to CSV files, for example.
`OLE DB`	Performs data access via an OLE DB provider.
`Raw File`	Imports data stored in the SQL Server `RAW` file format. It is a rapid way to import data that has perhaps been output by a previous package in the `RAW` format.
`XML`	Accesses data held in XML format.

Again in keeping with the open nature of the SSIS architecture, you can also write custom data sources, which I cover in Chapter 16.

Event Handlers

The Windows OS is, in many ways, driven by events. If an application window gets resized, a message is raised to notify the OS that a window-resize event has been fired. For ease of software development, constructs such as the .NET Framework encapsulate these OS messages and present them in an easy-to-handle event that can be captured and acted on. In.NET, for example, the `System.Windows.Forms.Form` class uses the `OnResize` event.

SSIS extends and exposes the event model further and offers the raising of events held in an instance of the `Microsoft.SqlServer.Dts.Runtime.DtsEventHandler` class.

Chapter 8 discusses event handlers in more detail.

Data Flow

I'm postponing the architectural discussion of the Data Flow engine until the next section in this chapter. It is an important and wide-ranging topic that requires the most diligent investigation and documentation. It's also a pretty advanced topic that seems to get more complex the deeper one probes into it.

Custom Data Flow Components

Custom Data Flow components is one of my favorite topics, simply because they empower the developer to produce any kind of transform by leveraging just a few interfaces defined in the SSIS object model. Chapter 16 discusses the creation of custom components in depth.

The Power of the Data Flow Architecture

Data Flow is both a logical and a physical construct that lives at the core of SSIS. It is the transport mechanism by which data passes between and within components, and it exists in the space between the source and destination of your package. To use an obvious analogy, if your data is water, Data Flow is the current that carries it along.

The term *Data Flow* can actually refer to more than one thing. SSIS offers the `Data Flow Task` as part of the Control Flow. You can design the contents of a Data Flow by double-clicking on the `Data Flow Task`, which opens the Data Flow tab. Components used within this task are handled as part of the Data Flow engine. The implementation of this Data Flow within SSIS manifests itself as a series of parallel or serial pipelines that facilitate the flow of data through the physical Data Flow, between components.

The components that live within your Data Flow hold a complementary relationship with the Data Flow engine. This is evident by virtue of each component having at least one input and at least one output—except for data sources and destinations, of course.

One of the key SSIS features and design decisions, in relation to Data Flow, is elimination of the necessity for *data staging*. Data staging is particular mostly to ETL and in some cases data-reporting functions. It is the practice of splitting an overall ETL operation into smaller parts that, possibly after each part has finished processing, temporarily store data in the database ready to be used by the next process. The rationale behind performing data staging probably has roots in memory limitations and performance optimization, but I think it goes deeper. It's entirely natural for our minds to *require* that staging be performed, because we like to have things broken up into smaller chunks with an easily visible start and end point.

SSIS throws that idea out of the window. Data can flow from one component to the next, both synchronously and asynchronously, without the need to output the data using any kind of staging, unless it's desired. This is achieved by the use of highly efficient and internally handled buffering of data.

Buffering, generally, is the concept of using an area of reserved memory to hold data before it is picked up by another process. As a concept it is nothing new, though it is certainly new to ETL and to the Microsoft ETL vision. The use of buffering vs. a staging strategy not only improves performance but also reduces the complexity of an ETL process. Staging requires interprocess communication (IPC) between the ETL processes and the database, but factors such as disk-access time and CPU usage also come into play.

In SSIS, buffers are reserved based upon how the server is configured, the amount of data involved, the column data types, and some definable settings. In many situations SSIS buffers can be used more like cache, providing a rapid-access repository for transient data. All buffer handling in SSIS is completely transparent to the developer.

If buffer size outweighs the amount of available memory, however, performance will be hit because SSIS implements a swapping strategy with the hard disk. This means it's important—as with most SQL Server performance issues—to ensure the fastest possible disk input/output (I/O) platform for your SQL Server instance. Also, ensure your server has plenty of RAM. (SQL Server can access the available memory; remember that 32-bit memory-addressing limits can be overcome by moving to a 64-bit platform.)

A Brief Word on Terminology

The population of the water-analogy-filled world of the Data Flow is about to increase by two. These new watery terms are a necessary addition to your SSIS vocabulary:

Upstream: This term refers to a component or transformation that exists *before* the current point in the Data Flow task.

Downstream: This refers to a component or transformation that exists *after* the current point in the Data Flow task.

Armed with an ability to describe the flow of data as it cascades through your Data Flow task, you're about to embark on a voyage further into the Data Flow architecture. All aboard the good ship SSIS!

Data Flow Transformations: Buffer-Usage Strategies

The way Data Flow components handle processing can be described with a combination of criteria. Management and use of buffers is controlled within the Data Flow engine to provide best performance by buffer reuse—where possible, reading and using existing data. Depending upon how the transformation component is constructed, the engine implements a suitable buffer-usage strategy. You can see that the matrix in Figure 2-5 includes rows to identify synchronous and asynchronous transformations, a distinction that bears heavily on buffer-usage strategy. Logically, the question of what makes a component synchronous or asynchronous is generally answered by examining its data inputs and outputs, or by identifying whether the transform must access anything outside of the Data Flow engine for processing reasons.

		Aggregate	Audit	Character Map	Conditional Split	Copy Column	Data Conversion	Data Mining Query	Derived Column	Export/Import Column	Fuzzy Grouping	Fuzzy Lookup	Lookup	Merge	MergeJoin	Multicast	OLEDB Command	Percent Sampling	Pivot/Unpivot	Row Count	Row Sampling	Script	Slowly Changing Dimension	Sort	Term Extraction	Term Lookup	PrintPage()
[-Blocking]	Streaming		✔	✔	✔	✔	✔		✔				✔			✔		✔		✔		✔					✔
	Row									✔			✔				✔					✔	✔				
[~Blocking]								✔						✔	✔				✔							✔	✔
[+Blocking]		✔									✔	✔									✔			✔	✔		
[Synchronous]			✔	✔	✔	✔	✔		✔	✔			✔			✔	✔	✔		✔		✔	✔				
[Asynchronous]		✔						✔			✔	✔		✔	✔				✔		✔			✔	✔	✔	✔

Figure 2-5. *Data Flow buffer-usage strategy matrix*

Note Transformations aren't the only Data Flow elements that are synchronous or asynchronous in nature. Data sources can also be classified as asynchronous, and Data Flow destinations are synchronous. Read more about this at the end of this chapter.

Physical examination of components within Business Intelligence Design Studio reveals concrete signs of how each component behaves with regard to buffer-usage strategy. Examine the value of the `SynchronousInputID` property on any output column of a transform to discover the component's nature. A value of `0` indicates an asynchronous output. A value other than `0` (which points to an input column with an ID matching the value) identifies the output as synchronous.

Row Transformations

As the name suggests, row transformations can offer the best performance, because the data required to perform the transform is available within each row.

Taking the concept a little further, you can see from the matrix in Figure 2-5 that row transformation–type components offer a single output row for each input row. The transformation takes place within the row construct, and although additional columns might be created, the row ratio of 1:1 remains constant from input to output. Maintaining this 1:1 ratio allows the transformation engine to reuse already created buffers containing existing data, again because all required input exists within that buffer.

Row transformations, because of the reasons behind the 1:1 ratio, are synchronous transformations.

Partially or Semiblocking Type

The partially or semiblocking transformation type is easily identified, logically, by examining the inputs and outputs. In contrast to row transformations, this type allows a disparity between the number of input rows and the number of output rows.

Take, for, example the `Merge` transformation. The number of output rows is the sum of the two merged sets of records, which in all likelihood does not equal the number of input records.

At buffer level—because no existing buffer holds this transformation result of more, fewer, or the same number of records—a new buffer must be created to hold the output. The copying of the output to a new buffer *could* create a new thread. This is discussed at the end of this chapter in the section on execution trees.

Partially (or semi) blocking transformations are classified as asynchronous transformations because of this non–1:1 ratio between input rows and output rows.

Blocking Type

With previous experience in mind, you can imagine the reasons for a type of transformation component that blocks processing. Certainly the processing behind the `Aggregate` and `Sort` components reveals this, because the reading of all records is required to perform, for example, an `Order By` on a set of records in SQL.

From a SQL perspective, `Aggregate` is the same type of operation in nature to the `Sort`, because a query needs to examine the whole result set to aggregate data. The flow cannot continue until this processing is complete. This is why `Aggregate` is a blocking transformation type.

Using the tried and tested technique of examining expected input rows and output rows, you can again see that this component type offers a non–1:1 ratio. For example, with the `Aggregate` component, the number of output rows will probably be less than or equal to the number of input rows. This disparity in ratio signifies that blocking transformations are also asynchronous transforms. As with semiblocking transformations, a new buffer is created and a new thread copies the output data to it.

Execution Trees Explained

You've probably seen execution-plan diagrams generated in Query Analyzer. Now it's time to get your hands dirty along similar lines with execution trees within your Data Flow tasks.

Execution trees are logical blocks that subdivide Data Flow tasks by the physical implementation of buffers and threads at runtime. The form of a given execution tree (or branch) is calculated by examining each component's buffer-usage strategy and branching, depending on synchronicity and blocking type.

Given the simple Data Flow in Figure 2-6, Figure 2-7 shows how its different buffer-usage strategies create different execution trees.

Because it uses only row-transformation components, the execution tree for the Data Flow in Figure 2-6 is kept relatively simple. (Full details on Data Flow are in Chapter 8.) You can see where the number of outputs matches the number of inputs, in keeping with the component's synchronous nature.

As the text in Figure 2-7 shows, two buffers are used to handle this Data Flow. One buffer contains the data read from the source file, which downstream undergoes a `Derived Column` transform and is fed to the `SQL Server Destination`:

```
Begin execution tree 0...
```

The second buffer is created to hold the error output from the data source, because data sources are asynchronous and therefore require a separate buffer for each output:

```
Begin execution tree 1...
```

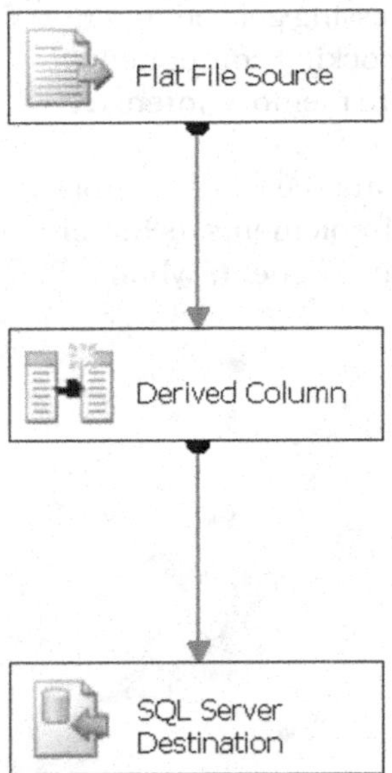

Figure 2-6. *A simple data flow*

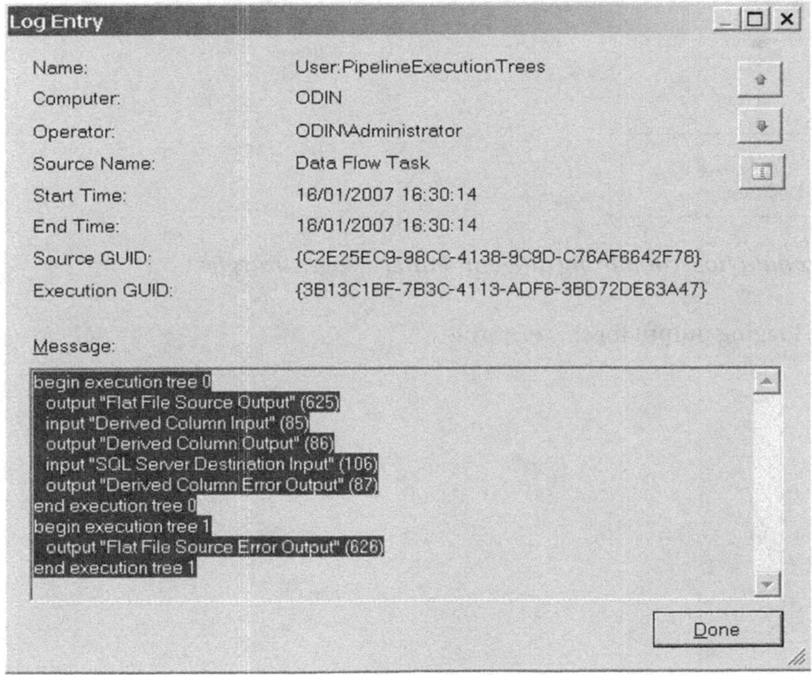

Figure 2-7. *Execution trees for Figure 2-6*

Now here's an example that demonstrates how complex SSIS processing gets behind the scenes: a Data Flow that contains a mixture of partially blocking and blocking components. In total, seven buffers are created, making for a more complex and more memory-intensive operation.

Figure 2-8 shows how, on the surface at least, the tasks performed are seemingly simple and straightforward. At a deeper level, it is interesting to see how SSIS implements its buffer-usage strategy, because buffering is an area that can provide performance benefits when optimized.

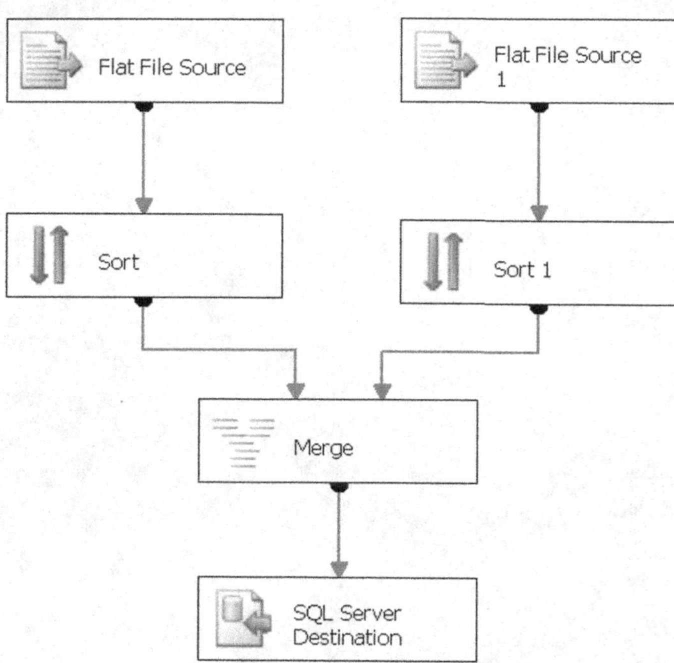

Figure 2-8. *A more complex data flow combining different buffer-usage strategies*

Figure 2-9 shows the logging output for this example.

```
Message:
begin execution tree 0
   output "Flat File Source Output" (625)
   input "Sort Input" (1402)
end execution tree 0
begin execution tree 1
   output "Flat File Source Error Output" (626)
end execution tree 1
begin execution tree 2
   output "Flat File Source Output" (1122)
   input "Sort Input" (1381)
end execution tree 2
begin execution tree 3
   output "Flat File Source Error Output" (1123)
end execution tree 3
begin execution tree 4
   output "Sort Output" (1382)
   input "Merge Input 2" (1112)
end execution tree 4
begin execution tree 5
   output "Sort Output" (1403)
   input "Merge Input 1" (1111)
end execution tree 5
begin execution tree 6
   output "Merge Output 1" (1113)
   input "SQL Server Destination Input" (106)
end execution tree 6
```

Figure 2-9. *A more complex execution tree*

An explanation of the output in Figure 2-9 in more straightforward terms will serve as a primer for the more-intensive discussion of optimization in Chapter 12. So let's look at the tree in detail:

```
BEGIN
   Allocate Buffer 0
      Read data from First Flat File Source and fill Buffer 0
      Pass Buffer 0 to first Sort Input component
   Allocate Buffer 1
      Read data from First Flat File Source Error Output
   Allocate Buffer 2
      Read data from Second Flat File Source and file Buffer 2
      Pass Buffer 2 to second Sort Input component
   Allocate Buffer 3
      Read data from Second Flat File Source Error Output
   Allocate Buffer 4
      Read data from First Sort Output
      Pass Buffer 4 to first Input on Merge component
   Allocate Buffer 5
      Read data from Second Sort Output
      Pass Buffer 5 to second Input on Merge component
   Allocate Buffer 6
      Read data from Merge Output
      Pass Buffer 6 to SQL Server Destination Input
END
```

This output is in keeping with the component-properties matrix in Figure 2-5: partially blocking and blocking component types need to initialize and use new buffers by nature.

As you can see from Figures 2-7 and 2-9, additional buffers (and therefore additional memory) are initialized, depending on the component's blocking type. As a consequence, additional threads *might* also be created to handle the processing, depending on the component's synchronicity. Optimizations and suggestions on strategy can be found in Chapter 12.

Summary

The architecture of SSIS is the most complex yet rewarding side of the technology to learn. Knowing the machinations that take place behind the scenes has enabled me on many occasions to perform genuinely revolutionary (to the client at least) optimizations that have dramatically improved package throughput in the most demanding of applications. As an SSIS specialist working with a deep and thorough understanding of the architectural framework, you can set yourself above your peers and provide real business value. For example, the ability not only to identify where bottlenecks occur, but also to predict and avoid them, will make you an SSIS hero.

Don't just take my word for it. SQL Server comes with a veritable profusion of tools and features for examining the underlying architecture of SSIS. My personal favorite tool of all time (well, it's on a par with Lutz Roeder's Reflector)—SQL Profiler—is invaluable for identifying calls made to the SQL engine, while the comprehensive logging facilities within SSIS allow the monitoring of buffers, pipelines, and many other components. Performance counters are a great way to keep an eye on buffer activity at a lower level, and Lutz Roeder's Reflector tool is perfect for taking a peek inside SSIS's various components.

The advances in ETL architecture that SSIS presents are substantial. Examining them has given you the opportunity to see why a straight comparison between a DTS package and an SSIS package is impossible. The architectures are fundamentally different, so performing ETL with SQL Server 2005 isn't just a case of loading up a legacy DTS package into SSIS and having it work as though nothing has changed. That said, SSIS does have provisions for upgrading and using DTS packages, which is the subject of Chapter 3.

CHAPTER 3

From DTS to SSIS

Chapters 1 and 2 have given you an overview of SSIS and the core architecture of both SQL Server and SSIS. This chapter is a guide to transitioning from DTS to SSIS. It explains

- How SSIS handles tasks you now do with DTS
- How you can do the same things more efficiently using some of SSIS's new features
- The best way to migrate your existing hard work with DTS into shiny new SSIS packages.

Although SSIS is an entirely fresh take on data integration/ETL, it retains enough familiarity for DTS users to recognize and use it instantly (in contrast, say, to the learning curve associated with moving from VB6 to Visual Basic .NET). But as you know from Chapter 1, and I will elaborate on here, SSIS is much more than an enhanced version of DTS.

Even readers without experience with DTS or other ETL tools can make use of content in this chapter. You'll learn more about Microsoft's changed approach to ETL and the level of commitment Microsoft has made to SSIS.

What's New?

SSIS's architecture and its tighter integration with the SQL Server Engine enable SSIS to outperform DTS in many ways that can benefit your business:

- **Processing:** With SSIS, you process more data and process it more quickly.
- **Scalability**: The SSIS components build on a common .NET architectural theme and leverage the rest of the .NET Framework in a similar way to most current-generation Microsoft technology. By comparison, DTS is architecturally immature, especially because it is not built on a common framework shared with SQL Server 2000.
- **Scope**: DTS was meant to be used for transforming data, and it's pretty good at it. It was fine for a little ETL here and there, but ETL was never DTS's main design purpose. It lacked the refinement and feature set to serve as a serious part of a valid ETL strategy. SSIS weighs in with enterprise-standard capabilities for performing tasks ranging from the simplest import/export, to complex transformations, to full ETL and data warehousing.

- **Customization**: Although SSIS offers the same capability set as DTS—on the surface at least—the amazing customization capabilities in SSIS are perhaps its biggest selling point. If what you want doesn't come in the box, you can make it yourself. With a minimum of effort and fuss, you can drop a high-performing, scalable, and architecturally sound custom component into SSIS that is limited only by your imagination. DTS's provision for custom functionality was much less realized; you could write scripts to interface with all sorts of components, but it was always a makeshift method and not exactly in the spirit of OOP.

SSIS also improves on DTS with a couple of completely unfamiliar features you'll learn more about in Chapters 7 and 8:

- **`For Loop` and `Foreach` Containers**: One of the uses of ActiveX Script in DTS is to perform iterative operations. A much neater and architecturally sound way in SSIS is to use the new `For Loop` and `Foreach` Control Flow containers. They provide a robust mechanism for iterative processing and plug nicely into SSIS Control Flow and Data Flow components.
- **Script Tasks**: Grab your Visual Basic .NET hat and write some custom code in a Script Task. This powerful and high-performance weapon in the SSIS armory leverages the .NET Framework, exposing the `ScriptObjectModel` and creating compiled code that is executed at package runtime.

I mean no disrespect to DTS by identifying these areas of improvement. DTS has been an incredibly useful tool over the years, but these are all compelling reasons to move forward with SSIS.

Preparing to Migrate Legacy DTS Packages

■Important Your DTS packages will work once they're migrated to SQL Server 2005, irrespective of their content or level of incompatibility with the SSIS architecture. In the first instance, the Package Migration Wizard attempts to translate your DTS package into an SSIS package by using SSIS-specific components that functionally mirror DTS counterparts—leaving you with an editable SSIS package that can be modified and updated. If this isn't possible, mechanisms are in place in SSIS to enable your package to run in a "black box" way. Everything will still work, and you can address upgrading of the DTS package to SSIS when time and resources allow.

Migrating to any new technology inevitably involves potential problems. In the case of SSIS, I can make you aware of the "standard" problems and upgrade issues, but each case and DTS package is different, so nothing is guaranteed. For this reason, I suggest that you perform an initial upgrade test on a backup of your database. You can do this even before upgrading to SQL Server 2005, which can attach and operate against your existing database files seamlessly. It is likely you will come across some sticky problems once you look beyond whether your tables/sprocs/triggers have been upgraded successfully.

With that in mind, let's take a look at the steps for performing an upgrade test.

Running SQL Server 2005 Upgrade Advisor

A great tool in your migration toolbox is the SQL Server 2005 Upgrade Advisor (see Figure 3-1). It should be in the `\Servers\redist\Upgrade Advisor` directory of your installation disc. The file is `SQLUASetup.msi`. You can run a check within the Upgrade Advisor for a more recent version, but you should check the Microsoft web site for one too, just to be sure.

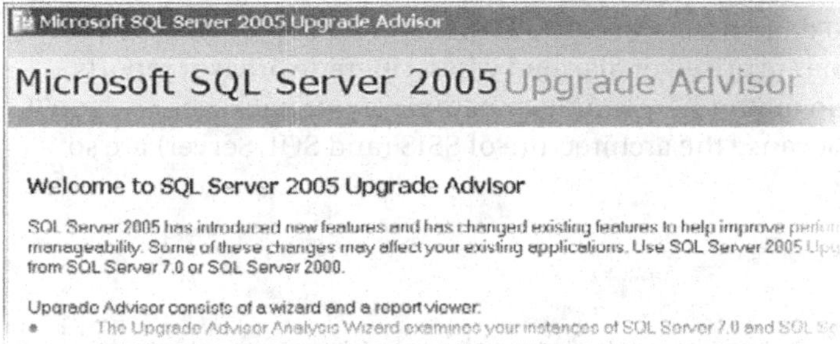

Figure 3-1. *The Upgrade Advisor welcome screen*

Upgrade Advisor performs checks to identify which areas throughout your SQL Server 7.0 or SQL Server 2000 database require more attention. Where SSIS is concerned, you are only interested in warnings regarding the migration of your DTS packages. This being the case, in this example I'm only going to tick the Data Transformation Services check box on the first Wizard step. (I'm not providing screenshots for every step of the process, including this one, because most of the actions to perform in the wizard are self-evident.)

Interestingly, the Upgrade Advisor comes with advice in textual format on the wizard's DTS Parameters page, as shown in Figure 3-2.

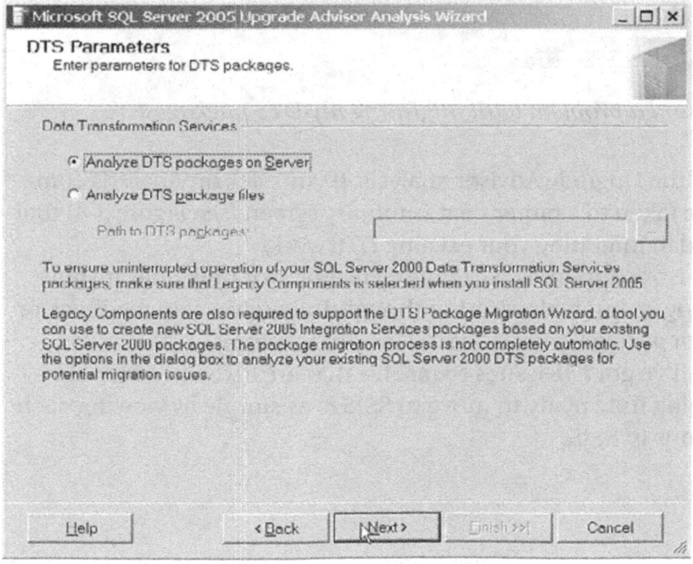

Figure 3-2. *Some words worth remembering from the Upgrade Advisor*

Kudos to Microsoft for providing a tool that not only advises on your migration but is also explicit in warning you that you should expect to take a personal hand in the process. A more generic tool with inexplicit and weak warnings would let you blunder on regardless and potentially destroy the hard work you put into creating DTS packages that could not be fully migrated.

Moving on, Figure 3-3 shows a message that—barring any miracles—you'll receive irrespective of the contents of your DTS package. The warning probably results from the location of the DTS package in your 7.0/2000 database, or because DTS has been deprecated, as shown in Figure 3-4. In other words, don't be surprised or alarmed when Upgrade Advisor reports problems with your DTS package. No matter how simple or complex your packages are, you'll see these generic warnings simply because the architecture of SSIS (and SQL Server) are so different from previous iterations.

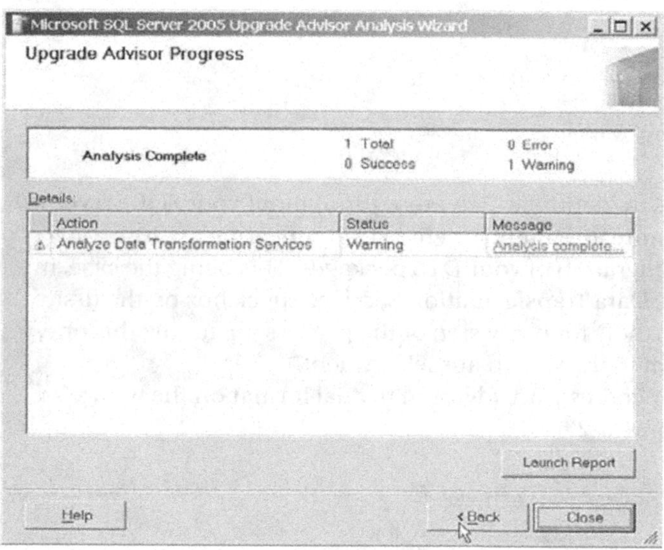

Figure 3-3. *Wow, Upgrade Advisor found a problem with migrating my DTS packages!*

Let's take a look at the results of the Upgrade Advisor analysis. If you click on Analysis complete... or Launch Report, you will be taken to a rather neat summary screen (see Figure 3-4) that lists and explains the issues expected in migrating your existing DTS work.

The level of detail Upgrade Advisor supplies is particularly useful. Not only does it show you what the problem/issue/warning is, but it also (rather thoughtfully) gives you feedback on its importance level and an indicator as to when you should look to resolve it.

As you can see from Figure 3-4, I've got five issues to resolve that are listed in order of *when* I should address the issue. Being fully ready to move to SSIS is as simple as viewing each issue to perform the necessary actions in SSIS.

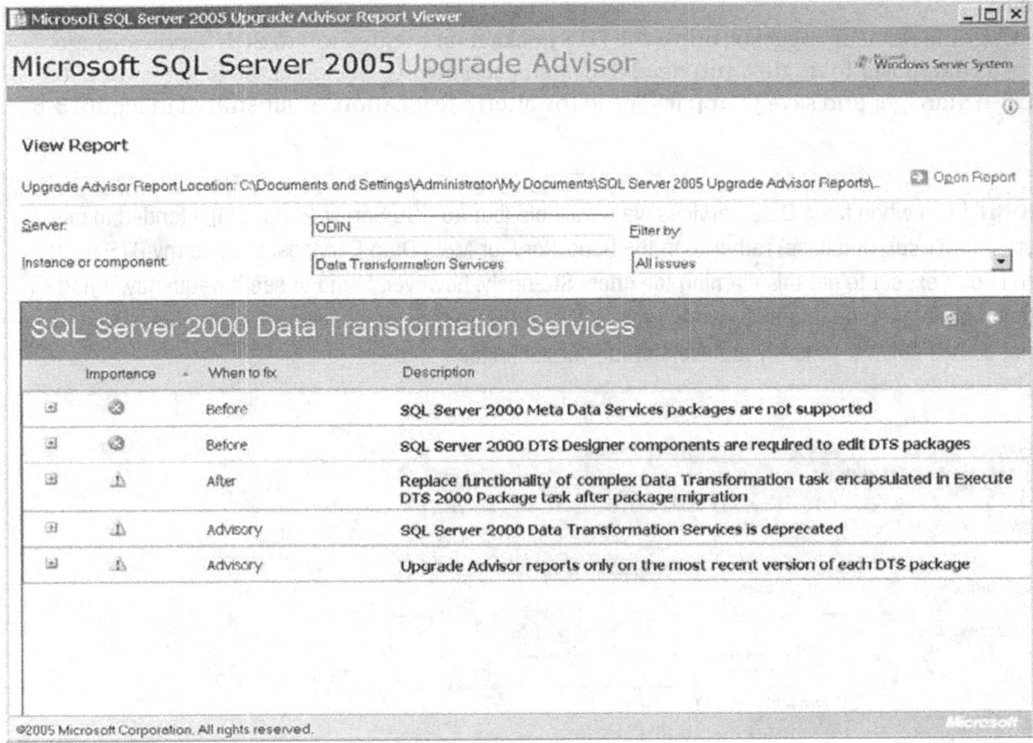

Figure 3-4. *The results of the Upgrade Advisor: there might be trouble ahead . . .*

Understanding Upgrade Advisor Warnings

Let's take a look at the issues Upgrade Advisor highlights in Figure 3-4 and at the recommended solutions. I am concentrating initially on these first few issues because they appear when I run the Upgrade Advisor against a server with a single, very simple DTS package. Later in this chapter you'll find a complete list of possible warnings you might receive upon running the Upgrade Advisor.

"SQL Server 2000 Meta Data Services packages are not supported"

Figure 3-5 shows an issue that the Upgrade Advisor commonly reports. This problem occurs because SQL Server 2005, like SQL Server 2000 before it, has deprecated Meta Data Services. Therefore your DTS packages cannot be held in a similar way once migrated.

Importance ▲ When to fix Description

Before SQL Server 2000 Meta Data Services packages are not supported

Existing Meta Data Services packages should be moved to SQL Server storage (in the msdb database) or to structured storage files before you upgrade. SQL Server 2005 does not install support for SQL Server 2000 Meta Data Services; therefore the Package Migration Wizard will be unable to access Meta Data Services packages after upgrade in the absence of the SQL Server 2000 Client Tools.

Show affected objects. (1 objects)

Tell me more about this issue and how to resolve it.

☐ This issue has been resolved.

Figure 3-5. *Resolving these issues makes using the Package Migration Wizard easier.*

Resolution

As the Upgrade Advisor suggests, move the DTS package(s) in question to SQL Server storage in the `msdb` database. To do this, you need to design each of your packages via SQL Server 2000 Enterprise Manager and save your package to the alternate location, as illustrated in Figure 3-6.

Caution Even when Meta Data Services was available (before SQL Server 2000 SP3), I tended to use SQL Server (the `msdb` database) rather than the Repository (or Meta Data Services) to store my DTS packages, so I don't expect to get this warning too often. Strangely, however, I tend to see it frequently, if not *every* time I perform some migration work, irrespective of the storage mechanism. Whether it's a valid warning or not comes down to where you have stored your packages.

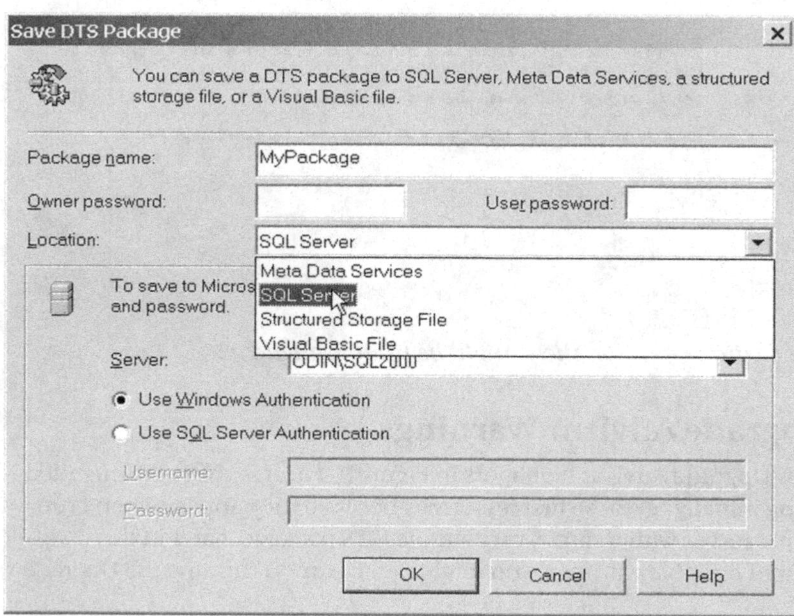

Figure 3-6. *Storing a DTS Package to the msdb database*

"SQL Server 2000 DTS Components are required to edit DTS Packages"

This issue message (detailed in Figure 3-7) is another one you will see regularly when running the Upgrade Advisor. It's a pretty stock issue and makes perfect sense, because the components are part of SQL Server 2000.

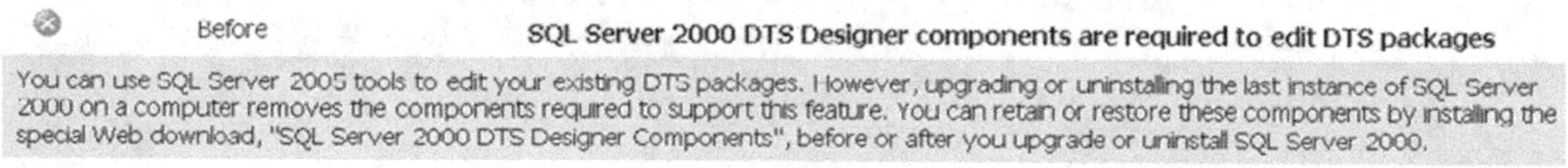

Before SQL Server 2000 DTS Designer components are required to edit DTS packages

You can use SQL Server 2005 tools to edit your existing DTS packages. However, upgrading or uninstalling the last instance of SQL Server 2000 on a computer removes the components required to support this feature. You can retain or restore these components by installing the special Web download, "SQL Server 2000 DTS Designer Components", before or after you upgrade or uninstall SQL Server 2000.

Figure 3-7. *Another common issue*

Resolution

Do as the message says and install the "special web download." Search on the Microsoft web site for *SQL Server 2000 DTS Designer Components* to yield a location (as shown in Figure 3-8) from which to download this additional component.

Microsoft SQL Server 2000 DTS Designer Components

The Microsoft SQL Server 2000 Data Transformation Services (DTS) package designer is a design tool used by developers and administrators of SQL Server 2005 servers to edit and maintain existing DTS packages until they can be upgraded or recreated in the SQL Server 2005 Integration Services package format. After installing this download, SQL Server 2005 users can continue to edit and maintain existing DTS packages from the Object Explorer in SQL Server 2005 Management Studio and from the Execute DTS 2000 Package Task Editor in Business Intelligence Development Studio, without needing to reinstall the SQL Server 2000 tools. The DTS package designer in this download was formerly accessed from the Data Transformation Services node in SQL Server 2000 Enterprise Manager.

Audience(s): **Customer, Developer**

X86 Package (SQLServer2005_DTS.msi) - 5083 KB

Figure 3-8. *Download SQL Server 2000 DTS Designer Components from the Microsoft web site.*

"Replace functionality of complex Data Transformation task encapsulated in Execute DTS 2000 Package after package migration"

In my experience, this warning (see Figure 3-9) appears whether the transformation is complex or a straightforward column mapping. That said, the complexity of your transformations directly relates to how much work you must do once you get your package migrated to SSIS. This is probably a good thing in any case, because it exposes you to the features of SSIS early rather than later, and your knowledge will grow more quickly as a consequence.

Resolution

This is merely a warning that you can't play around too much with your migrated package once it hits SQL Server 2005. That's okay—it'll still work—and you can reengineer it using SSIS at your convenience.

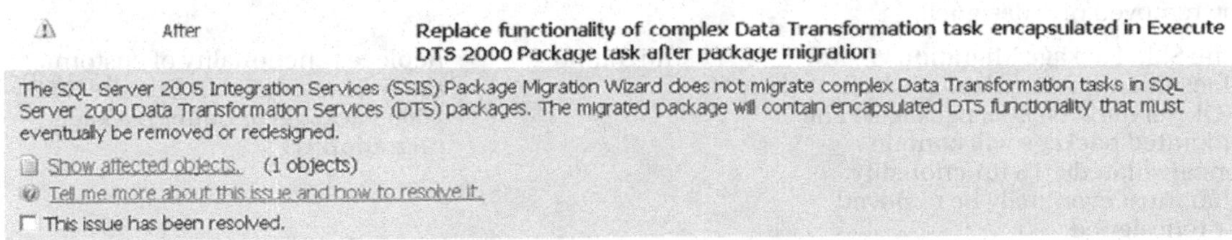

Figure 3-9. *If you have a transformation in your DTS Package, you will definitely see this.*

"SQL Server 2000 Data Transformation Services is deprecated"

There isn't much to say about this one. DTS no longer exists in SQL Server 2005, which is something you were already aware of.

Resolution

Use SSIS instead!

"Upgrade Advisor reports only on the most recent version of each DTS Package"

This is another warning message that really is only a reminder. So pay attention!

Resolution

It's just advice. Take heed but don't worry!

A Complete List of Possible Upgrade Advisor Messages

The Upgrade Advisor can detect and offer corrective advice for a large number of possible problems with your DTS packages. For example, you may have a package containing a Data Mining task or, more than likely, ActiveX scripting tasks. Upgrade Advisor generates specific messages if these task types are detected. Table 3-1 is a complete list of Upgrade Advisor warnings.

Table 3-1. *Migration Issues and Resolutions*

Issue Description	When to Resolve	Resolution
The SQL Server 2005 Integration Services (SSIS) Package Migration Wizard does not migrate ActiveX Script code that accesses the DTS object model via the `Parent` property of the `GlobalVariables` collection in SQL Server 2000 DTS packages. After migration, you must manually edit the resulting SSIS package to restore former package behavior.	Postmigration	Rewrite your ActiveX script after migration to access the DTS object model.
The SSIS Package Migration Wizard does not migrate the Analysis Services task in SQL Server 2000 DTS packages. The migrated package will contain encapsulated DTS functionality that must eventually be removed or redesigned.	Postmigration	Rewrite this part of your DTS Package using SSIS.
The SSIS Package Migration Wizard does not migrate custom tasks in SQL Server 2000 DTS packages. The migrated package will contain encapsulated DTS functionality that must eventually be removed or redesigned.	Postmigration	Replace functionality of custom task encapsulated in Execute DTS 2000 Package task after package migration.
The SSIS Package Migration Wizard does not migrate Data Driven Query tasks in SQL Server 2000 DTS packages. The migrated package will contain encapsulated DTS functionality that must eventually be removed or redesigned.	Postmigration	Replace functionality of Data Driven Query task encapsulated in Execute DTS 2000 Package task after package migration.

Issue Description	When to Resolve	Resolution
You must completely migrate existing SQL Server 2000 Data DTS packages to SQL Server 2005 Integration Services packages before support is withdrawn.	Advisory only	The features of DTS you are using simply don't have a parallel within SSIS. Consider rewriting at the first opportunity.
The SSIS Package Migration Wizard does not migrate the Data Mining Prediction Query task in SQL Server 2000 DTS packages. The migrated package will contain encapsulated DTS functionality that must eventually be replaced. SQL Server 2005 does not install support for the SQL Server 2000 Data Mining Prediction Query task; therefore the migrated package will not run after upgrade in the absence of SQL Server 2000 Analysis Services.	Postmigration	Replace functionality of Data Mining Prediction Query task encapsulated in Execute DTS 2000 Package task after package migration.
The SSIS Package Migration Wizard does not migrate Dynamic Properties tasks in SQL Server 2000 DTS packages. After migration, you must manually edit the resulting SSIS package to restore former package behavior.	Postmigration	Replace functionality of Dynamic Properties task after package migration.
Upgrade Advisor is unable to scan packages with password protection. To scan encrypted DTS packages, use the SSIS Package Migration Wizard, which is included with SQL Server 2005.	Advisory only	Remove any passwords from your DTS Packages.
Upgrade Advisor is unable to scan packages with invalid characters (/ \ : [ ] . =) in the package name.	Advisory only	Remove invalid characters from your package name.
To ensure uninterrupted execution of DTS packages after an upgrade, check the Advanced button on the Components to Install page of the Installation Wizard and make sure that DTS 2000 runtime support is selected on the Feature Selection page.	Premigration	Install backward-compatibility files to retain the ability to run and maintain your DTS packages after an upgrade.
You can use SQL Server 2005 tools to edit your existing DTS packages. However, upgrading or uninstalling the last instance of SQL Server 2000 on a computer removes the components required to support this feature. You can retain or restore these components by installing the special SQL Server 2000 DTS Designer Components web download, before or after you upgrade or uninstall SQL Server 2000.	Preupgrade	SQL Server 2000 DTS Designer components are required to edit DTS packages.
No DTS packages were found on the server that you selected to analyze.	Premigration	Point the Upgrade Advisor to the correct server.

Continued

Table 3-1. *Continued*

Issue Description	When to Resolve	Resolution
An error was encountered while creating objects referenced by the package. This error might have been caused by an unregistered custom task, or by the presence of Analysis Services Processing task in the package in the absence of an Analysis Server install on this machine.	Advisory only	Package contains unregistered custom task or Analysis Services Processing task.
The SQL SSIS Package Migration Wizard does not migrate Parallel Data Pump tasks in SQL Server 2000 DTS packages. The migrated package will contain encapsulated DTS functionality that must eventually be removed or redesigned.	Postmigration	Replace functionality of Parallel Data Pump task encapsulated in Execute DTS 2000 Package task after package migration.
Existing Meta Data Services packages should be moved to SQL Server storage (in the `msdb` database) or to structured storage files before you upgrade. SQL Server 2005 does not install support for SQL Server 2000 Meta Data Services; therefore the Package Migration Wizard will be unable to access Meta Data Services packages after upgrade in the absence of the SQL Server 2000 Client Tools.	Preupgrade	Move any DTS packages and anything else you have written from the Repository to the SQL Server `msdb` database
The SQL SSIS Package Migration Wizard does not migrate ActiveX scripts associated with steps in SQL Server 2000 DTS packages. After migration, you must manually edit the resulting SSIS package to restore former package behavior.	Postmigration	Replace functionality of ActiveX script attached to package steps after package migration.
You can use SQL Server 2005 tools to edit your existing DTS packages. However, upgrading or uninstalling the last instance of SQL Server 2000 on a computer removes the components required to support this feature. You can retain or restore these components by installing the special SQL Server 2000 DTS Designer Components web download, before or after you upgrade or uninstall SQL Server 2000.	Premigration	SQL Server 2000 DTS Designer components are required to edit DTS packages.
The SQL Server 2005 SSIS Package Migration Wizard does not migrate transaction settings in SQL Server 2000 DTS packages. After migration, you must manually edit the resulting SSIS package to restore former package behavior.	Postmigration	Reconfigure transaction settings after package migration.

Issue Description	When to Resolve	Resolution
Upgrade Advisor may be unable to scan a package for reasons that include a corrupt file, insufficient permissions, or other causes.	Advisory only	Resolve problems with your DTS Package: check access permissions and see if you can edit the package in SQL Server 2000 Enterprise Manager. Save the package again with a different name.
The SSIS Package Migration Wizard does not migrate Execute Packages tasks that load Meta Data Services packages. The migrated package will contain encapsulated DTS functionality that must eventually be replaced. SQL Server 2005 does not install support for SQL Server 2000 Meta Data Services; therefore the migrated package will not run after upgrade in the absence of the SQL Server 2000 Client Tools.	Preupgrade	Replace functionality of Execute Package task (with Meta Data Services package) encapsulated in Execute DTS 2000 Package task after package migration.
Upgrade Advisor reports only on the most recent version of each DTS package. To report on multiple versions of a DTS package, use the SSIS Package Migration Wizard.	Advisory only	Upgrade Advisor reports only on the most recent version of each DTS package.

Of the multitude of issues/warnings the Upgrade Advisor can raise, the ones that cause the most work are those related to ActiveX scripting. This makes sense, because the way the object model is manipulated and used is dramatically different between DTS and SSIS. This chapter doesn't address the rebuilding of your ActiveX script–based tasks. See Chapters 7 and 8 to learn how scripting is implemented in SSIS.

Using the Package Migration Wizard

By this point you should be ready to migrate your DTS packages. You will have used the Upgrade Advisor to identify potential problems and resolved them using the information I presented in the preceding section. Now it's time to perform the migration, so let's take a look at one migration option: the SSIS Package Migration Wizard.

You can access the Package Migration Wizard a few different ways—through SQL Server Management Studio, for example—but I recommend using Business Intelligence Development Studio (BIDS). The reason is that once the Package Migration Wizard has finished, you're left with a nice, neat `.dtsx` file in your project, ready to mess around with and fix/optimize as necessary.

So, having created a new SSIS project in the BIDS IDE, I'll start the Package Migration Wizard from the Project menu (see Figure 3-10).

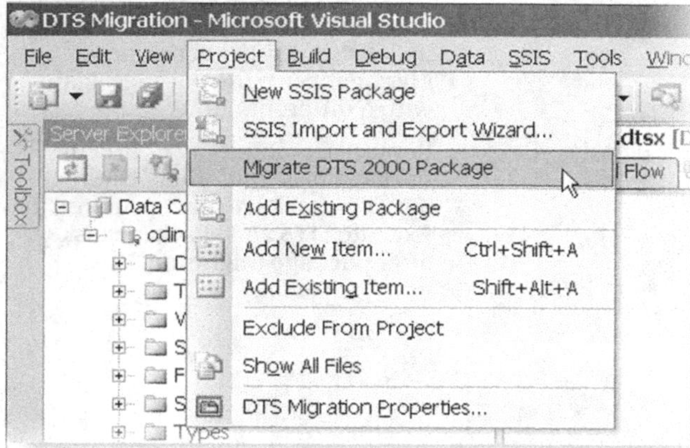

Figure 3-10. *Package Migration Wizard menu options*

The Package Migration Wizard process is straightforward, so you should be able to drill through it pretty quickly. After all, it's the product that comes out at the end that you're most interested in. Is it identical to your DTS equivalent? Will it work? Let's find out . . .

Figure 3-11 shows a screen that you will see only if you are following this migration method: a dialog box asking where to put the migrated `.dtsx` file.

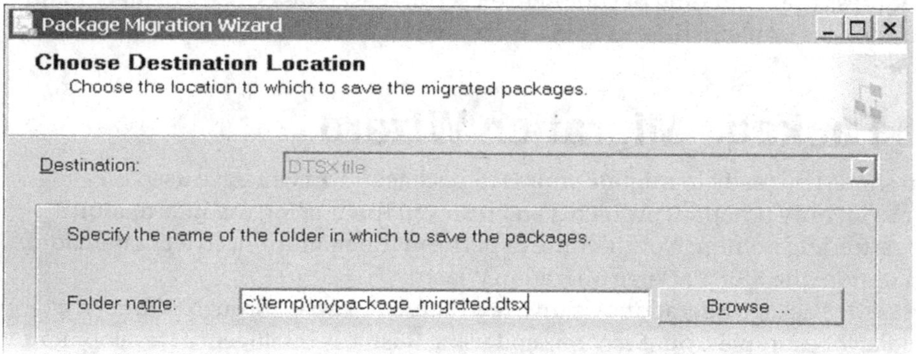

Figure 3-11. *It's a good idea to migrate your DTS Package to a .dtsx file.*

You can see from Figure 3-12 that you get a choice of which DTS packages you want to migrate. You must tick the ones you want. The package I've prepared for this example is there, so I select it and click Next.

This is where the Package Migration Wizard takes over. Having entered all the information it requires and selected the packages to migrate, you are presented with a summary screen that serves as your last chance to go back and make any changes (see Figure 3-13).

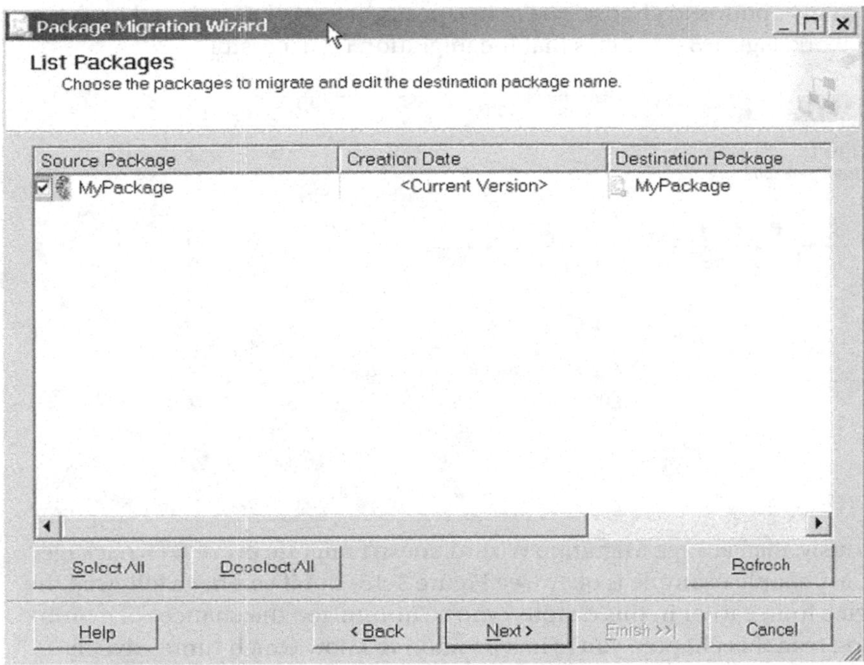

Figure 3-12. *Select the packages you want to migrate.*

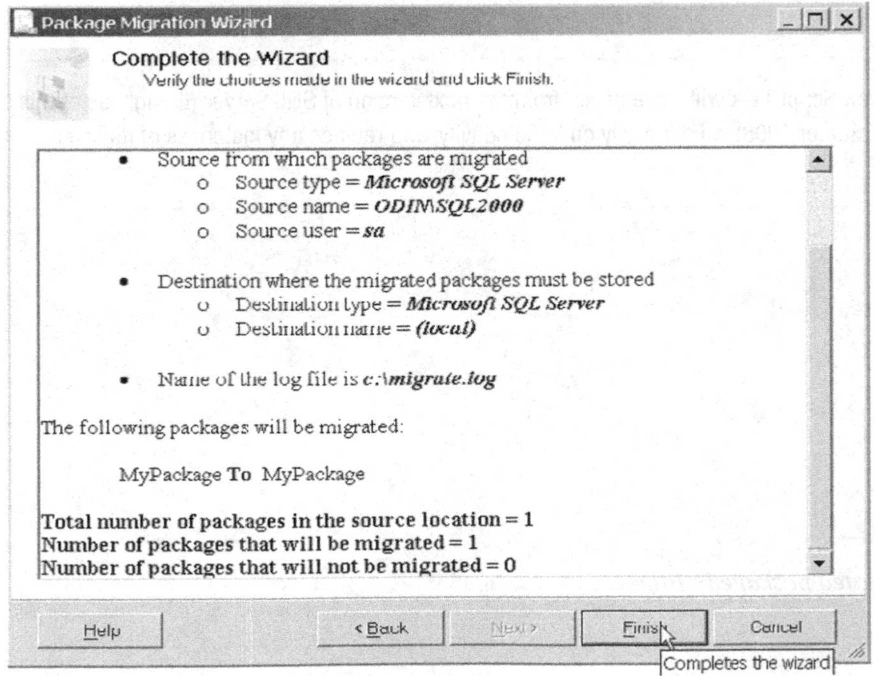

Figure 3-13. *Take a deep breath and click Finish.*

There aren't too many options to choose, so I'm in a position to click Finish and let the Migration Tool do its work. Figure 3-14 shows that the migration is successful.

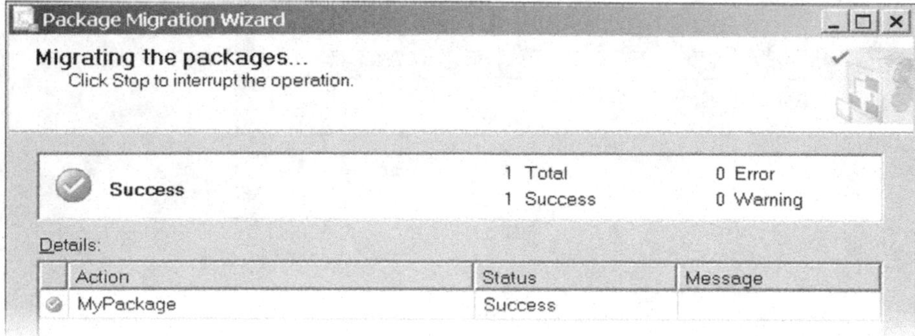

Figure 3-14. *Success*

As I stated previously, the Package Migration Wizard doesn't migrate every DTS package entirely successfully. My simple example is okay (see Figure 3-15) but if you have followed the Upgrade Advisor advice from earlier in this chapter, you've minimized the chances of a problem appearing. Having read this chapter, you're in a position to know which "unresolvable problems" (by this I mean unresolvable by the Package Migration Wizard) still exist even before you run the wizard—and why the problem has occurred—which means you are in a strong position to rewrite the task using SSIS when you have the opportunity.

■ **Warning** The ActiveX Script Task will be removed from the next version of SQL Server (though, as of this writing, it is still in SQL Server 2008), so don't rely on it too heavily, and replace any instances of its use at your convenience.

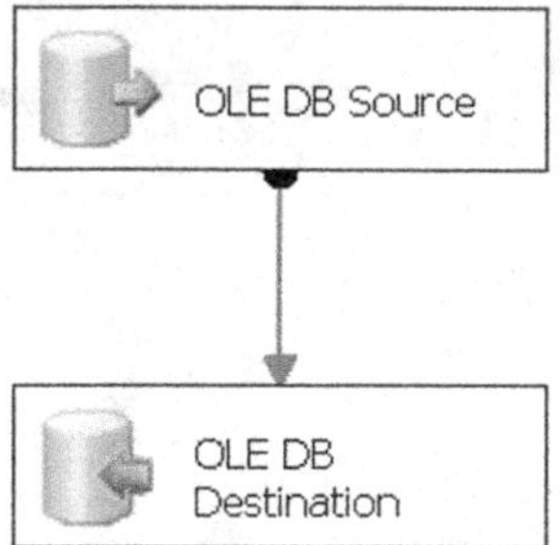

Figure 3-15. *The migrated package in BIDS*

Summary

It would be impossible to cover every potential issue you might encounter in migrating from DTS to SSIS. For this reason I've based the information in this chapter on the migration work I've done in the past few years, and I've avoided trying to provide specifics for every migration contingency. I've tried to cover everything that Microsoft considers to cause DTS-to-SSIS migration problems, and a few more things that I've discovered along the way.

Should you migrate your DTS packages? SQL Server 2005 handles legacy DTS constructions adequately enough that the more casual user can make do with calling DTS packages from within SSIS (or SQL Server 2005). The decision probably comes down to cost: it's cheaper in the short term to leave your DTS packages alone, but it could cost much more in the longer term, when drawbacks such as transactional costs and the cost of legacy knowledge skills are considered. Which route you take depends on your priorities.

The ideal solution to the migration question, in a world of limitless project funding at least, is to rewrite your DTS packages using SSIS. This way you get the best of all worlds—much better knowledge of SSIS and faster, more scalable packages.

CHAPTER 4

The IDE and Extending Visual Studio

A book on SSIS would be incomplete without a tour around the IDE provided with SQL Server 2005 for the development of BI projects. Microsoft has tied together the three non–database engine products that ship with SQL Server—SSIS, SSAS, and SQL Server Reporting Services (SSRS)—and provided a Visual Studio "lite" instance for developing projects for them: BIDS

BIDS illustrates how the concept of reuse at Microsoft goes well beyond programming and extends to development environments. The integration of Visual Studio into SQL Server as a development platform is not just welcome; it's a joy. Microsoft's common-IDE strategy opens a number of previously locked doors and makes switching from development in one language to another, and one from one Microsoft technology to another, a smooth experience.

This chapter is for two kinds of readers. Those of you approaching the subject of SSIS from the development discipline will already be familiar with the latest iteration of Visual Studio. For you the chapter is about how the IDE has been extended for developing SSIS solutions. For the more DBA-centric individual who has probably never seen or used Visual Studio, this chapter provides an introduction to this shiny and easy-to-use environment. The reality of working with SSIS will eventually require even DBAs to use the full Visual Studio as part of a SSIS development team. But even if you only ever use BIDS, the chapter is entirely relevant. All of the features of Visual Studio 2005 are available to the SSIS developer; BIDS users just can't write or open other project types.

A First Look at BIDS

As you can see from Figure 4-1, BIDS is made up of a number of panels in addition to the usual menu bar and row of icons. Hidden away to the side are a few pullout tabs that contain items such as servers and controls.

I'll examine the purpose and function of each part of the IDE, starting with a look at how project structure is handled in Visual Studio 2005. I won't explain each and every menu function and may even brush over the more important ones for now. I'm doing this to give some context to the functions the IDE exposes, rather than effectively identify each part as a standalone feature.

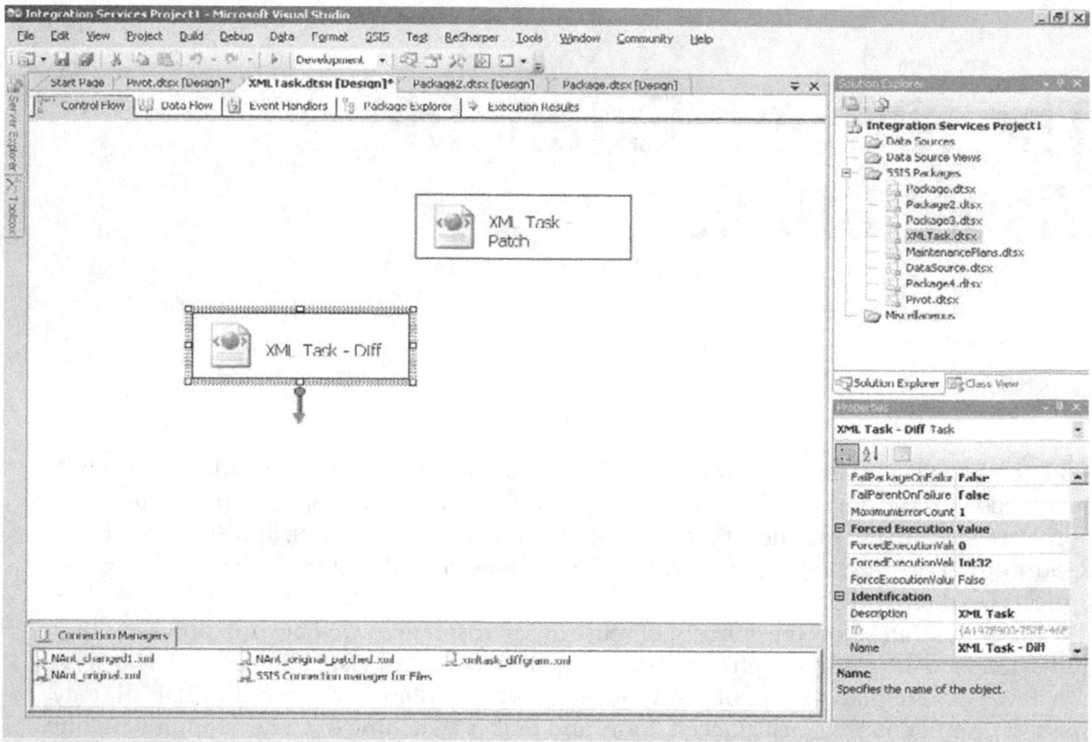

Figure 4-1. *This is BIDS.*

Projects and Solutions

Project structure in Visual Studio 2005 isn't a particularly complex topic, but it's easy to miss a feature or two when coming to the IDE for the first time.

A *solution*, in the Visual Studio context, groups together projects—be they class libraries or BizTalk orchestrations or Windows Forms applications—that bear some relation to one another. The relation might be that they are in the same logical layer, or even that they contain everything that solves a business problem.

In previous iterations of Visual Studio it was possible to have a project open without having a solution. This meant that it wasn't immediately obvious to developers that multiple projects could be open at once as part of a single Visual Studio instance. Visual Studio 2005 implements a solution-based structure by default, so although you can open a project without a solution, Visual Studio attempts to use solutions where possible.

It is quite unusual, architecturally, to use a single project in the fulfillment of a business requirement. Usually—certainly in Windows development, systems integration, and many other applications (or service-oriented solutions)—you deal with multiple components and tiers interacting with one another. In Visual Studio, the logical and favored approach is to keep these multiple projects as part of a single Visual Studio solution. In a Service Oriented Architecture (SOA) project, multiple solutions are used for each of the services being offered.

When using multiple projects, you need to start considering dependencies, build order, reference paths and other requirements generally connected to the sequential compilation of individual projects within a solution.

Solution Explorer

The Solution Explorer window is usually (and by default) docked on the right side of the IDE. It shows the solution and project structure in its entirety. On the most obvious level it provides a single location to view and edit files contained in the current solution. It also allows you to access the properties for each of the files (as project items) and manipulate them.

Figure 4-2 shows a solution called `myFirstSSISProject`, consisting of a single project. Figure 4-3 shows the Solution Explorer with multiple projects added. You can see I have created a solution called `ApressBook.Chapter4`, which I've set up as *test-driven* development. The test-driven approach to development is often used as part of an overall project management/ development paradigm known as *agile methodology*. Supporters of the agile approach will be pleased to learn that SSIS projects can easily be developed in the same manner. This topic is becoming more relevant as the various agile methodologies profuse throughout Windows software development.

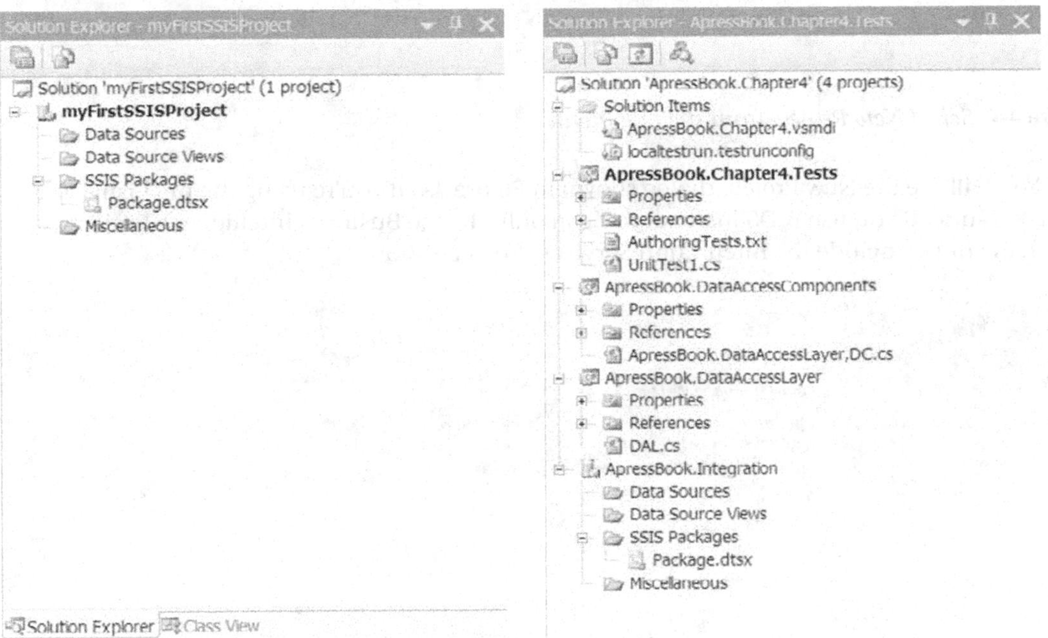

Figure 4-2. *The BIDS Solution Explorer*

Figure 4-3. *Solution Explorer with multiple projects added*

Before you can get to this stage, however, you need to know how to create projects and add projects to solutions.

Creating and Saving a Project

You can create a new Visual Studio project from the File ➤ New ➤ Project menu option, as shown in Figure 4-4.

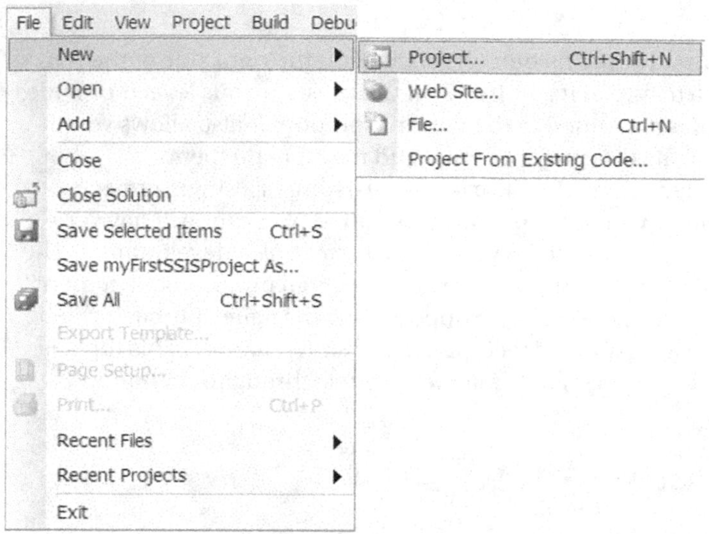

Figure 4-4. *Select New Project from the File menu.*

You will see the New Project dialog shown in Figure 4-5 if you're using the full Visual Studio 2005 suite. If you use BIDS instead, you can only choose Business Intelligence Projects, which of course include the Integration Services Project option.

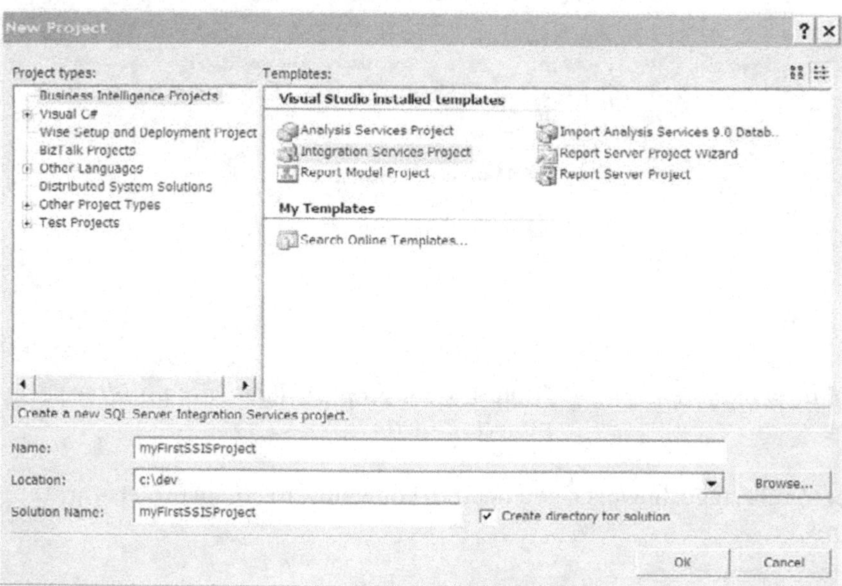

Figure 4-5. *Choose your project type in the New Project dialog (Visual Studio 2005).*

Alternatively, if you want to add a new (or existing) project to your solution, you can choose the File ➤ Add ➤ New/Existing Project menu option.

Populating a Solution

To create a solution containing different project types,

1. Select File ➤ New ➤ Project and from the New Project dialog and select Integration Services Project.

   At the beginning with a new SSIS project, you're presented with the familiar SSIS Control Flow design surface for the package (added by default as part of this project type template). The project is been placed inside a solution automatically, and you can see it in the Solution Explorer.

2. Right-click on the solution in the Solution Explorer. Select Add ➤ New Project, as shown in Figure 4-6.

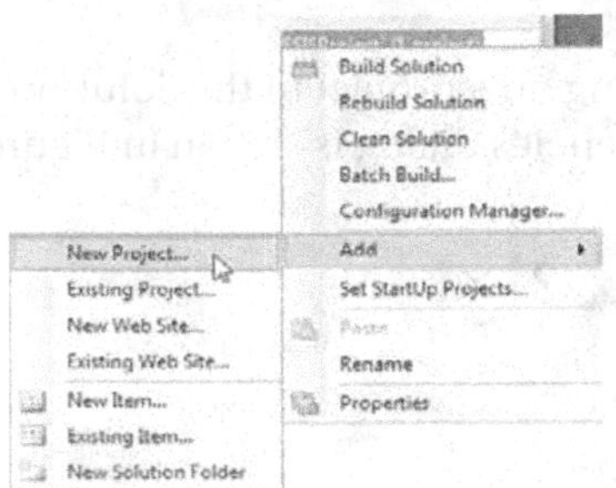

Figure 4-6. *Adding a new project to a solution*

3. Choose the project type you wish to add to your solution (see Figure 4-7).

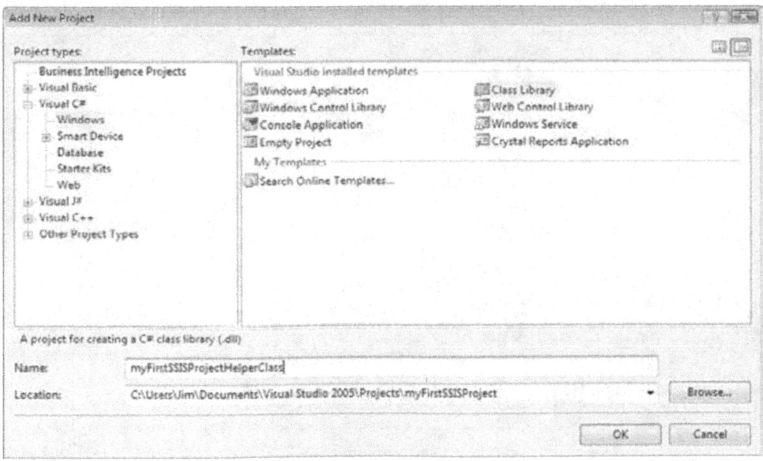

Figure 4-7. *Choosing a project type*

In this case I've chosen to add a C# Class Library as a helper in supporting my SSIS package.

4. Add other projects until you have a solution containing all of the different types of projects you anticipate needing (or add them later as necessary).

   Save your solution using either File ➤ Save or the icons shown in Figure 4-8.

Figure 4-8. *Tiny disks (how cute!)*

Clicking on the single-disk icon saves the file currently being edited, whereas clicking on the multiple-disk icon provides a full project/solution save.

Project Dependencies and Build Order

Once you have multiple projects in your solution with dependencies in place among them, Visual Studio takes care of the build order to ensure your projects are ready to be referenced by one another for compilation.

You can, however, alter the build order by right-clicking on a project in the Solution Explorer and selecting Build Order.... The Project Dependencies dialog is shown in Figure 4-9.

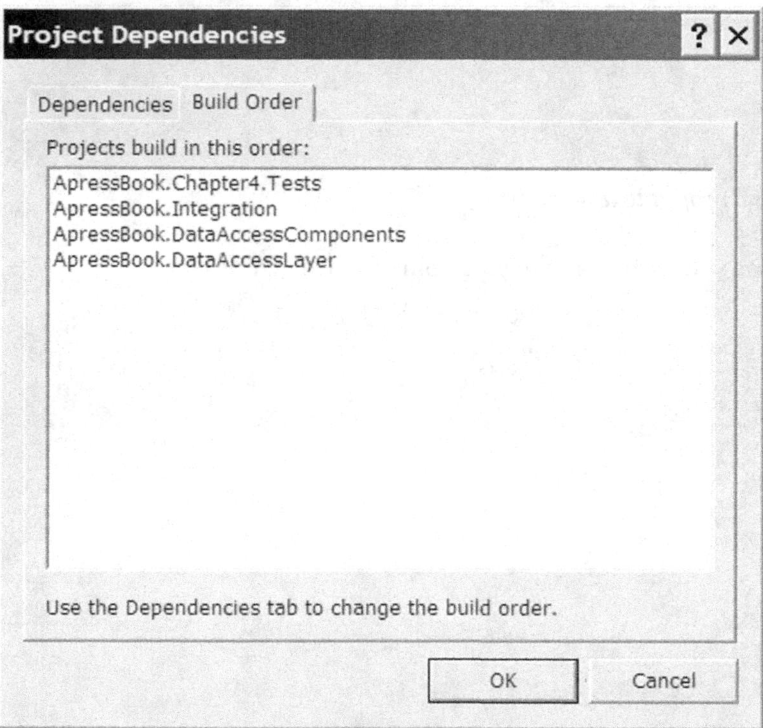

Figure 4-9. *Viewing and changing project dependencies and build order*

One thing worth remembering when you have multiple projects in a single solution is the build location of *assemblies*. An assembly is essentially a compiled version of the code, such as a `.exe` or `.dll` file. This isn't a consideration when it comes to BIDS and SSIS because the compilation destination is always SQL Server. When it comes to .NET assemblies, however, you can specify a build location, which by default is in a `/bin` directory under the project directory. This becomes relevant in projects where SSIS is not the only technology in use.

Sometimes an inexperienced project lead will stipulate a common build directory for your solutions. The requirement to have all compiled assemblies in one place isn't necessarily the problem; it's making Visual Studio try to compile your solution projects into the same directory. This can cause problems with compilation of assemblies that, as part of a project reference, are still in use when one of the subsequent assemblies is compiled. To avoid this issue and to fulfill the requirement of having all compiled assemblies in the same directory, you can specify a post-build event that copies the compiled DLL to a specified location. In this way no handles are left open during the compilation task.

At any point during the development of your SSIS project you can add a new and entirely separate SSIS package, as illustrated in Figure 4-10.

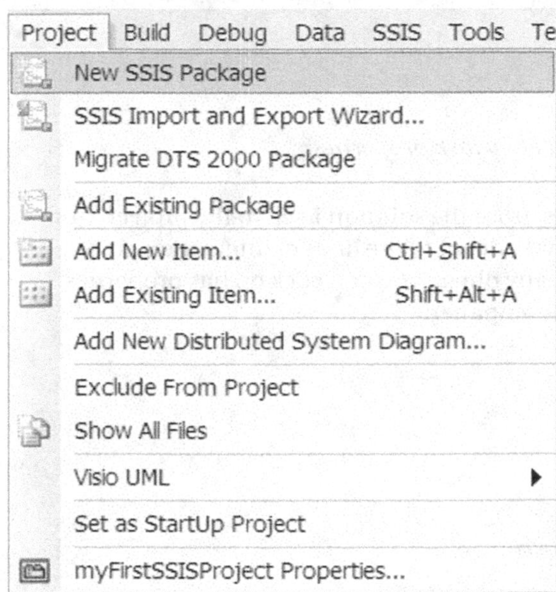

Figure 4-10. *Adding a new SSIS package to your project*

As a new part of your SSIS project, the contents and settings of the new package are entirely separate from any existing packages you might have.

Properties Explorer

Pretty much any object in the Microsoft development universe has a series of configurable attributes or properties that expose the object's inner values. At the object level these really are just public properties contained within the code of the object. Altering a property value through the use of the Properties explorer changes the object's behavior or look at either design time or runtime. Figure 4-11 shows the Properties explorer.

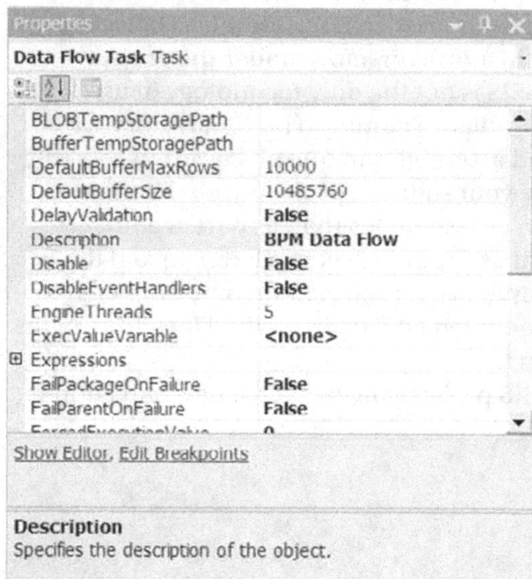

Figure 4-11. *The Properties window showing Data Flow task properties*

All levels of an SSIS solution have properties, from the solution itself to the project, from project items to individual components, all the way down to the lines of interaction among components (see Figure 4-12). Chances are that any object you can click on has properties, and they will be displayed in the Properties explorer pane.

Figure 4-12. *Most if not all project items have properties.*

The project itself has a number of properties. These properties pertain to the immediate project, to build settings, and to deployment settings (see Figure 4-13).

BIDS includes fewer project properties than you get with Visual Studio for some of the other project types. I'll take another look at these properties in Chapter 14, to discuss the impact they have on the running and debugging of your projects.

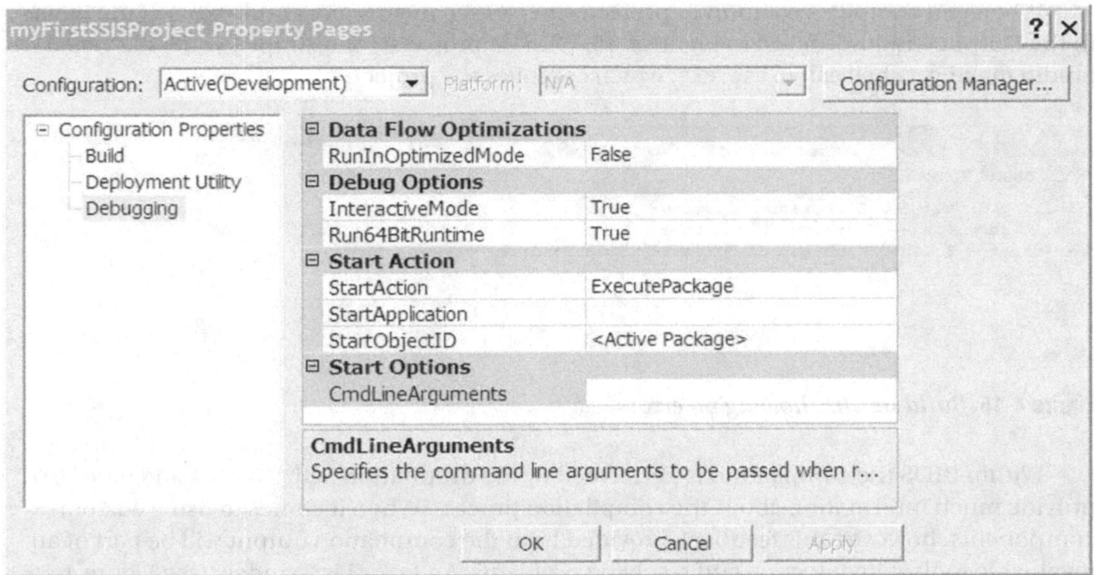

Figure 4-13. *Project properties, including build, deployment, and debugging*

Compilation, Running, and Debugging

For integration enthusiasts, the requirement to compile your packages or projects will be a new one. It need not be a stumbling block to anyone, since it's an entirely transparent process when you click the Run button. However it is useful—especially in multidiscipline integration projects—to take your skills further and know about compilation and compilation settings. Consider also that you may at some point get involved with agile development and possibly Team Foundation Server. It's always good to have more information than you need right now so you can disseminate your knowledge to your peers later on. Figure 4-14 shows how to compile a solution from the Build menu option.

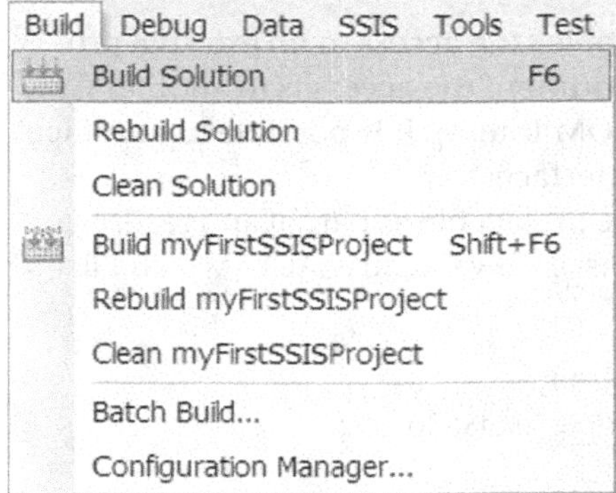

Figure 4-14. *You need to compile your packages or projects.*

When you compile a solution or project, you can see the progress and status of the build in the Output window, shown in Figure 4-15. With C# projects, for example, you'll see Visual Studio making a shell call to `Csc.exe`, which compiles the project.

```
Output
Show output from: Build
Build started: SQL Integration Services project: Incremental ...
Build complete -- 0 errors, 0 warnings
========== Build: 0 succeeded, 0 failed, 1 up-to-date, 0 skipped ==========
```

Figure 4-15. *Build results showing no errors*

Within BIDS the compilation is performed by the destination SQL Server—and it doesn't provide much information about the compilation process. When it comes to using custom components, however, this feedback provided from the compilation output will be part of an invaluable toolset in detecting and resolving problems. An Error List window (see Figure 4-16) is also available that contains errors, warnings, or message information.

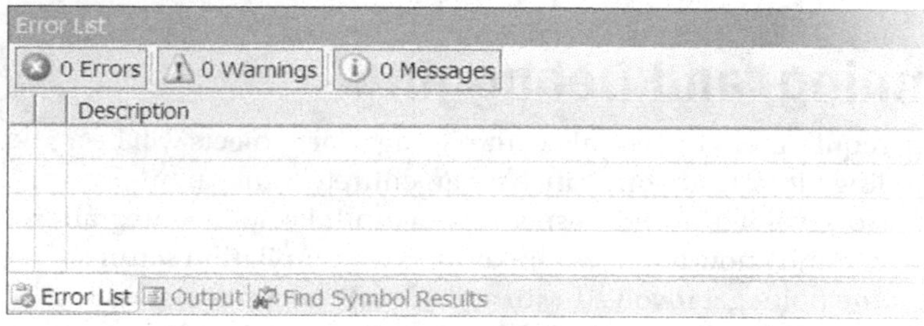

Figure 4-16. *The Error List shows errors, warnings, and messages.*

References

References are the encapsulation of a mechanism that enables the access to an external project's functionality and contents. Typically in a .NET environment the access is to another CLR object such as a class library, though through the use of COM Interop it is possible to interface with legacy objects that implement the necessary COM interfaces.

The reference declaration exists as metadata within the project file as part of an `ItemGroup`. This is how a reference to a component held in the Global Assembly Cache (GAC)—which I'll talk about in the next section—looks as metadata:

```
<Reference Include="Microsoft.SqlServer.DTSPipelineWrap,
Version=9.0.242.0, Culture=neutral, PublicKeyToken=89845dcd8080cc91,
processorArchitecture=MSIL" />
```

Notice that because this is a reference to a component held in the GAC, no value is held for the location of the file. Enough information is included to identify the reference subject uniquely and correctly within the GAC.

Adding references to a project is as easy as choosing Add Reference... from the Project menu (see Figure 4-17) or by right-clicking on the project and selecting Add Reference... (see Figure 4-18).

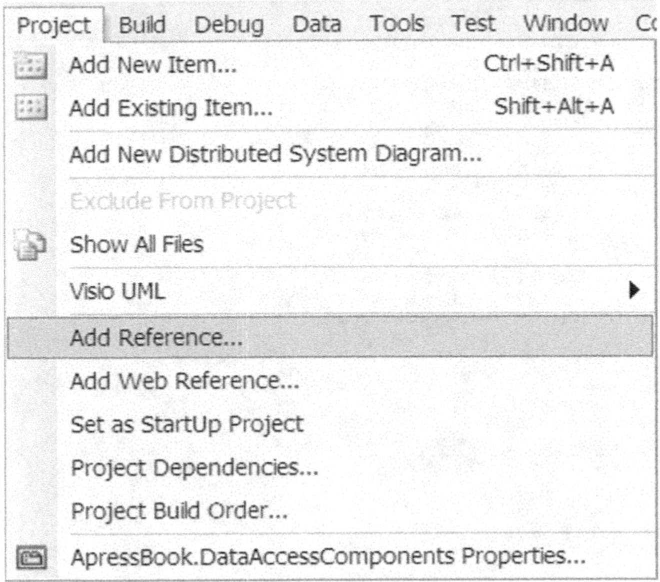

Figure 4-17. *Adding a reference from the Project menu*

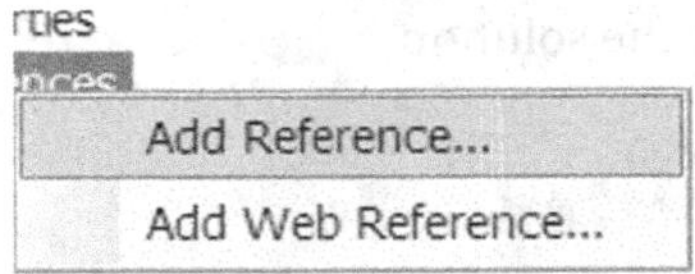

Figure 4-18. *Adding a reference in the Solution Explorer*

Four types of references are of interest: project references, file-based references, .NET references, and web references. Ultimately they all achieve the same goal—providing access to an external resource—but how they are implemented is subtly different.

.NET Reference

Adding a .NET reference is as simple as choosing an item (or items) from the .NET tab and clicking OK (see Figure 4-19). For an assembly to appear in this list, it must be in the Global Assembly Cache (GAC), and a copy should exist in the .NET Framework folder: `%WINDIR%\Microsoft.NET\Framework\<latest 2.x.x.x version>`. Copy it in there if it doesn't already exist.

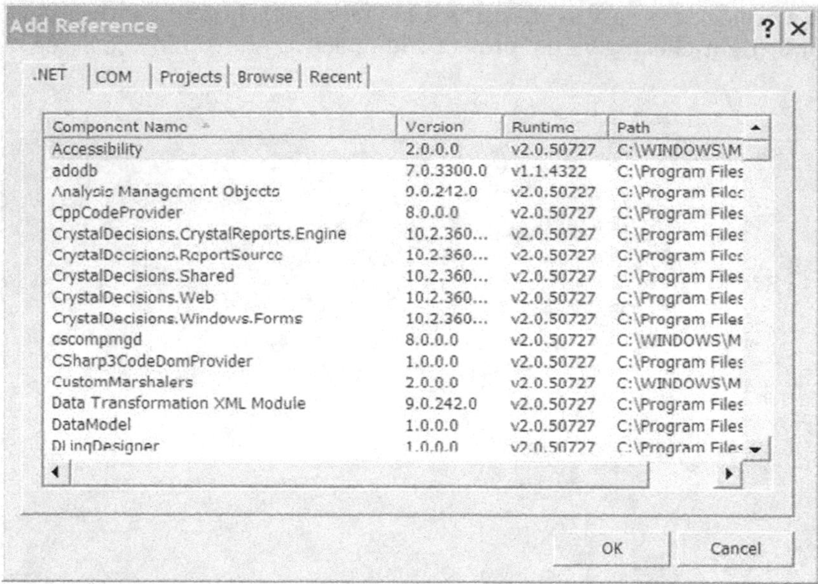

Figure 4-19. *Adding a .NET reference*

Project-Based Reference

The beauty of a project reference is that it refers to a project that is part of the same solution. This way, when a solution is compiled the reference is automatically updated as part of the build. This is very useful when you build and test a solution! Figure 4-20 shows how to select the Projects tab to choose a reference from a project that is part of the solution.

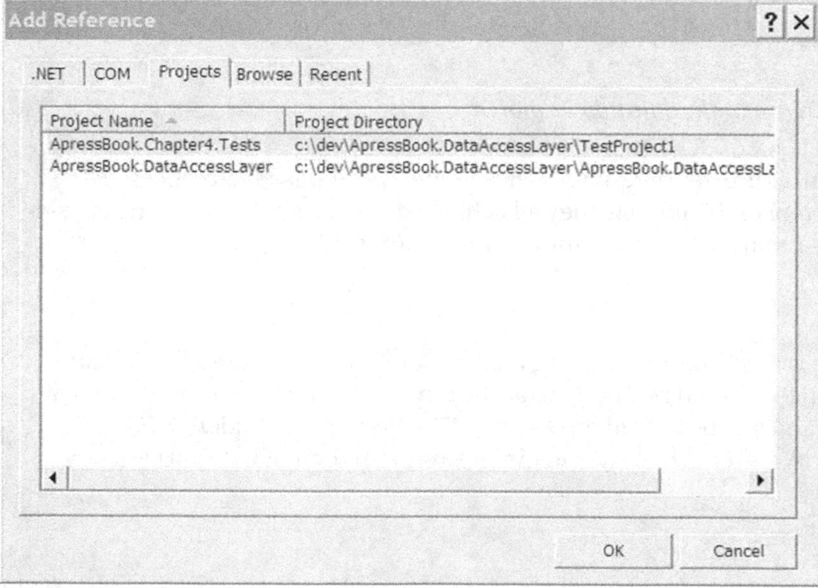

Figure 4-20. *Adding a project reference*

File-Based Reference

A file reference is a standard way of referencing an external assembly in cases where the reference subject is already compiled, isn't part of the GAC, and doesn't change. Examples include a third-party assembly or a previously built class library. Figure 4-21 shows that by using the Browse tab you can navigate to a DLL and select it as a reference.

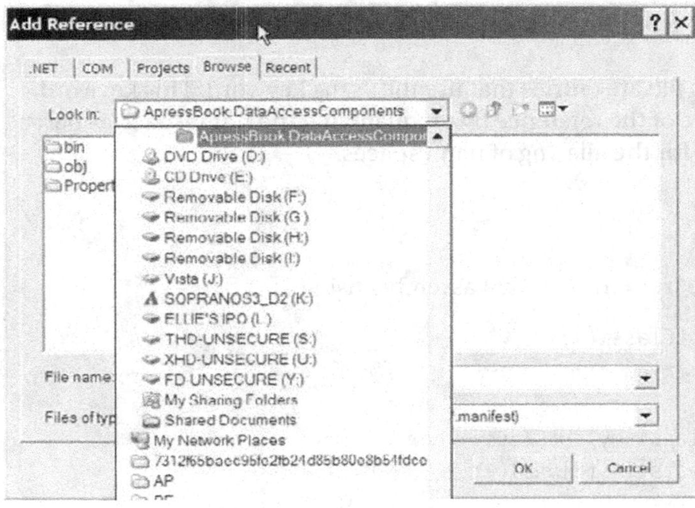

Figure 4-21. *Adding a file-based reference*

Web Reference

To consume a web service, a special kind of reference—a web reference—is required. From the Project menu, select Add Web Reference... to bring up the Add Web Reference screen, shown in Figure 4-22.

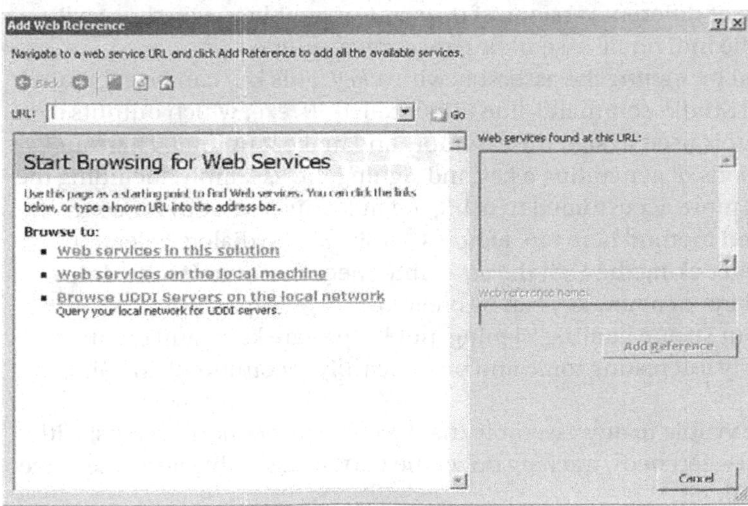

Figure 4-22. *Looking for web services to consume*

You enter the URL for the web service and, after connection to verify the available services, click OK to store the reference details in the project file.

Chapter 14 looks at web references in greater depth, including issues associated with using a web proxy.

Using a Reference in Code

Once a reference has been added to a project, the code to access its public properties and methods is intuitive.

At the very beginning of a class file are entries that use the `using` keyword. This keyword, similarly used in C++, allows the use of the reference by prequalifying the namespace as part of the `using` directive. It also allows for the aliasing of namespaces.

For example:

```
Using ApressBook.Chapter4.Tests;
```

means I can create a class reference from the external assembly using

```
TestClass1 myTestClass = new TestClass1();
```

instead of

```
ApressBook.Chapter4.Tests.TestClass1 myTestClass = new
        ApressBook.Chapter4.Tests.TestClass1();
```

Once the object reference has been created, it's then a simple matter of using the new variable to access public properties or call public methods:

```
Bool successStatus = myTestClass.Test1();
```

The GAC

The GAC is a special repository for storing and serving up assemblies for consumption. It allows the creation and storage of different versions of the same assembly—even those with the same filename—because the individual assemblies are *strongly named*.

A strong name is generated by *signing* the assembly with a *key*. This key can be generated manually by the use of a Visual Studio command-line utility called `SN.exe`, which outputs a `.snk` (Strong Name Key) file that is used to sign the assembly and make it unique. There are alternative—and easier—methods of generating a key and signing the assembly, including the Solution Properties dialog. I'm more accustomed to using the first approach, but for completeness I will detail the second method here too. Figure 4-23 shows the dialog. Selecting Signing on the left side and then ticking the Sign the assembly check box enables the drop-down list from which existing keys or a new key can be created.

There is much to read about strong naming, signing, public/private keys, and cryptography in general. It is an incredibly interesting topic and one I heartily recommend knowing more about.

Assemblies in the GAC are visible to any assembly that has the correct permissions; with non-strongly named file-based references, tracking down the correct assembly and guaranteeing the version can be more difficult.

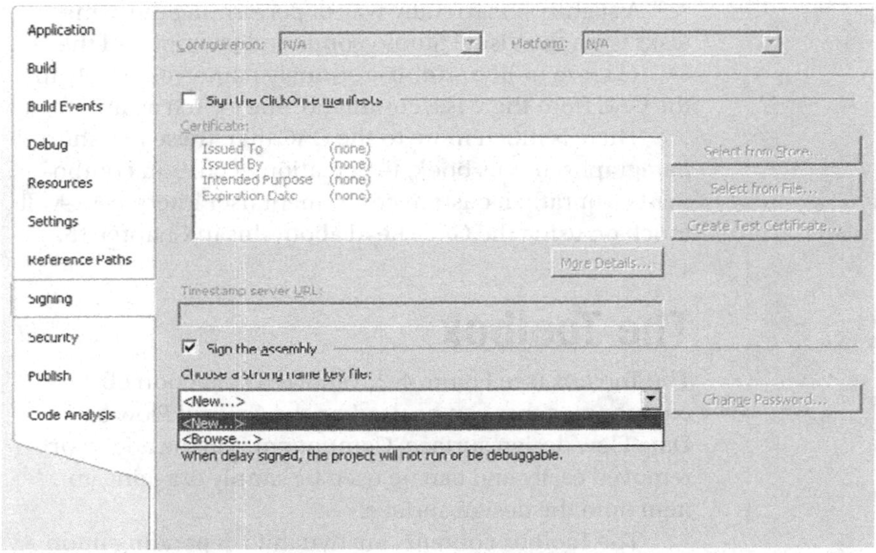

Figure 4-23. *Signing an assembly by specifying the creation of a new key*

The simplest way of viewing and managing the GAC's contents is to use the .NET configuration tool, hidden away under Administrative Tools in the Control Panel. It's called Microsoft .NET Framework 2.0 Configuration. Among other capabilities, it can list and manage items stored in the GAC, as shown in Figure 4-24.

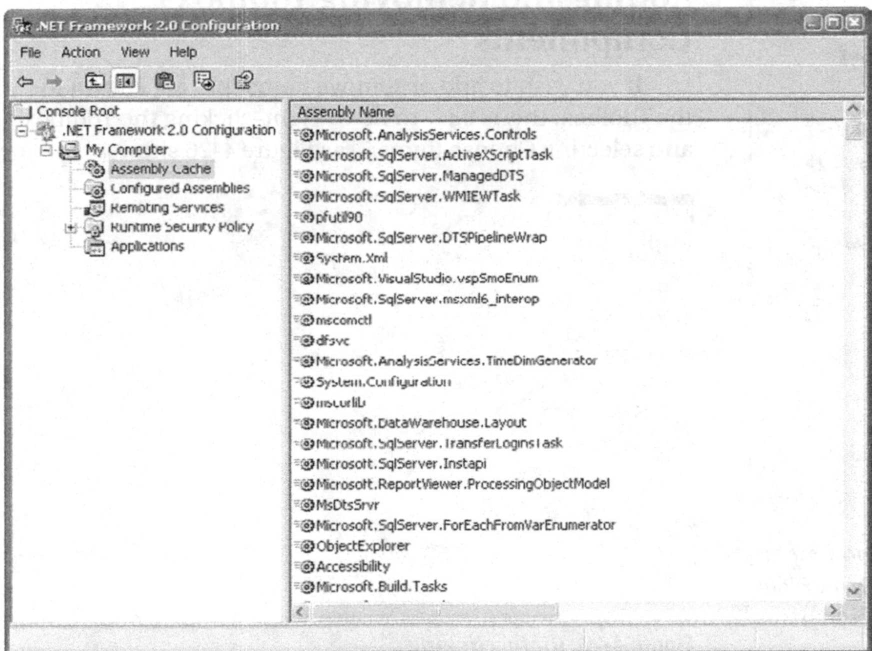

Figure 4-24. *The Microsoft .NET Framework 2.0 Configuration tool*

Figure 4-25. *The component Toolbox for both Control Flow and Data Flow components*

A slightly less friendly way of performing the same tasks is via the Visual Studio command prompt and the `GACUtil.exe` utility. Adding a strongly named assembly to the GAC from there is a command-line switch away!

There is much more to the GAC than these few short paragraphs. In this book, the creation of custom components—or rather, custom component user interfaces—will touch on using the GAC. Read about this in Chapter 15.

The Toolbox

The Toolbox (see Figure 4-25) shows a collection of components that can be used on the Control Flow or Data Flow design surface. Components can be added or removed easily and can be used by simply dragging an item onto the design surface.

The Toolbox contents are dynamic depending upon the subject of the main window in Visual Studio. The Toolbox shows Control Flow components when the Control Flow design surface is active and Data Flow components when the Data Flow design surface is active. You are not shown inappropriate components, which makes using the Toolbox simpler and easier.

Adding and Removing Toolbox Components

If you wish to add or remove items that are shown in the Toolbox, this is easy to do by right-clicking the Toolbox and selecting Choose Items..., as Figure 4-26 shows.

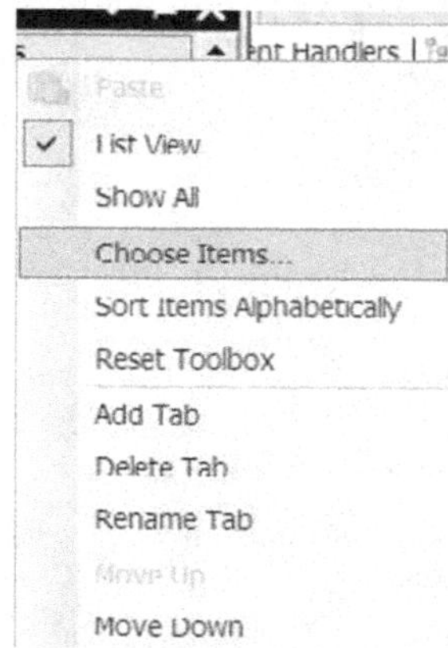

Figure 4-26. *Right-clicking on the Toolbox allows you to add items.*

To change the contents of the Toolbox, select the items you want from the Choose Toolbox Items dialog, shown in Figure 4-27.

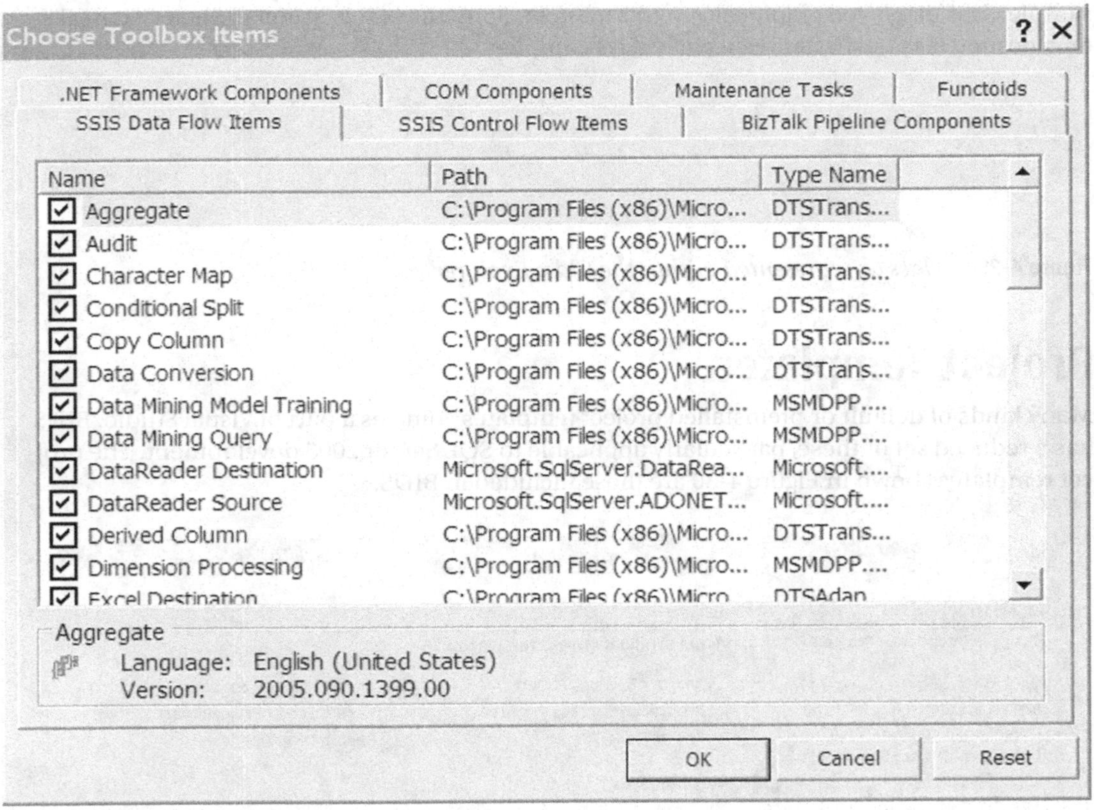

Choose Toolbox Items

.NET Framework Components | COM Components | Maintenance Tasks | Functoids
SSIS Data Flow Items | SSIS Control Flow Items | BizTalk Pipeline Components

Name	Path	Type Name
☑ Aggregate	C:\Program Files (x86)\Micro...	DTSTrans...
☑ Audit	C:\Program Files (x86)\Micro...	DTSTrans...
☑ Character Map	C:\Program Files (x86)\Micro...	DTSTrans...
☑ Conditional Split	C:\Program Files (x86)\Micro...	DTSTrans...
☑ Copy Column	C:\Program Files (x86)\Micro...	DTSTrans...
☑ Data Conversion	C:\Program Files (x86)\Micro...	DTSTrans...
☑ Data Mining Model Training	C:\Program Files (x86)\Micro...	MSMDPP....
☑ Data Mining Query	C:\Program Files (x86)\Micro...	MSMDPP....
☑ DataReader Destination	Microsoft.SqlServer.DataRea...	Microsoft....
☑ DataReader Source	Microsoft.SqlServer.ADONET...	Microsoft....
☑ Derived Column	C:\Program Files (x86)\Micro...	DTSTrans...
☑ Dimension Processing	C:\Program Files (x86)\Micro...	MSMDPP....
☑ Excel Destination	C:\Program Files (x86)\Micro	DTSAdap

Aggregate
Language: English (United States)
Version: 2005.090.1399.00

OK | Cancel | Reset

Figure 4-27. *Choose additional SSIS components from here.*

Class Explorer

Though not applicable to BIDS, the Class Explorer in the full Visual Studio can be incredibly useful for developing object-oriented components for your projects. It is a little hidden away in the IDE. Figure 4-28 shows what the Class Explorer looks like.

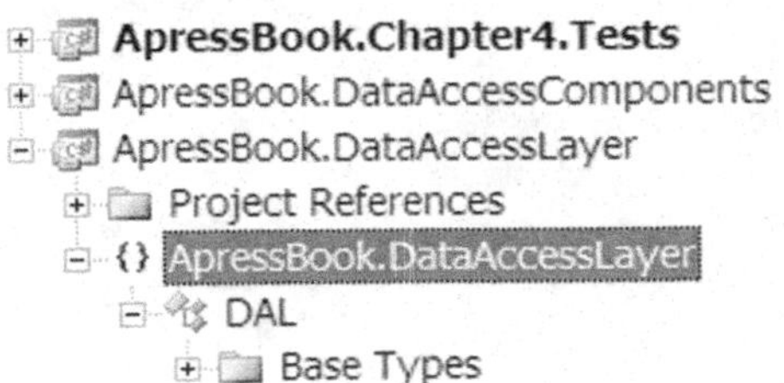

Figure 4-28. *Another tree view, this time for your classes*

Choosing the Class tab instead of the Solution tab on the Solution pane lets you explore code and projects from a different perspective, showing the classes instead of the files. A class diagram can also be created that represents the classes in the project. Figure 4-29 shows a sample class displayed graphically in this manner. Sometimes it is useful to get a visual take on a desired class structure, especially if it's complex.

Figure 4-29. *A class as represented within the Class Explorer*

Project Templates

Many kinds of default or preinstalled project templates come as a part of Visual Studio. BIDS has a reduced set of these, particularly applicable to SQL Server 2005 development. The project templates shown in Figure 4-30 are those included in BIDS.

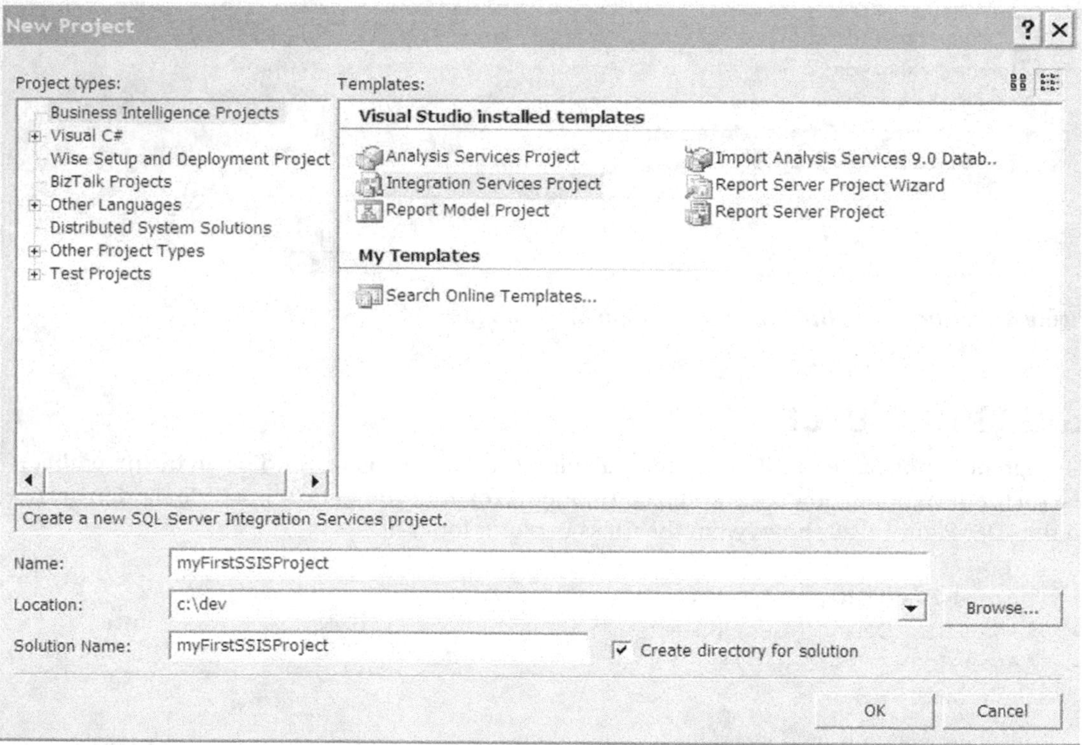

Figure 4-30. *BIDS project templates*

It is possible to create custom templates, as I have done many times on various projects. The most useful ones as relevant to SSIS are for custom Control Flow components and custom Data Flow components. You can download them from my site (http://www.ifoo.org).

In essence, a project template is an empty project that contains the minimum information required to create and build a project of the specified type. Within my SSIS Custom Component template, for example, the contents of the .vstemplate file includes

```
<VSTemplate Type="Project" Version="2.0.0"
    xmlns="http://schemas.microsoft.com/developer/vstemplate/2005">
    <TemplateData>
        <Name>SQL Server 2005 SSIS Data Flow Custom Component</Name>
          <Description>This is a template for creating a Data FlowCustom Component
for
          SSIS in C# without User Interface</Description>
          <Icon>TemplateIcon.ico</Icon>
          <ProjectType>CSharp</ProjectType>
    </TemplateData>
    <TemplateContent>
          <Project ReplaceParameters="true" File="SQL Server 2005 SSIS Custom
            Component.csproj" TargetFileName="$projectname$.dll">
            <ProjectItem ReplaceParameters="true">
              SSIS Custom Component.cs
            <ProjectItem>
            <ProjectItem ReplaceParameters="true">Licence.txt<ProjectItem>
            <ProjectItem>properties\assembly.info<ProjectItem>
          </project>
    </TemplateContent>
</VSTemplate>
```

The file holds information for which files to include (a minimal .cs file I've created) and special values enclosed in $ symbols. These are dynamic values that are replaced when an instance of the project type is created in Visual Studio.

The SSIS Menu

The SSIS menu becomes visible only when an SSIS-related page, such as one of the SSIS design surfaces, is showing in the main window. The SSIS menu offers options for logging, package configuration, digital signing, variables, working offline, event logging, and new connections.

Logging

As with most Microsoft technologies, it is possible to log events as they happen. In the case of SSIS, the logging is performed within an executing package (or packages). When you click the Logging menu option, a new window (see Figure 4-31) appears that lets you select the location of logging output and event types to log.

Providers and Logs | Details

Add a new log

Provider type: SSIS log provider for Text files | Add...

Select the logs to use for the container:

Name	Description	Configuration

Delete

Figure 4-31. *The screen to configure logging*

Logging can be enabled on a per-container basis, or the whole package can be selected. You configure this on the left side of the window under the Containers heading.

Information needs to be provided for the log-provider type. In Figure 4-30 I've gone for the SSIS log provider for Text files, which can itself be configured to define specifics such as file location.

Figure 4-32 shows how I've chosen an existing log connection.

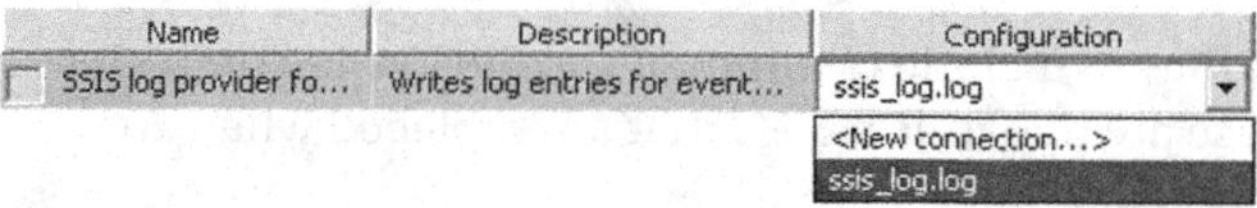

Figure 4-32. *Configuring a new log*

A number of different log providers are available, as shown in Figure 4-33; each can be configured through this interface.

SSIS log provider for Text files

SSIS log provider for Text files
SSIS log provider for SQL Profiler
SSIS log provider for SQL Server
SSIS log provider for Windows Event Log
SSIS log provider for XML files

Figure 4-33. *The different log providers available by default*

The details tab in Figure 4-34 is where the loggable events are shown and chosen. In addition, information that goes along with each event can be specified. Different containers and components expose a different number and different types of events.

☐ Events	☐ Comp...	☐ Operator	☐ SourceName	☐ SourceID	☐ ExecutionID	☐ MessageText	☐ DataBytes
☐ OnError	☐	☐	☐	☐	☐	☐	☐
☐ OnExecStatusChanged	☐	☐	☐	☐	☐	☐	☐
☐ OnInformation	☐	☐	☐	☐	☐	☐	☐
☐ OnPostExecute	☐	☐	☐	☐	☐	☐	☐
☐ OnPostValidate	☐	☐	☐	☐	☐	☐	☐
☐ OnPreExecute	☐	☐	☐	☐	☐	☐	☐
☐ OnPreValidate	☐	☐	☐	☐	☐	☐	☐
☐ OnProgress	☐	☐	☐	☐	☐	☐	☐
☐ OnQueryCancel	☐	☐	☐	☐	☐	☐	☐
☐ OnTaskFailed	☐	☐	☐	☐	☐	☐	☐
☐ OnVariableValueChanged	☐	☐	☐	☐	☐	☐	☐
☐ OnWarning	☐	☐	☐	☐	☐	☐	☐
☐ Diagnostic	☐	☐	☐	☐	☐	☐	☐

Figure 4-34. *Events exposed by the Flat File Source component*

It is easy to pick which events are of particular interest by selecting them individually or—should all events be required—a single click on the header row check box selects all. You can do the same with the individual event items within each event type. Figure 4-35 shows how the output of logged events appears in the Log Events window. This is visible at design time after the package has executed. It is easy to see that even the simplest of packages can generate a large number of events, depending on the logging configuration.

Log Events

Name	C	O.	S..	S..	E...	Message	Start Time	End Time
OnPreValidate	C..	C...	P...	{...	{9...		6/6/2007 ...	6/6/20...
OnPreValidate	C..	C...	D...	{...	{9...		6/6/2007 ...	6/6/20...
OnInformation	C..	C...	D...	{...	{9...	Validation phase is beginning....	6/6/2007 ...	6/6/20...
OnProgress	C..	C...	D...	{...	{9...	Validating	6/6/2007 ...	6/6/20...
OnProgress	C..	C...	D...	{...	{9...	Validating	6/6/2007 ...	6/6/20...
OnProgress	C..	C...	D...	{...	{9...	Validating	6/6/2007 ...	6/6/20...
OnPostValidate	C..	C...	D...	{...	{9...		6/6/2007 ...	6/6/20...
OnPostValidate	C..	C...	P...	{...	{9...		6/6/2007 ...	6/6/20...
PackageStart	C..	C...	P...	{...	{9...	Beginning of package executio...	6/6/2007 ...	6/6/20...
Diagnostic	C..	C...	P...	{...	{9...	Based on the system configura...	6/6/2007 ...	6/6/20...
OnPreExecute	C..	C...	P...	{...	{9...		6/6/2007 ...	6/6/20...
OnPreExecute	C..	C...	D...	{...	{9...		6/6/2007 ...	6/6/20...
OnPreValidate	C..	C...	D...	{...	{9...		6/6/2007 ...	6/6/20...
OnInformation	C..	C...	D...	{...	{9...	Validation phase is beginning....	6/6/2007 ...	6/6/20...
OnInformation	C..	C...	P...	{...	{9...	Validation phase is beginning....	6/6/2007 ...	6/6/20...
OnProgress	C..	C...	D...	{...	{9...	Validating	6/6/2007 ...	6/6/20...
OnProgress	C..	C...	D...	{...	{9...	Validating	6/6/2007 ...	6/6/20...
OnProgress	C..	C...	D...	{...	{9...	Validating	6/6/2007 ...	6/6/20...
OnPostValidate	C..	C...	D...	{...	{9...		6/6/2007 ...	6/6/20...
User:PipelineExecutionTrees	C..	C...	D...	{...	{9...	begin execution tree 0□□ o...	6/6/2007 ...	6/6/20...
User:PipelineExecutionPlan	C..	C...	D...	{...	{9...	SourceThread0□□ Drives: 1 ...	6/6/2007 ...	6/6/20...
OnInformation	C..	C...	D...	{...	{9...	Prepare for Execute phase is b...	6/6/2007 ...	6/6/20...
OnInformation	C..	C...	P...	{...	{9...	Prepare for Execute phase is b...	6/6/2007 ...	6/6/20...
OnProgress	C..	C...	D...	{...	{9...	Prepare for Execute	6/6/2007 ...	6/6/20...
OnProgress	C..	C...	D...	{...	{9...	Prepare for Execute	6/6/2007 ...	6/6/20...
OnProgress	C..	C...	D...	{...	{9...	Prepare for Execute	6/6/2007 ...	6/6/20...
User:PipelineInitialization	C..	C...	D...	{...	{9...	No temporary BLOB data stora...	6/6/2007 ...	6/6/20...
User:PipelineInitialization	C..	C...	D...	{...	{9...	No temporary buffer storage lo...	6/6/2007 ...	6/6/20...
OnInformation	C..	C...	D...	{...	{9...	Pre-Execute phase is beginning...	6/6/2007 ...	6/6/20...
OnInformation	C..	C...	P...	{...	{9...	Pre-Execute phase is beginning...	6/6/2007 ...	6/6/20...
OnProgress	C..	C...	D...	{...	{9...	Pre-Execute	6/6/2007 ...	6/6/20...

Figure 4-35. *Logging output*

Package Configurations

Package configurations in SSIS are akin to `app.config` files in ASP.NET or any other kind of configuration repository. Configurations are individual sets of information that pertain to packages, referring to internal properties. They can be updated at runtime as required and as such are a flexible way of changing variable values and other constituent values.

When the Package Configurations menu item is selected, the welcome screen of the Package Configuration Wizard is displayed (see Figure 4-36). (It can be turned off for future use.) It serves as an introduction to the wizard.

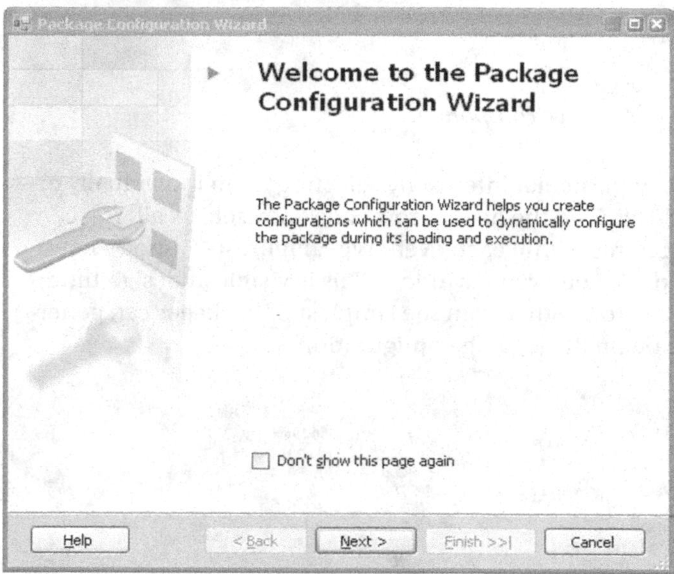

Figure 4-36. *The Package Configuration Wizard welcome screen*

A package by default has no package configuration defined. Configurations must be added as necessary to provide the level of configuration required. Figure 4-37 shows the initial settings required to create a configuration file.

Being a C# developer, I usually go for the XML configuration file type, simply because it's nice to have immediate visibility and maintainability of the package configuration. The actual location of the configuration file can be set here or referenced as Windows environment variable; again, I usually go for the latter option so maximum flexibility is maintained. In Figure 4-37 I've selected an XML configuration file but gone for a hard-coded file location for simplicity. The other configuration types are shown in Figure 4-38.

The next step of the wizard (Figure 4-39) offers the ability to select properties to export to the configuration type location. These properties are values that may, by necessity, change for the proper execution of a deployed package. This means of course that any property not exported cannot be altered at runtime. However, it's a simple matter to revisit the Package Configurations menu option and edit existing configuration-type settings to add or remove properties for export.

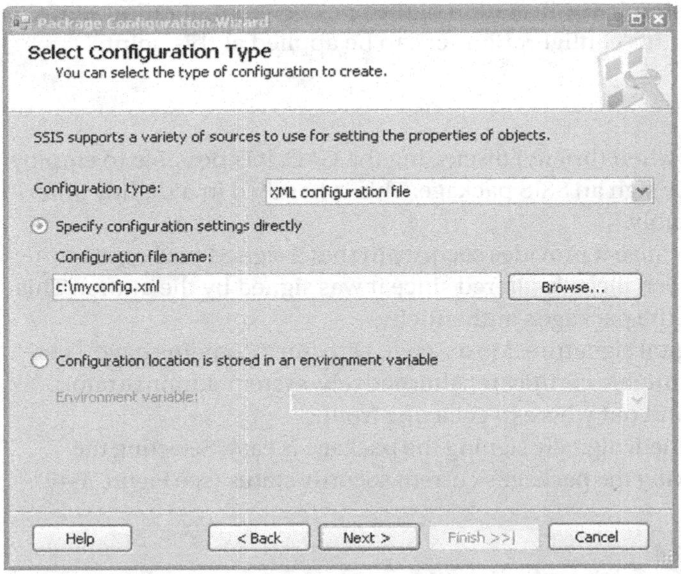

Figure 4-37. *Step one: selecting the configuration type*

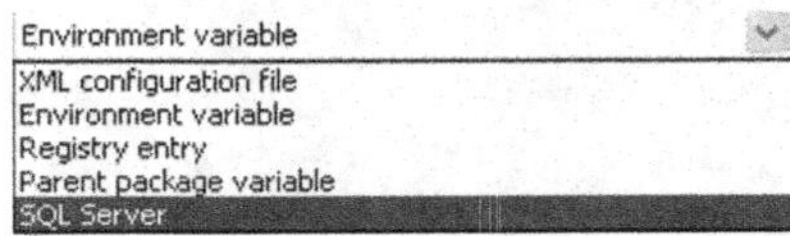

Figure 4-38. *Configuration types*

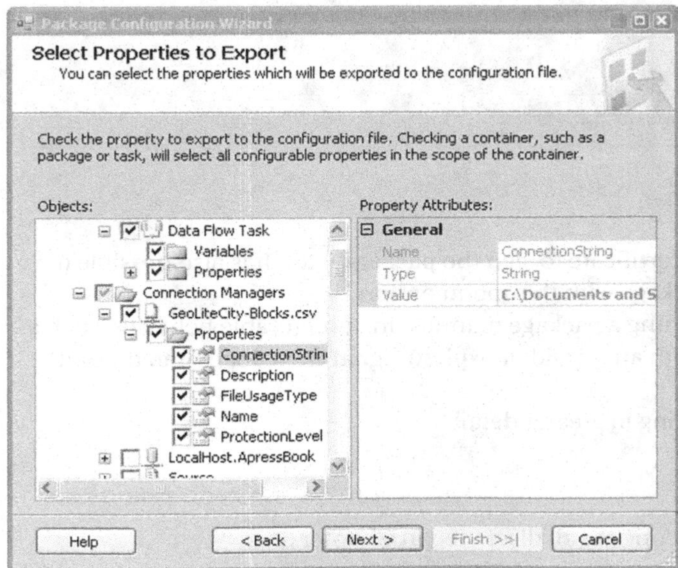

Figure 4-39. *Selecting configurable properties*

The final step in the wizard is a simple confirmation of the package-configuration settings that have been specified. A name for this configuration set can be applied at this point.

Digital Signing

As I described earlier in this chapter when (briefly) discussing the GAC, it is possible to employ cryptographic principles and digitally sign an SSIS package. This is handled in a slightly different way from the average .NET assembly.

Digital signing is a good idea because it provides security in that a signed package is confirmation that the package has not been illegally altered since it was signed by the author. This gives a certain level of confidence in the package's authenticity.

The first thing to acquire is a digital signature. Most Active Directory domains have a certification authority that can issue a suitable certificate. Alternatively, system administrators are usually a good starting point to find out where to get a one from.

Once a certificate has been obtained, digitally signing the package is easy. Selecting the menu option brings up a screen showing the package's current security status (see Figure 4-40).

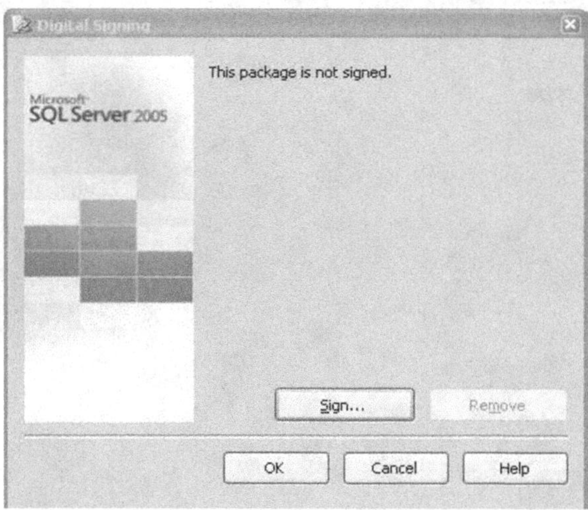

Figure 4-40. *This package is not signed!*

Select Sign... to choose a digital certificate to sign the package with. It is also possible to remove a digital signature from a package with this menu option.

The ramifications of digitally signing a package manifest in configurable behavior, such as whether to allow a package signed with an invalid or expired signature to load or to block it completely.

Chapter 13 discusses digital signing in greater detail.

Variables

Variables, variable namespace, and scope are all discussed in Chapter 5.

Work Offline

This option is included as a courtesy. Its purpose is simply to prevent too many error messages about connection failures when a connection is unavailable for some reason. Selecting this option still enables a package to be viewed or updated in this situation.

Log Events

The Log Events option simply displays the Log Events window inside the IDE so logged events can be viewed, as shown in Figure 4-41.

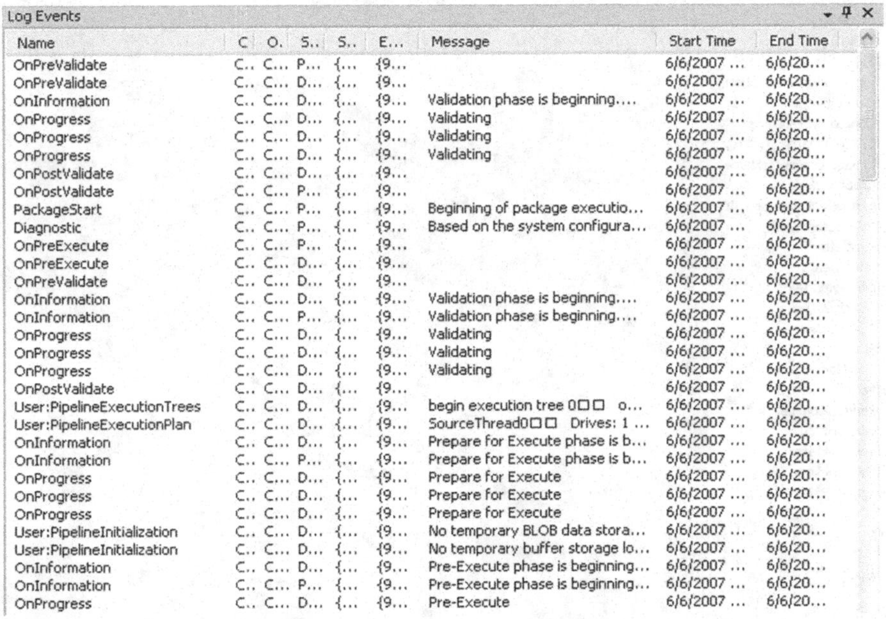

Log Events

Name	C	O.	S..	S..	E...	Message	Start Time	End Time
OnPreValidate	C..	C...	P...	{...	{9...		6/6/2007 ...	6/6/20...
OnPreValidate	C..	C...	D...	{...	{9...		6/6/2007 ...	6/6/20...
OnInformation	C..	C...	D...	{...	{9...	Validation phase is beginning....	6/6/2007 ...	6/6/20...
OnProgress	C..	C...	D...	{...	{9...	Validating	6/6/2007 ...	6/6/20...
OnProgress	C..	C...	D...	{...	{9...	Validating	6/6/2007 ...	6/6/20...
OnProgress	C..	C...	D...	{...	{9...	Validating	6/6/2007 ...	6/6/20...
OnPostValidate	C..	C...	D...	{...	{9...		6/6/2007 ...	6/6/20...
OnPostValidate	C..	C...	P...	{...	{9...		6/6/2007 ...	6/6/20...
PackageStart	C..	C...	P...	{...	{9...	Beginning of package executio...	6/6/2007 ...	6/6/20...
Diagnostic	C..	C...	P...	{...	{9...	Based on the system configura...	6/6/2007 ...	6/6/20...
OnPreExecute	C..	C...	P...	{...	{9...		6/6/2007 ...	6/6/20...
OnPreExecute	C..	C...	D...	{...	{9...		6/6/2007 ...	6/6/20...
OnPreValidate	C..	C...	D...	{...	{9...		6/6/2007 ...	6/6/20...
OnInformation	C..	C...	D...	{...	{9...	Validation phase is beginning....	6/6/2007 ...	6/6/20...
OnInformation	C..	C...	P...	{...	{9...	Validation phase is beginning....	6/6/2007 ...	6/6/20...
OnProgress	C..	C...	D...	{...	{9...	Validating	6/6/2007 ...	6/6/20...
OnProgress	C..	C...	D...	{...	{9...	Validating	6/6/2007 ...	6/6/20...
OnProgress	C..	C...	D...	{...	{9...	Validating	6/6/2007 ...	6/6/20...
OnPostValidate	C..	C...	D...	{...	{9...		6/6/2007 ...	6/6/20...
User:PipelineExecutionTrees	C..	C...	D...	{...	{9...	begin execution tree 0□□ o...	6/6/2007 ...	6/6/20...
User:PipelineExecutionPlan	C..	C...	D...	{...	{9...	SourceThread0□□ Drives: 1 ...	6/6/2007 ...	6/6/20...
OnInformation	C..	C...	D...	{...	{9...	Prepare for Execute phase is b...	6/6/2007 ...	6/6/20...
OnInformation	C..	C...	P...	{...	{9...	Prepare for Execute phase is b...	6/6/2007 ...	6/6/20...
OnProgress	C..	C...	D...	{...	{9...	Prepare for Execute	6/6/2007 ...	6/6/20...
OnProgress	C..	C...	D...	{...	{9...	Prepare for Execute	6/6/2007 ...	6/6/20...
OnProgress	C..	C...	D...	{...	{9...	Prepare for Execute	6/6/2007 ...	6/6/20...
User:PipelineInitialization	C..	C...	D...	{...	{9...	No temporary BLOB data stora...	6/6/2007 ...	6/6/20...
User:PipelineInitialization	C..	C...	D...	{...	{9...	No temporary buffer storage lo...	6/6/2007 ...	6/6/20...
OnInformation	C..	C...	D...	{...	{9...	Pre-Execute phase is beginning...	6/6/2007 ...	6/6/20...
OnInformation	C..	C...	P...	{...	{9...	Pre-Execute phase is beginning...	6/6/2007 ...	6/6/20...
OnProgress	C..	C...	D...	{...	{9...	Pre-Execute	6/6/2007 ...	6/6/20...

Figure 4-41. *The Log Events window is on the left side of the screen.*

New Connection

This menu option brings up the Add SSIS Connection Manager dialog. Everything to do with connections is handled through this Manager, which is why I have dedicated more space to it in Chapter 7.

Package Explorer

For an overview of a package, especially considering the various elements plugged into it that aren't immediately obvious from looking at the graphical design surface, there is no better tool than the Package Explorer.

Accessed via a tab along the top of the main screen, the Package Explorer lists containers, components, variables, and everything else associated with a package. You can see it in Figure 4-42.

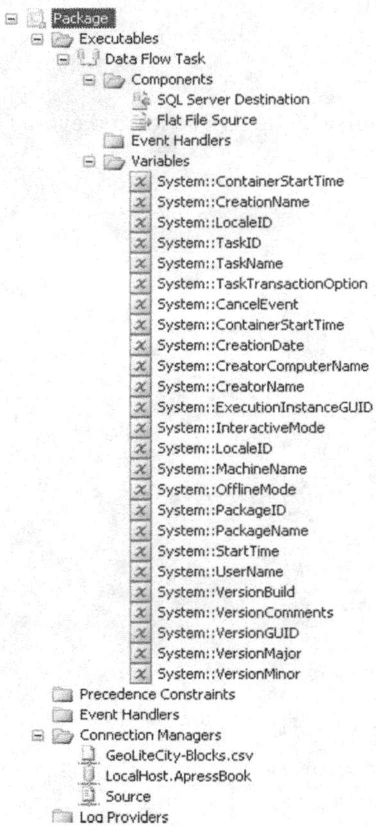

Figure 4-42. *The Package Explorer unwraps a package nicely!*

This tab comes in particularly useful when you're addressing problems in a package and some perspective is required to see just how deep the rabbit hole goes. When you take over another developer's work, having a one-stop-shop where all package facets are visible is invaluable for avoiding too much tail-chasing.

The Package Explorer naturally allows you to drill down into individual items contained in the view, which makes it even better.

Execution Results

The Execution Results tab shows detailed time-based information regarding the execution of a package. This runtime-generated view of proceedings is invaluable in identifying problems encountered during the process for rectification purposes, and also to supply details for optimization (which is covered in Chapter 12). Figure 4-43 shows sample contents of the tab.

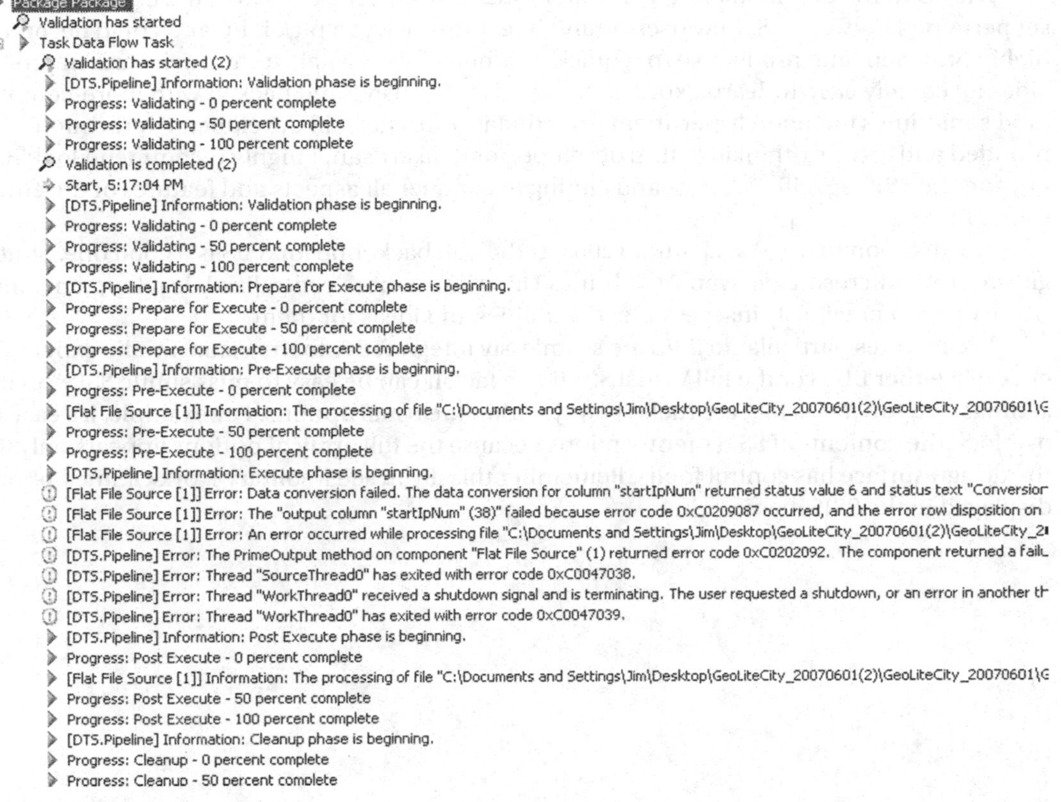

Figure 4-43. *Oops, I've left some errors in this one.*

Expect to return to this tab time and again to view and refine the execution of packages.

USEFUL IDE SHORTCUTS

Ctrl + Shift + B: Recompile from files
Ctrl + Shift + E: Exception monitoring
F5: Debug project
F9: Toggle breakpoint
F10: Code debug with step over
F11: Code debug with step into

Summary

This chapter has looked at the features BIDS and its big brother, the fully featured Visual Studio 2005. I've tried to highlight the most important and immediate aspects of the development environment for all users of SSIS.

With DTS the development environment was entirely self contained; the exposed feature set pertained only to DTS. New users found it relatively easy to pick it up and could become highly proficient and productive in it quickly. Although the Visual Studio environment provides an equally easy-to-learn experience, it is also expansive and packed with more-complex (and sometimes not entirely pertinent) functionality for the SSIS developer. For the more rounded and forward-thinking DBA, developer, or data artisan, I highly recommend looking beyond the SSIS-specific features and aiming to conquer all aspects and features of the environment.

The decision to use Visual Studio 2005 as the IDE backbone for SSIS is a good one. Strategically, from Microsoft's viewpoint, it brings DBAs into a more centralized development arena that can open previously inaccessible possibilities and ideas for them.

The features particular to SSIS are seamlessly integrated into the Visual Studio experience, via either BIDS or the full Visual Studio. In fact, it can be easy to miss subtle SSIS-specific settings and functions that are tucked away within the usual options. For example, it's easy to overlook the contents of SSIS menu options because the full array of options appears only if the design surface has control focus. Remember this if you see a solitary Work Offline option displayed in the SSIS menu.

CHAPTER 5

Package Hierarchy

Now that you're familiar with the development environment and with adding projects and packages, it's time to learn exactly what the conceptual and physical objects in an SSIS project are. Different types of project items—but not a great variety—can be added to an SSIS project.

I'm going to use the word *container* a lot in this chapter. SSIS package hierarchies are like Russian dolls. Each doll can hold another doll until you reach a solid doll that's too small to fit another inside. In SSIS, the box you keep your Russian dolls in is the package, and the dolls themselves are containers. The solid doll at the center is not a container; it's a *component* (or *executable*, to use Microsoft terminology).

In other words, the hierarchy in SSIS is incredibly flexible and allows containers (at least certain kinds) to hold other containers. Combining this image with Chapter 2's metaphor for the way data flows between components, a picture emerges of a fast-moving digital river being squirted out by differently sized Russian dolls . . . inside other Russian dolls. That's a weird thought. Figure 5-1 shows a more abstract image of the package hierarchy.

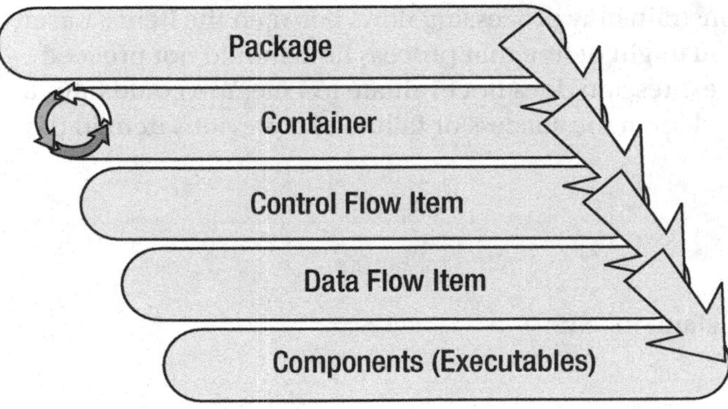

Figure 5-1. *The package hierarchy*

Because the fundamental, all-encompassing logical and physical container is the package, it is at some level within the package that you'll spend most of your time. For this reason, it's important to know how processing within SSIS is grouped. The SSIS package's hierarchical structure is reflected in the object model. This is worth bearing in mind should you wish to start poking around using Visual Studio and creating (for example) dynamic packages for your projects, custom components, or custom containers.

This chapter investigates packages, containers, components, and everything that relates to them, such as precedence and flow. By the end of the chapter you should know everything you need to know, both conceptually and in practice, about the structure of your work in SSIS.

Vocabulary

The key terms in the SSIS hierarchy are

Package: The root of the hierarchy. Although an SSIS solution can contain a number of packages, they are not held, logically or physical, in any kind of container.

Container: The level beneath the package can be either a container or some kind of executable (a Control Flow executable). A container is a logical construct that can hold other containers or components grouped together under the "super-container."

Executable: A component that implements the necessary SSIS interfaces and so makes itself available for use within SSIS. An example is the `Script Component`, which supports the running of Visual Basic.NET code within your package against contained Data Flow.

Scope: Scope (a concept familiar to anyone with programming knowledge) refers to the visibility and usability of a variable to a piece of code, based on where in the code the variable is defined. For example, a variable with global scope is defined at package level and is visible to and usable by any package, container, or component in the hierarchy beneath it. By contrast, a variable defined at Data Flow task level is visible only to that task and its subtasks.

Precedence constraints: In the Control Flow design surface it is possible, once you have multiple Control Flow items, to constrain how processing flows between the items, based on certain criteria. For example, you might define that process flow should not proceed from one package to another if an expression does not evaluate to `True`. You could have a simple constraint such as one based upon the success or failure of a previous item in the Control Flow.

Containers

Four container types are available by default in SSIS:

- `Task Host`
- `Foreach Loop`
- `For Loop`
- `Sequence`

The `Task Host` container is the default container that single tasks fall into. It isn't a container type you can select. Instead, if you do not specify a container, the task is wrapped in this default container type. This allows variables and event handlers to be extended to the contained task as usual. However, this container type cannot use precedence constraints. The other three container types can work with precedence constraints, event handlers, and variables.

Each of these containers, as Control Flow types, is discussed in Chapter 8.

Packages

Note that even a Control Flow task that isn't apparently part of a container is still contained within the `Task Host` container. It groups functionality in a single place. For example, you might have a package that fulfils a single purpose or provides a single service. How you group functionality is entirely your decision, though there are certain sensible and logical paths to follow—for example, not putting all of the functionality inside a single package. It definitely makes sense to split functionality up where possible, along those logical demarcation lines only you will be able to identify.

SSIS package structure can be confusing if you're transitioning directly from DTS. The package structure in DTS is one-dimensional in that every component is used within the same design surface. The flow of processing between components is all mixed together with the data. SSIS abstracts out the concepts of Control Flow and Data Flow and presents them as separate entities.

While it seems like a major departure, logically and physically, it really isn't all that different from DTS and really shouldn't present too many problems going forward. Consider SSIS to be an object-oriented version of DTS, if you like.

Package Properties

It's important to look at the properties exposed by the package—not only through the IDE but at the object level. These properties are discussed in their entirety in Appendix B. Increased knowledge of the properties will become more important when you develop custom controls.

Package Methods

It's also important to look a the methods exposed by the package object—again this is of particular interest when you develop custom controls. For a complete examination of these methods, see Appendix B.

Control Flow

Within the Control Flow a component can be a container or an executable. The Control Flow item itself can be within a container or within a package. See Chapter 8 for further details.

Data Flow

A Data Flow component or executable is at the very bottom level of the package hierarchy. See Chapter 9 for further details.

Checkpoints

Just like the mid-level checkpoints on console games that save players from replaying the entire level when they "die," SSIS checkpoints allow failed packages to continue on restart from predefined points.

The advantages are tremendous, certainly in the development and testing phases of a project. I have lost count of the times I have sat watching masses of data flow through a particularly long-running process, only to have everything fall apart directly afterwards. I'm not talking about SSIS or even DTS here. Every kind of development has these epic moments of processing that take an age to develop and test properly. This is why having a facility to create save points in the process tree is a real bonus and a great time-saving feature.

The use of checkpoints requires a little thought when you're conceptualizing or designing a package. This shouldn't come as much of a surprise, since everything in SSIS requires some thought before implementation. In the case of checkpoints, however, the temptation is to try to shoehorn them in at the last minute rather than plan their use from the start. This approach can cause a pretty major redevelopment cycle just to squeeze desired checkpoint functionality in. The reason for this revolves around solution structure. The creation of checkpoints by the SSIS runtime is available only at Control Flow task level.

Three basic properties need to be populated at package level for the use of checkpoints to be enabled:

- `CheckpointFileName`: Specifies a path and filename for the checkpoint file.
- `CheckpointUsage`
  - `Never` specifies that checkpoints should not be used.
  - `IfExists` specifies that checkpoints should be used if already in use.
  - `Always` specifies that checkpoints should always be used.
- `SaveCheckpoints`: Specifies whether checkpoints should be saved. The executing package saves checkpoints at points during processing in case of failure.

The checkpoint file saves the last position during execution, the value of variables, and the current operation. The checkpoint file does not save the value of variables of type `Object`, however, so care should be taken if using checkpoints is a requirement.

The final piece of checkpoint configuration is to identify the points within the solution from which you might want to recover processing. These points can be identified to the SSIS runtime by setting the `FailPackageOnFailure` property of each significant object. In a hierarchy of objects that all have the `FailPackageOnFailure` property set, processing resumes upon restart at the nearest checkpoint to the point of failure.

As a final note, remember that disk space is used to store the checkpoint file. Depending on the processing involved, the file can grow quite substantially.

Variables

SSIS provides support for strongly typed part–Common Type System (CTS)–compliant variables as a part of any container or package (which, as you know, is a container also). CTS is a fundamental part of .NET. It refers to a base set of data types that are independent of specific implementations in a programming language such as C# or a technology such as SSIS.

I use CamelCase variable names, having finally kicked the Hungarian-notation addiction some years ago. It seems that the recommended notation for variables in C# is CamelCase. I recommend the same for SSIS variables.

CamelCasing is the practice of capitalizing each word except the first one. For example, if I have a variable that holds a count of how many times `Lateralus` appears in a derived column, I might call it countOfLateralus. Notice that I haven't included the variable's data type in the name. Variables in SSIS are defined with the properties shown in Table 1-1.

Table 1-1. *Variable Properties in SSIS*

Property	Description
Name	A good variable name describes the semantic and not the type!
Scope	Scope is a read-only property when you are creating a variable. It is populated as a consequence of where in the package hierarchy you are defining it. (See the next section for a discussion of variable scope.)
Data Type	Available types are Boolean, Byte, Char, DateTime, DBNull, Double, Int32, Int64, Object, Int16, SByte, Single, String, UInt32, and UInt64
Value	The initial value of the variable on package execution.
Namespace	The namespace the variable belongs to.
Raise event on change	Signifies whether an OnVariableValueChanged event is fired when the value of the variable changes.

Variable Scope

A variable's scope can be understood by referencing the twin tenets of accessibility and visibility. In programming languages such as C#, a variable can be defined with an access level that, in conjunction with the declaration's location, defines where and how it can be accessed. SSIS handles scope definition less flexibly and much more simply, though the functionality offered can still be leveraged to give powerful control over variable scope.

Each container can have its own collection of variables. The scope of the variable can be defined as being within its parent container. For example, as in Figure 5-2, if I define a variable at the top container level, it can be accessed by and be visible to any object beneath it in the hierarchy.

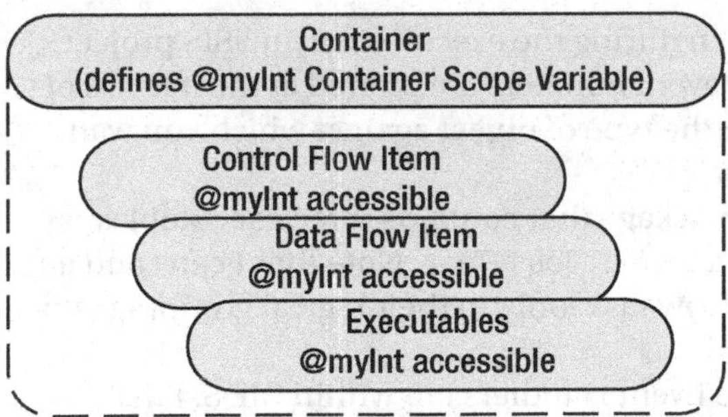

Figure 5-2. *Global variable scope*

Global variables are variables defined at the very top of the program hierarchy and are thus visible to everything beneath. By definition, they are accessible and visible in every scope. Why not use them all the time and not worry about scope? Why is use of global variables considered to be bad practice?

Those are fair questions. In theory, since SSIS provides the mechanism to support such an approach, there's no reason not to move forward with it. Only when due consideration is given to the potential benefits of having a more mature variable-usage strategy are valid reasons against a global approach found.

Viewing the problem from a purely performance-centric standpoint, variables defined at a global level are more memory hungry in their implementation. In terms of implementation, the variable can be modified from any point in the hierarchy, which means that it is much harder to ensure the value of the variable at any point. If your only indicator of a bug in the code is that the value of your variable is changed, you'll have more problems when trying to troubleshoot the issue.

In summary, a variable's scope can be defined by identifying the level within which it was declared. Because scope works from the top of the hierarchy down, the declared variable is also visible to any containers beneath the declaration level.

In the case illustrated in Figure 5-3, the `myFlowInt` variable is declared at the task level. This means only members of that task can see and access the variable.

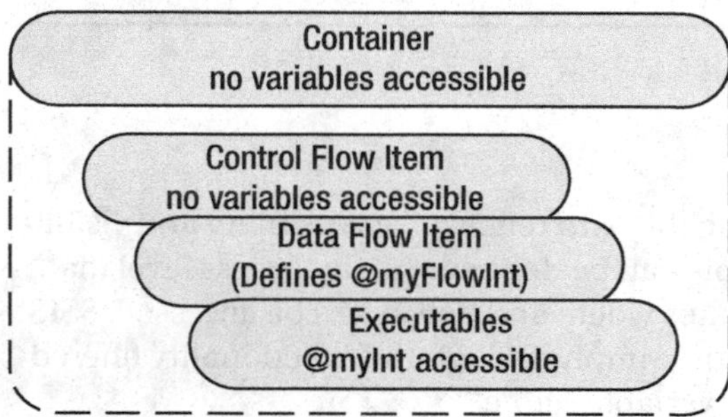

Figure 5-3. *Task scope variables*

Event Handlers

Events, as the word suggests, are things that happen during the execution of an SSIS project. In keeping with the utterly flexible nature of SSIS, event handlers are offered at most levels of the package hierarchy. Naturally, depending upon the type of object against which you want to handle events, the types of event handlers differ.

Taking the case shown in Figure 5-4, I have a package that contains three executables: `Check Database Integrity`, `Data Flow Task`, and `Transfer Jobs Task`. Note that I can't add an event handler to the executables within the Data Flow task, only to their logical grouping container against the Data Flow task itself.

To add or edit event handlers, you can use the Event Handlers tab within BIDS. First, in the left box marked Executable, select the object you wish to add a handler to. Then make a selection from the Event Handler box (see Figure 5-5).

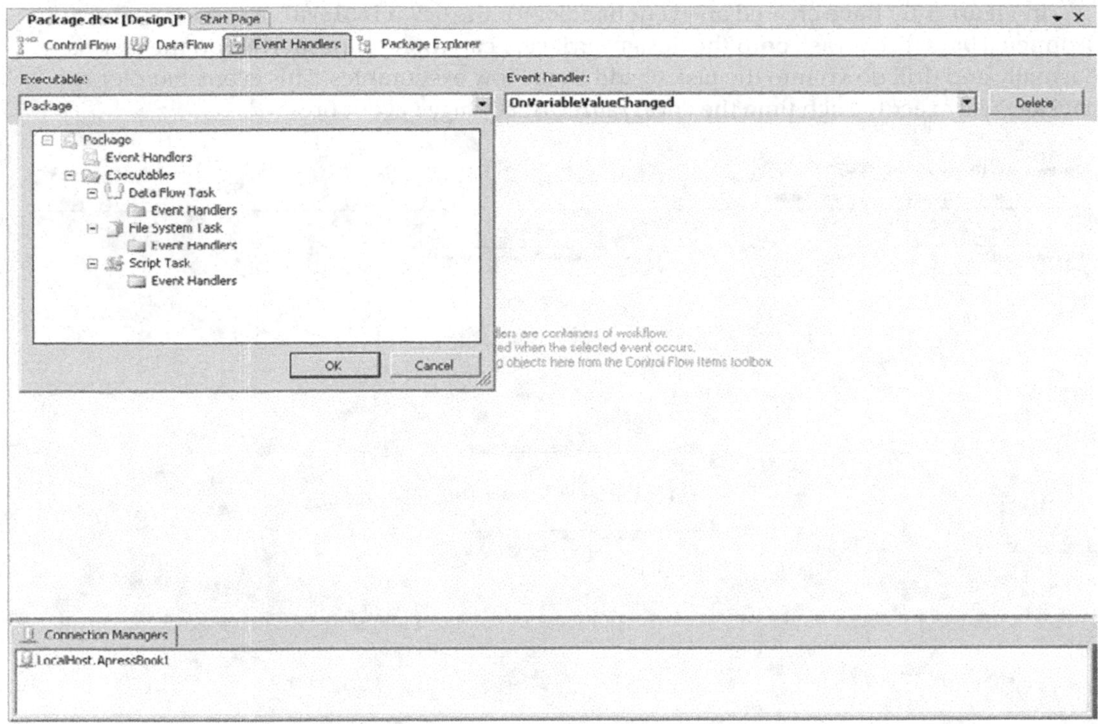

Figure 5-4. *Example event-handler window*

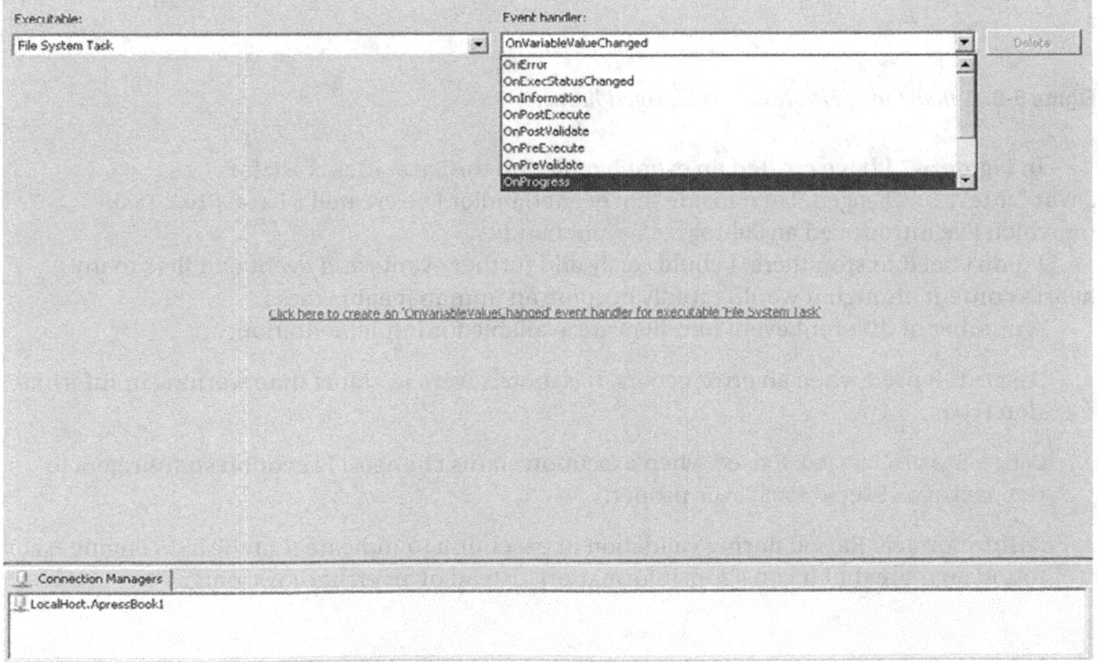

Figure 5-5. *Select executable, then select event handler.*

In Figure 5-6 I have created an event handler for the `OnVariableValueChanged` event and dropped a `Data Flow Task` onto the design surface. I can then set properties on the task as normally and drill down into the task to add Data Flow executables. This event-handler sub-package will execute each time the `OnVariableValueChanged` event fires.

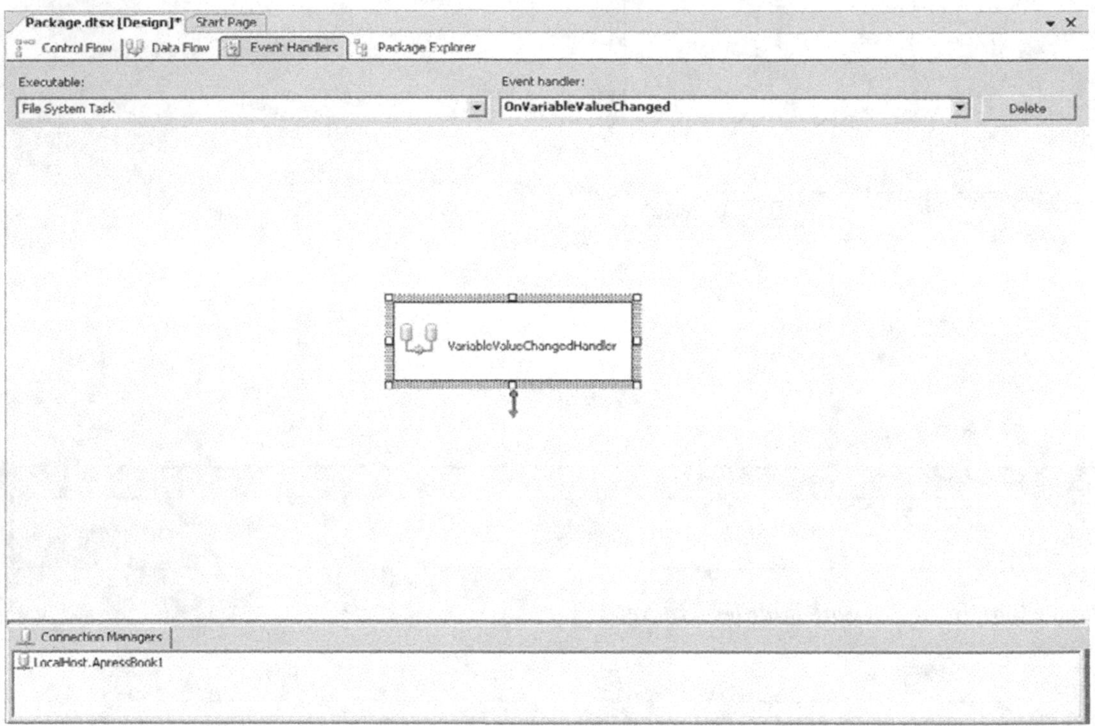

Figure 5-6. *A new OnVariableValueChanged handler*

In Figure 5-7 I have created an event handler on the `Data Flow Task` for `OnVariableValueChanged`. Then inside that event handler I've created a `Data Flow Task` for which I've introduced an `OnProgress` event handler.

I didn't need to stop there. I could easily add further events and event handlers to my heart's content, though it would rapidly become an unmanageable mess.

A number of different event handlers are available for implementation:

`OnError`: Raised when an error occurs. It is more severe in status than warning or information types.

`OnExecStatusChanged`: Raised when execution status changes. Execution status refers to the package's `ExecutionStatus` property.

`OnInformation`: Raised during validation or execution to indicate that the SSIS engine has found an issue that it considers information instead of an error or warning.

`OnPostExecute`: Raised once execution has completed.

`OnPostValidate`: Raised once validation has completed.

`OnPreExecute`: Raised immediately before the executable runs.

`OnPreValidate`: Raised when validation starts.

`OnProgress`: Raised when the executable makes progress. This allows the updating of progress bars and other feedback mechanisms.

`OnQueryCancel`: Raised to force a decision on whether processing should stop.

`OnTaskFailed`: Raised when a task fails during processing.

`OnVariableValueChanged`: Raised when the value of a variable changes. The raising of this event is dependent on whether the `RaiseChangeEvent` property is set to `True` when the variable is declared.

`OnWarning`: Raised during validation or execution to indicate that the SSIS engine has found an issue it considers a warning instead of an error or information.

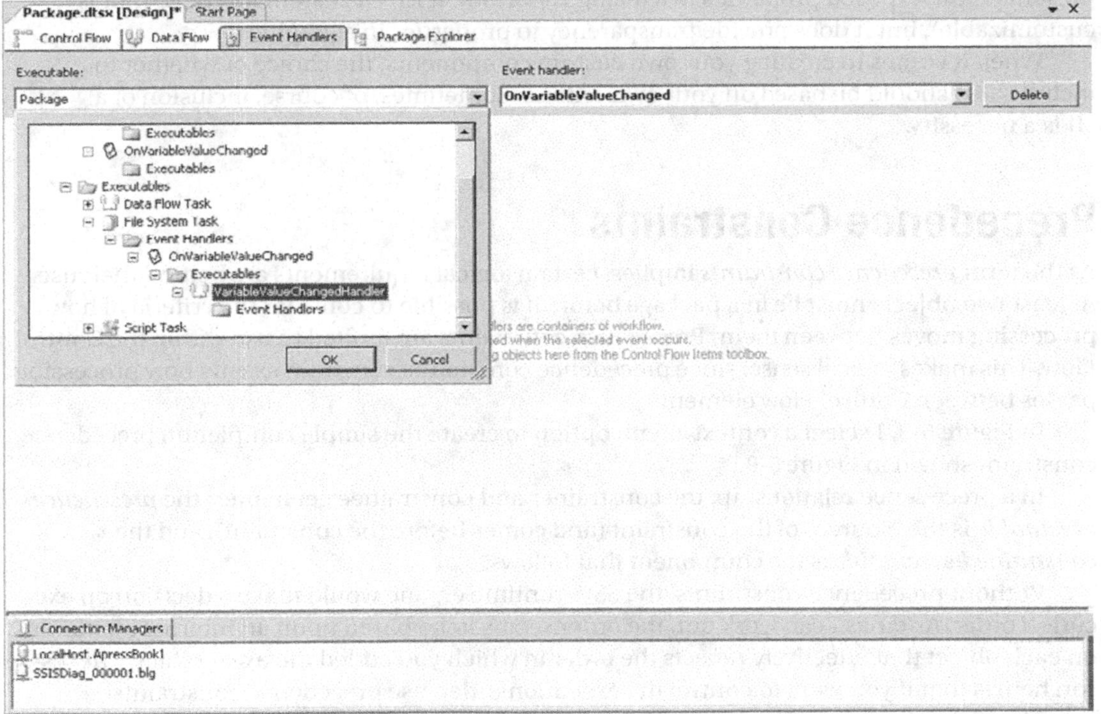

Figure 5-7. *Event handlers can have events too!*

Adding Components

Adding components is as simple as dragging the required component from the Visual Studio Toolbox and dropping it onto the design surface.

If the component you choose is a `Data Flow Task`, you can double-click on it, and you will find yourself suddenly on the Data Flow tab in the Designer. Alternatively, you can simply select the Data Flow tab at the top of the design surface.

Using Executable Designers

Some containers and components have designers and some just have properties. There doesn't seem to be a hard and fast rule as to which ones have which. Generally speaking, though, right-clicking on the item and selecting Edit—if the option exists—reveals all. Microsoft has apparently made a design decision to include a UI for almost all of the containers and executables—even where dynamic values can be set effectively and easily in the Properties pane—to provide a more friendly experience and shallower learning curve.

The story doesn't end there, however. Any SSIS component that exposes properties has a UI, even when it wasn't built with one; SSIS very kindly offers Advanced Properties, which presents these exposed properties in a dialog UI format. It isn't a custom interface (nor is it customizable), but it does provide transparency to properties in a graphical way.

When it comes to creating your own custom components, the choice of whether to include a UI should be based on your own criteria. Sometimes, of course, inclusion of a UI is a necessity.

Precedence Constraints

As the term *precedence constraints* implies, certain logical requirements are behind their use. At least two objects must be in a package before it is possible to consider the criteria of how processing moves between them. Precedence constraints are limited to use within the Control Flow. This makes logical sense, since precedence constraints constrain exactly how processing passes between Control Flow elements.

In Figure 5-8, I select a context-menu option to create the simple completion precedence constraint shown in Figure 5-9.

In a precedence relationship, the constrainer and constrainee get names: the *precedence executable* is the "source" of the constraint (and comes before the constraint), and the *constrained executable* is the component that follows.

Without precedence constraints, the SSIS runtime engine would make a decision on execution order. As far as I can work out, the order seems to be based upon an internal identifier on each object that effectively reflects the order in which you added the executables. The lesson here is that if you want to control the execution order, use precedence constraints!

The only other case where execution order is decided by the runtime is within a package with a branching Control Flow. Normal, orderly service resumes once the runtime comes across the next constraint.

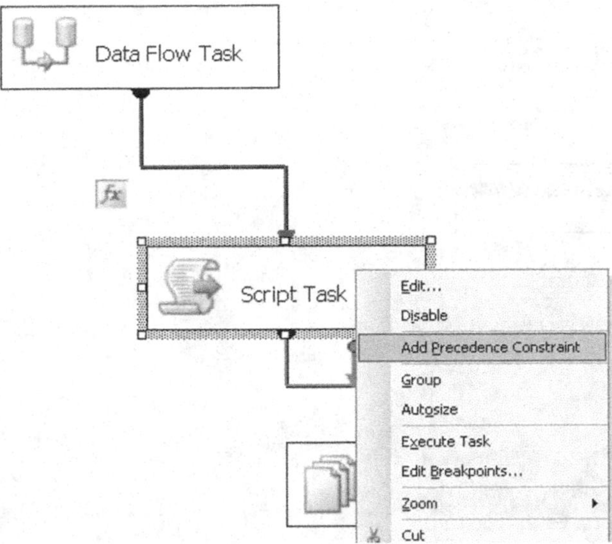

Figure 5-8. *Using context menu to add a precedence constraint*

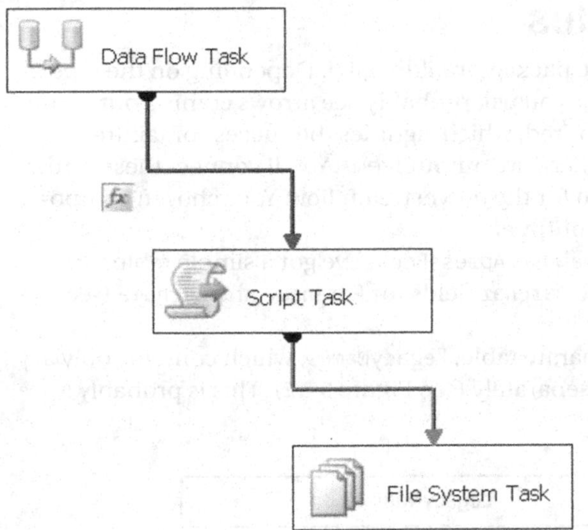

Figure 5-9. *A simple precedence constraint*

In this case, since I've already created the precedence constraint, I can edit the existing constraint by choosing Edit from the context menu. This opens the Precedence Constraint Editor, which shows in Figure 5-10 that I've chosen an expression as the evaluation operation. (Obviously, I've entered a spurious expression in Figure 5-10 that will never evaluate to `True`, but the principle is there.) Notice also the Multiple constraints section at the bottom of the window in Figure 5-10. This controls the behavior of how multiple constraints are evaluated.

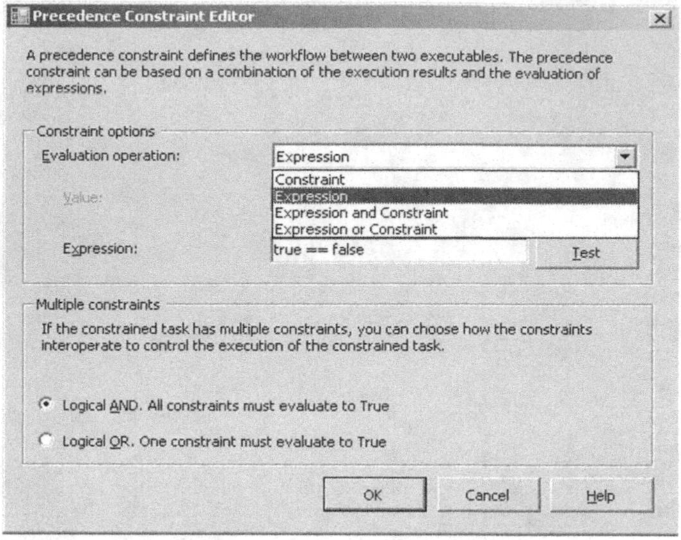

Figure 5-10. *Setting constraint options, in this case as an expression*

Flow Between Executables

Drag a component from the Toolbox onto the package-builder GUI. Depending on the type of component you drop onto the design surface, you will probably see arrows coming out of the bottom of it. Usually these arrows are green or red, which signifies the success or failure, respectively, of the component at runtime. These are output feeds. You'll connect these arrows to other components to provide a destination for the downstream flow. Your chosen component might have multiple inputs or multiple outputs.

Let's look at a simple example. In my database, `ApressBook`, I've got a simple table that contains a 32-bit integer primary key and two `varchar` fields for `Forename` and `Surname` (see Figure 5-11).

I need to make periodic updates to a separate table, `LegacyNames`, which contains only a `FullName` column, not `Forename` and `Surname` separately (see Figure 5-12). This is probably a familiar situation for most readers.

Names		
PK	NameID	int identity
	Forename Surname	varchar(50) varchar(50)

Figure 5-11. *Simple table: Names*

LegacyNames		
PK	LegacyNameID	int identity
	Fullname	varchar(100)

Figure 5-12. *The second simple table: LegacyNames*

Now (ignoring the fact that this could easily be done within a single query depending upon circumstances), I'll build a very simple SSIS package to do the transformation, using the `Derived Column` transform in this instance. Let's take a look at this step by step. I am going to assume you know how to create a new SSIS project by now; if you don't, refer to Chapter 4.

1. An empty Control Flow design surface is visible. If the Control Flow tab is not selected and showing for some reason, just click on the Control Flow tab and the design surface will appear.

2. Drag a `Data Flow Task` from the Toolbox onto the design surface.

3. Double-click on the `Data Flow Task` (see Figure 5-13) to open the Data Flow design surface.

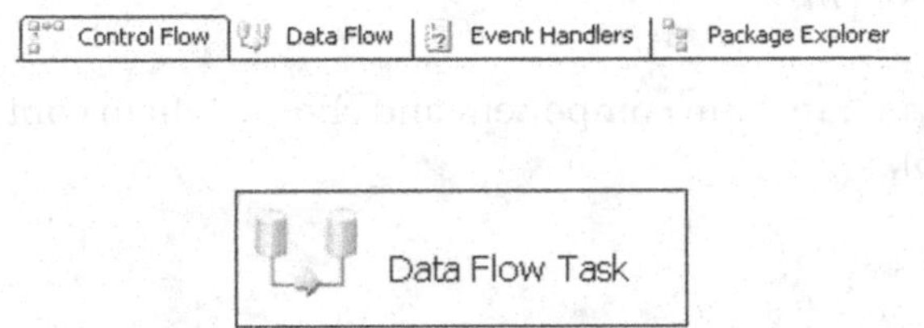

Figure 5-13. *The Control Flow designer shows the Data Flow Task.*

4. Right-click in the Connection Managers area, select New ADO.NET Connection, and configure the connection for your database.

5. Drag a `DataReader Source` component from the Toolbox onto the design surface.

6. Observe that the `DataReader Source` has a single green arrow and single red arrow protruding from the bottom of the component (see Figure 5-14). This illustrates the component's two outputs.

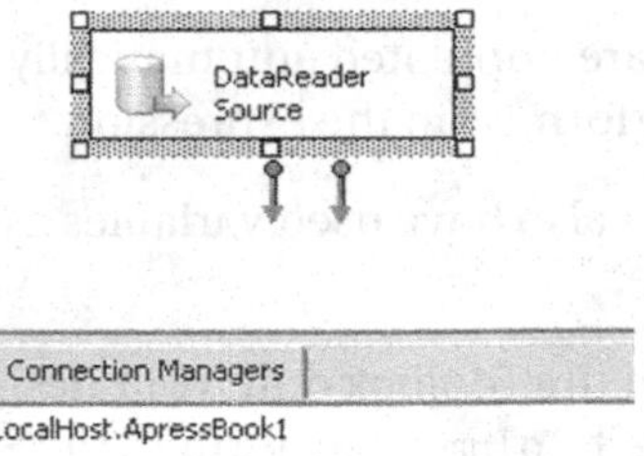

Figure 5-14. *The DataReader Source*

7. Configure the `DataReader Source`—specifically, the SQL statement—as `SELECT nameid, forename, surname FROM names`

8. Drop a `Derived Column` transform onto the design surface.

9. Drag the end of the green arrow from the `DataReader Source` onto the `Derived Column` transform (see Figure 5-15).

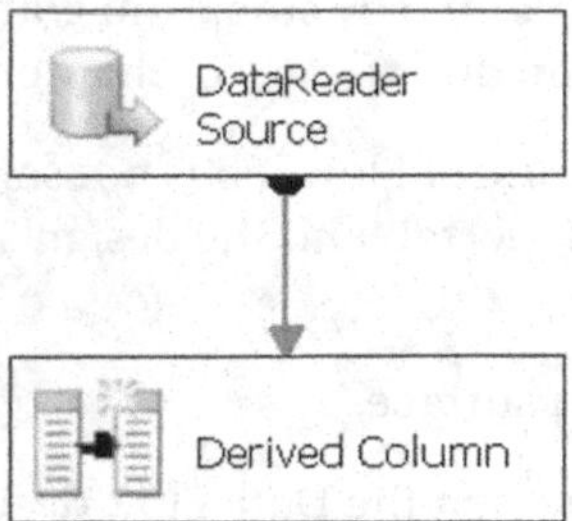

Figure 5-15. *Connecting the components*

10. Right-click on the `Derived Column` transform component and choose Edit to configure the component (see Figure 5-16).

Derived Column Name	Derived Column	Expression	Data Type	Length
Fullname	<add as new column>	forename + " " + surname	Unicode string [DT_...	50

Figure 5-16. *Configuring the Derived Column*

11. Choose a name for the `Derived Column`—I've chosen `Fullname` in Figure 5-16—and enter the required expression in the Expression field. In this case I want to concatenate the `Forename` and `Surname` fields from the input, so I've used:

```
forename + " " + surname
```

12. Notice how the Data Type properties and length are populated automatically based upon the input-column types and operations performed in the expression.

13. As you will notice from this edit screen, you could also have used variables as part of your expression.

14. Drop a `SQL Server Destination` component from the Toolbox onto your design surface and connect the green arrow from the `Derived Column` transform to the SQL Server destination.

15. Right-click on the `SQL Server Destination` and set the connection properties. I have chosen the `LegacyNames` table as the destination for this connection.

16. As a part of this component you will see Mappings, which you should click on.

You will see the mappings environment (see Figure 5-17), which illustrates an interesting point. Notice that the graphical representation on this dialog shows Available Inputs and not the name and contents of your source table. In this case, because we specified the output from the `DataReader Source` as being a SQL statement that selected `nameid`, `forename`, and `surname`, these are the fields we see as available.

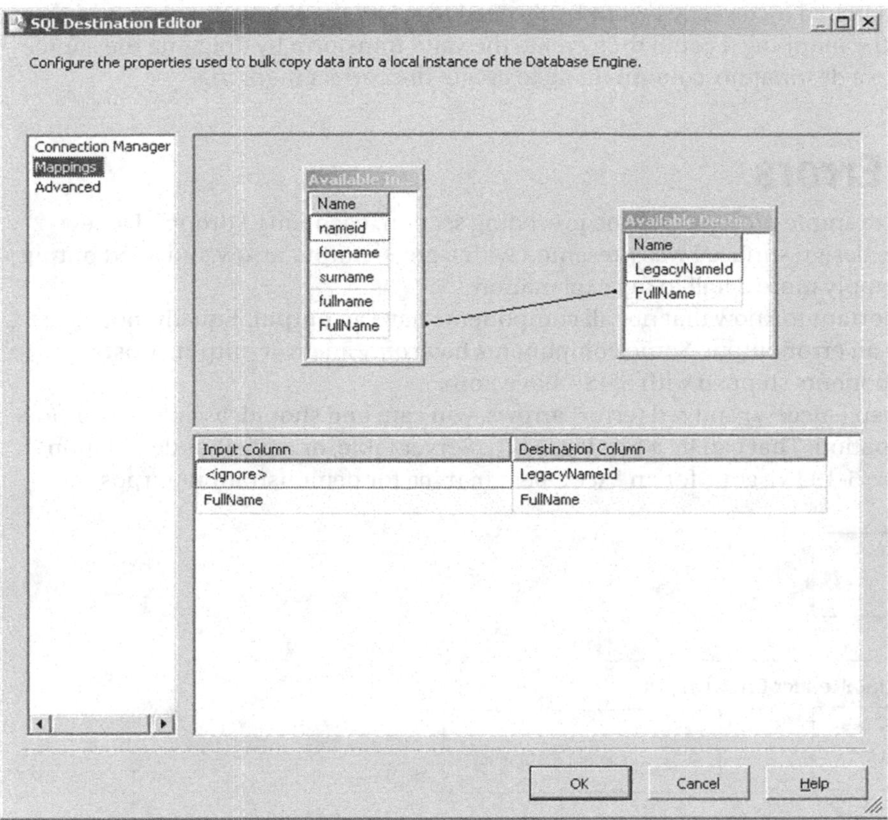

Figure 5-17. *Mapping columns*

If I go back and edit the `DataReaderSource` and remove `nameid` from the SQL, you can see how that column is removed from the Available Inputs in Figure 5-18.

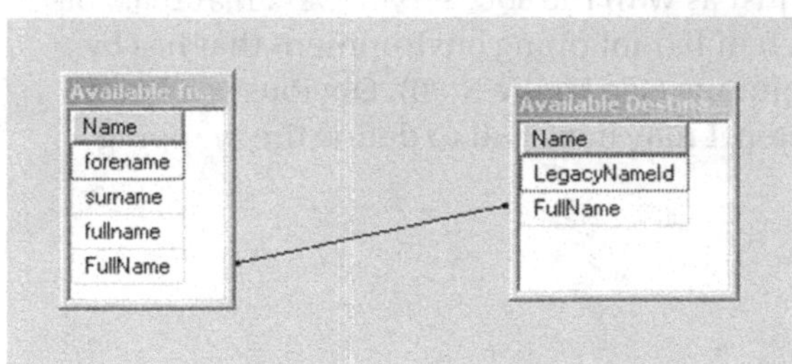

Figure 5-18. *The change is apparent.*

Notice that `Fullname` is also listed as an Available Input, as you would expect. This is the derived column you created in the upstream `Derived Column` component. As you can see, SSIS has automatically made the column mapping for us because the source (Available Inputs) and destination (Available Destinations) columns match by name.

If they were matched incorrectly I would only need to select the connecting line and press Delete to remove the mapping. I could then create the valid transform by dragging the source-column name onto a destination-column name to create the correct mapping.

Directing Errors

Going back to the example presented in the preceding section, each time I dropped a new component on the design surface I was presented with a green output arrow and a red output arrow. It's time to apply more detail to my explanation.

First, it is important to know that not all components have an output. Equally, not all components have an error output. Some components have *only* an error output. Most—certainly the components shipped with SSIS—have both.

With both green (success) and red (error) arrows, you can, and should, assign the outputs to a suitable destination. That can be a text log, a SQL Server table, or any other destination you fancy. In Figure 5-19 I've gone for an `Excel Destination` for demonstration purposes.

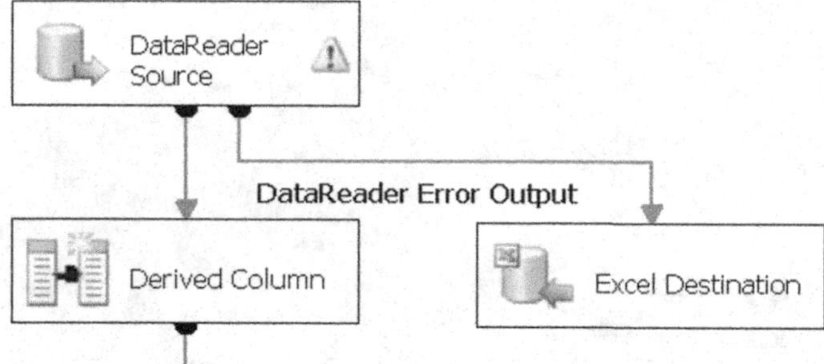

Figure 5-19. *Green arrow, red arrow*

Of course assigning the output isn't as simple as dropping the `Excel Destination` on the design surface: configuration requirements must be met!

You need to set the connection properties, just as with the `SQL Server Destination`. Following the dialog through to Mapping, we see a familiar mapping environment that has by default defined a 1:1 mapping for each of the columns (see Figure 5-20). Obviously, if I had tailored the destination values in the previous step, I may have had to define the mapping manually.

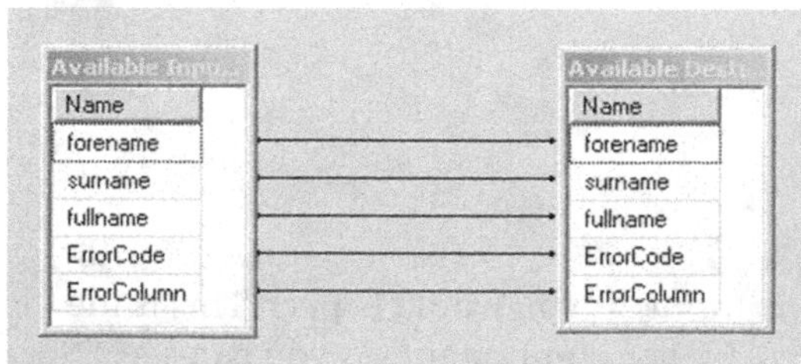

Figure 5-20. *A nice easy mapping*

When it comes to configuring components or whole packages for handling, it is probably a good idea to consider a unified exception strategy. Ask yourself, for example, what you would like to happen if a single row fails to be transformed. Would you expect to cancel processing for the entire package? Are you happy with ten errors but any more should cause cancellation of processing? Should execution continue? Should the data flow downstream to the next component? To prevent errors, should triggers still be fired on the destination? Should the table be locked? Do you need to keep identity values?

All of these configuration options and more are available by right-clicking on the `SQL Server Destination` component and selecting Edit ➤ Advanced to bring up the option dialog shown in Figure 5-21.

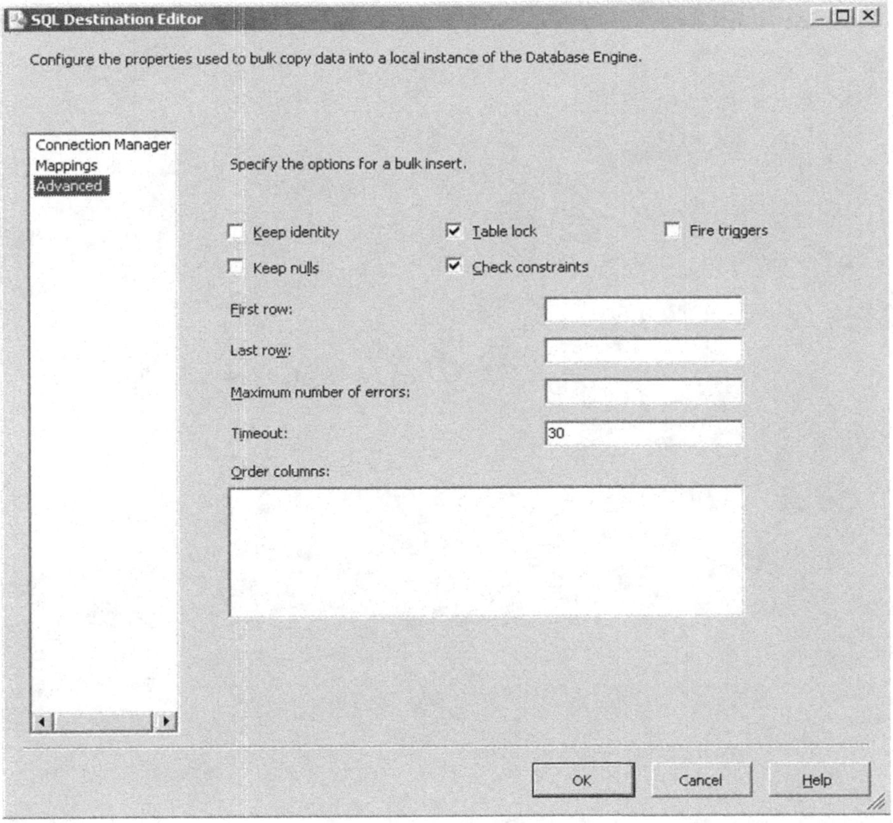

Figure 5-21. *Advanced options for fine-tuning*

SSIS provides settings for components, containers, and packages to cater to all of your error-handling requirements. The configuration shown for components generally applies only to Data Flow destination components, but these and other similar settings are available for your use.

Summary

As a fundamental part of using SSIS, knowing how packages and other containers work and interact with other SSIS constructs is important. When it comes to interpackage functionality, it's vital.

This chapter has discussed a variety of topics fundamental to a sound understanding of SSIS. Things should start falling into place, and the more astute SSIS user will be in a sound position to proceed with creating functional and, moreover, useful packages and solutions.

Although Control Flow and Data Flow components aren't discussed in this book until Chapters 7 and 8, it is a useful exercise to take a step back and review how data is being held and to see if optimizations can be made.

CHAPTER 6

Control Flow

As I discussed in Chapter 2, SSIS features a much more enterprise-ready architecture than was available through DTS. One feature of this architecture is the abstraction of the different logical layers one might find in any ETL or integration tool. To work as dynamically and with as much flexibility as possible, an ETL tool requires a number of constituent parts to work together in creating a whole. In SSIS, these parts are

- Control Flow
- Data Flow
- Precedence constraints
- Connection managers

Figure 6-1 is a diagrammatic representation of this structure.

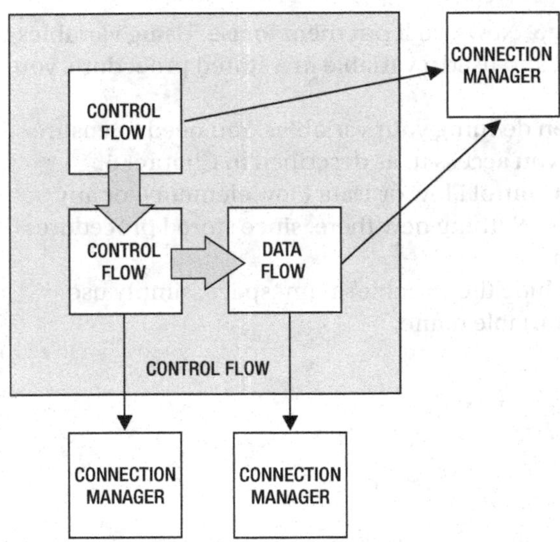

Figure 6-1. *A logical view of a possible SSIS package*

That these individual components are separate and yet interoperate with, and provide support for, one another is the key to why SSIS is such an impressive tool. Also impressive is the way in which this interoperability is provided and structured.

Where Does the Control Flow Fit?

Chapters 6, 7, and 8 concentrate on the main parts in this structure, starting with the Control Flow. The Control Flow design surface is the first thing you see when you create a new project in BIDS. Most of the executables that I'll discuss in this chapter and the next two have accurate and descriptive names. It won't take much for you to make an educated guess as to each one's purpose. That isn't the point, though. How they work and how they can be used in conjunction with other components is what counts.

Sometimes it's easy to avoid paying too much attention to the atomic detail of SSIS. I'd rather be overly obsessive and cover everything I can than leave possible gaps in your knowledge. Concept is nice, but putting it into practice can be the hardest part. The devil is in the details, as the saying goes. On the other side of the coin, it is definitely useful to have the fundamental precepts and concepts behind something before you go ahead with it.

I recommend you also check out the MSDN documentation on the components you intend to use as part of your solution. Obviously I'm not going to reproduce that content here, and it might have key information specific to your implementation. Using this chapter in conjunction with MSDN is a good idea.

What is this chapter then? Is it only for reference? Well, it isn't *purely* for reference purposes, although it does contain reference material. There's so much information to cover that I can't provide examples for every feature of the Control Flow. What I can do, however, is deliver some insight into the more-involved tasks and provide examples where appropriate.

By the end of this chapter you will have a solid understanding of everything necessary to master the Control Flow, *and* you'll also have reference content to use in the future.

A Note About Using Variables

Variables themselves were discussed in Chapter 5. Now you'll put them to use. Using variables is pretty straightforward. If you've ever declared and used a variable in a stored procedure, you know the drill.

Don't forget to consider variable scope when defining your variables. You need to ensure that the variable is visible to the point at which you access it, as described in Chapter 5.

When you use a variable as a property in a Control Flow or Data Flow element—or anywhere else—you must prefix it with the `@` symbol. Nothing new there, since stored procedures have used the same syntax since their inception.

What about the variable namespace? To include the variable's namespace, simply use square brackets and put two colons before the variable name:

```
[@myNamespace::theCounter]
```

It's that easy.

Transactions

Using transactions in SSIS is fairly simple, though the encapsulated functionality is actually quite complex and features technology such as the Distributed Transaction Coordinator (DTC).

There is always a point where a transaction starts and, naturally, where it ends. It is usually the end point that holds the most intrigue, since it can be a rollback or commit depending on the transaction's contents.

When transactions are used within a .NET application and reference `System.Transactions`, they are managed by the DTC, and it's easy for components to take part in cross-process and cross-component transactions.

The more simple form of transactional functionality is provided through the SQL Server engine as *native transactions*, using familiar keywords such as `BEGIN TRANSACTION`, `COMMIT TRANSACTION`, and `ROLLBACK TRANSACTION`. Native transactions are useful for self-contained transactional functionality or even subtransactions used as part of a larger overall transaction strategy.

The SSIS package and contained containers can take part in transactions almost transparently by specifying the value of the `TransactionOption` property on the component. Three options are provided for this property:

`Supported`: The container will join an existing transaction but will not create its own.

`Not Supported`: The container will not join an existing transaction nor create one.

`Required`: The container will join an existing transaction or create its own so one exists.

The transactional support on the Windows platform is incredibly impressive, and this extends into SSIS. The shame of it—in terms of geek cool—is that the complexity is encapsulated away.

The demarcation lines between where the DTC is used over native transactions is, in reality, fairly irrelevant. The rule tends to be about whether the same connection manager is used across the transaction, which means native transactions can be used, since they are at database-engine level.

Common Control Flow Properties

A large number of common properties are available against the Control Flow. I have extracted them and presented them as Appendix C. The Appendixes for this book are available to readers at `http://www.apress.com` in the Source Code/Download section. I highly recommend reviewing them at some point, since they do contain important configuration settings and other things that enable some exciting features.

Control Flow Tasks

SSIS includes 28 stock Control Flow tasks. The remainder of this chapter is the story of those tasks. Again, I can't present examples for each and every task, but I'll do my best to provide suitable detail in each case.

For Loop Container

The `For Loop Container` is a nice simple task to start with. It's a basic container that provides looping functionality. The difference between a `For` loop and, for example, a `While` loop is essentially in how the looping is controlled and the entry and exit conditions are evaluated. It's the simplest of all loop types, except perhaps `Do`. (But SSIS doesn't offer that kind of loop, at least not out of the box, so pretend I didn't mention it.)

A `For` loop contains a counter that usually increments (though it sometimes decrements), at which point a comparison is made with a constant value. If the condition evaluates to `True`, then the loop execution continues. An evaluation of `False` causes the loop to exit.

In C#, a `for` loop can be expressed like this:

```
int theMaximumValue = 100;

for (int theCounter = 0; theCounter < theMaximumValue; theCounter++)
{
// loop processing
Console.WriteLine(String.Format("Current Value: {0}", theCounter.ToString()));
}
```

The SSIS `For Loop Container` follows the same concept. With the SSIS `For Loop Container`, however, the initialization and assignment parts of the loop are entirely optional, which makes sense for simplicity.

When you right-click the `For Loop Container` and select Edit, you are presented with the screen shown in Figure 6-2.

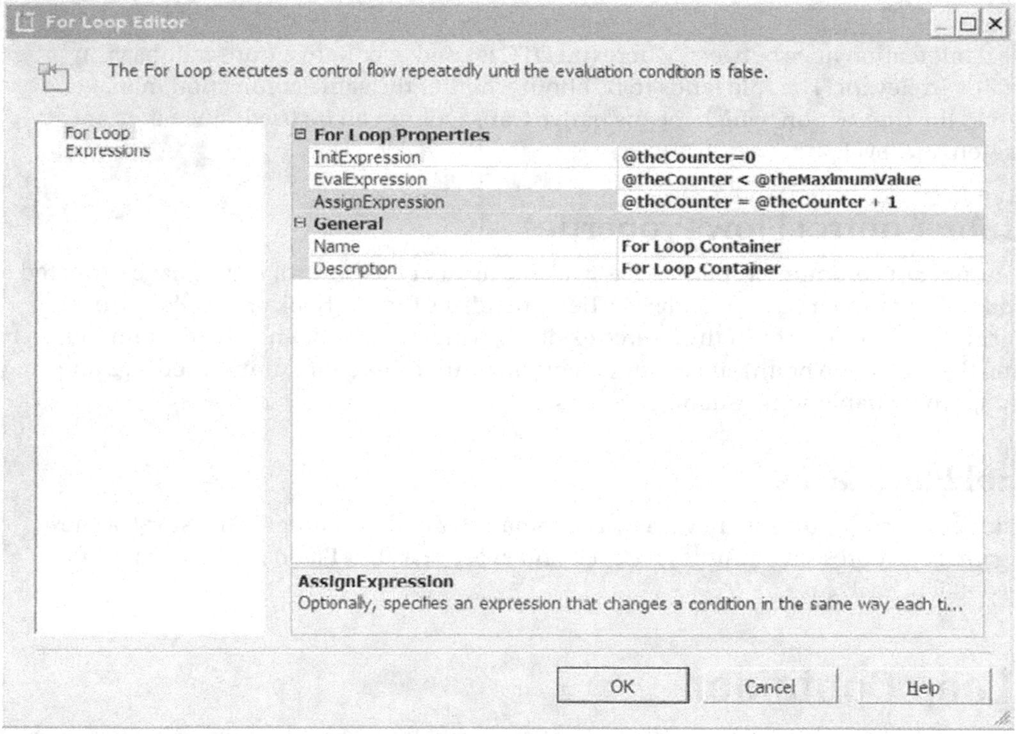

Figure 6-2. *For Loop editor*

I've configured the `For Loop Container` in Figure 6-2 to mimic the C# example I just gave you. To do this, I've set the container properties as follows:

```
InitExpression = @theCounter = 0
EvalExpression = @theCounter < @theMaximumValue
AssignExpression = @theCounter = @theCounter + 1
```

I've used two variables in this example: `@theCounter` and `@theMaximumValue`, both of type `Int32`. Of course I defined them before I got to this point and initialized them with values.

Properties

The SSIS `For Loop Container` offers the following configurable properties in addition to the common properties you'll find in Appendix C:

`AssignExpression`: Read/write property containing a valid expression to increment or decrement the `For` loop counter.

`EvalExpression`: Read/write property for an expression that is evaluated on each iteration of the loop. The expression should evaluate to `True` for the loop to continue.

`InitExpression`: Read/write property containing an expression that is used to initialize the loop.

Foreach Loop Container

The `Foreach Loop Container` is for situations where you have a collection of items and wish to use each item within it as some kind of input into the downstream flow.

The physical implementation is more than meets the eye. It looks like each of the enumerators, custom or otherwise, is instanced from a parent container. In effect, there is only a single kind of container (`Microsoft.SqlServer.Dts.Runtime.ForEachLoop`), but it can hold within it any compliant enumerator (`Microsoft.SqlServer.ManagedDts.ForEachEnumerator`).

The container object hierarchy within the framework is

```
System.Object
  Microsoft.SqlServer.Dts.Runtime.DtsObject
    Microsoft.SqlServer.Dts.Runtime.Executable
      Microsoft.SqlServer.Dts.Runtime.DtsContainer
        Microsoft.SqlServer.Dts.Runtime.EventsProvider
          Microsoft.SqlServer.Dts.Runtime.ForEachLoop
```

In a CLS language, the enumeration of any collection that implements the `IEnumerable` interface from the `System.Collections` base class can be leveraged using `foreach` syntax. An example in C# might be

```
XmlDocument theDocument = new XmlDocument();

theDocument.LoadXml(@"\\xmlserver\xmlshare\testfile.xml");

foreach (XmlNode aNode in theDocument.ChildNodes)
{
        // perform operation on 'each' Node
        aNode.InnerXml += "Operation Complete";
}
```

In SSIS, rather than implementing `IEnumerable` from `System.Collections`, a special alternate interface is defined called `ForEachEnumerator` (which in turn implements `IDTSForEachEnumerator`). This interface can be found in the `Microsoft.SqlServer.Dts.Runtime` assembly. Although it is similar in many ways to `System.Collections IEnumerable`, including the fact that it exposes a `GetEnumerator` method, it is an entirely separate implementation of the enumeration concept and as such is incompatible with `IEnumerable`.One big difference is that a call to `GetEnumerator()` returns a `System.Object` in the SSIS implementation, yet in the standard `System.Collections` version, the `IEnumerator` interface is returned.

There are specific implementations for each (no pun intended) of the different types of `Foreach` containers in SSIS. By default, the `Foreach` containers I cover in this chapter are installed, but if they don't fit your requirements, as I've said, just write your own; Chapters 15 and 16 discuss this in detail.

After you select the `Foreach LoopContainer` from the Toolbox and drop it on the design surface, the component reverts to its default setting of being a `Foreach File Enumerator` type. To alter the type and other settings, right-click the component and select Edit, as shown in Figure 6-3.

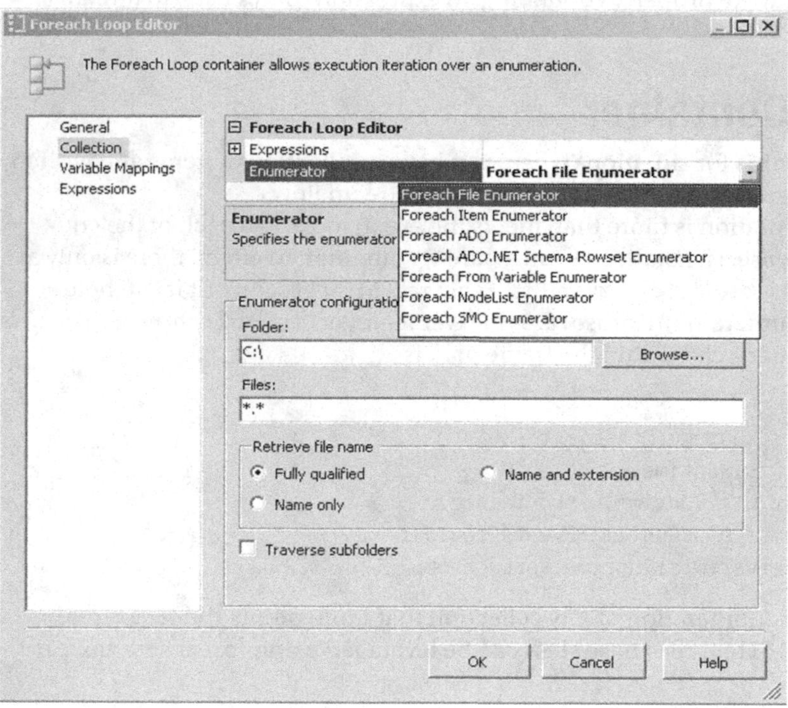

Figure 6-3. *Choosing the enumerator type*

Foreach ADO Enumerator

The `Foreach ADO Enumerator` enumerates each row in a row collection such as dataset, data table, or recordset. It can be used as an easy way of performing operations on each row in a collection, contained within the `Foreach Loop Container`. Figure 6-4 shows the configuration screen for this enumerator.

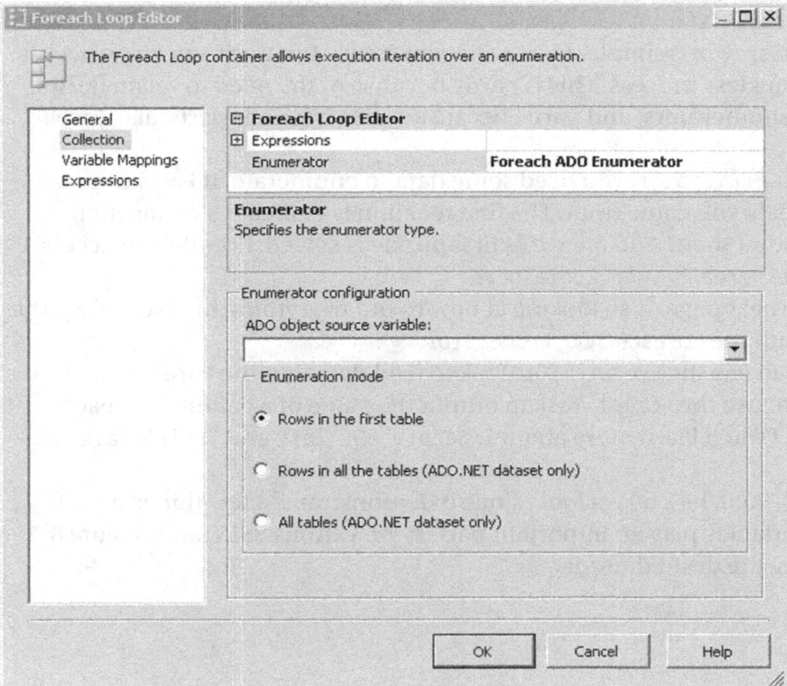

Figure 6-4. *The Foreach ADO Enumerator*

Collection Configuration

- **ADO object source variable**: This property specifies the name of the variable containing the data source.
- **Enumeration mode:**
    - `EnumerateAllRows`: When the variable contains a dataset, this setting enumerates all the rows in all the tables in the dataset. When the variable contains a datatable, this setting enumerates all the rows in the table. When it contains a recordset, it enumerates all the rows in the recordset.
    - `EnumerateRowsInFirstTable`: When the variable contains a dataset, this setting enumerates all the rows in the first table in the dataset. When the variable contains a datatable, it enumerates all rows in the table. When it contains a recordset, it enumerates all the rows in the recordset.
    - `EnumerateTables`: When the variable contains a dataset, this setting enumerates all the tables in the dataset. When the variable contains a datatable, it raises an error at runtime. When it contains a recordset, it enumerates all the rows in the recordset.

Usage

Using the Foreach ADO Enumerator is simple when you know how—but until you know how, it can be a frustrating and thankless process. This is partly because of the need to retain flexibility for supporting custom enumerators, and partly because . . . well, it's not particularly well designed or documented.

To use the Foreach ADO Enumerator, you need some data to enumerate. It isn't immediately apparent where this data will come from. The first reaction is to create a connection manager for the data, but what then? And once this first puzzle is solved, how do you access the retrieved data inside the Foreach Loop Container?

I'm going to spend the next page or so looking at how to put everything in place to use the Foreach Loop Container with the Foreach ADO Enumerator.

What I'm aiming for is to use the Execute SQL Task to feed data into the Foreach Loop Container, where I intend to use the Script Task to output the value of a column, for each row, to the output window. (You'll learn more about Excecute SQL Task and Script Task later in this chapter.)

Sounds easy, doesn't it? Well, let's take a look, since it demonstrates a few things to remember and also how variables play an important part in the various SSIS tasks. Figure 6-5 shows a package containing the desired results.

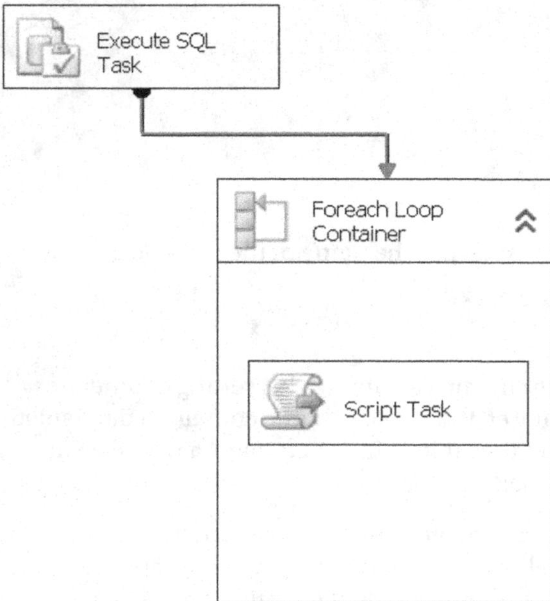

Figure 6-5. *The package you'll be creating*

A good starting point is to look at the data involved. Here I'm using a simple table from my ApressBook database. It has 1.6 million rows of data but is only three integer columns wide. Figure 6-6 shows the table structure.

	Column_name	Ty...	Computed	Length	Prec	Scale	Nullable	TrimTrailingBlanks	FixedLenNullInSource	Collation
1	startIpNum	int	no	4	10	0	yes	(n/a)	(n/a)	NULL
2	endIpNum	int	no	4	10	0	yes	(n/a)	(n/a)	NULL
3	locId	int	no	4	10	0	yes	(n/a)	(n/a)	NULL

Figure 6-6. *My simple table*

I want to output the value of one of the integer columns inside the Script Task. I'm going to assume that you either have a table with the same column names and datatypes or that you can create it in order to be able to follow the coming example. Listing 6-1 shows the table-creation script. If you need to create the table using the script, do so in whatever nonsystem database you are using for these examples. Ensure, however, that your task configurations also point to the database containing the created table.

Listing 6-1. *Table-Creation Script*

```
CREATE TABLE [dbo].[aTable]
(
        [startIpNum] [int] NULL ,
        [endIpNum] [int] NULL ,
        [locId] [int] NULL
)
```

Listing 6-2 is a script to populate the table with five rows of sample data. An alternative way of populating this table is to follow the example later in this chapter for the Bulk Insert Task. This example populates the table with a huge amount of data, which is ideal for learning how to use some of the other tasks described in this chapter.

Listing 6-2. *Script for Populating the Table*

```
INSERT INTO aTable ( startIpNum, endIpNum, locId)
VALUES (33996344, 33996351, 21530)

INSERT INTO aTable ( startIpNum, endIpNum, locId)
VALUES (50331648, 67276831, 223)

INSERT INTO aTable ( startIpNum, endIpNum, locId)
VALUES (67276832, 67276847, 3224)

INSERT INTO aTable ( startIpNum, endIpNum, locId)
VALUES (67276848, 67277023, 223)

INSERT INTO aTable ( startIpNum, endIpNum, locId)
VALUES (67277024, 67277031, 971)
```

Now that you have a populated table, follow these steps:

1. Create a new `OLE DB` connection manager and configure it to point to your local database (which in my case is `ApressBook`). I have called my connection manager `LocalHost.ApressBook`. For the sake of following the example, perhaps you could call yours the same.

2. With the connection manager in place, drop an `Execute SQL Task` from the Toolbox onto the design surface. You now need to configure it to retrieve the data you're interested in.

3. Right-click the `Execute SQL Task` and select Edit. You're presented with a screen similar to that shown in Figure 6-7.

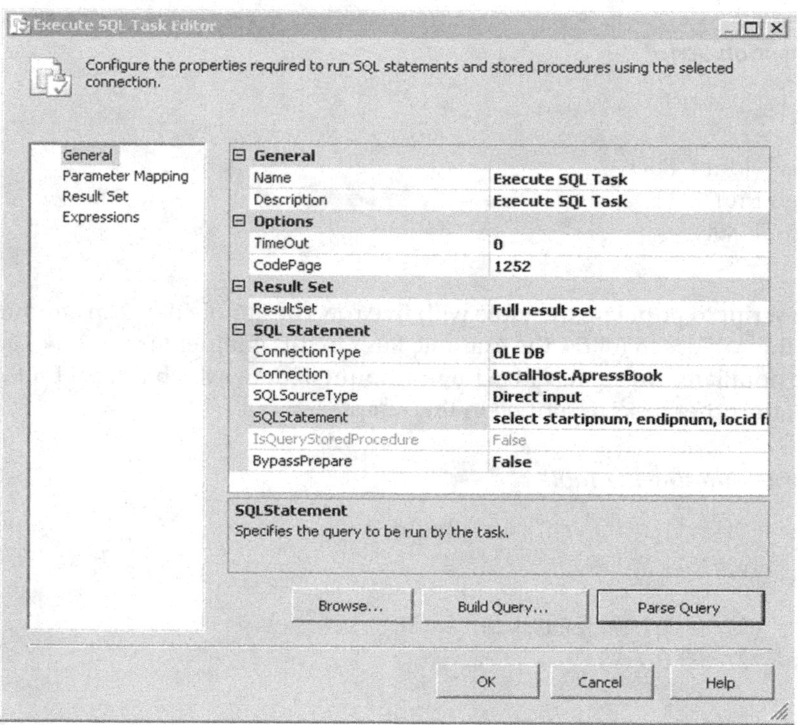

Figure 6-7. *First configuration steps*

4. You'll use a simple query here to get the rows you need. Populate the `SQLStatement` property with `SELECT startipnum, endipnum, locid FROM atable`.

5. Ensure the `Connection` property is populated by the name of the connection manager you created in Step 1 and then skip out of this configuration screen by clicking OK.

6. You need to add two variables, the first one of which—`myColVal4`—can be seen in Figure 6-8. This variable is for holding the value of the column you want on each iteration. Create the variable as package scoped and of type `Int32` to match the type of the `locid` column in the source table. This is the column you want to use for the `Script Task`. Remember that to create a package-scoped variable you must deselect the

Execute SQL Task in the designer by clicking elsewhere on the Control Flow design surface. Failure to do this causes the variable to be created at task level.

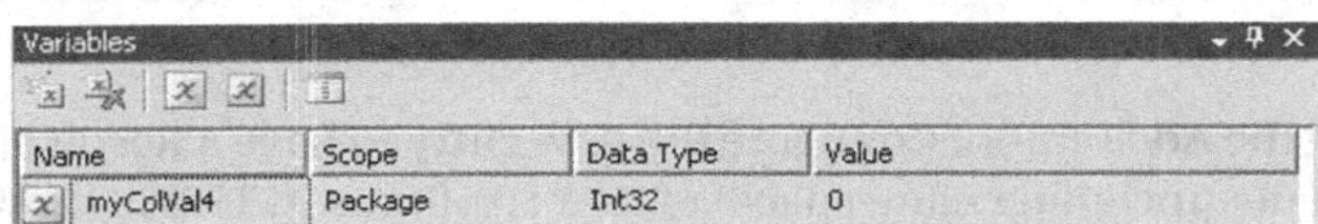

Figure 6-8. *The variable to hold the column value*

7. Add another package-scoped variable, which I'm calling myDataset, to hold the data returned from the Execute SQL Task (see Figure 6-9). Define the variable type as System.Object.

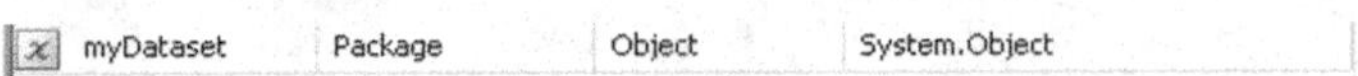

Figure 6-9. *The second variable to hold the dataset*

8. Go back to the Edit screen of the Execute SQL Task (see Figure 6-10). You can now configure everything you need to get the data out of the task and use it with the Foreach task. To return a result set from this component, you need to change the value of the ResultSet parameter—again, shown in Figure 6-10—to Full result set. The Foreach ADO Enumerator expects a setting of Full result set to operate.

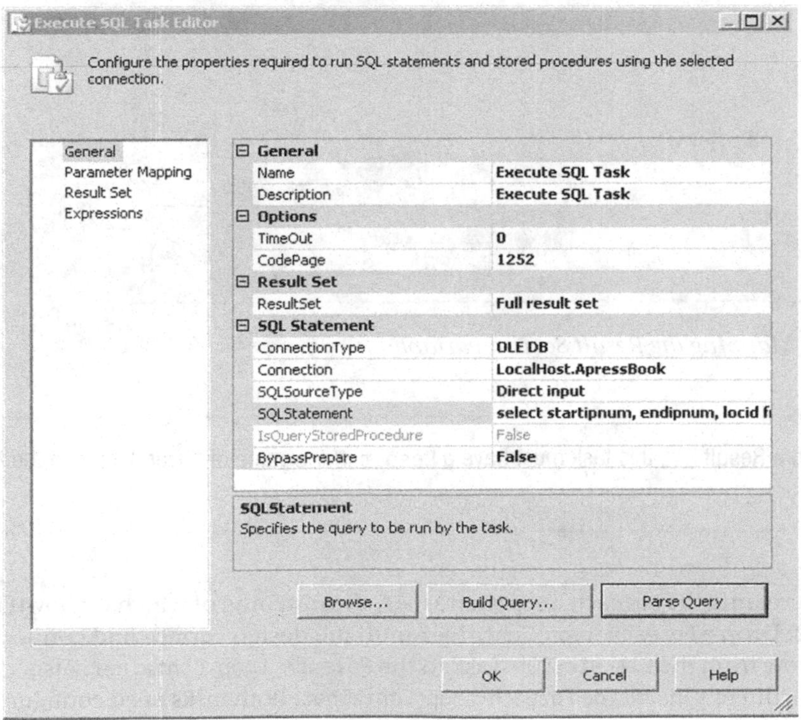

Figure 6-10. *Back to edit more properties.*

9. You're not done yet. You need to configure the task to assign the result set to a variable that will be used in the enumerator. To perform the assignment of the result set to a variable in this task, you need to look at the Result Set section of the editor. Select Result Set on the left side of the window.

10. Add a mapping using the Add button. Configure the new entry to have a Result Name of 0 and a Variable Name (including namespace) of `User::myDataset`. This is shown in Figure 6-11. The variable name refers to the `System.Object` typed variable, `myDataset`, that you declared earlier. This gets assigned as part of the task and is used to pass the `ResultSet` directly into the next task—with a little configuration of course.

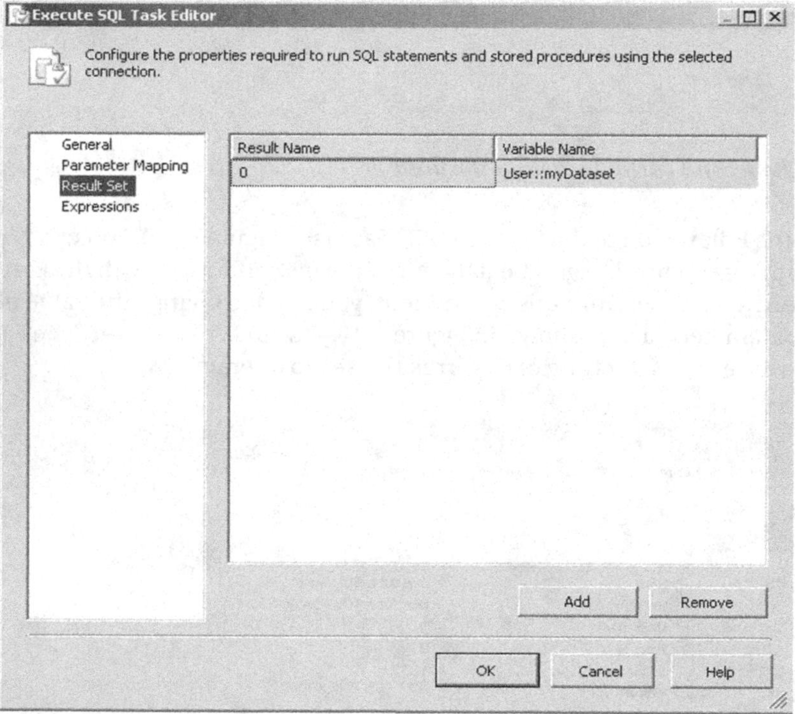

Figure 6-11. *Mapping the Result Set to a variable*

■ **Caution** To return a Result Set, this task must have a `Result Name` value of `0` (zero), or else the task will fail.

---

11. Next up is creating the `Foreach Loop Container`, the outcome of which is shown in Figure 6-12. Drop a `Foreach Loop Container` onto the design surface and connect the success arrow from the `Execute SQL Task` to the `Foreach Loop Container`. Also, drop a `Script Task` directly inside the `Foreach Loop Container`. Both tasks need configuring but let's go ahead and configure the `Foreach Loop Container` first. Figure 6-13 shows this.

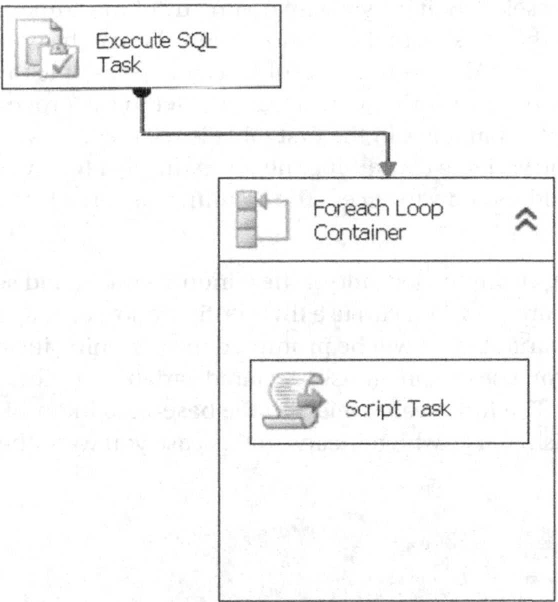

Figure 6-12. *Adding the Foreach Loop Container and Script Task*

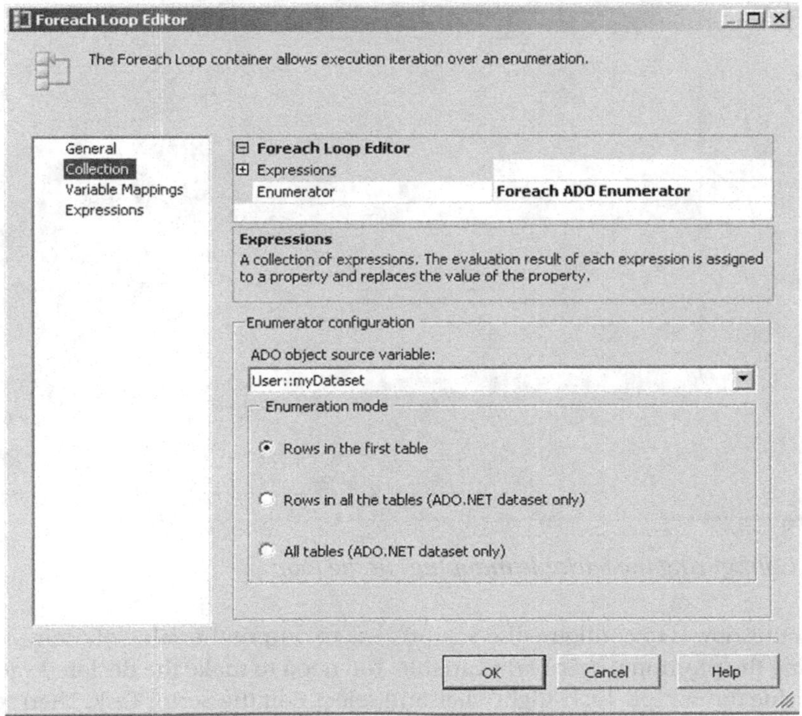

Figure 6-13. *Specifying the enumeration type and data-source variable*

12. Right-click the `Foreach Loop` and select Edit (as you can do on any of the containers or tasks). Select Collection from the left side of the window, then change the enumeration type to `Foreach ADO Enumerator`. Also set the ADO object source variable to `User::myDataset` so the task is populated with the data from earlier in the process. Ensure, under Enumeration mode, that Rows in the first table is selected. This correctly supplies the enumerator with the variable containing the data you wish to have enumerated, but you also need to address how to access the column value inside the `Script Task`.

13. After selecting Variable Mappings from the left side of the window, you should see a screen like the one shown in Figure 6-14. You can use this configuration area to assign a column from the dataset to a variable that will be promoted to everything inside the `Foreach` container. In this case you use the previously declared variable—`myColVal4`—and specify the Index value of 2. The Index value refers to the base-zero index of the column from the dataset you wish to use, which means in this case you want the third column (`locid`).

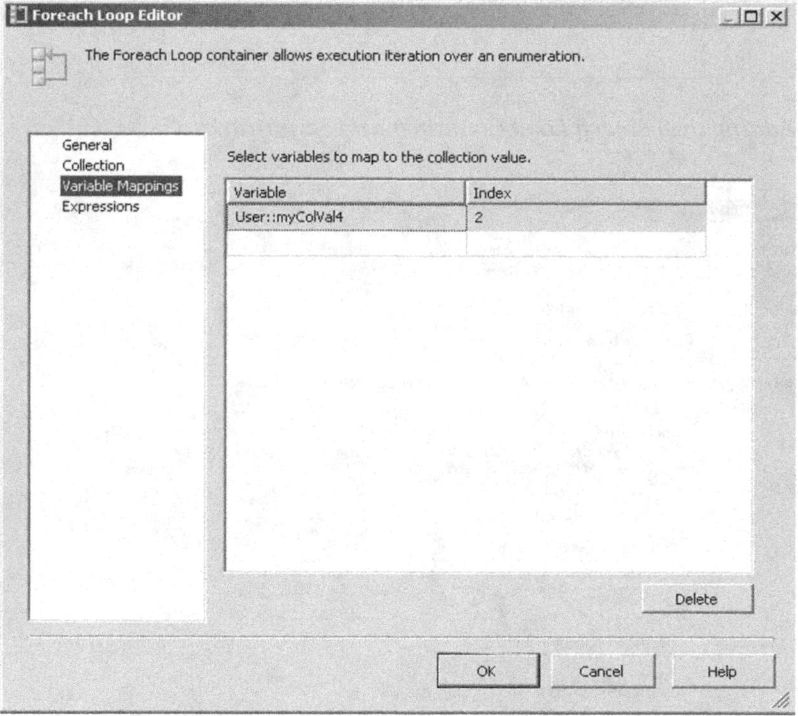

Figure 6-14. *Configuring the variable mappings in the loop*

14. All that remains now is to configure the `Script Task` to output the value of each `locid` column using the promoted `myColVal4` variable. You need to make the declared variables available inside the `Script Task`. Right-click and select Edit the Script Task. Then select Script on the left side of the window. You should then see a screen like Figure 6-15. The

ReadOnlyVariables property needs to be set to myDataset, and the ReadWriteVariable property should be set to myColVal4. This means that the myDataset variable is promoted for use inside the Script Task in a read-only fashion, and the myColVal4 variable is promoted as read/write.

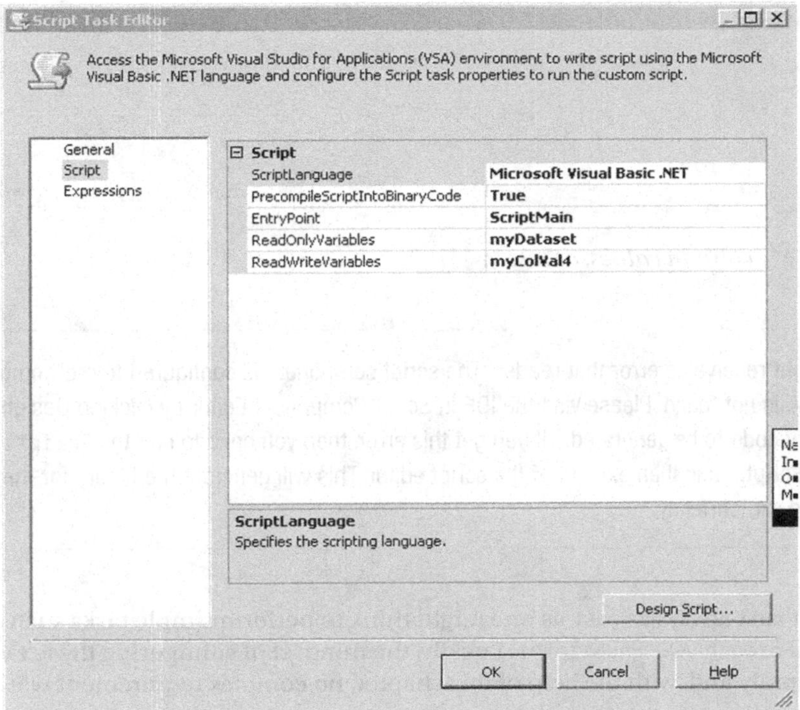

Figure 6-15. *Promoting variables for visibility inside the Script Task*

15. Set the PrecompileScriptIntoBinaryCode property to True. If you do this *after* clicking the Design Script... button, however, you'll have to go back in to design the script again so that a binary version of the code is produced. This is important because it can cause problems with execution.

16. Click Design Script... at the bottom of the window, which allows you to configure the script. You need to add some code, which I have highlighted in Figure 6-16. This code simply writes out the value of the myColVal4 variable to the debug output window in the IDE.

```
Public Sub Main()
    '
    ' Add your code here
    '

    System.Diagnostics.Debug.Print("Row: " & Dts.Variables("myColVal4").Value.ToString() &

    Dts.TaskResult = Dts.Results.Success
End Sub
```

Figure 6-16. *Using the Dts object to access promoted variables*

17. Run the package. You should get results like those in Figure 6-17. It looks like we have achieved what we set out to achieve—displaying the value of the `colid` column for each row of the returned (and enumerated) result set.

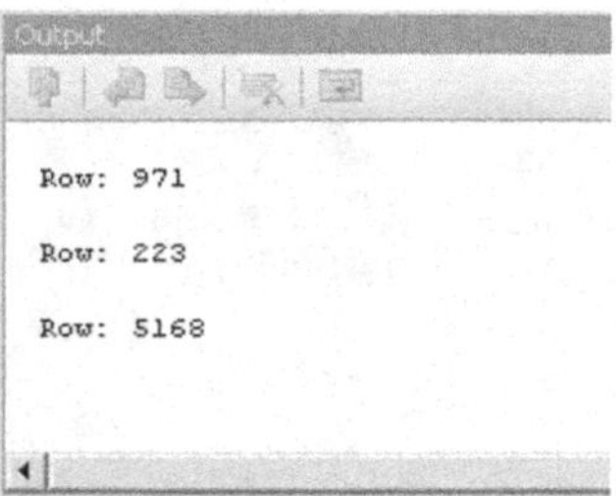

Figure 6-17. *My column values, at last*

■ **Warning** You might receive an error that reads: "The script component is configured to pre-compile the script, but binary code is not found. Please visit the IDE in Script Component Editor by clicking Design Script button to cause binary code to be generated." If you get this error, then you need to edit the `Script Task`, go back into Design Script... and then exit out of the script editor. This will generate the binary for the code, and everything should run perfectly.

In summary, it isn't always as easy as one might think to perform simple tasks such as implementing the `Foreach ADO Enumerator`. Luckily, the mindset of configuring these tasks correctly comes rapidly and, with the help of this chapter, no complex requirement will prove itself uncodeable.

Foreach ADO.NET Schema Rowset Enumerator

The `Foreach ADO.NET Schema Rowset Enumerator` is used to enumerate one of the schema information objects supported by the OLEDB provider used in a connection manager. Figure 6-18 shows the configuration screen once the `Foreach ADO.NET Schema Rowset Enumerator` value is selected as the Enumerator property value.

The collection-configuration screen prompts for two settings:

- **Connection**: The connection needs to be an `OLEDB` connection manager, such as `NativeClient`.
- **Schema**: A list of the available schema rowset objects for the OLEDB provider.

OLEDB providers implement support for any number of schema rowsets. The particular schema rowsets in use are down to whoever created the provider, which in turn depends on the features required of the provider. This is why a complete list of schema rowsets and possible *restrictions* is not available in this book. Think of restrictions as filters. Text values or variables can be used to filter the schema rowset based upon the restriction type chosen.

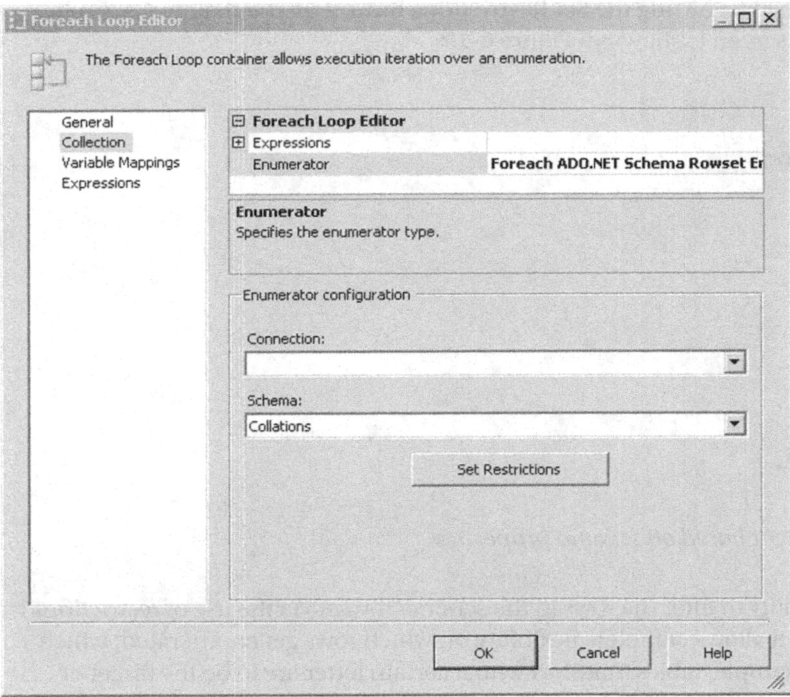

Figure 6-18. *Properties for the Foreach ADO.NET Schema Rowset Enumerator*

Table 6-1 is a sample list of schema rowsets and restrictions that are implemented in the native SQL OLEDB provider (`SQLNCLI.1`). The full list would be 36 entries long and would be valid only for this particular version of this particular OLEDB provider.

Table 6-1. *Schema Restrictions*

Schema	Available Restrictions
Asserts	CONSTRAINT_CATALOG CONSTRAINT_SCHEMA CONSTRAINT_NAME
Catalogs	CATALOG_NAME
Character sets	CHARACTER_SET_CATALOG CHARACTER_SET_SCHEMA CHARACTER_SET_NAME
Check Constraints	CONSTRAINT_CATALOG CONSTRAINT_SCHEMA CONSTRAINT_NAME
Collations	COLLATION_CATALOG COLLATION_SCHEMA COLLATION_NAME

You should review available documentation for the OLEDB provider in use to discover all possible enumerable schemas.

Restrictions are accessed by hitting the Set Restrictions button on the dialog. A sample restrictions-configuration screen is shown in Figure 6-19.

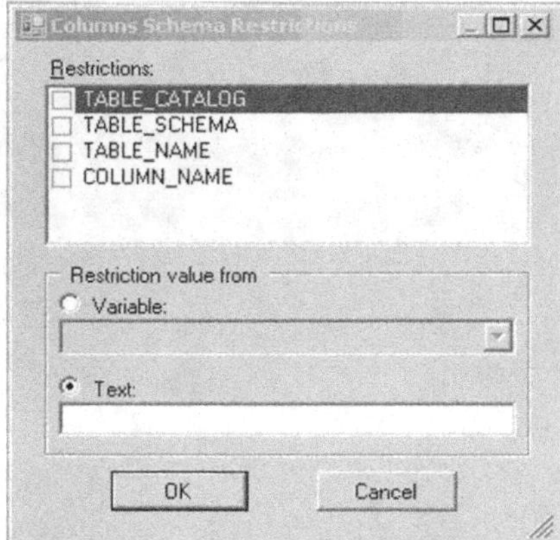

Figure 6-19. *Restricting content based on schema properties*

The inclusion of an ability to filter the rows in the schema rowset via the use of restrictions is important and very useful. It allows complete flexibility on which rows get enumerated, which is a good thing when, for example, tables that start with a certain letter are to be the target of enumeration. Without restrictions this would be much harder to implement.

Foreach File Enumerator

The `Foreach File Enumerator` evaluates the contents of a specified folder with a specified file filter and provides a collection of file objects to be iterated through. Figure 6-20 shows the main configuration screen. You configure this enumerator with settings shown in Table 6-2.

Table 6-2. *Foreach File Enumerator Properties*

Setting	Possible Value	Description
Folder		The name of the folder containing the files to enumerate
Files		The filename filter
Retrieve file name	Fully qualified	Retrieve full filename and extension, plus path information
Name and extension		Retrieve full filename and extension, excluding path information
Name only		Retrieve filename only, excluding extension and path information
Traverse subfolders		Specify whether to enumerate files in subdirectories below the folder specified in the Folder property

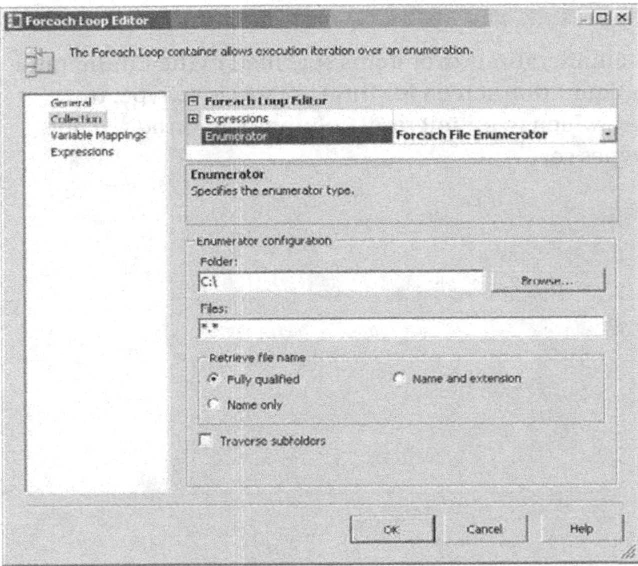

Figure 6-20. *Setting Foreach File Enumerator properties*

Foreach From Variable Enumerator

The `Foreach From Variable Enumerator` enumerates over the enumerable contents of a variable. The variable could contain, for example, an array or a dataset table, or any other kind of collection. Figure 6-21 shows the single configuration option available for this enumerator: specifying the name of the variable within which the enumeration is contained.

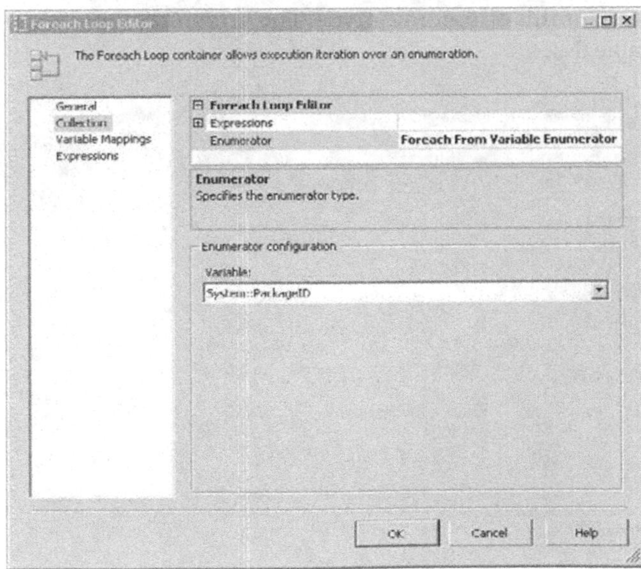

Figure 6-21. *Configuring the Foreach From Variable Enumerator*

Foreach Item Enumerator

The Foreach Item Enumerator performs enumerations over items specified in the Enumerator Configuration. Figure 6-22 shows the configuration screen for this Foreach Loop type. It prompts you to supply a list of values over which to enumerate. Columns can be added and removed for each list item and the datatypes set.

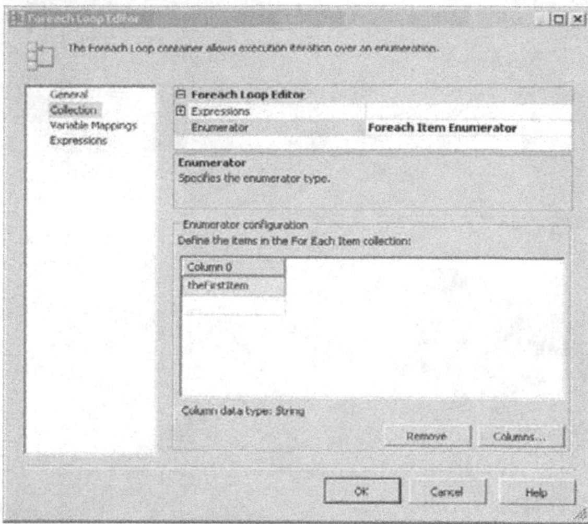

Figure 6-22. *Adding items to the Foreach Item Enumerator list*

Foreach Nodelist Enumerator

The Foreach Nodelist Enumerator enumerates the result set from an XPath expression. Figure 6-23 shows the configuration screen for this enumerator type. The screen prompts you to supply the properties shown in Table 6-3.

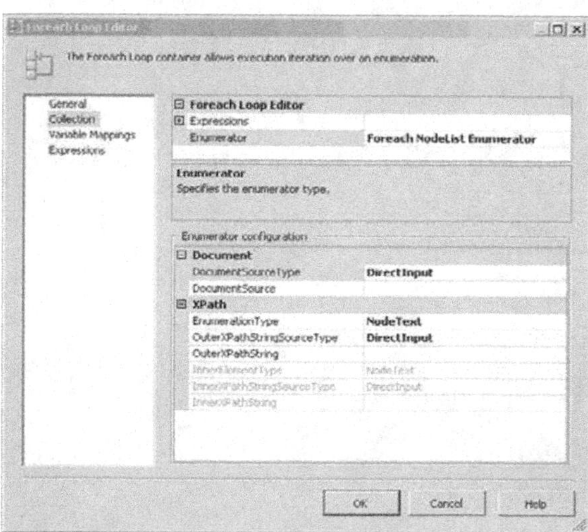

Figure 6-23. *The Foreach NodeList Enumerator editor*

Table 6-3. *Foreach Nodelist Enumerator Editor*

Properties	Possible Value	Description
DocumentSourceType		Tells the component where it should get the XML document from for processing
	FileConnection	Specifies that the DocumentSource property contains the name of a file connection containing the XML document
	Variable	The DocumentSource property contains the name of a variable that contains the
XML document		
	DirectInput	The DocumentSource property contains the XML document entered directly into the property
DocumentSource		Contains the name of a file, the name of a variable, or the XML document to process depending on the value of the DocumentSourceType property.
EnumerationType	ElementCollection	Enumerates element nodes
Navigator		Enumerates navigator objects
	Node	Enumerates nodes
NodeText		Enumerates node text
OuterXPathStringSourceType		Tells the component where it should get the outer XPath string from for processing
	FileConnection	Specifies that the OuterXPathString property contains the name of a file connection containing the outer XPath query
	Variable	The OuterXPathString property contains the name of a variable that contains the XPath query
	DirectInput	The OuterXPathString property contains the XPath query entered directly into the property
OuterXPathString		Contains the name of a file, the name of a variable, or the XPath query to use depending on the value of the OuterXPathStringSourceType property

Foreach SMO Enumerator

The `Foreach SMO Enumerator` enumerates SQL Server Management Objects (SMO) objects. Essentially this means any SQL Server object that is accessible via SMO. This is expressed as an SMO query that can be entered manually in the enumerator-configuration settings, as shown in Figure 6-24.

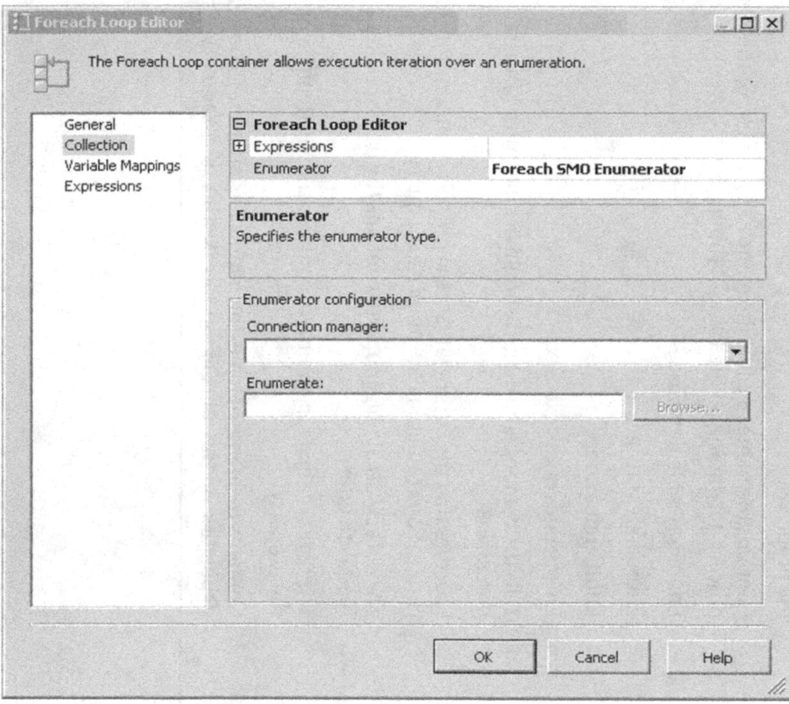

Figure 6-24. *Foreach SMO Enumerator configuration*

Configuration

- **Connection manager**: Specifies the connection manager to use for the enumeration.
- **Enumerate**: A string representing the SMO Query to enumerate against. An object-browse facility, accessed via the Browse button, can be used rather than entering an SMO query directly. This allows the selection of the objects you wish to enumerate, and the Enumerate property value gets populated by the results of the browse operation.

Sequence

Remember in Chapter 5 when I said that the root of the package-content hierarchy is a container? One special kind of container both conceptually and physically can hold any other type of container or Control Flow component. It's a *container container*, or supercontainer if you will. If you've ever used Microsoft BizTalk you'll recognize the concept of the Sequence component in the Group Shape.

There are a number of reasons why you would want to group Control Flow containers (or a series of Control Flow containers) inside a Sequence Container. The most obvious, superficially at least, is to provide a logical grouping to your processing. Dividing the processing into subsections feels good to the human mind, and it does tend to make things easier when you revisit your packages after an extended time and can immediately identify which parts of the package do which parts of the processing.

On a more technical and architectural level, the ability to transactionalize processing across multiple containers is important. This is certainly something that the Sequence Container provides too.

The enabling and disabling of individual Sequence Containers is useful in development and debugging stages of any project.

Properties and variables can be set at Sequence Container scope level that are propagated to all items contained within the container. This is useful for keeping variable state between contained containers.

ActiveX Script Task

If you are making the transition from DTS in SQL Server 2000, you may well be making use of this Control Flow task as an aid to migrating existing packages. If that is the case, you already know everything you need to know about ActiveX scripts.

If you don't know anything about ActiveX scripts, please move along in an orderly fashion. Nothing to see here . . . I say this only because ActiveX scripting is, as I mentioned in Chapter 3, deprecated and will be unavailable in the next version of SSIS. As Microsoft recommends, you shouldn't develop new functionality using ActiveX scripting!

It is my understanding that the version of SSIS shipping with the next version of SQL Server—Katmai or SQL Server 2008 as it is known—will continue to support ActiveX scripting. However, this is not guaranteed, and support could cease at any time come Release To Market (RTM) or with the release of a hotfix or Service Pack.

With all that said, the whole point of including the ActiveX Script Task is to provide legacy support; it has everything needed to get existing code to run. It is quite simple since, presumably, your ActiveX script has already been tested and works, so you can easily drop it into the ActiveX Script Task environment.

Check out Chapter 3 for more information on how to migrate old DTS packages to SSIS.

Now repeat after me: Use the Script Task . . . Use the Script Task.

Analysis Services Execute DDL Task

The Analysis Services Execute DDL Task executes Data Definition Language (DDL)–compliant content against an SSAS connection. XML for Analysis (XMLA) is the industry standard choice for DDL when it comes to "analysis services." SSAS is no exception.

The Analysis Services Execute DDL Task runs XMLA against an SSAS instance. This could be to create a new partition or dimension or other kind of SSAS object.

The latest XMLA standard—1.1—specifies two Simple Object Access Protocol (SOAP) methods: Execute and Discover.

The concepts surrounding the execution of DDL against SSAS are beyond this book's scope. They are very interesting, however, so I recommend learning more about this topic, especially if your SSIS knowledge is being gained for purposes of data analysis. Figure 6-25 shows the main configuration screen for the task.

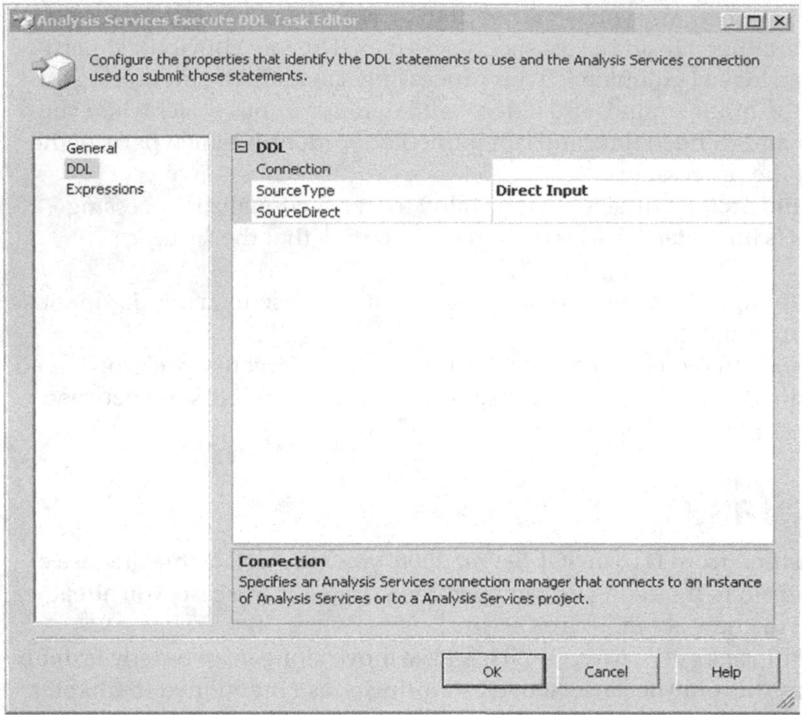

Figure 6-25. *Configuring the Execute DDL task*

DDL Configuration

Table 6-4 shows the configuration properties and possible values for the `DDL Configuration` task.

Table 6-4. *DDL Configuration*

Property	Possible Value	Description
`Connection`		Specifies the SSAS connection manager to use.
`SourceType`		Indicates to the component where the DDL can be found.
	`FileConnection`	Indicates that the `Source` property contains the name of a file connection that contains the DDL.
	`Variable`	Tells the component the `Source` property contains the name of a variable. The value of the variable is the DDL statement to use.
	`Direct Input`	Indicates that the `SourceDirect` property contains the actual DDL.
`Source`		Depending on the value of `SourceType`, this property will contain either the name of a file connection (which contains the DDL) or the name of a variable (the value of which will be the DDL).
`SourceDirect`		If the `SourceType` property value is `DirectInput`, then this property contains the DDL statement to use.

Analysis Services Processing Task

The `Analysis Services Processing Task` instigates analysis-services processing against SSAS objects such as cubes, dimensions, and mining models. This task will work only against SSAS 2005.

This task is useful, for example, when an ETL process has completed and SSAS objects need rebuilding to accommodate underlying data changes. It will usually come at the end of a set of ETL tasks, but another set of ETL tasks could follow the `Analysis Services Processing Task` also. Figure 6-26 shows the main configuration screen for the task.

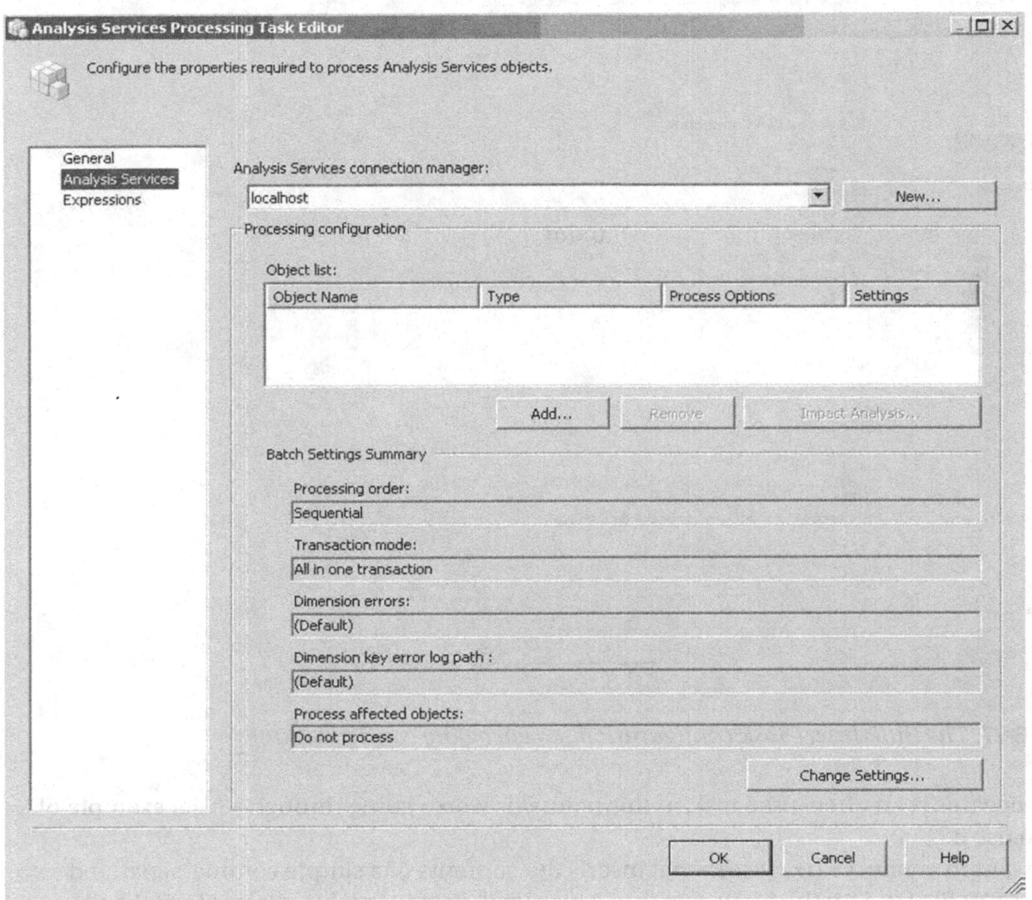

Figure 6-26. *Configuring the required operations*

Without delving too deeply into the features of SSAS . . . the properties exposed in this task all relate to the processing of these SSAS objects. Usefully, multiple operations can be specified, and you have a choice to process them sequentially or in parallel.

Bulk Insert Task

Importing flat-file data into a SQL Server doesn't get any faster than when you use a `Bulk Insert Task`. In reality this task is just a wrapper over the T-SQL `Bulk Insert` statement, as it was with DTS. Nonetheless, the performance has been tweaked and improved, and you should find this iteration of `Bulk Insert` to be much faster. With that said, there is little to see in terms of changes from the DTS version of this task. It's a staple component of DTS that you probably have used a million times before. Figure 6-27 shows the configuration screen.

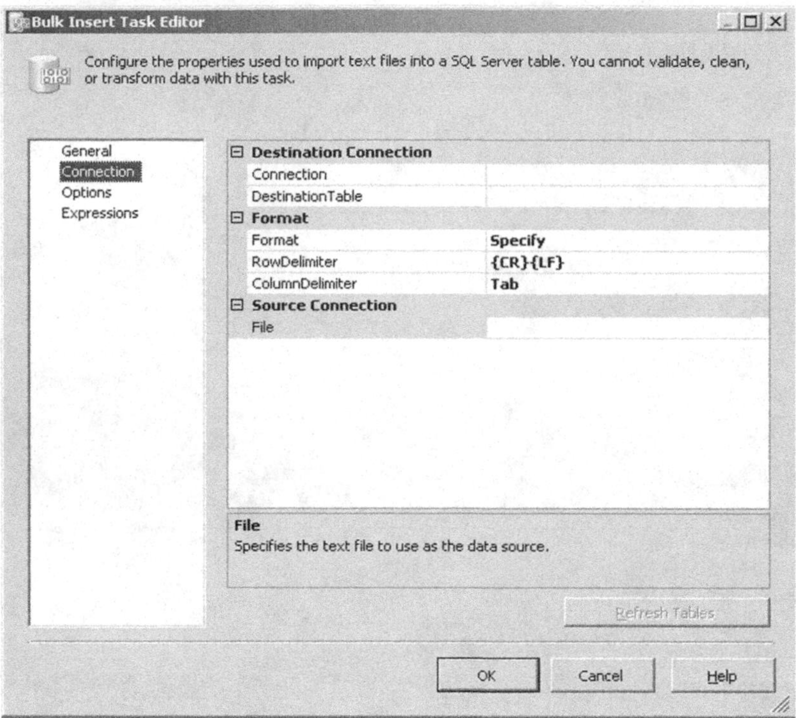

Figure 6-27. *The Bulk Insert Task configuration screen, before configuration*

Since this is an often-used task, at this point it is worth going through a brief example of how to use it.

I want to create a `Bulk Insert` that inserts the contents of a simple comma-separated value (CSV) file held on the filesystem into a new local database table. A sample of the file is in Listing 6-3. (The actual file is two million rows in length.) The file I've used, called `GeoLiteCity-Blocks.csv`, is released under the GNU Public License (GPL) for noncommercial use and is available from `http://www.maxmind.com/app/geolitecity`. Unzipped, it is around 100 MB.

Listing 6-3. *The bulkimport.fmt File*

```
<?xml version="1.0"?>
<BCPFORMAT xmlns="http://schemas.microsoft.com/sqlserver/2004/bulkload/format"
xmlns:xsi="http://www.w3.org/2001/XMLSchema-instance">
  <RECORD>
    <FIELD ID="1" xsi:type="CharTerm" TERMINATOR="," MAX_LENGTH="12"/>
    <FIELD ID="2" xsi:type="CharTerm" TERMINATOR="," MAX_LENGTH="12"/>
    <FIELD ID="3" xsi:type="CharTerm" TERMINATOR="\r\n" MAX_LENGTH="12"/>
  </RECORD>
  <ROW>
    <COLUMN SOURCE="1" NAME="startipnum" xsi:type="SQLINT"/>
    <COLUMN SOURCE="2" NAME="endipnum" xsi:type="SQLINT"/>
    <COLUMN SOURCE="3" NAME="locid" xsi:type="SQLINT"/>
  </ROW>
</BCPFORMAT>
```

Before I start configuring the task, I need to check the destination table to ensure the columns and datatypes are correct. The script for checking the table is in Listing 6-4.

Listing 6-4. *Table-Creation Script for the Destination Table*

```
CREATE TABLE [dbo].[csv_import_table_1]
(
          [startipnum] [int] NOT NULL,
          [endipnum] [int] NOT NULL,
          [locid] [int] NOT NULL
)
```

I optimized the import experience by using `Grep` to strip out the quotes around each value. And I removed first two rows temporarily just for this example:

```
Copyright (c) 2007 MaxMind LLC. All Rights Reserved.
startIpNum,endIpNum,locId
```

■ Caution For this example you should do as I did and remove the first two lines of the CSV file. Also, remove the quotes around each value in using `Grep` or a similar tool. Don't try and do it in Notepad or Wordpad, though, because the replace operation will take too long to complete.

Table 6-5 shows a sample of the data from the input file. Based on the data in Table 6-5, I used an XML format file for use with the bulk insert specifically created for this file. Create a new text file holding the contents of Listing 6-3 and save it as `bulkimport.fmt`.

Table 6-5. *Sample Data from Maxmind Input File*

startIpNum	endIpNum	locId
33996344	33996351	21801
50331648	67276831	223
67276832	67276847	3228
67276848	67277023	223
67277024	67277031	983
67277032	67277039	223
67277040	67277047	5170
67277048	67277055	3911
67277056	67277215	15953

Now, let's get the data from the file into the database. Ensure that the changes to the source CSV file (detailed above) have been made; otherwise the `Bulk Insert` will fail.

1. Drop a `Bulk Insert Task` from the Toolbox onto the Control Flow design surface.
2. Right-click the task and select Edit.
3. Click Connection on the left side of the screen to start configuring the task.
4. Since the desired destination for the bulk insert is the local SQL Server, you can use the OLE DB/SQL native client to get best performance. Select the <New Connection>... value in the Connection property box and create a new SQL Native Client connection to the database containing the destination table `csv_import_table_1`. Call this new connection `myConn`.
5. Set the `DestinationTable` value to point to the `csv_import_table_1` table.
6. Since we have an XML format file, set the Format value to `Use File`.
7. Change the `FormatFile` value to point to your format file (`bulkimport.fmt`, created above). In my case it is in `c:\temp\bulkimport.fmt`.
8. Select the <New Connection...> value in the File property box under the Source Connection section and create a new `File` connection manager that points to your copy of the `GeoLiteCity-Blocks.csv` file. Ensure the File property now reads `GeoLiteCity-Blocks.csv`; if it doesn't, select it from the drop-down list. With the Connection section fully configured, it should look just like Figure 6-28.
9. Now configure the Options settings. Click the Options item on the left side of the screen.
10. Set the `BatchSize` value to 10000. Ultimately this can be set to any sensible value but 10000 is fine for now.
11. Click the down arrow in the Options value box and uncheck the Check Constraints option. Ensure all other options are unchecked also. With the options for the task configured, it should look like Figure 6-29.

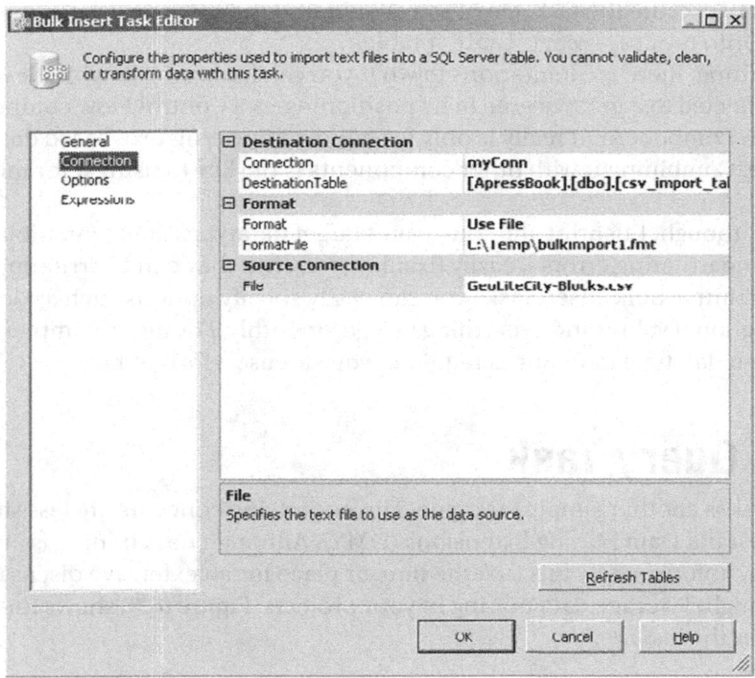

Figure 6-28. *The connection, all configured*

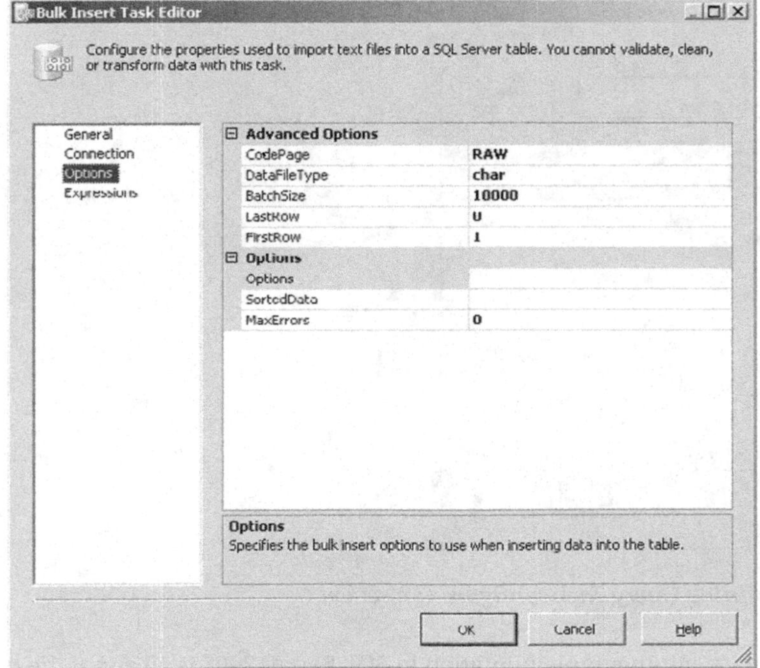

Figure 6-29. *Options settings, fully configured*

All that remains is to execute the task. Do it! You should find that the correct number of rows are bulk inserted into the `csv_import_table_1` table.

As is true of everything, there are limitations to what you can and can't do with the `Bulk Insert Task`. This is reflected to a great degree in its positioning as a Control Flow component rather than a Data Flow component. It really is only for rapidly importing text-based data into a SQL Server table. Combining it with other components is the key to using it for more-complex purposes.

The drill is simple, though. Ensuring the source and target datatypes are compatible is important for preventing irritating errors—easily fixable errors, but they can be irritating nonetheless. For more simple bulk-insert tasks you can easily specify options such as delimiter, line endings, and quoted value, and everything will go smoothly. For more-complex situations, such as when datatype mapping is required, you can use a format file.

Data Mining Query Task

`Data Mining Query Task` is another simple task type. The underlying concepts are less simple, requiring you to understand Data Mining Extensions (DMX). Although data mining is one of my favorite things ever, unfortunately this isn't the time or place for an extensive discussion of it or even of how you might leverage data mining in your projects. Figure 6-30 shows the main configuration screen for the task.

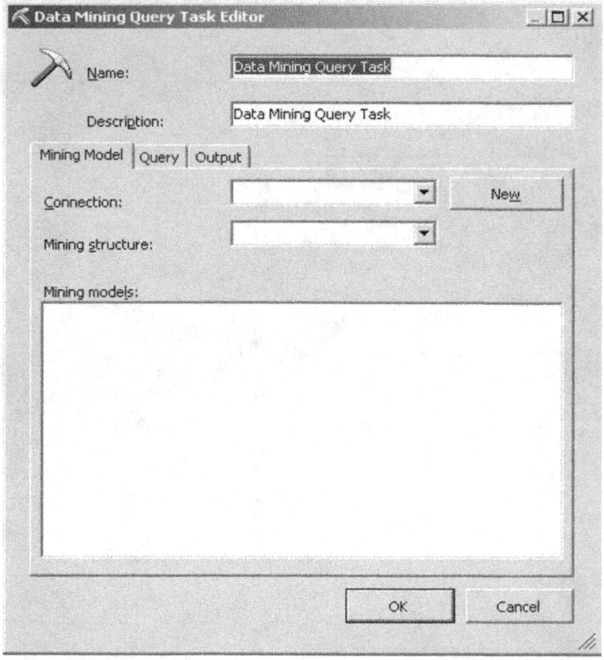

Figure 6-30. *The Data Mining Query Task configuration screen*

In a nutshell, the data-mining implementation in SQL Server 2005 is all about the discovery of factually correct forecasted trends in your data. This is configured within SSAS against one of the provided data-mining algorithms. In creating a DMX query you are requesting a predictive set of results from one or more such models built on the same mining structure. You may wish to retrieve predictive information about the *same* data but calculated using the different available algorithms.

I'll assume that if you are using the `Data Mining Query Task` you have at least one properly configured data-mining model within SSAS. If you've got that already, you will know all about DMX. The `Data Mining Query Task` handles the returning of both singleton queries and datasets.

Execute DTS 2000 Package Task

Unsurprisingly, the `Execute DTS 2000 Package Task` runs legacy DTS packages created using SQL Server 2000. Just as with the `ActiveX Script Task`, this is provided for support only and will probably be deprecated in the next release. It's really just a transparent, runnable container for your DTS package and as such no extension of functionality into SSIS exists. Figure 6-31 shows the configuration for the execution of the DTS 2000 Package Task.

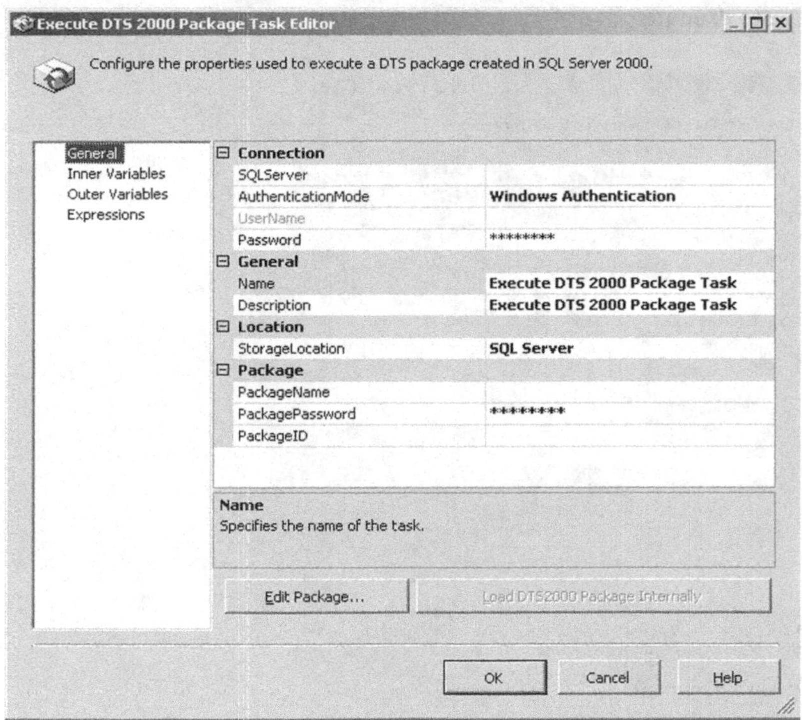

Figure 6-31. *Configuring the Execute DTS 2000 Package Task properties*

Perhaps you have already tried the DTS Migration Wizard and it hasn't worked. No? If you haven't tried to upgrade your legacy project yet, run along and try it now. I've written about it in Chapter 3. It might just save you from having to use this task type!

There are caveats and prerequisites to using the Execute DTS 2000 Package Task. You must, for example, have the DTS 2000 runtime engine installed, which some installers/DBAs disable because of its legacy status. If it isn't there you'll need to install it from the original media.

You can even edit your old DTS package using the Execute DTS 2000 Package Task editor, though you'll need to have SQL Server 2000 Tools installed to do so.

This task can run legacy packages stored in msdb, Meta Data Services, or files. Once configured, the Execute DTS 2000 Package Task can store the original package.

You can also use variables in your packages, at both task level (parent) called *outer variables*, and within the legacy DTS 2000 package (child) called *inner variables*.

Execute Package Task

You should carve up your SSIS Projects so they are made of individual, separate packages, each with a discrete function. You can then use the Execute Package Task to run these subpackages, making everything modular and easy to work with. As a bonus, this modularity lends itself to reuse, which is surely a design goal of everything we do. Figure 6-32 shows the configuration of the package to execute.

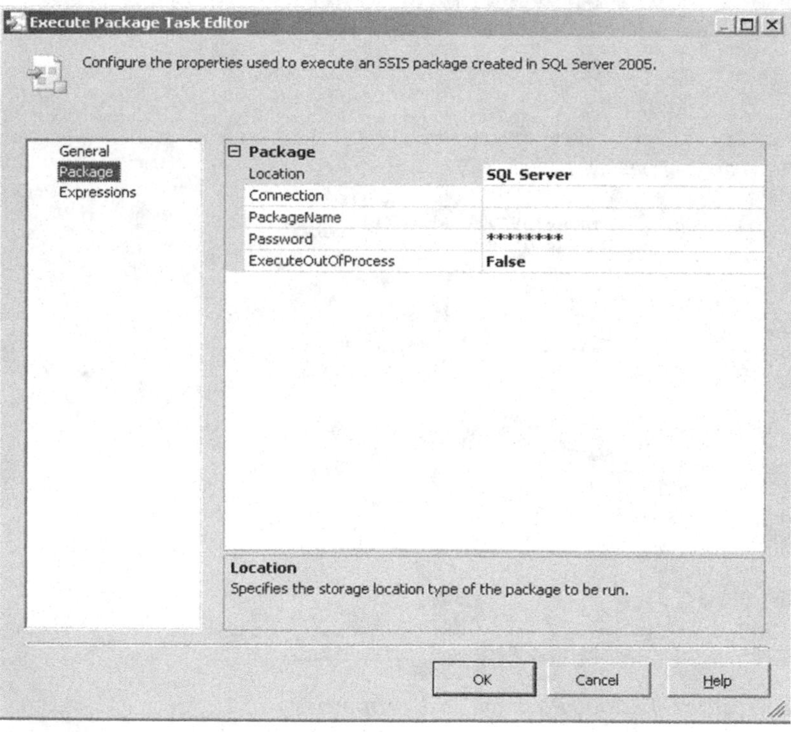

Figure 6-32. *Configure the package to execute*

Unlike the `DTS 2000 Package Task`, this task can't connect to SQL Server 2000 and run a package held in Meta Data Services. The `Execute Package Task` facilitates the running of an SSIS-created package that is held in either the filesystem or in the `msdb` database.

The `OLEDB` connection manager is used to connect to the configured SQL Server to access a package in the `msdb` database. A `File` connection manager is used to access filesystem-based packages.

Execute Process Task

Th `Execute Process Task` provides functionality to run a valid executable process as if from the command line. Nonetheless, when it comes to fully featured ETL processing, it can be very useful to make calls to external programs to perform additional tasks. Let's take a brief look at how this task can be configured. Figure 6-33 shows the configuration screen.

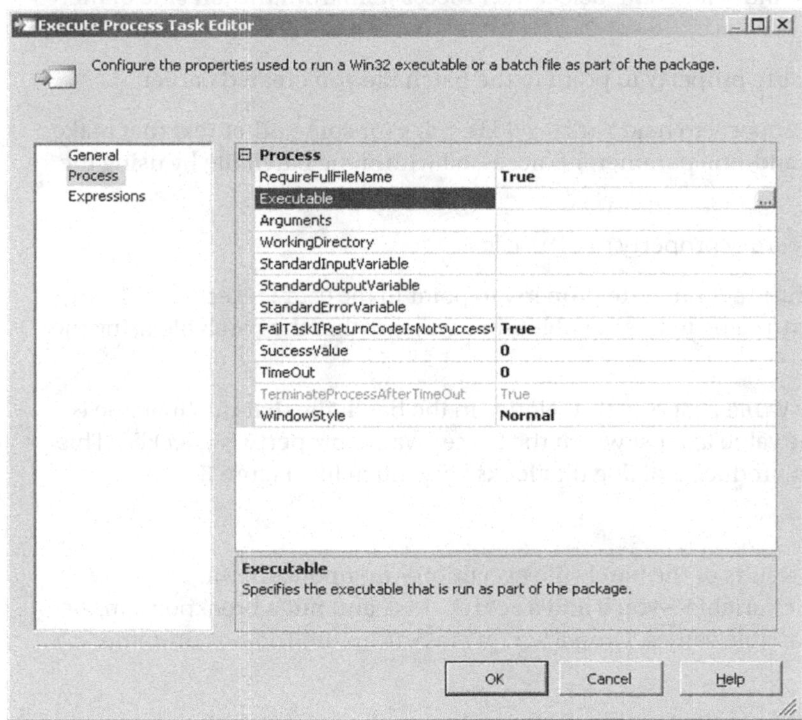

Figure 6-33. *Configuring the properties to execute an external process*

A few things need to be in place before you configure this task. Obviously, access to the executable file or batch file is needed for a start. In this example I'll describe how to execute a batch file, passing in a command-line argument, retrieving a variable from inside the batch file, and checking the return value for successful execution.

The first thing to create is the batch file. Create one called `MarkFileLogsAsComplete.bat` with the following contents:

```
@ECHO OFF
REM do some processing here, maybe?
ECHO %1 Done
RETURN 1
```

I'll describe the how and why of the batch file shortly. For now, let's move on and create the SSIS package. This example assumes that you know how to create a new package and that it is open in the IDE.

1. Drop an `Execute Process Task` from the Toolbox onto the design surface.
2. Add a new package-scope variable, `execVariableOutput`, of datatype `String`.
3. Right-click the task and select Edit. Select the Process item from the left side of the dialog.
4. Update the `Executable` property to point to the batch file you created earlier.
5. Set the `Arguments` property to read `Marking_File_Logs` (or some other text that makes sense). This command-line parameter is accessed within the batch file by using the `%1` syntax.
6. Set the `WorkingDirectory` property to `c:\windows`.
7. Update the `StandardOutputVariable` property to point to the `User::execVariableOutput Variable`. You assign a value to this variable—in a way—within the batch file using the `ECHO` command.
8. Update the `SuccessValue` property to 1. Notice in the batch file that the final line is `RETURN 1`.This is the value against which the `SuccessValue` property is checked. This final setting should produce a dialog that looks very much like Figure 6-34.
9. Click OK.
10. In order to see the results of the batch-file execution—an update of the `execVariableOutput` variable—you'll add a `Script Task` and put a breakpoint in there to view the variable values. Drop a `Script Task` from the Toolbox onto the design surface.
11. Connect the output from the `Execute Process Task` to the `Script Task`.
12. Right-click the `Script Task` and select Edit. Select the `Script` value from the left side of the dialog.
13. Set the `PrecompileScriptIntoBinaryCode` property to `True`. If you do this *after* clicking the Design Script... button, however, you'll need to go back in to design the script again so that a binary version of the code is produced. This is important because it can cause problems with execution. (See the Warning on page 106.)
14. Add `execVariableOutput` to the `ReadOnlyVariables` property value.

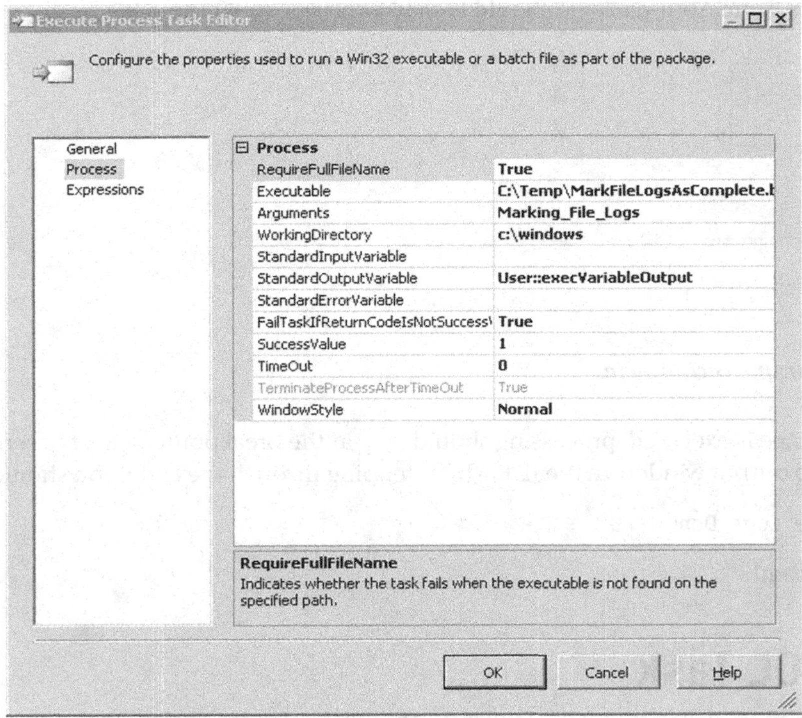

Figure 6-34. *Configured task properties*

15. Click the Design Script... button.
16. Add `Imports System.Diagnostics` to the Imports section at the top of the code.
17. Edit the `Main` method to match Listing 6-5.

Listing 6-5. *Edited Main Method*

```
Public Sub Main()

        Debug.WriteLine(vbCr)
        Debug.WriteLine("out: " & _
                Dts.Variables.Item("execVariableOutput").Value.ToString() & vbCr)

        Dts.TaskResult = Dts.Results.Success

End Sub
```

18. Set a breakpoint on the first `Debug.Writeline`.

That's it, you're done. Your package should look like the one in Figure 6-35.

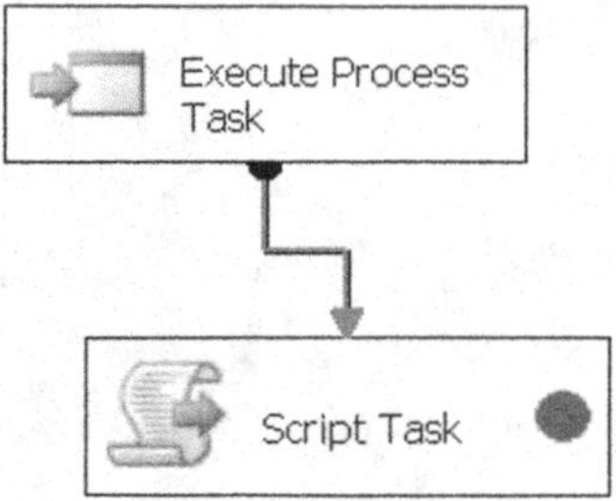

Figure 6-35. *The example is complete.*

Once the package is executed, processing should stop at the breakpoint inside the script. Taking a look at the output window in the IDE while stepping through the code, you should see:

```
out: Marking_File_Logs Done
```

It's as easy as that!

Execute SQL Task

Like `Execute Process Task`, `Execute SQL Task` is pretty self-explanatory. If you have a need to execute SQL against a connection, look no further. There are nuances, however, because the SQL to be executed could return a set of results or could be a call to a stored procedure.

This is also why this task allows the configuration of parameters: input, output, or return values. Figure 6-36 shows the task-configuration editor.

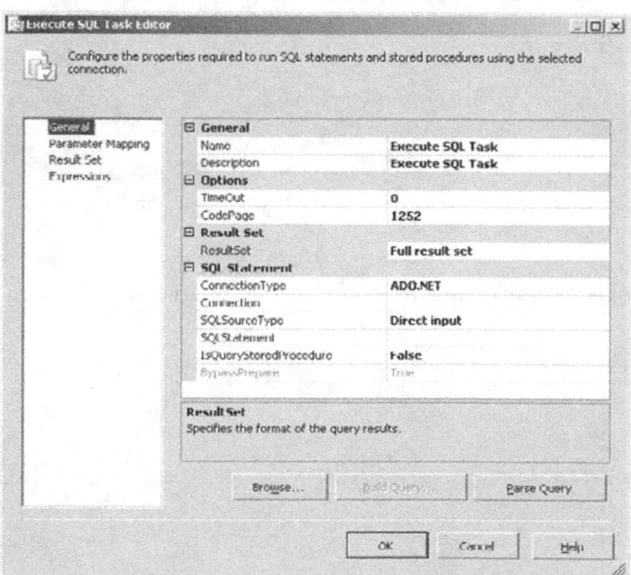

Figure 6-36. *The Execute SQL Task configuration editor*

When you execute a query that returns a result set, the `ResultSet` property should be set to `Full result set`. This also means that the Result Set section of the configuration needs to be correctly configured to receive the data. I've shown this in Figure 6-37.

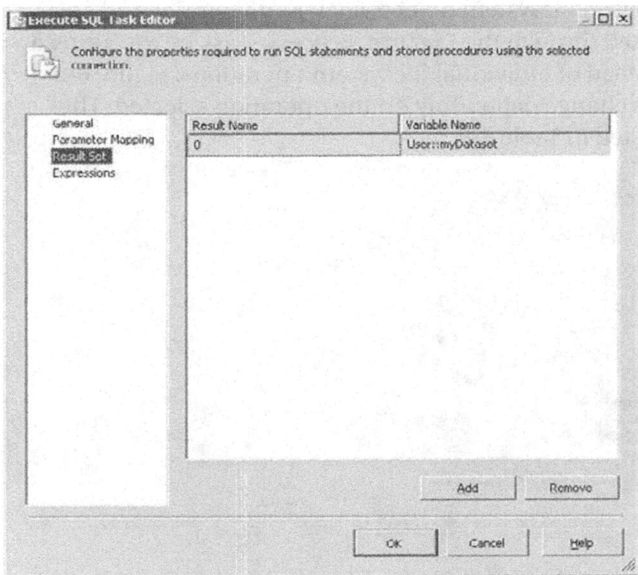

Figure 6-37. *Result Name 0? It must be a result set.*

As I described much earlier in this chapter, the correct configuration of the `Result Name` property should be to set it to `0` (zero) to retrieve a result set (or XML), with a variable of type `Object` being specified as the value of the Variable Name property.

When you use batched SQL statements—separated by `GO` statements, naturally—there are a few caveats to remember to ensure the task will work:

- Only one statement can return a result set, and it must be the first statement in the batch.
- If the result set uses result bindings, the queries must return the same number of columns. If the queries return a different number of columns, the task fails. However, even if the task fails, the queries that it runs, such as `DELETE` or `INSERT` queries, might succeed.
- If the result bindings use column names, the query must return columns that have the same names as the result-set names that are used in the task. If the columns are missing, the task fails.
- If the task uses parameter binding, all the queries in the batch must have the same number and types of parameters.
- When you map a variable to a result set with the `Single row` result set type, the variable must have a datatype that is compatible with the datatype of the column that the result set contains.

File System Task

Although the `File System Task` sounds similar to the `Execute Process Task`, at least in paraphrase, taken literally the name does describe the exact functionality offered. This task addresses common filesystem operations on filesystem objects such as directories and files.

Similar functionality can be replicated through the `Execute Process Task` by executing a batch file containing the operations, instead of individual filesystem operations. Figure 6-38 shows how `File System Task` properties change depending on the operation selected. The supported operations for this task are listed in Table 6-6.

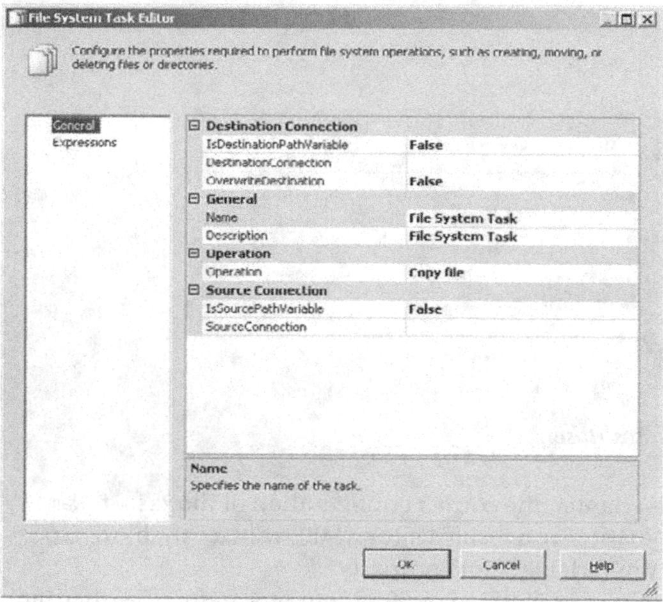

Figure 6-38. *The visible File System Task properties change depending upon the operation selected.*

Table 6-6. *Supported File System Task Operations*

Operation	Description
Copy directory	Copy entire directory
Copy file	Copy a file
Create directory	Create a directory
Delete directory	Delete a directory and its contents
Delete directory Content	Delete the contents of a directory, not the directory itself
Delete file	Delete a file
Move directory	Move a directory and its contents
Move file	Move a file
Rename file	Rename a file
Set attributes	Set the attributes of a file (such as Read Only)

FTP Task

The FTP Task is another handy SSIS component that gets used often in ETL environments. Sending the results of transformation or receiving input data via FTP, ever a popular file-transmission protocol, is well supported using this task. FTP doesn't really have a place in an SOA, but it does have a place. A surprising number of companies—even large companies like Ford—use FTP as part of certain ETL processes.

The task encapsulates and automates the tedious entering of FTP commands such as OPEN, USER, PASS, and GET. Figure 6-39 shows the configuration of an FTP operation. The supported operations for this task are listed in Table 6-7.

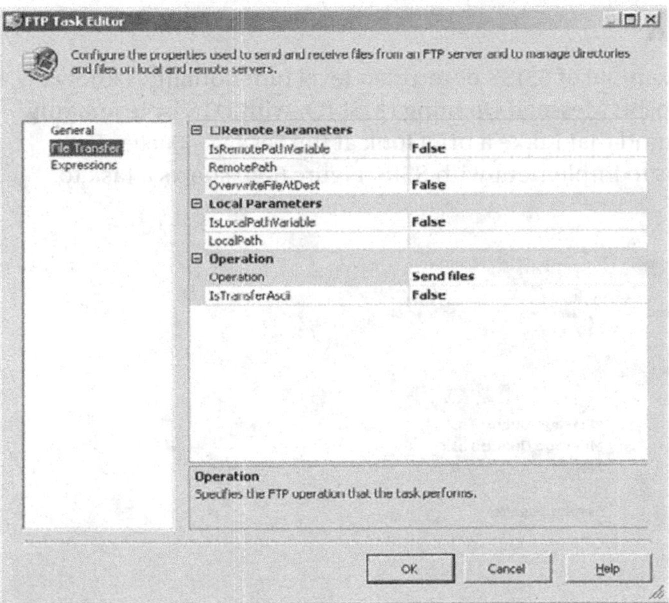

Figure 6-39. *Configuring an FTP operation*

Table 6-7. *Supported FTP Task Operations*

Operation	Description
Send files	Send files to remote server
Receive files	Receive files from a remote server
Create local directory	Create a local directory
Create remote directory	Create a remote directory
Remove local directory	Remove a local directory
Remove remote directory	Remove a remote directory
Delete local files	Delete files from a local directory
Delete remote files	Delete files from a remote server

Things to remember

- Wildcards are supported.
- When accessing a local file or a local directory, the FTP task uses a `File` connection manager or variable value. Multiple files can only be specified (by wildcard) when using a variable.
- When accessing a remote file or directory, the `FTP Task` uses the property or variable value.

Message Queue Task

The `Message Queue Task` is another example of SSIS's enterprise-level functionality. I know of at least two companies that use Microsoft Message Queuing (MSMQ) with DTS by leveraging ActiveX Scripting. It is with them in mind that I take a brief look at the `Message Queue Task` and show just how quick and easy it is to implement with SSIS. Figure 6-40 shows a task to configure MSMQ operations.

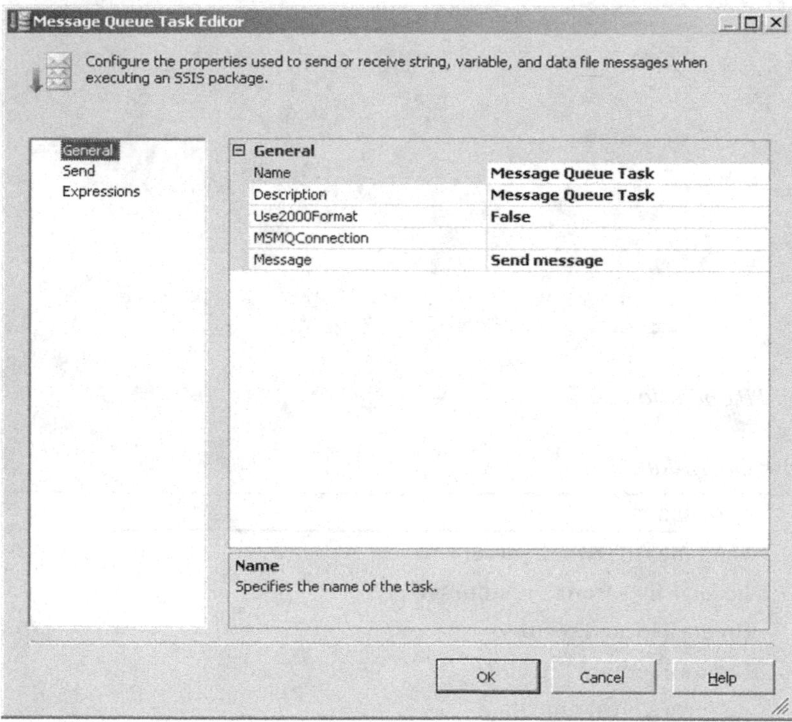

Figure 6-40. *A nice and neat task to configure MSMQ operations*

The cool thing about this task is that messages can easily be passed not only externally from SSIS but also internally, between packages. The message contents can be one of four kinds, as shown in Table 6-8.

Table 6-8. *Message Types*

Property	Description
`Data File`	The message is contained in a file.
`String`	The message is a `String`.
`String Message to Variable`	The source message, a `String`, has a destination type of `Variable`. This property is only supported on receive.
`Variable`	The message contains one or more `Variables`.

Script Task

The `Script Task` provides functionality to perform code-level processing using a familiar .NET language—Visual Basic.NET—and features of the .NET Framework. The `Script Task` configuration screen is shown in Figure 6-41.

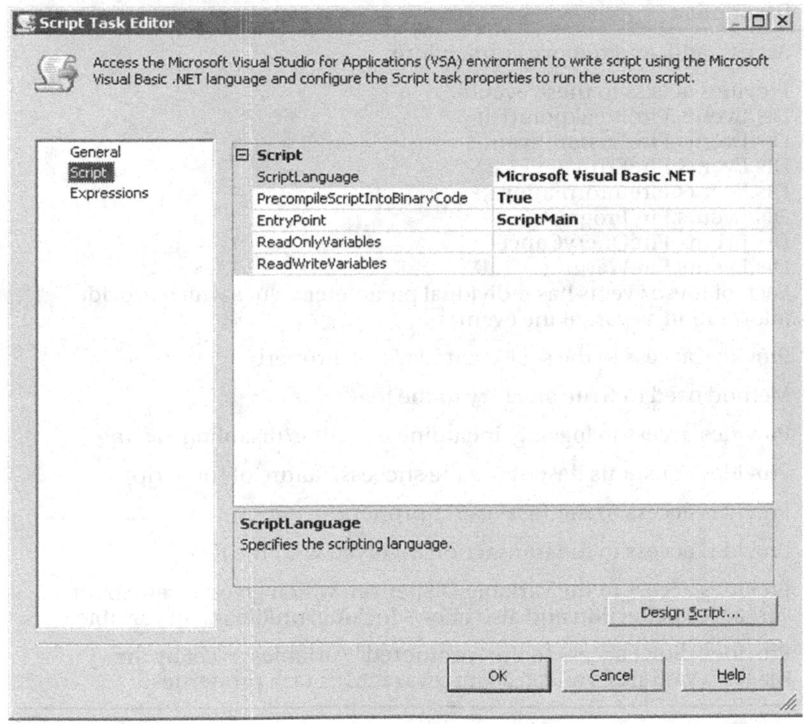

Figure 6-41. *The Script Task configuration dialog*

Scripting in SSIS is a suitably complex topic that is discussed in much greater detail in Chapter 14. To provide a very brief overview of an important feature of the task, Figure 6-42 shows some of the properties within the `Dts` object available to the `Script Task` coder.

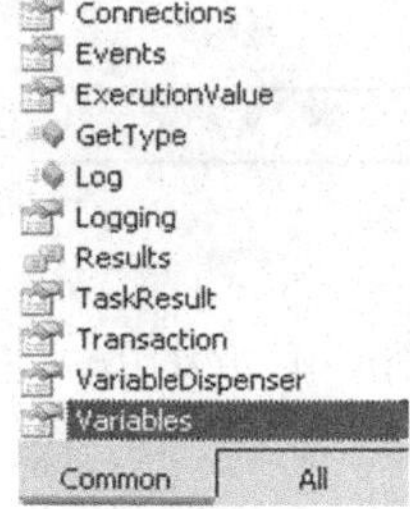

Figure 6-42. *The Dts object is incredibly useful.*

Within the `Script Task`, the static `Dts` object is exposed to provide access to the contents shown in Table 6-9.

Table 6-9. *Properties exposed by the Dts object in the Script Task*

Object Exposure	Description
`Dts.Connections`	Access, add, and remove connections.
`Dts.Events`	Provides access to these events: Dts.Events.FireBreakpointHit Dts.Events.FireCustomEvent Dts.Events.FireError Dts.Events.FireInformation Dts.Events.FireProgress Dts.Events.FireQueryCancel Dts.Events.FireWarning Each of these events has individual parameter values which provide information as part of the event.
`Dts.ExecutionValue`	Provides access to the set `ExecutionValue` property
`Dts.Log`	Method used to write an entry to the log
`Dts.Logging`	Provides access to logging, including enabling/disabling logging
`Dts.Results`	Provides constants describing the success/failure of the script
`Dts.TaskResult`	Provides access to the `TaskResult` property
`Dts.Transaction`	Provides access to the transaction involved with the task
`Dts.VariableDispenser`	Provides access to the Variable Dispenser, which gives access to the `Variables` collection and also allows locking/unlocking of variables
`Dts.Variables`	Provides direct access to the "promoted" variables as set by the `ReadOnlyVariables` and `ReadWriteVariables` task properties

Use Edit ➤ Design Script to edit the script. As you might expect, you can set breakpoints, which are hit when the task is running.

Send Mail Task

What can I say the Send Mail Task that isn't already implied by its name? It's a task that sends e-mail. Clever and useful!

No messing with things like Collaboration Data Objects (CDO) or SQLMail (remember that?) here. Just configure the Simple Mail Transfer Protocol (SMTP) connection, set a few properties, and your mail is gone. Figure 6-43 shows the main configuration screen.

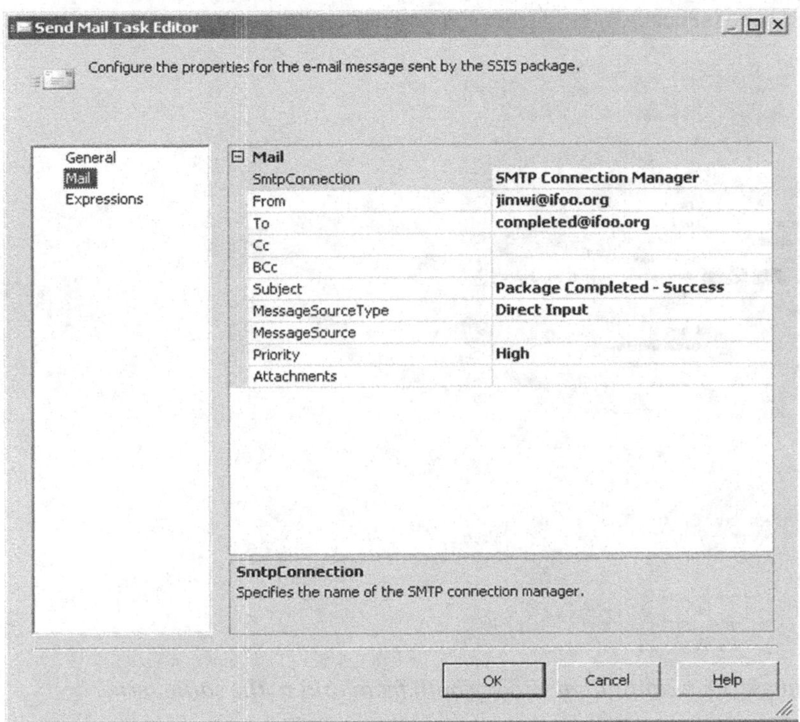

Figure 6-43. *Configuration of the Send Mail Task is straightforward.*

This task is useful for sending messages within, for example, the development environment, but it doesn't offer the flexibility of control and presentation that a more dedicated e-mail solution might. I guess it isn't meant to be anything more than basic.

Messages can be built up using a variable and perhaps a `Script Task` upstream in the Control Flow that would go some way toward producing content more suitable for reporting purposes. Alternatively, I would advise the creation and use of either a custom Control Flow component that incorporates your requirements, or a class library containing methods to support them.

The message text can be a string that you provide, a connection to a file that contains the text, or the name of a variable that contains the text. The task uses the `SMTP` connection manager to connect to a SMTP server.

Transfer Database Task

The `Transfer Database Task` is used to copy or move a database from one SQL Server to another. Transfers can take place between version 8 (SQL Server 2000) and version 9 (SQL Server 2005) database servers. This task can transfer only a single database as part of the operation. It is not possible to transfer SQL Server 2005–format databases to SQL Server 2000, however. SQL 2005 has many more features and the two formats just aren't compatible.

Figure 6-44 shows the task-configuration dialog, updated to make a copy of the `ApressBook` database called `ApressBookUAT`.

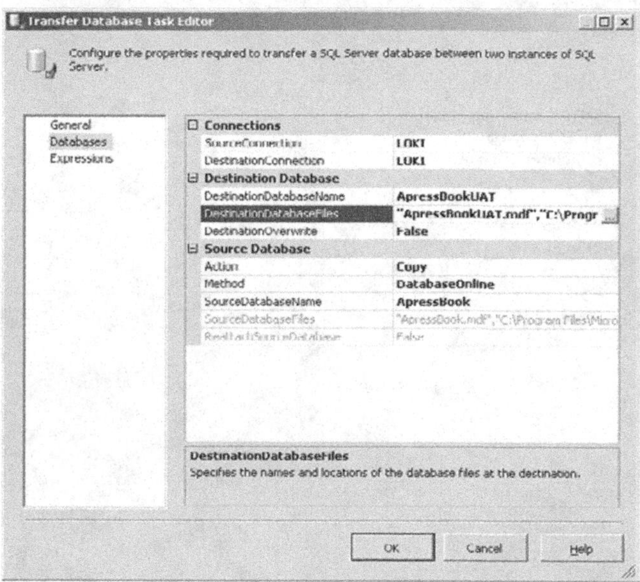

Figure 6-44. *A Transfer Database Task configured to copy both from and to the same server*

For operations such as copying a database from between environments—perhaps between the test environment and the production environment or during User Acceptance Testing (UAT) as a rapid way to clear down test data—this task is perfect and one you'll use time and again. Remember, however, that if you are transferring a database to the same server, the `.mdf` and `.ldf` files must be renamed if a separate copy is to be made.

When you use online-mode transfers, an `SMO` connection manager is required for both the source and destination servers, unless you're transferring databases to and from the same server. In this case only a single `SMO` connection manager is required.

Transfer Error Messages Task

The `Transfer Error Messages Task` transfers user-defined error messages between SQL Server instances. This is a pretty specialized task type. A DBA or someone else who has chosen not to transfer error messages as part of the `Transfer Database Task`, and realizes they should have also been copied, might use this task.

This task makes it easy to transfer all or some of the user-defined error messages from one server to another. This can be seen in Figure 6-45.

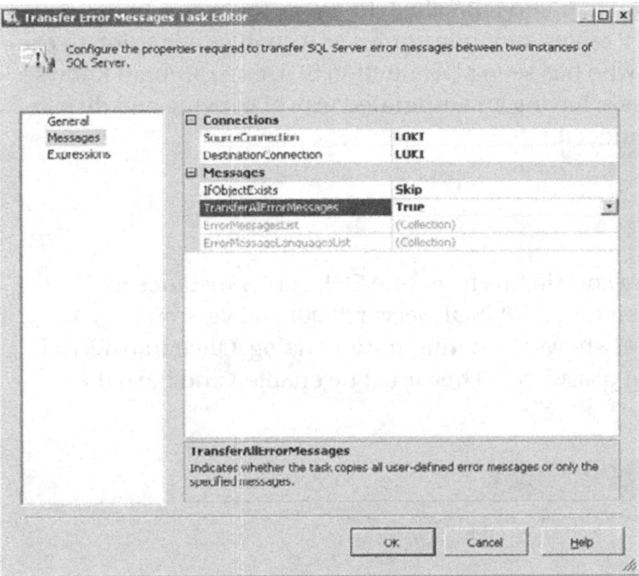

Figure 6-45. *These simple properties for the Transfer Error Messages Task need configuring.*

Transfer Jobs Task

The `Transfer Jobs Task` is used to copy SQL Server Agent jobs from one SQL Server instance to another. Transfers can take place between version 8 (SQL Server 2000) and version 9 (SQL Server 2005) database servers. An example of the configuration screen is in Figure 6-46.

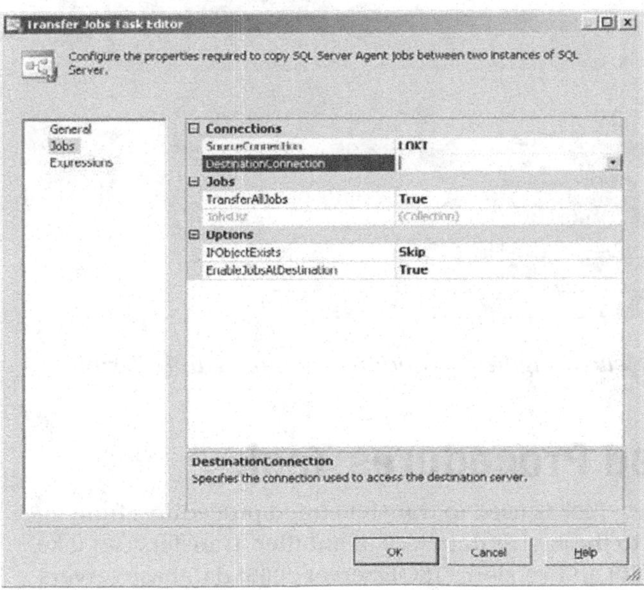

Figure 6-46. *Configuring the Transfer Jobs Task to copy jobs and enable them at destination*

This is a useful task for the SSIS developer and DBA alike. Imagine, for example, creating a package that distributes updates to OLTP tables and then copies and enables a SQL job to execute an OLAP-update package. Anyone who has seen a production SQL environment knows how many jobs get created on a daily basis; having an automated way of copying and distributing jobs around servers is very useful indeed.

Transfer Logins Task

The `Transfer Logins Task` is used to copy logins from one SQL Server instance to another. Transfers can take place between version 8 (SQL Server 2000) and version 9 (SQL Server 2005) database servers. Figure 6-47 shows the configuration dialog. Once transferred, the logins are disabled and have random passwords. They must be enabled and have their passwords changed to be useable.

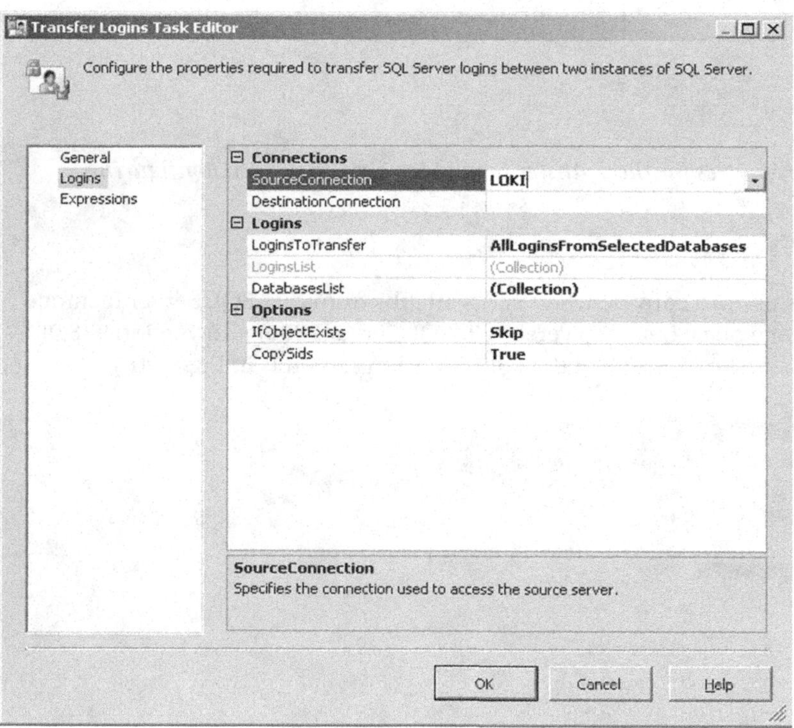

Figure 6-47. *The Transfer Logins Task has few configuration options, yet is incredibly flexible.*

Transfer Master Stored Procedures Task

The `Transfer Master Stored Procedures Task` is used to transfer stored procedures from the `master` database on one SQL Server to the `master` database of another. Transfers can take place between version 8 (SQL Server 2000) and version 9 (SQL Server 2005) database servers. Figure 6-48 shows a partially configured task.

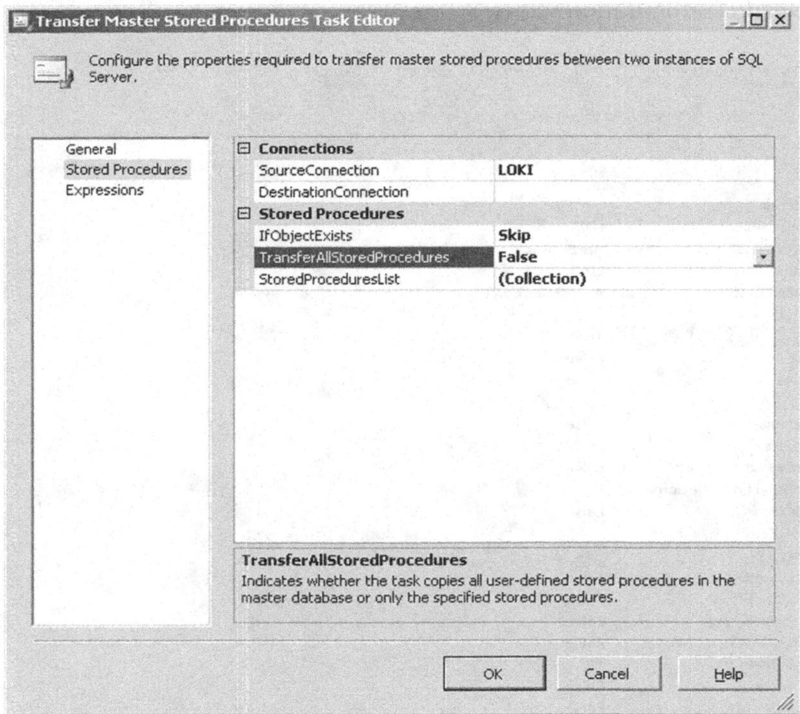

Figure 6-48. *Configuring the Transfer Master Stored Procedures Task*

Why would you want to transfer only master stored procedures? I can only think that, again, they might not have been copied for some reason during a database transfer. Or maybe there's a problem with a server's master stored procedures and they need refreshing from a different server. This is another task that is more DBA-oriented than developer-oriented.

Transfer SQL Server Objects Task

The `Transfer SQL Server Objects Task` is used to transfer SQL Server objects from one SQL Server instance to another. Transfers can take place between version 8 (SQL Server 2000) and version 9 (SQL Server 2005) database servers, depending on content.

The "depending on content" caveat is in place simply because some SQL Server objects are new to SQL Server 2005 and just don't exist on 2000. It makes complete sense that SQL 2005 features such as .NET assemblies won't transfer!

This task will be immediately familiar to any user with even basic DBA skills; the transfer of SQL Server objects through the SQL Server Management Studio is handled by this task type, with a nice friendly UI fronting the process.

Figure 6-49 shows the main configuration screen.

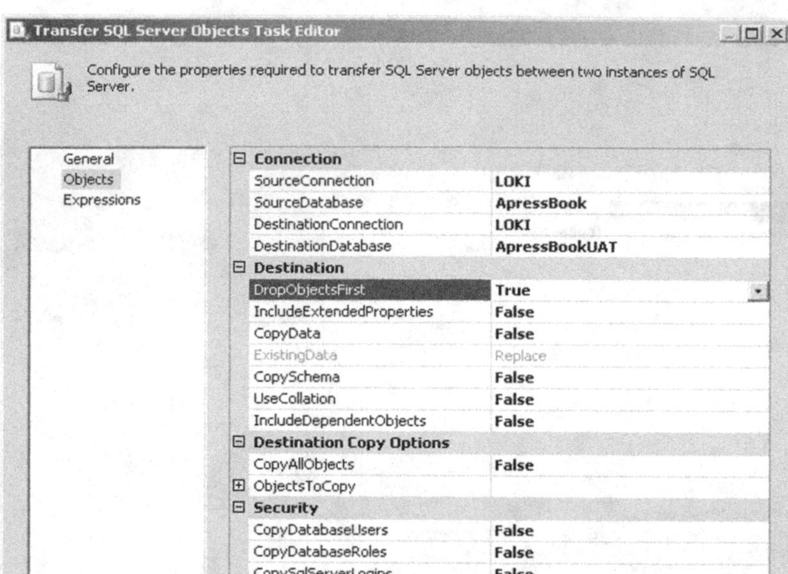

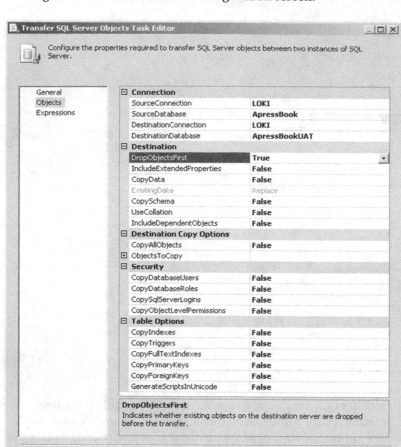

Figure 6-49. *The Transfer SQL Server Objects Task has lots of properties but is still straightforward.*

Web Service Task

The `Web Service Task` consumes a web service method. I anticipate this task will be widely used, so it warrants a detailed explanation and example.

As you might expect, this task takes care of all the hard work in consuming a web service. There is no messing around with building SOAP envelopes or the like. You simply configure the task to make the call.

Imagine a scenario where part of an SSIS solution requires a package that makes a web service call to retrieve information about a supplied ZIP code. In this case, I'm assuming access already exists to a suitable web service that serves such a request. I'll use a web service located on the `http://www.webservicex.net` web site that is freely available for low-usage requirements.

As usual, I am starting this example with a new package that contains no tasks, components, or other settings.

Let's work through the steps required to get our required functionality:

1. Drop a `Web Service Task` from the Toolbox onto the design surface.
2. Add a new package-scoped variable called `myWebMethodResult` of datatype `String`.
3. Right-click the `Web Service Task` and select Edit. You will see a screen similar to Figure 6-50. The first configuration options relate to accessing the desired web service.

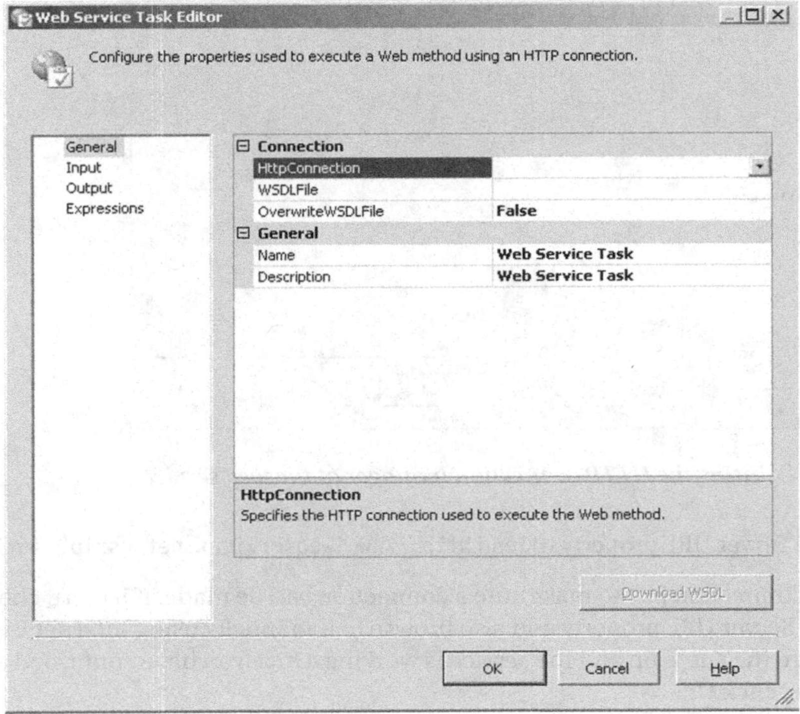

Figure 6-50. *The Web Service Task configuration screen, before configuration*

4. The next thing to do is to get the task to discover some information about the web service you wish to call. Luckily the web service specification includes the use of a Web Services Description Language (WSDL) file that, when accessed, provides information about how to communicate with the service and the web methods that are exposed for consumption. The first configuration screen is the place to tell the task where to find this file and download its contents. Click the ellipsis (...) button on the `HttpConnection` property and select < New Connection...> to display the screen shown in Figure 6-51.

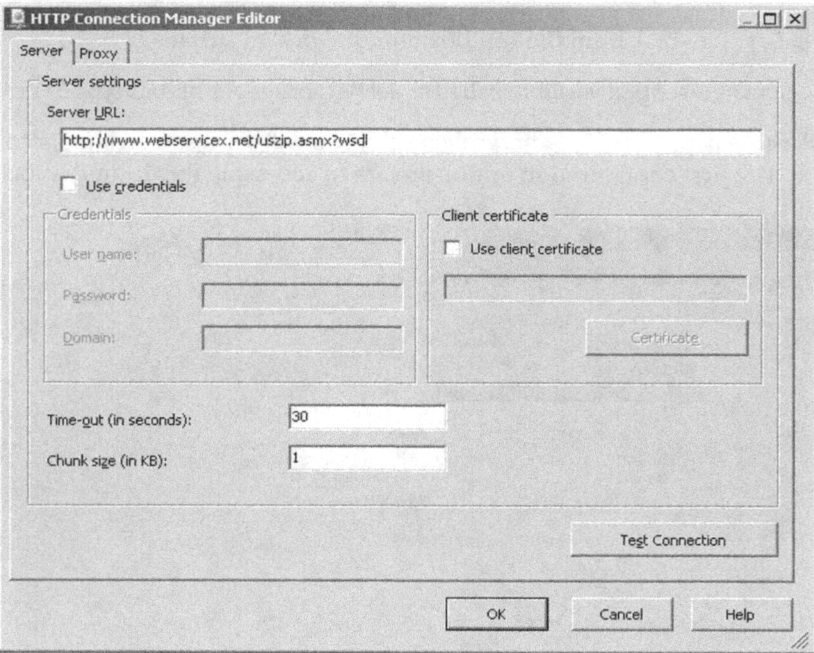

Figure 6-51. *Pointing the HTTP connection manager at the web service*

5. Change the Server URL property to read `http://www.webservicex.net/uszip.asmx?wsdl`.

6. Click Test Connection just to make sure a connection can be made. If it can't, check the URL in the Server URL property and also browse to it manually using Internet Explorer to make sure the site is up and the service is working. Once you have confirmed everything is fine, click OK.

7. Back on the main configuration screen, enter a path and filename to store a copy of the WSDL file. I have chosen `c:\temp\zipinfows.wsdl`, but it isn't important where it goes or what its name is, as long as security access is ensured. Your configuration screen should be looking similar to the one in Figure 6-52.

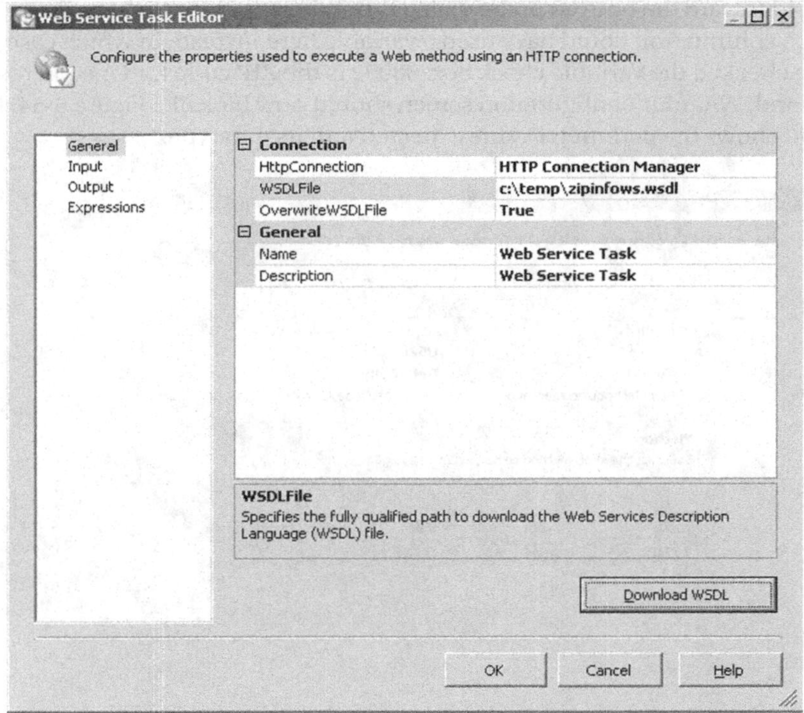

Figure 6-52. *Web Service Task configuration is beginning to come together.*

8. Click Download WSDL, which is located toward the bottom of the window. After a few moments the message shown in Figure 6-53 should appear.

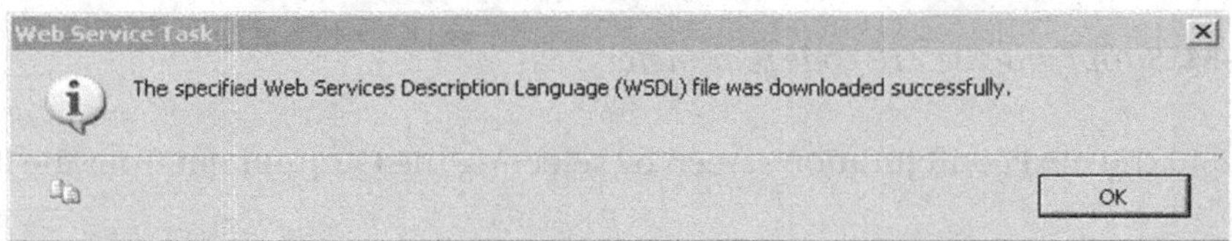

Figure 6-53. *The WSDL file has been downloaded.*

9. Select the item labeled Input from the left side of the dialog.
10. Click the Service property and select `USZip` from the drop-down list.
11. Click the Method property and select `GetInfoByZip` from the drop-down list.

12. Once the grid toward the bottom of the dialog is populated, enter 98052 as the value for the Value column. You could have used a variable here instead, in which case you would have checked the Variable check box. 98052 is the ZIP code for One Microsoft Way, Redmond, WA. Your configuration screen should now look like Figure 6-54. Notice how the grid shows the parameter value expected and its datatype.

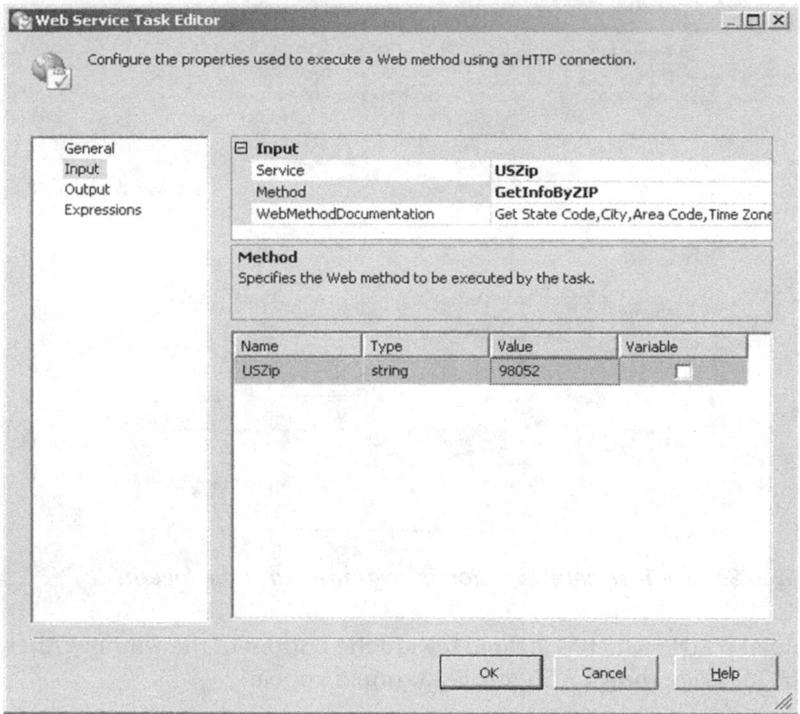

Figure 6-54. *Supplying the ZIP code parameter*

13. Move on to the next configuration screen by selecting the Output item from the list on the left.

14. Configuration on this tab is simple. Change the `OutputType` to `Variable`, and change the `Variable` property to the name of our variable—in this case `User::myWebMethodResult`. Figure 6-55 shows these configuration settings. Once everything is configured, click OK.

15. To get some feedback from the `Web Service Task`—that is, that the value held in the `myWebMethodResult` variable has changed—let's add a `Script Task`. Drop a `Script Task` from the Toolbox onto the design surface, somewhere below the `Web Service Task`.

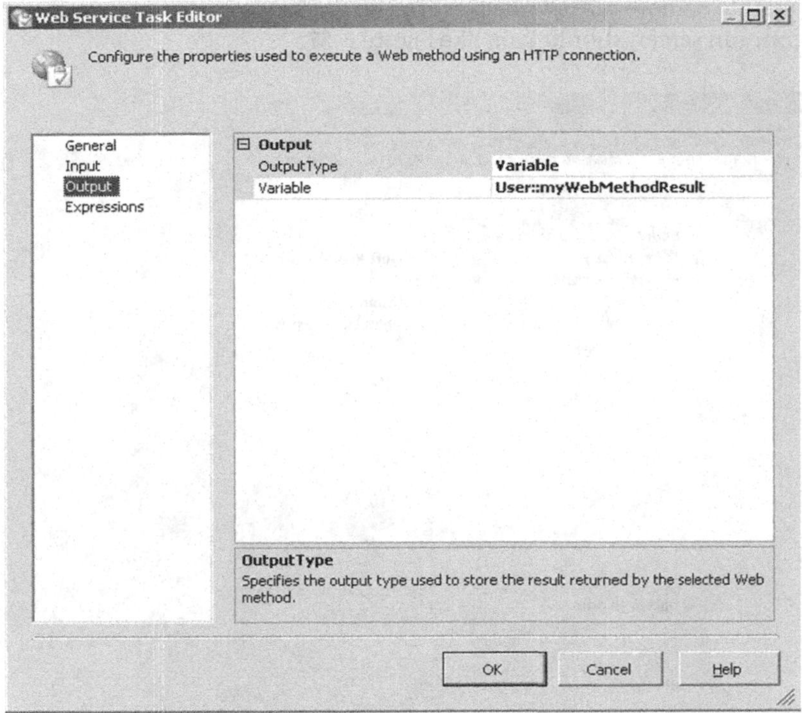

Figure 6-55. *Assigning the web method result to a variable*

16. Connect the success arrow from the bottom of the `Web Service Task` to the `Script Task`. Your Control Flow designer should look something like Figure 6-56.

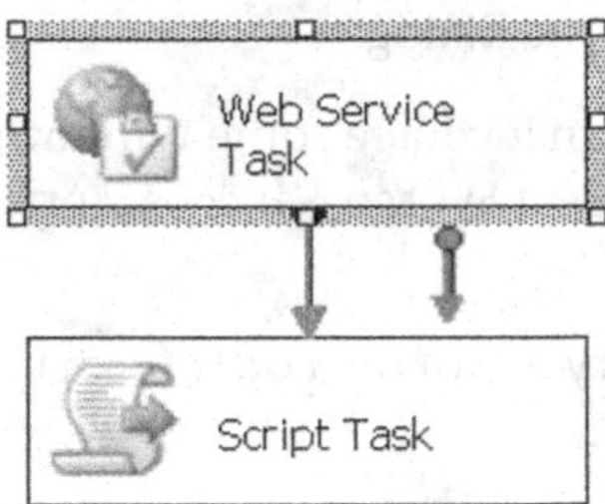

Figure 6-56. *Your Control Flow should look like this.*

17. Right-click `Script Task` and select Edit to configure it.

18. Select Script from the left side of the dialog, and set the `PrecompileScriptIntoBinaryCode` property to `True`. If you do this *after* clicking the Design Script... button, however, you need to go back in to design the script again so that a binary version of the code is produced. This is important because it can cause problems with execution.

19. Enter our variable name—`myWebMethodResult`—in the `ReadOnlyVariables` property. Your configuration screen should look like Figure 6-57.

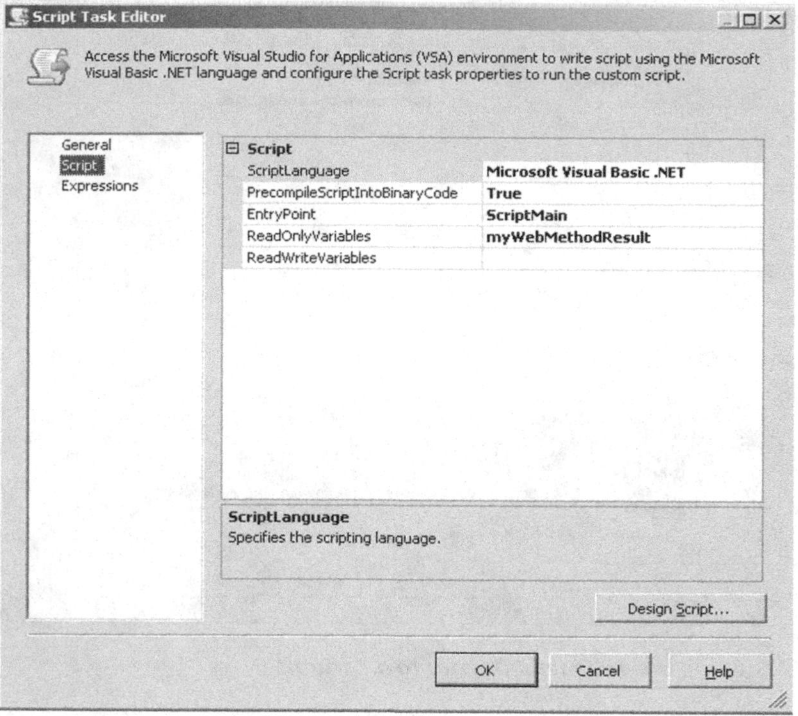

Figure 6-57. *The Script Task configuration*

20. Click the Design Script... button toward the bottom of the dialog.

21. Once the IDE has opened up, add a reference so you can leverage some Windows Forms methods. Go to Project ➤ Add Reference and select `System.Windows.Forms.dll` from the list presented. Click Add and then OK.

22. Add the following line to the Imports section at the very top of the code: `Imports System.Windows.Forms`.

Change the `Sub Main` section to match Listing 6-6.

Listing 6-6. *Edit Sub Main*

```
Public Sub Main()

    MessageBox.Show("The result is:" & vbCr & vbCr & _
    Dts.Variables.Item("myWebMethodResult").Value.ToString())

    Dts.TaskResult = Dts.Results.Success

End Sub
```

24. Your code should look like that contained in Figure 6-57. Assuming it is, save this code and get back to the package design by selecting File ➤ Close and pressing Return.

```
Imports System
Imports System.Data
Imports System.Math
Imports Microsoft.SqlServer.Dts.Runtime

Imports System.Windows.Forms

Public Class ScriptMain

    Public Sub Main()

        MessageBox.Show("The result is:" & vbCr & vbCr & _
            Dts.Variables.Item("myWebMethodResult").Value.ToString())

        Dts.TaskResult = Dts.Results.Success

    End Sub

End Class
```

Figure 6-58. *The code for the Script Task to display the variable value*

You are all done editing the package now. All that remains is to execute the package. If everything goes according to plan, you should see a message box that looks like Figure 6-59.

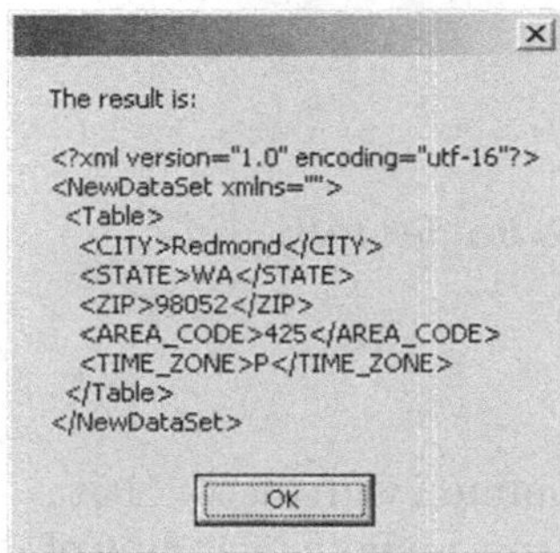

Figure 6-59. *So that's where Microsoft lives!*

This should give you a taste of how the `Web Service Task` can be used. It's pretty simple to configure, but there are a few ways to get caught out that can cause problems.

The first thing to ensure is that the HTTP Connection Manager URL is pointing to the WSDL file and not just the web service `.asmx` page. Also, on the first configuration screen for the task (Figure 6-52), you must enter the file name and location in the property box manually. Clicking the ellipsis shows the Open File dialog, but in most cases the WSDL file won't already exist and so will require downloading.

WMI Data Reader Task

The `WMI Data Reader Task` executes Windows Management Instrumentation (WMI) queries to return a set of results representing information about a computer. This task is another of those included with SSIS that serves as a bridge between SSIS and an external technology. There's much more to learn about WMI in order to use this task than there is to learn about SSIS.

Configuring the task is straightforward, though it does require knowledge of WMI Query Language (see Figure 6-60).

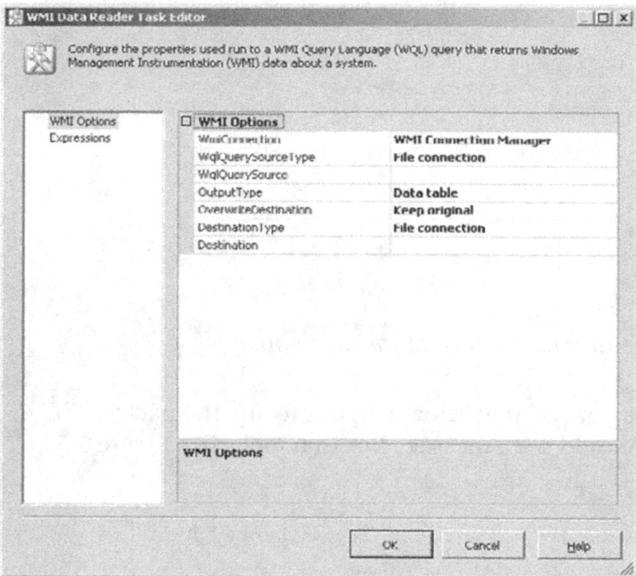

Figure 6-60. *Very few configuration steps are required for the WMI Data Reader Task.*

WMI Event Watcher Task

The `WMI Event Watcher Task` watches for a specific WMI event. In common with the `WMI Data Reader Task`, the necessary knowledge to configure this task comes from an understanding of WMI rather than the task itself.

In the configuration of this task, a WMI query is entered that identifies the particular WMI event to monitor for. A counter property (`NumberOfEvents`) is available that specifies the number of events to wait for before the task completes. Figure 6-61 shows the editor screen for configuring this task.

XML Task

The `XML Task` is the central point for dealing with XML in any and every way possible. Through a variety of configuration settings, this task allows the performance of transformations, validations, and all sorts of other XML-related operations. Figure 6-62 shows the main configuration screen, the contents of which change depending on the operation selected. The task is useful for a variety of operations on XML input, listed in Table 6-10.

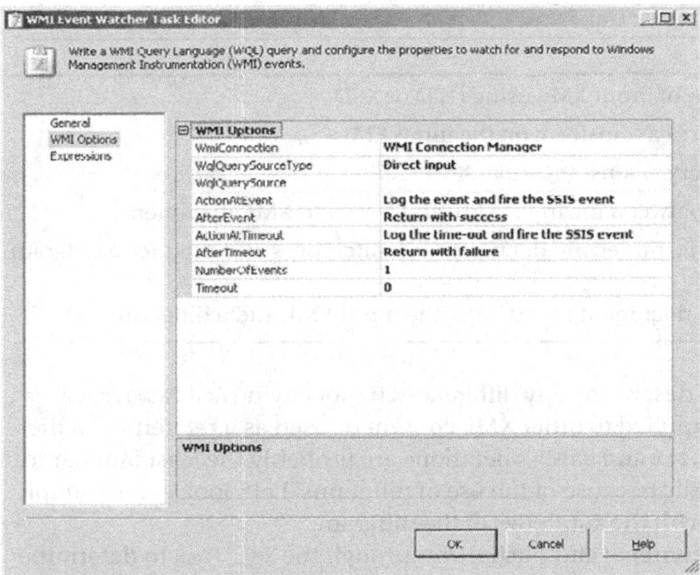

Figure 6-61. *Configuring the WMI Event Watcher Task*

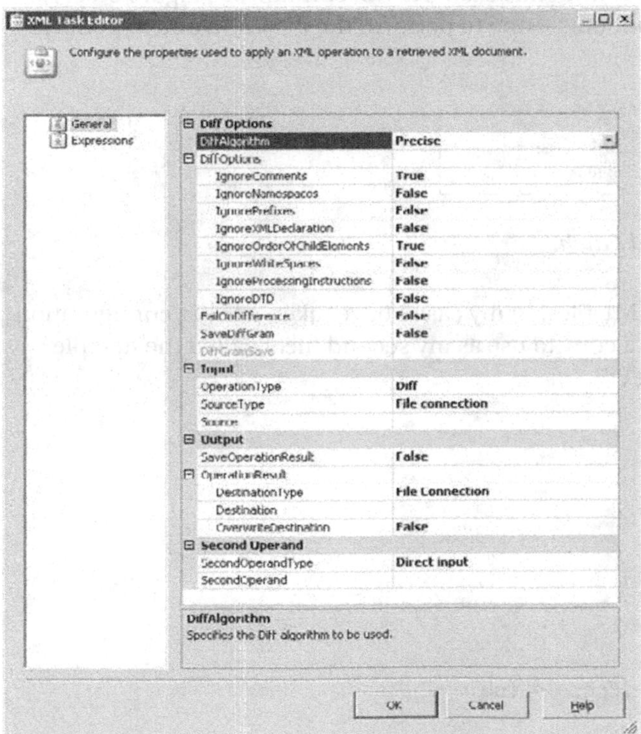

Figure 6-62. *The many options to configure the XML Task*

Table 6-10. *XML Task Operations*

Operation	Description
Validate	Perform validation of input XML using DTD or XSD
XSLT	Use XSLT to perform a transform on the input XML
XPath	Execute XPath query against the input XML
Merge	Perform a merge between the input XML and a second XML document
Diff	Analyze input XML and second document for differences and produce a diffgram of the differences
Patch	Re-create an XML document based upon the input XML and a diffgram

A *diffgram* contains metadata describing any differences by specifying Add, Remove, or Change elements that can then be applied to other XML content or used as a reference. Of the possible operations available, the Diff and Patch operations are probably the least familiar to the general SSIS developer, especially because of the use of diffgrams. Let's look at an example in order to become more familiar with the subtleties of the diffgram.

Let's take two similar XML documents and push them through the XML Task to determine the differences. This is quite a powerful example in that it is very simple and quick to work through, yet the operation performed is very useful, and comparable functionality is hard to find elsewhere.

Before I begin, to give a better idea of what this example will contain, see Figure 6-63. It shows two independent XML Task components—one to perform the Diff and one to perform the Patch.

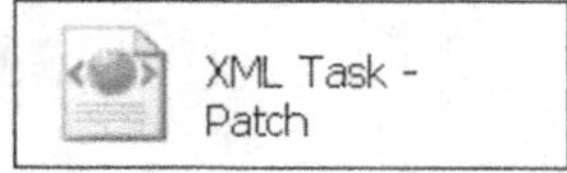

Figure 6-63. *Meet my two friends, Diff and Patch.*

The first thing to do is to find two XML files. In my case I have taken a NUnit configuration file as my first file and slightly modified a copy to use as my second file. I called the first file NAnt_original.xml. It's shown in Listing 6-7.

Listing 6-7. *NAnt_original.xml*

```
<?xml version="1.0"?>
<doc>
    <assembly>
        <name>NAnt</name>
    </assembly>
    <members>
        <member name="T:NAnt.Console.ConsoleStub">
            <summary>
            Stub used to created <see cref="T:System.AppDomain"/> and launch real
```

```
    <c>ConsoleDriver</c>
            class in Core assembly.
            </summary>
        </member>
        <member name="M:NAnt.Console.ConsoleStub.Main(System.String[])">
            <summary>
            Entry point for executable
            </summary>
            <param name="args">Command Line arguments</param>
            <returns>The result of the real execution</returns>
        </member>
        <member name="T:NAnt.Console.ConsoleStub.HelperArguments">
            <summary>
            Helper class for invoking the application entry point in NAnt.Core
            and passing the command-line arguments.
            </summary>
        </member>
        <member name="M:NAnt.Console.ConsoleStub.HelperArguments
.#ctor(System.String[],System.String)">
            <summary>
            Initializes a new instance of the <see cref="T:NAnt.Console.
ConsoleStub.HelperArguments"/>
            class with the specified command-line arguments.
            </summary>
            <param name="args">The commandline arguments passed to NAnt.exe.</param>
            <param name="probePaths">Directories relative to the base directory
of the AppDomain to probe for missing
assembly references.</param>
        </member>
        <member name="M:NAnt.Console.ConsoleStub.HelperArguments.CallConsoleRunner">
            <summary>
            Invokes the application entry point in NAnt.Core.
            </summary>
        </member>
        <member name="P:NAnt.Console.ConsoleStub.HelperArguments.ExitCode">
            <summary>
            Gets the status that the build process returned when it exited.
            </summary>
            <value>
            The code that the build process specified when it terminated.
            </value>
        </member>
    </members>
</doc>
```

The second file, against which I am going to compare the first file, I have called `NAnt_changed1.xml`. It's in Listing 6-8.

Listing 6-8. *NAnt_change1.xml*

```
<?xml version="1.0"?>
<doc>
    <assembly>
        <name>NAnt</name>
    </assembly>
    <members>
        <member name="T:NAnt.Console.ConsoleStub">
            <summary>
            Stub used to created <see cref="T:System.AppDomain"/> and launch real
<c>ConsoleDriver</c>
            class in Core assembly.
            </summary>
        </member>
        <member name="M:NAnt.Console.ConsoleStub.SSISTest(System.String[])">
            <summary>
            Entry point for SSIS Test executable
            </summary>
            <param name="args">Command Line arguments</param>
            <returns>The result of the real SSIS Package execution</returns>
        </member>
        <member name="M:NAnt.Console.ConsoleStub.Main(System.String[])">
            <summary>
            Entry point for executable
            </summary>
            <param name="args">Command Line arguments</param>
            <returns>The result of the real execution</returns>
        </member>
        <member name="T:NAnt.Console.ConsoleStub.HelperArguments">
            <summary>
            Helper class for invoking the application entry point in NAnt.Core
            and passing the command-line arguments.
            </summary>
        </member>
        <member name="M:NAnt.Console.ConsoleStub.HelperArguments.
#ctor(System.String[],System.String)">
            <summary>
            Initializes a new instance of the <see
cref="T:NAnt.Console.ConsoleStub.HelperArguments"/>
            class with the specified command-line arguments.
            </summary>
            <param name="args">The commandline arguments passed to NAnt.exe.</param>
            <param name="probePaths">Directories relative to the base directory
of the AppDomain to probe for missing assembly references.</param>
        </member>
        <member name=
"M:NAnt.Console.ConsoleStub.HelperArguments.CallConsoleRunner20">
```

```
            <summary>
            Invokes the application entry point in NAnt.Core.
This is the 2.0 version.
            </summary>
        </member>
        <member name="P:NAnt.Console.ConsoleStub.HelperArguments.ExitCode">
            <summary>
            Gets the status that the build process returned when it exited.
            </summary>
            <value>
            The code that the build process specified when it terminated.
            </value>
        </member>
    </members>
</doc>
```

Create both files somewhere on your local drive. I keep them in the `c:\temp` directory. I have made only a few changes to the original XML file to create the second file:

```
<member name="M:NAnt.Console.ConsoleStub.SSISTest(System.String[])">
      <summary>
          Entry point for SSIS Test executable
      </summary>
      <param name="args">Command Line arguments</param>
      <returns>The result of the real SSIS Package execution</returns>
</member>
```

I have also changed line 34 so the method name reads `CallConsoleRunner20` (I've added the 20), and on line 36 I have added `This is the 2.0 version` to the text. These aren't huge changes, but they are pretty difficult to identify manually. I have used relatively small files for this example for convenience, though in reality smaller files are unusual, and actual files can be many orders of magnitude larger.

We finally have everything necessary to start the example. As usual I'm writing this from the perspective of expecting a newly created and empty package file, with the empty Control Flow sitting in the IDE in front of you. If you do not have this already, create a new package now, then follow this sequence of steps:

1. Drop two `XML Task` components from the Toolbox onto the Control Flow design surface. Rename the first one `XML Task - Diff` and the second `XML Task - Patch`.

2. Right-click the `XML Task - Diff` component and select Edit (or double-click the task).

3. Change the `SaveDiffGram` property to `True`. (Make sure that the `OperationType` is set to `Diff` or else this option won't appear!)

4. Set the `DiffGramDestinationType` property to `FileConnection` if it isn't already set as such.

5. Click the down arrow in the `DiffGramDestination` property box and select *<New File connection...>*.

6. On the File Connection screen, change the `Usage Type` value to `Create File`. Enter the full path and desired file name of the to-be-created diffgram file in the File property box. I have used `c:\temp\xmltask_diffgram.xml`. This is the file that gets created to detail the differences between the two XML input files.

7. Under the Input section, ensure the `SourceType` property is set to `FileConnection`.

8. Click the down arrow on the `Source` property box and select <New File connection...>.

9. On the File Connection screen, change the `Usage Type` value to `Existing File`. Enter the full path and filename of the source XML file in the File property box. I have used `c:\temp\NAnt_original.xml`. This is the first of the XML files detailed above.

10. Under the Second Operand section, you need to repeat the process of pointing to the task to a file. This time it is the second XML file against which the first file will be compared. Set the `SecondOperandType` property to `FileConnection` if it isn't already set as such.

11. Click the down arrow in the `SecondOperand` property box and select <New File connection...>.

12. On the File Connection screen, change the `Usage Type` value to `Existing File`. Enter the full path and filename of the second XML file in the File property box. I have used `c:\temp\xmltask_changed1.xml`. Again, this is the file that you are requesting be compared to the file specified in the Input section. Your configuration screen for this XML Task should now look like the one in Figure 6-64.

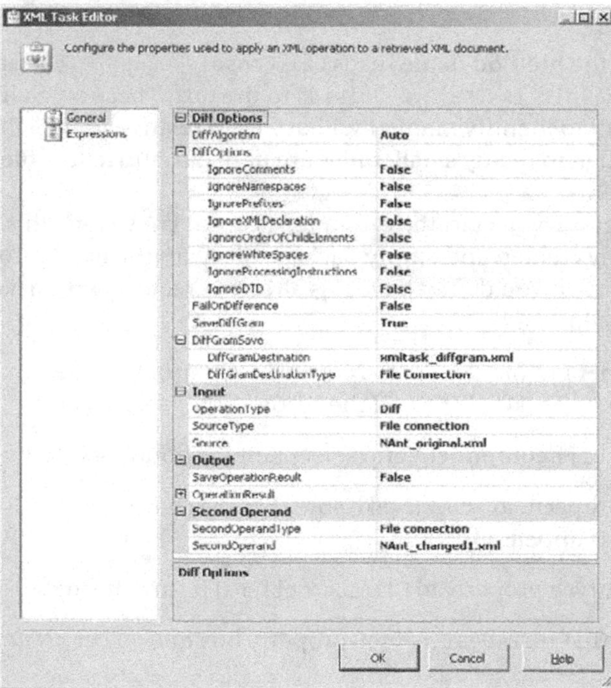

Figure 6-64. *Your task configuration should look like this.*

13. Click OK to execute the `XML Task - Diff` task. You should find a new file called `xmltask_diffgram.xml` that has been created in your specified directory. If everything has gone to plan, it should look like the file shown in Listing 6-9.

Listing 6-9. *The diffgram File*

```
<?xml version="1.0" encoding="utf-16"?>
<xd:xmldiff version="1.0" srcDocHash="10170752643863270339" options="None"
fragments="no" xmlns:xd="http://schemas.microsoft.com/xmltools/2002/xmldiff">
  <xd:node match="2">
    <xd:node match="2">
      <xd:node match="1" />
      <xd:add>
        <member name="M:NAnt.Console.ConsoleStub.SSISTest(System.String[])">
          <summary>
            Entry point for SSIS Test executable
            </summary>
          <param name="args">Command Line arguments</param>
          <returns>The result of the real SSIS Package execution</returns>
        </member>
      </xd:add>
      <xd:node match="5">
        <xd:change
match="@name">M:NAnt.Console.ConsoleStub.HelperArguments.CallConsoleRunner20</xd:cha
nge>
        <xd:node match="1">
          <xd:change match="1">
            Invokes the application entry point in NAnt.Core. This is the 2.0
version.
            </xd:change>
        </xd:node>
      </xd:node>
    </xd:node>
  </xd:node>
</xd:xmldiff>
```

So far so good. It looks like the `XML Task - Diff` has picked up on the differences between the two files and created a nice diffgram file for us to use.

Now it's time to perform a `Patch` operation on the original XML file to bring it in line with the structure of the second file, `NAnt_changed1.xml`. This is a good exercise because it also validates the results of the first `XML Task` operation:

1. Right-click the `XML Task - Patch` component and select Edit (or double-click the task).

2. Under the Input section, set the `OperationType` property to `Patch`.

3. Ensure the `SourceType` property is set to `FileConnection`.

4. Click the down arrow on the `Source` property box and select `NAnt_original.xml`. Again, this is the first of the XML files detailed above.

5. Under the Output section, set the `SaveOperationResult` property to `True`.
6. Ensure the `DestinationType` property is set to `FileConnection`.
7. Click the down arrow on the `Source` property box and select <New File connection...>.
8. On the File Connection screen, change the `Usage Type` value to `Create File`. Enter the full path and desired filename of the to-be-created output file in the File property box. I have used `c:\temp\NAnt_original_patched.xml`. This is the file that gets created as the result of applying the diffgram to the original XML file.
9. Under the Second Operand section, set the `SecondOperandType` property to `FileConnection` if it isn't already set as such.
10. Click the down arrow in the `SecondOperand` property box and select `xmltask_diffgram.xml`. Your configuration screen should look like Figure 6-65.

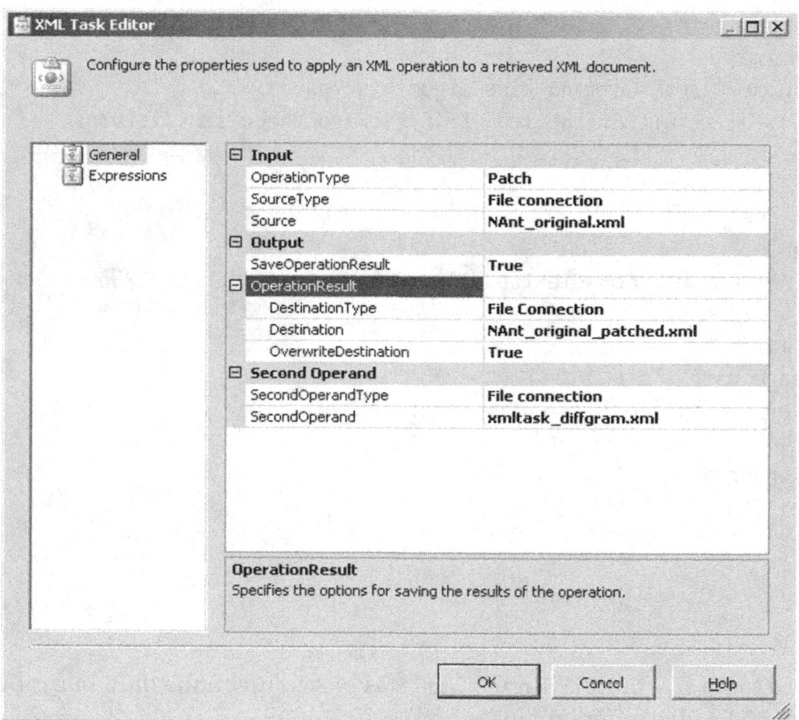

Figure 6-65. *Configuring the Patch operation*

11. Click OK to execute the `XML Task - Patch` task. You should find yet another file in your specified output directory: `NAnt_original_patched.xml`.

Although I'm not going to reproduce its contents here, if you take a look at the file generated by the task, you'll see it now contains the changes that were identified as a part of the `Diff` operation.

In fact, this is easily verifiable using the `XML Task - Diff` task. All you need to do is delete the `NAnt_original.xml` and `xmltask_diffgram.xml` files, rename the `NAnt_original_patched.xml` file to `NAnt_original.xml`, and then execute the `XML Task - Diff`.

When the diffgram file—`xmltask_diffgram.xml`—is generated this time, it contains some information, but notice that it contains no metadata that specifies that any changes are necessary. This is a good thing. The `Diff` and `Patch` operations have worked as expected and everything is right with the world.

Summary

This has been a big chapter. A huge chapter. It has lots of information about everything to do with the Control Flow, and not all of it will be relevant to every user. For the more developer-minded, tasks such as transferring logins or SQL Server objects really aren't going to apply.

It has probably struck the more-discerning reader of this chapter that there are . . . well . . . still some janky old things going on in Microsoft ETL world. I don't mean that there are serious flaws in SSIS, just that the implementation of some of the Control Flow components (and the maintenance and Data Flow components) could be a little better.

Taking the `Web Service Task` in particular, it could certainly be more powerful and more logical in its approach, but it is made to be flexible and for mass consumption. If you have particular needs that you feel the task doesn't address, I'll see you later in Chapter 14, where we can look at how to build a replacement.

As I'm not one to complain, I rewrote a number of the Control Flow tasks to better suit my purposes and to be a little more in keeping with the flexibility of the rest of the toolset. I suggest that anyone wanting to get more out of the SSIS experience do the same.

CHAPTER 7

Maintenance Plans

In the main, the maintenance tasks included with SSIS are wrappers, presented in a graphical format, for T-SQL statements that perform maintenance tasks. What's nice about these components is that they encapsulate fairly complex statements for you, with all necessary parameters. As such the tasks form a pragmatic though essential toolset for performing maintenance tasks through SSIS.

Even though these components are generally of more use to DBAs and others with an administrative bent, it's worth taking a look at them irrespective of your background or role. This chapter is concise and feels more like a pure reference because the maintenance tasks don't have any great depth and are pretty much entirely self contained.

As a rule, the maintenance tasks I've included should be configured using the component's edit UI. That's great for packages you develop with the SSIS designer, of course, but knowing which properties do what is important too.

The maintenance tasks all seem to implement a common interface that exposes a core set of properties. In most cases these properties simply don't apply to the maintenance component in question, which can be rather confusing. In those cases the properties, such as `ResultSetType`, can be set to any value because the component doesn't use them. In this chapter, I'm including only properties pertinent to and valid for the configuration of each component.

Appendix D contains a detailed property reference for all maintenance-plan tasks. The appendixes for this book are available to readers at `http://www.apress.com` in the Source Code/Download section.

Back Up Database

The `Back Up Database Task` is used to back up SQL Server databases. Essentially it's a wrapper for the T-SQL `BACKUP` statement.

I've used this task in a number of different scenarios. In development projects the task can be a useful alternative to checkpoints, where a backup is performed at the end of intensive processing tasks to provide a restart point. For pure maintenance purposes, I have created packages that contain various data-cleanup tasks followed by a `Back Up Database Task`. This is a nice way to consolidate maintenance functions into a single controllable location, and the package can be easily called using the SQL Agent, on a schedule.

Maintenance is probably the most common use for this task. When used in conjunction with the other maintenance tasks in this chapter, it can help you create an incredibly powerful set of packages to control and maintain your database.

Figure 7-1 shows the main configuration screen for this task. The similarity to the backup function within SQL Server Management Studio is striking. Figure 7-2 shows the familiar Management Studio version.

Figure 7-3 shows the options that are available as part of the SQL Management Studio Back Up Database function.

As you can see from comparing the two interfaces, they are pretty much identical in terms of functionality. My point is that if you've ever backed up a database in SQL Server, you'll feel entirely at home with the SSIS `Back Up Database Task`.

Since it will help when you look at the `History Cleanup Task` later in the chapter, I'll take you through a quick example of how to configure the `Back Up Database Task`. I am assuming you have created a new package for use with this example and you have your SSIS IDE open showing the Control Flow design surface.

1. Drop a `Back Up Database Task` component onto the Control Flow design surface.
2. Double-click the task or right-click it and select Edit.
3. The next thing to do, as usual, is to add a connection manager. Click the New... button after the Connection drop-down list and create a connection that points to the server on which a database suitable for backup resides.
4. Ensure the Backup type property is set to `Full`.
5. Click the Database(s) drop-down list. In the panel that is presented, select a specific database from the bottom-most list.
6. Under the Backup component property, select `Database`.
7. Ensure the Backup set will expire property is unchecked.
8. Set the Back up to property to `Disk`.
9. Ensure the Create a backup file for every database property is set. Under the Folder property, ensure the location is set to a suitable disk location. This should be the case automatically.
10. Check the Verify backup integrity checkbox.
11. Select OK.
12. Check the folder location specified in the Folder property of Step 9. You should find a backup (`.bak`) file has been created for the database you selected in Step 5.

A record of this backup has been made in the `backupfile` table of the `msdb` system database on the server. It's worth checking this table, just for reference, to observe where the record is kept. This information might be useful in the future.

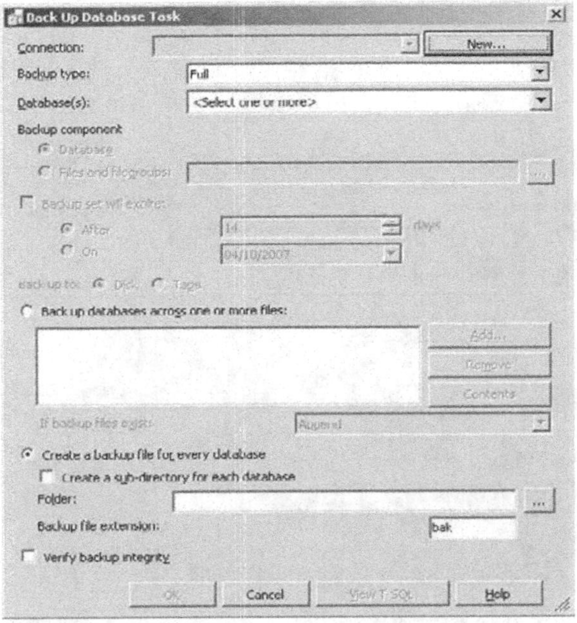

Figure 7-1. *Back Up Database Task configuration*

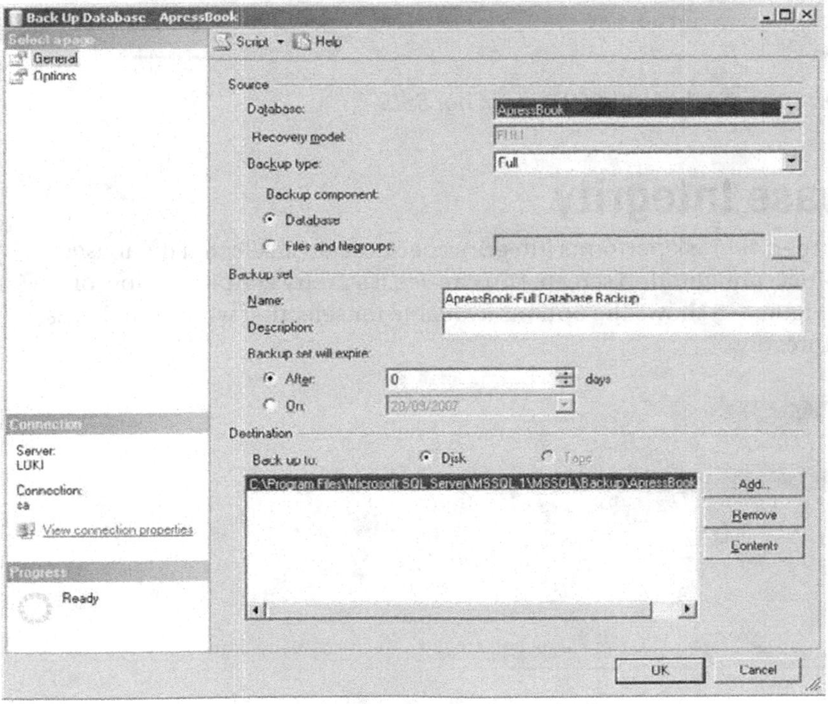

Figure 7-2. *The main backup window in SQL Management Studio*

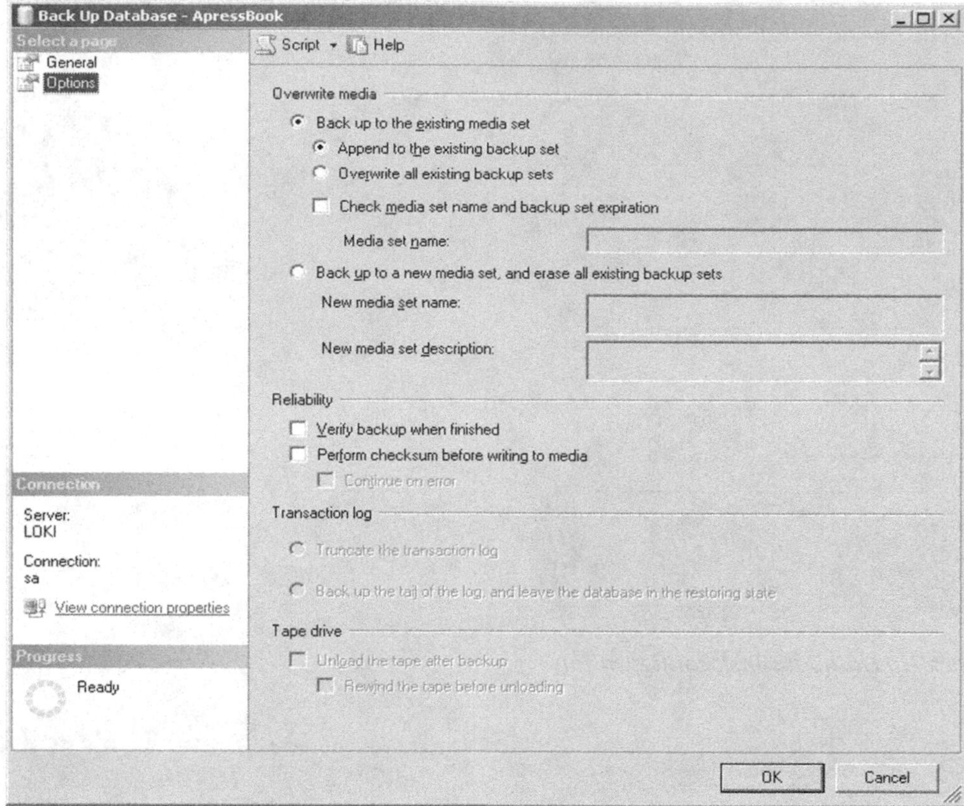

Figure 7-3. *Additional options—again from SQL Server, not SSIS*

Check Database Integrity

The `Check Database Integrity Task` performs integrity checks against selected databases. Figure 7-4 shows the initial configuration screen. You can see it's pretty simple and low on configuration options. Figure 7-5 shows the options available for selecting which databases should be checked for integrity.

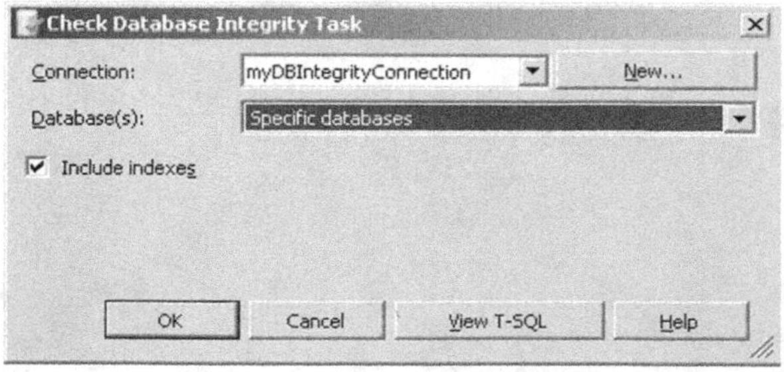

Figure 7-4. *Setting Check Database Integrity Task properties*

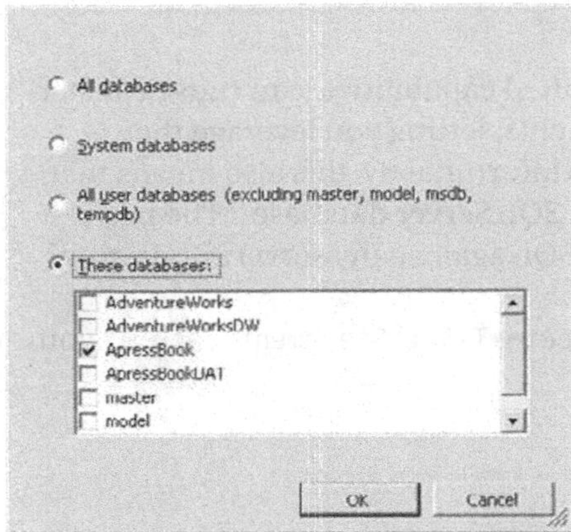

Figure 7-5. *Selecting the databases for which integrity will be checked*

As is suggested by the button shown in Figure 7-4, you can view the T-SQL that gets generated for execution. In this particular case it is a pretty simple `DBCC CHECKDB WITH NO_INFOMSGS` statement. Checks are performed against all objects within the selected database(s).

As a part of the `CHECKDB` operation, `CHECKALLOC`, `CHECKTABLE`, and `CHECKCATALOG` are also executed, in addition to the validation of Service Broker data and the contents of all indexed views.

Upon execution, the task returns a success status if the integrity check completes without error. If problems are encountered with the check, then the task fails.

Execute SQL Server Agent Job

The `Execute SQL Server Agent Job Task` runs SQL Server Agent jobs. As with executing any SQL job, even outside of SSIS, the SQL Server Agent must be running for jobs to run.

Figure 7-6 shows the configuration screen for this task. As is the case with most of the maintenance tasks, the configuration options are limited and simple in nature. The list contains an entry of each of the available SQL Server Agent jobs. Simply check the Select checkbox for each job you wish to execute.

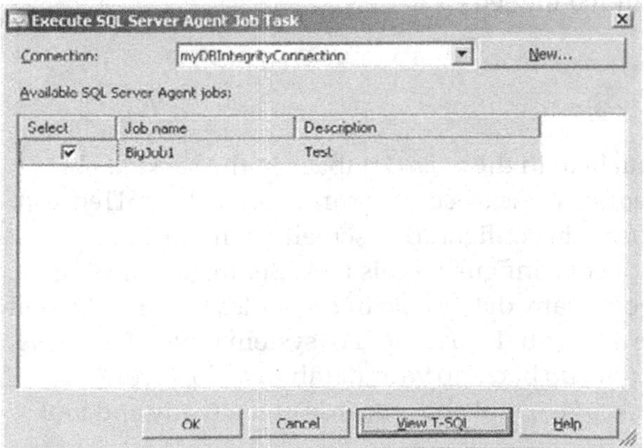

Figure 7-6. *Setting which jobs to run as part of the task*

Execute T-SQL Statement

The Execute T-SQL Statement Task, another task with limited capabilities, can cause consternation if due care is not paid. This task runs T-SQL statements, letting you leverage the enhancements that T-SQL provides over traditional SQL. Unfortunately, this also means that this task can be used to execute statements only against a SQL Server database. (The news isn't *all* bad, however. The Execute SQL Task lets you run SQL against any server supporting standard SQL.)

Figure 7-7 shows the configuration screen for the Execute T-SQL Statement Task. As you can see, there aren't many options available to configure.

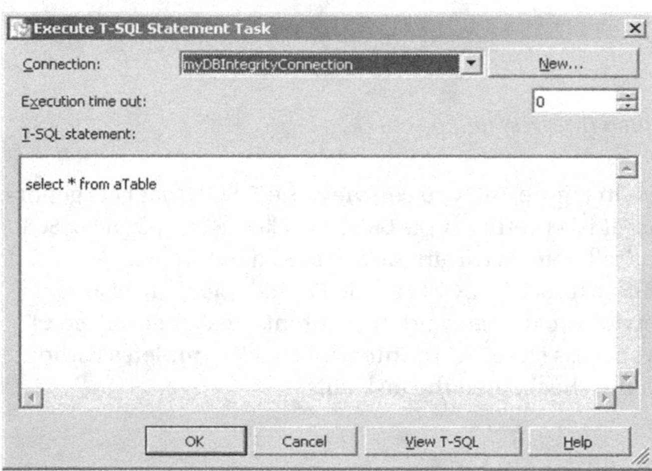

Figure 7-7. *Remember, this is the T-SQL task!*

Rather than take a closer look at this task to identify how it works and how objects such as stored procedures can be executed, I recommend that you not use this task at all. If you want to do anything beyond executing the simplest of T-SQL statements, use the Execute SQL Task, which is part of the Control Flow components collection. That task lets you use parameters and assign results to variables and all the other good things that go along with database queries. By contrast, this T-SQL task is very limited indeed.

History Cleanup

The History Cleanup Task deletes history data held in the msdb database in the backupfile, backupfilegroup, backupmediafamily, backupmediaset, backupset, restorefile, restorefilegroup, and restorehistory tables. Figure 7-8 shows the main configuration screen for this task.

It's worth running through a quick example of configuring this task. Before performing the example's history cleanup, however, find out if any data exists in the tables that get cleaned out so you can observe the task's effects. Take a look in the backupfile system table of the msdb database. It probably contains some records (you *do* back up your databases, don't you?) that you can delete as part of this example. My backupfile table has records in it already and looks like Figure 7-9.

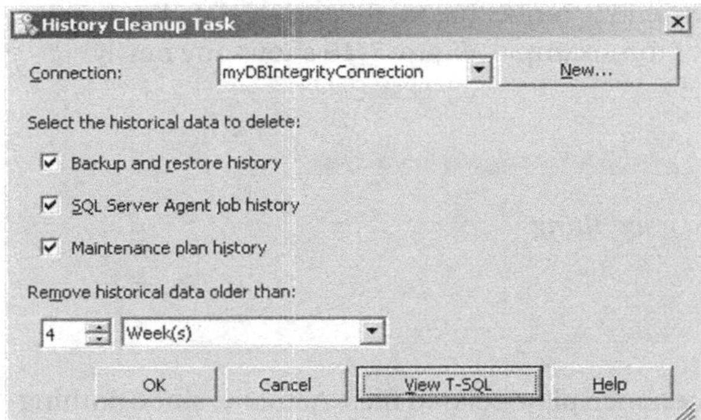

Figure 7-8. *Main configuration screen for the History Cleanup Task*

	backed_up_page_co...	file_type	source_file_block_size	file_size	logical_name	physical_drive	physical_name
1	36200	D	512	296747008	ApressBook	C:\	C:\Program File
2	2	L	512	437649408	ApressBook_log	C:\	C:\Program File

Figure 7-9. *My backupfile table has records.*

If no records exist in your `backupfile` table, look in any of the other tables that get cleaned out by this task. Or you could follow the example earlier in the chapter for the `Back Up Database Task`. That example performs a backup that automatically populates the `backupfile` table for you as an audit that the backup took place. You need to leave at least an hour between performing the backup and working with this example, however, or else the `backupfile` table will still contain data.

Now you'll configure an example package that clears out this history. Then you can check to make sure everything has executed as expected. I am assuming you have created a new package for use with this example and you have your SSIS IDE open showing the Control Flow design surface.

1. Drop a `History Cleanup Task` from the Toolbox onto the Control Flow design surface.
2. Double-click the task or right-click it and select Edit.
3. Add a connection manager. Click the New... button after the Connection drop-down list and create a connection that points to the server on which you want to perform this task.
4. Make sure the Backup and restore history, SQL Server Agent job history, and Maintenance plan history options are all checked.
5. Change the Remove historical data older than property to read `1 Hour(s)`.
6. Select OK.
7. Execute the task.

You should find, upon examining the `backupfile` table, that the historical data has been cleared out. This is the point of the task and of this example. Figure 7-10 shows my newly cleansed `backupfile` table.

Figure 7-10. *An empty backupfile table: this is a good thing.*

Maintenance Cleanup

The `Maintenance Cleanup Task` deletes maintenance plan–related files. Actually, since nothing marks files as particularly maintenance related, this task could realistically be called the "Delete Files Task."

You can configure this task to delete either a specific file or a group of files from a particular folder (and first-level subfolders) based upon a specified file extension. Figure 7-11 shows the configuration properties available for the task.

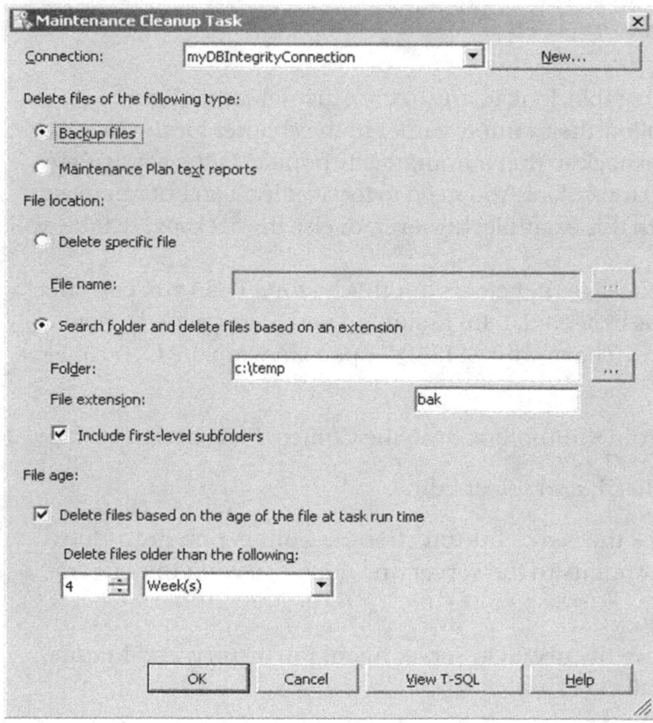

Figure 7-11. *Clean up those unsightly maintenance files.*

As with the `History Cleanup Task`, a time limit can be imposed on the task to specify the age of a file being considered for deletion.

Notify Operator

The `Notify Operator Task` sends notification messages to SQL Server Agent operators. Database Mail must be configured for this task to be used, because mail-enabled accounts must exist on the server. Figure 7-12 shows the main configuration screen.

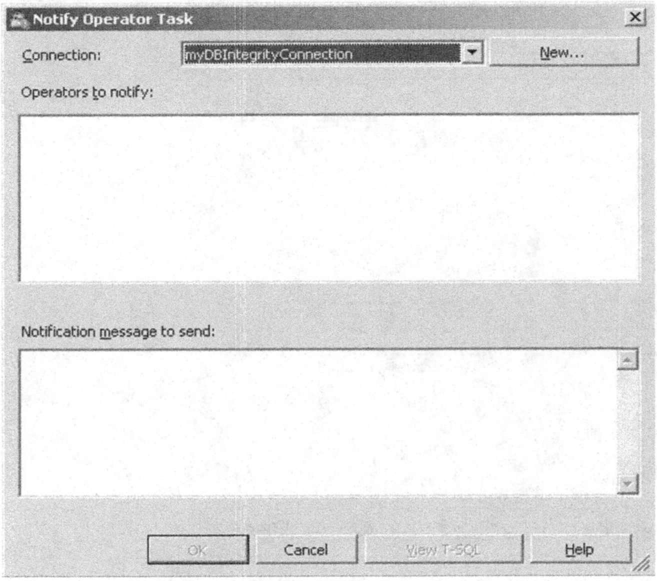

Figure 7-12. *Anyone there? Operator?*

I don't have any users with an e-mail address configured, so when I try to edit the task, I get the message shown in Figure 7-13.

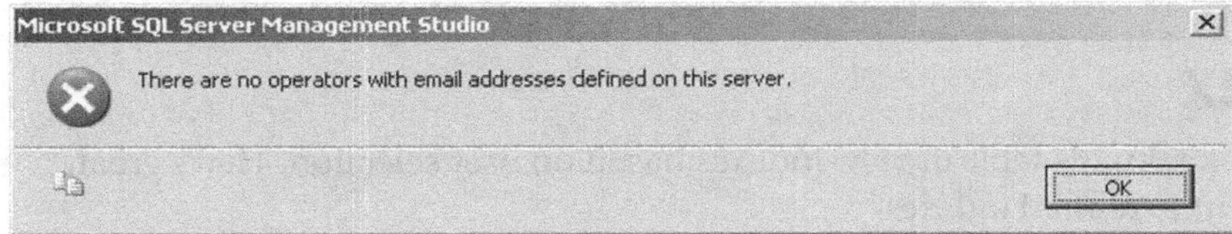

Figure 7-13. *No operators have been configured.*

You can configure Database Mail using the SQL Server Management Studio under the Management branch of the server tree. You can create individual mail-enabled users by choosing to configure Database Mail from this point. Figure 7-14 shows the screen for creating and editing mail-enabled users on the selected server.

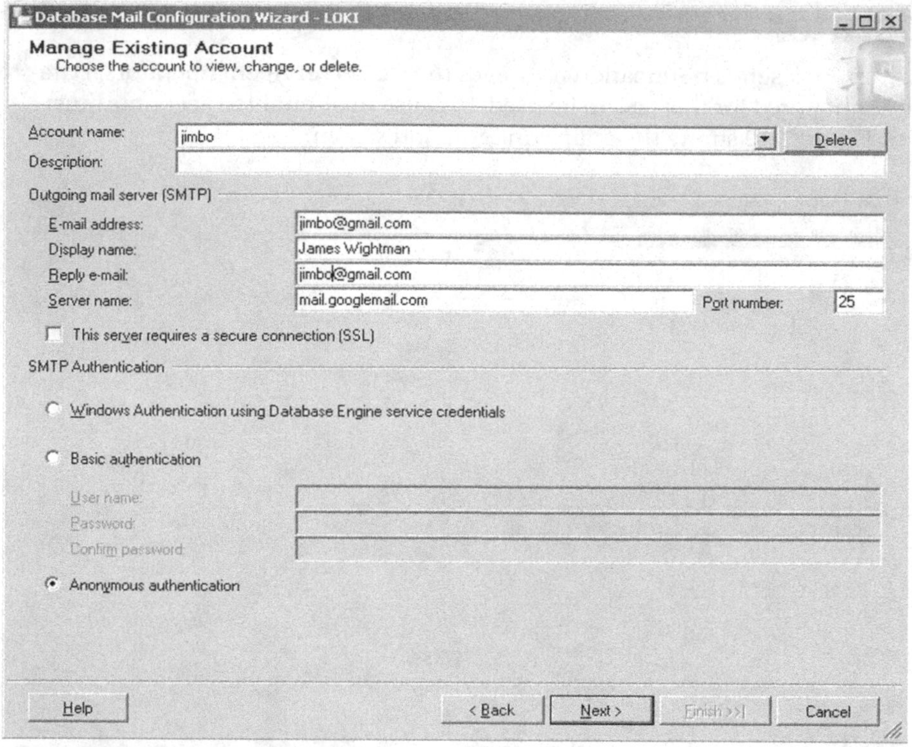

Figure 7-14. *Managing an existing Database Mail user*

Using this task isn't as simple as dropping it on the design surface and expecting everything to get taken care of. You also need some knowledge of how to send mail from within SQL Server.

Rebuild Index

The `Rebuild Index Task` rebuilds table or view indexes based on user selection. That's great, but why would you *want* to rebuild indexes?

As you probably know, indexes are automatically maintained by the SQL Server Engine. This means that any changes to the underlying data are handled automatically. So far so good. But problems can arise as a consequence of these index updates in much the same way that data being written to a hard disk can become fragmented because of how free space is distributed.

An index rebuild produces the most benefit in situations where the index(es) concerned are more than about 30% fragmented. When less fragmentation is detected, consider using the `Reorganize Index Task` instead.

Figure 7-15 shows the configuration screen for the `Rebuild Index Task`. Notice that the task does not give an indication of index fragmentation—something that might be quite useful to know.

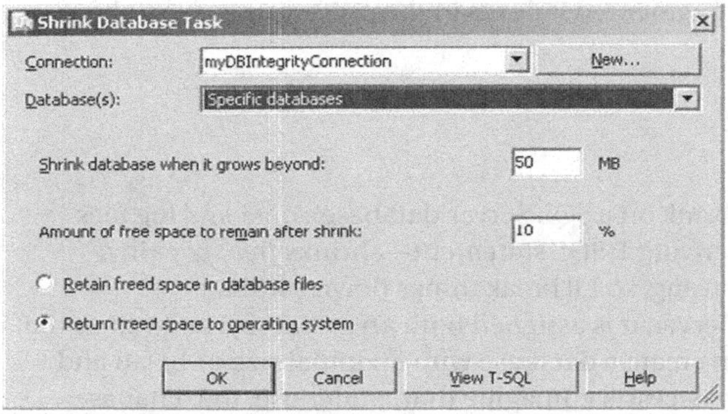

Figure 7-15. *Rebuild Index Task configuration*

The fragmentation value of a particular index can be retrieved using a little T-SQL trickery:

```
SELECT  stattable.index_id,
                indextable.[name],
                stattable.avg_fragmentation_in_percent as fragpercent
FROM     sys.dm_db_index_physical_stats (DB_ID(), OBJECT_ID(N'theMasterTable'),
               NULL, NULL, NULL) AS stattable
INNER JOIN sys.indexes AS indextable ON stattable.object_id = indextable.object_id
AND       stattable.index_id = indextable.index_id
```

This query returns a list of indexes and a percentage figure for each that shows the fragmentation. To point the query at an alternate table, simply change the value contained in the `OBJECT_ID()` parameter.

For particularly large tables, the rebuilding of indexes can take a considerable amount of time. For this reason, avoid rebuilding *all* indexes in a database at once.

Reorganize Index

The `Reorganize Index Task` reorganizes table or view indexes to reduce fragmentation. Typically it is used when the fragmentation percentage is less than 30% on a particular index. Figure 7-16 shows the configuration screen for the task. Notice it has fewer configuration options than the `Rebuild Index Task`, simply because this task works with existing data.

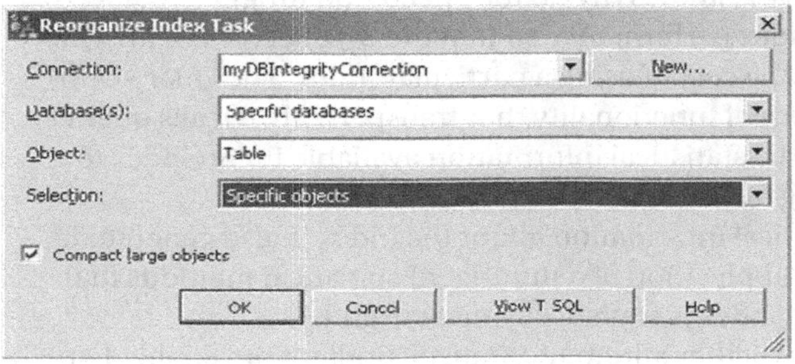

Figure 7-16. *Reorganizing indexes*

You'll find more information about fragmented indexes in the preceding section about the `Rebuild Index Task`.

Shrink Database

The `Shrink Database Task` performs a shrink on a SQL Server database's data and log files. More accurately, this task—and the underlying T-SQL statement—shrinks *free space* in a database. The concept can be quite confusing, so I'll break things down a little.

When a database is created in SQL Server, it is assigned both an initial size and values that designate growth rate. For example, I can create a database with an initial size of 10 GB and specify that it should grow by 5 GB when necessary. Imagine that, under use, the database grows once but holds just over 10 GB of data. This means that more than 4 GB of space has been allocated but isn't yet in use.

A shrink operation reduces the amount of free space—that is, space allocated but not yet in use—to a user-specified level. Figure 7-17 shows the main configuration screen for the `Shrink Database Task`.

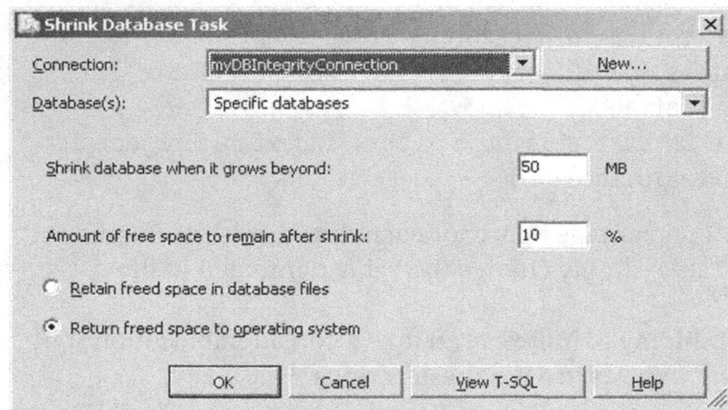

Figure 7-17. *Shrinking a bloated database*

Update Statistics

The `Update Statistics Task` updates database statistics. These statistics exist against columns, indexed tables, or views and relate to the statistical distribution of values.

"But what *are* statistics?" I hear you ask, and, "Why do they need updating?"

Statistics are all about measuring index performance so that the SQL Server Engine Query Optimizer can make calculations about the cost of using a particular index. The Query Optimizer itself is a clever and intriguing piece of functionality that transparently tweaks queries automatically. It does, however, rely on the statistical information available for an index to make the most-valid decisions regarding index usage.

When an index is created, the statistical information about the index is also generated. This information is created through the application of a number of statistical methods that provide insight into when leveraging the index is statistically most useful.

When data changes, depending on whether automatic statistic updates are enabled on the database, the statistics can become out of date and provide bad advice to the Query

Optimizer. The Query Optimizer will then use an index where it may have been more prudent not to. In these cases, the statistics need updating. Studying the execution plan for a particular query can highlight problems with statistics that might mean an update is advisable.

This task can be used to instigate a statistics update. Figure 7-18 shows the task's configuration screen.

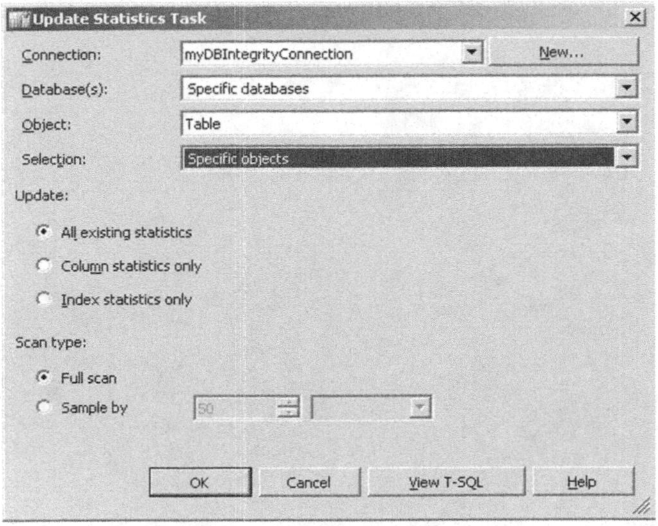

Figure 7-18. *Selecting the objects and types of statistics to update*

Summary

Even though maintenance tasks are, in the main, likely to be used only by the DBAs among us, everyone can learn a lesson here. With repeated ETL tasks, a database often tends to grow bloated with extraneous and redundant supporting files. Everyone needs some tender loving care occasionally, and the more TLC a database receives the better it will perform.

Perhaps these maintenance tasks should be considered a vital part of *everyone's* SQL Server repertoire. Perhaps this is something else that SSIS teaches us all.

This chapter marks the end of discussions of Control Flow tasks and components, but your journey is only just beginning. Starting with the next chapter, you'll see what delights await you after you drill through the Control Flow into the Data Flow.

Summary

CHAPTER 8

■ ■ ■

Data Flow Data Sources

Now we're talking. No more messing around with containers and the like—it's time for straightforward data manipulation! Now you will see the true power of the fully operational battle station that is SSIS.

The components available to the Data Flow design surface via the Toolbox form the ETL capabilities of SSIS:

- **Extract**: Data Flow sources
- **Transform**: Data Flow transformations
- **Load**: Data Flow destinations

This chapter is all about data sources. While they are an integral part of the Data Flow design, they do form the E in ETL and warrant a chapter of their own.

It's worth remembering that data staging is unnecessary as part of the Data Flow, because transformations are handled "in memory." You can still drop data into staging tables if you want to, but it's probably entirely unnecessary.

By far the coolest part of using the Data Flow is that, after you use it for a short while, everything begins to click into place, make sense, and start to feel natural, almost organic. The realization soon hits that there is probably an easier and more efficient method of getting the desired result, and within a breath the flow evolves. Further glory comes when you execute the package and see task after task turn green in mere moments, even though many millions of rows are being processed by the pipelines.

Did I mention I'm a big fan of SSIS?

Let's get into the thick of things by looking at the different kinds of default data sources SSIS provides. As I introduce each data-source component in this chapter, I'll indicate the number of outputs available by default. Outputs, you probably remember, are shown as arrows extending out of the bottom of components on the design surface. They are generally either green arrows, which signify the standard output, or red arrows, which signify error output.

DataReader Source

1 output, 1 error output

The `DataReader Source` uses an `ADO.NET` connection manager to read data from a `DataReader` and channel it into the Data Flow. Figure 8-1 shows the initial configuration screen for this component.

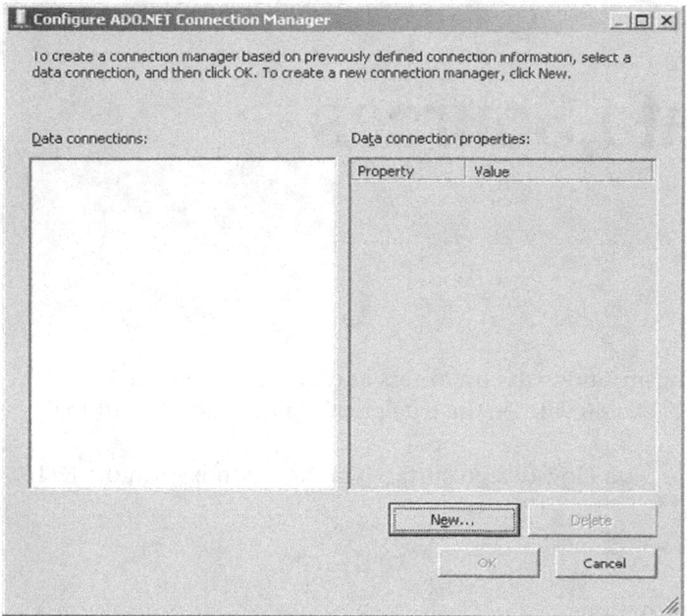

Figure 8-1. *Specifying the connection manager to use*

I'll head straight into an example. Suppose you want to create a standard `DataReader Source` component that reads the data from a local database table and places it into the Data Flow.

Start by making sure that everything is in place to complete the example. If you followed the Control Flow `Bulk Insert Task` example in Chapter 6, you should have a large table in a database somewhere that contains sample data downloaded from MaxMind. I'm assuming you still have this resource available. If you don't, see my examination of the `Flat File Source` component that follows this section. I go through an example there of how to use that data source type to import the same MaxMind data.

The final prerequisites for this example are that you create a new package, drop the `Data Flow Task` component from the toolbox onto the Control Flow design surface, and head over into the Data Flow design surface (by double-clicking the Data Flow component or selecting the Data Flow tab at the top of the main IDE window).

With those preliminaries taken care of, the first thing you need to do is add an `ADO.NET` connection manager:

1. Right-click in the Connection Manager area of the IDE window and select New ADO.NET Connection.... This will bring up the screen for configuring an ADO.NET connection manager.

2. Select New... to create a new connection manager. You're presented with the screen shown in Figure 8-2.

3. Fill out the connection settings on the Connection Manager screen to point to the relevant database (the database that contains your version of the `CSV_IMPORT_TABLE_1` table used in Chapter 6). Click Test Connection to ensure the manager can connect. Once done, click OK.

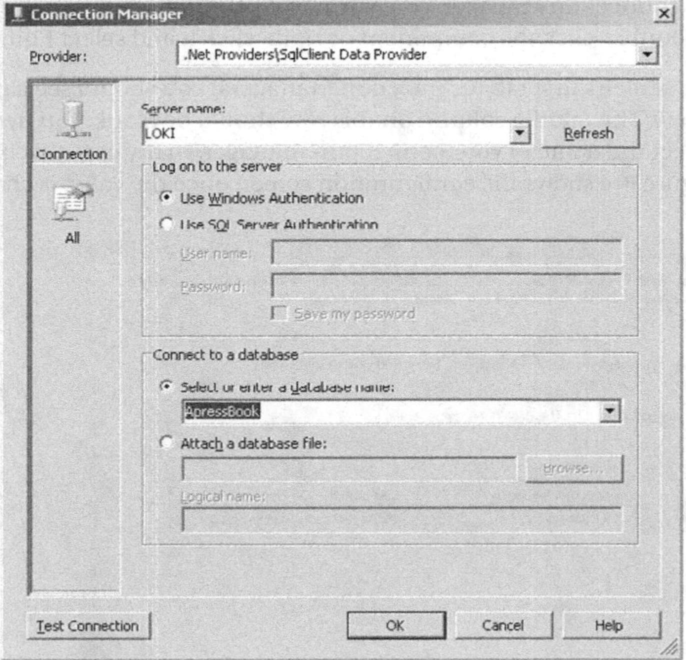

Figure 8-2. *Provide settings to connect to your database server.*

4. You should find yourself back at the Configure ADO.NET Connection Manager screen. It should now list your newly created connection manager on the left side of the screen and look similar to Figure 8-3.

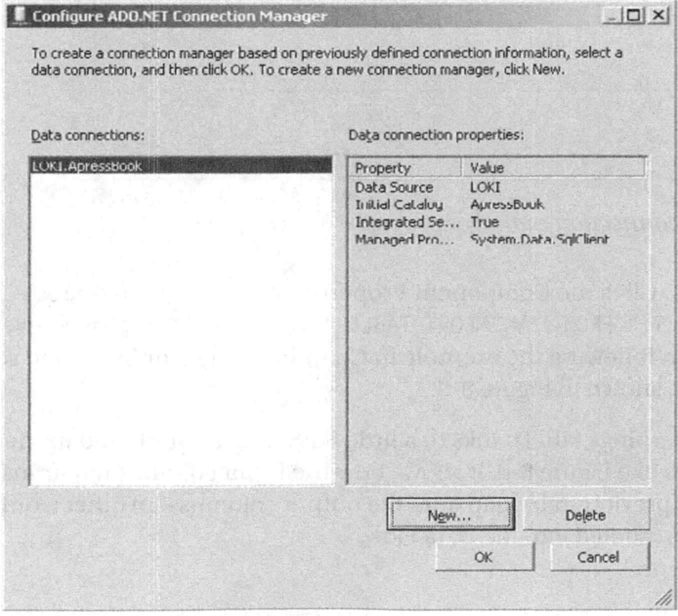

Figure 8-3. *Thar she blows . . . the connection manager is listed.*

5. Now that you have a connection manager, you can start to configure the `DataReader Source` component. Double-click the component or right-click it and select Edit.

6. On the configuration screen's first tab (Connection Managers) you should see a grid containing a single row. The middle column on this row should be blank. You need to change this to reflect the name of your connection manager. In my case this is `LOKI.ApressBook`. Figure 8-4 shows the configuration screen once the value is changed.

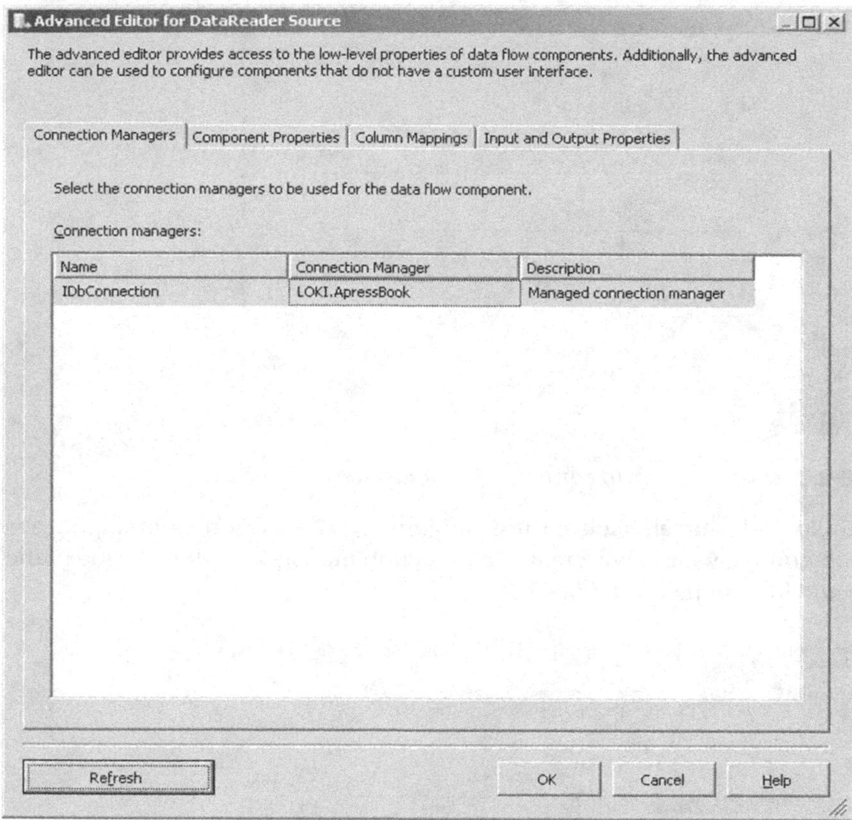

Figure 8-4. *Setting the connection manager property*

7. You can now move on. Click the Component Properties tab and update the `SQLCommand` property to read `SELECT * FROM CSV_IMPORT_TABLE_1` (or, `SELECT * FROM` whatever you called your table when following the example in Chapter 6). The configuration screen should look like mine, shown in Figure 8-5.

8. Select the Column Mappings tab. Thanks to a little SSIS magic you should immediately see a screen that looks like Figure 8-6. It shows how the input columns (columns from the `SQLCommand` on the previous tab) map onto the output columns—in other words, the columns that will be presented into the Data Flow.

Advanced Editor for DataReader Source

The advanced editor provides access to the low-level properties of data flow components. Additionally, the advanced editor can be used to configure components that do not have a custom user interface.

Connection Managers | Component Properties | Column Mappings | Input and Output Properties

Specify advanced properties for the data flow component.

Properties:

Property	Value
Common Properties	
ComponentClassID	{DF01D463-7089-41EE-0F05-0A6DC17CE633}
ContactInfo	Extracts data from a relational database by using a .NET pr
Description	Extracts data from a relational database by using a .NET pr
ID	1
IdentificationString	component "DataReader Source" (1)
IsDefaultLocale	True
LocaleID	English (United Kingdom)
Name	**DataReader Source**
PipelineVersion	0
UsesDispositions	True
ValidateExternalMetadata	True
Version	2
Custom Properties	
CommandTimeout	30
SqlCommand	SELECT * FROM CSV_IMPORT_TABLE_1
UserComponentTypeName	Microsoft.SqlServer.Dts.Pipeline.DataReaderSourceAdapter

SqlCommand
Specifies the SQL statement used by the component to extract data.

Refresh | OK | Cancel | Help

Figure 8-5. *Component properties configured in step 7*

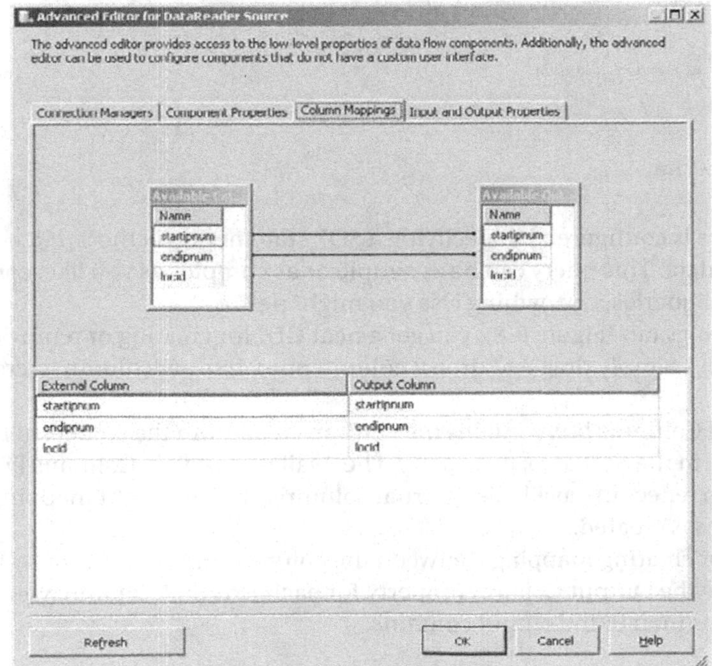

Figure 8-6. *Magic column mapping, thanks to SSIS*

9. That's it for now. You're not interested at this point in the Input and Output Properties tab. Simply select OK and you will be returned to the Data Flow design surface.

That's it—example over—the `DataReader` Data Source is configured. As you now appreciate, this process isn't particularly complex and can be completed in moments. After you have configured a few hundred data-source components it really will become second nature!

Now that you've taken a run through creating a `DataReader Source`, let's take a closer look at some of the concepts and configuration settings it presents. Figure 8-7 takes you back to the Component Properties tab of the component configuration.

Connection Managers | Component Properties | Column Mappings | Input and Output Properties

Specify advanced properties for the data flow component.

Properties:

Property	Value
Common Properties	
ComponentClassID	{BF01D463-7089-41EE-8F05-0A6DC17CE633}
ContactInfo	Extracts data from a relational database by using a .NET pr
Description	Extracts data from a relational database by using a .NET pr
ID	1
IdentificationString	component "DataReader Source" (1)
IsDefaultLocale	True
LocaleID	English (United Kingdom)
Name	**DataReader Source**
PipelineVersion	0
UsesDispositions	True
ValidateExternalMetadata	True
Version	2
Custom Properties	
CommandTimeout	30
SqlCommand	SELECT startipnum, endipnum, locid FROM atable
UserComponentTypeName	Microsoft.SqlServer.Dts.Pipeline.DataReaderSourceAdapte

SqlCommand
Specifies the SQL statement used by the component to extract data.

Figure 8-7. *Component properties*

The `DataReader Source` is configured by specifying a SQL statement (via the `SqlCommand` property) that returns the data. This query can be as simple or as complex as you like, containing inner or outer joins, subqueries, or anything else you might desire.

On the Column Mappings tab (Figure 8-8), you get a neat GUI for creating or removing mappings between columns. Simply drag and drop a column onto another column to create the mapping.

The Available External Columns box contains the columns read from the source, in this case the columns specified in the `SqlCommand` property. The Available Output Columns box is automatically populated to reflect the available external columns, and a straight mapping between matching columns is created.

By deleting, moving, or creating mappings between the columns in the boxes, or by using the data grid to manipulate the Output Column property for each External Column, you can alter how the input columns map to the output columns.

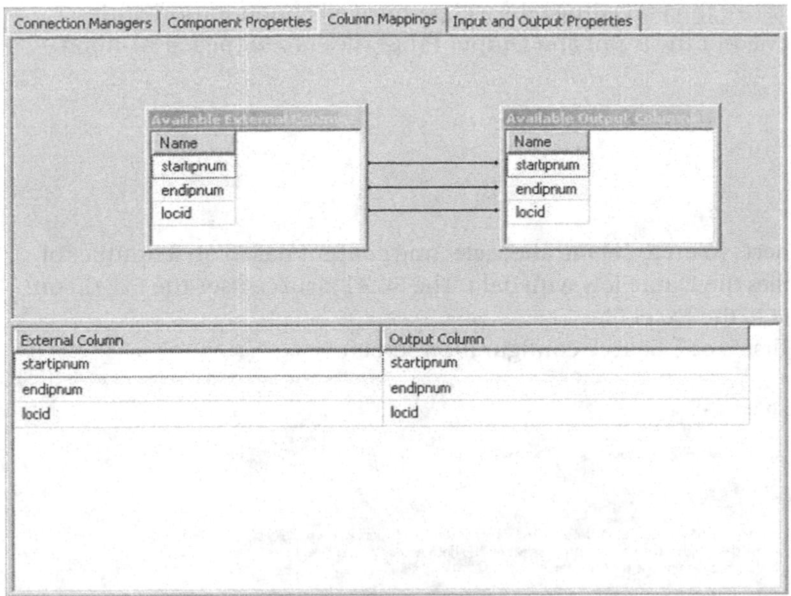

Figure 8-8. *Specifying column mappings*

Finally, the Input and Output Properties tab (Figure 8-9) shows the configuration screen for the available outputs—both normal output and error-output streams. On closer examination you can see a logical, textual representation of the columns that are presented to the output stream and to the error stream where each output and the columns it contains can be configured individually.

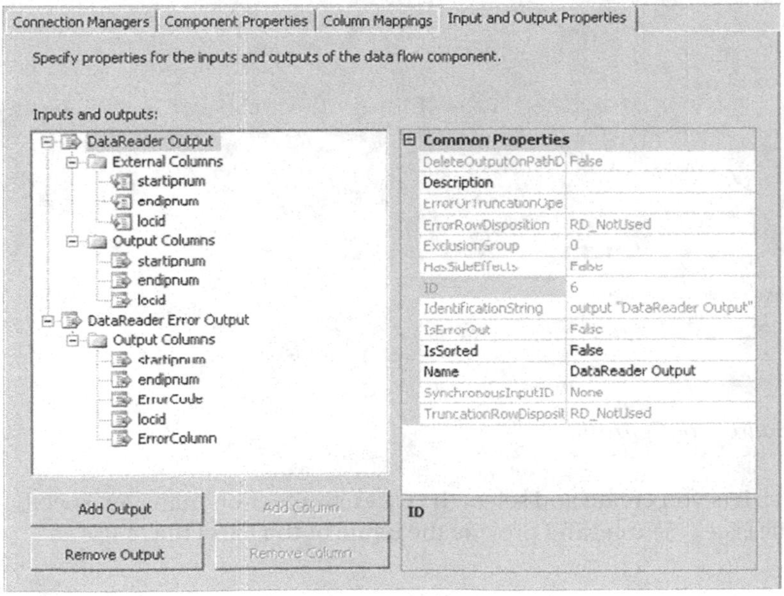

Figure 8-9. *Input/output properties*

In the vast majority of cases, the preceding tabs will perform all configuration duties, necessitating only a brief review of the Input and Output Properties tab for peace-of-mind purposes.

Excel Source

1 output, 1 error output

The `Excel Source` connects to an Excel file and, selecting content based on a number of configurable settings, supplies the Data Flow with data. The `Excel Source` uses the `Excel` connection manager to connect to the Excel file.

Figure 8-10 shows the first `Excel Source` configuration screen.

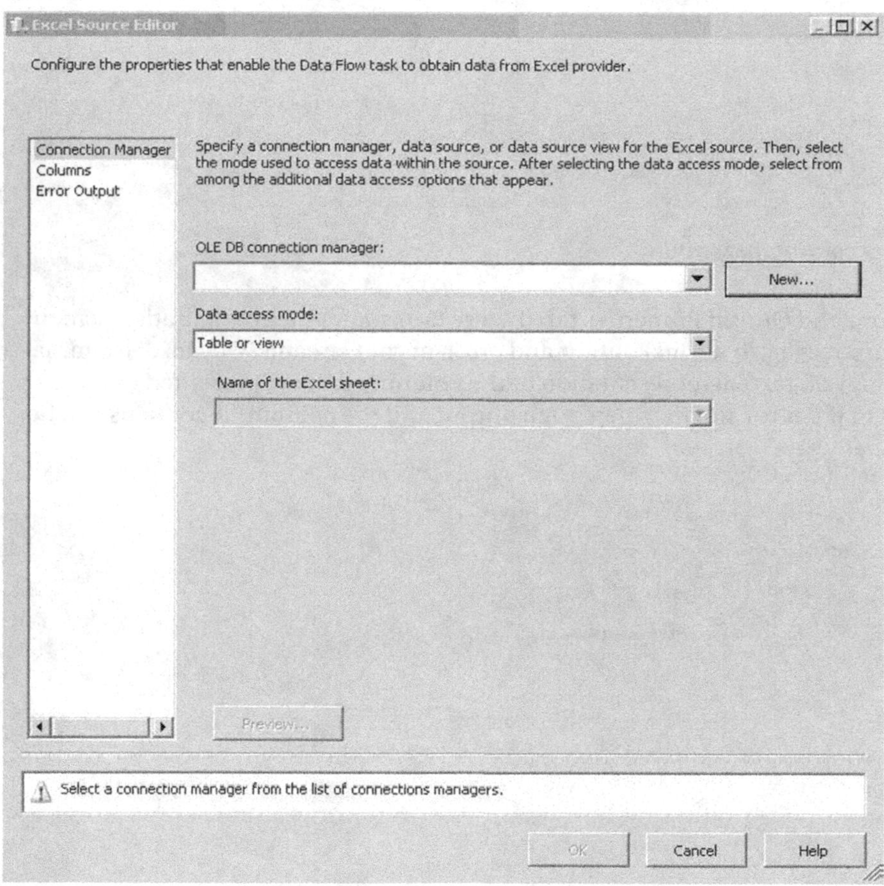

Figure 8-10. *The basic Excel Source configuration*

The configuration screen lets you create and select the `Excel` connection manager, specify how data is selected from the `Excel Source`, and provide the name of the Excel file to use as the source.

The `Excel` Connection Manager configuration screen, shown in Figure 8-11, lets you select the Excel file location, specify the Excel format used to create the file, and indicate whether the first row of data contains column names.

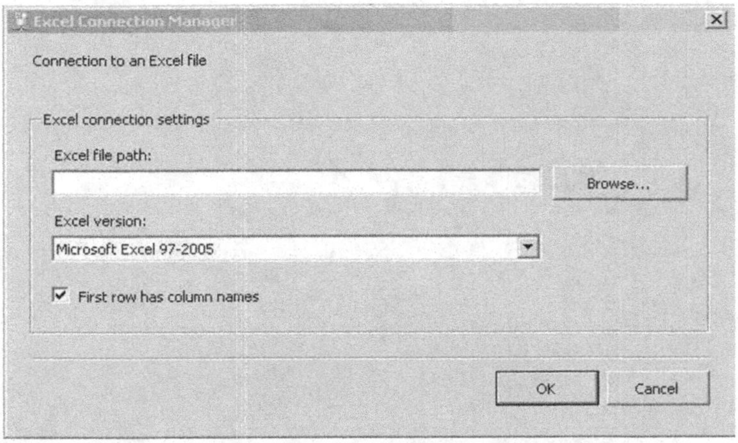

Figure 8-11. *Specifying the Excel file particulars*

It's useful to take a look at the data this source is expecting to use. Click Preview on the Connection Manager area of the data source configuration to display a screen like the one in Figure 8-12.

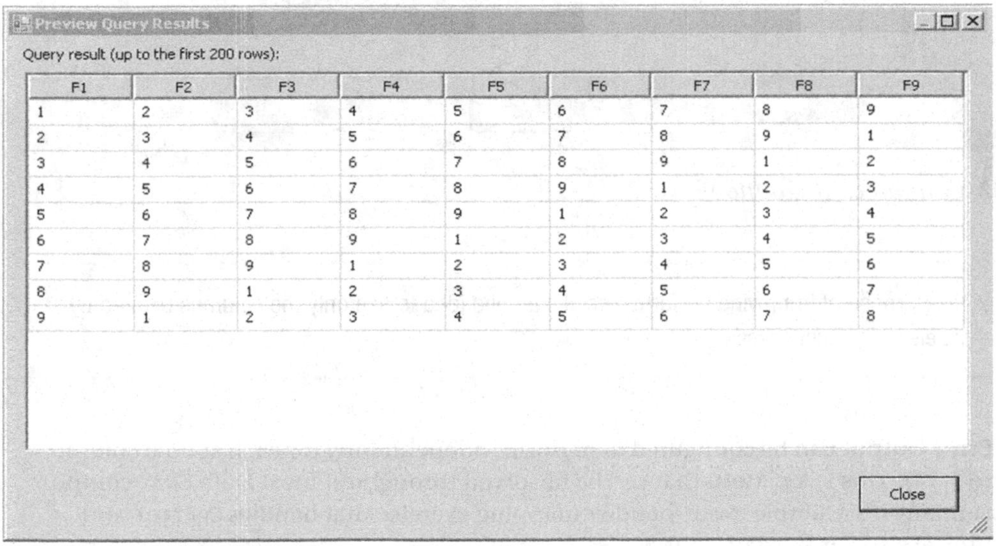

Figure 8-12. *Previewing the Excel source data*

The Columns part of the data source configuration shows the columns that are available and selectable from the source file. By default all columns are selected, though the selection can be changed to suit requirements. This is shown in Figure 8-13.

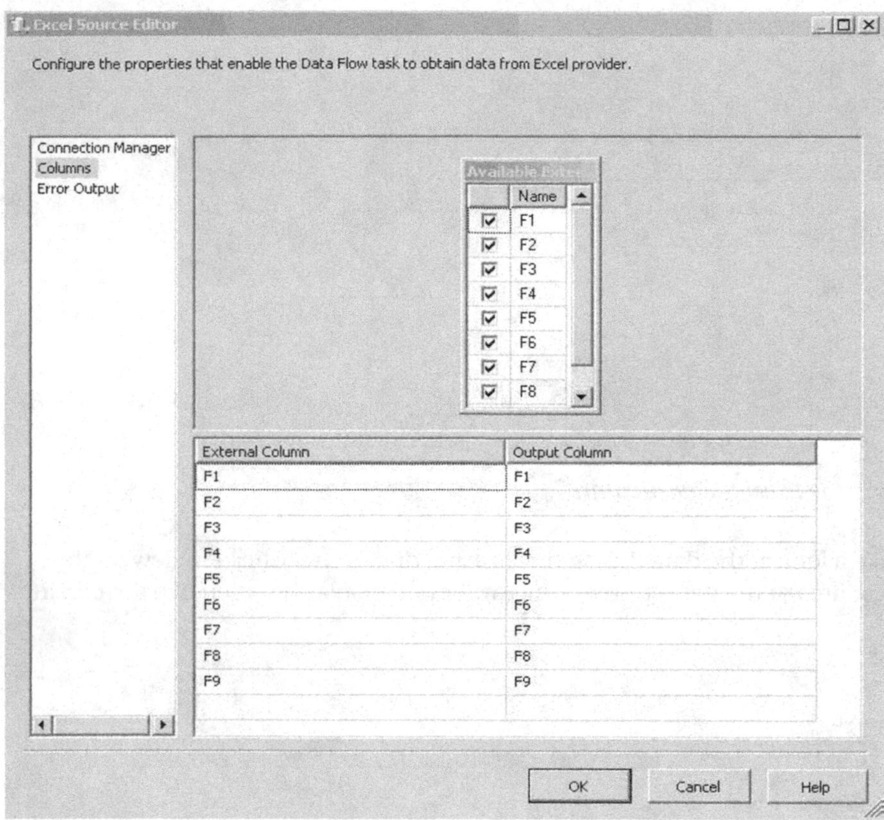

Figure 8-13. *Column configuration*

Note For the purpose of improving performance, it's a good idea to use only the columns needed by excluding—deselecting—unnecessary columns.

The Error Output can be configured to perform independently for each source column (see Figure 8-14). This is a pattern that can be observed throughout most Data Flow components. Essentially it's a simple event-handler mapping exercise that handles `OnError` and `OnTruncation` events for the data source.

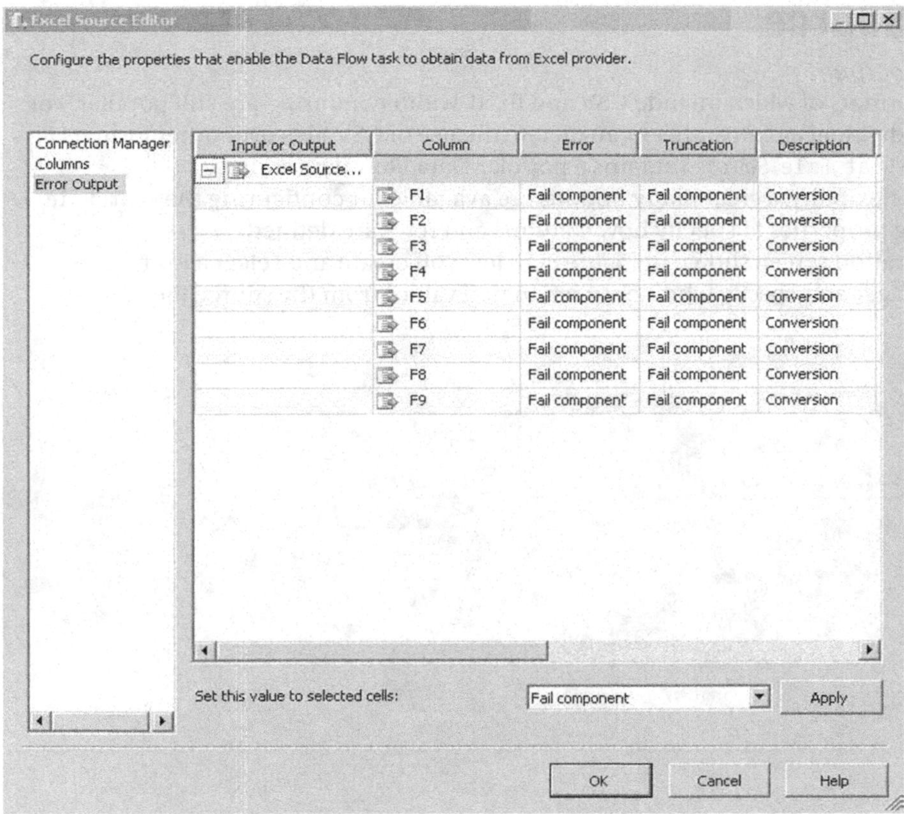

Figure 8-14. *Configuring error output*

Possible values for both the Error and Truncation properties are shown in Table 8-1.

Table 8-1. *Available Property Values*

Property Value	Description
Ignore Failure	Ignore the fact that an exception of some kind has occurred and continue to the next event.
Redirect Row	The source row that caused the failure is routed into the error stream rather than the main process stream.
Fail Component	If an error occurs, fail the component.

Flat File Source

1 output, 1 error output

Flat files—formats of which include CSV and fixed-width columns—are still popular. For many reasons individual circumstances can dictate the use of CSV files over other formats, which is why the Flat File Source remains a popular Data Flow data source.

To maintain flexibility, a great many options are available for configuring the Flat File Source, including properties to specify how columns and rows are defined.

The configuration screen shown in Figure 8-15 lets you create and select a Flat File connection manager and specify whether to retain null values from the source file.

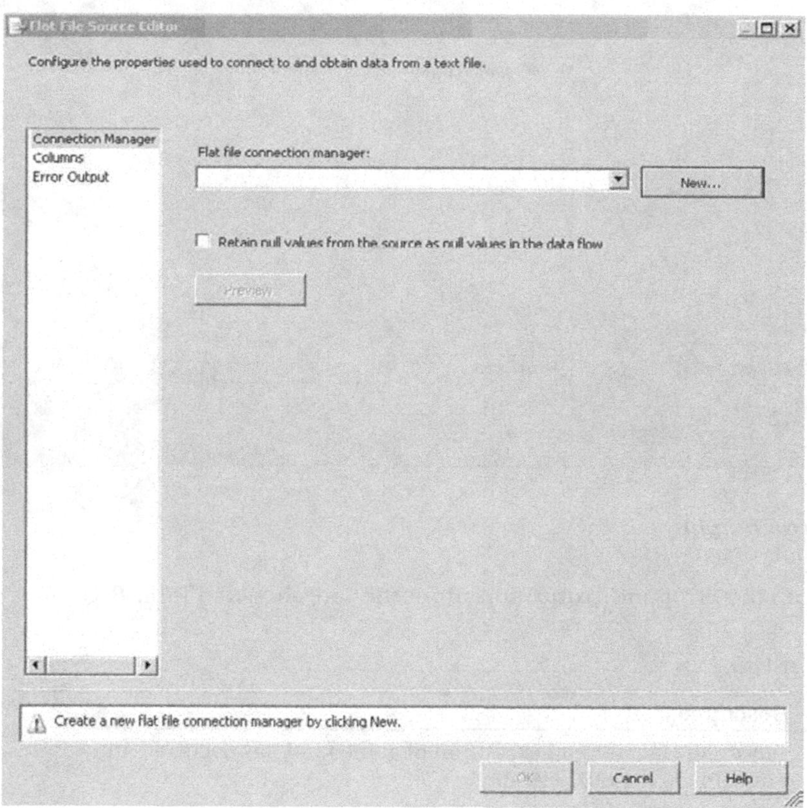

Figure 8-15. *Configuring the connection manager to use for this Data Source*

The crux of the configuration to define how the source file is handled is actually within the Flat File connection manager. Its configuration screen is shown in Figure 8-16.

It's worth mentioning here that if multiple files are required, the MULTIFLATFILE connection manager should be used instead of the Flat File connection manager. It allows the selection of multiple files and handles the consecutive opening of the files. Figure 8-17 shows the selection of the MULTIFLATFILE connection manager type.

For delimited format files, the Columns configuration screen is used to specify row and column delimiters. Changing these values and then selecting Reset Columns reflects how the input file is interpreted based upon the delimiter selections.

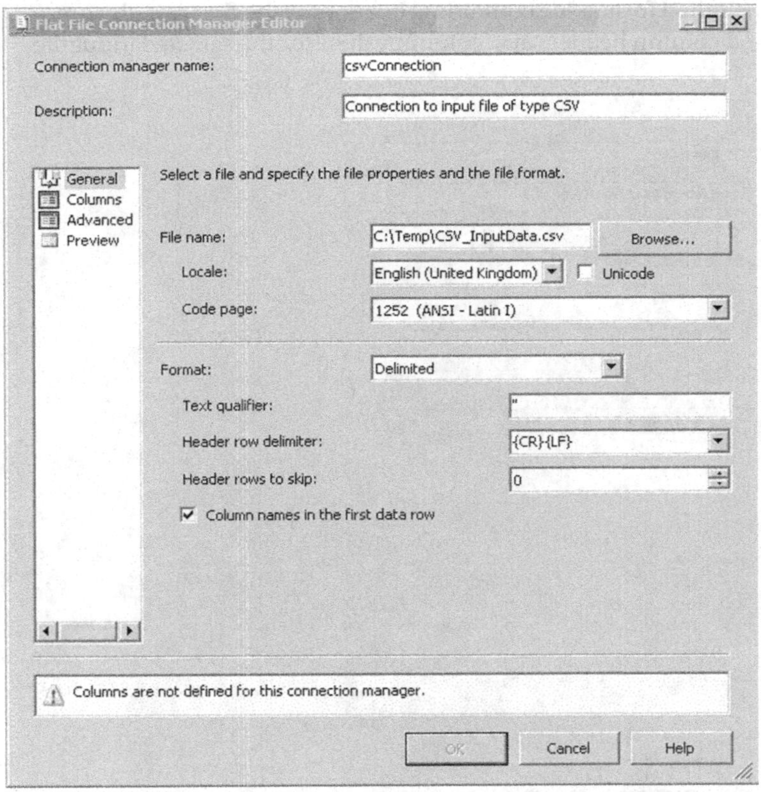

Figure 8-16. *Setting the specific input-file properties*

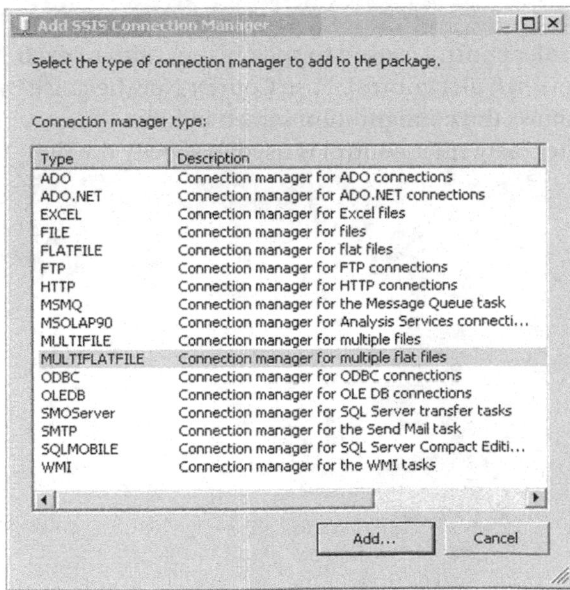

Figure 8-17. *The MULTIFLATFILE connection manager type*

As in Figure 8-18, with a delimited format file containing headers as the first row, the preview grid should reflect expected column headers and column values for the selected input file.

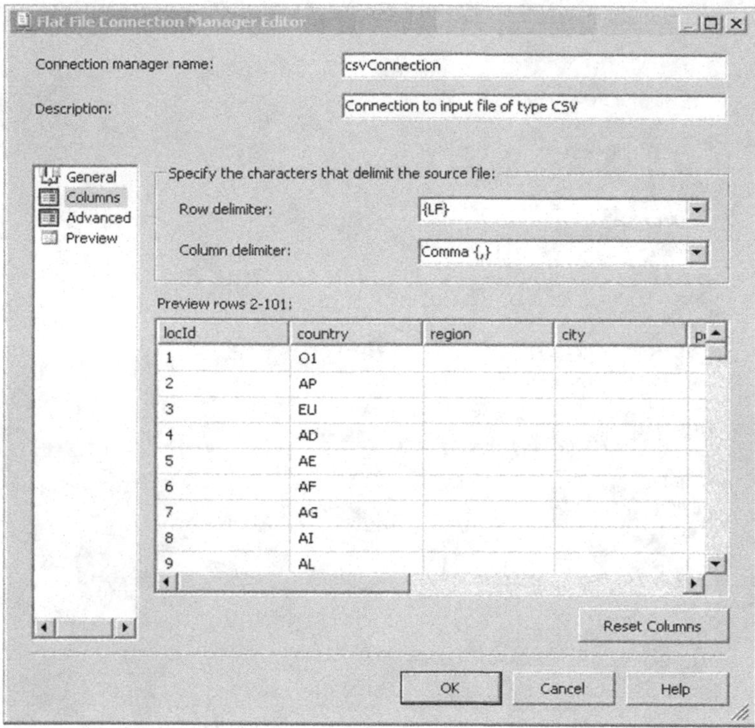

Figure 8-18. *Preview data to ensure settings are correct (delimited format).*

For fixed-width format files a rather tasty ruler control is used to specify the width of each column. The font setting relates only to the preview/ruler control. I use Courier New because I'm an old-fashioned kind of guy. Figure 8-19 shows the configuration screen in full.

For ragged-right format files the same rather tasty ruler control is used to specify the file properties, as shown in Figure 8-20.

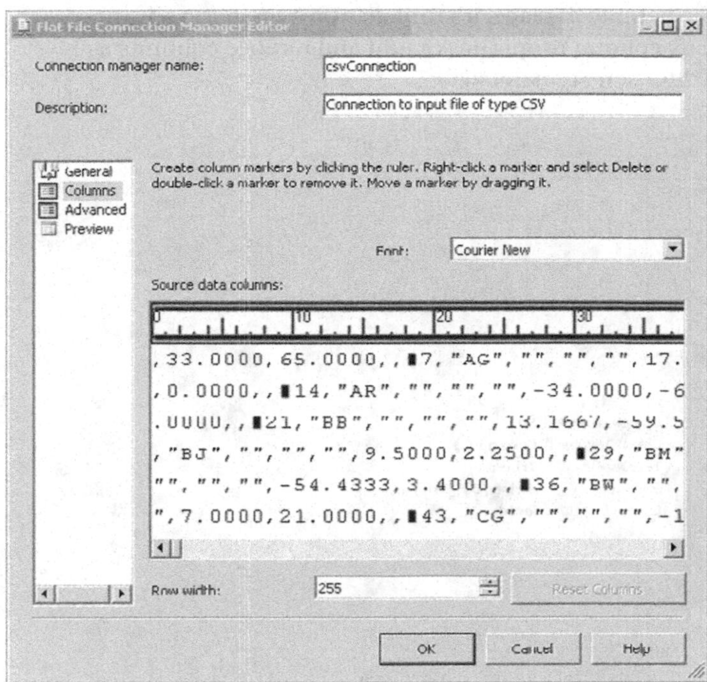

Figure 8-19. *Previewing data for the fixed-width format*

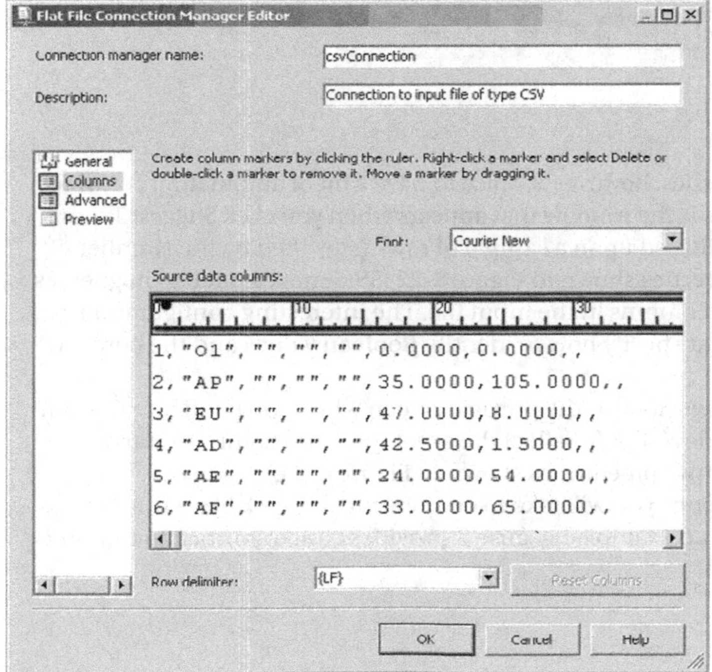

Figure 8-20. *Previewing data for the ragged-right format*

Once the source file settings are happily in place, it's time to move on to the advanced settings. From here it's easy to specify column properties or add and remove columns as necessary. Figure 8-21 shows this editor screen in detail.

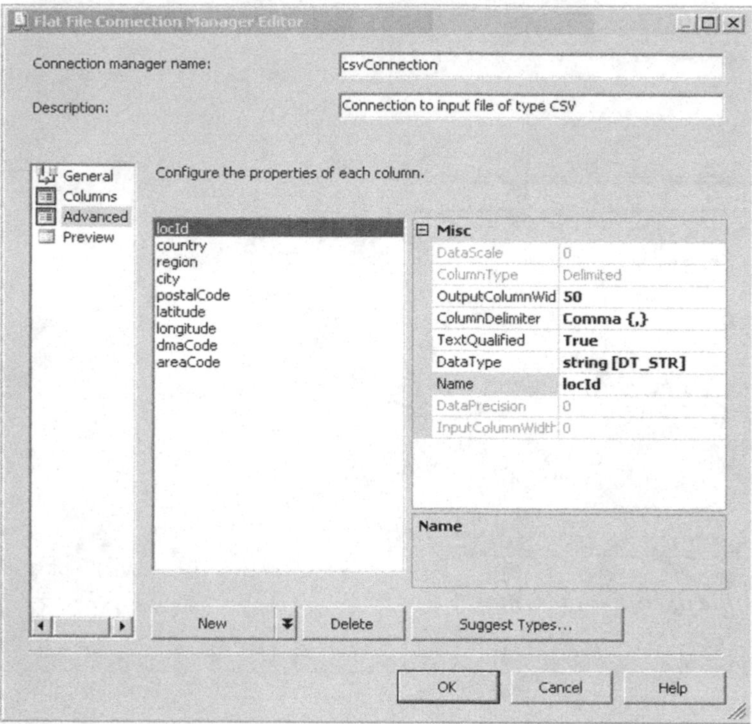

Figure 8-21. *Setting column data types*

When it comes to these properties, however, it's nice to have a bit of automation . . . which leads me nicely to Figure 8-22. This is the window that appears when you click Suggest Types . . .

I really like this functionality. Based upon a sample of rows (specified by the Number of rows property) and the other properties shown in Figure 8-22, SSIS makes intelligent guesses as to the data types of each of the columns in the input file. The interesting configuration properties here are the settings that specify how to identify Boolean values and the percent-padding option.

Finally, it's always worth taking a look at the preview screen when you configure the connection manager. By now the preview should reflect the exact rows and columns that are required to be supplied into the input pipeline, as shown in Figure 8-23.

Although I have every confidence you will take to configuring this task like a duck to water, it's pertinent to go through an example because it provides a nice contrast to the `Bulk Insert Task` example in Chapter 6.

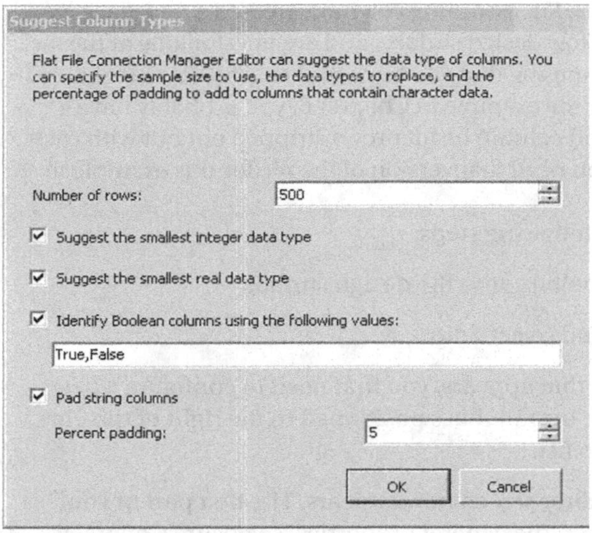

Suggest Column Types

Flat File Connection Manager Editor can suggest the data type of columns. You can specify the sample size to use, the data types to replace, and the percentage of padding to add to columns that contain character data.

Number of rows: 500

☑ Suggest the smallest integer data type

☑ Suggest the smallest real data type

☑ Identify Boolean columns using the following values:

True,False

☑ Pad string columns

Percent padding: 5

OK Cancel

Figure 8-22. *Priming the Suggest Types function*

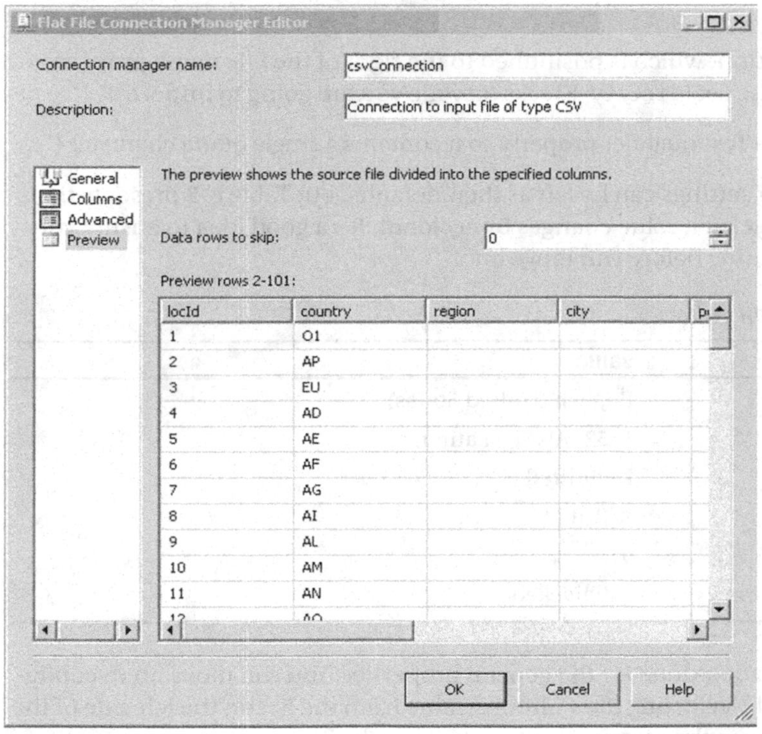

Figure 8-23. *Previewing the output*

As with the earlier example in this chapter, I'm assuming you have created a new package, dropped a `Data Flow Task` onto the Control Flow design surface, and are now looking at the empty Data Flow design surface. I am also assuming that you have the `GeoLiteCity-Blocks.csv` file in an accessible location. If you did follow the example in Chapter 6, you probably have a copy of the file with the copyright message and column header rows stripped out but with each value still surrounded by quote characters. You need that version of the file for this example to configure it successfully as the source.

Begin this bulk-insert exercise with the following steps:

1. Drop a `Flat File Source` from the Toolbox onto the design surface.
2. Double-click the task or right-click and select Edit....
3. On the Flat File Source Editor screen that appears, you first need to configure a new connection manager. Click the New... button that's positioned to the right of the `Flat File` connection manager drop-down list.
4. The Flat File Connection Manager Editor screen now appears. The first part of your configuration effort will concentrate on the general properties, so ensure General is selected from the list on the left side of the screen. Enter a name for the new connection manager against the Connection manager name property. I have called mine `myFlatFile`.
5. Click the Browse... button, which is positioned to the right of the File name property box, and navigate to the `GeoLiteCity-Blocks.csv` file you are going to import.
6. Modify the value of the Text qualifier property so it contains a single quote character (").
7. Most of the remaining settings can be left as their defaults, but Table 8-2 presents them so you can double-check if a value changes by accident. It's a good idea to ensure your values correlate with mine before you move on.

Table 8-2. *Default Configuration Values*

Property	Value
Locale	English (United States)
Code page	1252 (ANSI – Latin I)
Format	Delimited
Header row delimiter	{CR}{LF}
Header rows to skip	0
Column names in the first data row	Unchecked

8. That's all the configuration done for the general properties. You can move on to configure the columns now by selecting the Columns value from the list on the left side of the screen. Figure 8-24 shows the screen you're be presented with.
9. Ensure the Row delimiter value is set to `{CR}{LF}` and the Column delimiter value to `Comma {,}`.
10. The Preview rows 1-100 window should show a grid containing the first 100 values from the CSV file, just as in Figure 8-24.

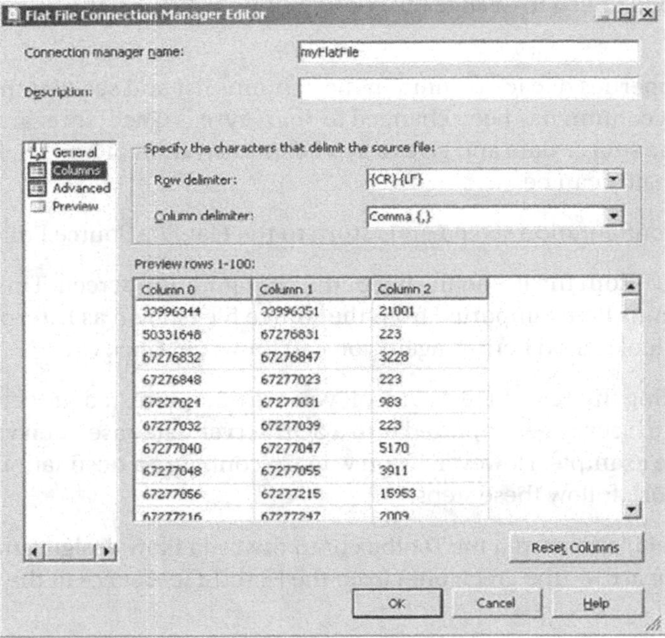

Column 0	Column 1	Column 2
33996344	33996351	21001
50331648	67276831	223
67276832	67276847	3228
67276848	67277023	223
67277024	67277031	983
67277032	67277039	223
67277040	67277047	5170
67277048	67277055	3911
67277056	67277215	15953
67277216	67277247	2009

Figure 8-24. *My columns-configuration screen*

11. Now you can move on to the advanced configuration. Select Advanced from the list on the left side of the configuration screen. You're presented with a list of the three columns being imported and a pane showing their properties to the right.

12. Here's where you can use the Suggest Types functionality to autonomously configure the data types for each column. Click Suggest Types... and you will be presented with the screen shown in Figure 8-25. This screen allows you to provide information that can help increase the accuracy of the suggestions being made.

Suggest Column Types

Flat File Connection Manager Editor can suggest the data type of columns. You can specify the sample size to use, the data types to replace, and the percentage of padding to add to columns that contain character data.

Number of rows: 200

☑ Suggest the smallest integer data type

☑ Suggest the smallest real data type

☑ Identify Boolean columns using the following values:

True,False

☐ Pad string columns

Percent padding: 0

OK Cancel

Figure 8-25. *Tweaking settings for more-accurate suggestions*

13. For this example you don't need to change the configuration values on this screen. Just click OK.

14. You can review the properties of each column in the columns list and see that the Data Type property for each column has been changed to `four-byte signed integer`. This is entirely accurate for the source data and gives a brief demonstration of how useful the Suggest Types functionality can be.

15. Click OK to close the configuration screen and return to the Flat File Source Editor.

16. Select the Options value from the list on the left of the configuration screen. This screen shows the columns being imported from the source file (shown as External Columns). Everything looks good here so again you can move on. Click OK.

You're now done configuring the `Flat File Source`. If you are not interested in seeing the data specified by the `Flat File Source` get imported into a SQL Server database, then you can skip the next set of steps in the example. However, if you want to configure a destination for the data and perform the import, follow these steps:

1. Drop a `SQL Server Destination` from the Toolbox onto the Data Flow design surface and connect the output arrow (the green one) from the `Flat File Source` to the new component.

2. Double-click the `SQL Server Destination` component or right-click it and select Edit.

3. Ensure the Connection Manager item is selected on the left side of the configuration screen. Create a new `OLE DB` connection manager that points to your local database server by clicking the New... button that lives to the right of the `OLEDB` connection manager property drop-down list.

4. Click the New... button to the right of the Use a table or view property drop-down list. This lets you create a new table in which to hold your CSV data. In the small script window that appears, change the script so the name of the new table is `CSV_IMPORT_TABLE_2`. Click OK.

5. Select the Mappings item from the list on the left of the configuration screen. This gives a graphical display—just like Figure 8-26—of automatically generated mappings (based upon column name, essentially) between the source data (displayed as Input Columns) and the destination table (displayed as Destination Columns).

6. Configuration is complete, so click OK.

7. Execute the package.

You will find, once processing is complete, that a large number of rows have been copied from the source CSV file to the destination table in SQL Server. Figure 8-27 shows the Data Flow design surface after processing has completed.

If you compare the functionality of this task with the Control Flow `Bulk Insert` task, you'll notice how much more configurable this data source is for connecting to a flat file. I concede that an extra step is required to get the source data to its destination, but the extra configuration options actually make it a much easier operation to complete. The cost is that using the Data Flow data source ➤ Data Flow data destination method isn't quite as fast in practice—though it is considered a bulk insert by the SSIS engine.

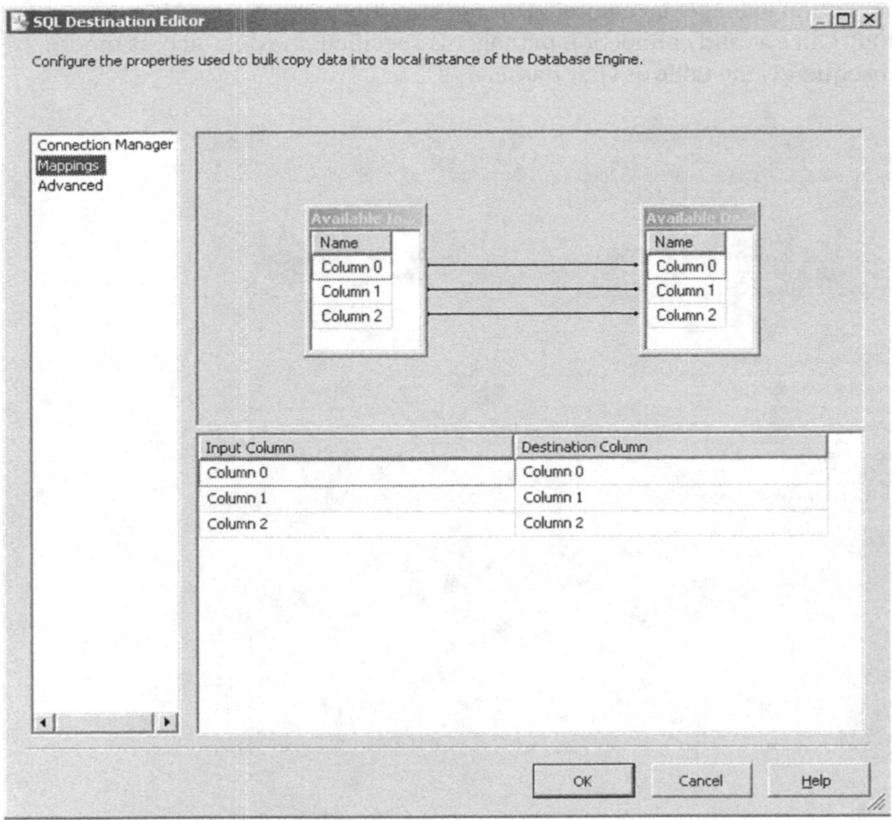

Figure 8-26. *Basic mapping performed by SSIS automatically*

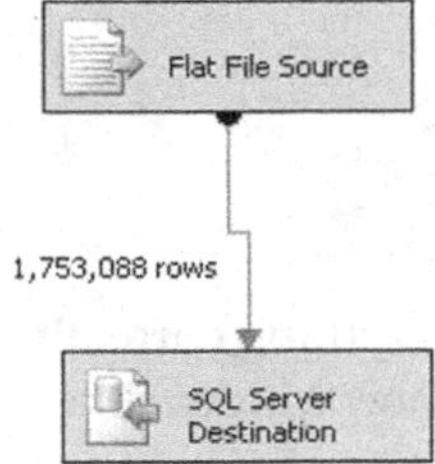

Figure 8-27. *Success! The bulk insert is complete.*

OLEDB Source

1 output, 1 error output

The `OLEDB Source` is used when the data access is performed via an OLE DB provider. It's a fairly simple data source type, and everyone is familiar with OLE DB connections.

As usual, a connection manager is required. You can specify or create one using the screen shown in Figure 8-28. Once a valid connection manager is specified, the data-access mode can be set, and subsequently the table or view name.

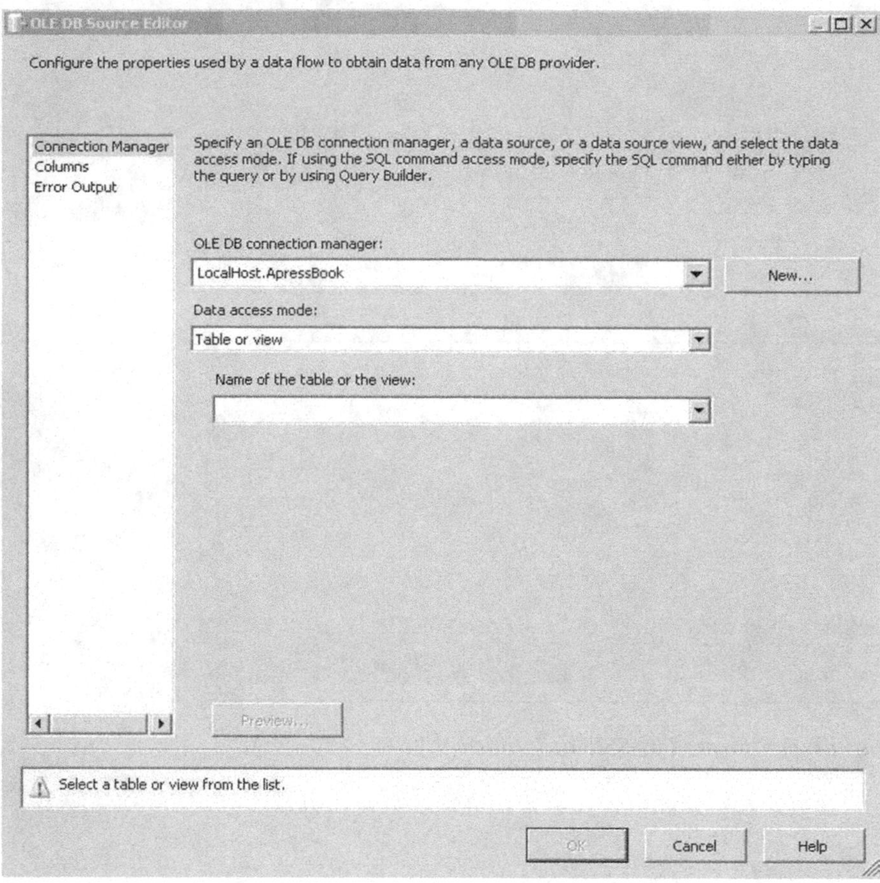

Figure 8-28. *Setting connection and content*

As part of my development routine I like to make sure I've configured everything correctly so far. I check this by clicking the Preview button. The results are shown in a new window like the one in Figure 8-29.

Moving swiftly onward to the Columns screen, you can select or deselect columns as necessary, as shown in Figure 8-30.

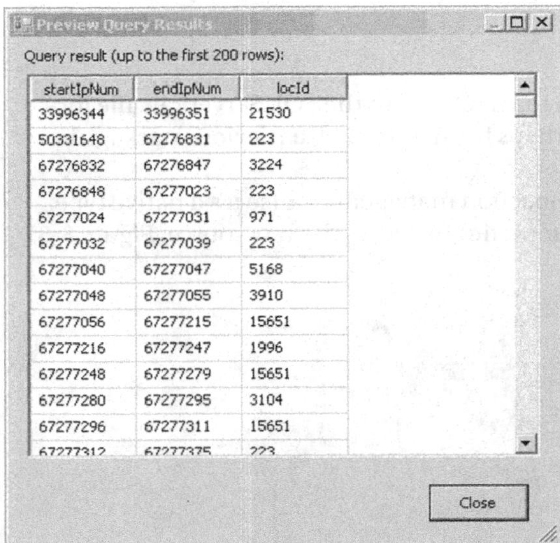

Figure 8-29. *Previewing the results of the settings*

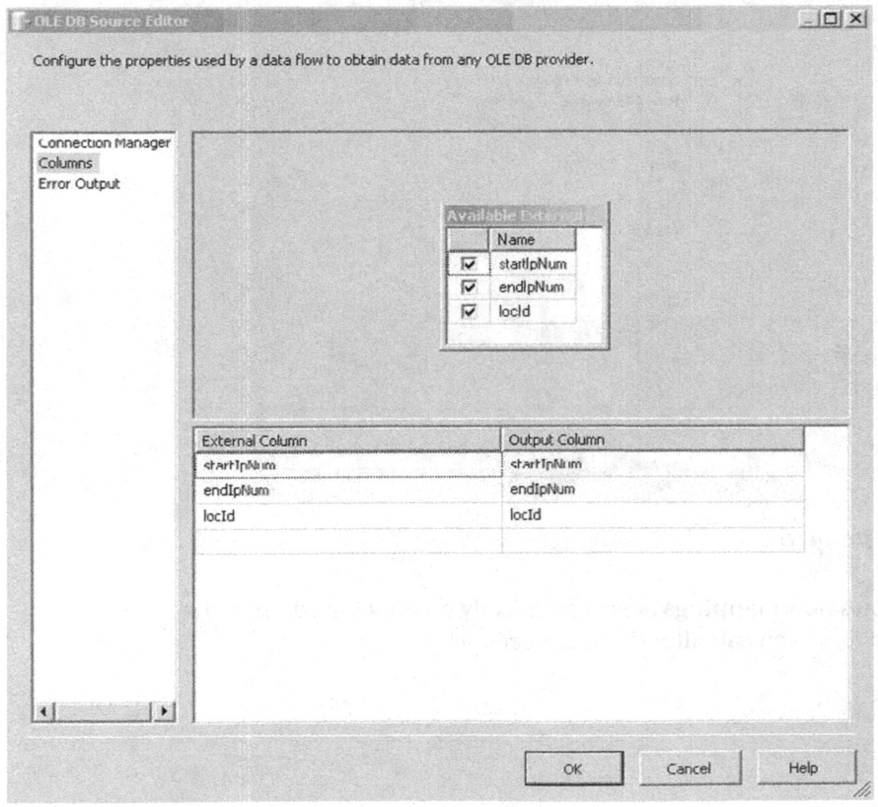

Figure 8-30. *Column configuration*

Raw File Source

1 output, 1 error output

The Raw File Source is used to import data that is stored in the SQL Server raw file format. It is a rapid way to import data that has perhaps been output by a previous package in the raw format.

The Raw File Source does not require a connection manager because it's a native type. For this reason it's simply a case of setting the properties to access the raw source. Figure 8-31 shows the first configuration screen for the task.

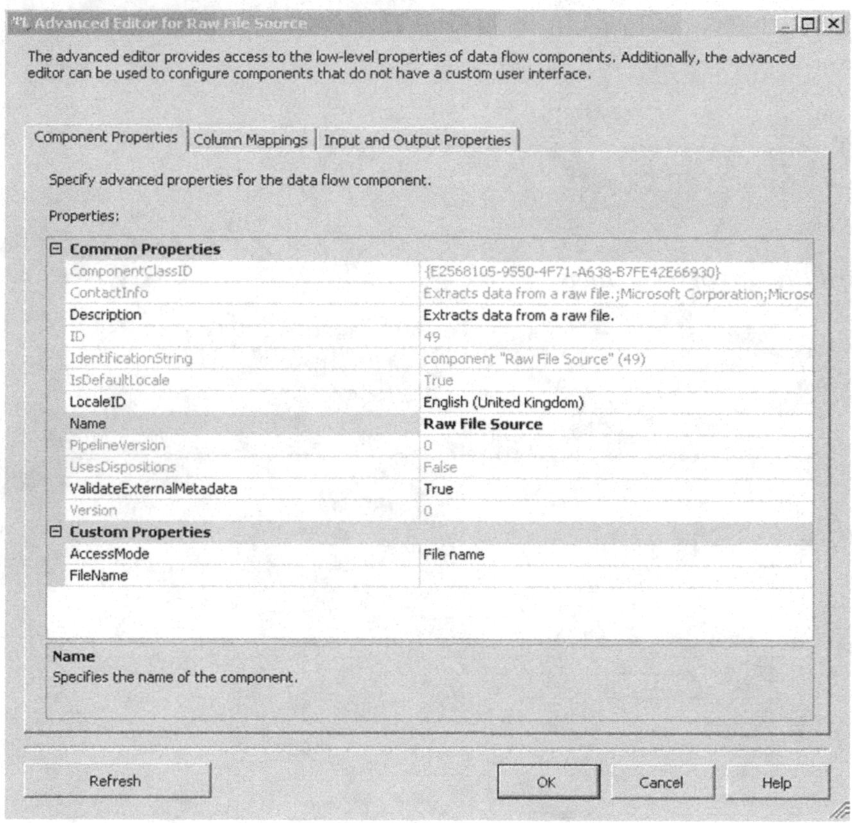

Figure 8-31. *Raw file properties*

Figure 8-32 shows how mappings are automatically created based upon the available input columns. Of course you can alter these as necessary.

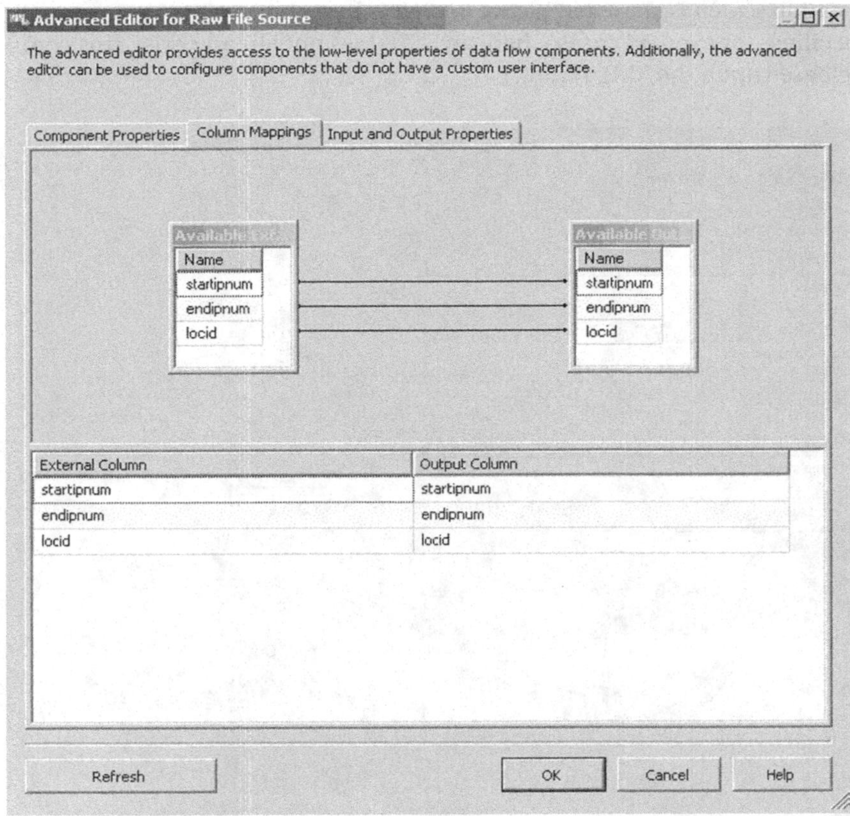

Figure 8-32. *Mappings, based on input columns*

XML Source

1 output, 1 error output

The XML Source is quite complex, at least when used in a real-world manner to consume XML content featuring collections or hierarchies of information. The XML Source requires an XML Schema Definition (XSD) file, which is really the most important part of the component because it describes how SSIS should handle the XML document.

To handle the potential complexity and subtlety of XML data, this data-source type is incredibly clever, particularly in relation to hierarchical data. In a parent/child hierarchy described in XML data, this component creates *two* outputs. The first output is for the parent data in the structure. The second output is for the child data in the structure. Also, an extra column is added to the child columns collection, identifying the parent to which the child data belongs.

As a consequence of this, for each output created as a by-product of the XML structure, an error output is also created. This gives complete control over the handling of streams as described by the XML source.

It should be noted that the XSD is included only to provide structural information to the component. No validation is performed at any stage.

The basic configuration screen is shown in Figure 8-33. It is here that the XML source and related XSD can be specified—or even, in cases where an XSD does not already exist, this component can create one based upon the XML input.

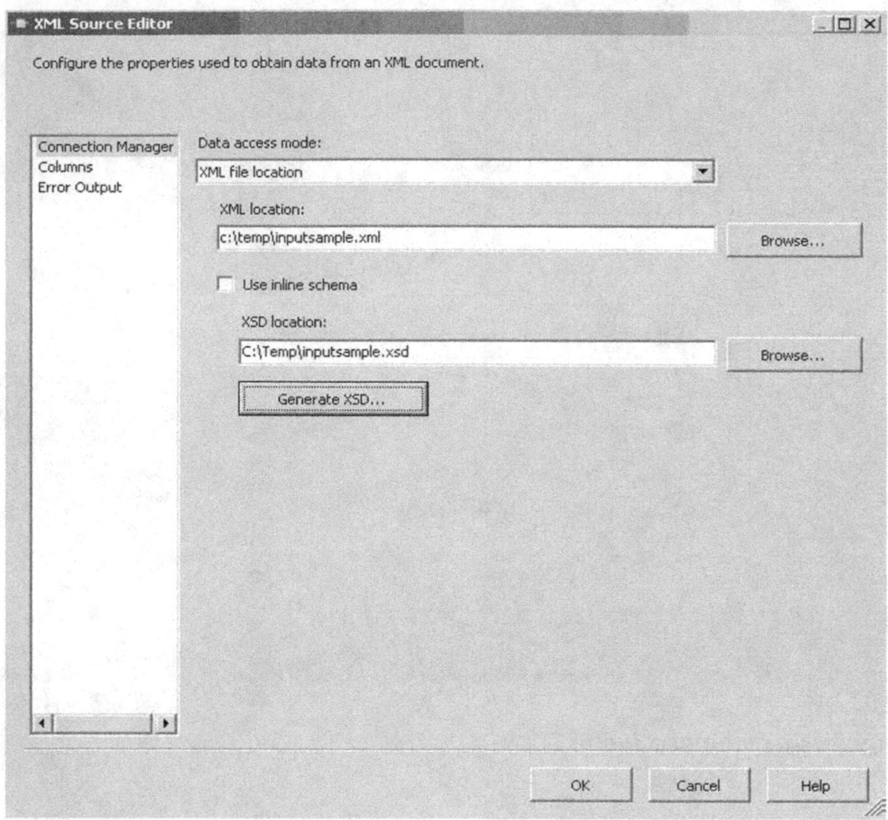

Figure 8-33. *XML Source configuration*

The example in Figure 8-34 shows the input columns available to the component.

The error-output configuration screen, shown in Figure 8-35, can be configured just like the error output from the other data-source components.

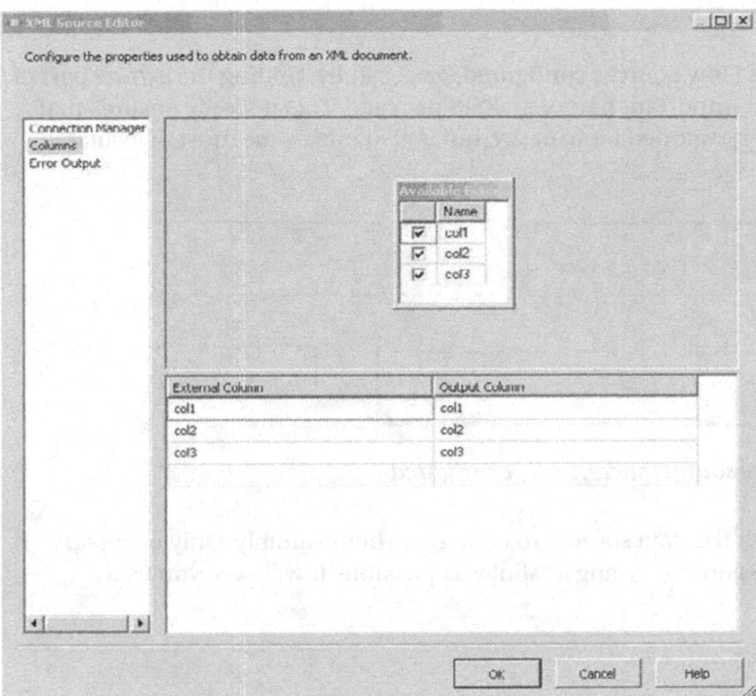

Figure 8-34. *Column configuration*

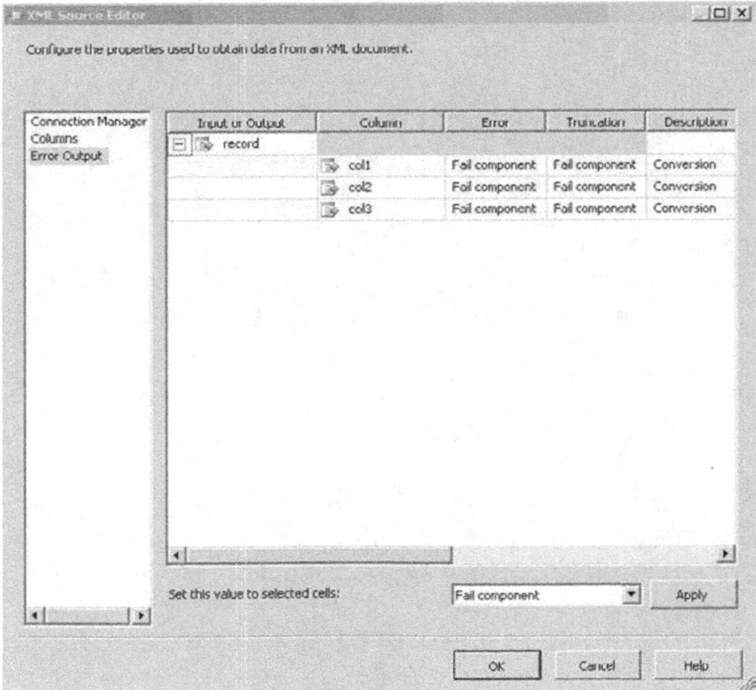

Figure 8-35. *Error output configuration*

Summary

Figure 8-36 shows all the Data Flow Sources configured successfully. Getting the *extract* part of ETL right is probably the most important part of an SSIS package. This not only ensures that the rest of the package can be developed more easily, but it also makes the most of available performance.

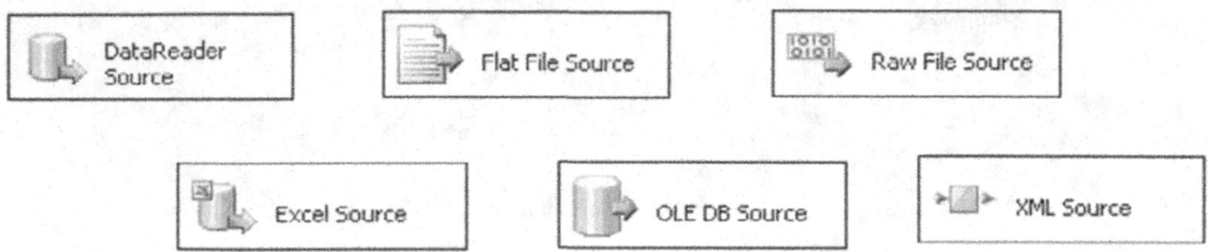

Figure 8-36. *All of the Data Flow sources successfully configured*

Time should be taken with the data sources to configure them suitably. Only necessary columns should be selected. Keep everything as slinky as possible. It will save you from headaches later.

CHAPTER 9

Basic Data Flow Transformations

Transformations are the meat—or the mycoprotein—in the ETL sandwich. Although it's vitally important to ensure the data sources in a package are configured correctly, the actual handling of data via transformations takes pole position when it comes to package development.

I have split Data Flow transformations into two chapters—basic and advanced—primarily for readability. The split is a logical one too. Data Flow transformations consist of the kind that are used every day and the kind that get used in more advanced and complex situations. This chapter covers the following basic transformations:

- `Audit`
- `Character Map`
- `Conditional Split`
- `Copy Column`
- `Data Conversion`
- `Derived Column`
- `Export Column`
- `Import Column`
- `Lookup`
- `Merge`
- `Merge Join`
- `Multicast`
- `OLE DB Command`
- `Percentage Sampling`
- `Row Count`
- `Row Sampling`
- `Sort`
- `Union All`

So this chapter serves as a more gentle introduction to the Data Flow than being instantly thrown to the lions with something like the `Slowly Changing Dimension` transform. For reference purposes, I'll start with a word on SSIS data types and data viewers.

SSIS Data Types

Developing with the Data Flow will introduce you to a number of new concepts. One of them is the use of SSIS-specific data types and how they map to established SQL Server types.

Certain tasks require either the input- or output-column data types to be of a certain kind. One example is the `Fuzzy Grouping` task (discussed in Chapter 10); to use the fuzzy-match type, the columns involved must be `DT_STR` or `DT_WSTR`. This maps nicely onto the SQL Server `CHAR`, `VARCHAR`, `NCHAR`, and `NVARCHAR` types.

It makes sense in this case, because the fuzzy algorithm is text based. On some levels, describing the types using the SSIS data types introduces what some might call unnecessary complexity. Those familiar with the SQL Server data types, however, will take to it all like another of those metaphorical ducks to the metaphorical water.

Table 9-1. *Comparison of SSIS to SQL Server Data Types*

SSIS Data Type	SQL Server Data Type
DT_BOOL	BIT
DT_BYTES	BINARY, VARBINARY, TIMESTAMP
DT_CY	SMALLMONEY, MONEY
DT_DATE	
DT_DBDATE	
DT_DBTIME	
DT_DBTIMESTAMP	DATETIME, SMALLDATETIME
DT_DECIMAL	
DT_FILETIME	
DT_GUID	UNIQUEIDENTIFIER
DT_I1	
DT_I2	SMALLINT
DT_I4	INT
DT_I8	BIGINT
DT_NUMERIC	DECIMAL, NUMERIC
DT_R4	REAL
DT_R8	FLOAT
DT_STR	CHAR, VARCHAR
DT_UI1	TINYINT
DT_UI2	
DT_UI4	
DT_UI8	
DT_WSTR	NCHAR, NVARCHAR, SQL_VARIANT, XML
DT_IMAGE	IMAGE
DT_NTEXT	NTEXT
DT_TEXT	TEXT

Data Viewers

A useful testing and debugging tool lives inside the Data Flow. *Data viewers* are views of data in the Data Flow at any point between the output of one component and the input of another. The view is composed of the column collection that exists in the Data Flow as populated as the output of the previous upstream component. Figure 9-1 shows a data viewer after the addition of the Pivot transform.

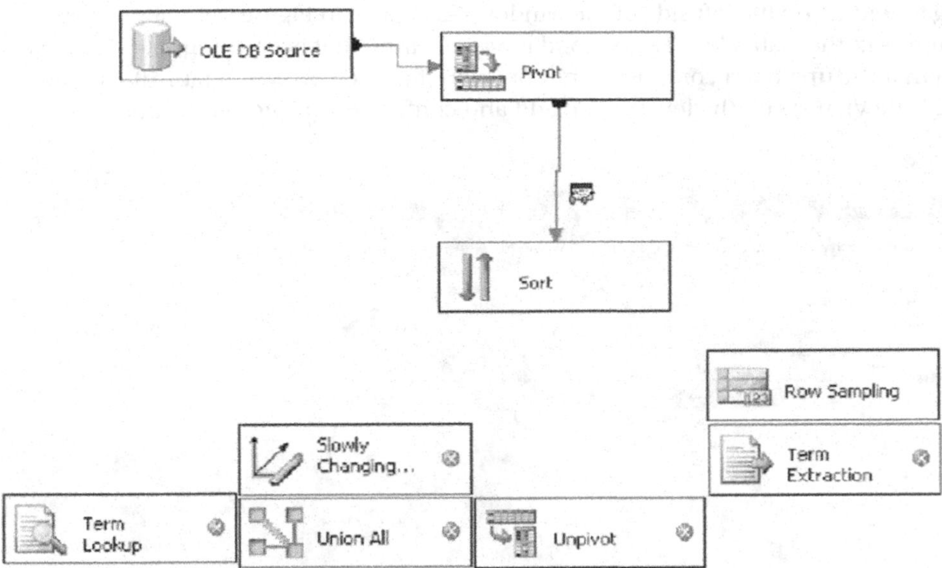

Figure 9-1. *A data viewer I've added after the Pivot transform*

To add a data viewer, simply right-click a connected Data Flow arrow and select Data Viewers.... This displays the configuration window shown in Figure 9-2.

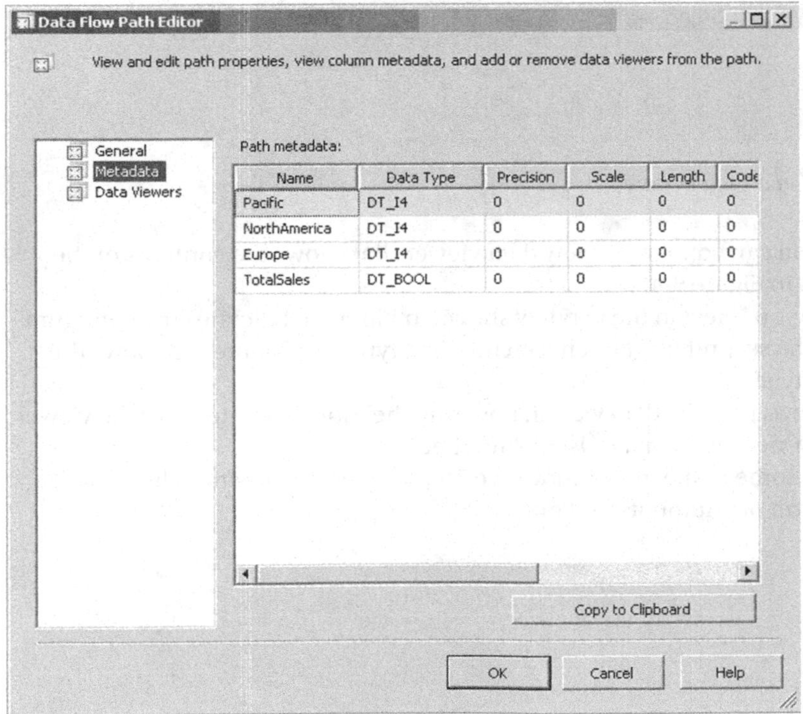

Figure 9-2. *The Metadata option shows the contents of the column collection.*

Selecting Metadata on the left side of the window—as I have in Figure 9-2—shows the available columns in the Data Flow. This is good for confirming that everything is working as expected and that the upstream component has been configured correctly. Figure 9-3 shows that selecting Data Viewers on the left lets you add and configure data viewers at this point of the Data Flow.

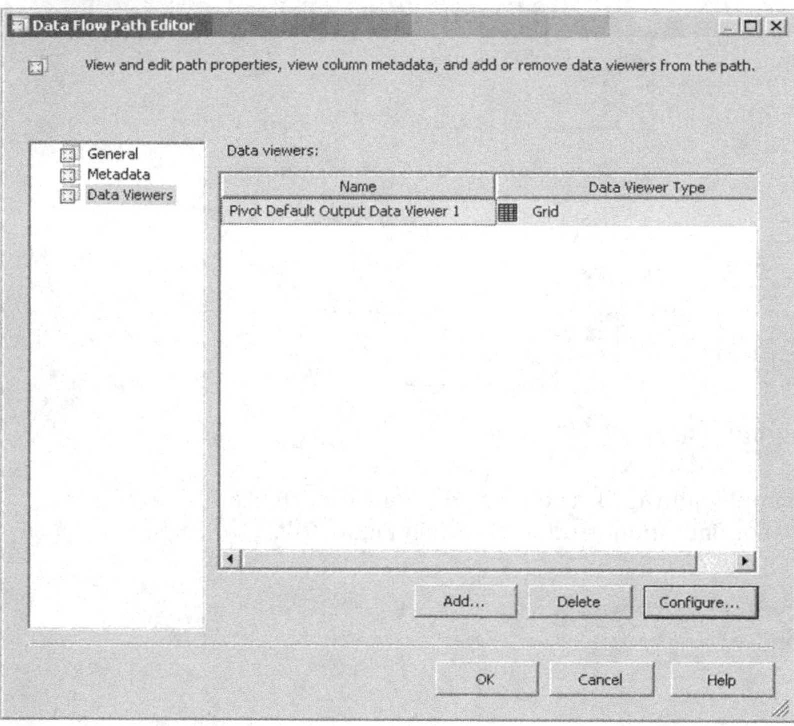

Figure 9-3. *I've already added a viewer here.*

By choosing Add..., you can configure a new data viewer that shows the contents of the Data Flow at this point, as in Figure 9-4.

The data-viewer type you select in the window shown in Figure 9-4 dictates the configuration options available in the second tab. I've chosen the Grid type, and Figure 9-5 shows the options available for that type.

At runtime, as data flows past the data viewer, hovering the mouse pointer over the viewer icon shows the configured view of the data. Useful? You bet.

Now, here we go with some of the most innovative and truly useful functionality in SSIS. It's time to get our transform on! Autobots, roll out.

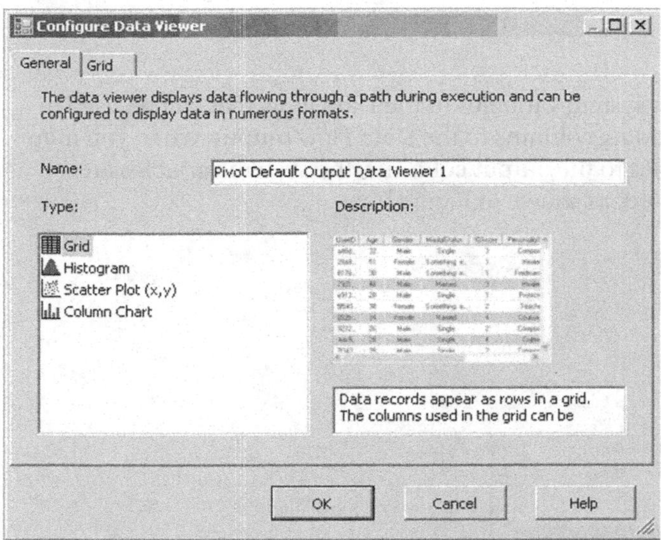

Figure 9-4. *The data viewer can show just the numbers or pretty pictures.*

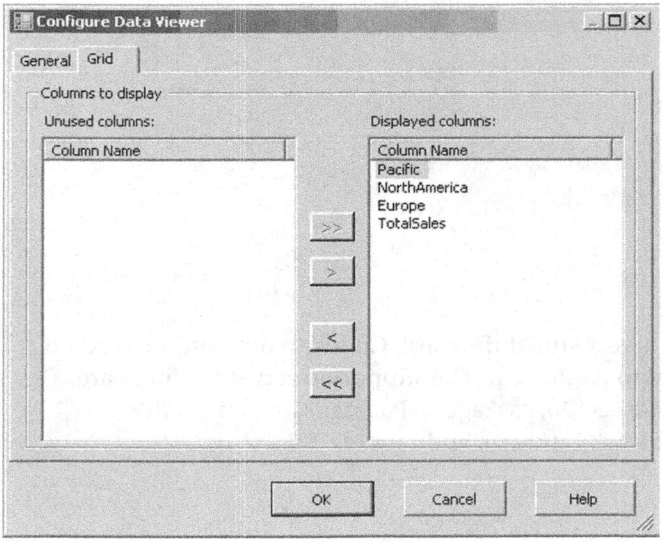

Configure Data Viewer
General
Grid
Columns to display
Unused columns:
Column Name
Displayed columns:
Column Name
Pacific
NorthAmerica
Europe
TotalSales
>>
>
<
<<
OK
Cancel
Help

Figure 9-5. *Select the columns to show in the viewer grid.*

Audit

1 input, 1 output, 0 error outputs

The Audit transformation exposes system variables to the Data Flow that can be used in the stream. This is accomplished by adding columns to the Data Flow output. When you map the required system variable or variables to the output columns, the system variables are introduced into the flow and can be used, as shown in Figure 9-6.

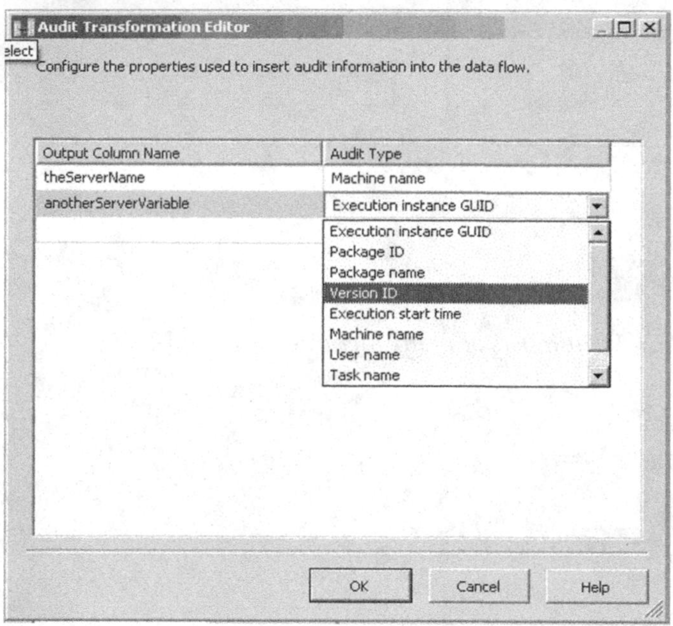

Figure 9-6. *Specifying new output columns*

The edit screen for the Audit task is very straightforward. Choose a new output-column name and the system variable required to populate it. The supported server variables are ExecutionInstanceGUID, ExecutionInstanceGUID, PackageID, PackageName, VersionID, ExecutionStartTime, MachineName, UserName, TaskName, and TaskId.

Character Map

1 input, 1 output, 1 error output

Got a string column? Want to manipulate it? Use this ambiguously named task. A character map is something I'd usually expect to find in the Windows Control Panel, but the Character Map task is something else entirely: it performs string manipulations on input columns. Figure 9-7 shows the main configuration screen.

You populate the lower grid in the configuration screen by selecting the columns to perform transformations on. A number of properties are available to manipulate for each row.

It should be remembered that the same column can be operated on by multiple transformations and so be added to the output collection multiple times (with different output-alias values).

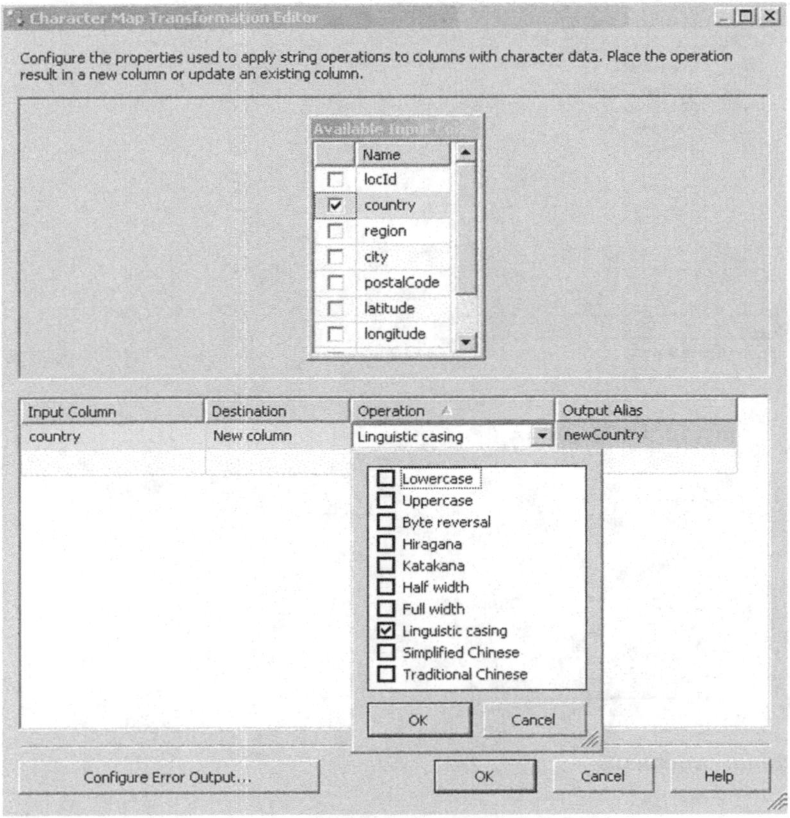

Figure 9-7. *Setting Character Map transform properties, per column*

Conditional Split

1 input, at least 1 output, 1 error output

The `Conditional Split` task splits Data Flow based on a condition. In many ways you could consider it a business process management (BPM) task in that, depending upon the results of an evaluated expression, data is routed as specified by the developer.

In a situation where multiple conditional statements are supplied, the data is routed based on the first expression to evaluate to `True`. As a consequence, there's also a default route for the data that falls through conditional processing without triggering a `True` result.

The configuration screen for this task is shown as Figure 9-8. Based on variables or columns, an expression can be entered to create different output streams. Each defined condition requires three pieces of information. Table 9-2 provides more explanation.

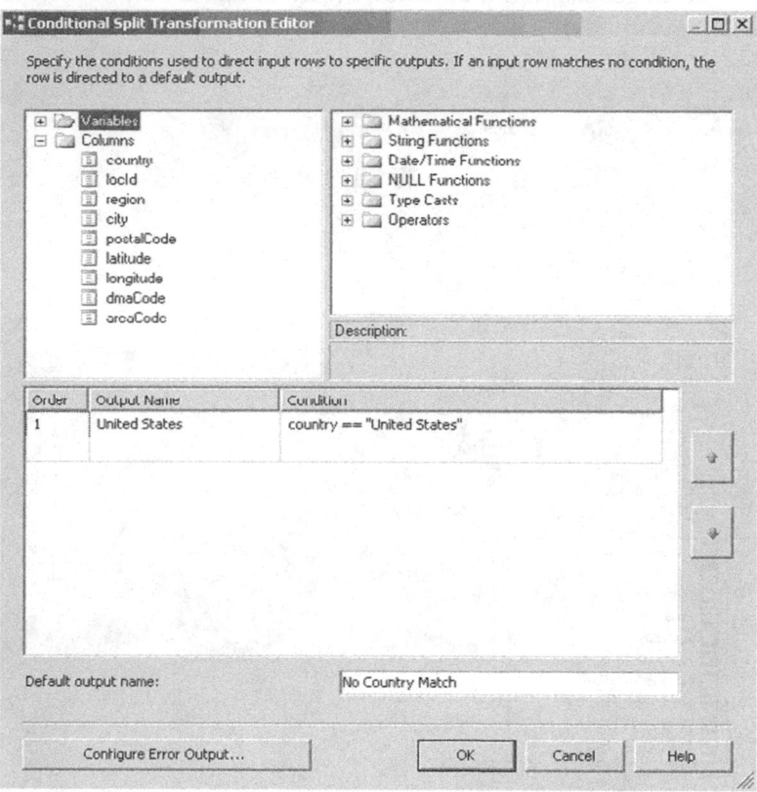

Figure 9-8. *Specifying conditional statements*

Table 9-2. *Condition Properties*

Property	Description
Order	The order in which the conditions are evaluated. Arrows to the right of the window move conditions up and down in precedence.
Output Name	The name of the output to create based upon the `True` result of the conditional statement.
Condition	A valid conditional expression that evaluates to `True` or `False`.

The Condition property for each output takes a value as a valid expression. The available syntax and functions are shown in a navigable format at the top right side of the configuration screen.

The `Conditional Split` task also has a default output for any data in the stream that does not meet any of the conditional requirements. The name of this default output can be specified on the configuration screen. Figure 9-9 shows how the `Conditional Split` can look. I have created a single conditional statement that splits the input based upon the value of a column.

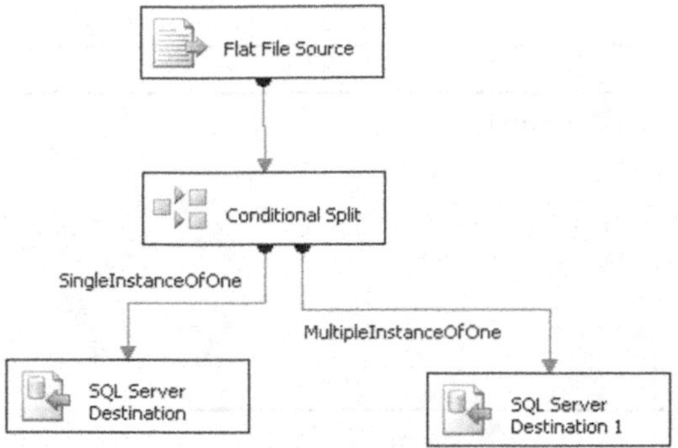

Figure 9-9. *The Conditional Split*

Now you'll take a more detailed look at this example and re-create it here. It's a good point from which to start becoming more familiar with Data Flow tasks.

Essentially this package splits a single set of data into two destination tables based upon the number of "1" characters detected within the first column of data in each row.

For this example you need to have created a new package, dropped a `Data Flow Task` onto the Control Flow design surface, and have clicked through into the Data Flow. Once again you'll use the `GeoLiteCity-Blocks.csv` file, so ensure you have it to hand. If you followed the `Bulk Insert Task` example in Chapter 6 and the `Flat File Source` example in Chapter 8, you have a copy of the file with the copyright message and column header rows removed and with each value surrounded by quote characters. This is the version of the file you need to use in this example to configure it successfully as the source.

1. Drop a `Flat File Source` from the Toolbox onto the design surface.

2. Double-click the task or right-click and select Edit. . . .

3. On the Flat File Source Editor screen that appears, you first need to configure a new connection manager. Click the New... button that's positioned to the right of the `Flat File` connection manager drop-down list.

4. The Flat File Connection Manager Editor configuration screen now appears. The first part of your configuration effort will concentrate on the general properties, so ensure General is selected from the list on the left side of the screen. Enter a name for the new connection manager against the Connection manager name property. I have called mine `myFlatFile`.

5. Click the Browse... button that's positioned to the right of the File name property box and navigate to the `GeoLiteCity-Blocks.csv` file you are going to import.

6. Modify the value of the Text qualifier property so it contains a single quote character (`"`).

7. Most of the rest of the settings can be left as their defaults, but Table 9-3 presents them so you can double-check if a value changes by accident. It's a good idea to ensure your values correlate with mine before you move on.

Table 9-3. *Default Configuration Values*

Property	Value
Locale	English (United States)
Code page	1252 (ANSI – Latin I)
Format	Delimited
Header row delimiter	{CR}{LF}
Header rows to skip	0
Column names in the first data row	Unchecked

8. That's all the configuration done for the general properties. You can move on to configure the columns now by selecting the Columns value from the list on the left side of the screen. Figure 9-10 shows the screen you're presented with.

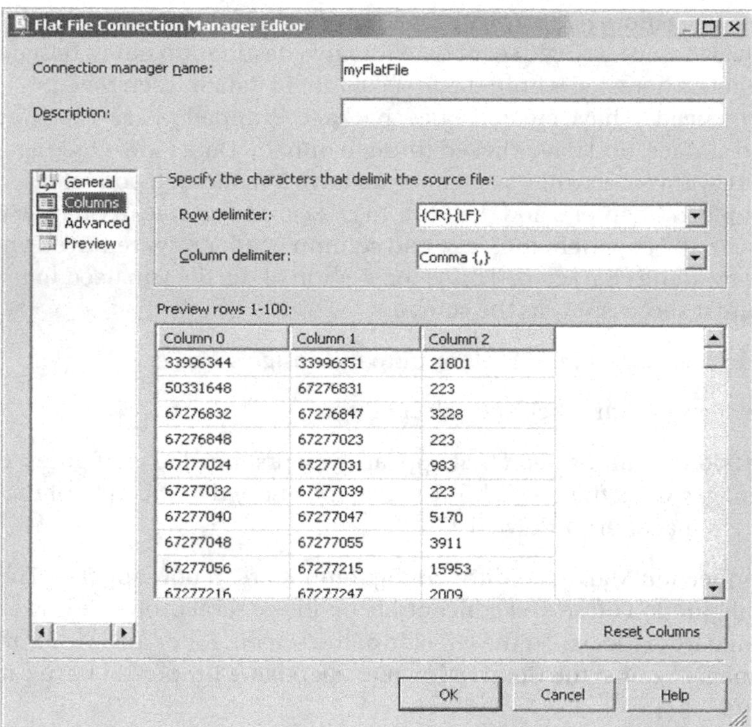

Figure 9-10. *My columns-configuration screen*

9. Ensure the Row delimiter value is set to `{CR}{LF}` and the Column delimiter value to `Comma {,}`.

10. The Preview rows 1-100 window should show a grid containing the first 100 values from the CSV file, just as in Figure 9-10.

11. Now you can move on to the advanced configuration. Select Advanced from the list on the left side of the configuration screen. You're presented with a list of the three columns being imported and a pane showing their properties to the right.

12. Here's where you can use the Suggest Types functionality to configure the data types autonomously for each column. Click Suggest Types... and you will be presented with the screen shown in Figure 9-11. This screen allows you to provide information that can help increase the accuracy of the suggestions being made. For this example you don't need to change the configuration values on this screen. Just click OK.

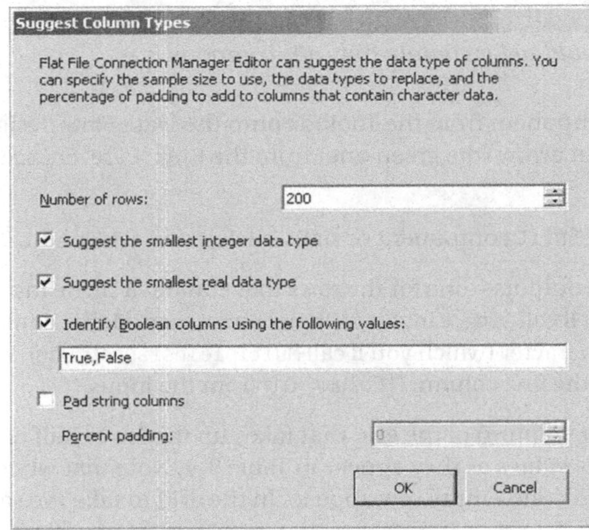

Figure 9-11. *Tweaking settings for more-accurate suggestions*

13. You can review the properties of each column in the columns list and see that the Data Type property for each column has been changed to `four-byte signed integer`. This is entirely accurate for the source data sampled and gives a brief demonstration of how useful the Suggest Types functionality can be. However, I happen to know that the values in `[Column 0]` and `[Column 1]` get significantly larger in this file, and so the number of rows sampled is insufficient. You can either increase the Number of rows value to `4,000,000`, just to make sure, or you can manually alter the data type for each column to `Numeric`. This data type is sufficiently large to allow all data to be imported.

14. Click OK to close the configuration screen and return to the Flat File Source Editor.

15. Select the Options value from the list on the left of the configuration screen. This screen shows the columns being imported from the source file (shown as External Columns). Everything looks good here, so click OK.

    Your Data Flow design surface should now look like Figure 9-12, containing only the configured Data Flow component. You can now move on to use the `Conditional Split` component.

Figure 9-12. *Your Data Flow should so far contain only one component.*

16. Drop a `Conditional Split` component from the Toolbox onto the Data Flow design surface and connect the output arrow (the green one) from the `Flat File Source` to the new component.
17. Double-click the `Conditional Split` component or right-click it and select Edit....
18. For this example you want two outputs—one for the rows that contain a single instance of the "1" character (which you'll call `SingleInstanceOfOne`) and a second that contains multiple instances of the "1" character (which you'll call `MultipleInstanceOfOne`). You're concerned only with values in the first column (`[Column 0]`) from the input.
19. Click in the first cell (the Order column) of the grid that takes up the lower half of the configuration screen. Enter the values as they appear in Table 9-4. Note that when you enter values in the first row, a second empty row appears in the grid to take the second set of values.
20. Click OK.

Table 9-4. *Configuring Conditional Outputs*

Order	Output Name	Condition
1	`SingleInstanceOfOne`	`FINDSTRING((DT_STR,10,1252)[Column 0],"1",1) == 1`
2	`MultipleInstanceOfOne`	`FINDSTRING((DT_STR,10,1252)[Column 0],"1",1) > 1`

It may come as a surprise to learn that this is the entire configuration required for the `Conditional Split` component. Any number of outputs can be defined on this grid very easily using valid expressions. The conditions for each output use the `FINDSTRING` expression syntax to perform a count of character instances for each row. For the purposes of this example, you aren't interested in any input rows that don't have the "1" character in the `[Column 0]` column. But if you were, you could just use the default output in whichever way you wanted.

Now you'll configure the destination components for the example:

1. Drop two SQL Server Destination components from the Toolbox onto the design surface.

2. Drag the output (green) arrow from the bottom of the Conditional Split component onto the first SQL Server Destination component. You will be presented with the window shown in Figure 9-13. As I described earlier in this section, this screen is used to specify which of the Conditional Split outputs to use as the input to the SQL Server Destination.

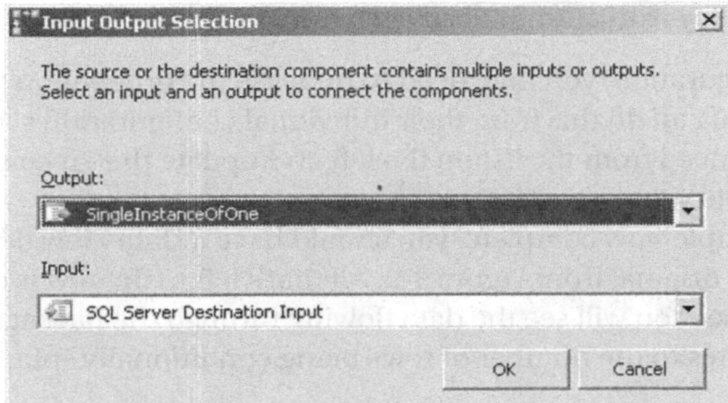

Figure 9-13. *Selecting the output from the Conditional Split*

3. Select the SingleInstanceOfOne value from the Output drop-down list.

4. Drag the unused output (green) arrow from the bottom of the Conditional Split component onto the second SQL Server Destination component. Again, you are presented with the window in Figure 9-13, except this time select MultipleInstanceOfOne as the value from the Output list.

5. Double-click the first SQL Server Destination component or right-click it and select Edit....

6. Ensure the Connection Manager item is selected on the left side of the configuration screen. Create a new OLE DB connection manager that points to your local database server by clicking the New... button that lives to the right of the OLE DB connection manager property drop-down list.

7. Click the New... button to the right of the Use a table or view property drop-down list. This lets you create a new table in which to hold the SingleInstanceOfOne data. In the small script window that appears, change the script so the name of the new table is CSV_SINGLE_INSTANCE_OF_ONE. Click OK.

8. Select the Mappings item from the list on the left of the configuration screen. This gives a familiar graphical display with automatically generated mappings. Click OK.

9. Double-click the second SQL Server Destination component or right-click it and select Edit....

10. Ensure the Connection Manager item is selected on the left side of the configuration screen. Create a new `OLE DB` connection manager that points to your local database server by clicking the New... button that lives to the right of the `OLE DB` connection manager property drop-down list.

11. Click the New... button to the right of the Use a table or view property drop-down list. This lets you create a new table in which to hold the `MultipleInstanceOfOne` data. In the small script window that appears, change the script so the name of the new table is `CSV_MULTIPLE_INSTANCE_OF_ONE`. Click OK.

12. Select the Mappings item from the list on the left of the configuration screen. This gives a familiar graphical display with automatically generated mappings. Click OK.

Depending on your server configuration, you may need to increase the timeout on the `SQL Server Destination` components. You can do this from their individual configuration screens in the Advanced section. Select Advanced from the list on the left and update the `Timeout` property so it contains a more suitable value—such as `360` seconds.

With the work to create the example now complete, you should have a Data Flow design surface that looks very much like the original from Figure 9-9. All that's left to do now is execute the package to make sure it works. You will see the data flowing through the package and giving a figure as it executes that relates to the number of rows being conditionally split. You can see this in Figure 9-14.

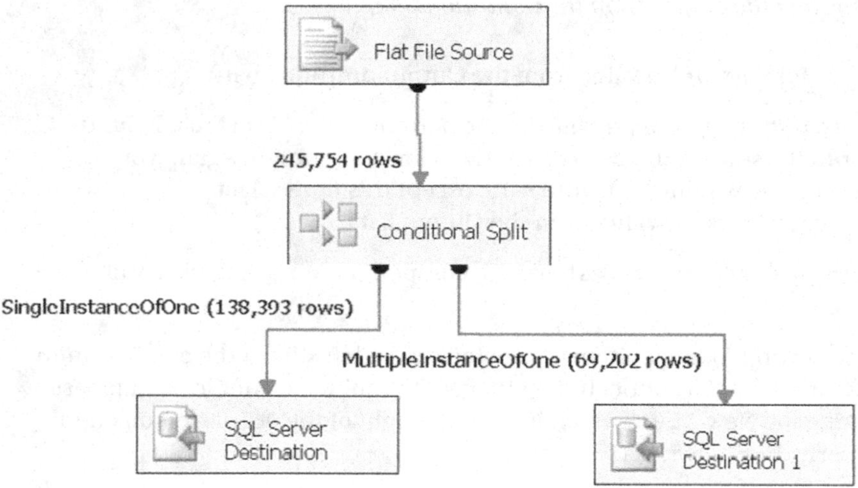

Figure 9-14. *The example Data Flow during execution*

Copy Column

1 input, 1 output

The `Copy Column` task makes a copy of a column contained in the input-columns collection and appends it to the output-columns collection. It's a nice easy way to create "safe" copies of existing columns or to provide working copies of a column. Figure 9-15 shows the main configuration screen.

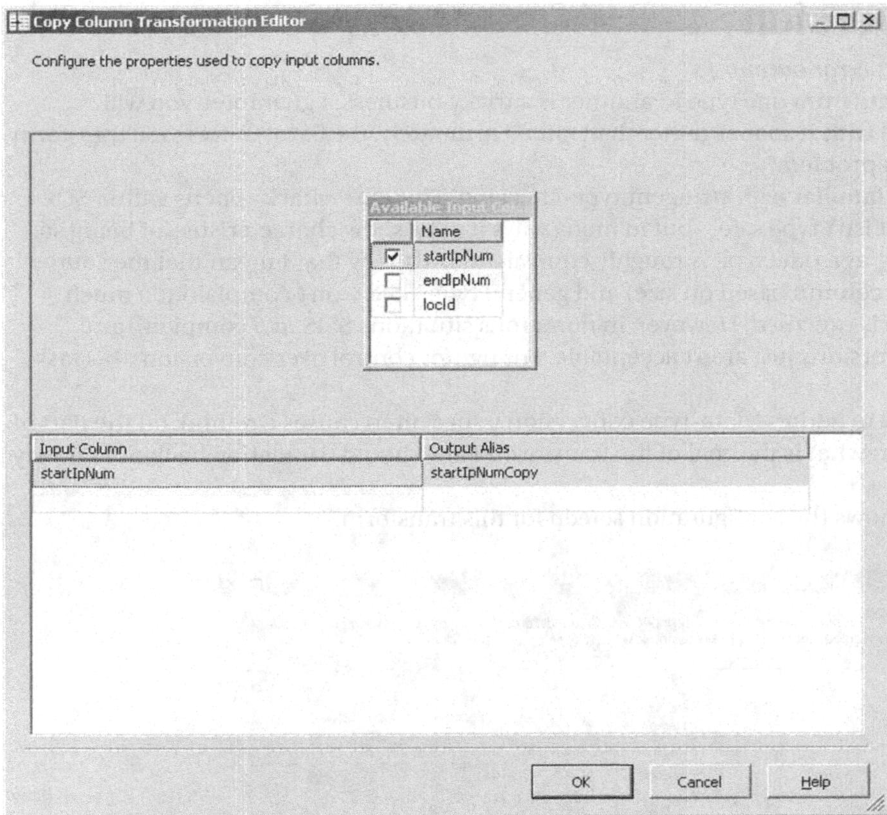

Figure 9-15. *Configuring the column from the input to copy*

In comparison to the tasks and components you've seen so far, the configuration screen for this task isn't exactly clear, particularly in terms of listing the columns that will form the output. I feel this makes the proposed content of the output ambiguous: does it contain the original input columns *and* the column(s) selected on this screen, or does this screen simply select the columns from the input to serve as the output?

To make it clear, any columns selected on this configuration screen are added to the output collection in addition to those from the input collection. In the case shown in Figure 9-15, the actual output collection looks like Table 9-5.

Table 9-5. *The Output-Columns Collection*

Column	Source
`startIpNum`	Input collection
`endIpNum`	Input collection
`locid`	Input collection
`startIpNumCopy`	Added by `Copy Columns` component

Data Conversion

1 input, 1 output, 1 error output

Converting data from one type to another is a tricky business. I guarantee you will become frustrated with it sooner rather than later. Fortunately, the `Data Conversion` transform addresses just this problem.

You might be familiar with stringent type-checking. This isn't what happens within SQL Server—because it isn't type safe—but in many ways it does show characteristics of being so. Essentially, so long as a data type is roughly equivalent in size (by that I mean that the source fits into the target column based on size) and general type, SSIS won't complain too much when the package is executed. However, in numerous situations SSIS *will* complain, and implicit type conversions just aren't acceptable. For tighter control over conversion, this task is ideal.

Also, the need to address data-type conversion issues often causes a rethink on the part of the SSIS developer: what is the goal of the transform? How should truncation be handled? Very useful indeed.

Figure 9-16 shows the configuration screen for this transform.

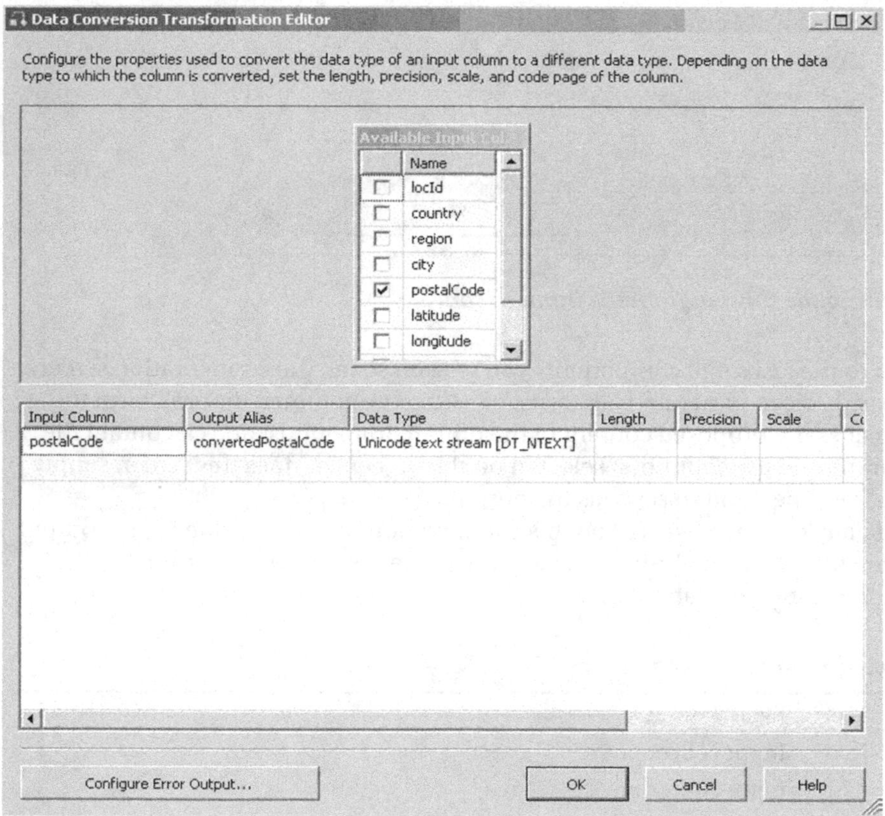

Figure 9-16. *A Unicode conversion in practice*

Column conversions can take place on a single column, many columns, or all columns from the input-columns collection. An alias name is given that is used at the output, and detailed conversion parameters such as length, precision, and scale can be specified.

Derived Column

1 input, 1 output, 1 error output

The `Derived Column` task is one I find myself returning to time after time. One or more new columns are appended to the output-columns collection based upon the work performed by the task, or the result of the derived function replaces an existing column value.

Figure 9-17 shows the configuration screen to define the derived columns.

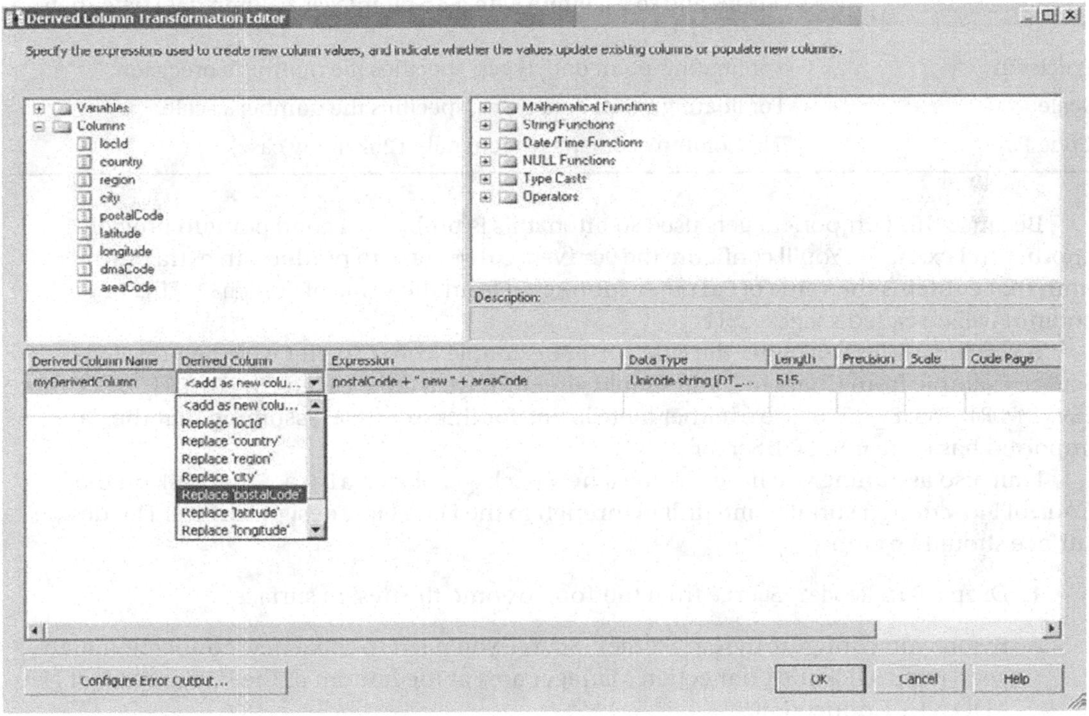

Figure 9-17. *Creating a derived column*

Expressions are again used in this task, the results of which form the values that find their way into the output stream. Each derived column is defined using the series of properties defined and described in Table 9-6.

Table 9-6. *Derived Column Properties*

Property	Description
Derived Column Name	The name to give the newly derived column in the output-columns collection.
Derived Column	States the requirement either to append a new column to the output-columns collection, or to replace the value of an existing column.
Expression	The valid expression used to create the derived value. The example in Figure 9-17 simply concatenates two existing input columns.
Data Type	The column's data type, usually computed automatically via background evaluation of the entered expression.
Length	The column's length, usually computed automatically via background evaluation of the entered expression. For example, a 32-bit integer is 4 bytes and so a column with a 32-bit integer-column data type shows a length of 4.
Precision	For floating-point data types, specifies the number's precision.
Scale	For floating-point data types, specifies the number's scale.
Code Page	The column's code page (generally 1252 in my case).

Because this component gets used so often, this is probably a good point to provide another full example. You'll configure the `Derived Column` task to produce an extra output column that contains the value of `Column 1` subtracted from the value of `Column 2`. This new column will be called `rangeResult`.

If you have followed either the `Bulk Insert` example from Chapter 6 or the `Flat File Source` example from Chapter 7, you should already have a table called `CSV_IMPORT_TABLE_1` or `CSV_IMPORT_TABLE_2`. The use of either table is fine for this example, assuming that the data imported has gone into SQL Server.

I am also assuming you have created a new package, placed a `Data Flow Task` on the Control Flow design surface, and drilled through to the Data Flow design surface. The design surface should be empty.

1. Drop a `DataReader Source` from the Toolbox onto the design surface.

2. Before you configure the `DataReader Source` you need to add a new connection manager. Right-click the Connection Manager area at the bottom of the IDE and select New ADO.NET Connection....

3. Click New... and configure a new connection to your database (the one that holds the `CSV_IMPORT_TABLE_1` or `CSV_IMPORT_TABLE_2` table) that uses the `SqlClient Data Provider`. My connection manager is called `LOKI.ApressBook` but obviously yours will be different.

4. Double-click the `DataReader Source` component or right-click it and select Edit....

5. On the configuration screen that appears, you first need to tell the component to use the connection manager you created in Step 3. Figure 9-18 shows this screen, where I have updated the connection-manager value. As you can see, the value to be updated is in the Connection Manager column of the configuration grid. Mine now reads `LOKI.ApressBook`.

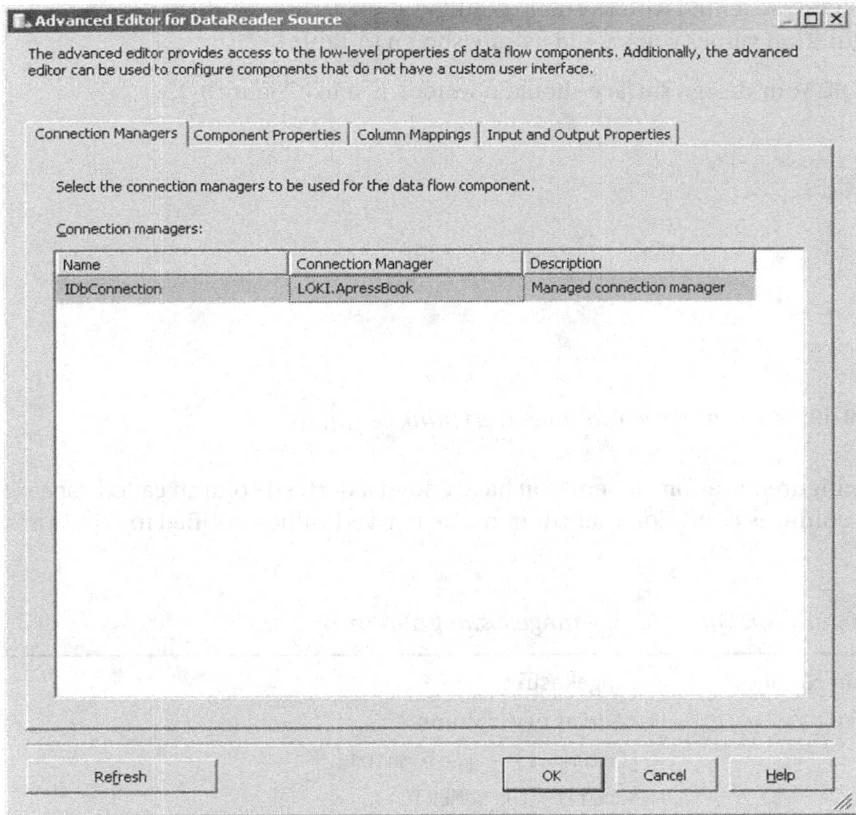

Figure 9-18. *Specifying the newly created connection manager*

6. Select the Component Properties tab. Update the SQL Command property to read `SELECT * FROM CSV_IMPORT_TABLE_1` (or `CSV_IMPORT_TABLE_2`, depending on which table you have available). Select the Column Mappings tab just to make sure everything is as expected.

7. Select OK at the bottom of the configuration screen. You should see your correctly configured `DataReader Source` sitting happily on the design surface.

8. Drop a `Derived Column` component from the Toolbox onto the design surface, somewhere below the `DataReader Source`.

9. Connect the output arrow from the bottom of the `DataReader Source` to the `Derived Column` component.

10. Double-click the `Derived Column` component or right-click it and select Edit....

11. You will be presented with the main configuration screen, similar to Figure 9-17. The configuration values you should use are shown in Table 9-7.

12. Click OK. Your design surface should now look just like Figure 9-19.

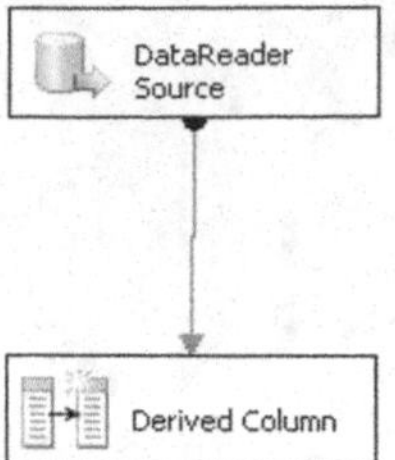

Figure 9-19. *The completed example, everything configured*

You've configured the component! You have added a derived column called `rangeResult` to the output-columns collection that contains the derived value specified in the expression in Table 9-7.

Table 9-7. *Configuration Values for the rangeResult Column*

Derived Column Name	`rangeResult`
Derived Column	<Add as new column>
Expression	`[Column 1] - [Column 0]`
Data Type	`Numeric (DT_NUMERIC)`
Length	`18`
Precision	`0`
Scale	
Code Page	

Export Column

1 input, 1 output, 1 error output

The purpose of the `Export Column` transformation task will come as no great surprise. It is used to extract data from within the input stream and write it to a file. There's one caveat: the data type of the column or columns for export must be `DT_TEXT`, `DT_NTEXT`, or `DT_IMAGE`. Figure 9-20 shows the main configuration screen.

This process is performed by the configuration of a few simple properties. The structure of the properties allows a separate file to be specified for each exported column via the File Path Column property. The properties for each export column are shown in Table 9-9.

Table 9-8. *Properties for Each Export Column*

Property	Description
Extract Column	The column in the input-columns collection to export to a file.
File Path Column	The valid file path and name to which the export should be directed.
Allow Append	Identifies whether a file, if it exists, should be appended to with the contents of the exported column.
Force Truncate	Identifies whether the file destination for the exported column should be overwritten if it exists.
Write Byte-Order Mark	The byte-order mark is only written when the column's data type is `DT_NTEXT` and when the export file is truncated (should it exist).

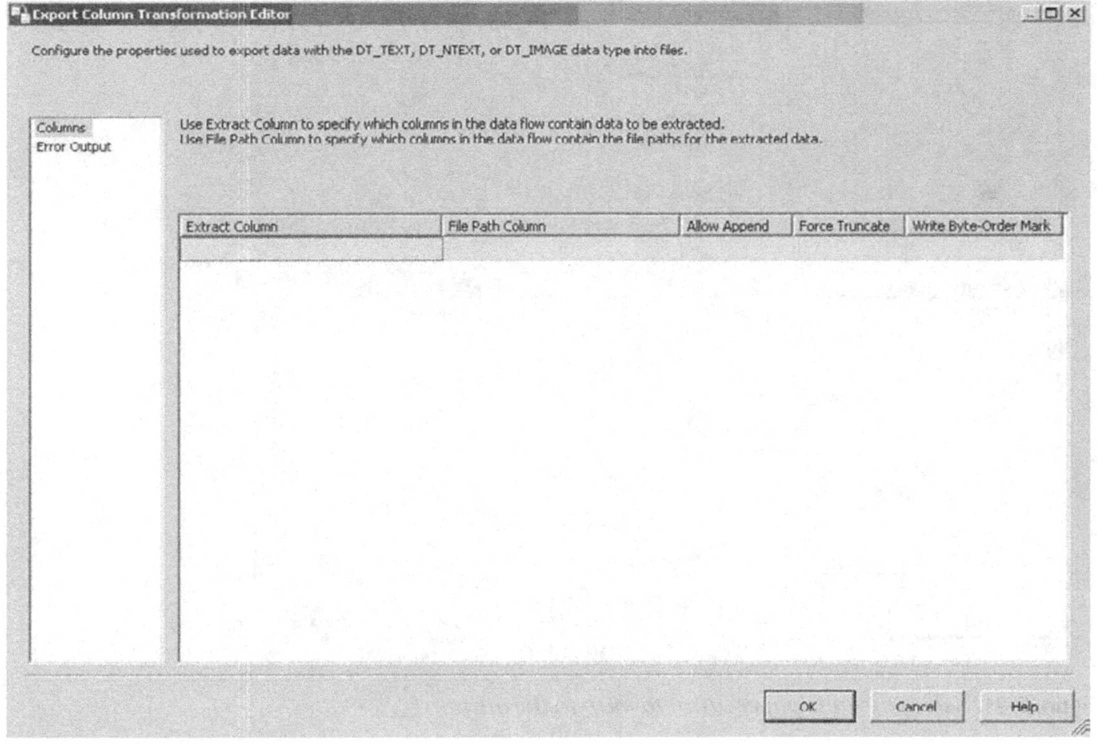

Figure 9-20. *The Export Column editor*

Import Column

1 input, 1 output, 1 error output

The `Import Column` task is the sister transformation of the `Export Column` task, though this time it's about getting data into the Data Flow from external files. Surprisingly, however, the editor for the task is less straightforward, clear, and complete than for the `Export Column` task.

Figure 9-21 shows the configuration screen's Input Columns tab, where most of configuration for the task takes place.

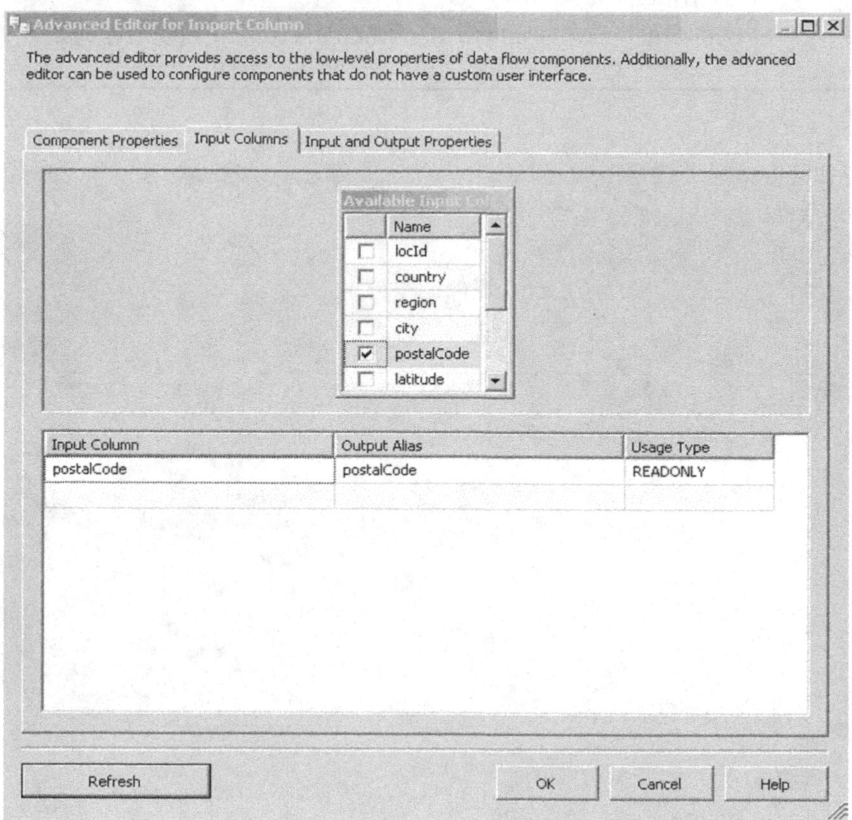

Figure 9-21. *Selecting an input column to map to the output*

The only other configuration is performed through the Input and Output Properties tab. Again, this is unlike the `Export Task` editor, which allows for more-visible property manipulation.

Using the Input and Output Properties tab, as shown in Figure 9-22, you can set the property for whether a byte-order mark (BOM) is expected for the imported data. Output and error-output properties can also be directly manipulated from this screen.

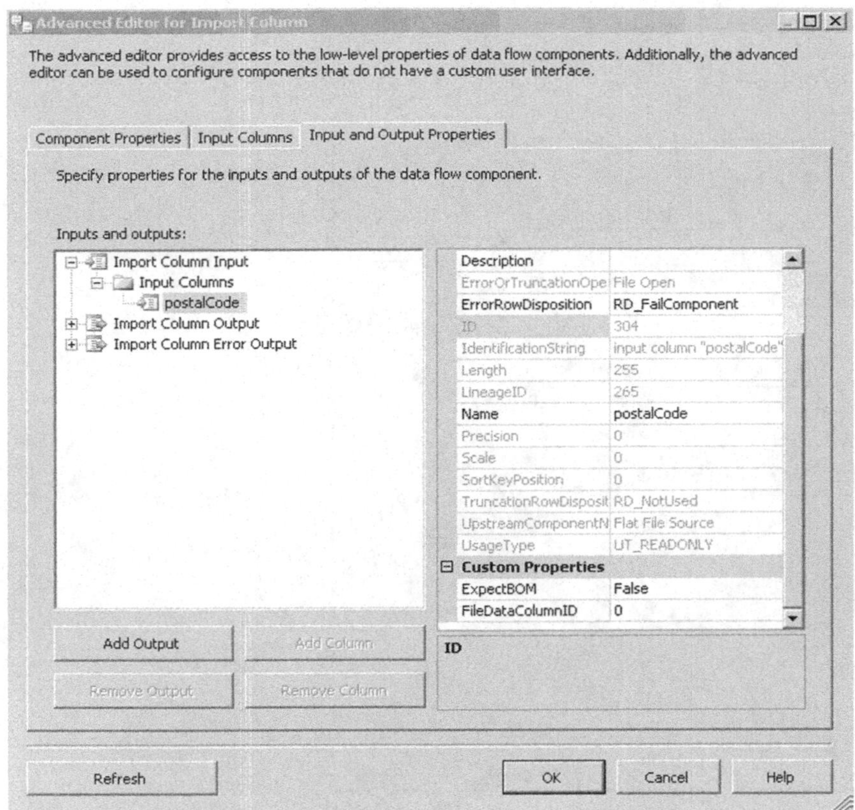

Figure 9-22. *A few good properties*

Lookup

1 input, 1 output, 1 error output

Like the `Fuzzy Lookup` (described in detail in Chapter 10), the `Lookup` task leverages reference data and joins between input columns and columns in the reference data to provide a row-by-row lookup of source values. This reference data can be a table, view, or dataset (generated by a SQL statement).

As always, it is important to specify the basic settings before getting into the more-complex ones. Figure 9-23 is the first screen presented when you edit the component, and on the first tab you can set the reference table's source.

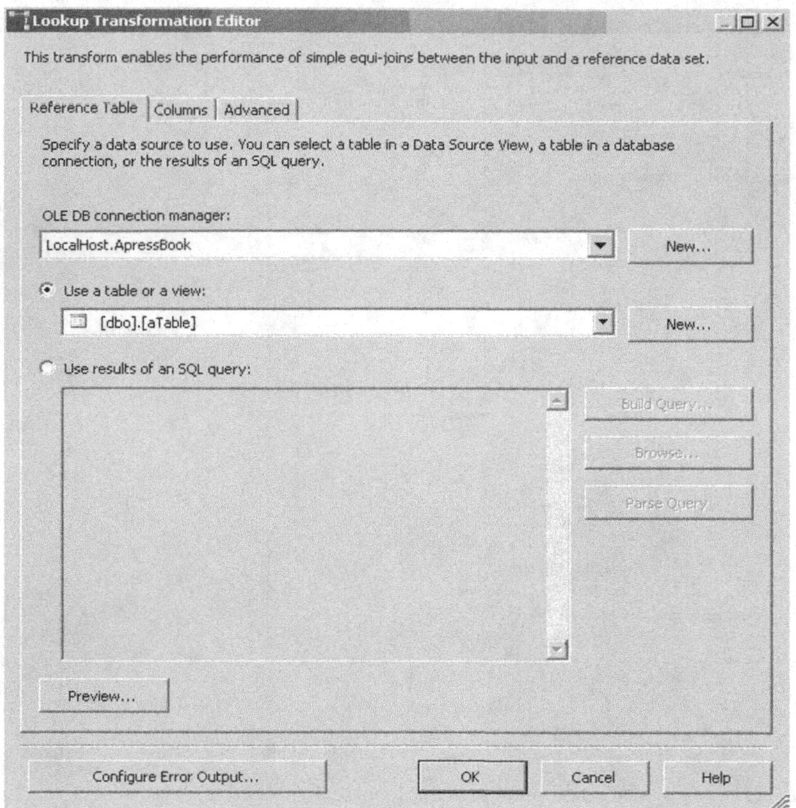

Figure 9-23. *Set the reference-table source first.*

When you use a SQL query as the source, you can configure an additional property (exposed on the Advanced tab) that contains the SQL generated by the component for caching purposes. This query is not optimized, but for optimum performance you can edit it manually via the Advanced tab configuration value.

Things start to get more interesting with Column tab, where you set the mapping for the join desired and specify what to do with the desired reference-table column as it relates to the output.

Figure 9-24 shows how I have joined the `locId` column from Available Input Columns to the `locId` column in the Available Lookup Columns. By checking the `startIpNum` column in the reference table on the right I have added it to the output Data Flow. Note, however, that columns of type `DT_TEXT`, `DT_NTEXT`, or `DT_IMAGE` cannot form the join.

Selecting a name from the Available Lookup Column list adds it to the grid in the bottom half of the window. The type of lookup operation—see Table 9-9—and the output alias can be set here.

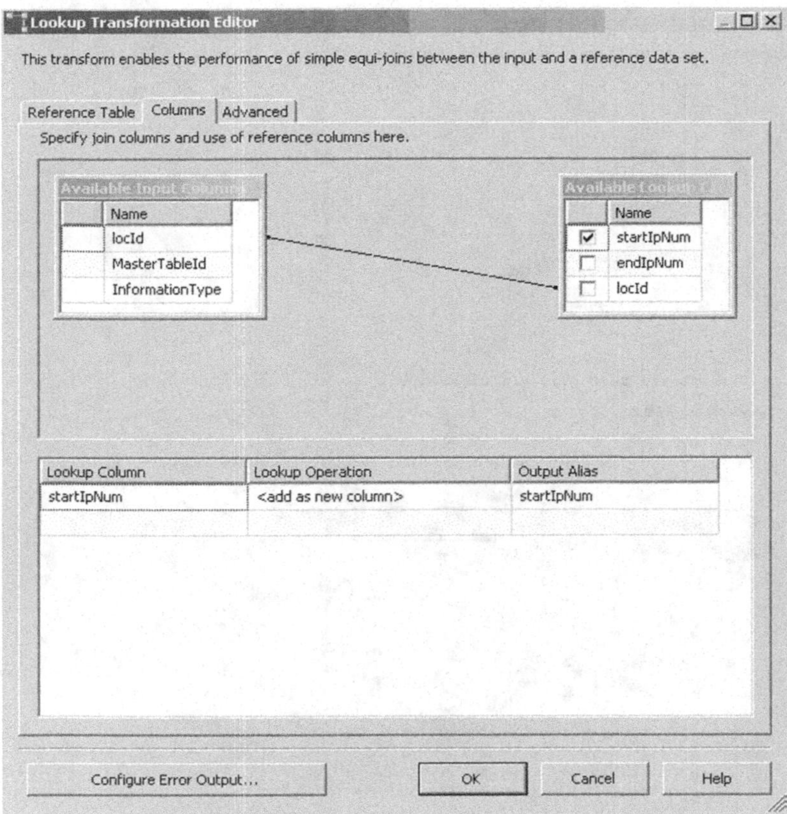

Figure 9-24. *Using locId as the join and replacing output values*

Table 9-9. *Lookup Operation Property Values*

Possible Value	Description
<add as new column>	The value of the column in the reference table is appended to the output as a new column.
<replace [Column Name]> (multiple)	Where [Column Name] is a list of source columns with data types compatible with the reference column, specifies that the value found in the selected reference-table column should replace the value held in [Column Name] in the Data Flow.

The Advanced configuration tab, shown in Figure 9-25, lets you perform optimizations and tweak settings. Depending on memory-usage requirements, a number of additional properties are on this tab. By default the `Lookup` task reads the reference table into memory and performs lookup operations from there. This is good for performance, but obviously, depending upon the size of the reference table, an amount of memory is allocated for task use.

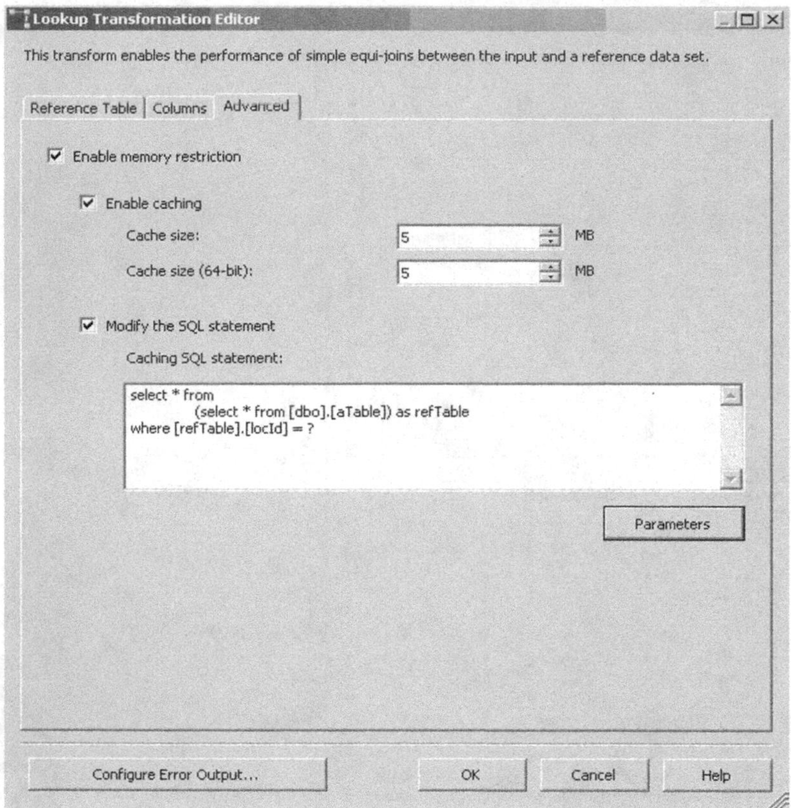

Figure 9-25. *Tweak, tweak*

It is possible to tweak the cache settings (or turn off the caching completely) by using the CacheType property, which is exposed via the task properties pane. Table 9-10 shows possible CacheType values.

Table 9-10. *CacheType Property Values*

Possible Value	Description
None	Caching of the reference table is disabled. As a consequence, the task will fail if it matches columns that contain NULL.
Partial	Caching is configurable via the additional properties explained in Table 9-11. As a consequence, the task will fail if it matches columns that contain NULL.
Full	The reference table is copied into memory in its entirety.

Table 9-11 shows additional properties that can be configured if the CacheType property is set to Partial.

Table 9-11. *Additional Properties Available When CacheType Is Partial*

Property	Description
`MaxMemoryUsage`	A measurement in megabytes of the maximum memory the task should use in a 32-bit environment. Limited to 3,072 MB.
`MaxMemoryUsage64`	A measurement in megabytes of the maximum memory the task should use in a 64-bit environment. Unlimited in value.

Merge

2 inputs, 1 output

The `Merge` task combines two separate sorted datasets into a single dataset that is expressed as a single output—a simple concept but a useful one!

Note that this task is a *combination* of data, not a *union* of data. The combination is based on keys in the data and as such is more complex than a union select. Requirements sometimes dictate the use of a union rather than a `Merge`. In those cases, the `Union All` task should be used instead. In addition, the `Merge` task is limited to two inputs; the `Union All` task accepts any number of inputs.

I'm sure it doesn't need saying but I'll say it anyway: merging columns of different fundamental types can't be done directly. If this is a requirement, a `Data Conversion` transform should be used upstream. However, it's acceptable to merge *similar* types—strings, for example—but truncation cannot occur, so the target column must be at least as large as the source.

Figure 9-26 shows the configuration screen for this task.

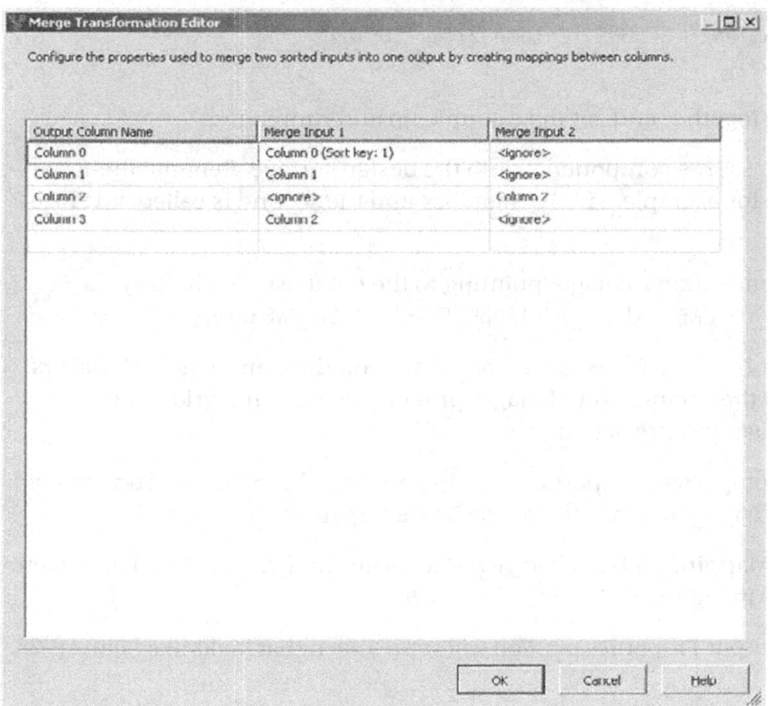

Figure 9-26. *Configuring the Merge Transform. Rather sparse!*

Both inputs connected to the Merge need to be sorted before the Merge transform will accept them for use. You can do this either with a Sort transform upstream, or by specifying within the previous upstream component that the output is sorted, using the component's Input and Output Properties tab.

A merge could be required upstream of a number of different tasks, so I'll present an example using the Merge task that specifies that the data is sorted without using an additional Sort transform.

Assuming you have followed at least one of the previous examples in this book, you know the drill for these examples by now: just create a new package, drop a Data Flow task on the Control Flow surface, and drill through to the Data Flow design surface.

This example uses the two tables created in the Conditional Split transform example, but to illustrate better how columns are marked as sorted (and how the Merge transform works), I'm renaming the columns in the two tables. You can run the following script to do this—assuming you already have these tables in your database, of course:

```
sp_rename 'CSV_SINGLE_INSTANCE_OF_ONE.[Column 0]', 'ipStart1'
GO
sp_rename 'CSV_SINGLE_INSTANCE_OF_ONE.[Column 1]', 'ipEnd1'
GO
sp_rename 'CSV_SINGLE_INSTANCE_OF_ONE.[Column 2]', 'locId1'
GO
sp_rename 'CSV_MULTIPLE_INSTANCE_OF_ONE.[Column 0]', 'ipStart2'
GO
sp_rename 'CSV_MULTIPLE_INSTANCE_OF_ONE.[Column 1]', 'ipEnd2'
GO
sp_rename 'CSV_MULTIPLE_INSTANCE_OF_ONE.[Column 2]', 'locId2'
GO
```

Now let's put everything together and get the example up and running:

1. Drop two DataReader Source components onto the design surface. Rename them so the first one is called, for example, Single Instance and the second is called Multiple Instance.

2. Create a SqlClient connection manager pointing to the database that holds your CSV_SINGLE_INSTANCE_OF_ONE and CSV_MULTIPLE_INSTANCE_OF_ONE tables.

3. Configure the Single Instance DataReader Source and, on the Connection Managers configuration tab, set the Connection Manager property value in the grid to point to the connection manager you created in Step 2.

4. Click over onto the Component Properties tab. Update the SqlCommand property to read SELECT * FROM csv_single_instance_of_one ORDER BY ipStart1.

5. Click to the Column Mappings tab to check whether everything looks okay. The screen should look like mine in Figure 9-27.

6. Click the Input and Output Properties tab. You will see a screen that looks like Figure 9-28.

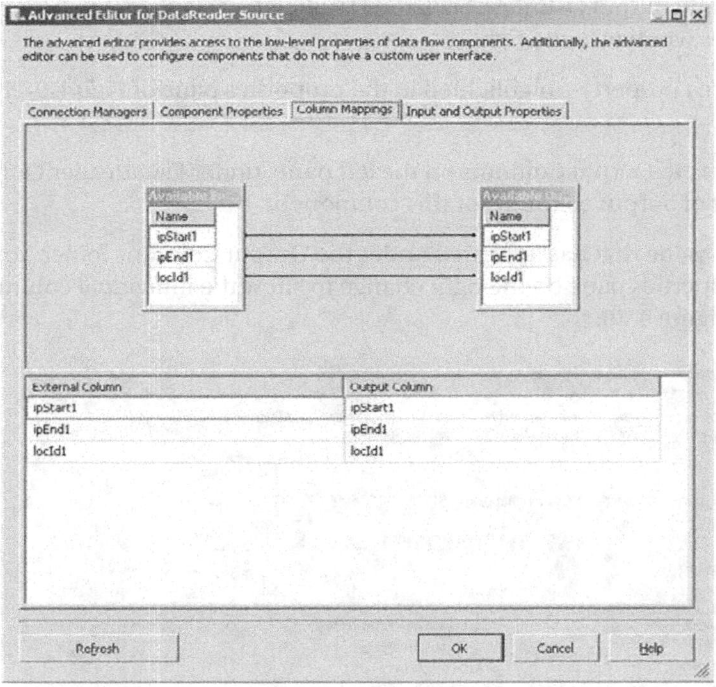

Figure 9-27. *Correct column mapping*

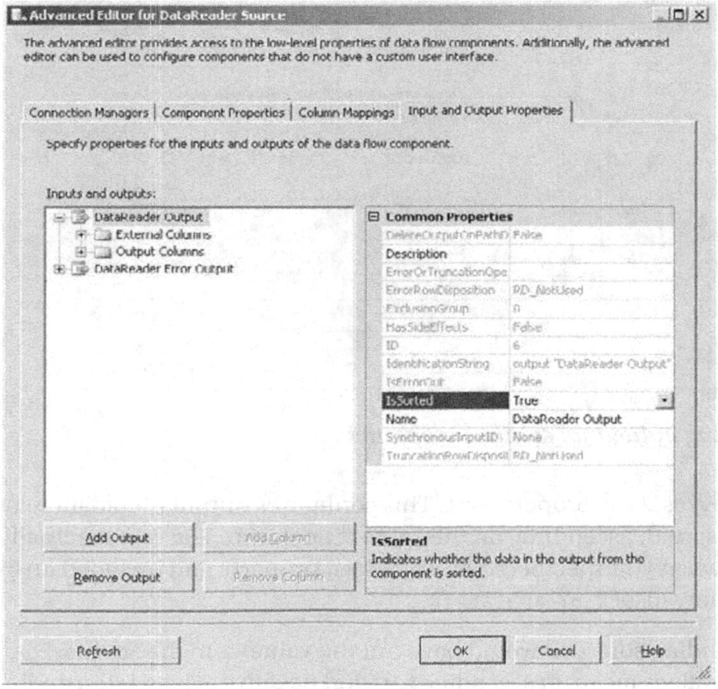

Figure 9-28. *Time to configure the output properties*

7. Under the Inputs and outputs window, click the DataReader Output value. This populates the properties window to the right.

8. Update the `IsSorted` property—highlighted in the properties pane of Figure 9-28—to read `True`.

9. Click the + icon next to Output Columns on the left pane, under DataReader Output. This shows the list of output columns for this component.

10. Click the `ipStart1` value that has appeared under the Output Columns folder. You should see the properties pane on the right change to show the individual column properties, as in Figure 9-29.

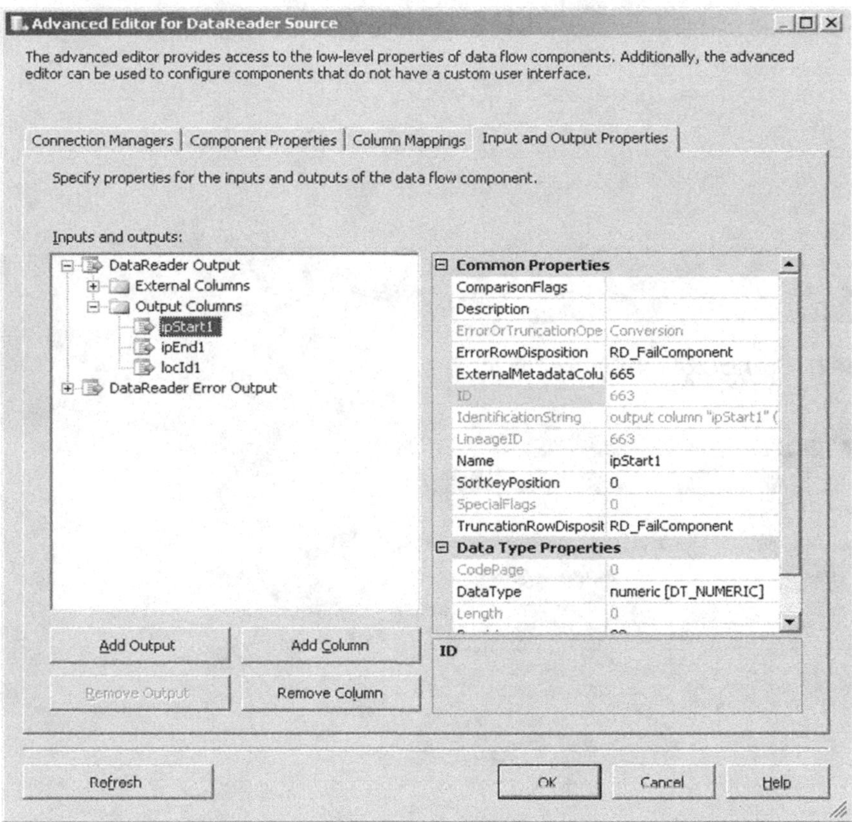

Figure 9-29. *Updating individual column properties*

11. Update the `SortKeyPosition` property to `1`. This configures output metadata to indicate that the output is sorted, ascending, on the `ipStart1` column. The sort is actually configured in Step 4, when you specified the `SqlCommand` property and included an `ORDER BY` clause in the query (`ORDER BY ipStart1`).

    To specify a descending sort, you would have put the value `-1` in the `SortKeyPosition` property. (Positive values mean an ascending sort and negative values a descending one.)

To include an `ORDER BY` that included more than one column, you would also have updated the `SortKeyPosition` property for each output column. For example, if you had used the query `SELECT * FROM csv_single_instance_of_one ORDER BY ipStart1, ipEnd1 DESC, locId1`, then you would had to have used the values in Table 9-12 instead.

Table 9-12. *Hypothetical SortKeyPosition Values*

Column Name	SortKeyPosition Value
ipStart1	1
ipEnd1	–2
locId1	3

12. Click OK to exit the configuration screen and save the values.
13. Configure the `Multiple Instance DataReader Source` and, on the Connection Managers tab, set the Connection Manager property value in the grid to point to the connection manager you created in Step 2.
14. Click over onto the Component Properties tab. Update the `SqlCommand` property to read `SELECT * FROM csv_multiple_instance_of_one ORDER BY ipStart2`.
15. Click the Column Mappings tab to check that everything looks okay.
16. Click the Input and Output Properties tab.
17. Under the Inputs and outputs window on this configuration screen, click the DataReader Output value. This populates the properties window to the right.
18. Update the `IsSorted` property—look at Figure 9-28 for a reminder—to read `True`.
19. Click the + icon next to Output Columns on the left pane, under DataReader Output. This shows the list of output columns for this component.
20. Click the `ipStart2` value that has appeared under the Output Columns folder. You should see the properties pane on the right change to show the individual column properties (just like earlier, in Figure 9-29).
21. Update the `SortKeyPosition` property to `1`. This configures output metadata to indicate that the output is sorted, ascending, on the `ipStart2` column. The sort is actually performed in Step 14, when you specified the `SqlCommand` property and included an `ORDER BY` clause in the query (`ORDER BY ipStart2`).
22. Click OK to save and exit the configuration screen. You now have two completely configured (but different) data sources for use with the `Merge` transform.
23. Drop a `Merge` component from the Toolbox onto the design surface, somewhere below the `DataReader` sources.

24. Connect the output arrow from the bottom of the `Single Instance` source to the `Merge` transform. You will be presented with a pop-up screen like Figure 9-30.

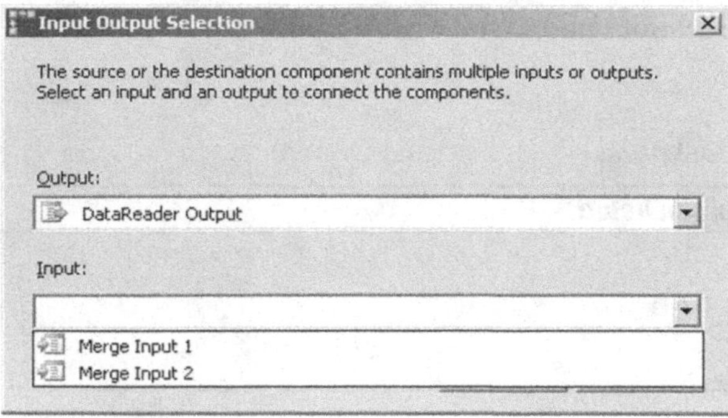

Figure 9-30. *Choosing which input to use*

25. Select Merge Input 1 from the Input drop-down list.

26. Connect the output arrow from the `Multiple Instance DataReader Source` to the `Merge` transform. You are not presented with a choice of inputs this time, because only one input remains for this transform type.

27. Double-click the `Merge` transform or right-click it and select Edit....

28. Configure the values contained in the grid based upon Table 9-13.

Table 9-13. *Merge Configuration Values*

Output Column Name	Merge Input 1	Merge Input 2
`mergedIpStart`	<ignore>	`ipStart2 (Sort key: 1)`
`mergedIpEnd`	`ipEnd1`	<ignore>
`mergedLocId`	`locId1`	<ignore>

Your configuration screen should look like mine, shown in Figure 9-31.

Configuring the Merge transform in this way gives three output columns—`mergedIpStart`, `mergedIpEnd`, and `mergedLocId`—which have been merged from two input datasets. The `ipStart2` column comes from the `Multiple Instance DataReader Source`, while the `ipStart1` and `locId` columns come from the `Single Instance` columns.

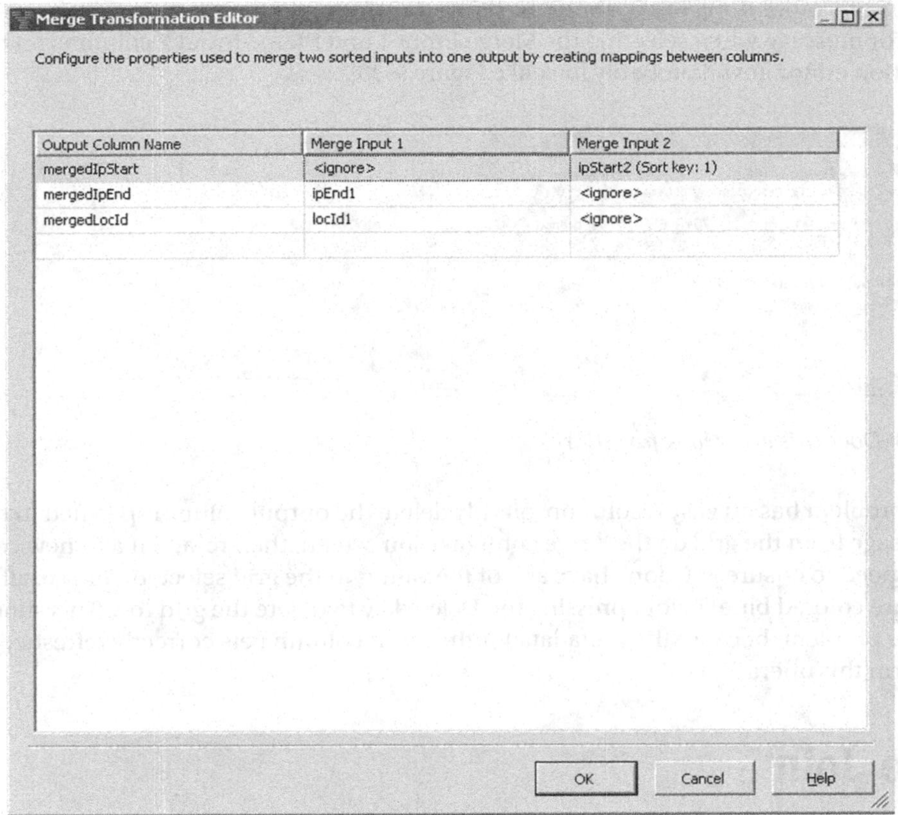

Figure 9-31. *The Merge transform configured for this example*

29. Click OK to be returned to the Data Flow design surface. Your Data Flow should now look like Figure 9-32.

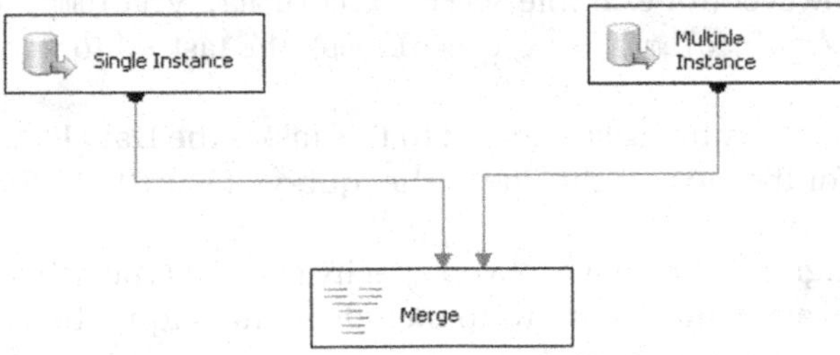

Figure 9-32. *The completed example*

There's one more thing to say about the `Merge` transform. Sometimes you will get an unexpected error message when selecting the Merge Input 1 and Merge Input 2 columns on the configuration editor. It will probably look like Figure 9-33.

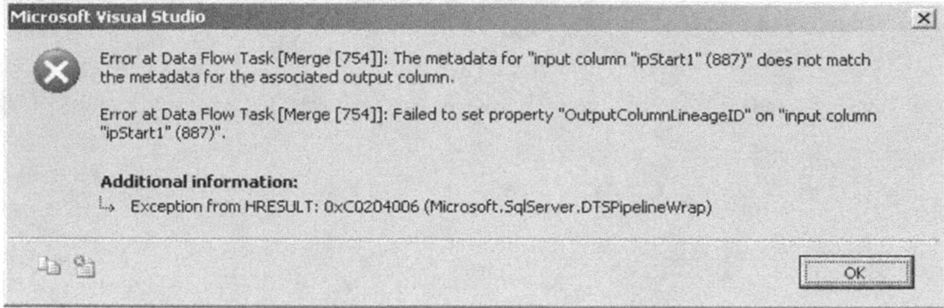

Figure 9-33. *Does this error look familiar?*

This problem has an easy resolution. Simply delete the output column specified in the error message from the grid on the `Merge` configuration screen, then re-add it as a new column. You need to ensure you don't have any of the values in the grid selected (and so, all columns are colored blue) before pressing the Delete key to delete the grid row. This should resolve the problem, because the metadata for the input column gets correctly refreshed when you perform this operation.

Merge Join

2 inputs, 1 output

Joins in SQL are great, aren't they? I've written more joins than I've had hot dinners. I've probably written a query *containing* more joins than I've had hot dinners. Let's face it, it's rare to write a query without a join of some kind in it. I'm going to assume, therefore, that anyone reading this book is entirely familiar and comfortable with the concepts involved.

The `Merge Join` transform uses joins to generate output. Rather than requiring you to enter a query containing the join, however (for example `SELECT x.columna, y.columnb FROM tablea x INNER JOIN tableb y ON x.joincolumna = y.joincolumnb`), the task editor lets you set it up graphically.

When the two inputs are specified—by being connected to this task—the Data Flow Designer asks whether the input is for the left or right side of the "query." Figure 9-34 shows how the choice is presented.

Figure 9-35 shows how the configuration options let you specify the join type, which columns in each input form the join, and which columns to include in the output. Both inputs need to be sorted before they will be accepted for use by the `Merge Join` transform.

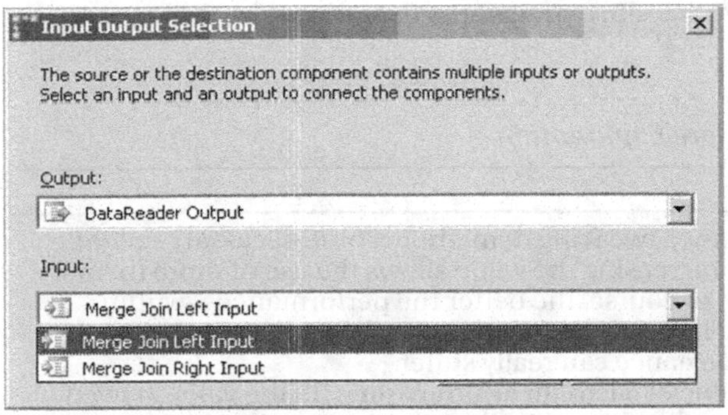

Input Output Selection

The source or the destination component contains multiple inputs or outputs. Select an input and an output to connect the components.

Output:
DataReader Output

Input:
Merge Join Left Input
Merge Join Left Input
Merge Join Right Input

Figure 9-34. *Which input would you like me to be today?*

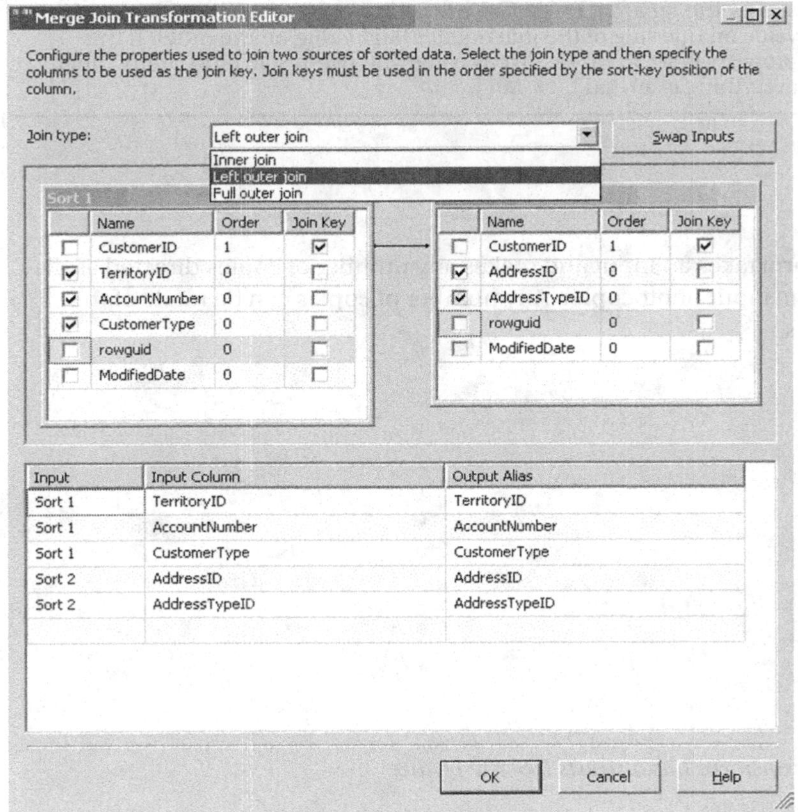

Figure 9-35. *Specifying the join*

In addition to the settings shown in Figure 9-35, extra properties, shown in Table 9-14, require some focus.

Table 9-14. *Merge Join Properties Requiring More Explanation*

Property	Description
`MaxBuffersPerInput`	As part of performance tweaking, it might become necessary to fiddle with this property. Increasing the value allows the use of more memory. The more memory, of course, the better the performance—within reason. Decreasing it means less memory is allowed per input, but as a consequence performance can really suffer. Also, the default value of 5 isn't an arbitrary one. It's the value arrived at by extensive testing and tweaking by Microsoft to give the best performance in the average scenario.
`TreatNullsAsEqual`	Does `Null == Null`? It might surprise you to learn that it doesn't! By setting the `TreatNullsAsEqual` property to `True`, you can make a `Null` value on one side of the join equal a `Null` value on the other. If this property is set to `False`, just as when you use T-SQL (and pretty much everything else), `Null != Null`.

Multicast

1 input, 1 or more outputs

The `Multicast` transform takes an input and makes any number of copies directed as distinct outputs. Consider it an input photocopier. Any number of copies can be made of the input, as Figure 9-36 shows.

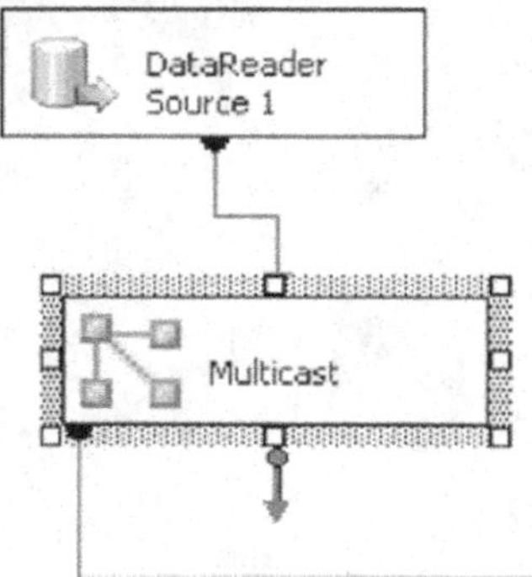

Figure 9-36. *The Multicast transform has outputs like the Hydra.*

The number of outputs that the `Multicast` transform generates is set entirely by the user. Like the mythical Hydra, for each output that gets assigned, another green arrow appears to make another output available. (I guess it's not quite like the Hydra then.)

OLE DB Command

1 input, 1 output, 1 error output

The OLE DB Command transform executes a SQL statement for each row in the input stream. It's kind of like a high-performance cursor in many ways. A familiar syntax for specifying parameters lets you use values from columns within the input stream as part of the SQL statement. Figure 9-37 shows the configuration screen for this task.

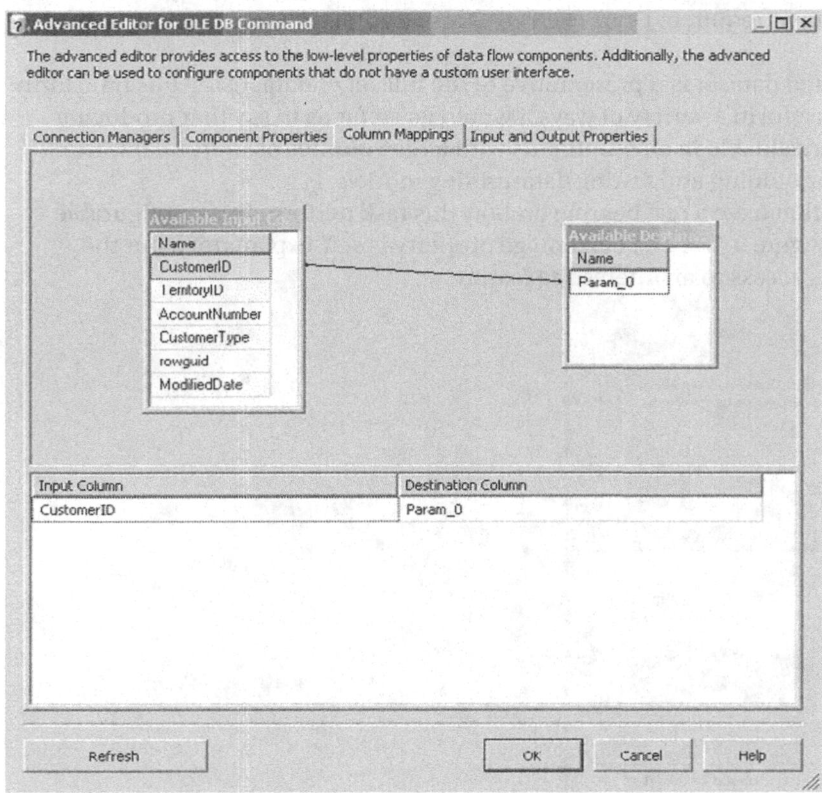

Figure 9-37. *Specifying the column value that populates the parameter*

To illustrate how this transform works, I've set the SQLCommand property to `SELECT * FROM Sales.Customer WHERE CustomerID = ?`.

In this case I have used the AdventureWorks sample database and a simple query with only one parameter. Obviously, the parameter value here is specified using the ? character. I could have included as many parameters as I wanted by just including them as part of the WHERE clause.

In the Columns Mapping tab on the editor screen in Figure 9-37, I'm presented with the input columns from the Data Flow. On the right of the tab, however, is a list of the parameters that need to be mapped from the input to populate the parameter values. Depending on conditions and matching types, the editor attempts to perform the mapping automatically. In cases where this does not happen, simply dragging the Available Input Column name onto the parameter name does the job.

Percentage Sampling

1 input, 2 outputs

The `Percentage Sampling` transform generates and outputs a dataset into the Data Flow based on a sample of data. The sample is entirely random to represent a valid cross-section of available data. As the task name suggests, the number of rows in the generated dataset is a set percentage of the source-input rows.

It's worth noting that the number of rows returned will rarely be precisely equal to the specified percentage of rows required. Don't even give this another moment of thought. It is unimportant.

Because the generated dataset is representative of the full set of data, using this transform to produce a sample is useful in a variety of ways. I would go so far as to say that producing these subsets of data is invaluable in environments with large volumes of source data. The task is also often used for training and testing data-mining models.

The two properties that have a real bearing on how this task performs are configurable from the editor screen (Figure 9-38). The Percentage property is self-explanatory, but the random-seed value gives access to an interesting feature.

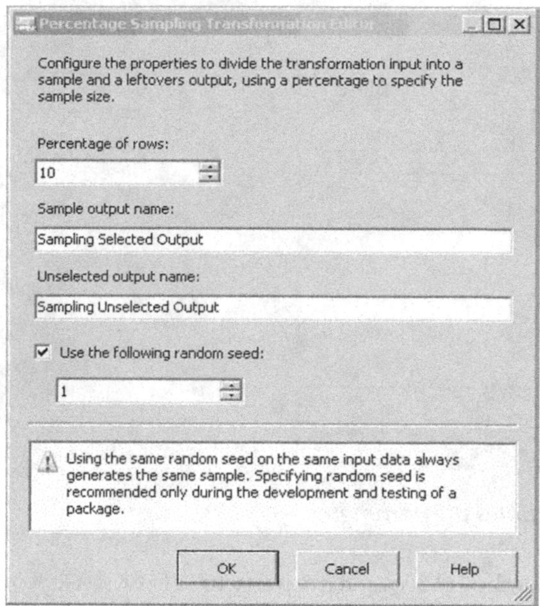

Figure 9-38. *Few properties, but they're perfectly formed*

The method by which random rows are selected for the data sample is based on a seed value—and is therefore only pseudorandom. The seed value in general task operations is gathered from the operating system, in this case uptime expressed as a number of ticks. This generates a pseudorandom number instead of a truly random one because using the same value as the seed gives the same set of random numbers. This method of creating pseudorandom numbers has gone unchanged since the early days of computing.

This transform exposes a property for the seed value for purposes of generating the same "random" set of rows each time. This can be very useful when testing, among other things. It is, naturally, a good idea to unset this property by unticking it when moving to a production environment to reinstate a more "random" level of randomness.

Row Count

1 input, 1 output

The `Row Count` task counts the number of rows as they flow through the component. It uses a specified variable to store the final count. It is a very lightweight component in that no processing is involved, because the count is just a property of the input-rows collection.

Because of the almost-transparent nature of the component, it is very useful in applications such as performing package optimizations. More information on optimization can be found in Chapter 12.

Figure 9-39 shows the configuration screen for the component. The one configurable custom property, as Figure 9-22 illustrates, is the `VariableName` property. It holds the name of the variable in which the calculated row count should be held.

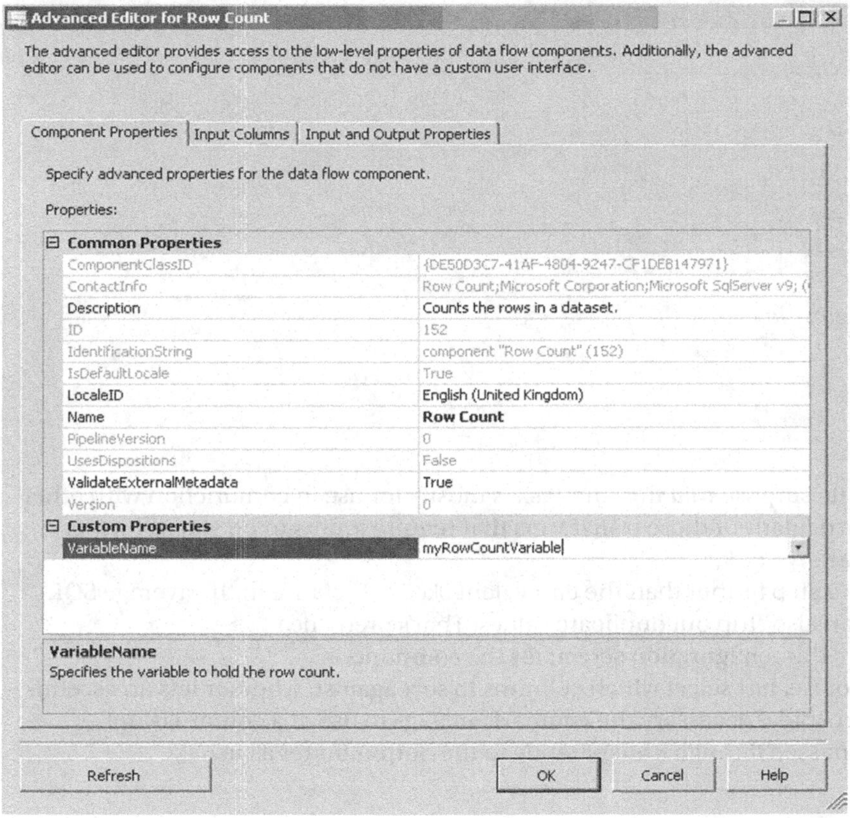

Advanced Editor for Row Count

The advanced editor provides access to the low-level properties of data flow components. Additionally, the advanced editor can be used to configure components that do not have a custom user interface.

Component Properties | Input Columns | Input and Output Properties

Specify advanced properties for the data flow component.

Properties:

Property	Value
Common Properties	
ComponentClassID	{DE50D3C7-41AF-4804-9247-CF1DE8147971}
ContactInfo	Row Count;Microsoft Corporation;Microsoft SqlServer v9; (
Description	Counts the rows in a dataset.
ID	152
IdentificationString	component "Row Count" (152)
IsDefaultLocale	True
LocaleID	English (United Kingdom)
Name	**Row Count**
PipelineVersion	0
UsesDispositions	False
ValidateExternalMetadata	True
Version	0
Custom Properties	
VariableName	myRowCountVariable

VariableName
Specifies the variable to hold the row count.

Refresh | OK | Cancel | Help

Figure 9-39. *The only custom Row Count property is the variable to hold the row count.*

Row Sampling

1 input, 2 outputs

The `Row Sampling` task, in a similar manner to the `Percentage Sampling` transform I discussed earlier, is used to create a (pseudo) random selection of data from the Data Flow.

This transform is very useful for performing operations that would normally be executed against a full set of data held in a table. In very high-volume OLTP databases, however, this just isn't possible at times. The ability to execute tasks against a representative subset of the data is a suitable and valuable alternative.

Figure 9-40 shows the component's configuration screen. Just as with the `Percentage Sampling` task, a random seed is used to create a subset of data to use as the output.

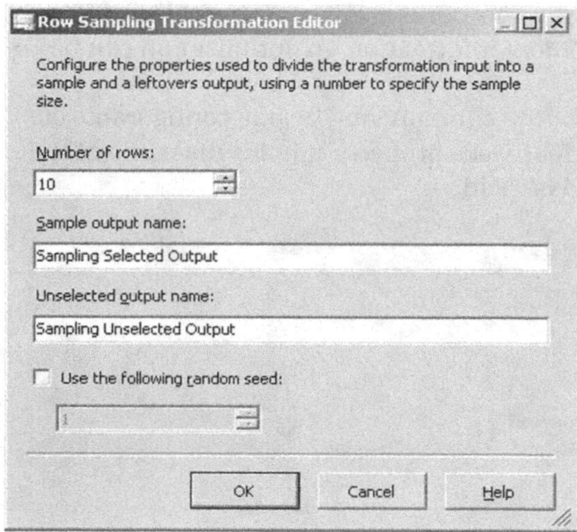

Figure 9-40. *Easy configuration*

Sort

1 input, 1 output

It will come as little surprise that the `Sort` task is mostly for use in conjunction with other tasks. I'm thinking particularly of those transforms that require inputs to be sorted further upstream, such as the `Merge` task.

This transform is a step further than the equivalent `ORDER BY` clause in the average SQL statement in that it can also strip out duplicate values. That's pretty neat.

Figure 9-41 shows the configuration screen for the component.

It's an easy task to use. Just select which columns to sort against, whether it is an ascending or descending sort, and if necessary the comparison flags to use. If a column is not selected for sort, it is passed through transparently to the output buffer as usual.

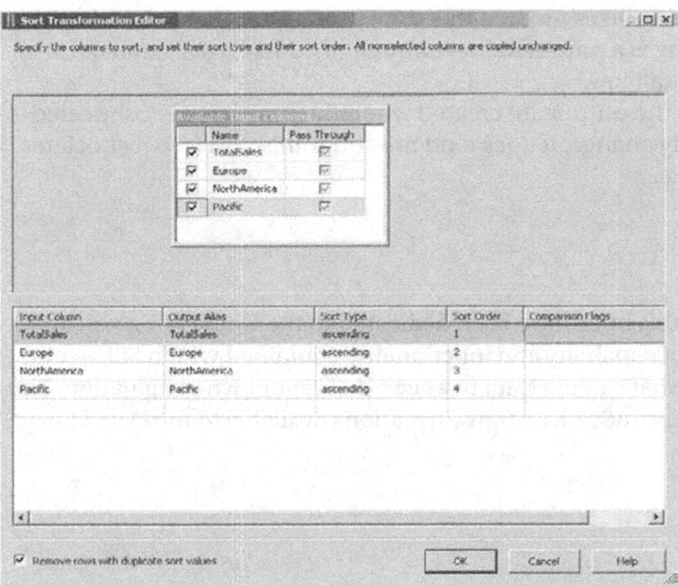

Figure 9-41. *Notice the Sort Order value in this multiple-column sort.*

Union All

2 or more inputs, 1 output

Just like a `Union All` statement in SQL, the `Union All` task combines any number of inputs into one output. Figure 9-42 shows this component's editor screen.

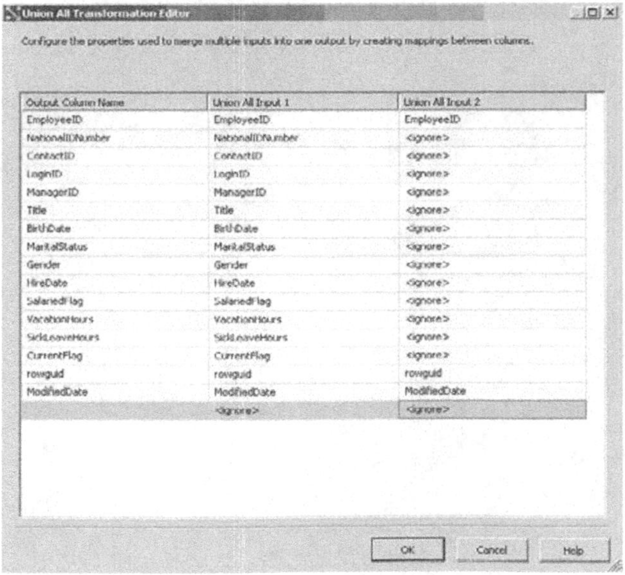

Union All Transformation Editor

Configure the properties used to merge multiple inputs into one output by creating mappings between columns.

Output Column Name	Union All Input 1	Union All Input 2
EmployeeID	EmployeeID	EmployeeID
NationalIDNumber	NationalIDNumber	<ignore>
ContactID	ContactID	<ignore>
LoginID	LoginID	<ignore>
ManagerID	ManagerID	<ignore>
Title	Title	<ignore>
BirthDate	BirthDate	<ignore>
MaritalStatus	MaritalStatus	<ignore>
Gender	Gender	<ignore>
HireDate	HireDate	<ignore>
SalariedFlag	SalariedFlag	<ignore>
VacationHours	VacationHours	<ignore>
SickLeaveHours	SickLeaveHours	<ignore>
CurrentFlag	CurrentFlag	<ignore>
rowguid	rowguid	rowguid
ModifiedDate	ModifiedDate	ModifiedDate
	<ignore>	<ignore>

OK Cancel Help

Figure 9-42. *Configuring Union All mappings*

Unlike in the `Merge` task, no sorting takes place in this transformation. Go back and read the section on the `Merge` task if sorting is a requirement—though of course a `Sort` transform *could* be used downstream in the Data Flow.

The columns and data types for the output are created when the first input is connected to the task. If the inputs subsequently change, it does tend to send things awry, so just delete the `Union All` task and add a new one.

Summary

That two lengthy chapters (so far) in this book have been dedicated to the Data Flow gives an indication of the depth and breadth of capability and functionality contained within SSIS—but that's not all. The only limitation on what can the Data Flow can do is your own imagination. The next chapter describes some of the more advanced transformations available to the Data Flow.

CHAPTER 10

Advanced Data Flow Transformations

In this second part of the discussion of Data Flow transformations, I'll continue to make deep inroads into each component. This chapter covers the following advanced Data Flow transformations:

- Aggregate
- Data Mining Query
- Fuzzy Grouping
- Fuzzy Lookup
- Pivot
- Script Component
- Slowly Changing Dimension
- Term Extraction
- Term Lookup
- Unpivot

It has been a relatively easy ride so far, but these components get much more complex quickly, especially when it comes to handling unstructured text. Some of the concepts in this chapter won't make sense until you gain practical, hands-on experience. Some of the transforms, by their very nature, won't produce the expected output the first time. It'll take some tweaking and repeated testing and configuration to get them right.

I'll spend much less time in this chapter discussing the Connection Manager tab and other more basic topics that I've already covered in other chapters. You can refer to previous chapters (Chapter 9 in particular) if you're unsure of any of the more basic material.

The data types used in SSIS and how they relate to native SQL Server data types are discussed in depth at the start of Chapter 9.

Aggregate

1 input, 1 or more outputs

SQL offers a number of aggregate functions that can be performed against data as part of a query statement. The `Aggregate` transformation component essentially encapsulates this functionality as part of the Data Flow. It's a relatively simple transformation component, although it does have a few welcome performance-related surprises. The aggregation can take place at transform level or at output level, depending on requirements.

This component is asynchronous, which, as you'll remember from Chapter 2, means that the data is not processed in a row-by-row fashion, and new buffers are not created during use.

You can define any number of output collections in the upper part of the configuration window, as shown in Figure 10-1. The transform can produce any number of different outputs, each with its own self-contained aggregation operation. You can see these by clicking the Advanced tab.

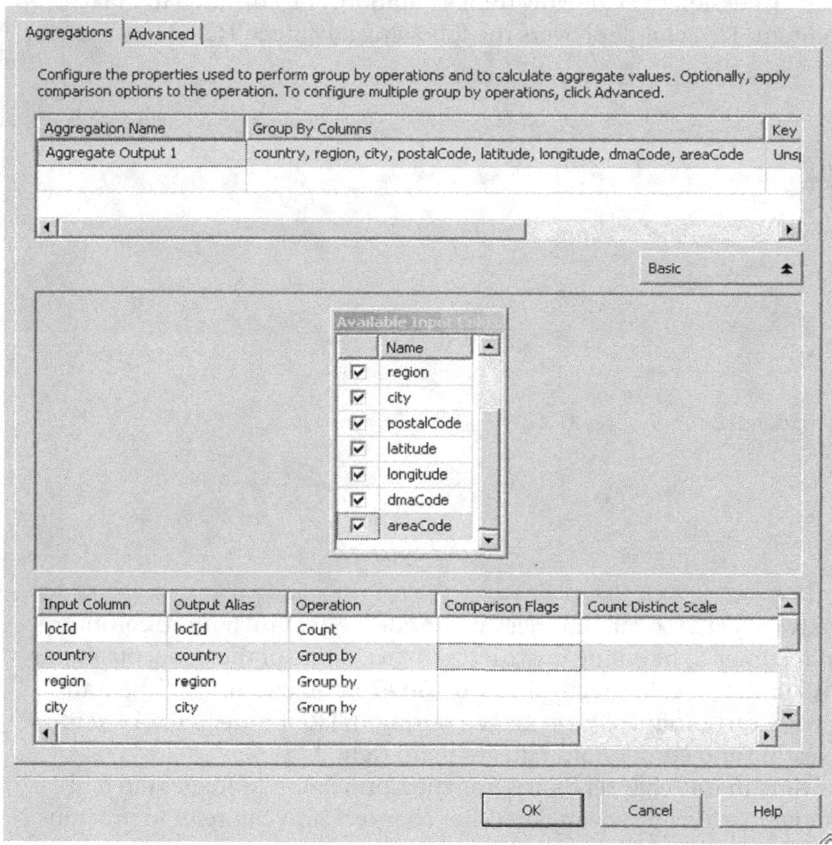

Figure 10-1. *Configuring the aggregation by operation type*

Each output has properties for key scale and number of keys, which are user-entered estimates that allow the task to optimize itself for expected data volumes. Table 10-1 shows these properties and their potential values.

Table 10-1. *Configuration for Each Aggregation Output*

Property	Possible Values	Description
Key scale		Advises the task to expect an approximate number of keys.
	Unspecified	Unused
	Low	The task can write about 500,000 keys.
	Medium	The task can write about 5,000,000 keys.
	High	The task can write more than 25,000,000 keys.
Number of keys		Specifies the exact number of keys to expect. If populated, its value takes precedence over key-scale value.

Once this task has a connected data source—and therefore a collection of columns to work against—it's easy to choose the required columns from the list of available ones. As Figure 10-1 illustrates, each input column has a number of configurable properties. This means that these configuration options are set at column level, entirely separate from output or task-level settings. Table 10-2 shows these column properties.

Table 10-2. *Aggregation Properties per Column*

Property	Possible Values	Description
Input column	Any of the input columns	Name of the input column selected for use
Output alias		An alias for the transformed column
Operation		Aggregation operation being performed
	Count	
	Count distinct	
	Sum	
	Average	
	Minimum	
	Maximum	
Comparison flags		Options that alter how two values are compared, such as whether to ignore casing.
	Ignore case	
	Ignore kana type	
	Ignore nonspacing characters	
	Ignore character width	
Count distinct scale		Optimizes the transformation by prespecifying the expected number of distinct values the task can write.
	Unspecified	Unused
	Low	The task can write about 500,000 keys.
	Medium	The task can write about 5,000,000 keys.
	High	The task can write more than 25,000,000 keys.
Count distinct keys		Specifies the exact number of values to expect. If populated, its value takes precedence over count distinct scale value.

Transformation component-level configuration is found on the editor screen's Advanced tab, as shown in Figure 10-2. Again, a number of properties are configurable from this point whose correct values aren't immediately obvious.

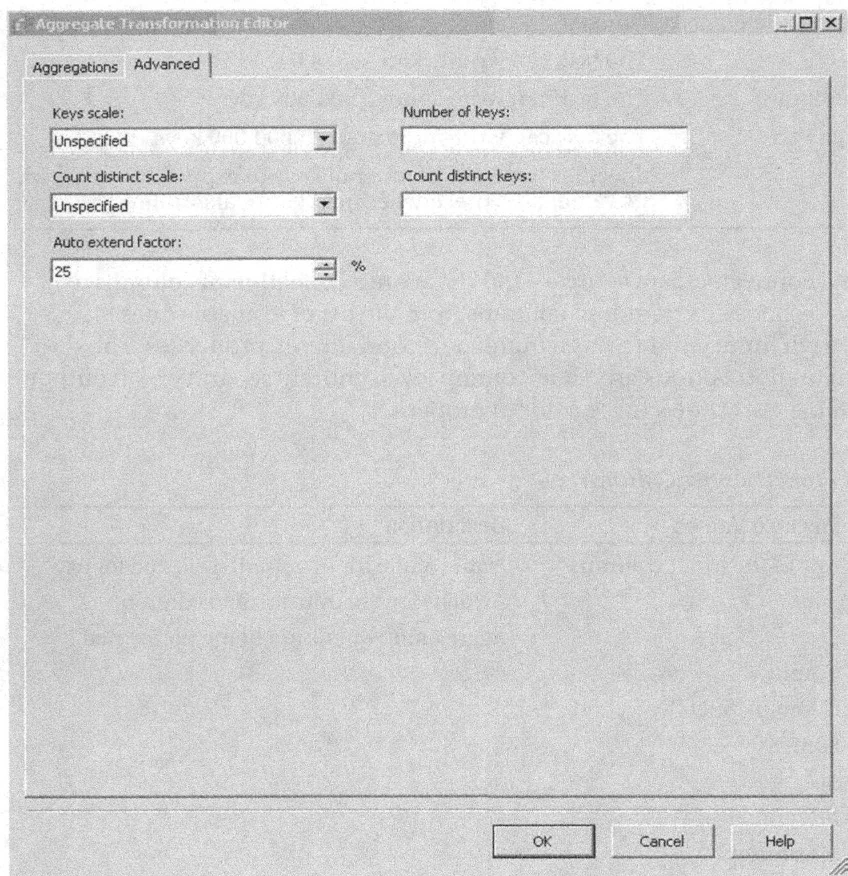

Figure 10-2. *Advanced properties—scary stuff!*

The properties and potential values for the Advanced tab are shown in Table 10-3. Remember that this configuration is for the transformation component as a whole, not for each defined operation or individual column.

Table 10-3. *Transformation-Level Configuration*

Property	Possible Values	Description
Key scale		Advises the task to expect an approximate number of keys.
	Unspecified	Unused
	Low	The task can write about 500,000 keys.
	Medium	The task can write about 5,000,000 keys.
	High	The task can write more than 25,000,000 keys.

Property	Possible Values	Description
Number of keys		Specifies the exact number of keys to expect. If populated, its value takes precedence over the key-scale value.
Auto extend factor	25% by default	Specifies the percentage by which memory can be extended to support the aggregation operation.
Count distinct scale		Optimizes the transformation by prespecifying the expected number of distinct values the task can write.
	Unspecified	Unused
	Low	The task can write about 500,000 keys.
	Medium	The task can write about 5,000,000 keys.
	High	The task can write more than 25,000,000 keys.
Count distinct keys		Specifies the exact number of values to expect. If populated, its value takes precedence over count distinct scale value.

Data Mining Query

1 input, 1 output

The first question to answer is: why is `Data Mining Query` part of Data Flow *and* the Control Flow? That's easy—it depends on what the specified Data Mining Extensions (DMX) query is for. For complete flexibility the task is included as both a Control Flow task and as a Data Flow transformation component.

In a nutshell, the data-mining implementation in SQL Server 2005 is all about the discovery of factually correct forecasted trends in data. This is configured within SSAS against one of the provided data-mining algorithms. The DMX query requests a predictive set of results from one or more such models built on the same mining structure. It can be a requirement to retrieve predictive information about the *same* data calculated using the different available algorithms.

For further information, see entry on the `Data Mining Query` task in Chapter 6.

Fuzzy Grouping

1 input, 1 output

The `Fuzzy Grouping` transformation is one of my personal favorites. Straight out of Microsoft Research Labs comes this crazy, intriguing, and initially unpredictable functionality . . . that gives me a headache when I think about how it must work—and the fact that it can be used as a transformation in an enterprise-level ETL tool!

In the broadest sense, `Fuzzy Grouping` is for use in cleansing data. By setting and tweaking task properties, you can achieve great results because the task interprets input data and makes "intelligent" decisions about its uniqueness. Upon finding a "group" of what it considers "identical" data, it selects a single canonical row to represent the group. These "unique" rows are routed out as task output. Figure 10-3 shows the configuration screen for this component.

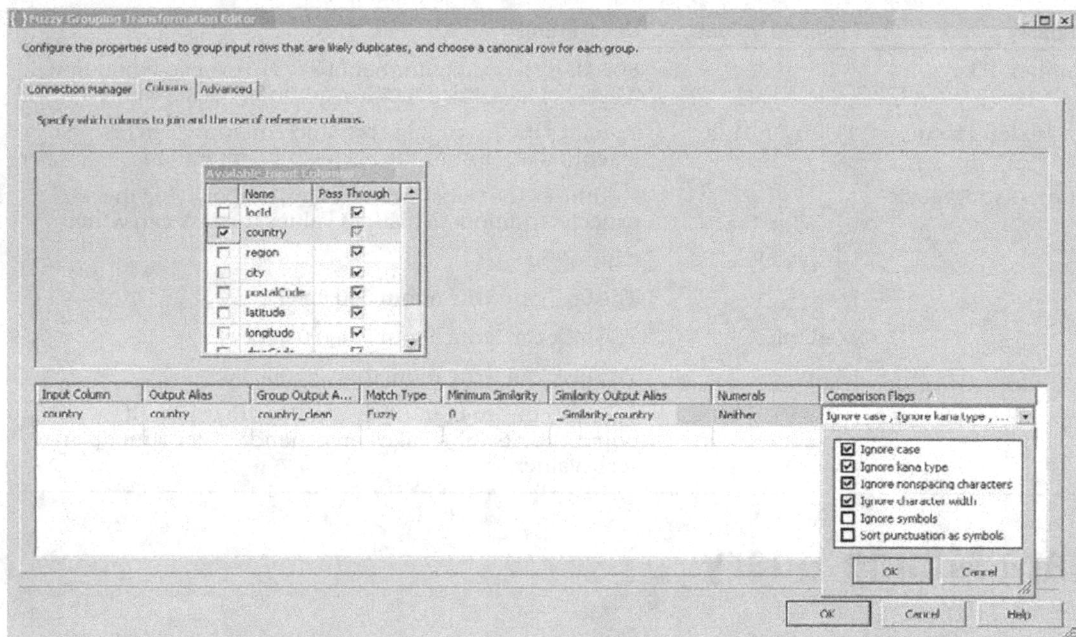

Figure 10-3. *A deceptively simple configuration screen for specifying columns*

Based upon a fuzzy-matching algorithm, all columns are processed and grouping is based on a given *similarity index*—a calculated value between 0 and 1. (You can think of it as a score.) A similarity index of 1 means values are identical.

When selecting columns to use from the Available Input Columns list, the Pass Through property indicates that the column should be copied into the output-columns collection directly and untouched. Table 10-4 shows the per-column properties available for configuration.

Table 10-4. *Fuzzy Match Operation Properties, per Column*

Property	Potential Values	Description
Input column		Name of the selected column that is suspected of containing duplicate values.
Output alias		Name of the column once it gets added to the output stream.
Group output alias		Name of the column that will contain the canonical value.
Match type		A mixture of fuzzy and exact-match types can be used across the selected columns. An exact match is preferable for performance benefits and accuracy. Leveraging columns that can be compared directly can help the fuzzy matching by narrowing the potential results on which the fuzzy match is attempted.
	Fuzzy	Only columns of data type `DT_WSTR` and `DT_STR` can be analyzed.
	Exact	Any data type except `DT_TEXT`, `DT_NTEXT`, and `DT_IMAGE` can be matched.

Property	Potential Values	Description
Minimum similarity		Designates the minimum acceptable value of the similarity index from the fuzzy-match algorithm.
Similarity output alias		Supplying a name in this property adds the value of the similarity index as a new column into the output stream. An empty value means the new column is not created.
Numerals		Indicates how numerals are handled when part of the column value.
	Neither	Ignore leading and trailing numerals.
	Leading	Only leading numerals are significant.
	Trailing	Only trailing numerals are significant.
	LeadingAndTrailing	Both leading and trailing numerals are significant.
Comparison flags		Options that alter how two values are compared, such as whether to ignore casing.
	Ignore case	
	Ignore kana type	
	Ignore nonspacing characters	
	Ignore character width	

Further task tweaks are available in the Advanced configuration properties tab, shown in Figure 10-4.

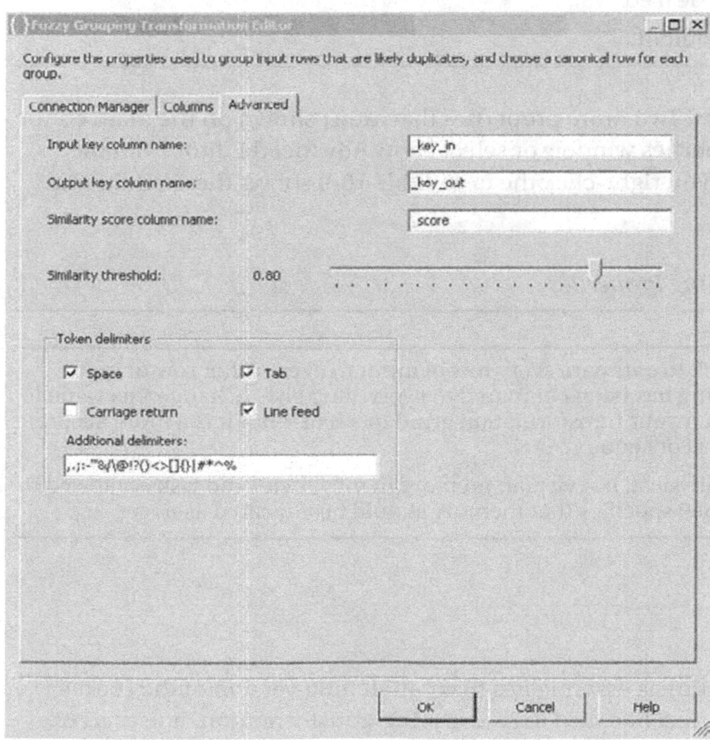

Figure 10-4. *Further Fuzzy Grouping configuration offering useful tweaks*

The configuration options on the Advanced tab are for the component and not for the columns chosen on the previous tab. These properties are described fully in Table 10-5.

Table 10-5. *Fuzzy Grouping Advanced Properties*

Property	Possible Values	Description
Input key column name		Value is set to `_key_in` by default, but the column to which it refers is a column that uniquely identifies each row.
Output key column name		Value is set to `_key_out` by default, but the column to which it refers is a column that identifies a group of rows identified as duplicates. Actual value of this column is the value of the `_key_in` column in the canonical data.
Similarity score column name		Value is set to `_score` by default and refers to the column that holds the similarity index of the canonical row.
Similarity threshold		Sets the minimum allowable similarity index for a match to be considered valid.
Token delimiters		
	Space	
	Tab	
	Carriage return	
	Line feed	
	Additional	

Sneaky hidden properties alert! Two more properties that aren't shown on the main editor appear if you look in the task properties window or select Show Advanced Editor from the context menu that displays when you right-click the task. Table 10-6 shows these additional properties.

Table 10-6. *Additional Fuzzy Grouping Properties*

Property	Description
Exhaustive	Forces the task to compare every row of input to every other row of input until everything has been compared to everything else. (Change this value to `True` and watch your transformation grind to a halt—but it is a more accurate operation as a consequence.)
Max memory usage	Amount of (physical, not virtual) memory in megabytes the task is allowed to use. A value of 0 specifies that memory should be allocated as necessary.

Fuzzy Lookup

1 input, 1 output

The `Fuzzy Lookup` transformation is essentially a fuzzy-matching version of the `Lookup` task described in detail Chapter 9. Just like the `Fuzzy Grouping` transformation, it uses a configurable fuzzy-matching algorithm to make intelligent matches. This task, however, uses a reference (or lookup) table to find suitable matches. The reference table needs to be available and selectable as a SQL Server 2005 table.

Figure 10-5 shows this component's configuration screen. The task uses indexes to produce results, so the configuration options of interest include selecting the index to use, whether to use an existing index, and how it should be maintained.

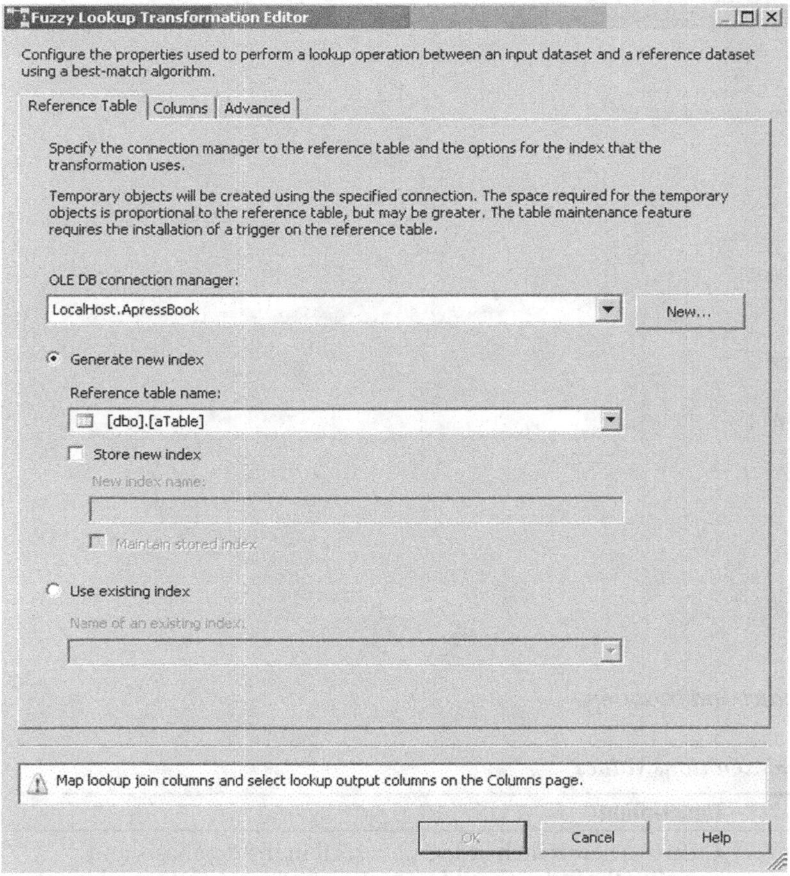

Figure 10-5. *Specifying connection manager and index options*

When this transform is first executed—the first run—a direct and exclusive copy is made of the specified reference table for use only with this task. Once this is done, the copied table is altered to include an integer key column and an index added based on this key.

The input-column values are tokenized and the results are stored in another new index, the *match index*, which is again built against the copied reference table. These generated tokens are the values actually used to match against in the task. Be warned, however: if the indexes are set to be maintained—more on this shortly—then this task might lock the reference table, making it temporarily unavailable.

On subsequent executions, the transform either can use the existing match index or can be asked to regenerate it. Regenerating the index on each run has its own limitations in terms of performance, so luckily some options allow the index to be maintained as values are added to the reference table.

Figure 10-6 shows the task's properties window, which includes the property that sets how the match index should be used. The `MatchIndexOptions` property can have the values described in Table 10-7.

Figure 10-6. *Tweaking the match index options*

Table 10-7. *Possible MatchIndexOptions Values*

Value	Description
`GenerateAndMaintainNewIndex`	Creates a new match index, persists it in the database, and specifies the index should be maintained when data is added to the base reference table by using triggers.
`GenerateAndPersistNewIndex`	Creates a new match index and persists it in the database. No maintenance is performed if the base reference table changes.
`GenerateNewIndex`	Creates a new match index each time the task is executed.
`ReuseExistingIndex`	In conjunction with the `MatchIndexName` property, specifies that an existing match index should be used.

Figure 10-7 shows the Columns tab of the configuration screen. When you select the columns to map, the data types of the columns concerned must be (as with the `Fuzzy Grouping` transformation) `DT_WSTR` or `DT_STR` types.

Figure 10-8 shows the component's advanced configuration options, and Table 10-8 looks at the properties you can configure through the Advanced tab.

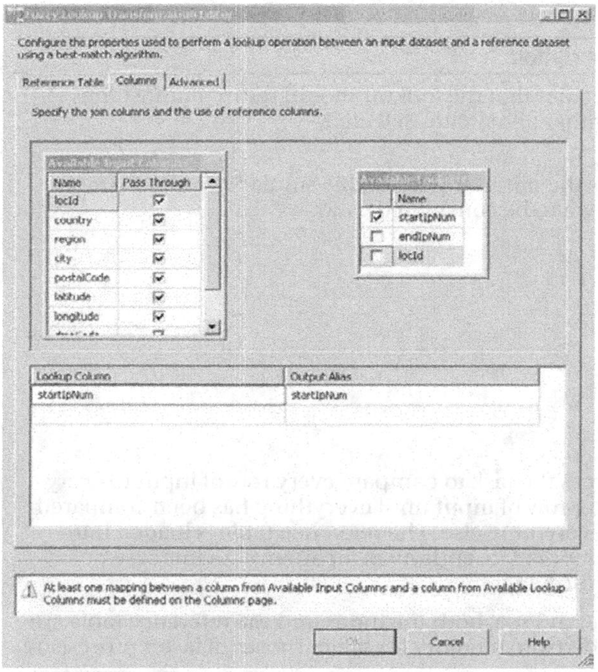

Figure 10-7. *Fuzzy column matching ahoy!*

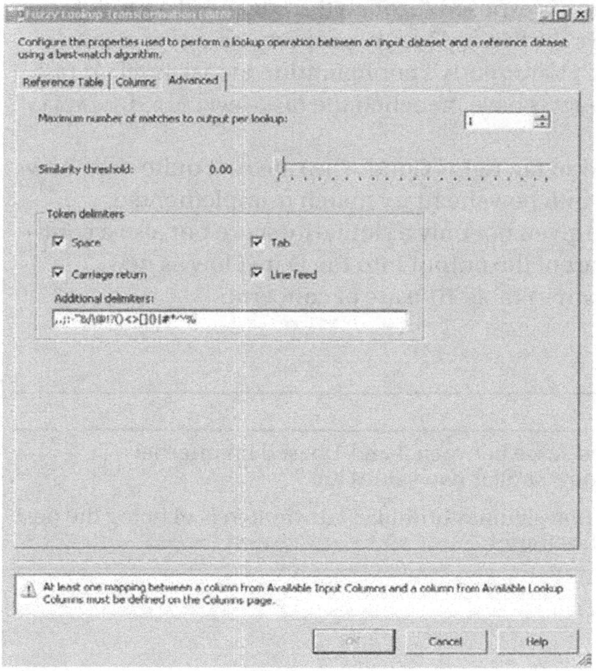

Figure 10-8. *Further properties to tweak the fuzzyness*

Table 10-8. *Advanced Fuzzy Lookup Properties*

Property	Possible Values	Description
Maximum number of matches to output per lookup		Specifies that the lookup should return at most the number of matches selected.
Similarity threshold		Sets the minimum allowable similarity index for a match to be considered valid.
Token delimiters		
	Space	
	Tab	
	Carriage return	
	Line feed	
	Additional	
Exhaustive		Forces the task to compare every row of input to every other row of input until everything has been compared to everything else. The reference table is loaded into memory in its entirety in an attempt to increase performance.
Warm cache		If set to `True`, both the index and the reference table are loaded into memory for the purposes of faster processing.

The similarity threshold can be set at task *and* join level. To set the join-level threshold, the match type between columns must be fuzzy—understandably.

The join level minimum-similarity setting is exposed through the advanced editor's Input and Output Properties tab. Figure 10-9 shows the `MinSimilarity` property being set at join level, and Figure 10-10 shows the `MinSimilarity` property's configuration at task level. At task level, fuzzy matches are made only when *all* rows have breached the task-level `MinSimilarity` threshold level.

Everything seems pretty straightforward so far, right? Good. The ride isn't quite over, however, because it's time to look a little deeper into how the fuzzy match is implemented.

When fuzzy matches are made, they are given not only a similarity score but also a confidence score. These values are included as part of the output into the Data Flow as new columns. Per match, the two properties shown in Table 10-9 are of concern.

Table 10-9. *Per-Match Properties*

Property	Description
Similarity score	A numerically expressed score between 0 and 1 based on internal algorithms, to express how similar two values are
Confidence score	Value between 0 and 1 that signifies how likely the match is of being the best match among all matches found

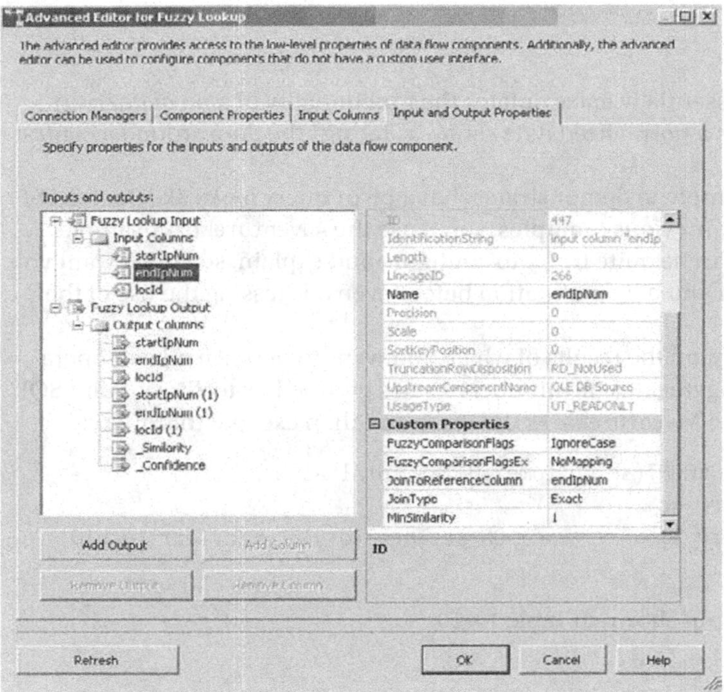

Figure 10-9. *Setting the MinSimilarity threshold at join level*

Figure 10-10. *Setting the MinSimilarity value at task level*

Pivot

1 input, 1 output, 1 error output

The Pivot transformation essentially encapsulates the functionality of a *pivot query* in SQL. A pivot query denormalizes a normalized data set by "rotating" the data around a central point—a value.

It's best if I start with an example to demonstrate what a pivot query looks like. Instead of using the output from one of the previous examples, you'll use the AdventureWorks sample database. The Pivot transform can be quite tricky to configure and explain, so I don't want you to be fiddling with table creation and data population before even addressing the use of the component.

First let's look at a SQL query, on the results of which you want to perform a pivot operation. This fairly standard query aggregates the number of sales grouped by territory. Point SQL Server Management Studio at the AdventureWorks database and then execute this query:

```
SELECT          st.[Group], COUNT(sc.CustomerID) AS TotalSales
FROM           Sales.Customer sc
INNER JOIN Sales.SalesTerritory st          ON st.TerritoryID = sc.TerritoryID
GROUP BY        st.[Group]
```

The query produces the output shown in Table 10-10.

Table 10-10. *SQL Statement Output*

Group	TotalSales
Europe	5623
NorthAmerica	9931
Pacific	3631

If you want this data expressed in a single row instead, with the Group values as columns instead of rows, you need to modify the query somewhat to pivot the table based upon the Group:

```
SELECT          'Total Sales' AS TotalSales, [Europe] as Europe, [NorthAmerica]

as NorthAmerica, [Pacific] as Pacific
FROM
(SELECT          st.[Group] AS Territory, sc.CustomerID as CustID
            FROM       Sales.Customer sc inner join Sales.SalesTerritory st
                 ON st.TerritoryID = sc.TerritoryID) AS Source
PIVOT
(
           COUNT(CustID)
           FOR Territory IN (Europe, NorthAmerica, Pacific)
) AS PivT
```

This modified query produces the same data as the original but in a different format: this time the Groups are produced as columns, not rows. The SalesTotal for each territory is stored in the column value, as Table 10-11 shows.

Table 10-11. *Query Output*

	Europe	NorthAmerica	Pacific
Total Sales	5623	9931	3631

Now you'll see how the Pivot task performs the same operation on the AdventureWorks data. (I should note here that configuration of this task is unnecessarily complex. If you have a requirement for frequent use of pivot functionality, you should consider writing your own transform component to replace this one. See Chapter 15 for details on the steps to take to create a custom component.)

As always with the examples in this book, make sure you have created a new package with a single Data Flow Task added to the Control Flow design surface. Switch over to the Data Flow design surface before starting the following steps:

1. Configure a SqlClient DataReader Source to use the query in Listing 10-1 (by populating the SqlCommand property):

Listing 10-1. *SQL Statement to Retrieve Data*

```
SELECT          st.[Group], COUNT(sc.CustomerID) AS TotalSales
FROM                  Sales.Customer sc
INNER JOIN Sales.SalesTerritory st             ON st.TerritoryID = sc.TerritoryID
GROUP BY         st.[Group]
```

2. Drop a Pivot component from the Toolbox onto the design surface, somewhere below the DataReader Source.

3. After connecting the DataReader Source output arrow to the Pivot transform, edit the Pivot task.

4. Skip ahead to the Input Columns tab. Select both available columns—Group and TotalSales—as the input columns to use, as shown in Figure 10-11.

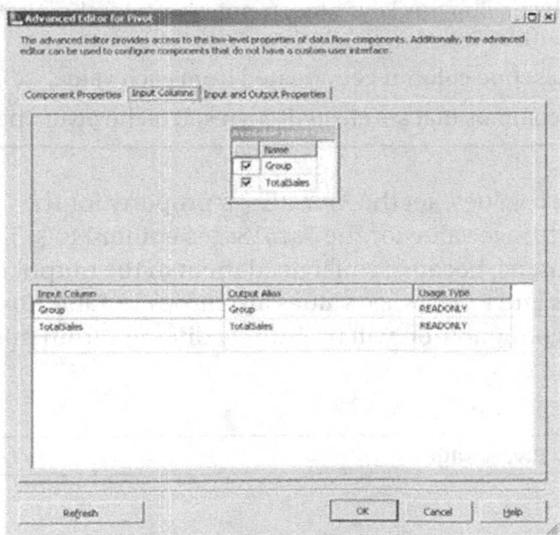

Figure 10-11. *Choose input columns from those available.*

5. Switch to the Input and Output Properties tab. Expand the list on the left side of the window to reveal all Pivot Default Input columns, then Input Columns. You should see the `Group` and `TotalSales` columns nestling underneath, as in Figure 10-12. These two input columns need configuring to indicate how the pivot should work. Possible `PivotUsage` property values are presented in Table 10-12.

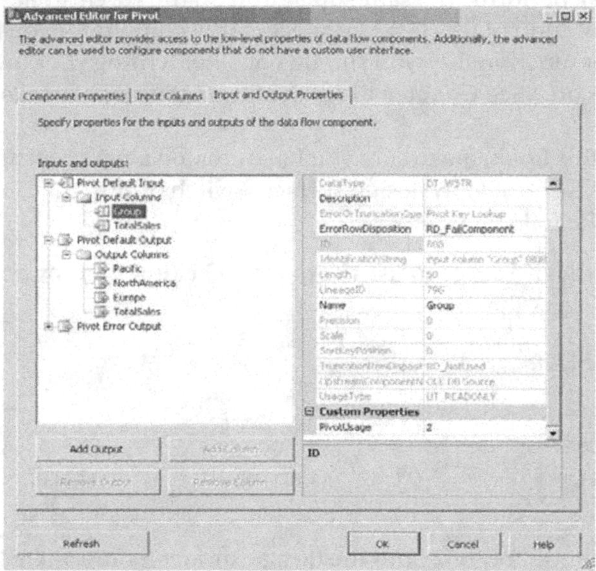

Figure 10-12. *Configuring the input and output columns to create the pivot*

Table 10-12. *Potential PivotUsage Values*

Value	Description
0	The column is not pivoted, and the column value should pass through to the output.
1	The column is part of a set defined by having this key value. Input rows with the same set key are combined into a single output row.
2	The column is a pivot column. At least one column gets created from each value.
3	Values from this column are used as columns that are created as a result of the pivot operation.

6. To create the pivot around the `Group` values, set the `PivotUsage` property for the `Group` input column to be `2` and the `PivotUsage` value for the `TotalSales` column to `3`. Take note of the `LineageID` for both columns, because you'll need them in the output column configuration. My `LineageID`s and `PivotUsage` values are shown in Table 10-13. Note that the `LineageID`s for your configuration will be entirely different from mine.

Table 10-13. *My LineageIDs*

Column Name	LineageID	PivotUsage
Group	31	2
TotalSales	34	3

7. Add new output columns as per Table 10-14. To do this, expand the list on the left side of the window to reveal all Pivot Default Output columns, then Output Columns. There should be no columns under Output Columns.

8. With the Output Columns branch of the list selected, click the Add Column button. This adds a new entry under the branch and populates the properties for the entry to the right of the screen. Configure the values for each new column from Table 10-14 (using the `LineageID`s you noted in the previous step, rather than mine.)

Table 10-14. *New Output Columns*

Column Name	PivotKeyValue	Source Column
`Pacific`	`Pacific`	`31` (`LineageID` for `Total Sales`)
`NorthAmerica`	`NorthAmerica`	`31` (`LineageID` for `Total Sales`)
`Europe`	`Europe`	`31` (`LineageID` for `Total Sales`)
`TotalSales`		`-1`

Figures 10-13, 10-14, 10-15, and 10-16 show the values I entered for these new columns. Table 10-15 describes properties important to the pivot operation.

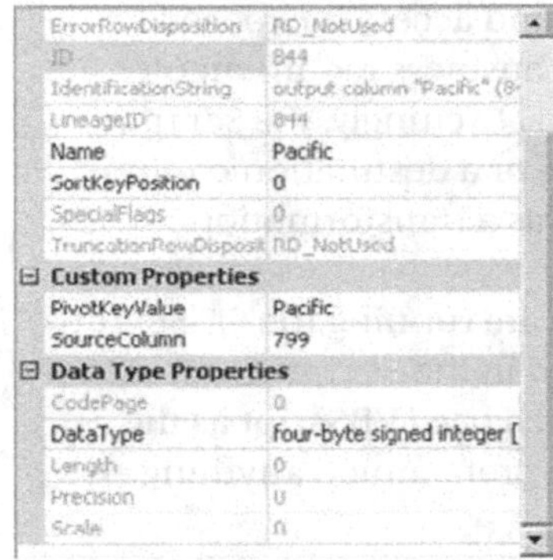

Figure 10-13. *The Pacific column*

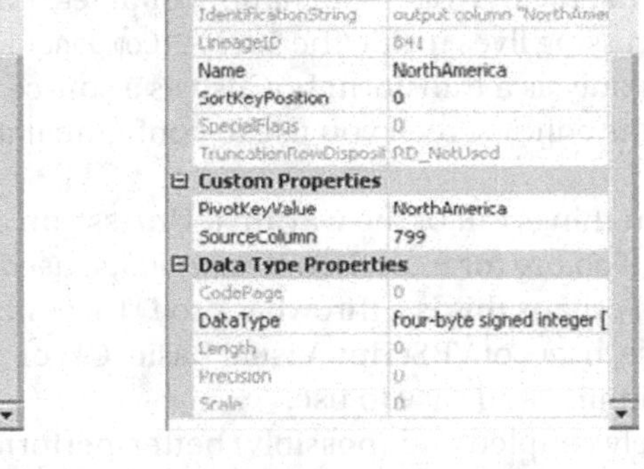

Figure 10-14. *The NorthAmerica column*

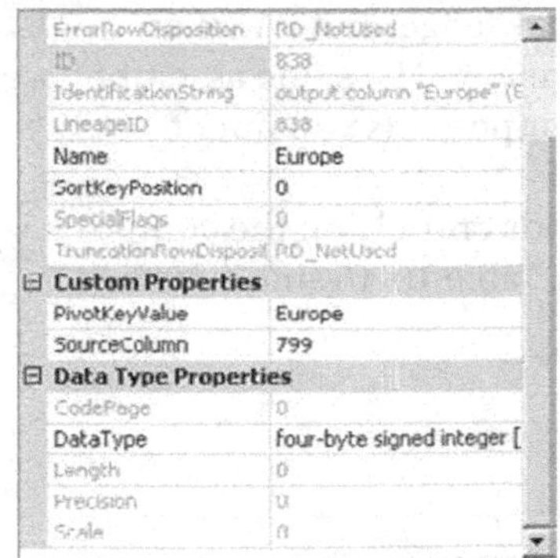

Figure 10-15. *The Europe column*

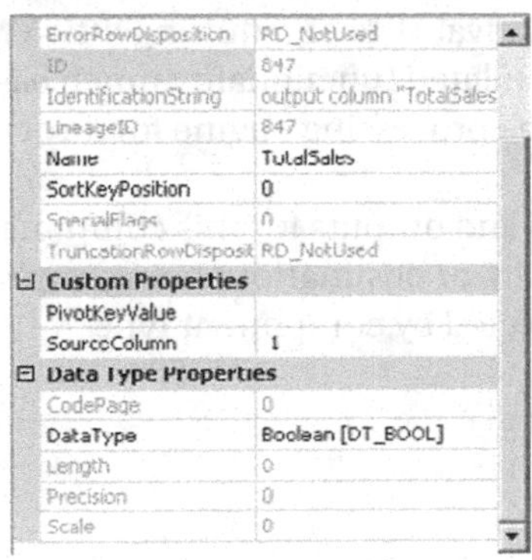

Figure 10-16. *The TotalSales column*

Table 10-15. *Important Pivot Properties*

Property	Description
`PivotKeyValue`	For each output, holds the value the pivot operation will group on.
`SourceColumn`	Holds the `LineageID` for the input column to use as the source.

9. Click OK to be returned to the Data Flow design surface. Configuration is complete!

With the `Pivot` transform, I can only suggest that hands-on use will give you a better idea of how it works. I definitely suggest that before you configure this transform, you create a suitable SQL pivot query to provide the basis of, and a reference to, the pivot the task is supposed to perform.

Script Component

0 or 1 inputs, 1 or possibly multiple outputs

The `Script Component` is a big one—one of two features ensuring that SSIS can be used for *any* purpose (the other, of course, being custom components). It's so big that Chapter 14 is dedicated to the scripting functionality.

I can't even begin to suggest how this task might be used, because it really has no limit. The Data Flow is available on a row-by-row basis inside this task, and access is exposed to each column in the flow. That means that imagination, or at least business requirements, really do dictate what processing lives inside the `Script Component`. Excitingly, the `Script Component` can be used not only as a transform but also as a source or a destination component. Figure 10-17 shows the editor screen you use to configure it as a transformation component.

I'll get some important things out of the way first. Unless you are running the `C# Script Component` (available from iFoo.org for free) then the language used in the `Script Component`—this task type—is VB.NET. Perhaps this is a throwback to DTS, which used VBScript as the script language. In any case, users of VBScript, Visual Basic, C#, or pretty much anything else will rapidly find VB.NET familiar and easy to use.

To create a more loosely coupled and (possibly) better-performing solution, I advise you to implement an external and reusable .NET assembly within which to house processing. This way the `Script Component` forms the function of a stub that makes the actual call to the external assembly. This has the advantage of requiring little VB.NET knowledge, and it makes maintenance of the encapsulated functionality much easier and neater. The same assembly can also be used to form the processing engine for any custom components you might develop in future.

The number of inputs and outputs for this component depends entirely on the component type (source, transform, or destination) being implemented. Table 10-16 shows how inputs and outputs are affected by component type.

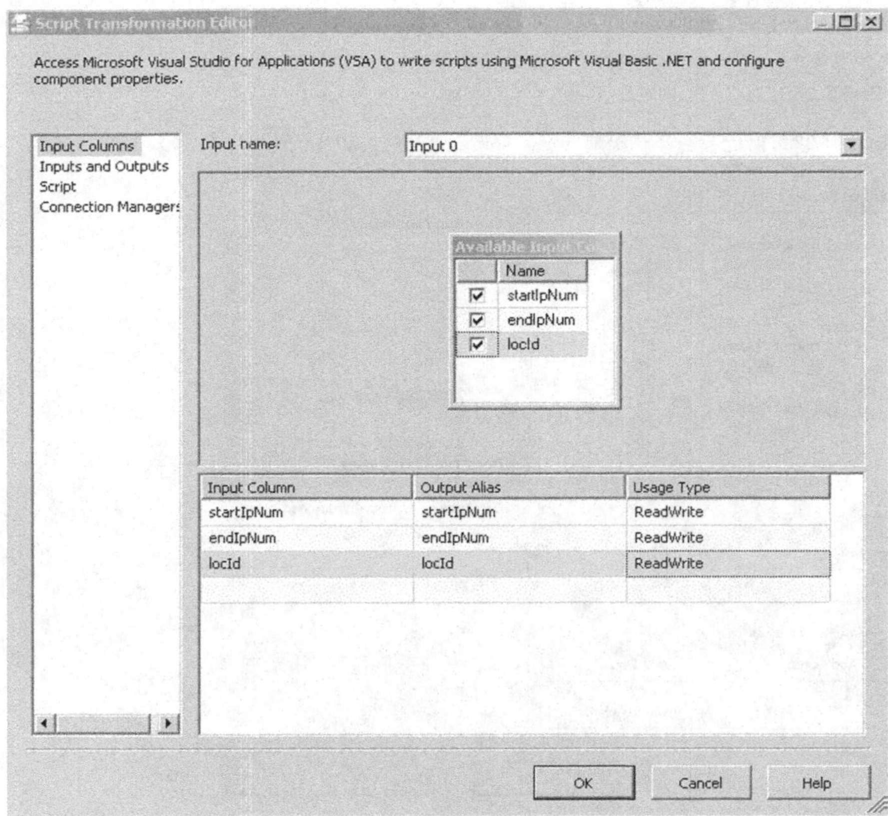

Figure 10-17. *Nothing unusual, just specifying input columns*

Table 10-16. *Script Component Inputs and Outputs by Component Type*

Component Type	Number of Inputs	Number of Outputs
Source	0	Multiple
Transform	1	Multiple
Destination	1	1

Although proper configuration of this task requires something a little more hardcore than simply setting a few properties, a number of important configuration options are exposed.

Don't expect to see a property that instructs the task to be a source or a transform or a destination. Instead, this is decided by the implementation of input and output columns via the Inputs and outputs configuration area of the component, shown in Figure 10-18.

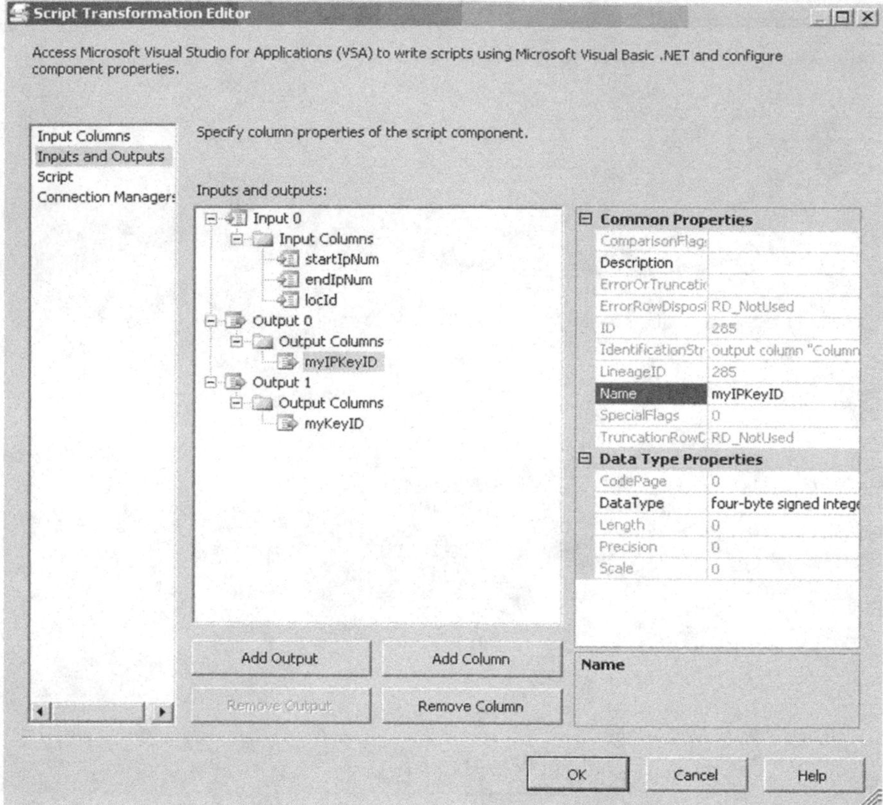

Figure 10-18. *Specifying the implementation of input and output flow*

In the example in Figure 10-18, I've attached an input to the component and created an additional output. By doing this I'm using the task as a transformation that, within the script, can have output assigned to it and thus become part of the Data Flow.

The more obvious properties exposed are shown in Figure 10-19. Three of the more important ones are described in Table 10-17.

Table 10-17. *Important Script Component Properties*

Property	Description
`PreCompile`	Sets whether a compiled copy of the script should be stored. The next time the script is called, the compiled version will be executed. This is faster but requires more space for storage. On 64-bit machines, this property must be set to `True`.
`ReadOnlyVariables`	A comma-separated list of variables for read-only use within the script. They can then be accessed via the object model in the script using the `Variables` collection.
`ReadWriteVariables`	A comma-separated list of variables for read/write use within the script. They can then be accessed via the object model in the script using the `Variables` collection.

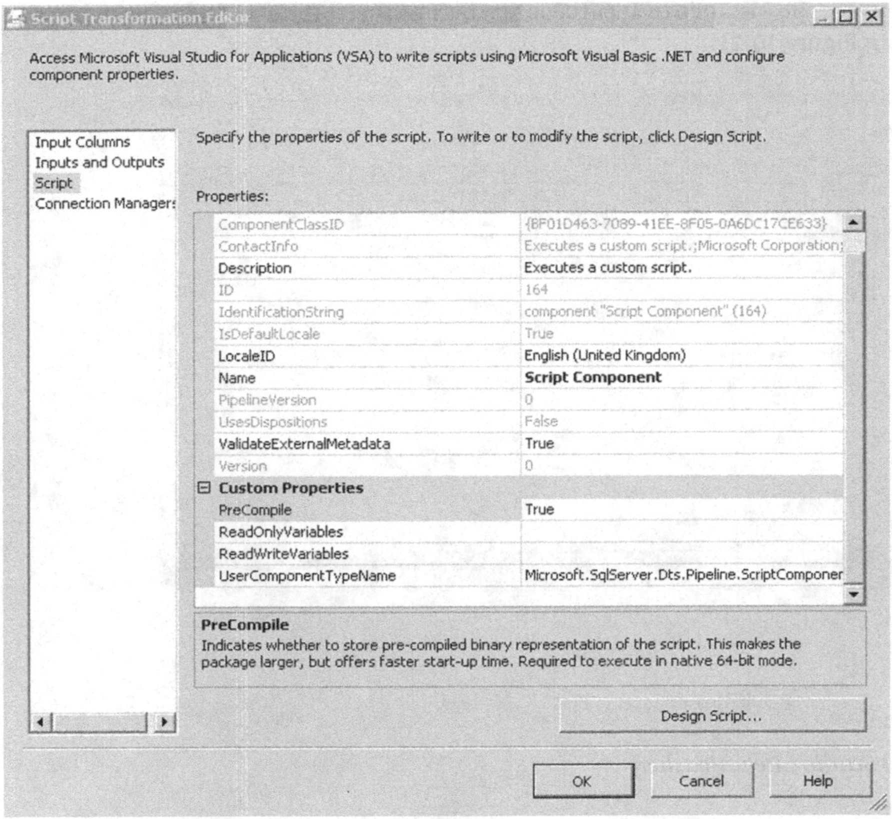

Figure 10-19. *Only a few properties, but they're useful*

In one of the examples in Chapter 6, I note that errors can be created if you change the PreCompile property value without revisiting the Design Script environment. You can avoid this problem by ensuring you click the Design Script... button after you change the property.

Figure 10-20 shows what happens when Design Script... is clicked. Visual Studio for Applications (or Visual Studio Lite as I call it, jokingly) appears, and code editing can begin.

Again, I'll cover scripting in more detail in Chapter 14, but for now I'll highlight the important bits that pertain to this task. The task generates code to handle the defined inputs via a class called ScriptMain. This is the entry point into the code from the task. A variable of type Input0Buffer called Row is passed into the [InputName]_ProcessInputRow method, where [InputName] is the name of the defined input.

Manipulating the underlying object model of the Input0Buffer class gives you access to the input columns and therefore to the data contained within them. Any instance of an input-buffer class contains properties relating to the columns contained within it.

You can create a script like this one, for example, within Input0.ProcessInputRow(...):

```
If (Row.locId > 10001) Then
    Output1Buffer.Column = Row.locId
    Output1Buffer.AddRow()
End If
```

The script accesses the instance of `Input0Buffer`, by `Row`, the contents of which can be seen enumerated in Figure 10-21.

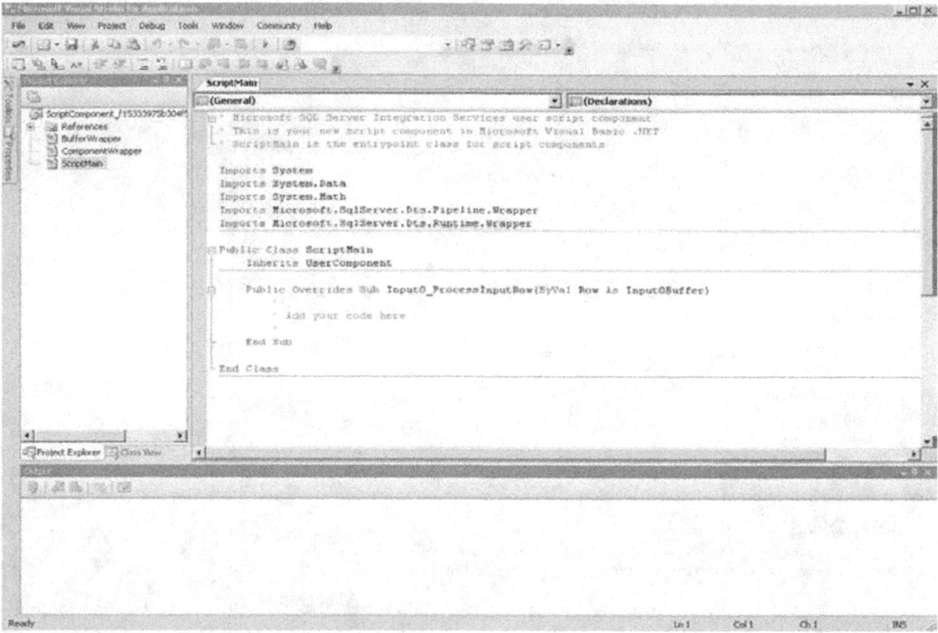

Figure 10-20. *Visual Studio Lite unleashed*

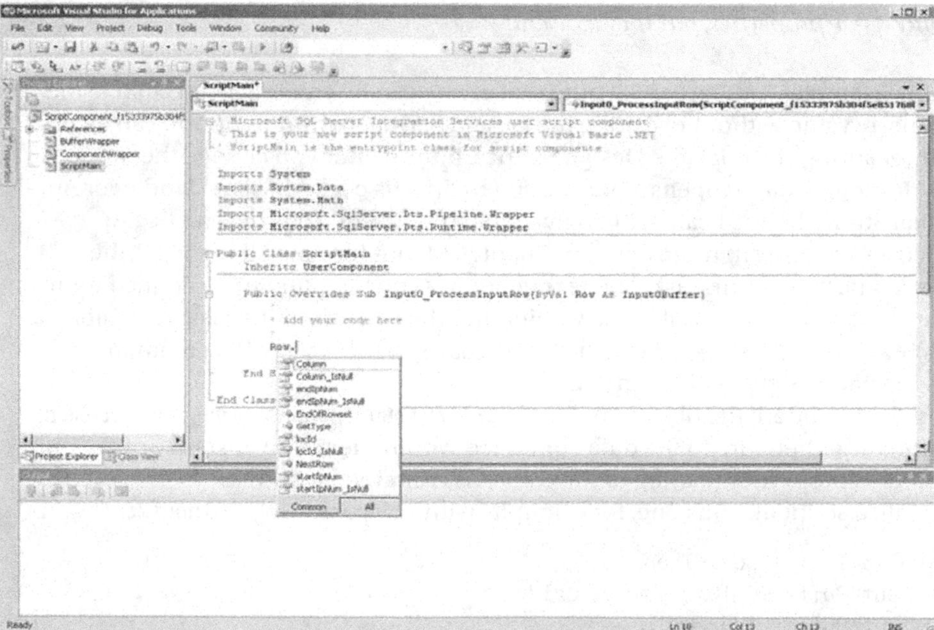

Figure 10-21. *The Row enumeration, showing the contents of the Input0Buffer class*

Based upon some simple logic, the script creates a conditional statement that sets the value of a column in one of the output buffers and adds `Row` to the downstream Data Flow. In reality you could do anything you want here. And in Chapter 14 I'll show you how.

Slowly Changing Dimension

1 input, up to 6 outputs

The `Slowly Changing Dimension` task is used to maintain dimension tables held in data warehouses. It is a highly specific task that acts as the conduit between an OLTP database and a related OLAP database. I could easily devote another whole book to the concepts connected to this component. I'll do my best to describe this task's purpose and properties without relying too much on OLAP or SSAS terminology and expertise.

As this transformation's name implies, it is concerned with the updating of dimensions stored in an OLAP database. The reason it refers to *slowly changing* dimensions is that, well, some dimensions just don't change too often. Dimensions such as surname and marital status don't change very often, but they can change. When they do change, what should be done with the old values? Fear no more: the `Slowly Changing Dimension` (SCD) transform is great for performing these updates in a simple and configurable way.

The different types of updates available have a large bearing on how the task will be configured. There are two main types *and* additional types that aren't so prevalent. I won't cover the additional types in this book The two main types are

- **Changing attribute change (Type 1)**: This type overwrites the specified dimension without tracking the change.
- **Historical attribute change (Type 2)**: This type creates a new record containing the dimension change while preserving the historical record and marking it as noncurrent. It's not hard to imagine that this is the most popular SCD update type. Who wants to throw away historical data?

As usual, you have two ways to configure this task. The easiest and most accessible way is to use the Slowly Changing Dimension Wizard. Despite its inconsistency with how the other tasks are configured, this is the best way to go about getting the SCD settings just right. Figure 10-22 shows the wizard's initial welcome screen.

I don't usually like wizards. I feel as if I'm abstracted away from everything going on behind the scenes, and that troubles me. In this case, however, I don't mind, because getting an SCD update going with the wizard takes mere moments. That doesn't mean it does everything or that no further configuration is necessary . . . but I'll come to that later.

Figure 10-23 shows the wizard's first (proper) configuration step. This step allows you to configure the connection properties and specify how the input columns join to the dimension columns. The key type offers the option to set the match as a business key. Selecting the input columns that match the relevant dimension columns tells the SCD task how to match the dimension table record with the source system record.

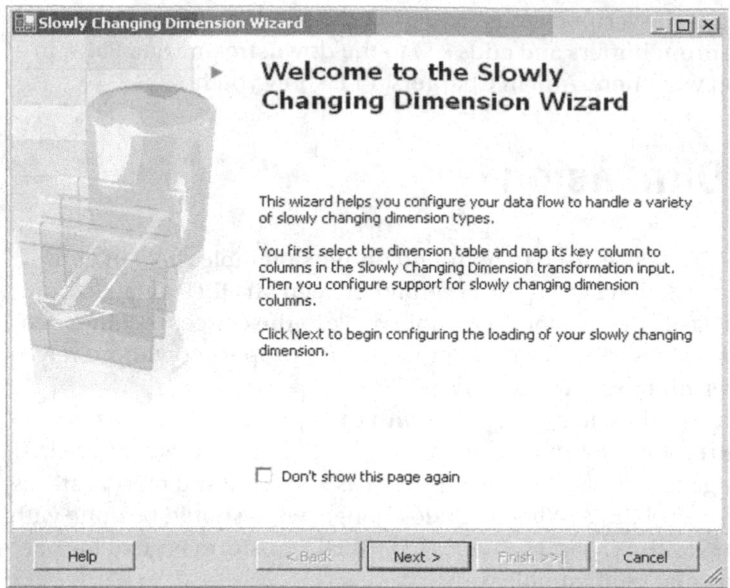

Figure 10-22. *The welcome screen. Happy days!*

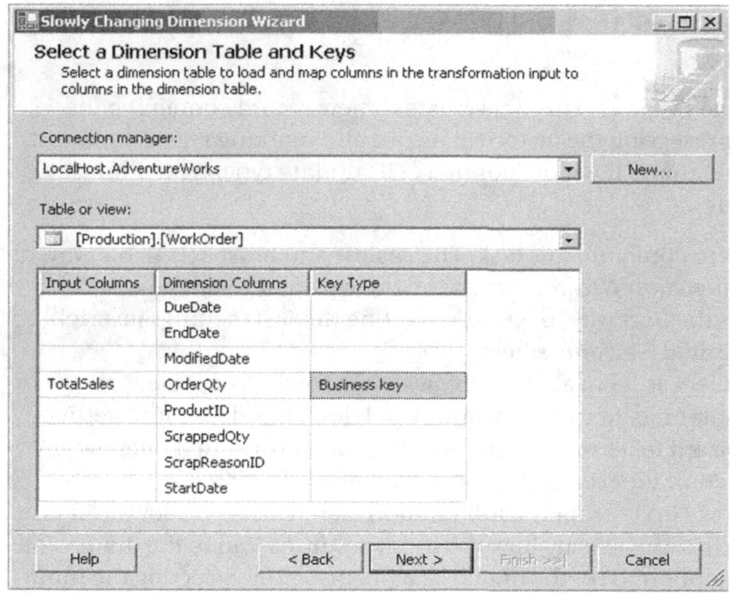

Figure 10-23. *The first step: setting connections and matching key*

■ **Caution** Null business keys are not allowed. Ensure the column does not contain any null values by using a conditional split upstream.

The wizard's next page (Figure 10-24) is where you can define the changes to dimension columns. You can also specify the type of change here. The three available types of change (listed on the wizard screen) are summarized in Table 10-18.

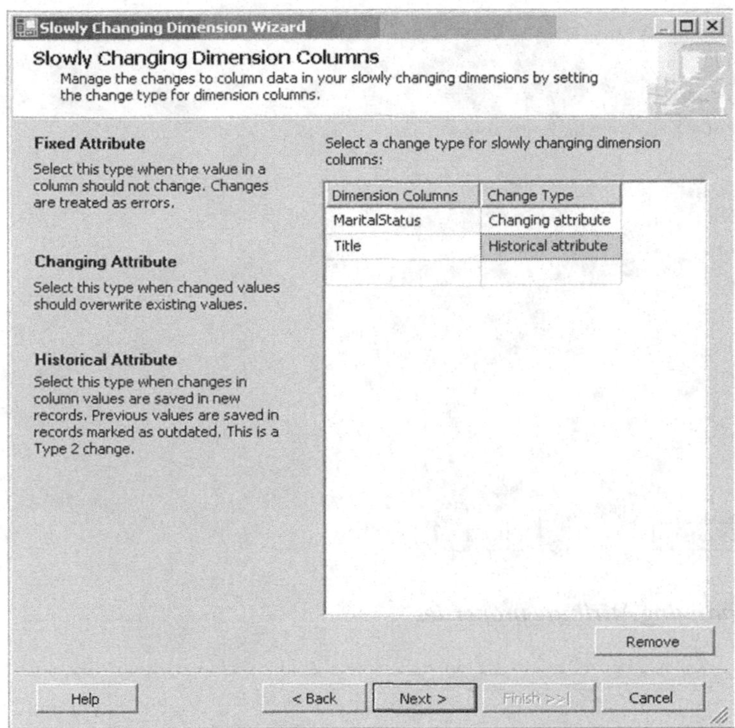

Figure 10-24. *Select those SCDs here.*

Table 10-18. *Possible Change Types*

Change Type	Description
Fixed attribute	Specifies that the value in the column should not change. Changes are treated as errors.
Changing attribute	Specifies that any changes should overwrite existing values.
Historical attribute	Specifies that a copy of the data should be made before changes are made. The original data is marked as noncurrent.

The wizard's next step (Figure 10-25) shows the options available for fixed or changing attributes. When you use a Historical attribute change, additional columns are used to signify that a record is no longer current. These indicators can be an existing column specified on the screen shown in Figure 10-26. You can specify start/end dates also. Further configuration can be made with respect to inferred dimension members (see Figure 10-27).

Clicking Finish on the final step of the wizard makes some craziness appear on your nice clean Data Flow design surface, as Figure 10-28 shows. Six different kinds of output—potentially—get added and configured in the Data Flow that gets generated. They're shown in Table 10-19.

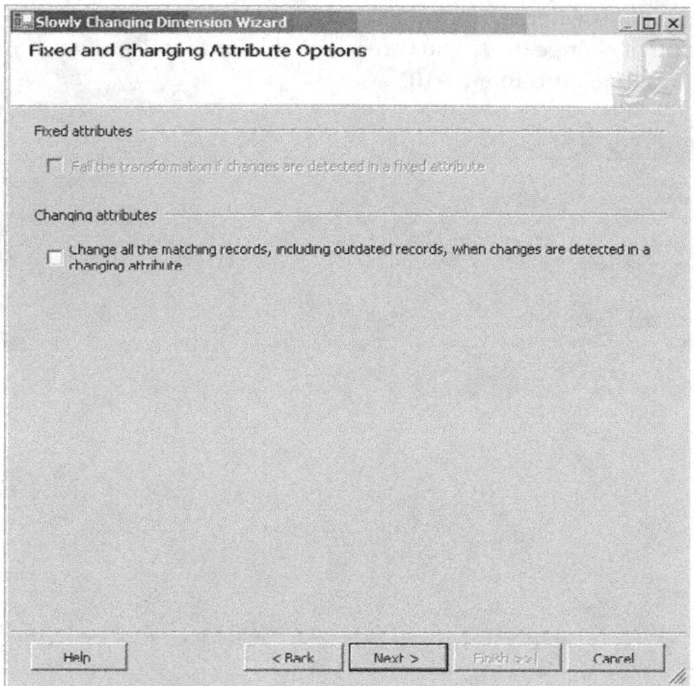

Figure 10-25. *Setting Fixed and Changing Attribute properties*

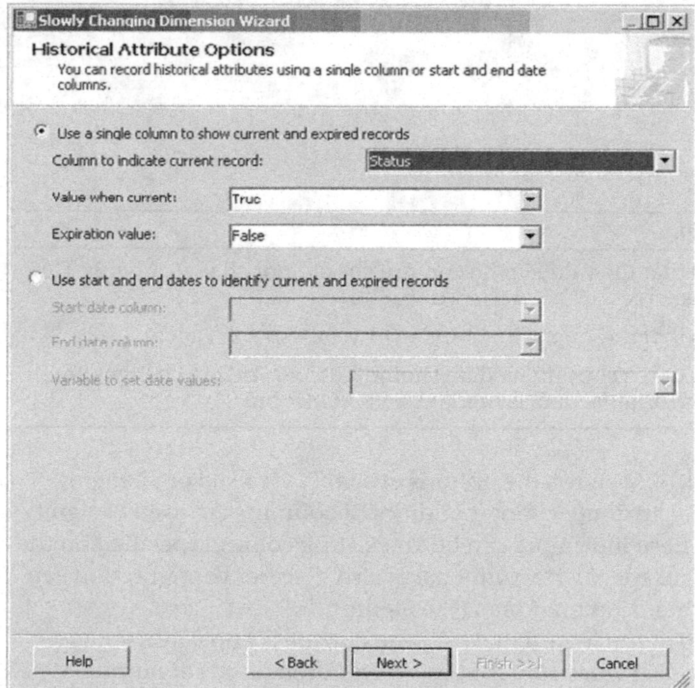

Figure 10-26. *Setting Historical attribute options*

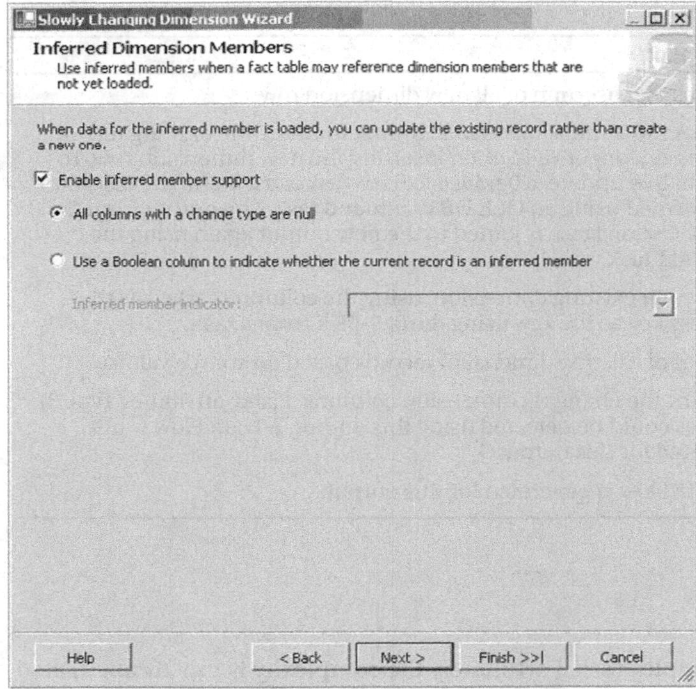

Figure 10-27. *Almost finished. Inferred member not loaded?*

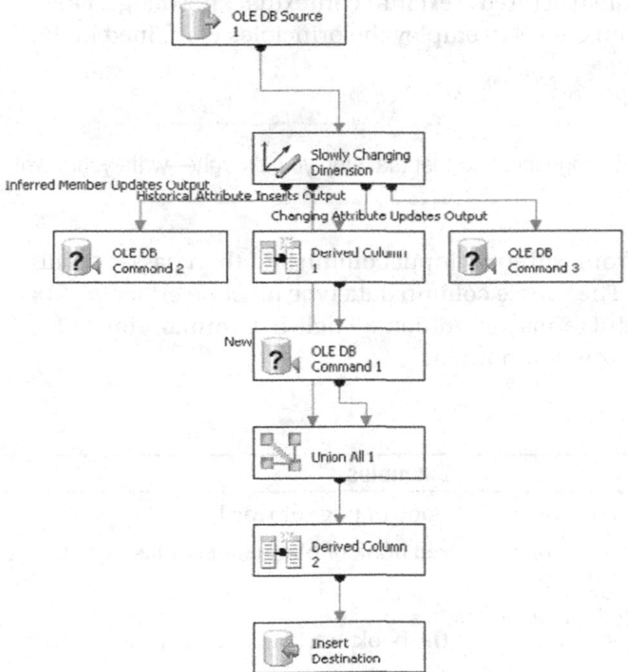

Figure 10-28. *Where did all this come from!?*

Table 10-19. *Possible Output Types*

Output Type	Description
New output	Handles the insertion of all new dimension rows.
Historical attribute	Handles the dimension change by first marking the existing record as being no longer valid, then inserting the new dimension row. To perform this update, a `Derived Column` task is used and the insertion is performed using an OLE DB command task. The output from the `OLE DB Command` task is joined to the new output again using the `Union All` task.
Changing attribute updates	Updates an existing dimension, using the column marked as the business key as the key, using the `OLE DB Command` task.
Inferred member updates	Updates of existing dimension records based on source values.
Fixed attribute	Contains the changing dimension columns. Fixed-attribute (Type 3) changes could be detected using this output. A Data Flow is not generated for this output.
Unchanged	No Data Flow is generated for this output.

Term Extraction

1 input, 1 output, 1 Error output

`Term Extraction` is another complex task. Fortunately the complexity is mostly abstracted away from the developer, but the concepts and implementation of the task makes for hearty conversation at any dinner party.

Unstructured text is what it's all about. One of my favorite topics of all time is the investigation into how to process "natural" or "unstructured" text into contextual knowledge. One way of extracting content and context from data is to employ the principles contained in the `Term Extraction` task.

■ **Note** This task is built to use only the English language. Don't let that stop you, though—write your own!

This transformation extracts terms from within an input column and then passes them into the Data Flow as an output column. The source column data type must be either `DT_STR` or `DT_WSTR`. Table 10-20 defines some useful terms in traditional English grammar, some of which are used in the property values for this component.

Table 10-20. *Common Terms*

Term	Description	Examples
Noun	Word designating an object or "thing"	**book** or **page** or **word**
Noun phrase	A noun modified by an adjective or a determiner or other structure	**red book** or **blank page** or **last word**
Article	A noun modifier signifying the type of reference being made by the noun	**the** book or **a** blank page or **the** last word
Pronoun	A word that can replace a noun in a sentence	**he** or **her** or **it**

Term	Description	Examples
Gerund	Action noun corresponding to a verb	**waiting** (corresponding to **wait**)
Token	A defined element within text against which meaning can be attributed	any word in a sentence
Adjective	Word whose purpose is to modify nouns and other constructs	**small** car or **young** girl
Proper noun	The name of a one-of-a-kind person, place, or thing	**Redmond** or **Donald** or **Chrysler**

The configuration consists of selecting the columns from which to extract terms (Figure 10-29), the specification of where to find term exclusions, and properties that specify how the extraction is performed.

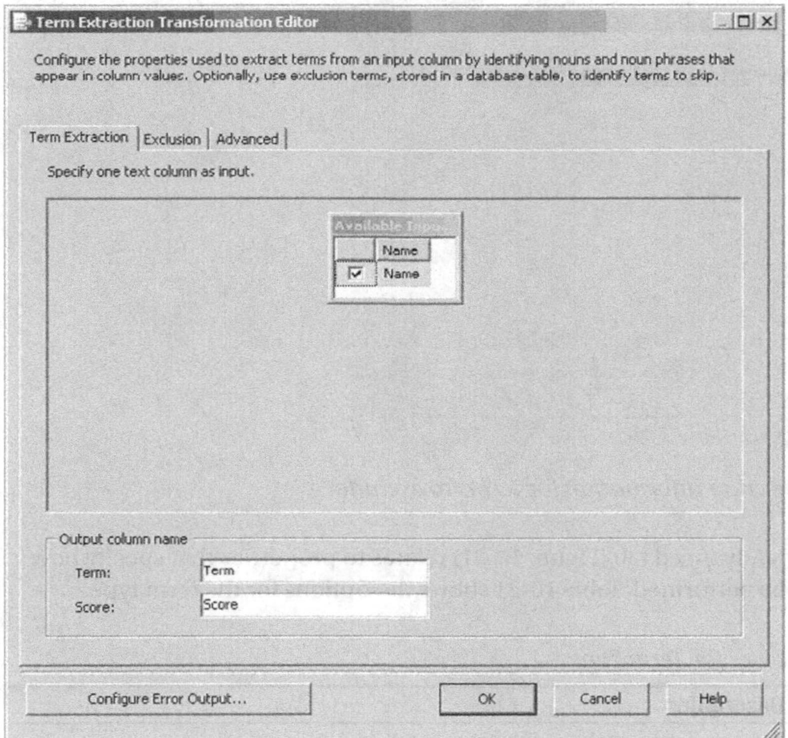

Figure 10-29. *Select the columns from which to extract terms.*

As with other advanced transformations such as the fuzzy-match tasks, an extracted term gets a "score" value when extracted that signifies the confidence the extraction engine has that the extracted value is a valid term. The output from this transform consists of only two columns, the names of which are specified on the first tab of the task editor:

`Term`: Name to use for the column containing an extracted term.

`Score`: Name to use for the column containing the extracted term score.

The Exclusion tab (Figure 10-30) shows that a connection can be made to a table containing exception values. When the term extraction process takes place, the terms in the exclusion lookup table are ignored. This table is loaded into memory by the task to provide better performance. When the term-extraction engine processes a noun phrase, if any part of it contains a value on the exclusion list, the entire term is excluded.

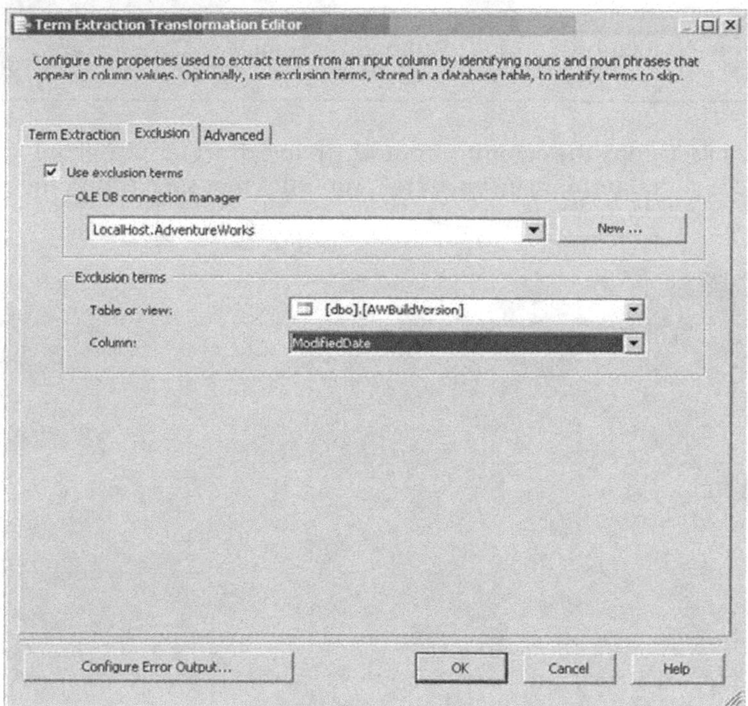

Figure 10-30. *Providing connection information for terms to exclude*

The component editor's Advanced tab (Figure 10-31) relates to properties that specify how the term extraction should be performed. Table 10-21 shows the options for the term type.

Table 10-21. *Advanced Properties for Term Type*

Possible Value	Description
Noun	The term extraction engine extracts only nouns.
Noun phrase	The term extraction engine extracts only noun phrases.
Noun and noun phrase	The term extraction engine extracts both nouns and noun phrases.

Irrespective of the term type selected, articles and pronouns are not extracted. This means that in a column that contains, for example, *the book*, only *book* is extracted. In addition, the engine extracts the singular form of the noun as long as the value exists in the internal dictionary. Gerunds are also treated as nouns if they are in the dictionary.

The next three advanced properties, their possible values, and descriptions are presented in Table 10-22.

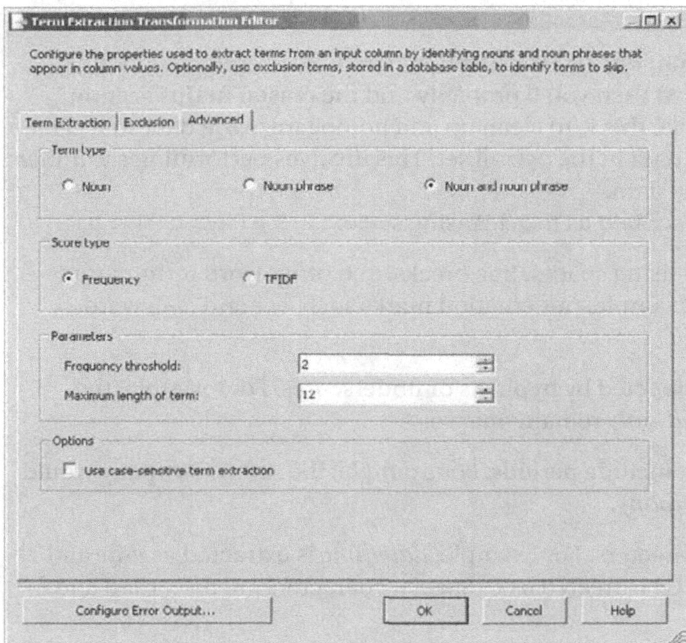

Figure 10-31. *Now we're talking: extraction properties*

Table 10-22. *The Last of the Advanced Properties*

Property	Possible Values	Description
Score type		Specifies the technique to use to calculate the score.
	Frequency	Specifies that a "raw frequency" is used to score the extracted term. Essentially this is just a count of how many times the term appears. This setting ties in with the frequency threshold property.
	TFIDF (term frequency–inverse document frequency)	Specifies that a TFIDF algorithm should be used to calculate the score for the term. This calculation is performed by dividing the number of rows by the number of times the term occurs, then taking a logarithm of the quotient.
Parameters		Extra properties that further tweak the `Term Extraction` operation.
	Frequency threshold	The number of occurrences of a term must breach the value of this property to be extracted as a term.
	Maximum length of term	The term being extracted must be smaller or equal in length to the value held in this property to be extracted.
Options		By default the transformation is case insensitive in that differently cased examples of the same word are treated as the same term. Proper nouns and words that are not listed in the internal dictionary are not treated with case insensitivity; they are treated literally.
	Use case-sensitive term extraction	The extraction engine treats differently cased words as different words. *Book* and *book* are extracted as separate terms, for example.

How It Works

The way in which this task works is not only interesting but incredibly useful to know. Certainly if it isn't performing as expected then you'll probably find the reason in this section.

The first operation in any task like this is to clean up and homogenize the data so it can be more accurately compared to other data in the overall set. This involves performing a number of steps across multiple passes of the data.

First-pass processing can be described as the cleansing stage:

- Separating text into words by using spaces, line breaks, and other word terminators in the English language. For example, punctuation marks such as *?* and *:* are word-breaking characters.
- Preserving words that are connected by hyphens or underscores. For example, the words *copy-protected* and *read-only* remain one word.
- Keeping intact acronyms that include periods. For example, the *A.B.C* Company would be tokenized as *ABC* and *Company*.
- Splitting words on special characters. For example, *date/time* is extracted as *date* and *time*, *(bicycle)* as *bicycle*, and C# is treated as C. Special characters are discarded and cannot be lexicalized.
- Recognizing when special characters such as the apostrophe should not split words. For example, *you're* is not split into two words and yields the single term *you* (noun).
- Splitting time expressions, monetary expressions, e-mail addresses, and postal addresses. For example, the date *January 31, 2004* is separated into the three tokens *January*, *31*, and *2004*.
- Removing *s* from nouns and pronouns. For example, *bicycles* becomes *bicycle*.
- Removing *es* from nouns and pronouns. For example, *stories* becomes *story*.
- Retrieving the singular form for irregular nouns from the dictionary. For example, *geese* becomes *goose*.

The second pass provides grammatical context to values:

- Once the cleansing has been performed, each term is reexamined and tagged with its grammatical type.
- Anything not handled by the transformation (whether configured to ignore or otherwise) is discarded.

The third pass separates data into sentences by checking for line-termination characters:

- ASCII line-break characters 0x0d (carriage return) and 0x0a (line feed). To use this character as a sentence boundary, there must be two or more line-break characters in a row.
- Hyphen (-). To use this character as a sentence boundary, neither the character to the left nor to the right of the hyphen can be a letter.

- Underscore (_). To use this character as a sentence boundary, neither the character to the left nor to the right of the underscore can be a letter.
- All Unicode characters that are less than or equal to 0x19, or greater than or equal to 0x7b.
- Combinations of numbers, punctuation marks, and alphabetical characters. These could mean, for example, *A23B#99* returns the term *A23B*.
- The characters, %, @, &, $, #, *, :, ;, ., , , !, ?, <, >, +, =, ^, ~, |, \, /, (,), [,], {, }, “, and ‘.

The fourth (and final) pass separates the data into individual words (or tokens) by looking for the following word boundaries:

- Space
- Tab
- ASCII 0x0d (carriage return)
- ASCII 0x0a (line feed)

This leaves a number of tokens for each value that the `Term Extraction` engine can process and decide to retain as terms or be discarded.

Of course, it is entirely possible to write a completely original term-extraction engine by writing a new custom component, even if it inherits parts of the original component to perform the basic processing.

Term Lookup

1 input, 1 output

Just when you thought it was safe to go back into the water . . . here is another term-based transformation: `Term Lookup`.

This task wraps the functionality of the `Term Extraction` transform and uses the values extracted to compare to a reference table, just like the `Lookup` transform. To get a better idea of how this all works, especially since it is such an integral part of the task, read the preceding section on the `Term Extraction` component. Figure 10-32 shows how you specify the column mapping for the lookup.

The Term Lookup tab of the task editor allows the selection of pass-through columns and the mapping of columns from the available input columns to the available reference columns specifying how to perform the lookup.

In terms of function, the transform extracts the terms and then performs a lookup against values in a specified reference table. A count is performed to see how many times a match occurs between the input term and the reference table, which gets written to the task output. A column is added to the output containing the extracted term, and another is added containing the number of occurrences. These new columns are called `Term` and `Frequency`. The reference table is cached in memory for performance reasons.

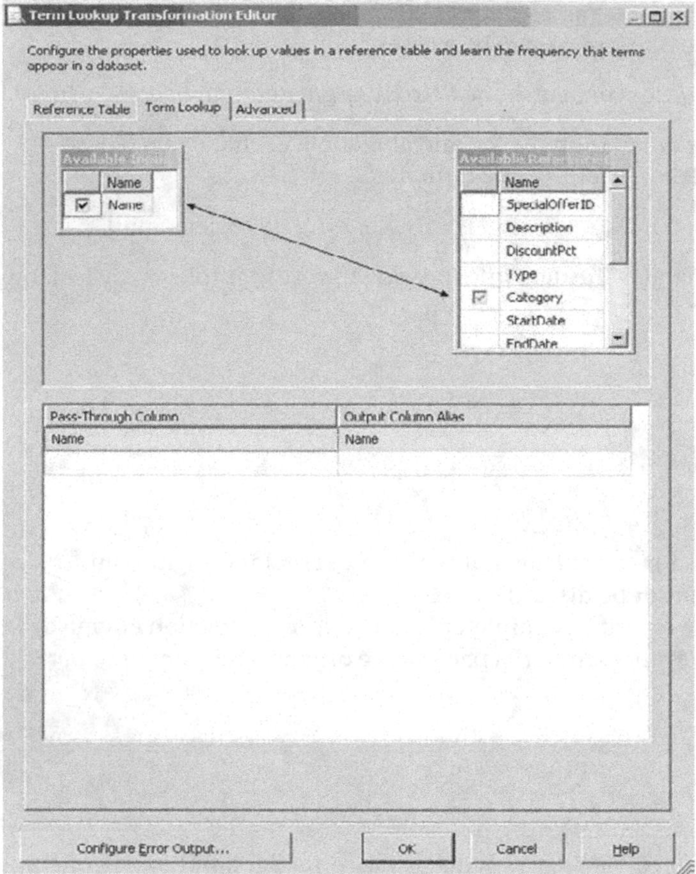

Figure 10-32. *Specifying the column mapping for the lookup*

You need to remember certain rules when you use this component:

- A noncapitalized word can be matched with a word that is capitalized at the beginning of a sentence. For example, the match between *student* and *Student* succeeds when *Student* is the first word in a sentence.
- If a plural form of the noun or noun phrase exists in the reference table, the lookup matches only the plural form of the noun or noun phrase. For example, all instances of *students* are counted separately from the instances of *student*.
- If only the singular form of the word is found in the reference table, both the singular and the plural forms of the word or phrase are matched to the singular form. For example, if the lookup table contains *student*, and the transformation finds *student* and *students*, both words are counted as a match for the lookup term *student*.
- If the text in the input column is a lemmatized noun phrase, only the last word in the noun phrase is affected by normalization. For example, the lemmatized version of *doctors appointments* is *doctors appointment*.

- When a lookup item contains terms that overlap in the reference set—that is, a subterm is found in more than one reference record—the `Term Lookup` transformation returns only one lookup result.
- The `Term Lookup` transformation can match nouns and noun phrases that contain special characters, and the data in the reference table may include these characters. The special characters are : %, @, &, $, #, *, :, ;, ., , , !, ?, <, >, +, =, ^, ~, |, \, /, (,), [,], {, }, “, and ‘.

Finally, each input column has an `InputColumnType` property that signifies how the column is handled as part of the task (see Figure 10-33).

Figure 10-33. *My solitary input column InputColumnType = 2*

The possible `InputColumnType` values are described in Table 10-23.

Table 10-23. *InputColumnType Values*

Value	Description
0	The column is not used in the lookup and is passed through to the output.
1	The column is used only by the lookup operation.
2	The column is used by the lookup operation and is also passed through to the output.

Unpivot

1 input, 1 output, 1 error output

Everything I wrote about the Pivot task is also true here, except in reverse of course—with some of the options removed.

This task essentially encapsulates the functionality of an *unpivot query* in SQL. An unpivot query increases the normalization of a less-normalized or denormalized data set by "rotating" the data back around a central point—a value.

I'll take you through an example that performs the reverse operation from the one I explained with the Pivot query. It uses the AdventureWorks sample database again. The following query is the source for this operation:

```
SELECT          'Total Sales' AS TotalSales, [Europe] as Europe, [NorthAmerica] as

NorthAmerica, [Pacific] as Pacific
FROM
(SELECT             st.[Group] AS Territory, sc.CustomerID as CustID
                    FROM            Sales.Customer sc inner join Sales.SalesTerritory
st
                              ON st.TerritoryID = sc.TerritoryID) AS Source
PIVOT
(
            COUNT(CustID)
                FOR Territory IN (Europe, NorthAmerica, Pacific)
) AS PivT
```

As a reminder, this query produces the result shown in Table 10-24: the Groups are produced as columns, not rows, and the SalesTotal for each territory is stored in the column value.

Table 10-24. *Pivoted Values*

	Europe	NorthAmerica	Pacific
Total Sales	5623	9931	3631

I want to get the data back into the normalized form I had in the Pivot example before the pivot operation. It aggregates the number of sales grouped by the territory, as in the output shown as Table 10-25.

Table 10-25. *Normalized Data*

Group	TotalSales
Europe	5623
NorthAmerica	9931
Pacific	3631

You need to unpivot the data set back around the Group column. Easy! To configure the task to perform the unpivot operation, the following steps need to be taken. As always, make sure you have created a new package with a single `Data Flow Task` added to the Control Flow design surface. Switch over to the Data Flow design surface before beginning with Step 1:

1. Configure a `SqlClient DataReader Source` to use the query in Listing 10-2 (by populating the `SqlCommand` property).

Listing 10-2. *SQL Query for Selecting Pivoted Data*

```
SELECT              'Total Sales' AS TotalSales, [Europe] as Europe, [NorthAmerica]

 as NorthAmerica, [Pacific] as Pacific
FROM
(
SELECT             st.[Group] AS Territory, sc.CustomerID as CustID
FROM                Sales.Customer sc inner join Sales.SalesTerritory st
                       ON st.TerritoryID = sc.TerritoryID
) AS Source
PIVOT
(
              COUNT(CustID)
             FOR Territory IN (Europe, NorthAmerica, Pacific)
) AS PivT
```

2. Drop an `Unpivot` component from the Toolbox onto the design surface, somewhere below the `DataReader Source`.

3. After connecting the `DataReader Source` output arrow to the `Unpivot` transform, right-click the transform and select Show Advanced Editor.... The basic edit functionality just doesn't cut it for this transform.

4. Switch to the Input Columns tab. Put checkmarks against all columns except `TotalSales`, as shown in Figure 10-34.

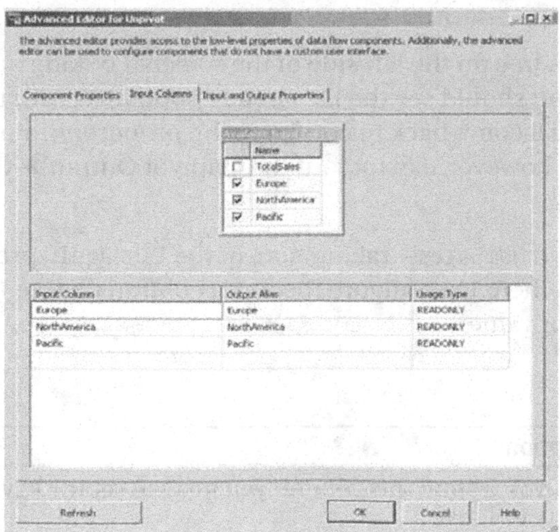

Figure 10-34. *Choose input columns from those available.*

5. Switch over onto the Input and Output Properties tab, shown in Figure 10-35. Let me assure you that your worst fears are indeed realized: you will again be playing `LineageID` roulette.

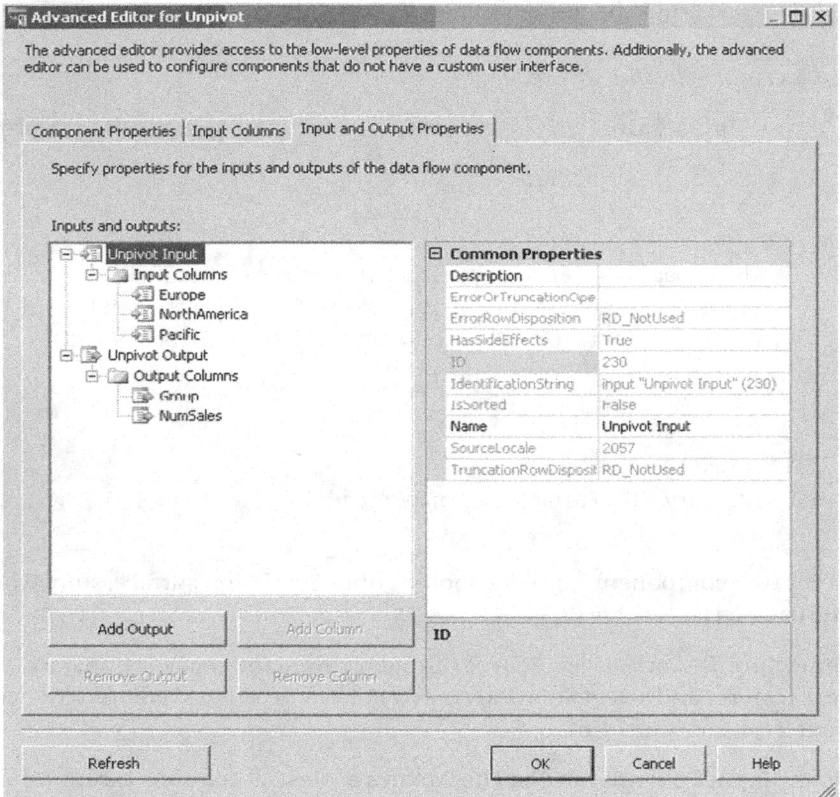

Figure 10-35. *Configuring the input and output columns to create the unpivot*

6. Expand out the inputs-and-outputs tree on the left side of the screen. Looking under Unpivot Input ➤ Input Columns, you should see the list already populated with the columns you selected in Step 4. You'll come back to configure the properties for these columns shortly. While you're here, however, expand out the Unpivot Output ➤ Output Columns branch too.

7. Add two output columns—`Group` and `NumSales`—taking note of the `LineageID` property values for both because you'll need them to configure the input columns. Table 10-26 shows the properties to set and their values.

Table 10-26. *Output Columns Properties*

Column	PivotKey	Description
Group	`True`	To unpivot around this column you need to set the `PivotKey` property to `True`.
NumSales	`False`	

Figures 10-36 and 10-37 show the properties window for each of the configured output columns.

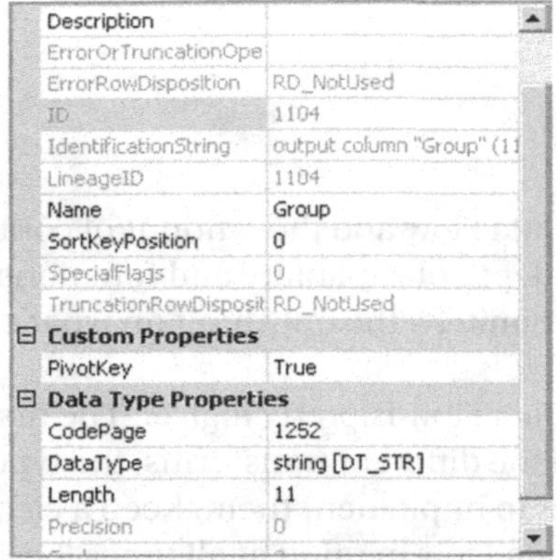

Figure 10-36. *The Group output column*

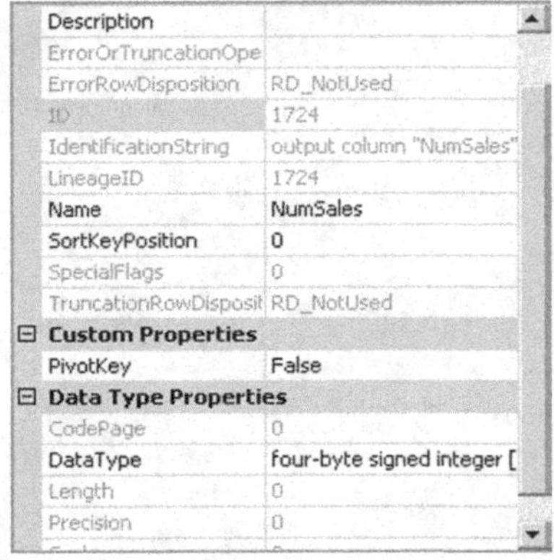

Figure 10-37. *The NumSales output column*

8. Go back to the Unpivot Input columns branch and configure the columns that you Selected in Step 4. Table 10-27 shows the configuration values for the columns.

Table 10-27. *Configuration Values*

Column Name	Destination Column	Pivot Key Value
Europe	`LineageID` for `NumSales` output column (1724 in Figure 10-37)	`Europe`
NorthAmerica	`LineageID` for `NumSales` output column (1724 in Figure 10-37)	`NorthAmerica`
Pacific	`LineageID` for `NumSales` output column (1724 in Figure 10-37)	`Pacific`

That's it—the example is completely configured. You can, optionally, create some kind of destination component now and attach it to the Data Flow to see the results.

Once again, with the `Unpivot` transform I can only suggest that hands-on use will give you a better idea of how it works. I definitely suggest that before you configure this transform, you create a suitable SQL unpivot query to provide the basis of, and a reference to, the unpivot the task is supposed to perform.

Summary

The number of chapters in this book devoted to the Data Flow and the amount of content contained in each accurately reflects the Data Flow's depth of capability and functionality—but that's not all. The Data Flow can be expanded indefinitely: the only limit on what can be produced is your imagination.

The best advice I can give when it comes to the Data Flow is pretty logical. The first thing to do is to learn the principles and practice of each of the different transforms, the types of input and output available to each, and the best times to implement them. Keep a clear and consistent idea of what you're trying to do with the Data Flow in mind at all times, because it can be easy to lose focus on the end goal when so many transformation options are on offer.

CHAPTER 11

Data Flow Destinations

As the final piece of the ETL puzzle, Data Flow destinations form perhaps the most vital function of all—delivering data to its destination. These Data Flow end points can be targets such as a database table, a flat file, an XML document, or all sorts of other storage media. All destination components share a common structure in that they have inputs (usually a single input) and no outputs.

Of course a Data Flow could require multiple destinations. This is entirely possible to achieve by using multiple destination components. Data can be piped into a destination component at any point of the Data Flow, and a `Multicast` transform lets you pipe the same Data Flow to multiple destinations.

This is the final chapter about the Data Flow. I'll tie up loose ends and address the all-important destination components in detail. By the end of this chapter your ETL destiny, at least as far as SSIS goes, will be in your own hands. You'll be able to take data from a source, transform it (perhaps many times and in many different ways), and drop it into a destination.

Data Mining Model Training

1 input

The `Data Mining Model Training` destination component trains data-mining models using sorted data contained in the upstream Data Flow. The received data is piped through the SSAS data-mining algorithms for the relevant model.

The first configuration task is to provide connection details for the required SSAS instance on the component editor screen's Connection tab, shown in Figure 11-1. On the same tab you then choose the mining structure the required mining model resides in.

The Columns tab (shown in Figure 11-2) lets you specify the mapping between the input columns and the columns in the mining structure.

You need to pay attention to the sort order of Data Flow entering this component, whatever the underlying structure of the mining model in use. Any structure using the content types of `KEY TIME` or `KEY SEQUENCE` must be sorted on that column before hitting the model, or else the processing of the model can fail.

This task will probably only make sense to anyone using the data-mining functionality in SSAS. The more of you who fit that description the better, considering its power and usefulness.

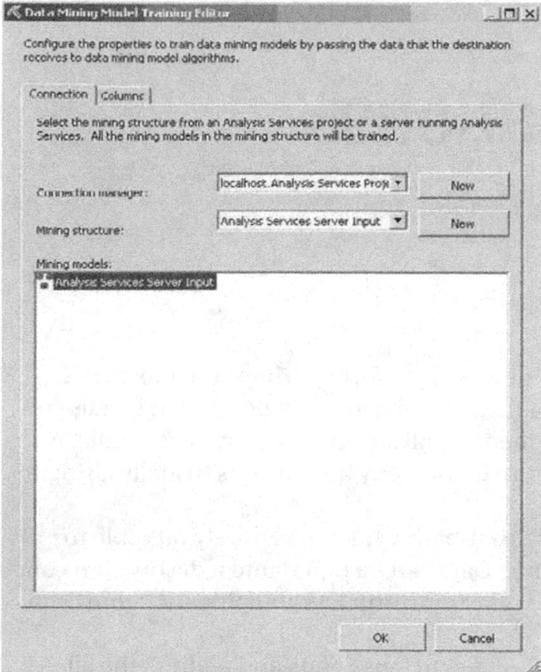

Figure 11-1. *Selecting the mining model to train*

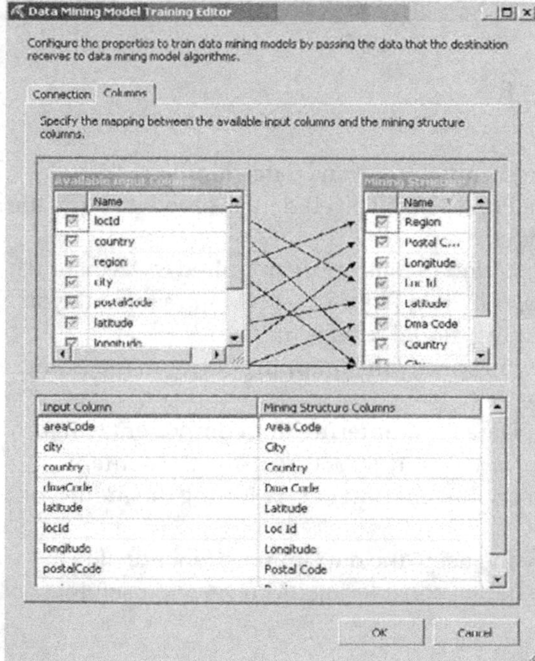

Figure 11-2. *Defining column mappings*

DataReader Destination

1 input

The `DataReader Destination` serves up the Data Flow for external consumption via an ADO.NET `DataReader`. This means, for example, that the results of an SSIS package executed from a .NET assembly can be consumed by connecting to the `DataReader Destination`.

Task properties can be set using the main configuration screen, shown in Figure 11-3.

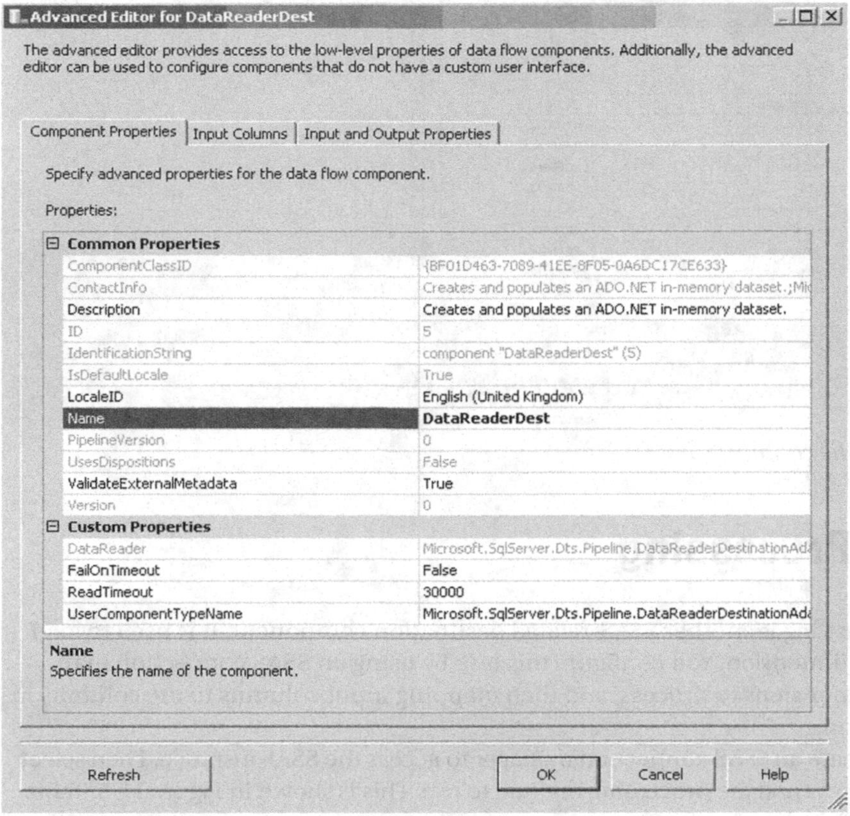

Figure 11-3. *Setting DataReader task properties*

The Input Columns tab (see Figure 11-4) lets you select columns to use at the destination from available input columns. You can specify each column as read only or read/write via the exposed `UsageType` property.

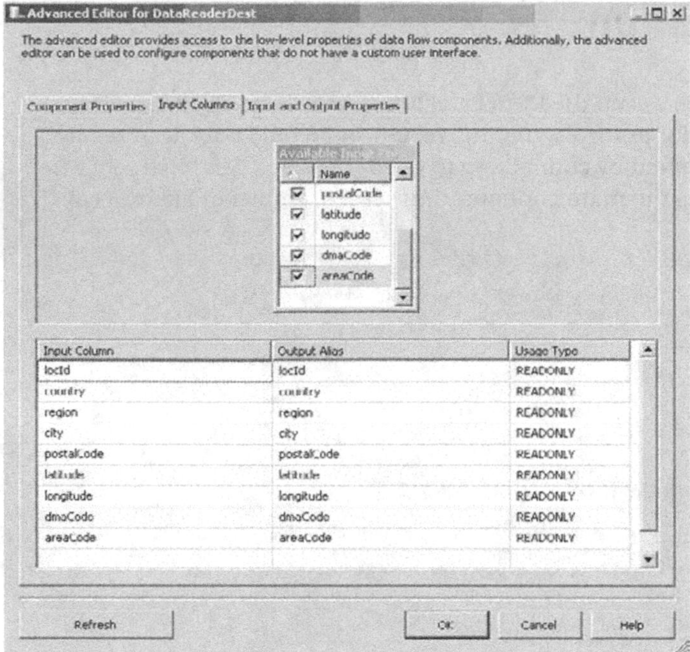

Figure 11-4. *Selecting the columns to use*

Dimension Processing

1 input

Dimension Processing is another SSAS-related destination component. It is used to load and process an SSAS dimension. You configure this task by using an SSAS connection manager, selecting the dimensions to process, and then mapping input columns to the columns in the selected dimension.

First, select or create an SSAS connection manager to access the SSAS instance. Then select the dimension to process and the processing method to use. This is shown in Figure 11-5. Table 11-1 shows the possible values for the Processing method property.

Table 11-1. *Processing Method Values*

Value	Description
Add (incremental)	Adds new dimension data in an incremental fashion.
Full	Processes the dimension by truncating all data then reprocessing it.
Update	Processes the dimension by rereading the data and updating the dimension.

The next step in configuring this task is to provide the mapping between the input columns and the destination dimension columns, as in Figure 11-6. Naturally, the data type and length should be compatible between the input and dimension columns.

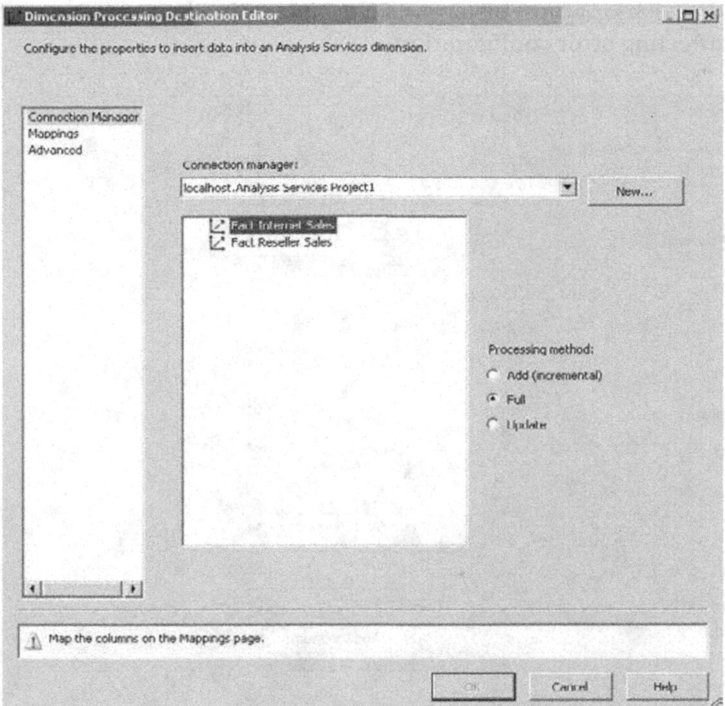

Figure 11-5. *Selecting the dimension to process*

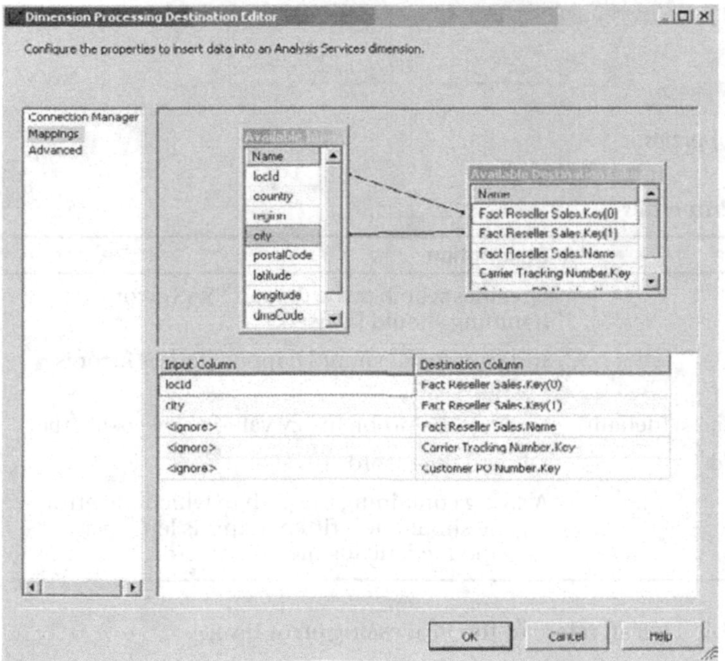

Figure 11-6. *Mapping between input and dimension columns*

The error configuration for this task is comprehensive, as can be seen in Figure 11-7. Table 11-2 shows the properties affecting error configuration.

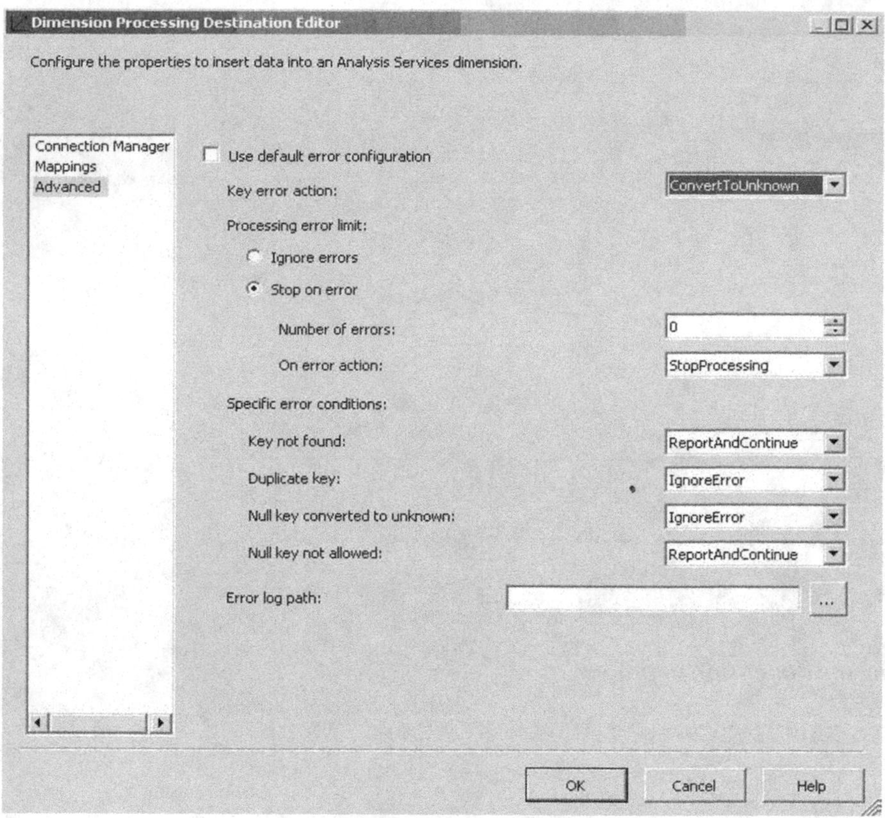

Figure 11-7. *Configuring error properties*

Table 11-2. *Error-Configuration Properties*

Property	Possible Value	Description
Use default error configuration		Specifies whether the default SSAS error handling should be used.
Key error action		Indicates what should happen if a key error is encountered.
	`ConvertToUnknown` (default)	Convert the problem key value to `UnknownMember`.
	`DiscardRecord`	Discard the record.
Error log path		A string containing the path to which the error log file should be written. If this is left unpopulated, no log file is generated.

The properties shown in Table 11-3 all relate to the Processing error limit.

Table 11-3. *Processing Error Limit Properties*

Property	Possible Value	Description
Ignore errors		All errors should be ignored.
Stop on error		Action should be taken on error.
Number of errors		The number of errors to permit before throwing an error.
On error action		The action to take upon throwing an error.
	`StopProcessing`	Processing of the dimension should stop.
	`StopLogging`	Any error logging should stop.

The final group of error configuration properties, listed in Table 11-4, all relate to Specific error conditions.

Table 11-4. *Specific Error Conditions*

Property	Possible Value	Description
Key not found		
	`IgnoreError`	The error should be ignored and processing should continue.
	`ReportAndContinue`	The error should be reported and processing should continue.
	`ReportAndStop`	The error should be reported and processing should stop.
Duplicate key		
	`IgnoreError`	The error should be ignored and processing should continue.
	`ReportAndContinue`	The error should be reported and processing should continue.
	`ReportAndStop`	The error should be reported and processing should stop.
Null key converted to unknown		
	`IgnoreError`	The error should be ignored and processing should continue.
	`ReportAndContinue`	The error should be reported and processing should continue.
	`ReportAndStop`	The error should be reported and processing should stop.
Null key not allowed		
	`IgnoreError`	The error should be ignored and processing should continue.
	`ReportAndContinue`	The error should be reported and processing should continue.
	`ReportAndStop`	The error should be reported and processing should stop.

Excel Destination

1 or more inputs, 1 error output

The `Excel Destination` component delivers data from the Data Flow into an Excel worksheet, using the `Excel` connection manager. The configuration editor for this component is shown in Figure 11-8.

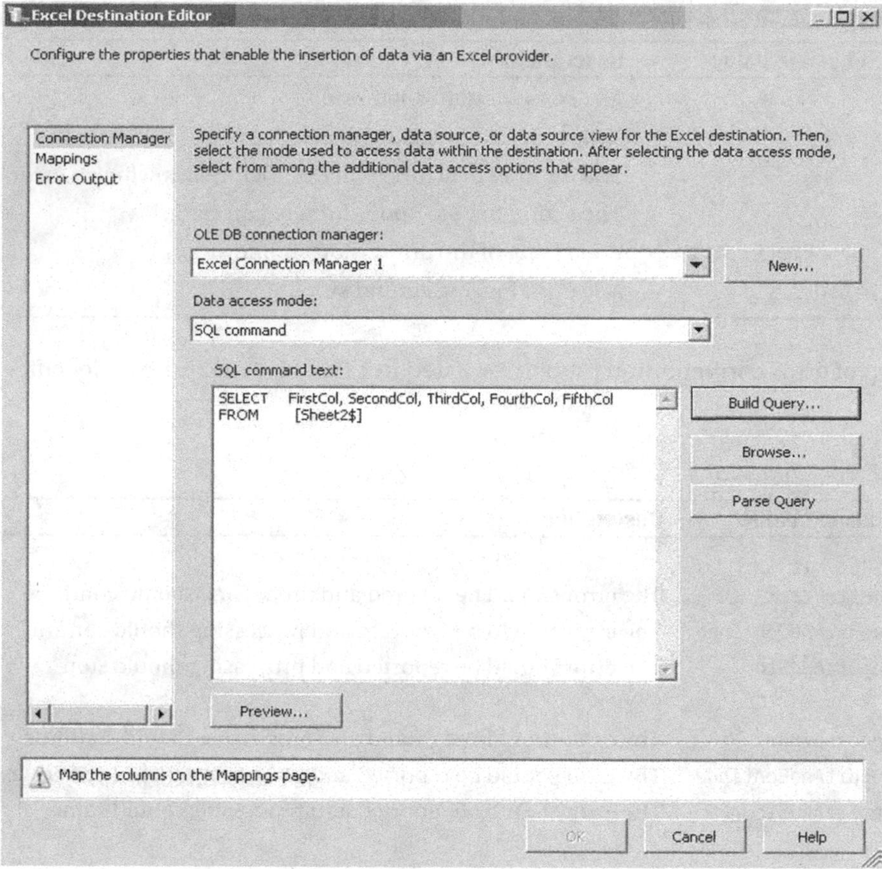

Figure 11-8. *Excel Destination configuration dialog*

The `Excel Destination` has a number of options for how the destination Excel file should be accessed. The exposed Data access mode property lets you select this method. Potential values for this property are shown in Table 11-5.

Table 11-5. *The Data Access Mode Property*

Possible Value	Description
Table or view	Specifies that a particular worksheet or range should be used as the destination in the Excel file.
Table name or view name variable	Specifies that a variable is used to specify the name of the worksheet or range name to use as the destination in the Excel file. The variable name in use must be specified in the `VariableName` property.
SQL command	Specifies that a pseudo-SQL query must be used (as specified in the SQL command text property).

The SQL command option that is offered as a data-access mode must contain a valid SQL statement to select the columns that serve as the destination in the Excel file. Figure 11-9 shows how I've used the Query Builder to generate the query. I selected Add Table on the Query Builder screen to add the possible Excel document contents to the upper window. From there it was a simple task to select the columns I wished to use as the destination.

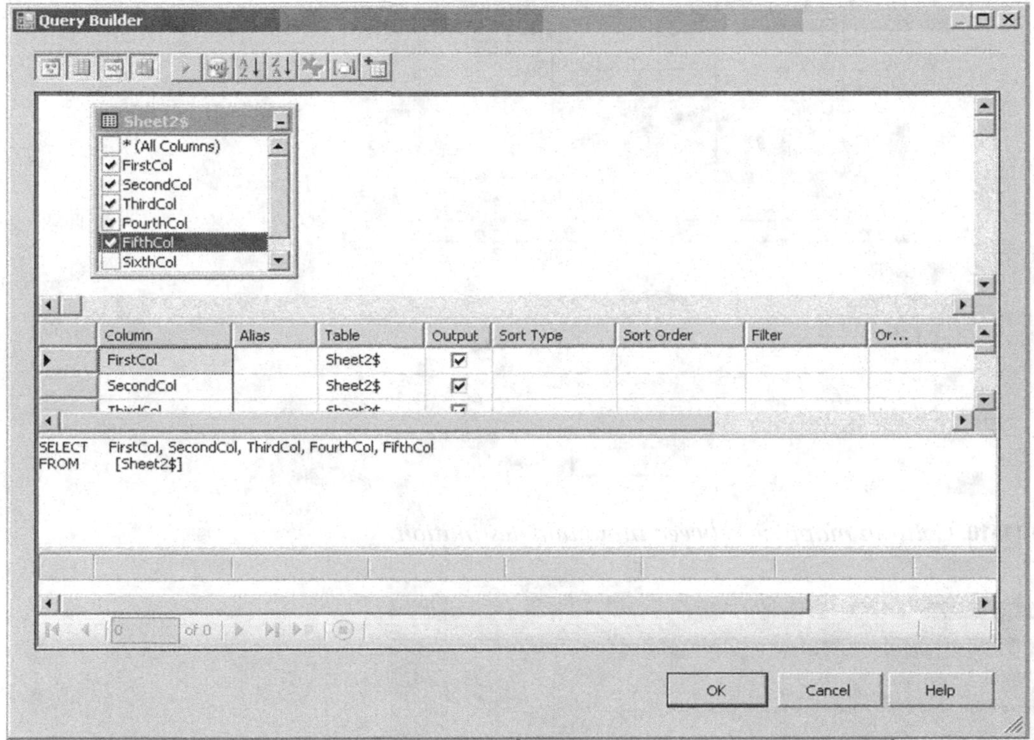

Figure 11-9. *The easy way of choosing destination columns*

The SQL statement generated as a consequence of my selections is shown at the bottom of the screen in Figure 11-9. The only obvious difference in the statement from the usual SQL format is the use of `[Sheet2$]` in the `FROM` clause. (Obviously, if the worksheet had a different name, that would be used here instead.)

Once the destination has been fully configured, you can perform the mappings by moving to the next section on the editor screen. This is shown in Figure 11-10.

The component attempts to perform column mapping between the input and destination columns where possible, based upon column name. You can map additional columns by dragging a column from the Input Column collection to the Destination Column collection.

If the destination columns' data types haven't been set in the Excel document already, you can set them by using the advanced editor for this task. Selecting the Input and Output Properties tab yields the screen shown in Figure 11-11.

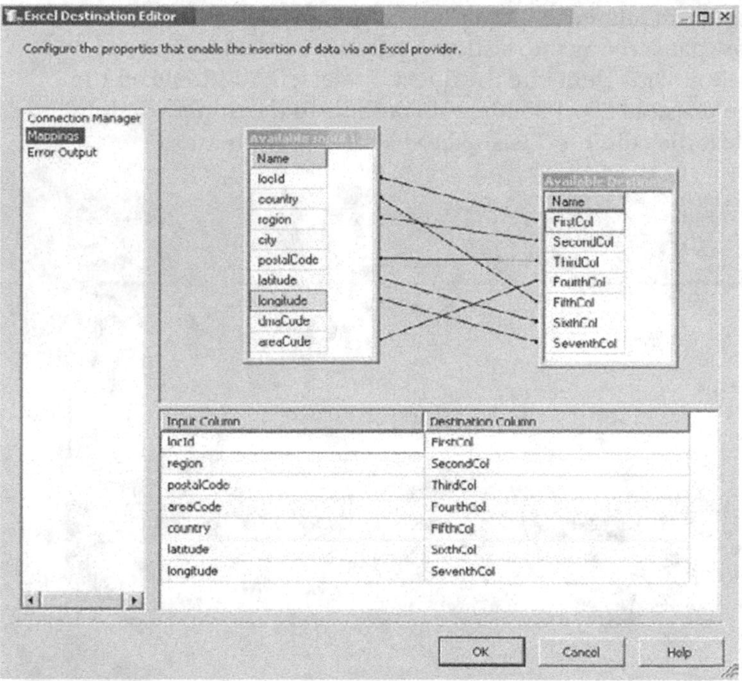

Figure 11-10. *Column mapping between input and destination*

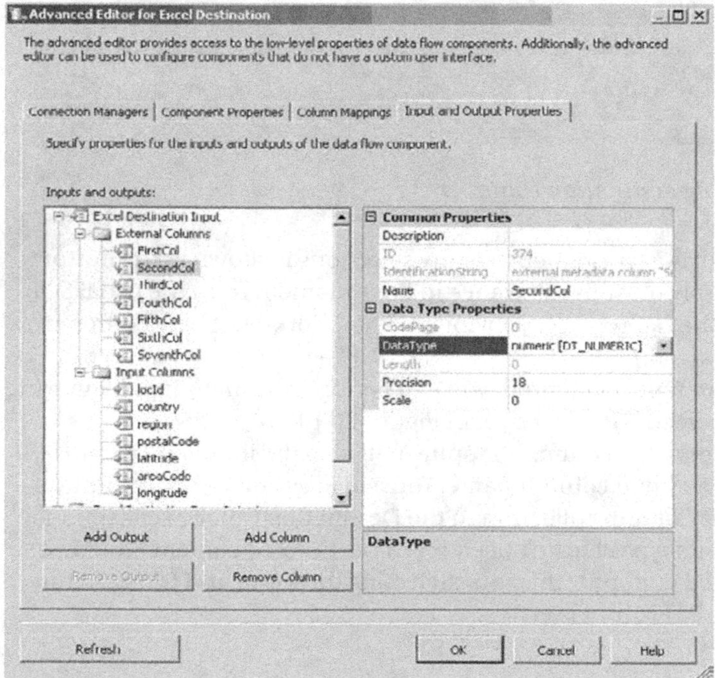

Figure 11-11. *Advanced editing: setting column data types*

By expanding out the Excel Destination Input tree on the left side and viewing each of the values under External Columns, you can easily set the data type for each of the columns from the Data Type Properties window.

■ **Note** Excel files created with Microsoft Office 2007 must be accessed using the OLEDB connection manager—for now, at least. Alternatively, check out Chapter 15 and write a custom connection manager.

Flat File Destination

1 input

The Flat File Destination component writes data out to a text file in one of the standard flat-file formats: delimited, fixed width, fixed width with row delimiter, or ragged right.

Selecting Edit... for the Flat File Destination presents a fairly simple and familiar configuration screen, as shown in Figure 11-12.

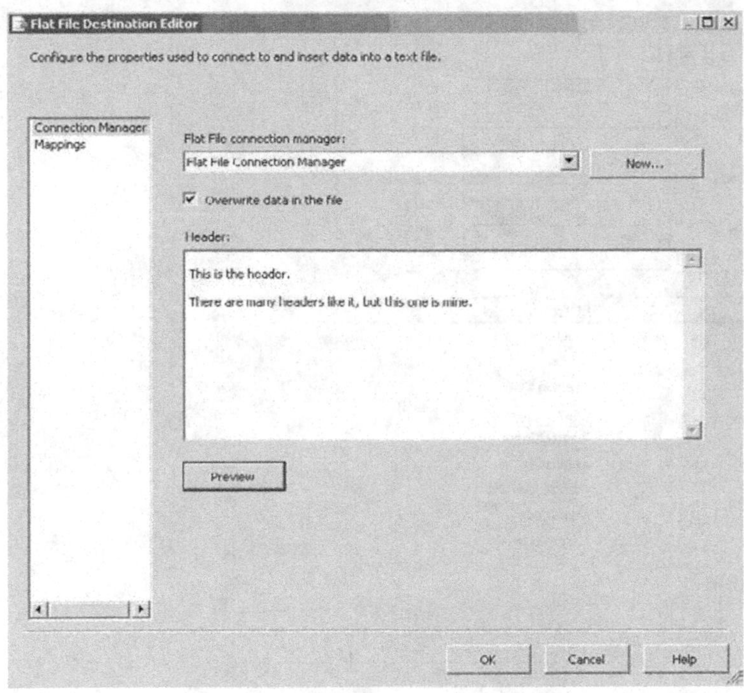

Figure 11-12. *Configuring the connection manager*

A new or existing Flat File connection manager must be defined first. Then you can set the two additional configuration options described in Table 11-6.

Table 11-6. *Basic Flat File Destination Properties*

Property	Description
Overwrite data in the file	Specifies whether the destination file should have its contents overwritten.
Header	Allows entry of a header that will appear at the very start of the destination file. It could include column headings or some kind of introductory text.

Figure 11-13 shows the column-mapping screen in the editor. The component attempts to perform column mapping between the input and destination columns where possible, based on column name. You can map additional columns by dragging a column from the Input Column list to the Destination Column list.

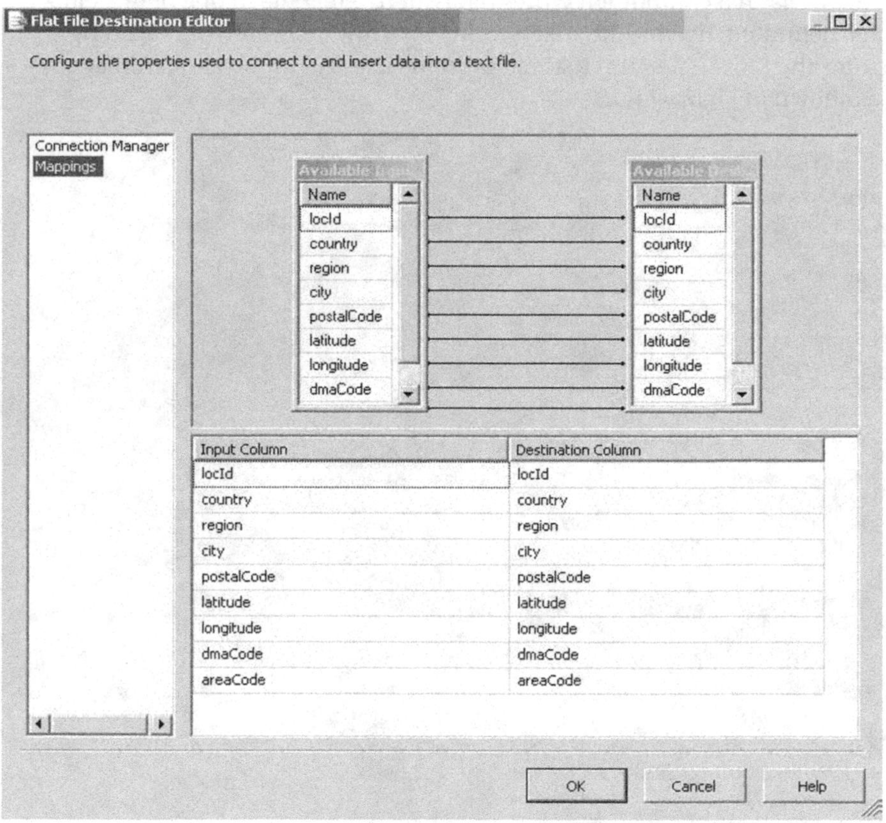

Figure 11-13. *Column mapping for the Flat File Destination*

OLE DB Destination

1 input

The `OLE DB Destination` component inserts data into any OLE DB–compliant data source.

As is usual with Data Flow destinations, the first thing to do is to create a new OLE DB connection manager for the executable to use or to select an existing one. Additional options are available to tailor the destination to best suit requirements.

The first of these options is the Data access mode, as shown in Figure 11-14. The first two possible values for this property are described in Table 11-7. This list is completed later in this section.

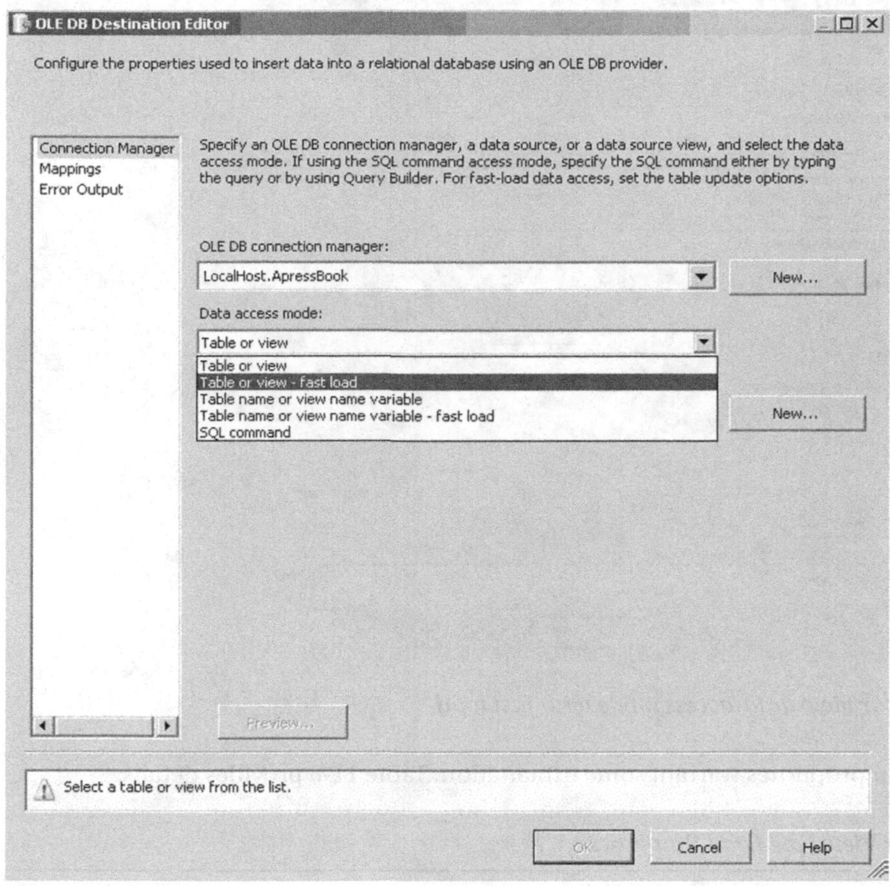

Figure 11-14. *Data access mode, including fast load*

Table 11-7. *Data Access Mode Values*

Value	Description
Table or view	Means that the related TableOrViewName property needs populating with the name of the table or view to use. Alternatively, a new table can be created.
Table or view – fast load	Specifies that the TableOrViewName property will contain the name of the table or view to use (or allows a new table to be created) and that fast load (bulk insert) will be used to write the input data to the destination.

Specifying Table or view – fast load as the Data access mode property exposes a further clutch of properties, as shown in Figure 11-15.

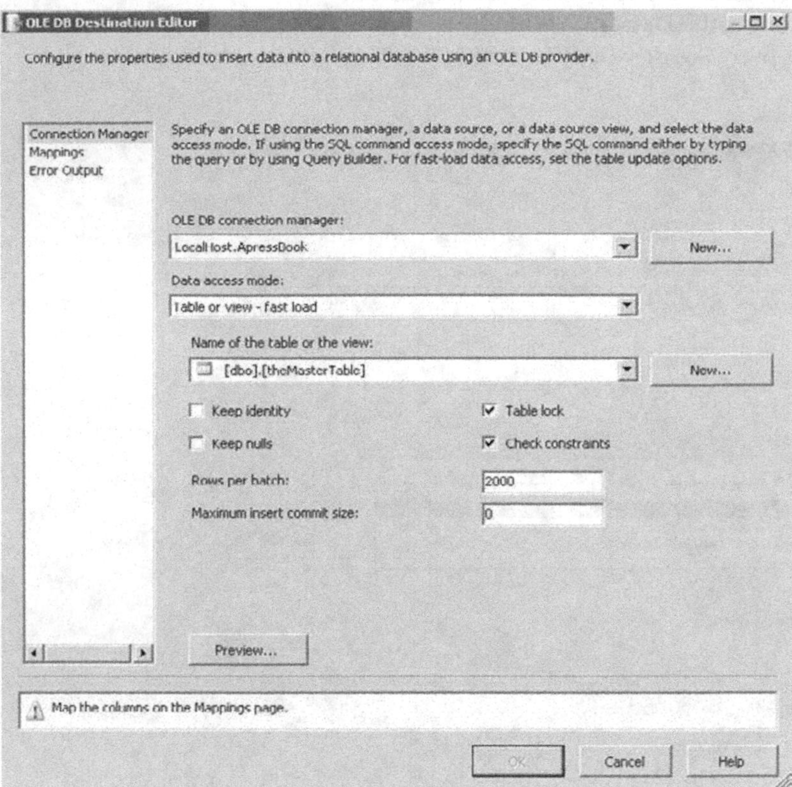

Figure 11-15. *Table or view data-access mode with fast load*

The additional properties warrant some explanation. Table 11-8 provides details.

Table 11-8. *Table or View Fast Load Properties*

Property	Description
Keep identity	Indicates whether identity values from the input columns should be retained at the destination (`true`) or that new SQL Server–generated values should be used (`false`).
Table lock	Indicates whether a table-level lock should be acquired for the duration of the operation.
Keep nulls	Indicates whether null values in input columns should be retained.
Check constraints	Specifies whether constraints are checked at the destination.
Rows per batch	Specifies the number of rows in a batch.
Maximum insert commit size	Specifies the size of the batch the component will attempt to commit. The default value of zero indicates that rows should be committed only after all rows are processed.

Two values for Data access mode offer the use of a variable. Table 11-9 describes them.

Table 11-9. *Data Access Modes with Variable*

Value	Description
Table name or view name variable	Specifies that the table or view name to use resides in a variable. This variable is specified in the `VariableName` property.
Table name or view name variable – fast load	Like a combination of the previous two Data access mode types, this option (as shown in Figure 11-16) is a bulk-insert type.

Figure 11-16 shows that the configuration screen remains incredibly similar when the data-access modes in Table 11-9 are selected. This time, however, a variable is used to hold the name of the table or view to use and is stored in the `VariableName` property.

The final possible value for Data access mode is SQL command. Predictably, choosing this option gives you the ability to enter a SQL statement that selects the columns to use from a destination table or view as the destination.

Once the connection, input, and destination configurations are set, the next section of the editor is for mapping the input columns to the destination columns (see Figure 11-17). Any columns from the input not mapped to destination columns are marked as <ignore>.

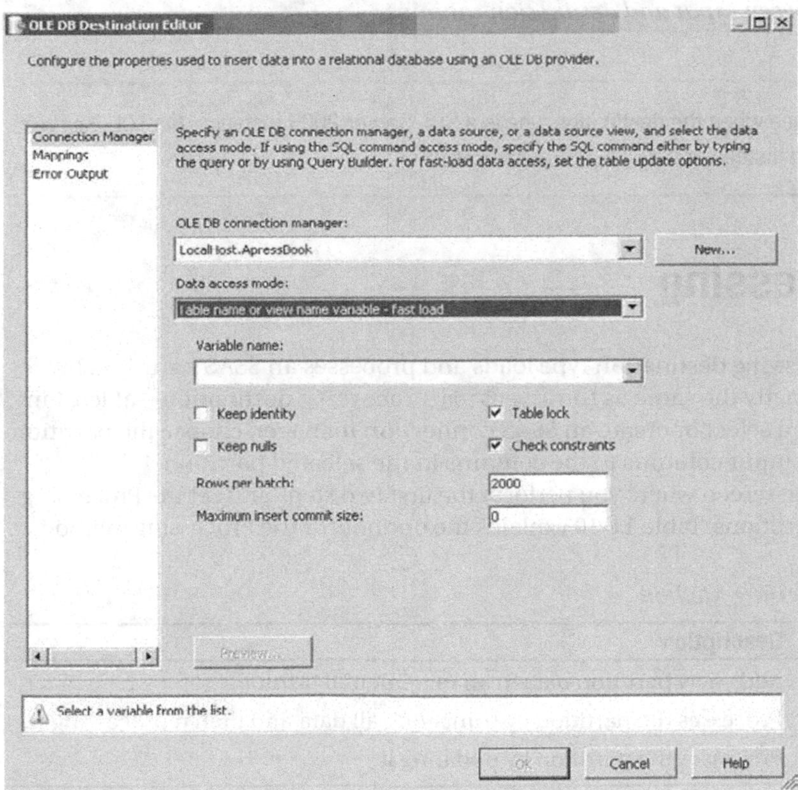

Figure 11-16. *Choosing to use a variable to express the table or view name with fast load*

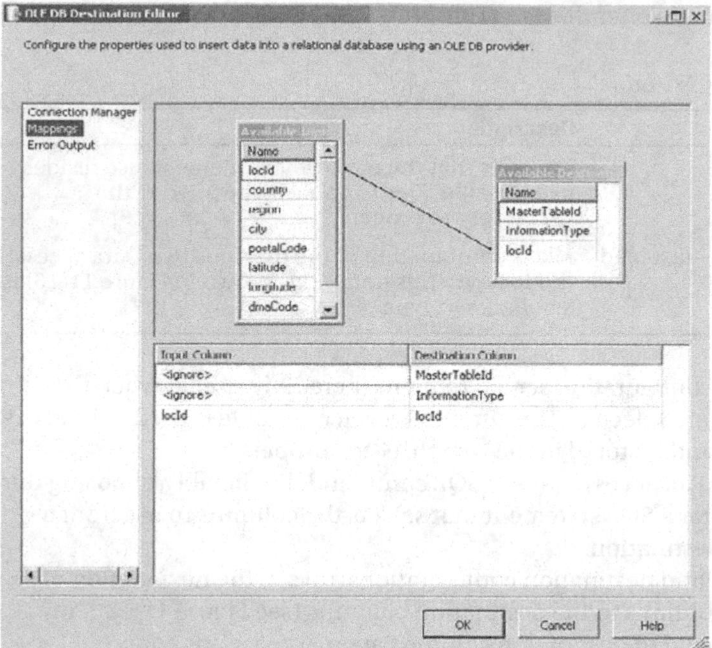

Figure 11-17. *Mapping between input and destination columns*

■ **Note** For better performance when the destination type is a SQL Server 2005 instance, the `SQL Server Destination` should be used instead of the `OLE DB Destination`.

Partition Processing

1 input

The `Partition Processing` destination type loads and processes an SSAS partition. In many ways it is almost exactly the same as the `Dimension Processing` destination—at least in terms of configuration. You select or create an SSAS connection manager, choose the partition to process, and then map input columns to the columns in the selected partition.

Figure 11-18 shows the screen where you perform the first two steps and set the Processing method to use with the partitions. Table 11-10 explains the options for the Processing method.

Table 11-10. *Partition Processing Method*

Value	Description
Add (incremental)	Adds new partition data in an incremental fashion.
Full	Processes the partition by truncating all data and then reprocessing it.
Data only	Processes the partition by updating it.

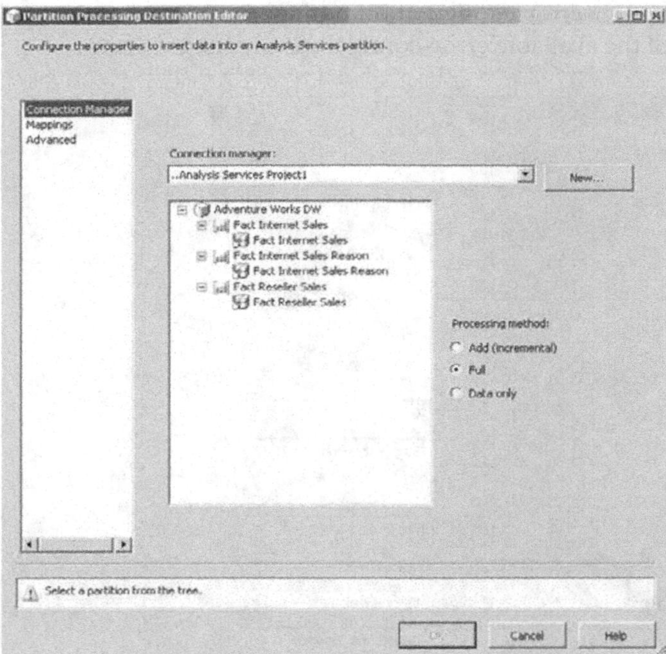

Figure 11-18. *Selecting the partition to process*

The next configuration step is to provide the mapping between the input columns and the destination partition columns, as in Figure 11-19. The data type and length should be compatible between the two sets of columns.

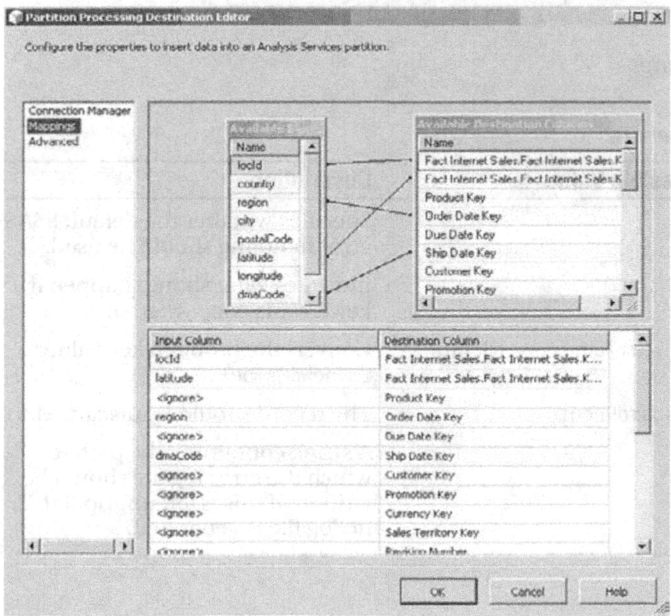

Figure 11-19. *Mapping between input and partition columns*

Figure 11-20 shows the comprehensive error-configuration settings for this task. Tables 11-11, 11-12, and 11-13 look at each of the available error-configuration settings in turn.

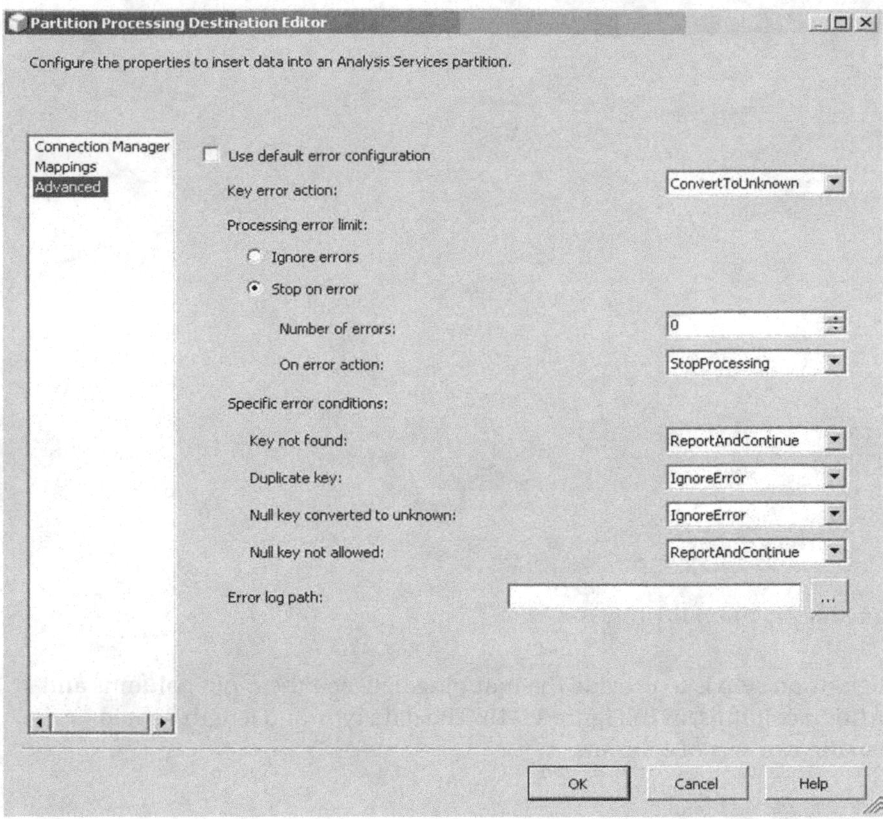

Figure 11-20. *Configuring error properties*

Table 11-11. *Error-Configuration Properties*

Property	Possible Value	Description
Use default error configuration		Specifies whether the default SSAS error handling should be used.
Key error action		Indicates what should happen if a key error is encountered.
	`ConvertToUnknown` (default)	Convert the problem key value to `UnknownMember`.
	`DiscardRecord`	The record should be discarded.
Error log path		A string containing the path to which the error log file should be written. If this is left unpopulated, no log file is generated.

The next collection of properties all relate to the Processing error limit. They are shown in Table 11-12.

Table 11-12. *Processing Error Limit Properties*

Property	Possible Value	Description
Ignore errors		All errors should be ignored.
Stop on error		Action should be taken on error.
Number of errors	The number of errors to permit before throwing an error.	
On error action	The action to take upon throwing an error.	
	`StopProcessing`	Processing of the dimension should stop.
	`StopLogging`	Any error logging should stop

The final group of error-configuration properties all relate to Specific error conditions and are listed in Table 11-13.

Table 11-13. *Specific Error Conditions*

Property	Possible Value	Description
Key not found		
	`IgnoreError`	The error should be ignored and processing should continue.
	`ReportAndContinue`	The error should be reported and processing should continue.
	`ReportAndStop`	The error should be reported and processing should stop.
Duplicate key		
	`IgnoreError`	The error should be ignored and processing should continue.
	`ReportAndContinue`	The error should be reported and processing should continue.
	`ReportAndStop`	The error should be reported and processing should stop.
Null key converted to unknown		
	`IgnoreError`	The error should be ignored and processing should continue.
	`ReportAndContinue`	The error should be reported and processing should continue.
	`ReportAndStop`	The error should be reported and processing should stop.
Null key not allowed		
	`IgnoreError`	The error should be ignored and processing should continue.
	`ReportAndContinue`	The error should be reported and processing should continue.
	`ReportAndStop`	The error should be reported and processing should stop.

Raw File Destination

1 input

The Raw File Destination is all about raw speed. It is an entirely native format and can be exported and imported more rapidly than any other connection type, in part because the data doesn't need to pass through a connection manager.

Figure 11-21 shows the configuration screen for this component. There are only a few custom settings to be concerned with. Table 11-14 examines the settings under Custom Properties in detail.

The Input Columns tab on the editor (Figure 11-22) lets you select the input columns that should be diverted to the Raw File Destination.

Table 11-14. *Raw File Destination Custom Properties*

Property	Possible Value	Description
AccessMode		Indicates which property will be used to access the file.
	File name	Specifies that the destination raw-file path and filename is specified via the FileName property.
	File name from variable	Specifies that a variable, the name of which should be stored in the VariableName property, holds the path and filename of the destination raw file.
FileName		The file path and filename of the raw file to use.
VariableName		The variable name containing the path and filename of the file to use.
WriteOption		Indicates how file creation or overwriting should be handled.
	Append	Specifies that the raw-file data should be appended to the existing destination file if it exists. The structure of the current data must match that of the data that already exists in the file.
	Create always	Specifies that a new destination file should always be created.
	Create once	Specifies that the destination file should be created only once, and that if it already exists to fail the component.
	Truncate and append	This option specifies that the raw-file data should be appended to the existing destination file only after truncating the contents. The structure of the current data must match that of the file.

Advanced Editor for Raw File Destination

The advanced editor provides access to the low-level properties of data flow components. Additionally, the advanced editor can be used to configure components that do not have a custom user interface.

Component Properties | Input Columns | Input and Output Properties

Specify advanced properties for the data flow component.

Properties:

Common Properties	
ComponentClassID	{E2568105-9550-4F71-A638-B7FE42E66933}
ContactInfo	Loads raw data into a file.;Microsoft Corporation;Microsoft
Description	Loads raw data into a file.
ID	77
IdentificationString	component "Raw File Destination" (77)
IsDefaultLocale	True
LocaleID	English (United Kingdom)
Name	Raw File Destination
PipelineVersion	0
UsesDispositions	False
ValidateExternalMetadata	True
Version	2
Custom Properties	
AccessMode	File name
FileName	c:\temp\rawfile_ch11.raw
WriteOption	Create Always

AccessMode
Specifies the mode used to access the file.

Refresh | OK | Cancel | Help

Figure 11-21. *Very few configuration settings*

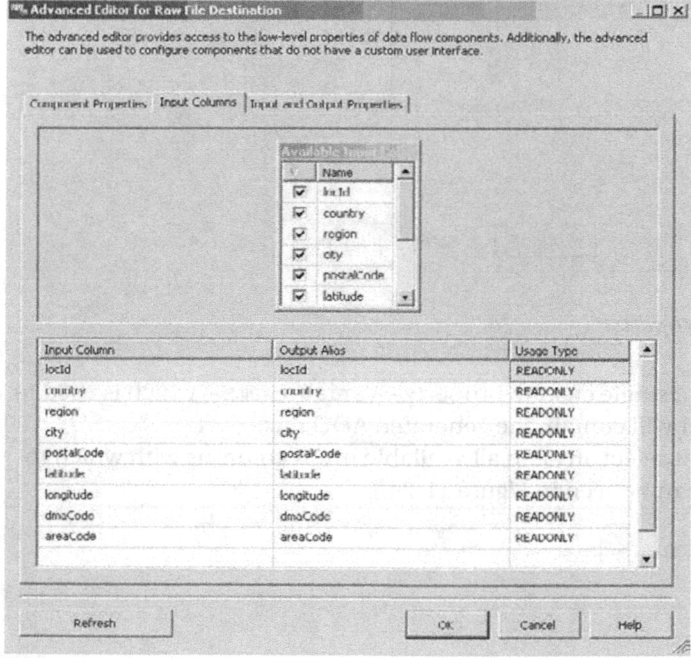

Figure 11-22. *Selecting from available input columns*

Recordset Destination

1 input

The `Recordset Destination` creates an instance of an ActiveX Data Objects (ADO) recordset and populates it with data from specified input columns. Figure 11-23 shows the configuration editor for this component.

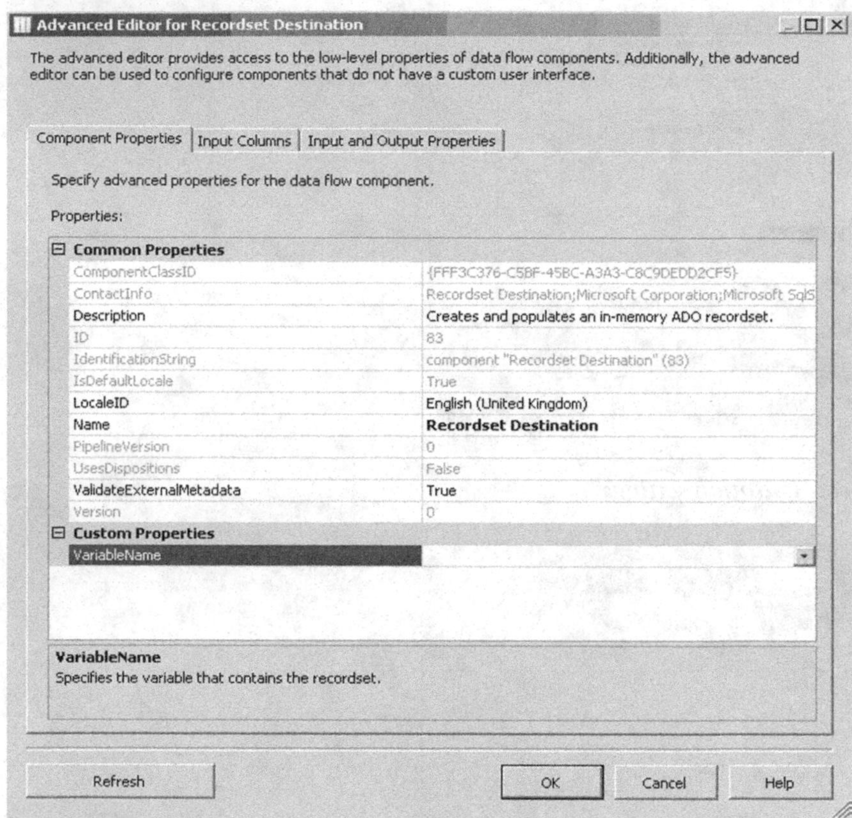

Figure 11-23. *Only a single custom property!*

This component exposes only a single custom property—`VariableName`—which is used to assign the name of the variable that will contain the generated ADO recordset.

The Input Columns tab lets you select any and all available input columns with which to populate the ADO recordset. This can be seen in Figure 11-24.

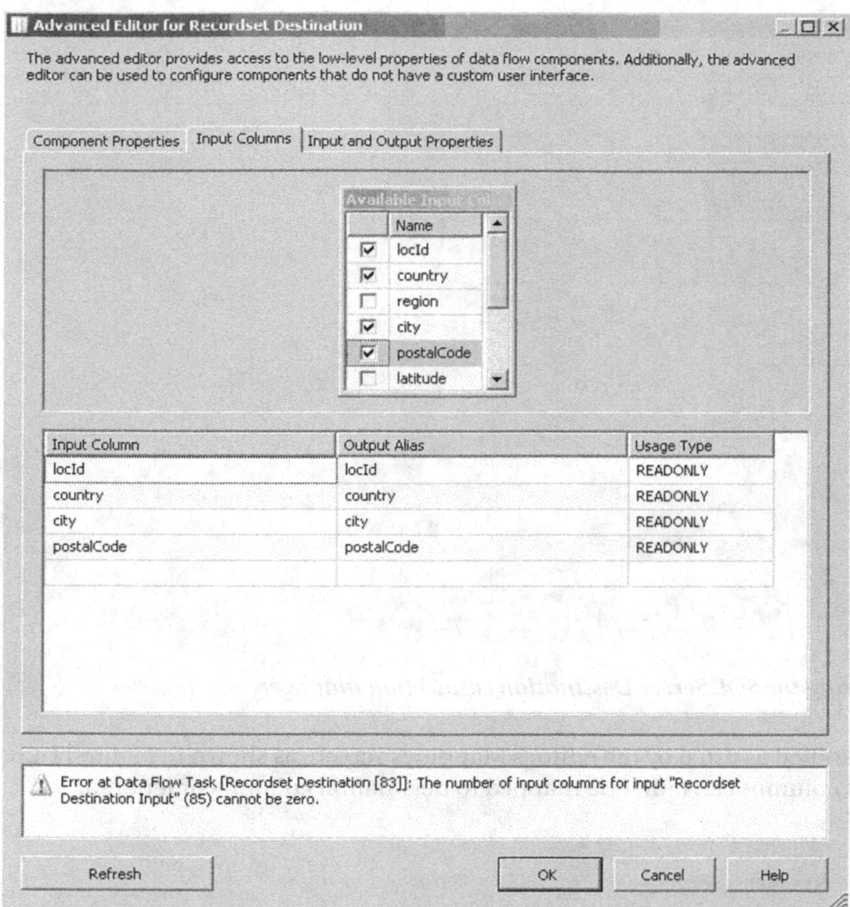

Figure 11-24. *Choosing the input columns with which to populate the recordset*

SQL Server Destination

1 input

The `SQL Server Destination` provides a connection to a SQL Server database. Selected columns from the input data are bulk inserted into a specified table or view. In other words, this destination is used to populate a table held in a SQL Server database.

Figure 11-25 shows the configuration editor, where the first task is to populate connection values. Once the OLE DB connection manager is created or selected, a table or view contained in the connection can be selected or created.

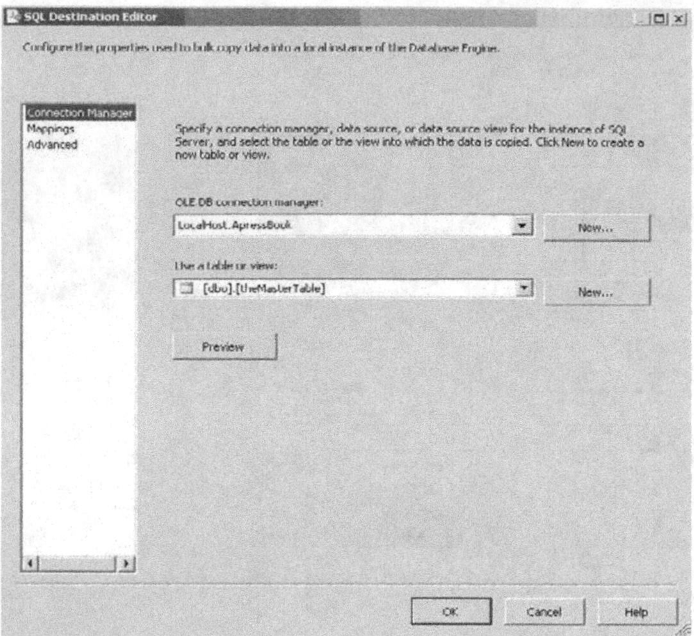

Figure 11-25. *Configuring the SQL Server Destination connection manager*

Mappings are handled as usual by the editor's Mappings screen, as shown in Figure 11-26. Here, available input columns can either be mapped to destination columns or ignored.

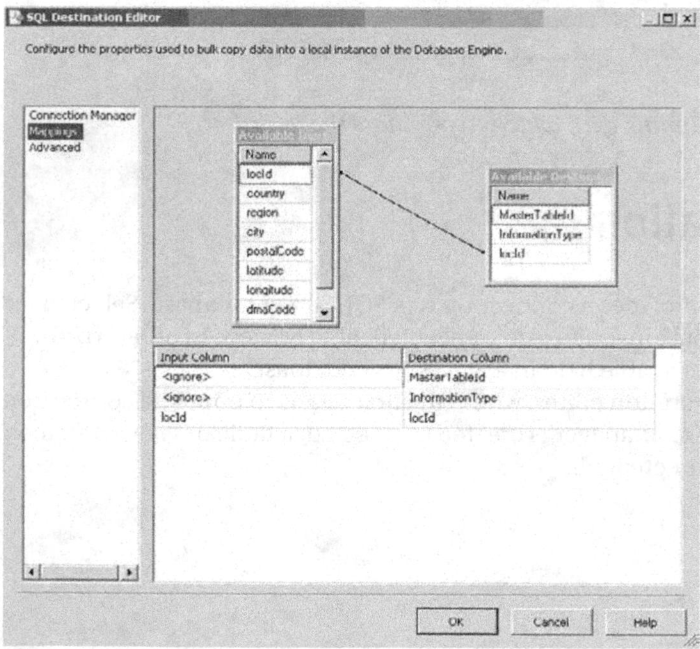

Figure 11-26. *Defining mappings*

Finally, the editor's Advanced screen (Figure 11-27) exposes a number of configurable settings that can be used to alter bulk-insert properties. Table 11-15 examines these properties.

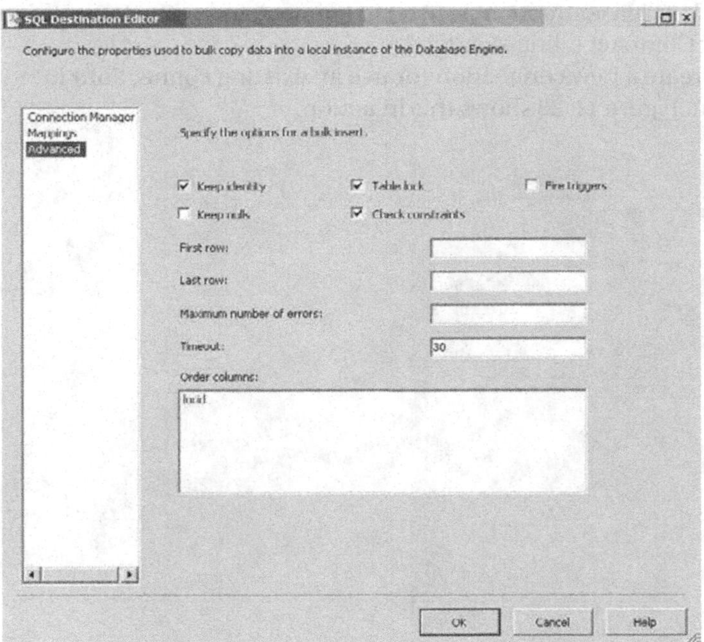

Figure 11-27. *Configuring advanced properties for bulk insert*

Table 11-15. *Bulk-Insert Properties*

Property	Description
Keep identity	Indicates whether identity values from the input columns should be retained at the destination (`true`) or that new SQL Server–generated values should be used (`false`).
Table lock	Indicates whether a table-level lock should be acquired for the duration of the operation.
Fire triggers	Indicates whether triggers are fired at the destination.
Keep nulls	Indicates whether null values in input columns should be retained.
Check constraints	Specifies whether constraints are checked at the destination.
First row	Specifies the first row to insert.
Last row	Specifies the last row to insert.
Maximum number of errors	Specifies the maximum number of errors to allow before the operation halts.
Timeout	Specifies the timeout (in seconds) of the operation.
Order columns	A delimited list of sort columns.

SQL Server Mobile Destination

1 input

The `SQL Server Mobile Destination` component is used to connect and write data to a SQL Server Mobile (or SQL Server Compact Edition) database.

The first task, as usual, is to create a new connection (or use an existing connection) to the SQL Server Mobile destination. Figure 11-28 shows this in action.

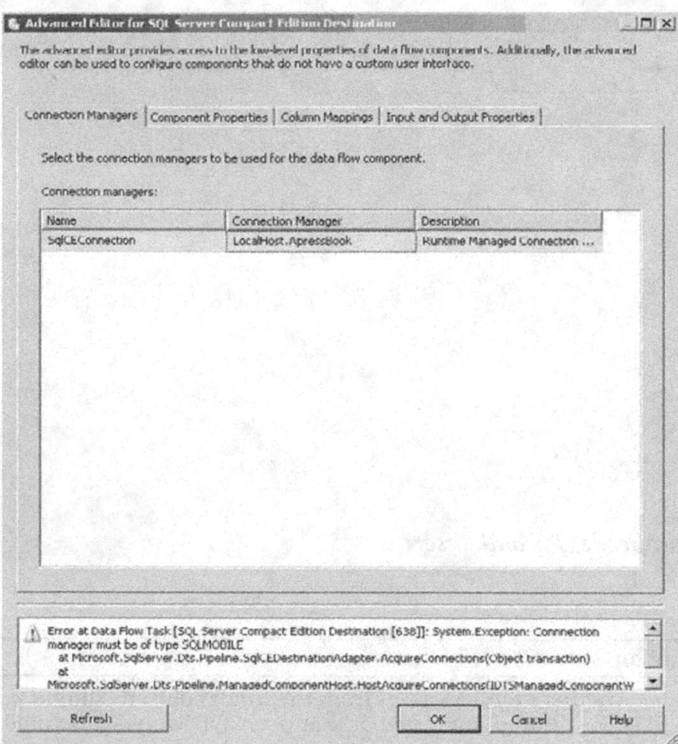

Figure 11-28. *Another day, another connection manager*

On the Component Properties tab, the properties exposed by this destination can be configured. These can be seen in Figure 11-29.

This simple destination component has only two properties. Only one of them—Table Name—is really configurable; it specifies the table into which the data in the flow should be directed. Changing the `UserComponentTypeName` can have dramatically undesirable results, so it's not really a configurable property.

Figure 11-30 shows the Column Mappings tab, another simple mapping screen. You simply map input columns onto available destination columns.

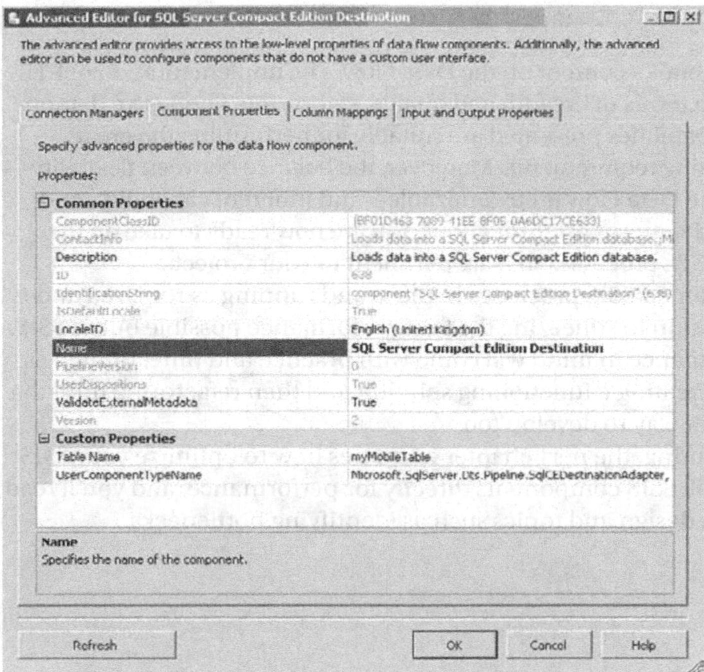

Figure 11-29. *Configuration properties*

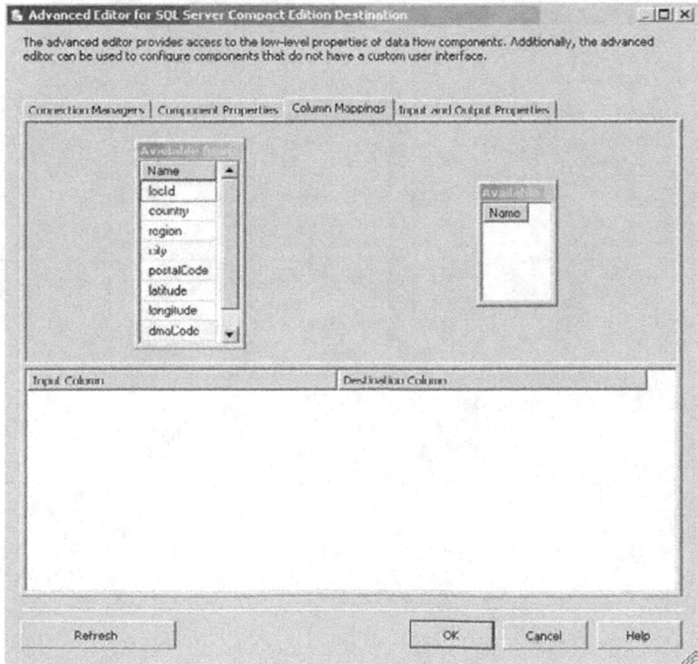

Figure 11-30. *Column-mapping time again*

Summary

This chapter marks the last of this book's content on the Data Flow. The implementation of ETL functionality in the Data Flow is, in terms of breadth and quality, staggering. I hope I've demonstrated that, out of the box, the capabilities presented are suitable for performing the great majority of even the most demanding requirements. Moreover, the balance between flexibility—in that every component part of the Data Flow is customizable—and inherent capability (and configurability) is maintained for the most part throughout. You are now ready to take on the task of producing successful SSIS ETL processes that are pertinent to your project.

Once you have suitably developed SSIS processes in place and running as required and expected, you can turn your attention to squeezing the best performance possible out of SSIS. Developing packages with performance in mind will come with practice and time, though as the Agile methodology suggests, creating a functioning solution and then refactoring until the optimal result is achieved is a great way to develop too.

In the spirit of Agile programming, the next chapter examines how to optimize your SSIS solutions. You'll learn how to tweak SSIS components directly for performance, and you'll read about more SSIS-friendly schema design and topics such as identifying bottlenecks.

CHAPTER 12

Optimization for SSIS

To build the most efficient, performance-driven SSIS solution, you must perform a suitably complex mix of SQL-based and SSIS-specific optimizations. Some obvious optimization techniques should already be under consideration as part of schema or query design, but others are less obvious and rely on an understanding of the underlying SSIS architecture. (See Chapter 2 for an architectural overview.)

That said, database purists should probably look away now. I'm about to plunge into discussing the rights and wrongs of database schema development. It might not be pretty, and it might not be the "correct" way of doing things, but this chapter is a discussion of my experiences in squeezing the best performance out of SSIS. Besides, in my view database and query optimization are entirely subjective. They're subjective because the criteria for successful optimization are genuinely dependent only upon your personal and project goals.

I concede that for the most part, I use *optimize* in the typical way as a substitute for "make it go faster." What might make a database "go faster" for general use, however, doesn't necessarily have the same effect when it comes to manipulating the data in SSIS. Fortunately, you can employ a number of different optimization techniques.

I am not a complete database philistine. I understand completely the need for a smart and shiny Third Normal Form (3NF) structure to your OLTP database. Part of what I'll be suggesting in this chapter is that you could consider a few concessions during the design phase to allow a smoother integration between your schema and SSIS.

This brings to mind a 1990 episode of the American television comedy *Cheers*. Sam Malone is challenged to a game of chess by a vastly more experienced player. To overcome his deficiencies, Sam cheats by using a radio link to friends sitting at a computer running a chess program in a back room. Sam does well until the computer crashes. Unbeknownst to Sam, his opponent has been fully aware of the ongoing cheating but is thrown when the crash causes Sam's game to veer from a classic grand-master strategy. In just a few random moves, Sam wins the game without any assistance because of his unorthodox, unique, and undocumented approach.

Decisions: The Basics

This section details some initial—and more-basic—considerations for optimizing your SSIS solutions. These are things you should take into account while developing your packages that might make a difference. As usual, I'll avoid giving too many specific examples, only because the massively wide variety of issues and flavors of solution that SSIS can address. You should be able to take the broad information I present and apply it to the specifics of your SSIS projects.

Real-time Processing vs. Preprocessing

Overnight processing can be a pain. In 2005 I was lucky enough to inherit (or should that be "be stitched up with"?) an overnight-processing job in SQL Server 2000. The first problem that needed addressing was the fact that the data was available only every other day, because the processing actually took close to 30 hours.

Neither the schema nor the data itself was particularly complex. The schema consisted of effectively five entities. Three entities held data in a relational format, and the other two were structured to hold a pivoted result based on the other three. The overnight job was concerned with pivoting the source data and, subsequently, the recursive processing of the result. I won't bore you with the details.

Part of the problem was the Windows Server 2003 box running SQL Server 2000. Essentially it was a standard desktop PC with extra memory (only a little extra) and extra disk space. However, I felt that 30 hours was a little excessive to perform a relatively simple data transformation, even based on a data volume that was constantly accumulating via other processes. Having little visibility of the strategic approach for this particular project at that time, I could only suggest and advise on possible paths to take to reduce processing time.

After a brief discussion with Microsoft UK, I replaced SQL Server 2000 on the server with SQL Server 2005. After making sure everything was still working, I fired up SSIS. With a little effort I managed to reduce the processing time from 30 hours to less than 1 hour—a massive increase in performance by any standards. Admittedly it isn't really a fair comparison because it wasn't a like-for-like copy of functionality from SQL Server 2000 to SQL Server 2005, but it does demonstrate that if you know what you're doing you can perform the unexpected.

That isn't the point of this little story, however. Back when I was looking at ways to reduce the processing time—during the project-briefing meeting, in fact—my mind was wandering to what I expected to find and how I might go about resolving any issues. My first port of call was to consider using the hosted CLR inside SQL Server, simply to cut down on interprocess communication. The next thing I thought about—and this is at the opposite pole from overnight processing—is real-time processing.

Once I had optimized the overnight processing and everyone was happy, I implemented phase two, which I had pegged as introducing real-time processing. The requirements of this particular project leaned quite nicely toward making real-time processing applicable (which it's important to remember isn't true of all projects).

The rationalization for this shift in processing paradigm was stated simply in terms of the volume of data concerned. Most of the data would never be accessed or viewed, and certainly never updated. Taking into consideration the SOA that it was hoped could be factored into the solution, it made sense to provide an "on-demand" processing model.

This polar shift in paradigm didn't take long to implement. By providing an SSIS package that took a starting point (a record identifier) and via the underlying recursion processing returned a properly formatted XML result for *just the information required*, I delivered an exponential reduction in required processing time and resource.

Considering the energy and materials saved, I also arguably provided an environmental service that day.

Normalization and Denormalization

Normalization is the standard database process of removing redundant columns from a table and putting them in secondary tables linked to the primary table by primary-key and foreign-key relationships.

The theory behind "normal form" and related relational rationale is interesting, but in my opinion the end result should always be a balance between normalization and ensuring a high-performance database environment. Reducing the amount of data held so nothing is replicated via the use of keys and other methods is great, but at the same time I like to keep half a mind toward integration performance.

The way I see it is this. I'm not so concerned about disk space or even necessarily holding the same data multiple times in my database. If it helps performance (and sometimes it does), then do it. If you can save even a millisecond per row of data, across billions of rows you're going to save substantial time and money. Indexes, don't forget, are a form of denormalization too, proving that sometimes a denormalized approach can be worthwhile.

Most readers of this book will be coming to projects that have already started. And SQL Server being what it is, by its very essence it encourages developers to create their own data models. This would be superb if all developers had the first clue what makes a database that performs well. Try as they might, all but the best developers still include nasty structures such as requiring six outer joins just to get a particular customer's forename.

If you can't get permission to throw away a month's worth of development effort to remodel the database properly, you're going to have to work with what you've got and include a few tweaks here and there that don't have an impact on the existing model.

For DBAs I'm sure this is all old news. But most DBAs have more than one database to look after. Given the choice, would a DBA go for a model that is easier to look after, or one that performs to the maximum level possible but is really difficult to maintain? Experience says that the first option is king: a database that is easier to look after has got to be the priority from the DBA viewpoint, which can be at odds with the drive for increased performance.

SQL Server Partitioning

Partitioning gives the professional optimizer a number of options and techniques to use, some of which are more complex than others.

Partitioning is the practice of subdividing a table to reduce the amount of processing required when it is accessed. Logic and sense tell us that a query that runs against a subdivision of a set of data will run much more quickly than it will against the entire set. The same is true when it comes to building or rebuilding indexes.

■ **Note** Partitioned tables and indexes are available only in the SQL Server 2005 Enterprise and Developer editions.

Deciding how to slice the data in a table to provide the partitions is the first thing to do. You might wish to partition a large table into monthly groups or by a particular identifier. The decision depends entirely on specific requirements.

I'll be sticking to an overall conceptual view of partitioning simply because it's an expansive topic about which I could write at least three chapters. Besides, the actual implementation is quite simple; it's the conceptual planning that takes the most thought!

You can choose among three kinds of partitioning: *hardware partitioning, horizontal partitioning*, and *vertical partitioning*.

Hardware Partitioning

Hardware partitioning is an interesting topic that requires substantial knowledge of non-SQL Server techniques and technology. The central theme of hardware partitioning is to leverage the hardware on which the solution is running. It might entail fully utilizing a multiprocessor architecture, or leveraging a RAID array, or anything else particular to the solution server.

Obviously, knowing something about hardware architecture, such as ensuring disks are on different I/O channels and are set to use maximum bandwidth, is useful here. Not everyone has these additional skills.

Take the example of creating a new SQL Server filegroup on a separate drive so you can use it to hold a large table that's related to other tables stored on the existing filegroup. This sounds like a good idea in principle, because the disk reads will be in parallel and data will therefore be returned more rapidly. But if the new filegroup you created is on a different partition of the same disk, rather than on a different physical disk, performance won't be affected (at least not positively). Having the knowledge to understand the server's physical architecture definitely makes a difference.

Horizontal Partitioning

Horizontal partitioning is the practice of dividing a single table into multiple tables, each containing a specific cut of the original data. Horizontal partitioning is the most popular partitioning type and in my opinion the most effective. In the true spirit of Sun Tzu, divide and conquer is the order of the day. It stands to reason that a table with 5 billion rows will react more quickly and be more manageable than a table with 15 billion rows. If you access the other 10 billion rows only occasionally, then you're wasting performance capacity.

Deciding how to partition the data requires the most thought. Depending on the data concerned, you might base partitioning on a date, for example, or on some kind of status flag. Whatever you choose as the basis for the partitioning, it should mean that less frequently accessed data is abstracted away, leaving the most pertinent data in a much more performance-friendly environment. Access to abstracted data can be simplified by creating a view containing `UNION` queries. This itself can cause performance issues, so define your partitions carefully!

Vertical Partitioning

Vertical partitioning is the concept of dividing a table based on column rather than row. Vertical partitioning divides a table into multiple tables that contain fewer columns. The two types of vertical partitioning are normalization and row splitting.

Row splitting divides the original table vertically into tables with fewer columns. Each logical row in a split table matches the same logical row in the others. For example, joining the tenth row from each split table re-creates the original row.

Like horizontal partitioning, vertical partitioning lets queries scan less data. This increases query performance. For example, a table that contains seven columns, of which only the first four are usually referenced, might benefit from splitting the last three columns into a separate table. This is of course entirely dependent on individual circumstances such as the use of indexes.

Vertical partitioning should be considered carefully, because analyzing data from multiple partitions requires queries joining the tables. It also could affect performance if partitions are very large.

Looking at ways of addressing more-general performance issues is fine, but in most cases specific problems need resolutions. The next section takes a look at identifying performance issues and tracking them to their root causes.

Identifying Performance Issues

This section covers the methods and tools available to the SSIS developer to pinpoint and measure the performance of all aspects of SSIS processing.

It is important to remember that SSIS sits on top of the SQL Server engine. Ultimately, whenever an SSIS package accesses data, the access is in the form of a SQL statement routed through the query processor. This is the reason why I have included reference to different ways of leveraging SQL and SQL Server engine optimizations.

As a core part of SSIS, the Data Flow is the area most likely to contribute to performance issues. It could be that the data sources need optimizing, or the destination configuration isn't as tight and efficient as it could be. It could be the transform components involved or it could be the server running out of resources.

With all this in mind, the starting point for any performance investigation must be to identify the points at which performance is suffering. A number of tools, not least within BIDS itself, can be used to identify bottlenecks and other areas that might need addressing. As I stated in the introduction to this chapter, SSIS-specific areas aren't the only ones that might require fine-tuning; our old friend the SQL statement is involved at times too, and traditional query tuning can yield excellent results.

Performance Metrics

If you're going to start to drill down and identify areas of inefficiency in a Data Flow task, you need to isolate and retrieve performance measurements for each of the task's parts in turn. Figure 12-1 shows a Data Flow task's constituent parts.

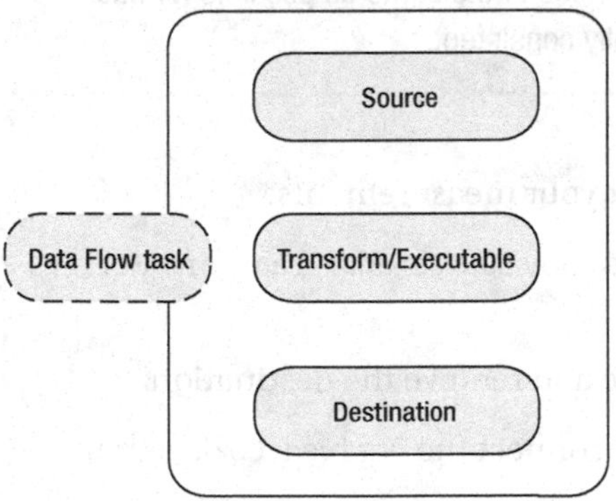

Figure 12-1. *The constituent parts of a Data Flow task*

Figure 12-2 shows an example Data Flow that I'll use to begin to illustrate some of the optimization principles. For the purposes of this example I have removed the error-output destination.

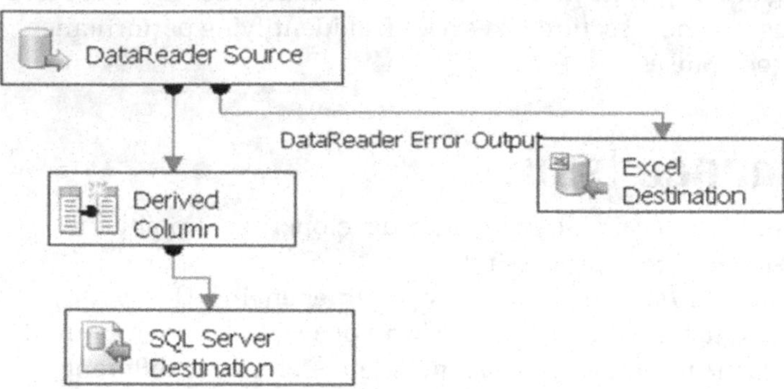

Figure 12-2. *How things look on the Data Flow design surface*

In the Data Flow task in Figure 12-2, it's easy to see the source, the transform, and the destination parts. I need to get figures for the execution time for each of these. For clarity I'll use the following syntax:

a is the execution time of the whole package.

b is the execution time for the source.

c is the execution time for the Derived Column transform.

d is the execution time for the destination.

■ **Note** In the case of any experiment, particularly with a piece of software that sits on top of an operating system that sits on a hardware layer that uses I/O to communicate with devices, the level of validity is always relative. It's essential to make sure the environment is as close to the same as possible for each stage of the measurements and that starting conditions are equally consistent.

Now you're ready to put the pieces in place to gather your measurements:

1. Take two copies of the original package. Name one copy `Source and Transform Metrics` and the other `Source Only Metrics`.
2. Open the `Source and Transform Metrics` package and remove the destination.
3. Add a `Row Count` executable to the Data Flow and connect the `Derived Column` transform to it.

4. Save the package.
5. Open the Source Only Metrics package and remove everything but the DataReader source.
6. Add a Row Count executable to the Data Flow and connect the source to it.
7. Save the package.

Having three packages, you can now run each of them to get the measurements for each, feed them into a simple formula, and have some data to begin analyzing. The Execution Result tab shows details of the package execution, including elapsed time and other statistics. Figure 12-3 shows the text in the Execution Results tab that details the complete package execution time. Thus, *a* = the execution time of the whole package = 00:08:42.922.

```
[DTS.Pipeline] Information: "component "SQL Server
Finished, 15:38:58, Elapsed time: 00:08:42.922
Task Execute SQL Task
```

Figure 12-3. *Whole package execution time*

Figure 12-4 shows the execution-results content for the Source and Transform Metrics package.

```
Progress: Cleanup - 100 percent complete
Finished, 15:49:44, Elapsed time: 00:00:15.484
Task Execute SQL Task
```

Figure 12-4. *Source and Transform Metrics execution*

You now know, as Figure 12-4 shows, that the time taken for the Source and Transform Metrics package to execute is 00:00:15.484, so this data can be applied to our equation:

d= the execution time for the destination = *a* – execution time for the Source and Transform Metrics package

And so:

d= 00:08:42.922 – 00:00:15.484

d= 00:08:27.438

Hmm—that's a suspiciously long time for the destination adapter . . . but for now let's turn our attention toward Source Only Metrics, the execution results for which are shown in Figure 12-5.

```
Progress: Cleanup - 100 percent complete
Finished, 15:55:45, Elapsed time: 00:00:09.343
Task Execute SQL Task
```

Figure 12-5. *The Source Only Metrics metrics*

Finally, you also have the figures for the source: *b* is the execution time for the source = 00:00:09.343.

Given this information, I'm sure you can guess what is coming next: You can now apply a simple formula to get the transform time:

c = the execution time for the derived Column Transform = *a* – *b* – *d*.

And so:

c= 00:08:42.922 – 00:00:09.343 – 00:08:27.438

c= 6.141 seconds

The answers, then, based upon measurements collected in an environment as consistent as possible for all tests, are shown in Table 12-1. It's quite useful—just this once at least—to view the results in a graph too. Figure 12-6 shows this graph in all its Excel-generated glory.

Table 12-1. *Results for a Simple Derived Column Package*

b **(Source Time)**	***c*** **(Transform Time)**	***d*** **(Destination Time)**	***a*** **(Total Time)**
00:00:09.343	00:00:06.141	00:08:27.438	00:08:42.922

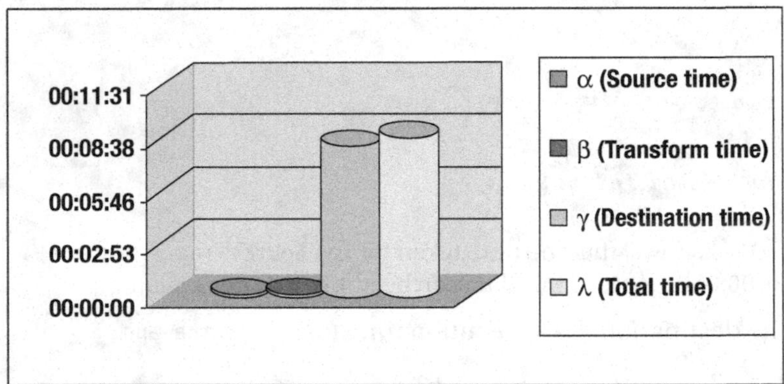

Figure 12-6. *Graph display of execution times*

Figure 12-6 indicates that the destination part of the package might need some investigation, given that it is taking so long to execute.

The example I've supplied here is pretty simple and doesn't consider real-life situations where you've chained a number of transforms together. To quantify the performance of those components you should isolate each of them as I've done in this example. Breaking the problem down into individual quantifiable units is the way problems get solved.

To understand the reasons behind a detected problem, further investigation must of course take place. A variety of tools—including but not limited to BIDS—can assist in this investigation. Next you'll look at these tools, how to use them, and the exact meaning of the information they collect.

The Hacker's Toolkit

Finding out what goes on under the covers of SSIS (or any software for that matter) can be a tricky process. It's important to remember, however, that you're not trying to see *how* SSIS is doing what it's doing. Instead you're looking purely for the effects its processing has on system resources and interactions between components. This makes the task much easier (and much more legal) and requires no knowledge of things like disassemblers or x86 assembly language. We're not here to intrude.

Three tools that can be leveraged to provide insight into performance issues:

- Windows Task Manager
- Performance/System Monitor (Perfmon)
- SQL Server Profiler

Windows Task Manager

The first thing I always check when encountering a performance issue is Windows Task Manager (on the Windows Server running SQL Server 2005). It offers a nice and quick view of CPU and memory usage and might give an early indication of a problem.

It can be accessed a number of ways. I usually open it by pressing Ctrl+Alt+Del and selecting Task Manager. You can also right-click the Windows Task Bar and select Task Manager. Figure 12-7 shows the Performance tab on Windows Task Manager. Figure 12-8 shows the Processes tab.

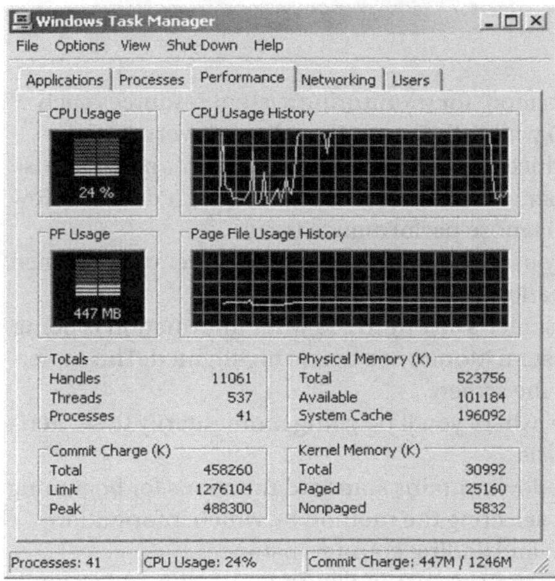

Figure 12-7. *Task Manager's Performance tab shows CPU-usage spikes.*

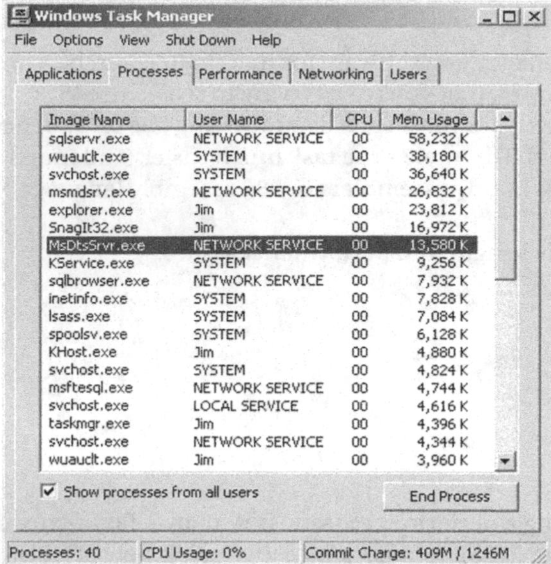

Figure 12-8. *Keeping an eye on SQL Server and SSIS processes*

Very high CPU usage against the running SQL Server process, large spikes in memory usage taking free memory to very low levels, and large paging-file usage increases all require further diagnosis. For that you can use Perfmon.

Performance/System Monitor (Perfmon)

Initial impressions of Perfmon might be that it's more for monitoring system resources such as CPU and memory usage than anything to do with SQL Server. In reality it is very useful, because applications can, at install time, introduce new monitoring types (or *counters*) for use with Perfmon. SQL Server installs a large number of these counters, which give a detailed view of exposed performance values and help you diagnose performance issues.

Figure 12-9 shows Perfmon in its (generally useful) default guise. SQL Server performance objects need to be added to provide the information you need.

First, take a quick look around the default screen's layout to see what information is being presented. On the left side of the screen, the System Monitor option is highlighted. This generates and displays the graph on the right side of the screen.

Counter Logs, another option on the left, is where you'll be going momentarily to set Perfmon to capture everything you need for diagnosis.

The toolbar across the top of the main window contains standard functions for beginning a new monitoring session, clearing the display, selecting the method by which information should be presented (graph type or text report), and adding counter instances.

To add performance-objects counters, click the + shown in Figure 12-10. The Add Counters configuration screen appears (see Figure 12-11) that lets you select appropriate and available performance objects.

The Add Counters configuration screen uses the value `Processor` as the default performance object. Having processor information displayed on the main screen is a good thing in conjunction with other, more-specific counters.

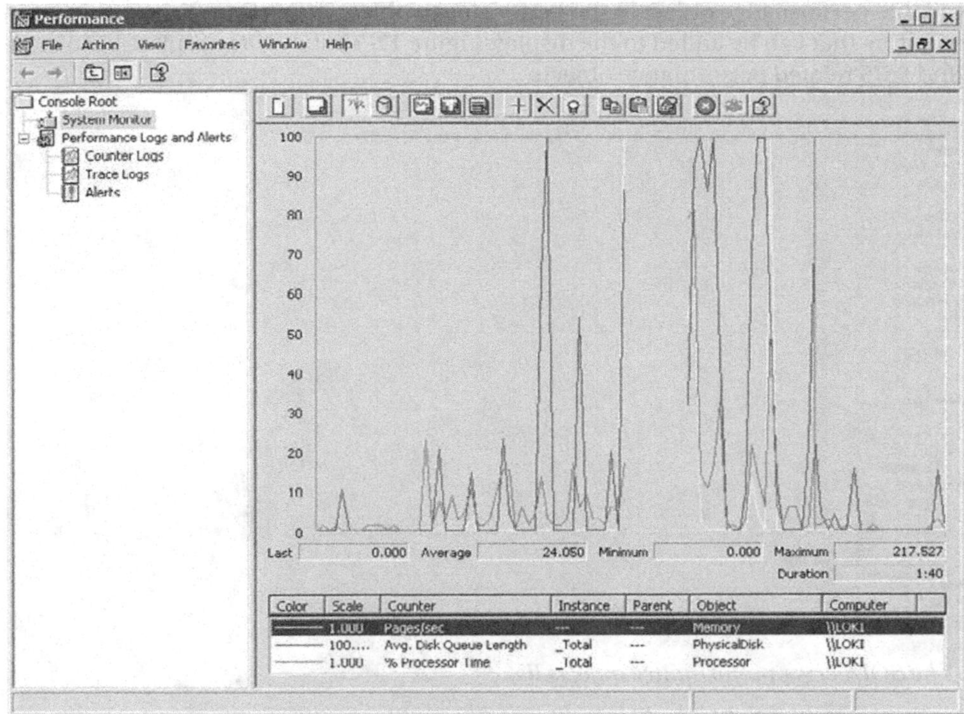

Figure 12-9. *The default Perfmon window*

Figure 12-10. *Add performance objects to Perfmon with this icon.*

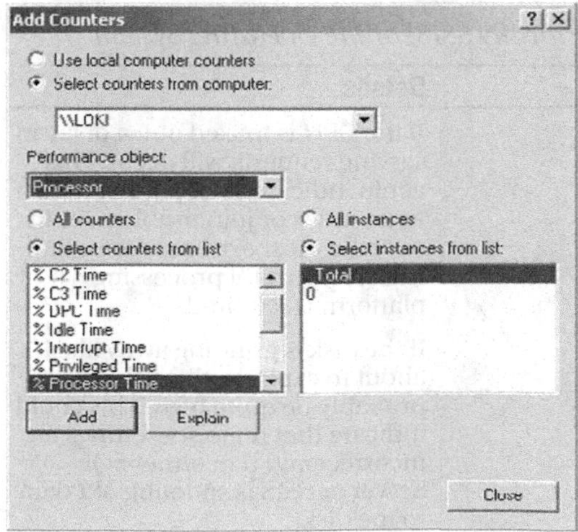

Figure 12-11. *Selecting performance objects in Perfmon*

Each available performance object in the Performance object drop-down list exposes a number of counters that can be added to the display. Figure 12-12 shows a complete list of SQL Server and SSIS related performance objects.

Figure 12-12. *The SQL Server performance objects list*

At this point it's worth suggesting you perform a trace using the same performance objects before executing the package. Although Perfmon captures only some of the counters (because they aren't being invoked by SSIS when the package isn't running), having a baseline trace is useful for comparison purposes. If, for example, the % Processor time counter is already at 90% without even touching SSIS, this would indicate the problem lies elsewhere and would need resolving before you attempt to measure package performance.

Tables 12-2 and 12-3 show the performance objects most pertinent to performance troubleshooting.

Table 12-2. *Counters Relating to SQL Server (Not Specifically SSIS) or the Operating System*

Performance Object	Counter	Details
Processor	% Processor time	If the CPU is maxed out, a delay in serving requests will occur. This could indicate a deeper issue such as an index or join problem, or in only the most extreme cases, that a more powerful processing platform is required.
PhysicalDisk	% Disk time	If the disk is grinding away like it's about to explode, this value will probably be quite high. This could indicate that memory settings are incorrect and that either SQL Server or SSIS is spooling out data to the disk.

Performance Object	Counter	Details
	Avg disk queue length	This value shouldn't generally exceed 2 for each physical disk over a period of time. If it does, this indicates a potential disk I/O issue in that data cannot be handled by the disk controller quickly enough.
System	Processor queue length	A value exceeding 2 for each processor in a system over a period of time indicates a CPU bottleneck. This could be because too many threads are awaiting execution.
SQLServer:Access Methods	Full Scans/Sec	A value exceeding 2 over a period of time could indicate that too many full scans are being performed and possibly that a more robust indexing strategy should be identified.
	Index Searches/Sec	A higher value shows that indexes are being hit. This is probably a good thing but only if it was intentional!
SQLServer:Buffer Manager	Free Pages	This value is the total number of pages free for buffer use.
	Stolen Page Count	The number of pages reclaimed from the buffer cache. This could indicate memory issues.
SQLServer:Memory Manager	Memory grants pending	This is the number of processes waiting for SQL Server to grant a memory request. Should be kept as low as possible.
	Total server memory	A figure signifying the amount of memory committed from the buffer pool. A high value indicates high buffer usage.
SQLServer:Databases	Transactions/sec	The higher the value, the more transactions are being processed. This could be a good thing so long as they are completing in a timely manner . . . but it could also indicate that too many transactions are taking place at once.
SQLServer:Locks	Number of Deadlocks/sec	This value, which should be low, reveals the number of lock requests that resulted in deadlock.
SQLServer:Wait Statistics	Lock Waits/Average wait time	The lower the wait time for a lock, the better. A high value indicates contention of some kind.

Continued

Table 12-2. *Continued*

Performance Object	Counter	Details
SQLServer:SQL Statistics	Sql Compilations/sec	This figure needs to be as low as possible since it is a count of statement compilations.
	Sql Re-Compilations/sec	This figure, a count of statement recompilations, should be kept as low as possible.
SQLServer:Plan Cache	Cache-hit ratio	This is a ratio of cache hits to misses. The value should be high since this indicates efficient caching in SQL Server.

Table 12-3. *SSIS-Specific Performance Objects*

Performance Object	Counter	Details
SQLServer:SSIS Pipeline	BLOB bytes read	Useful to keep an eye on to manage BLOB buffer usage.
	BLOB bytes written	This value can be used to manage BLOB buffer usage.
	BLOB files in use	This important counter gives an indication that the SSIS execution engine is running out of RAM and so needs to spool BLOB file content out to a disk location.
	Buffer memory	Represents total memory used by buffers. The larger the value, the more buffer space is being used. This could indicate a perfectly healthy buffer-usage strategy in your Data Flow. It could also indicate there is trouble ahead. A high value means high memory usage. See the Buffers spooled counter for further information.
	Buffers in use	If the number of buffers in use is high, this is probably caused by the particular buffer-usage strategy employed. It may well be by design. If you are attempting to reduce asynchronous tasks, this figure should decrease if your approach is working.
	Buffers spooled	This is a particularly important counter. It gives an indication that the SSIS execution engine is running out of RAM and so needs to spool buffer content out to a disk location.
	Flat buffer memory	This counter can provide an insight into the size of the data passing through the pipeline.
	Flat buffers in use	If this value is particularly high, especially when compared to the value of Flat buffer memory, this could be a sign of efficient use of asynchronous tasks.

Performance Object	Counter	Details
	Private buffer memory	Private buffers are usually used by the execution engine to store lookup data temporarily, for example. High private buffer usage might indicate that a review of lookup or sort tasks is in order.
	Private buffers in use	Again, new buffers are created because the previous one is full or because its contents cannot be shared for some reason. A high number might indicate that the use of lookup or sort tasks needs review.

Let's take this step by step. You'll use Perfmon to identify the particular part of SQL Server, SSIS, or the operating system that is causing the problem in an underperforming SSIS package:

1. Fire up Perfmon using your preferred method. I usually open a Run dialog (Windows key+R or `Run...` from the Start Menu) and type `perfmon`. The program file can be found in the Windows\System32 directory and is called `Perfmon.exe`.
2. Right-click Counter Logs and select New Log Settings. Give the new settings a name.
3. On the Log Configuration screen (see Figure 12-13), select Add Counters....

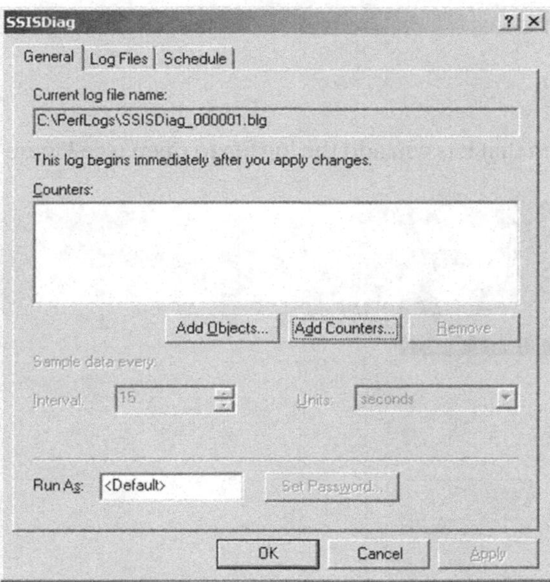

Figure 12-13. *Log configuration. Add counters here.*

4. Select the desired counters from the list presented in Table 12-3.
5. Be sure to set the Sample Interval low so everything that needs to be captured gets captured.
6. Click OK.

7. Right-click the newly created Counter Logs file and select Start, as in Figure 12-14.

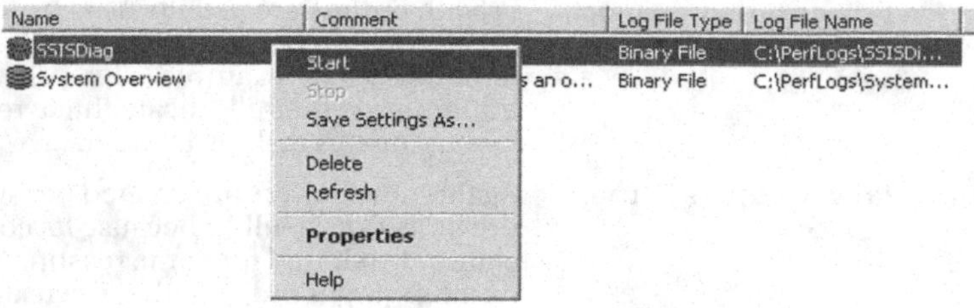

Figure 12-14. *The new Counter Log is ready to go.*

8. Run your underperforming SSIS package.
9. Once the SSIS package has finished, wait a few moments and then right-click the Counter Log file and select Stop.
10. Select System Monitor from the left of the Perfmon screen.
11. Click the View Logs icon on the toolbar (see Figure 12-15).

Figure 12-15. *The View Logs button*

12. You're now presented with a screen that lets you add the log file to open (see Figure 12-16).

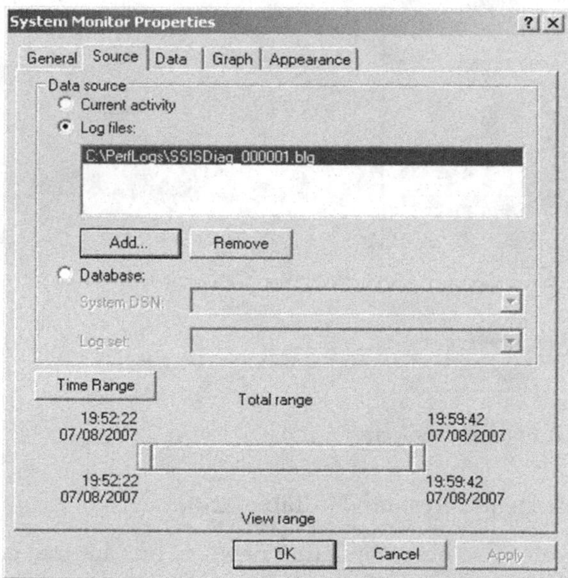

Figure 12-16. *Add the Log File location and set Time Range to view the log.*

13. Click OK and view the log, which should be just like mine in Figure 12-17.

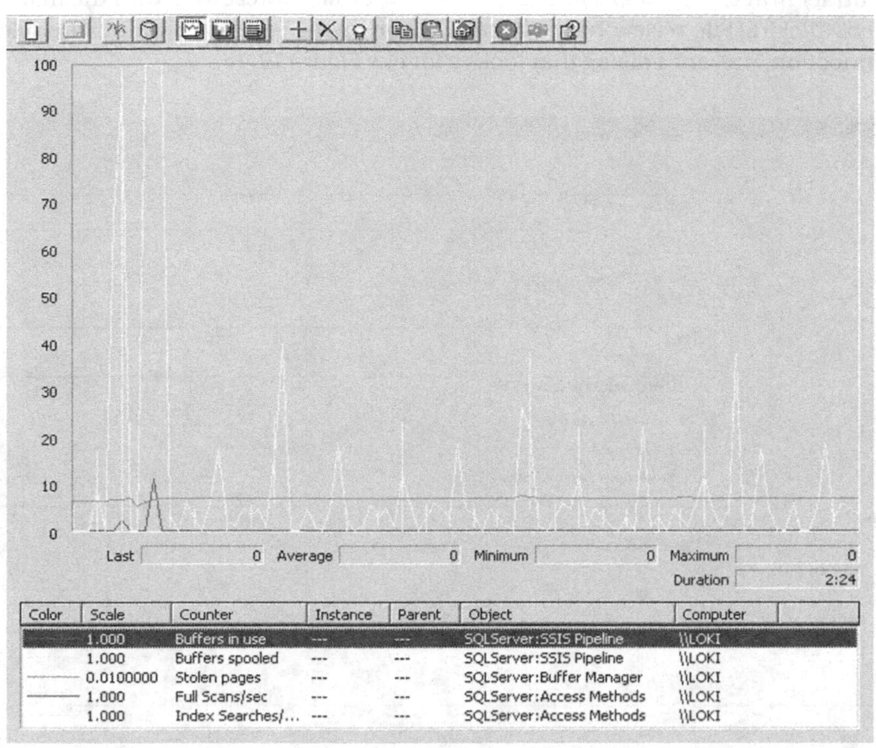

Figure 12-17. *Everything looks pretty good for my package.*

Obviously, some packages will show problems against the performance counters specified. Using the information in Tables 12-2 and 12-3 against each of the counter types, you can highlight the cause of a particular issue, which gives you more information with which to investigate the problem.

Having identified that there is a performance issue with a particular aspect of the database server, it's time to drill down yet further. If the issue is query related—that is, a long-running query or an index-related problem—using SQL Profiler to see the executing query causing the problem is the next step.

If, however, the Perfmon results indicate a particularly SSIS-related issue, such as buffer usage, you can go straight to looking at some fixes and optimizations that relate specifically to SSIS.

SQL Server Profiler

How much do I love SQL Profiler? It's useful in so many ways, not least for spotting poorly performing SQL statements being fired at the database engine. You're probably already familiar with this tool, so I'm going to illustrate how to configure it just to capture the events we are looking for.

SQL Server Profiler is installed as part of SQL Server 2005. To open it, look in the `Performance Tools` folder under `Start/Programs/SQL Server 2005`. You will be presented with the main Profiler screen. Clicking File ➤ New Trace or the first icon on the toolbar will, after you select the database connection, present a dialog that looks a lot like Figure 12-18.

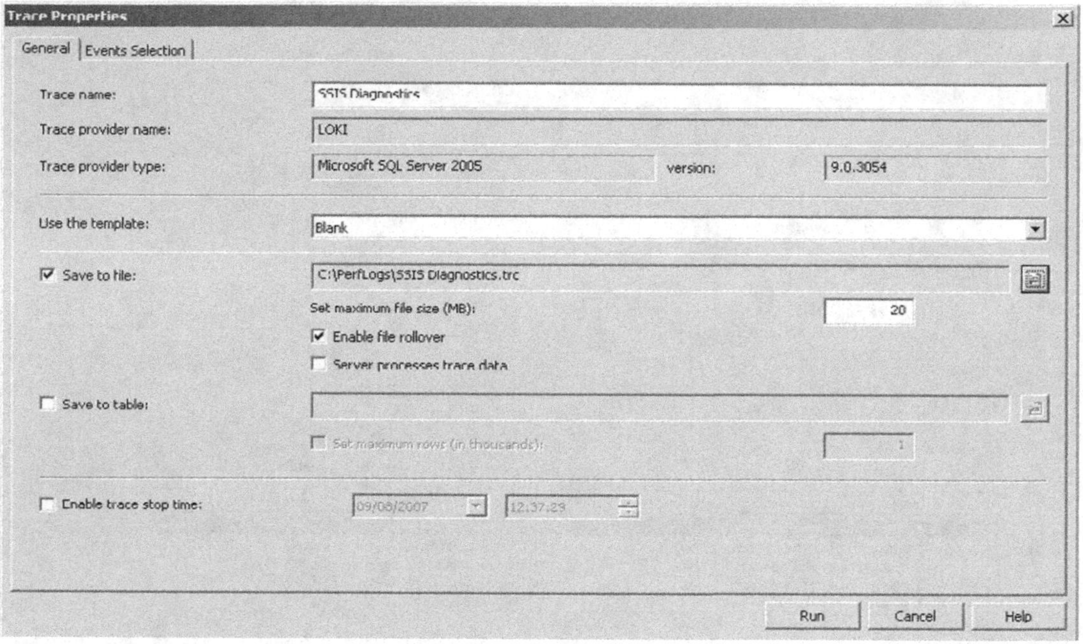

Figure 12-18. *Setting standard trace properties*

I usually just configure Trace name and set the trace to Save to file on this screen. I do, however, set the Use the template value to Default, since it gives basic coverage of T-SQL and stored-procedure events. Additional event types added by the template can be removed.

Figure 12-19 shows the Events Selection tab, from which any kind of event can be selected for monitoring.

Although there are literally dozens of different events to capture, fortunately you need only concentrate on the two shown in Table 12-4.

Table 12-4. *Important Profiler Event Types*

Event	Description
Stored Procedures/RPC:Completed	Indicates that a stored procedure has completed execution.
TSQL/Batch Completed	Indicates that a T-SQL statement has completed execution.

I'll select these event types to demonstrate the kind of data that gets reported, which you can see in Figure 12-20.

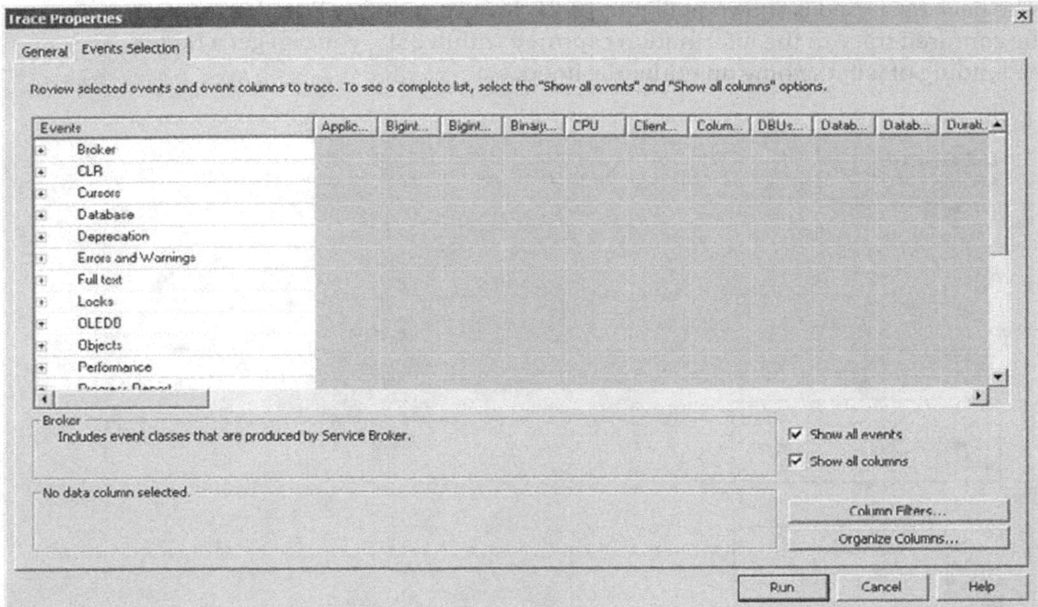

Figure 12-19. *Selecting the events to capture*

EventClass	TextData	ApplicationName	NTUserName	LoginName	CPU	Reads	Writes	Duration	ClientProcessID
Trace Start									
SQL:BatchCompleted	SET NO_BROWSETABLE ON	Microsoft® V...	Jim	LOKI\Jim	0	0	0	0	2712
RPC:Completed	declare @p1 int set @p1=1 exec sp_prepare @p1 output,NULL,N...	Microsoft® V...	Jim	LOKI\Jim	0	0	0	0	2712
RPC:Completed	exec sp_unprepare 1	Microsoft® V...	Jim	LOKI\Jim	0	0	0	0	2712
RPC:Completed	exec [ApressBook].[sys].sp_columns_90_rowset N'SourceIncludin...	Microsoft® V...	Jim	LOKI\Jim	16	114	0	24	2712
RPC:Completed	exec [ApressBook].[sys].sp_columns_90_rowset N'SourceIncludin...	Microsoft® V...	Jim	LOKI\Jim	0	114	0	6	2712
SQL:BatchCompleted	SET NO_BROWSETABLE ON	Microsoft SQ...	Jim	LOKI\Jim	0	0	0	0	2516
RPC:Completed	declare @p1 int set @p1=1 exec sp_prepare @p1 output,NULL,N...	Microsoft SQ...	Jim	LOKI\Jim	0	0	0	0	2516
RPC:Completed	exec sp_unprepare 1	Microsoft SQ...	Jim	LOKI\Jim	0	0	0	0	2516
RPC:Completed	exec [ApressBook].[sys].sp_columns_90_rowset N'SourceIncludin...	Microsoft SQ...	Jim	LOKI\Jim	16	114	0	21	2516
RPC:Completed	exec [ApressBook].[sys].sp_columns_90_rowset N'SourceIncludin...	Microsoft SQ...	Jim	LOKI\Jim	16	114	0	74	2516
RPC:Completed	exec sp_reset_connection	Microsoft SQ...	Jim	LOKI\Jim	0	0	0	0	2516
RPC:Completed	exec [ApressBook].[sys].sp_columns_90_rowset N'SourceIncludin...	Microsoft SQ...	Jim	LOKI\Jim	16	114	0	4	2516
RPC:Completed	exec [ApressBook].[sys].sp_columns_90_rowset N'SourceIncludin...	Microsoft SQ...	Jim	LOKI\Jim	15	114	0	12	2516
SQL:BatchCompleted	exec [sys].sp_oledb_ro_usrname	Microsoft SQ...	Jim	LOKI\Jim	0	4	0	6	2516
SQL:BatchCompleted	select collationname(0x0904D00034)	Microsoft SQ...	Jim	LOKI\Jim	0	0	0	0	2516
SQL:BatchCompleted	select * from Person.Contact	Microsoft SQ...	Jim	LOKI\Jim	15	569	0	8129	2516
SQL:BatchCompleted	BULK INSERT [SourceIncludingFullname] FROM 'Global\DTSQLIMPOR...	Microsoft SQ...	Jim	LOKI\Jim	1437	1253	747	30409	2516
Trace Stop									

Figure 12-20. *The results of the capture*

The package I used is shown in Figure 12-21. It's a very simple Data Flow but, by comparing the captured trace to the information captured within SSIS, you can get a better understanding of what's going on under the hood.

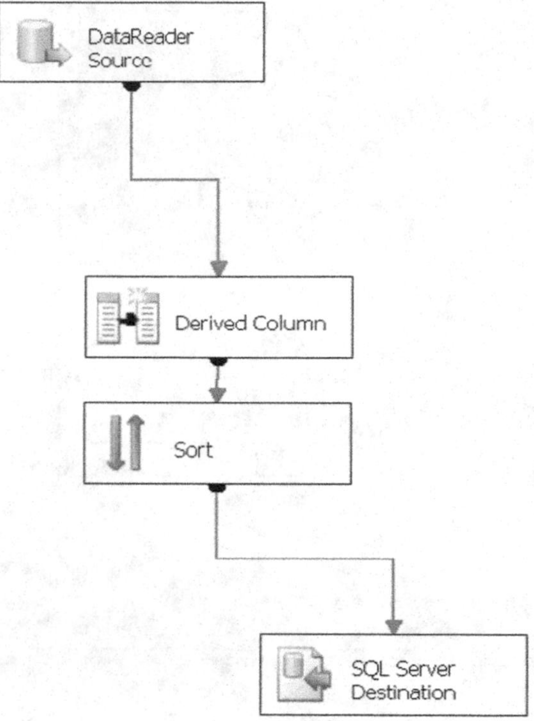

Figure 12-21. *My simple package*

So let's take a look at the Data Flow. I've got two transformation components in there that, as Chapter 2 will remind you, are nonblocking, streaming, and synchronous (in the case of the `Derived Column`) and blocking and asynchronous (in the case of the `Sort`). In terms of buffer usage, the Data Flow presents the information in Figure 12-22.

I've dipped back into the SSIS development environment here to take a look at some of the logging that can be captured—in this case around the pipeline execution tree. I won't go into too much detail here, but the information presented by the execution tree and the other information that can be logged when a package executes proves useful in identifying potential optimizations. I discuss these topics a little later in this chapter.

Getting back to the SQL side of package execution: as often happens, inefficient queries can form the basis of poor performance. The inefficiency could be a result of poor or corrupt indexing, disk issues, or any number of other causes that one would associate with typical SQL Server performance problems. Using SQL Profiler should, however, reinforce the discovery of the source of the problem and, in turn, this suggests that query optimization should take place—or that there is a larger problem at hand.

It's beyond this book's scope to look in any great depth at query optimization. Several tools that are a part of SQL Server 2005 can identify and rectify SQL Server engine–related issues. One of them is SQL Server Management Studio.

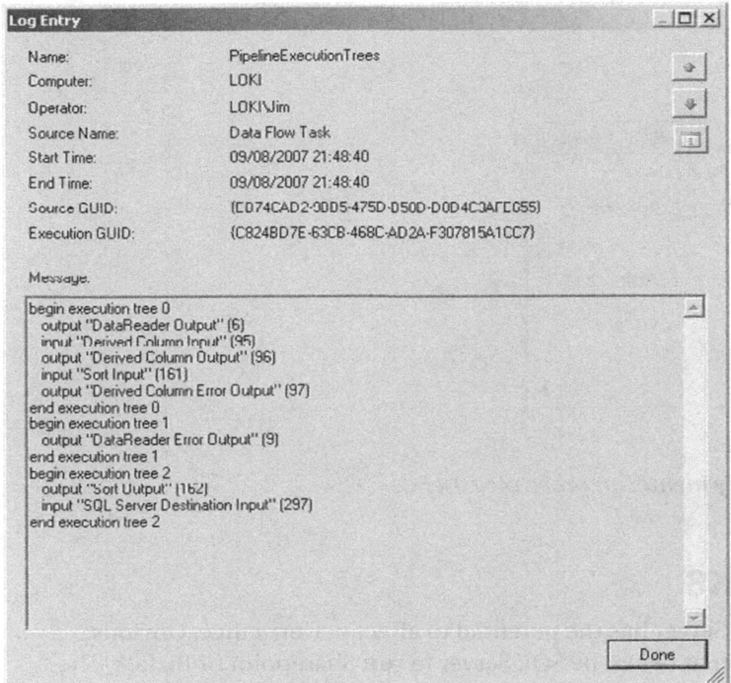

Figure 12-22. *The execution tree of my Data Flow*

SQL Server Management Studio

The first stop on this epic journey of optimization was to isolate the SQL queries that are being performed. Extracting the queries out and ensuring, on an individual basis, that they are executing with maximum efficiency is a very productive way of increasing performance.

SQL Server Management Studio gives you the ability to look over and optimize queries where necessary. Under Query in the menu options are a number of options that relate to gathering more information about your SQL queries. Again, gathering measurements from each part of the query will help you to identify areas needing optimization. Luckily, SQL Server Management Studio (like Query Analyzer before it) performs the measurements on demand and even compares them to previously collected performance data and measurements. You can use the Display Estimated Execution Plan functionality inside the Query menu (see Figure 12-23) to identify bottlenecks in the execution plan of a particular query.

Also, using the Database Engine Tuning Advisor—an option also shown in Figure 12-23—aids optimization by automatically identifying possible tuning measures. Again, going into any great depth on this topic is beyond the scope of this chapter, especially since the automated tuning advisor gives the same advice I would be giving here.

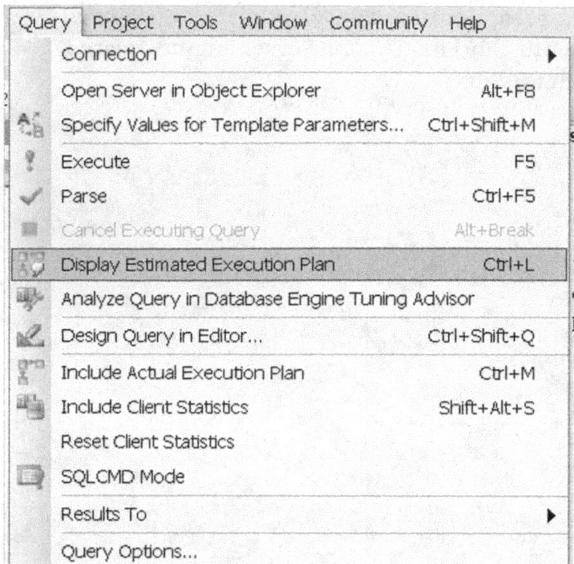

Figure 12-23. *Options in the Query menu can prove very useful.*

SQL Server Tweaks

Anything that runs against SQL Server has the potential to affect performance. Obvious impediments include replication or using the SQL Server to run Sharepoint or Biztalk. The less-obvious ones include implementing a "heavy" recovery model or more-intensive logging options. Also ensure that memory options are sufficient so that SQL Server has enough to operate but also that SSIS gets a good share.

Remember that the SQL Server engine and SSIS are entirely separate entities.

Reviewing your SQL Server settings is certainly well worth considering. Generally speaking, however, these settings will get reviewed when it comes to promoting packages to the production environment anyway, so I'm probably preaching to the converted.

Platform Tweaks

I don't have much to say about platform tweaks, except to suggest using SQL Server on a database server rather than an application server. Don't install other server applications on there that can hinder performance. Preferably, use the 64-bit version of Windows Server and SQL Server 2005 on a 64-bit processor platform, with lots and lots of memory.

Another option, depending on network utilization, is to abstract out the SQL Server instance and SSIS to different servers. This is a pretty dramatic move, to be sure, but at least this way the RAM on each server is dedicated (excluding the operating system of course) to an assigned task, whether running SQL Server or running SSIS.

It's time to take a look at optimization that is specific to SSIS. The next section discusses the topic and explores the various methods and configuration settings available.

SSIS-Specific Optimizations

The most obvious "quick win" for optimizing SSIS components is to check through each source component, each transformation component, and each destination component and make sure all configuration settings are as optimal as possible. Extraneous columns should be discarded; data types and column sizes should be accurately defined.

The key to identifying additional areas to address is to keep a keen eye on any warnings generated by the development environment. Usually this is as simple as a warning that a certain column involved in a transformation component is unused . . . so take the advice and remove it. If the transformation involves only a small number of rows, these tweaks to ensure a streamlined package will mostly go unnoticed. With larger amounts of data, however, the small savings will soon add up and make for a bigger performance benefit.

A number of "features," some idiosyncratic, also need consideration and handling to ensure they are not adversely affecting performance (or indeed, to ensure they are assisting in producing better performance!). I'll present as many of these individual optimizations as I can think of and have heard of from around the SSIS community. Not all of the recommendations, tweaks, and tricks will apply to every piece of your solution. Simply pick out those parts that seem most relevant.

One of the first things that come to mind is taking a more parallelized approach within the Data Flow. I'll talk about this at the end of this section. The same goes for buffer-usage settings and strategies.

One of the things that often catch out developers is that they forget that performance overheads are inherent in debugging a solution. This isn't just true of SSIS; general .NET development, C++ development, and any other kind of development experience this to different degrees. Sometimes it comes as a direct consequence of the IDE offering real-time debugging (and so a debugger is attached to running code, reducing performance) and sometimes it's because logging and debugging information is (explicitly or implicitly) being written out by the executing code.

This means that performance issues can present themselves in a development environment when, perhaps, a production environment would not experience the same issues. A number of alternate ways to test the execution of a package, whether for the collection of performance statistics or otherwise, give a more realistic picture.

Detaching the package from the IDE entirely makes the most difference, but it is possible to go some way toward this by (as Figure 12-24 shows) choosing Start Without Debugging from the IDE's Debug menu. Don't be surprised, however, if the performance is pretty much the same as before. Again, this isn't the ideal way to execute a package for performance.

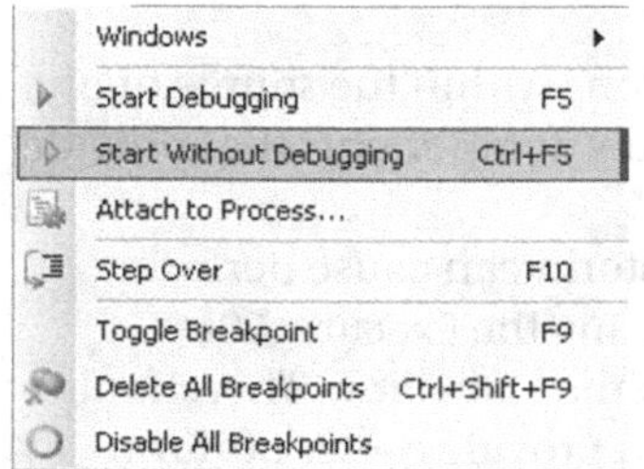

Figure 12-24. *Start Without Debugging = better performance*

As I said, the way to ensure the best performance is to execute the package without any IDE or debugging overhead. You can do this in a number of ways, depending upon whether you want to set foot outside of a GUI and use a DOS command line. The method also depends on where your package is stored—but I'll assume it's within the SSIS Package Store for now.

If you want to use the command line, you can use `DTExec.exe` or its more GUI brother `DTSExecUI.exe`. `DTExec.exe` is in the SQL Server installation directory under `\90\DTS\Binn`, and `DTSExecUI.exe` is under `\90\Tools\Binn\VSShell\Common7\IDE`.

Now I'll move on to more specific tuning methods. A great number of individual tweaks and methods can be implemented that aren't immediately apparent during general SSIS development. Some apply to the package as a whole, some to data sources and, last but not least, some to the Control Flow and Data Flow.

Component and Component-Query Tweaks

Earlier in this chapter I looked at using SQL Server Profiler to identify queries that are being executed from within SSIS. If you have a Data Flow that uses the `Lookup` component, you would have noticed (unless you had already modified the value) during the Profiler trace that during execution a `select * from ReferenceTable` query is executed. (`ReferenceTable` is the name of the lookup table to use, of course.) Using the `select *` syntax is wasteful, particularly when the query runs against a table with multiple and/or large columns. This query should be replaced with one that selects only the required columns. In addition, creating an index on the reference table can help enormously.

Data-source components that feature a data-access mode property are deceptive in that performance can suffer depending upon the mode selected. The `OLE DB Source Adapter` is one such component. Selecting the Table or View or Open Rowset access modes (or their respective From Variable variants) is actually slower than entering a SQL statement. This is especially true when the SQL statement selects only columns pertinent to and in use in the Data Flow.

The sorting of data is sometimes a requirement for using certain downstream Data Flow components, as Chapters 9 and 10 explain, and naturally having sorted data is a requirement in other instances. Using the `Sort` transform as part of the Data Flow can prove expensive; fortunately an alternative is available in some cases. If possible, include an `ORDER BY` clause as part of the source query, because it is much faster than using the `Sort` transform. There is additional work to do however: you need to tell the Data Flow that the data is sorted.

As part of the Data Flow data source, using the Advanced Editor, set the `IsSorted` property of the Source Output node to `True`. Having done this, drill down in the view and modify the source columns that are part of the `ORDER BY` clause, setting the `SortKeyPosition` value to the relevant sort position value.

If possible, also include any `JOIN`, `GROUP BY`, and `UNION` operations within the source query too, since again this will result in better performance over individual components that provide the same function.

While I'm on the subject of OLE DB: the `OLE DB Command` transform can cause performance issues that are due to its inherent row-based approach. Try using the `Execute SQL Control Flow` task instead, and use the generated recordset within the Data Flow. This should provide a performance boost. The `OLE DB Destination` adapter can provide better performance, where applicable, if you set the `Data Access Mode` property to `Fast Load` and consider appropriate usage of the other exposed properties, such as commit size.

In addition—and I'm sure this is one of those pieces of advice you've read absolutely everywhere—try to use the SQL Server Destination component where possible. By its very nature it executes in-process with the SQL Server instance, thereby reducing unnecessary overheads.

The Control Flow Script Task and Data Flow Script Component can perform much better when precompiled. The Script Task exposes the PrecompileScriptIntoBinaryCode property, and the Script Component exposes PreCompile. In both cases, set these properties to True.

Note On the 64-bit platform, precompilation is not a choice but a requirement!

Going back to indexes again for a moment, you need to consider two questions:

- Does creating an index on a table help when it comes to the data source?
- Are existing indexes causing performance problems when it comes to data destinations?

Indexes can be disabled in SQL Server 2005 (rather than just dropped as in previous versions), and the opportunity to do so can be beneficial at times, such as before large insert/update operations.

Be smart when using the Lookup components. If the operation against the reference table uses the same key and retrieves the same value time and again, use Partial Cache mode. Use Full Cache only when the entire reference table will be accessed and the table itself is relatively small. Alternatively, where possible, use the Merge Join transform instead.

Bulk Inserts/Text Files

Reading text files from a disk can be an intensive process. Leveraging in-built optimization settings can reap dramatic benefits here. Setting the Fast Parse property to True for each output column on the Flat File source (and indeed the Data Conversion Data Flow transform) will provide an incredible increase in performance. There are caveats to using Fast Parse. For example, the data must not be locale specific, and only the most common date formats are supported.

When you define source columns, performance is improved slightly when only relevant columns have their data types assigned. Leave unused columns as the default String data type. If a source column can be left as a String type, leave it as a String.

A Note on Buffers and Memory Usage

You can detect and monitor buffer and memory usage using the techniques I describe in the early part of this chapter. It isn't necessarily as simple as "the fewer buffers used the better" or "the least memory used the better the performance." It is more a case (although it sounds obvious) of tweaking buffer usage to fit server capacity, development resources, and cost restrictions. Voltaire said, "The perfect is the enemy of the good," and it is true for optimizing SSIS performance.

Using asynchronous transforms where possible is a good thing in the right circumstances. Those circumstances involve the tight configuration of SQL Server and a multiprocessor 64-bit server with plenty of RAM. If I weren't using a multiprocessor server or were limited on RAM, however, I'd try to use more synchronous transforms instead.

What really should be avoided is creating a situation where all available memory is eaten up by buffers. This causes the buffers to be written out to the disk temporarily and, of course, this has a big performance impact.

Ultimately it is not always possible to ensure that buffers do not get spooled to the disk. Even the most aggressive buffer strategies using the most memory-efficient components can be tripped up by a solution requirement necessitating the use of a more memory-intensive operation. In those cases, having the buffer spooling out to a disk on a separate high-speed channel can have a suitable performance difference. To change the spooling location, two properties of the Data Flow task must be modified—`BufferTempStoragePath` and `BLOBTempStoragePath`.

With careful and appropriate use, increasing the size of the buffers can yield a performance increase. The problem is that careless use will dramatically degrade performance because buffers start to get spooled to the disk. Buffers are governed by a number of properties exposed at Data Flow level, shown in Table 12-5. Careful thought should be given to changing these values, because they can directly cause negative performance. On the other side of the coin, changing these settings can have dramatic performance benefits.

Table 12-5. *Exposed Buffer Properties*

Property	Description
`DefaultBufferSize`	Maximum size in bytes of an individual buffer. Set by default to 10,485,760 bytes.
`DefaultBufferMaxRows`	Maximum number of rows that can be held in an individual buffer. By default the value is set to 10,000, though this figure will be reduced if (based on row size estimates) the memory consumption would be greater than the `DefaultBufferSize`.
`MaxBufferSize`	Upper limit for the `DefaultBufferSize` property. Has a value of 100 MB and cannot be changed.
`MinBufferSize`	Minimum allowable buffer size. The `DefaultBufferMaxRows` value will be automatically increased to accommodate extra rows to push the memory use in the buffer above the `MinBufferSize` threshold.

A pretty major operation to optimize Data Flow is to consider replacing synchronous components with alternate, asynchronous components. This isn't always possible, but where it *is* possible significant performance benefits become available. The next subsection looks at ways of implementing such a change—and parallelizing the Data Flow.

Data Flow Parallelization

The principle of parallelization is simple, at least in theory. The concept of doing multiple things at the same time is as old as . . . patting your head and rubbing your stomach simultaneously. SSIS features tasks that are both synchronous (wait until you've finished patting your head before you rub your stomach) and asynchronous (both at the same time). Some tasks are also nonblocking, semiblocking, or fully blocking (see Chapter 2). As I explained earlier in this chapter, the introduction of one kind or the other is dependent entirely on circumstance, but this doesn't mean we can't discuss how things would be in a more ideal world. In keeping with the (theoretical) idea of "many digital hands make light work," this subsection is all about how to use asynchronous tasks in your Data Flow and to optimize buffer usage.

The asynchronous execution of tasks is limited by, essentially, one property. `MaxConcurrentExecutables` is held at package level. By default its value is –1, which equates to "total number of logical processors + 2." This value might be fine, but it might need to be increased based upon the contents of the package. Give it a tweak and retest performance is my advice.

To discuss memory-usage optimization, a very brief recap of Data Flow component types is in order. This serves as a summary and reminder of some of the information in Chapter 2.

Nonblocking: Data is maintained in-place in one set of buffers throughout the lifetime of the pipeline.

Semiblocking: Output data produced as a consequence of semiblocking transformations is going to differ in terms of quantity from the input set. Because of this, new buffers need to be created to accommodate the newly created set.

Fully blocking: Buffers must be created to hold all the data, since every row is required before the transformation can be applied.

It stands to reason that memory usage is minimized by avoiding the use of fully blocking transforms. As a general rule, irrespective of whether memory is an issue or not, it will prove a wise decision to employ nonblocking or semiblocking components where possible.

Summary

This chapter has presented a detailed overview of structural considerations and optimization techniques both of the underlying SQL and of SSIS packages. I have purposely avoided too much depth simply because entire volumes have been written about SQL Server optimization. It would be easy to create a similar book that concentrates solely on SSIS optimizations. This isn't that book.

Instead I have tried to present documentation that identifies the most common areas where performance bottlenecks occur and remedies to address them. Most SSIS users will never need to optimize for their 60 TB datastores, which in many respects is a shame because it is great fun squeezing every last ounce of performance out of a database server.

In this age of consumer-driven "some is good, more is better" attitudes, it's all too easy to upgrade your hardware to bring performance in line with expectations. When you are already operating on the edge of hardware performance capabilities, however, you need to look at alternate ways of optimizing what you are doing.

Although I don't want to spoil your enjoyment of the later chapter on custom components, I've got to tell you about something really exciting to do with producing custom code for use in your packages. This approach will probably be frowned upon by the "reuse" purists, but I guess it depends on how extreme you need performance to be. Most of the components that ship with SSIS are produced in such a way as to be reusable in many different packages. This means that they can't perform as well as they would if they were produced for one specific application. They aren't coded poorly, but they do need to have a certain amount of open-endedness and so cannot perform processing in the most efficient and tight way. If you find yourself in a situation where you simply must have better performance from a particular component, consider rewriting it with the emphasis away from reuse and on performance, or inherit from an original SSIS component and override the poorly performing method(s).

My advice is to squeeze every ounce of performance from the hardware you've got before you take the easy option. It will pay off, trust me. When your integration project suddenly has to scale up from two million rows a day to one hundred million, you can look your boss in the eye and say "no problem."

CHAPTER 13

SSIS Security

You can look at SSIS security in many different ways, though essentially—and based upon the idea that security *should* be implemented—you have two opposite approaches to choose from.

One approach is to make security considerations an integral part of SSIS package development. This means identifying potential areas of insecurity and investigating methods within the operating system, SQL Server, and SSIS to resolve them. This is probably the least-used approach in solutions development, though it really shouldn't be.

The second approach is to engage in package development without considering security until functionality has been completed. This means retrofitting security into an already completed model, which is never ideal. Not only will it make for less intrinsic and integrated security, but it will probably also require much more development time. This approach is, sadly, the one that is used most often.

Back in the early days of (popular) computing, security was never a real concern. Distinguished industry pioneer Richard Stallman didn't even want to include password protection on operating systems and did everything in his power at MIT to prevent passwords from being introduced. Even today, computer security isn't taken as seriously as it should be by corporations, individuals, and even law enforcement. I foresee huge challenges that will result from this relaxed attitude, especially in a world where legislators, law-enforcement officials, and even the general public have little or no understanding of security concepts.

This state of affairs leaves developers and other technically gifted specialists vulnerable to poorly formed and poorly understood legislation. Actions that seem perfectly innocuous to most techies (for example, sending source code via e-mail or a ZIP file containing the results of a query) have the potential to be misinterpreted by the layperson, with possibly serious consequences.

If not for the protection of systems and data, we should consider security to be of paramount importance as a way of protecting ourselves and our colleagues against recrimination. Maybe it shouldn't be that way, but it is. As the technology industry grows and sucks in more people who didn't grow up learning assembly language, the more some of these people will be exposed to situations in which they can make a quick buck from someone else's work. Make sure you don't get implicated in something sinister by protecting yourself with every security method available.

This chapter looks at introducing security because it's necessary. Whatever your reasons, read on and make your SSIS solutions watertight.

SSIS Security Options

You can implement security in SSIS solutions in a number of different ways, depending on circumstance and requirements. All are easy enough to implement, and all configuration is performed through familiar tools. Ultimately the choice of how much or how little security to implement is up to you, but packages can be secured at a variety of levels. Let's take a look at what you can do.

Before I go much further, it is worth noting that cooperation with your local systems administrator (sysadmin) will help in creating a more holistic approach to security. Sysadmins generally have a greater level of system access and understand topics such as NTFS, group security policies, and folder-sharing permissions. Because of the nature of SSIS, most security configuration will take place directly as part of SSIS, but some of it can be at the level of the filesystem and user-account permissions.

The basis of a secure SSIS solution is not rooted in SSIS, in just the same way that *any* application running on any operating-system platform ultimately relies on other factors to be secure. This begins with a secure hardware platform upon which the Windows Server operating system is installed. A complex piece of software, especially one as function rich as Windows Server, has a staggering number of configuration options that can create an insecure environment if they're incorrectly set. This environment in turn supports the applications installed on it, such as SQL Server 2005, and of course SSIS sits on top of that too.

So, it's not enough to just concentrate on securing SSIS. Before considering SSIS security requirements, the securing of hardware, operating system, and SQL Server installation are all prerequisites; otherwise the securing of SSIS is essentially pointless.

Approaching SSIS security with a clear idea of what is necessary and expected will help you not only achieve the required level of security but also implement it in as rapid a manner as possible. This includes considerations such as who should be able to view a package, who can change it, and who can execute it. How sensitive is the data being manipulated by the package? What are the particularly insecure points along the path of package execution that need particular attention?

From a more formal perspective, the questions to be addressed are

- Do you need to digitally sign your package to avoid hacking attacks?
- Does a package or a part of it need to be encrypted?
- Who should access your packages?
- Should your packages be secured at server level?
- Do you need to implement custom security for your packages?

This chapter provides the information you need to implement measures that answer each of these questions.

Digitally Signing Packages (Or, Do You Need to Know If a Package Has Been Changed?)

Just like a handwritten signature but impossible to forge, a *digital signature* marks an SSIS package as being, at the point of signing, legitimate and from a *trusted source*. If a package is changed, the digital signature is broken, and the detection of any change is therefore possible by checking the signature.

The first requirement to enable the signing of a package is to obtain a special file called a *certificate*. The first step is to select Digital Signing . . . from the SSIS menu in the IDE to display the screen shown in Figure 13-1.

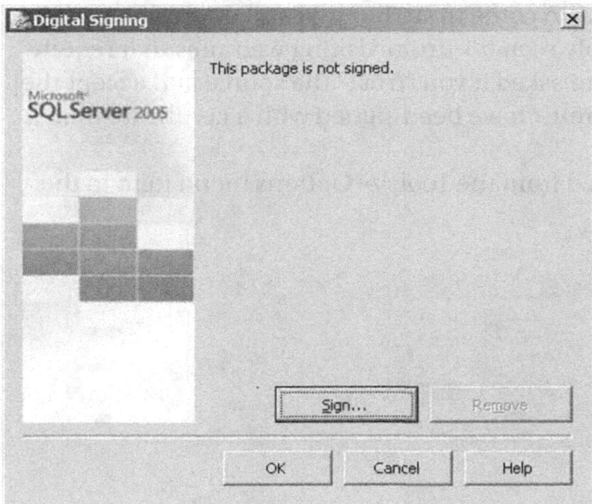

Figure 13-1. *The Package Signing introduction screen*

A certificate can be requested from a Certificate Authority (CA). This authority might be a third party (used more to get certificates for Internet use) or a Windows Server on your local network that acts as a CA. Certain prerequisites apply to certificates for use with SSIS.

Certificates are assigned one or more *purposes*. For SSIS use, the Code Signing purpose must be among these assigned purposes. In addition, the certificate root authority must be a trusted publisher. Finally, the certificate should be available in the current user's Personal Store for SSIS to pick it up; otherwise you'll see an empty list of certificates (see Figure 13-2).

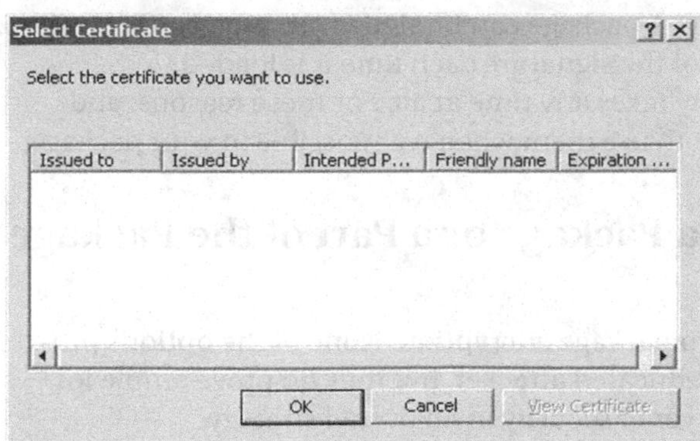

Figure 13-2. *I don't have any certificates in my Personal Store.*

Of course, it isn't expected that the digital signature should be checked manually before each execution. SSIS provides native management of this. It is required, however, that the `CheckSignatureOnLoad` property be set on the package. If everything checks out—the certificate is valid and from a trusted source—then the package loads transparently. If problems are encountered, however, the SSIS runtime highlights them.

This brings the issue of *trust* into the equation. A digital signature is only an indication that the package comes from whom it purports to come from, but that still doesn't mean it comes from a trusted source. You have probably seen this from visiting web sites that require the download of signed ActiveX controls: you're asked if you "trust" the source and accept the download. In the very same way, the package must have been signed with a certificate that comes from a trusted source.

Additional options in this area are accessed from the Tools ➤ Options menu item in the IDE (see Figure 13-3).

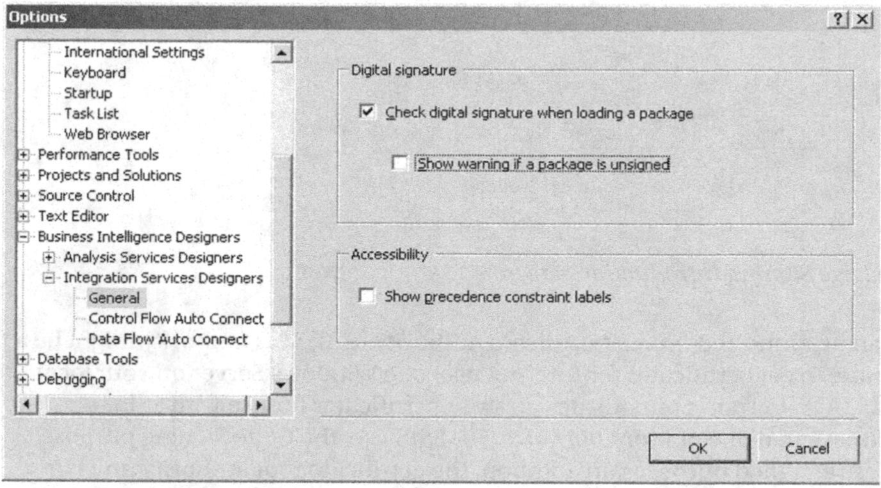

Figure 13-3. *Some more options hidden away!*

With these settings, the circle is complete. A package can be signed, and the configuration properties can be set to enable the checking of the signature each time it is loaded.

Using digital signatures is easy and hardly takes any time at all. For these reasons, and because of their security benefit, I advise you to use them whenever possible in your packages.

Package Encryption (Or, Does a Package or a Part of the Package Need to Be Encrypted?)

SSIS offers a number of options with regard to package encryption. None of the options provides sufficient protection against the more-educated attacker, but they do prove ample for most internal purposes or as an additional layer of security in an overall strategy.

Two exposed package properties are noteworthy. The first, `PackagePassword`, is used in conjunction with the second property, `ProtectionLevel`. `ProtectionLevel` has six possible values. Discussing them brings up a few additional concepts to learn and issues to address.

The first of these concepts is the *user key*. All you really need to know is that it's a security value assigned to individual user accounts by the operating system, created at the point the account itself is created. It is a public key that is unique to the particular instance of the user account—which means a user account of the same name could be created, but its user key would be entirely different. A change of password for the user account is also irrelevant to the user key.

Herein lies the first problem. Because the user key is generated from the user account, those wishing to gain access to anything secured with the user key need only log into the account. This *could* be considered to be a good thing, but outside of the development environment don't forget that the user key will be different even for an account with the same name (if it is created in a different environment). A *different* key is generated when the account is created in *each* environment.

Administrators can change the account password and log in, and encrypted files are decrypted and available to them. Also, a nasty surprise can come if the user account is lost or deleted. Without proper contingency planning, the user key can be lost, and access to encrypted files will be forsaken and irrecoverable through legitimate means.

The user key is used in other encryption operations such as use of the Encrypting File System (EFS) in Windows.

The security measures offered natively through SSIS and SQL Server are vulnerable to attack. They can be breached successfully with a little effort and knowledge. Vigilance through usage monitoring and effective security policy can limit the effectiveness of attacks, especially because most intrusions will be brute-force based and by definition require repeated access attempts to succeed. This is where consultation with your trusty sysadmin will pay dividends.

Fortunately, within SSIS additional security measures can be implemented at package level to provide extra protection. The following package-protection levels can be specified:

`DontSaveSensitive`: Saves the package with all sensitive information, such as passwords, removed.

`EncryptSensitiveWithUserKey`: Sensitive data is encrypted using the user key. Other users can open the package, but any sensitive data will be cleared. Only the user who created and saved the package (and therefore encrypted it using their user key) can see the sensitive data.

`EncryptSensitiveWithPassword`: Sensitive data is encrypted using the password entered in the `PackagePassword` property. This isn't as secure as encrypting with the user key but is more portable.

`EncryptAllWithPassword`: This option encrypts the entire package and contents using the `PackagePassword` value. This makes the package portable and moderately secure.

`EncryptAllWithUserKey`: The entire package is encrypted using the user key. Obviously, this makes the package much less portable, because it is tied to a specific user account. It does, however, make it more secure.

`ServerStorage`: Security considerations are deferred to SQL Server. Care should therefore be taken to ensure SQL Server security is adequately configured! This option is available only if the package is saved to SQL Server instead of the filesystem.

Sensitive data, such as passwords, is stored in the package as clear text unless expressly specified otherwise. When a property is marked as sensitive in a component, an XML attribute is used in the actual package file to identify it as such to SSIS. The `Sensitive` attribute—and attributes in general—gets more coverage in Chapter 15.

I have to repeat something about the use of user keys here. There is no legitimate way of recovering data—SSIS packages included—that is encrypted with user keys if access to the very same user account that created the data is lost. Notice that I said no *legitimate* way. There are some pretty quick and easy ways to get around this user key–based security but, obviously, I have no wish to propagate knowledge that could be used for system intrusion.

Also, a word to the wise: it is widely rumored that EFS, like most commercial security products, has a back door that is left open primarily for law-enforcement reasons. In fact, I have been told as much by a senior police official. This might be a good thing in terms of crime detection, but it does leave the door open for the determined criminal to exploit.

By way of illustration, I have created two packages and specified different security methods. The first example (Figure 13-4) shows the XML representation of a package file with a `ProtectionMethod` value of `EncryptSensitiveWithUserKey`.

```
PerformanceIssues1.dtsx - Notepad
File Edit Format View Help
<?xml version="1.0"?><DTS:Executable xmlns:DTS="www.microsoft.com/SqlServer/
pointFileName"></DTS:Property><DTS:Property DTS:Name="SaveCheckpoints">0</D
<DTS:ConnectionManager><DTS:Property DTS:Name="DelayValidation">0</DTS:Prope
<DTS:ConnectionManager><DTS:Property DTS:Name="DelayValidation">0</DTS:Prope
<DTS:ConnectionManager><DTS:Property DTS:Name="DelayValidation">0</DTS:Prope
<DTS:ConnectionManager><DTS:Property DTS:Name="DelayValidation">0</DTS:Prope
<DTS:LogProvider><DTS:Property DTS:Name="ConfigString">new trace.trc</DTS:Pr
<DTS:PackageVariable><DTS:Property DTS:Name="PackageVariableValue" DTS:Data
  &lt;diagram fontclsid="{0BE35203-8F91-11CE-9DE3-00AA004BB851}" mouseiconc
    &lt;font&gt;
      &lt;ddsxmlobjectstreamwrapper binary="01010000900180380100065461686f6
    &lt;/font&gt;
    &lt;mouseicon&gt;
      &lt;ddsxmlobjectstreamwrapper binary="6c7400000000000" /&gt;
    &lt;/mouseicon&gt;
  &lt;/diagram&gt;
  &lt;layoutmanager&gt;
    &lt;ddsxmlobj /&gt;
  &lt;/layoutmanager&gt;
  &lt;ddscontrol controlprogid="DdsShapes.DdsObjectManagedBridge.1" tooltip
    &lt;control&gt;
      &lt;ddsxmlobjectstreaminitwrapper binary="000800000e0e00008c040000" /
    &lt;/control&gt;
    &lt;layoutobject&gt;
      &lt;ddsxmlobj&gt;
        &lt;property name="LogicalObject" value="{EB74CAD2-9BB5-475D-B50D-D
        &lt;property name="ShowConnectorSource" value="0" vartype="2" /&gt;
      &lt;/ddsxmlobj&gt;
    &lt;/layoutobject&gt;
    &lt;shape groupshapeid="0" groupnode="0" /&gt;
  &lt;/ddscontrol&gt;
&lt;/dds&gt;&lt;/dwd:Layout&gt;&lt;/dwd:DtsControlFlowDiagram&gt;&lt;/Packa
<DTS:PackageVariable><DTS:Property DTS:Name="PackageVariableValue" DTS:Data
  &lt;diagram fontclsid="{0BE35203-8F91-11CE-9DE3-00AA004BB851}" mouseiconc
    &lt;font&gt;
      &lt;ddsxmlobjectstreamwrapper binary="01000000900144420100065461686f6
    &lt;/font&gt;
    &lt;mouseicon&gt;
      &lt;ddsxmlobjectstreamwrapper binary="6c7400000000000" /&gt;
```

Figure 13-4. *A very open package that could be easily copied*

The second example (Figure 13-5) shows the same package with a `ProtectionMethod` value of `EncryptAllWithPassword`.

Figure 13-5. *A package encrypted with password. Much better!*

It's very easy to choose the protection method required and from there, SSIS and the IDE handle the implementation of that method seamlessly.

Caution The more determined individuals among us will find decrypting a package, even without the password or user key, child's play. Make additional security preparations and don't even think about e-mailing packages that must remain secure, without using SSL or another security protocol.

Package Access (Or, Who Should Access Your Packages?)

The question of package access comes down to two considerations that define your interpretation of "access." The first consideration is who should be able to execute your packages. The second is who should be able to edit them. Limiting access in either scenario is easy enough and can be performed by a variety of means—including, in part, the security options specified in the preceding subsection.

Ultimately though, the practice of how to secure package access depends on factors such as where it is stored, the development and production environments, team structure, and project architecture.

Evaluating and using the tools at your disposal is always a good idea. In this particular instance, SSIS, SQL Server, and NTFS security options are available to leverage.

Leverage NTFS Security

If your packages are stored as .dtsx files in the filesystem, leveraging the features of NTFS security is one option to take. As a mature and robust technology, NTFS security serves nicely in providing user-based access via folder or file permissions for any kind of file.

Although it is might be a familiar practice to most readers, it's a good idea to have a brief review of how to set up and configure NTFS permissions. Also, you should ensure your approach segues into the rest of your organization. This is another instance when speaking with your sysadmin is a good idea.

Configuring permissions can start with individual user accounts or, more properly, with a user group or group policy. By way of demonstration I'm first going to configure my package folder to allow access only to a particular user.

Figure 13-6 shows the user accounts on my local development machine.

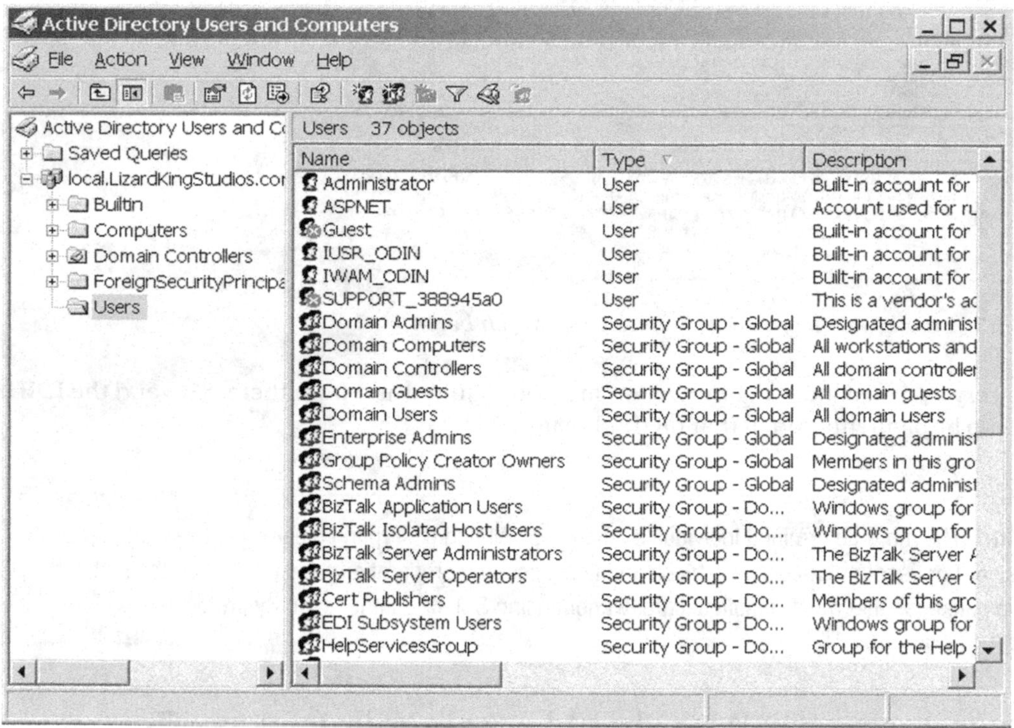

Figure 13-6. *My local and domain user accounts*

I could easily just configure the package folder to allow access only to my own user, but that would mean other users could not access my packages or execute them. This might be just the solution you're looking for . . . but it's unlikely. Perhaps a better way would be to create some new user accounts to use specifically for this purpose.

I'm going to create two new users. I'll assign read-only permissions on the package folder to the first user, SSISPackageReadOnly. The second user, SSISPackageReadWrite, will have full read/write permissions allowing the editing and alteration of the package. The user names here are entirely arbitrary so feel free to choose your own if you're following along.

Figure 13-7 shows how to add a new domain user.

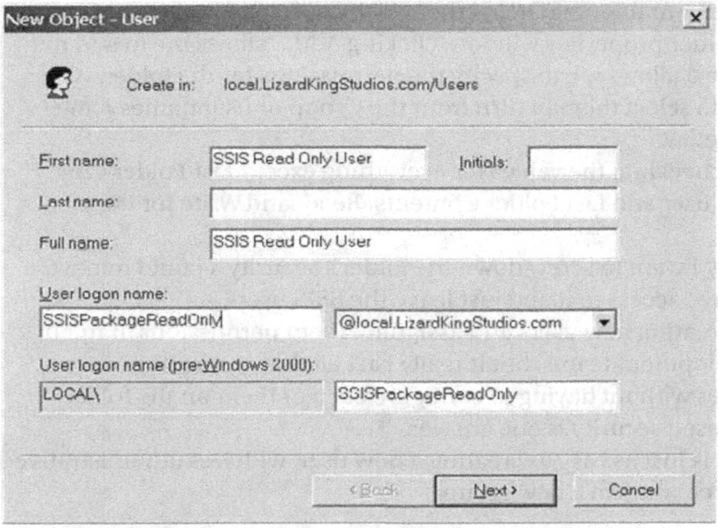

Figure 13-7. *Adding a new domain user*

With the accounts created I'm now going to look at folder permissions by right-clicking the folder in a Windows Explorer instance, selecting Properties, and then looking at the Security tab (Figure 13-8).

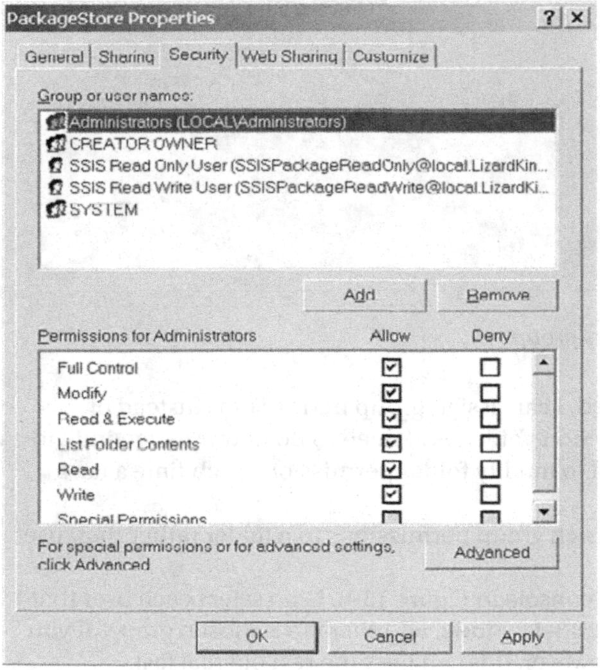

Figure 13-8. *Folder security properties*

Notice that I'm looking at permissions on the containing folder rather than individual .dtsx (package) files. It is possible to set the permissions on each package file, but as far as I'm concerned, limiting access to the container that holds them is the way to go.

On the Security tab of the folder properties window, clicking Add... allows me to add my two new SSIS package users. It also allows me to specify the permissions for the folder. With the two users I've added, I need to select them in turn from the Group or user names pane, then choose their permissions below.

I start by deselecting (or unchecking) the values for everything except List Folder Contents and Read for the read-only user and List Folder Contents, Read, and Write for the read/write user.

Depending upon how tightly I want to screw down the folder's security, I could remove the other groups or users that have access to it and just leave the SSIS users.

There are obvious flaws to creating new users and assigning them permissions. It might be fine to do this in smaller development teams, but it really isn't all that secure, is it? Somehow keeping assigned user names without having to configure each of them on the folder would be a good thing. Group-based security is one answer.

Creating user-group objects is just as easy as creating a new user, with less administrative overhead. Figure 13-9 shows the creation of a new group.

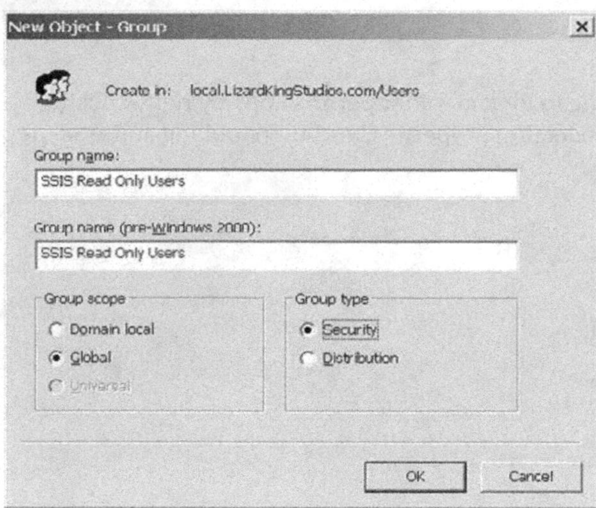

Figure 13-9. *Creating an SSIS Read Only Users group*

With a new custom-made group created, I can assign group permissions instead of assigning user permissions on the Package Store folder. All I need to do now is assign individual users to the group, and I no longer need to modify folder permissions each time a user needs access to a folder.

Figure 13-10 shows the operation to assign group permissions to a folder rather than user permissions.

Going back to the user-administration console in Figure 13-6, I can select each user that I want to add to my new group and, as Figure 13-11 shows, add them to a chosen group. If you have more than a couple of users to add, however, this can become real old real fast.

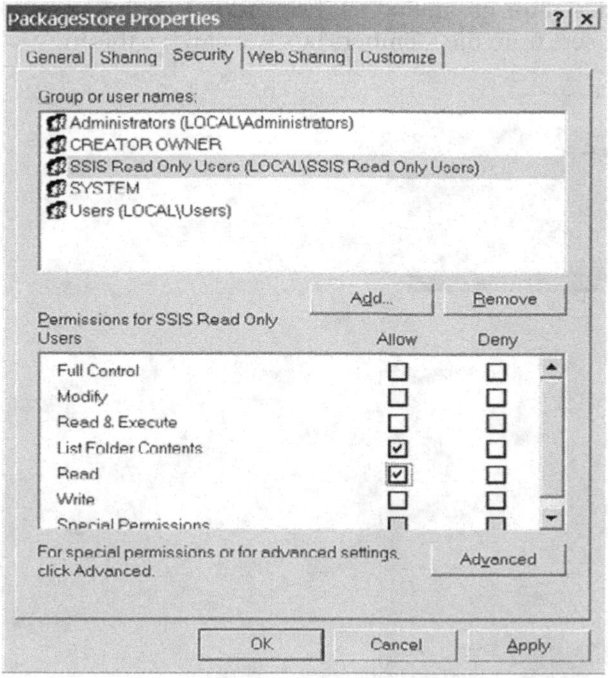

Figure 13-10. *Assigning group permissions*

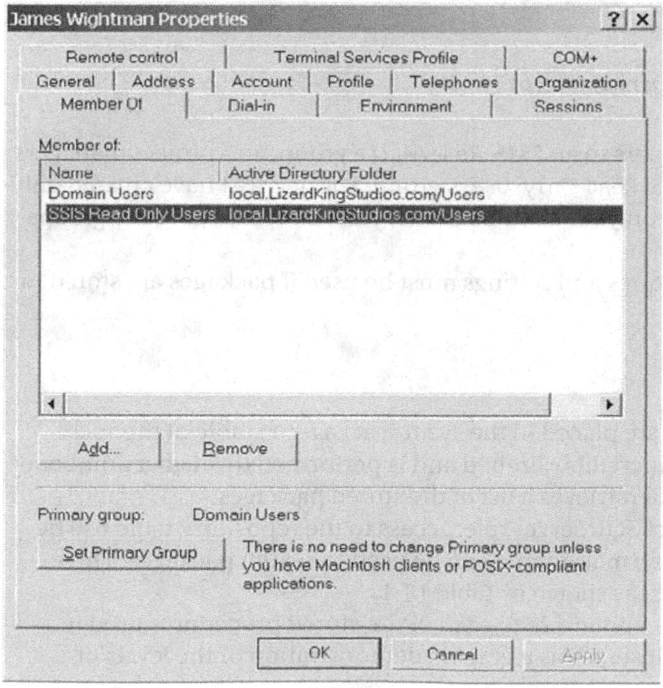

Figure 13-11. *Adding groups to users individually*

An alternative is to look at the properties of the group that has been added—in my case `SSIS Read Only Users`—and add relevant users from the Members tab. You can see this in Figure 13-12.

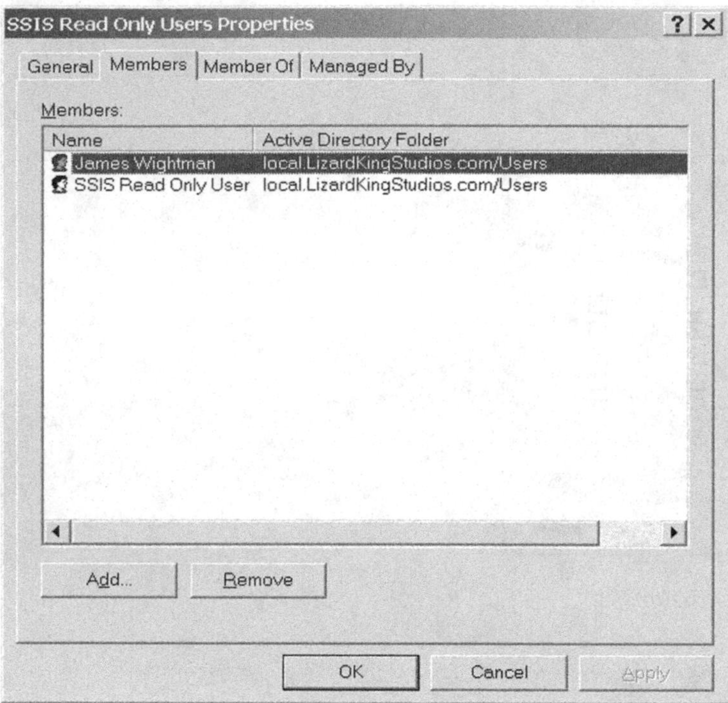

Figure 13-12. *The easy way: assigning users to groups*

And we're done. I can add developers to an `SSIS Read/Write` group, and project managers or other lower-access users to the `SSIS Read Only Users` group. For brevity I have created only two groups, but of course, depending on your circumstances, you can create as many groups as you need.

An entirely different set of techniques and settings must be used if packages are stored in SQL Server.

Leverage SQL Server Security

When stored in SQL Server, packages are placed in the `sysdtspackages90` table of the `msdb` database. Access to this repository is incredibly limited and is performed through a number of stored procedures—including one that retrieves a list of the stored packages.

Without assignment to the correct SQL Server role, access to the repository table will be denied. This is handy to know—it's information that can be used to secure packages. Three `msdb` database roles control this access, as shown in Table 13-1.

Table 13-2 shows the permissions applicable to each of the stored procedures used to access the SQL Server Package Store. It serves as a graphic demonstration of the levels of access available to each role.

Table 13-1. *SSIS-Specific Database Roles*

Database Role	Description
db_dtsoperator	Allows only the most basic of operations: retrieve a list of packages and execute a package.
db_dtsltduser	Allows retrieval of the list of packages, and allows the creation and modification of packages.
db_dtsadmin	Allows all operations: listing, creation, modification, and execution of packages.

Table 13-2. *SSIS Administrative Stored-Procedure Permissions*

Stored Procedure Name	Database Role	Protection
sp_dts_addfolder	db_dtsadmin	Grant
	db_dtsltduser	Grant
sp_dts_addlogentry	db_dtsadmin	Grant
	db_dtsltduser	Grant
sp_dts_checkexists	db_dtsadmin	Grant
	db_dtsltduser	Grant
	db_dtsoperator	Grant
sp_dts_deletefolder	db_dtsadmin	Grant
	db_dtsltduser	Grant
sp_dts_deletepackage	db_dtsadmin	Grant
	db_dtsltduser	Grant
	db_dtsoperator	Grant
sp_dts_getfolder	db_dtsadmin	Grant
	db_dtsltduser	Grant
	db_dtsoperator	Grant
sp_dts_getpackage	db_dtsadmin	Grant
	db_dtsltduser	Grant
	db_dtsoperator	Grant
sp_dts_getpackageroles	db_dtsadmin	Grant
	db_dtsltduser	Grant
sp_dts_listfolders	db_dtsadmin	Grant
	db_dtsltduser	Grant
	db_dtsoperator	Grant
sp_dts_listpackages	db_dtsadmin	Grant
	db_dtsltduser	Grant
	db_dtsoperator	Grant
sp_dts_putpackage	db_dtsadmin	Grant
	db_dtsltduser	Grant
	db_dtsoperator	Grant
sp_dts_renamefolder	db_dtsadmin	Grant
	db_dtsltduser	Grant
sp_dts_setpackageroles	db_dtsadmin	Grant
	db_dtsltduser	Grant

It is also possible—and at times desirable—to secure individual packages rather than the SQL Server store as a whole. Figure 13-13 shows the Package Roles dialog. You access it through the `msdb` store by right-clicking the package and selecting Package Roles… from the context menu.

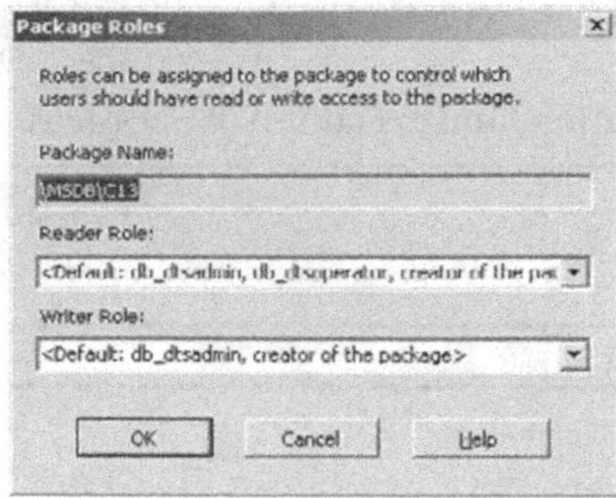

Figure 13-13. *Setting package permissions*

Changing the values in the Reader and Writer role drop-down lists will mean access is limited to those roles specified. That being the case, additional roles can be created (just as when I created new user groups for NTFS) that have more clearly defined permissions *and* inherit permissions from the stock `db_dts*` roles.

Creating a new role using the SQL Server Management Studio is easy enough. Imagine I want to create a role for the development team and one for the deployment team in my organization.

After opening SQL Server Management Studio and navigating to Roles under the Security node of the Database Server, I see a screen similar to Figure 13-14. I have right-clicked on Database Roles in this instance, so I can see the New Database Role... context-menu item.

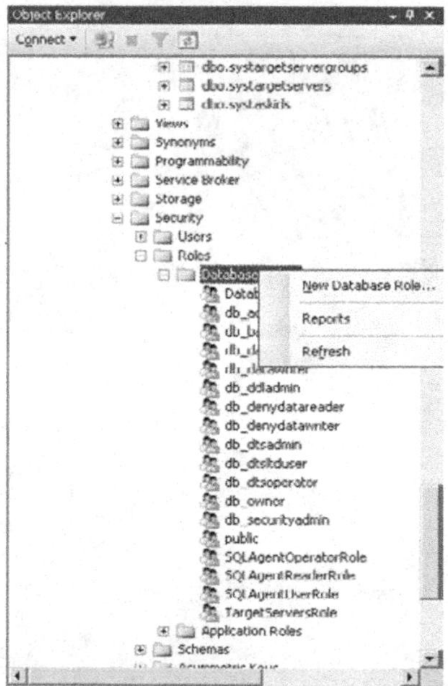

Figure 13-14. *Ready to add a new database role*

Now I'm going to create a new role just for developers, featuring only the permissions such a role would require. Figure 13-15 shows the screen for configuring new roles.

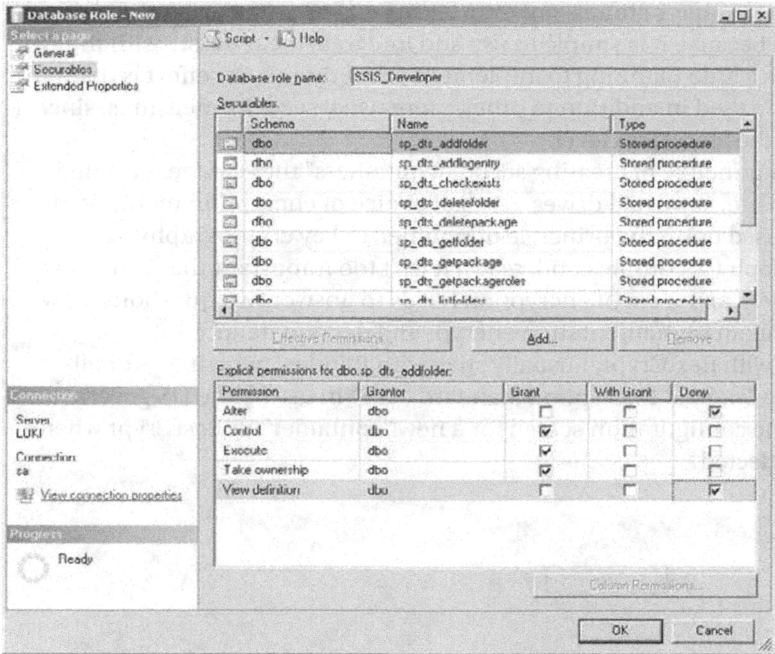

Figure 13-15. *My new SSIS_Developer role*

Having created a new role, I can go back to the Package Roles dialog (Figure 13-13) and configure the reader or writer to use my newly created role.

Custom Security Options

Since it is possible to create SSIS packages programmatically, consideration could be given to implementing custom security the same way. Admittedly this method could prove to be quite convoluted, and certainly a large amount of flexibility would be lost—but how far you need to go depends on business requirements.

Custom Launcher

You could simply create a secure "Package Launcher" application that adds additional layers of security on top of NTFS and interfaces with SQL Server and SSIS package security.

Jetico BestCrypt

There are times when the ultimate level of security is required. The best product I've ever used to provide this is from a Finnish company called Jetico (`http://www.jetico.com`). Jetico offers a wide range of personal and corporate security products, including a military-grade file shredder

(BCWipe) and a data encryption tool (BestCrypt) that implements US government–approved encryption. I'm not on their payroll but I can't help gushing at how much I appreciate the work Jetico has put into this product.

I have used BestCrypt a number of times, not only because of its amazing speed and security characteristics, but because it is simple to use and integrates seamlessly with the Windows filesystem. It does take a little planning to implement properly, but the effort is definitely worth it. BestCrypt should be used in addition to other, more usual security measures, since it provides protection only at the filesystem level.

BestCrypt works on the principle of creating secure "containers" that can be mounted, through the BestCrypt interface, as virtual drives. A select choice of encryption methods are available, all of which are based upon the principle of symmetric-key cryptography.

The subject of cryptography is complex and, really, it isn't too important that you know the inner workings. Ultimately, any form of encryption needs to answer two questions: how secure is it? How quickly does an implementation encrypt and decrypt data?

Of the choices on offer with BestCrypt, I usually stick with Rijndael, which is—for all intents and purposes—the Advanced Encryption Standard (AES) in use by the US government. Figure 13-16 shows the configuration screen for a new "container" in BestCrypt where the encryption method is selected.

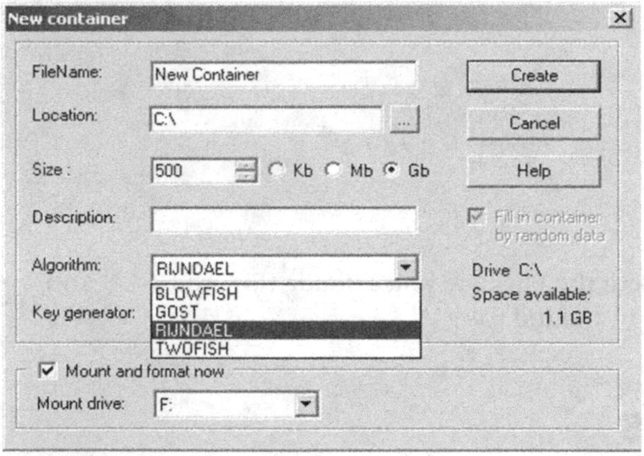

Figure 13-16. *Choosing container properties*

I'll take you through one of my previous solutions in which I used BestCrypt. The client requirement on this particular project was that the highest levels of operating-system and application security should be implemented. So far, so good. However, the sensitivity of the data concerned required additional measures.

The security model I proposed was that the database should be mounted and available only when absolutely necessary. This meant when the retrieval of data was required or when data manipulation, through SSIS, was taking place. In addition, SSIS packages needed to be in a (logically) separate secure location for development and maintenance purposes, though the location should be equally secure.

I created two encrypted containers using BestCrypt. One held the SQL Server database files (database and logs), and the other was for the SSIS packages. I set the BestCrypt containers to use Rijndael encryption. Pretty secure!

I then wrote a number of command-line scripts to mount the encrypted containers as virtual drives and mount the database files subsequently in SQL Server. I also created scripts to perform the opposite operation to dismount the containers cleanly and secure them once processing was complete.

This worked well. BestCrypt enforces the entry of the key each time a device is mounted, the value of which should obviously remain closely guarded. The key was subsequently changed once my work was completed, meaning only a handful of people had access to the data.

A big boost to BestCrypt's security comes inherently as a consequence of its design. Should the server be powered off for any reason (including being stolen), the containers remain unmounted at next boot, because the secure containers must be mounted before they can be used, and the mount operation requires entry of the key. This makes the holder of the key—rather than the technology supporting it—the weakest point of the security chain.

Summary

As always, the correct strategy to take is the one that best fits your individual requirements. Demonstrating and specifying best practice is great, but it isn't always possible to implement every security measure in every environment.

I will summarize this chapter, however, by saying that I cannot stress enough how important security is. I personally fitted night-vision closed-circuit television cameras to my house, which in many respects is overkill—I live in a nice neighborhood and already have an alarm fitted—but I would rather do too much than be left with regret and a house emptied of its contents.

The same is true of computer systems, though for whatever reason the security of data isn't taken as seriously across the technology industry. Perhaps the problem stems from the time it takes to implement security properly, or maybe it's an underestimation of the capabilities and prevalence of criminals in this industry. Whatever the reason, the time to make a difference is right now. Plan for a secure solution and stop the offenders in their tracks.

The next chapter focuses on scripting in .NET, which will give you the tools and knowledge to leverage some of the .NET base classes within SSIS, including those that handle encryption and cryptography.

CHAPTER 14

Scripting, .NET Style

This chapter, along with Chapter 15, goes black-ops on the programming aspects of SSIS. This chapter covers scripting in SSIS along with topics such as object-oriented programming (OOP), .NET, debugging, and many more. Since it deals with the conceptual elements of programming with SSIS, it doesn't cover C# or Visual Basic .NET in any great detail.

You'll read about

- **Principles of object-oriented (OO) design**: C# and VB.NET are OO languages, and .NET is built on OO principles.
- **Common .NET concepts**: The Common Language Runtime (CLR), Microsoft Intermediate Language (MSIL), the Common Type System (CTS), are the fundamental .NET elements.
- **Using the** `Script Component`: You'll learn about the component's classes and work through an implementation example.

This chapter serves as a primer to Chapter 15, where you'll apply everything you learn here to the creation of custom components for use in SSIS.

Development Environments

Before I start, I'll say a quick word about development environments. I'm talking about platform and tools installation rather than the IDE, which Chapter 4 discusses in detail.

The traditional approach to the developer's working environment is to install everything on a single development machine. I used to do that too. I would install so many development tools on my PC that it would be pretty useless for anything else because of all the background support services running. Also, of course, it's another of those all-eggs-in-one-basket situations: if the PC fails, it's game over for the entire development environment. I've since found a much better alternative: virtual machines (VMs).

Microsoft Virtual PC is cool and affordable, but I use VMware, primarily because I think it is a more-robust, enterprise-level product with many more features. Figure 14-1 shows my main VMware screen.

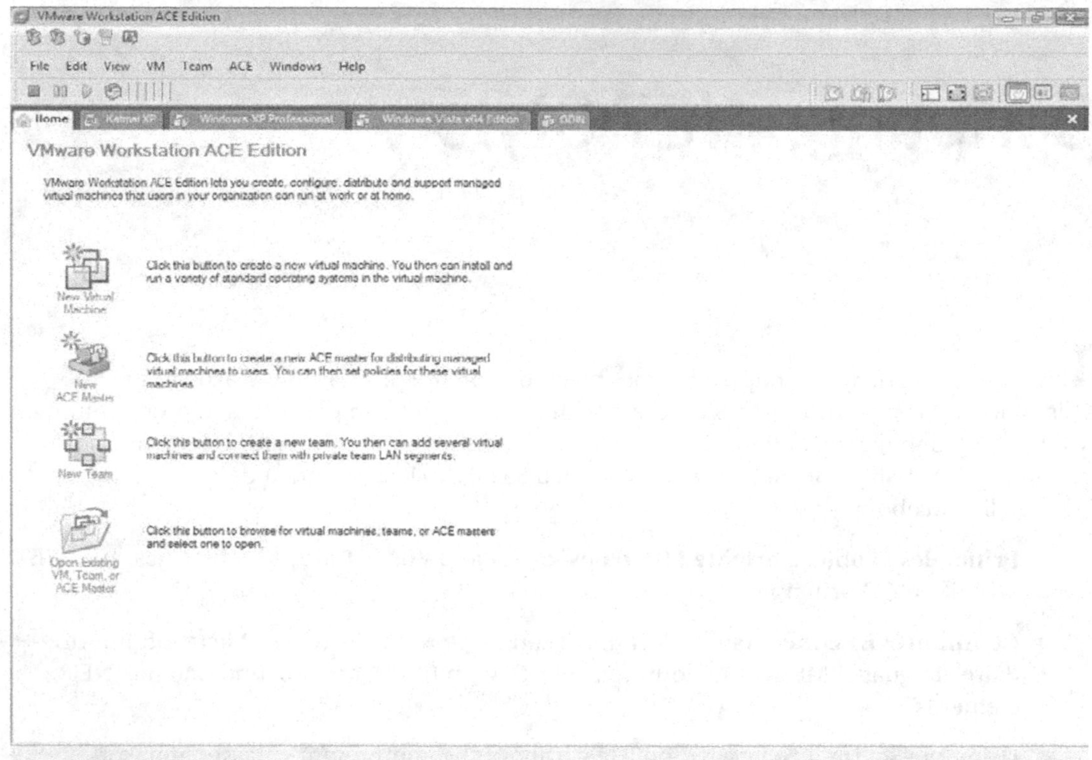

Figure 14-1. *The VMware Workstation main screen. Each tab is a VM I have open.*

Using a VM setup brings many advantages, and it isn't as time consuming to configure as one might imagine. Essentially you create a single VM on which you install your operating system. The VM software (well, VMware at least) can then create standalone clones of the original, and individual environments can then be configured. I have separate environments for Visual Studio 2005, Orcas, Katmai, BizTalk, Sharepoint, and even Linux. I back them up regularly to avoid nasty surprises.

The final bonus of using VMs is that the files are portable. I can take them from PC to PC (so long as the PC is licensed of course) and start developing immediately.

OOP

When I first came across C++ in about 1986, I just didn't get it. More accurately, I didn't see the point or understand the use of these "new" things called classes. In my defense, I was only ten years old at the time and my background was in Z80 Machine Language, 6502 Assembly Language, and C. I'm not looking to be excused, however, because I should have identified the potential of OOP right away. It wasn't too long, though, before I was just head over heels about C++ and OOP in general, and I've stayed that way ever since.

Depending on your background and organizational role, you may or may not have experience with OOP. You will certainly have had limited exposure (if any) to OOP if your skills are rooted in SQL Server alone. SQL Server programmability was procedural-only until the release of SQL Server 2005. Even with SQL Server 2005, most programming is inside standard stored procedures, which remain non-OO in nature.

So you've managed to get along quite nicely in SQL Server without OOP until now. Why the change? What's the point? What does it give you?

The Benefits of OOP

OOP is a useful tool for expressing the interaction between objects and for creating concrete implementations of conceptual models. OOP promotes more code reuse than other methodologies and produces a higher level of code maintainability. (One thing I never forget, however, is that I was writing perfectly serviceable, efficient, reusable, and highly maintainable code before I'd even heard the term *object oriented*.)

.NET is a technology with its roots deep within OO principles. Visual Basic .NET is an OO language, as are C# and C++. This makes the question of whether OOP is a good or bad thing utterly irrelevant to the general developer. If you are using SSIS and using the `Script Task/Script Component`, or want to use custom components, you will be touching on some or all OO principles.

OOP is, fundamentally, just another methodology. It's more flexible than some and less flexible than others. The concept of using objects in OOP means that features such as *encapsulation, inheritance*, and *polymorphism* can be leveraged—but these concepts are just another means to the same end: reuse and maintainability.

OOP 101

OOP is a complex and far-reaching topic that can't be adequately covered in a few short pages, but you will learn enough to work with the scripting component in this chapter and with custom components in Chapter 15.

Not surprisingly, OOP is based upon the concept of *objects*. An object can be anything. This page is an object. You are an object. The eyes with which you read this text are objects. Everything and anything can be expressed in terms of an object.

Objects in OOP are really quite rich—they have *properties* (much like, say, a train object has wheels) and *methods* (like a train object can start and stop) and can interact with other objects in a variety of ways as defined by OOP principles.

Let's look at a simple example using the train object from the preceding paragraph. This example will also give you insight into how easy it is to produce a poorly designed object model—and how to avoid doing so. I'll illustrate this and subsequent examples using the Visual Studio class-diagram viewer.

Classes and Interfaces

Before I get to the example, you need to understand two important new concepts: the class and the interface.

Classes are the building blocks of OOP. They are used to contain logical groupings of methods and properties. If that sounds simple, that's because it is. Any complexity comes from the concepts I'll discuss later in this section.

Object interaction at runtime is performed through creating an *instance* of a class. Instancing is a process whereby a physical in-memory structure is created that represents the logical class model. All methods and properties of the class relate to the created instance.

Classes, unless they are defined as *abstract* (explained in the next paragraph) implement a *Constructor* (or *ctor* as some call it). This special method is called whenever an instance of the class is made, and it can be used to initialize the class in whichever way you see fit.

A class can implement properties and methods directly or can be defined as abstract. An abstract class cannot be instantiated; instead a class must inherit from this abstract class, so in many respects an abstract class is like a template.

A class can implement an *interface*—a type of object that contains definitions for properties and methods (without content) but for which an instance cannot be created and instead must be implemented by a class. In C# the syntax for this is `public class myClass : myInterface`, and in VB.NET it's `Public Class myClass Implements myInterface`. Essentially, an interface details, in terms of methods and properties, a contract to which any class that implements it must adhere. This means that a class implementing an interface must contain at least the methods and properties defined in the interface.

Finally, classes can also be defined as *static*. This means that an instance of the class cannot be created, and instead access is shared: the properties and methods of the class can be accessed without an instance being created.

Figure 14-2 shows one way an `ITrain` interface could be expressed. The examples in this section use interfaces rather than classes because this is the way to work with OOP in .NET today. For the purposes of the following examples and diagrams, assume that although I am defining interfaces, the implementing classes are identical in their implementations.

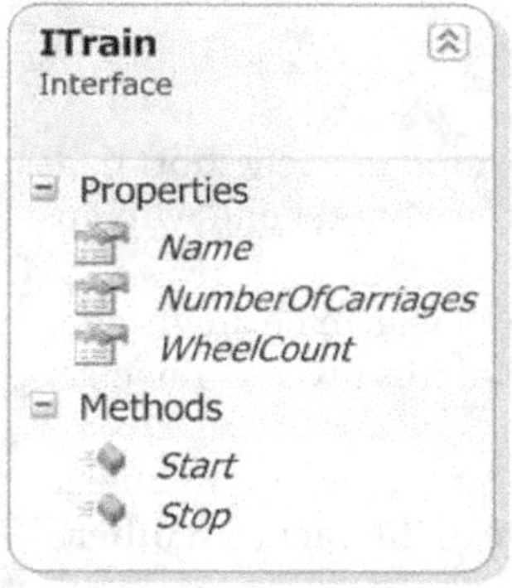

Figure 14-2. *ITtrain interface*

This interface seems to make sense, because it has a series of properties to express the `Name`, `NumberOfCarriages`, and `WheelCount`, and two methods that provide functionality to `Start` and `Stop` the train.

In theory there doesn't look like too much is wrong with this object model. In practice, however, it is very limited and not very OO in nature. The limitations become apparent when I want to extend the scope of my requirements. Imagine for a moment that I needed to define additional vehicles within my model. Not a problem: I can create a new interface for the new vehicle type. Figure 14-3 shows the definition.

Now I have two interfaces that share some of the same properties and methods but exist entirely separately from each other. This means that code is implemented in two separate locations to perform the same tasks—something that goes against the idea of using OO to promote code reuse and increase maintainability.

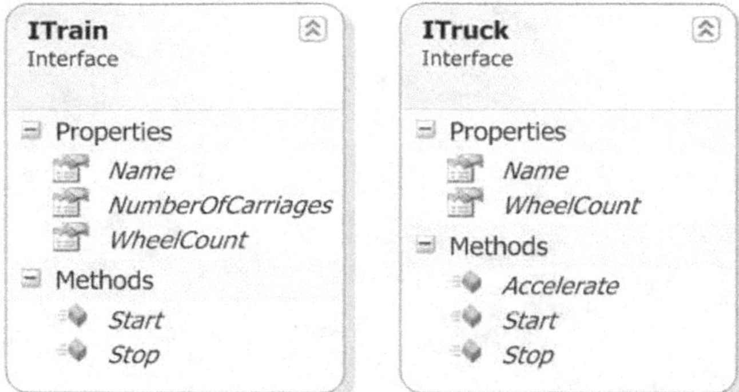

Figure 14-3. *ITrain and ITruck, similar but not identical*

I'll take another look at the problem, keeping OO in mind. I've got two classes that share some properties and some methods but also have extra properties and methods depending on the class. This sounds like the ideal opportunity to look at inheritance.

Inheritance

Any object in the real world can be usually be defined and classified as being constructed from a more generic "parent" object. The most generic object from which subsequent objects can be derived can be considered the *base class*—the construct that is the lowest common denominator of all subsequent child objects (or at least the most *sensible* lowest common denominator; taking the concept too far defeats its purpose).

For example, if you wanted to create an OO model of all life on our planet, your aim would be to identify a base object that could succinctly describe all life and be used to describe and define subsequent diversity. Depending upon how literally you wanted to take the term "all life on our planet," you could go all the way back to the classification of kingdom, through phylum, and all the way to specific species such as human or dog or *Rhododendron macrophyllum*. For the purpose of brevity however, a more reasonable starting point might be at the level of *animal*.

All animals share certain common, base properties such as movement, respiration, sensitivity, growth, reproduction, excretion, and nutrition. Using animal as the base class, a structure can be built up that accurately describes each level in the hierarchy. Eventually you find yourself with an object at the very bottom that, based on the objects preceding it (and the specific properties that are relevant only to the object itself) describes a human or a dog or whatever else.

Most OO designs aren't as complex as trying to map the entirety of planetary life, however. And this brings me back to the original train and truck problem. It should be possible to introduce a more generic object that contains the properties and methods shared between a truck and a train and any other kind of vehicle you might care to mention.

So I can define a base interface that contains the properties and methods that relate to all classes that are derived from it. I'll call it `IVehicle`. Figure 14-4 shows a representation of the `IVehicle` interface.

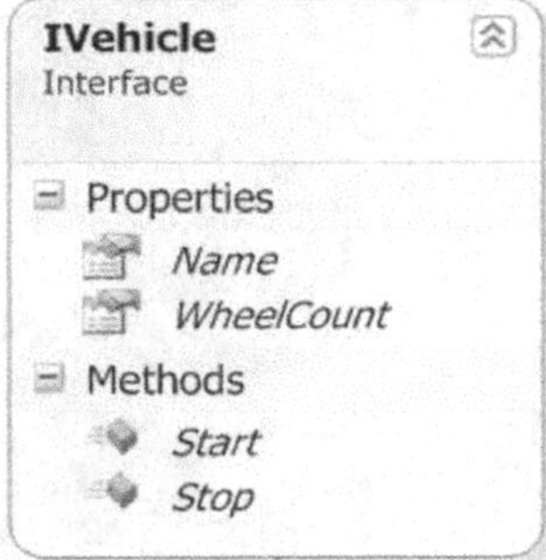

Figure 14-4. *The base interface contains common properties.*

This is a great first step, but it doesn't explain how this relates to the train and truck classes. Thanks to inheritance—one of the main features of OO—you can specify that your child interfaces derive (inherit) from a base interface (or any other interface, in fact), in addition to the interface's own properties and methods.

With this in mind, a more OO way of addressing the problem can be seen in Figure 14-5. You can see from Figure 14-5 that the `ITruck` and `ITrain` interfaces now only have additional properties defined in them, even though they clearly derive from `IVehicle`. Thanks to inheritance, the properties and methods from the base interface are exposed by the individual train and truck interfaces as if they were explicitly defined in each interface.

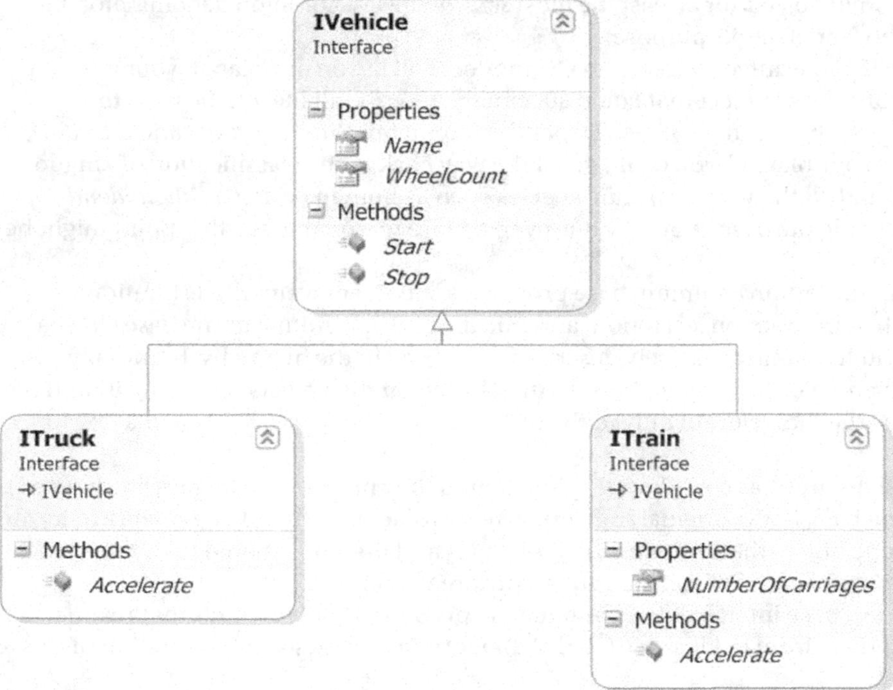

Figure 14-5. *Better use of OO using the IVehicle interface*

If I create a `Train` class by implementing the `ITrain` interface, all the properties and methods in `IVehicle` are exposed by a reference to a created instance of the `Train` class, as you can see in Figure 14-6.

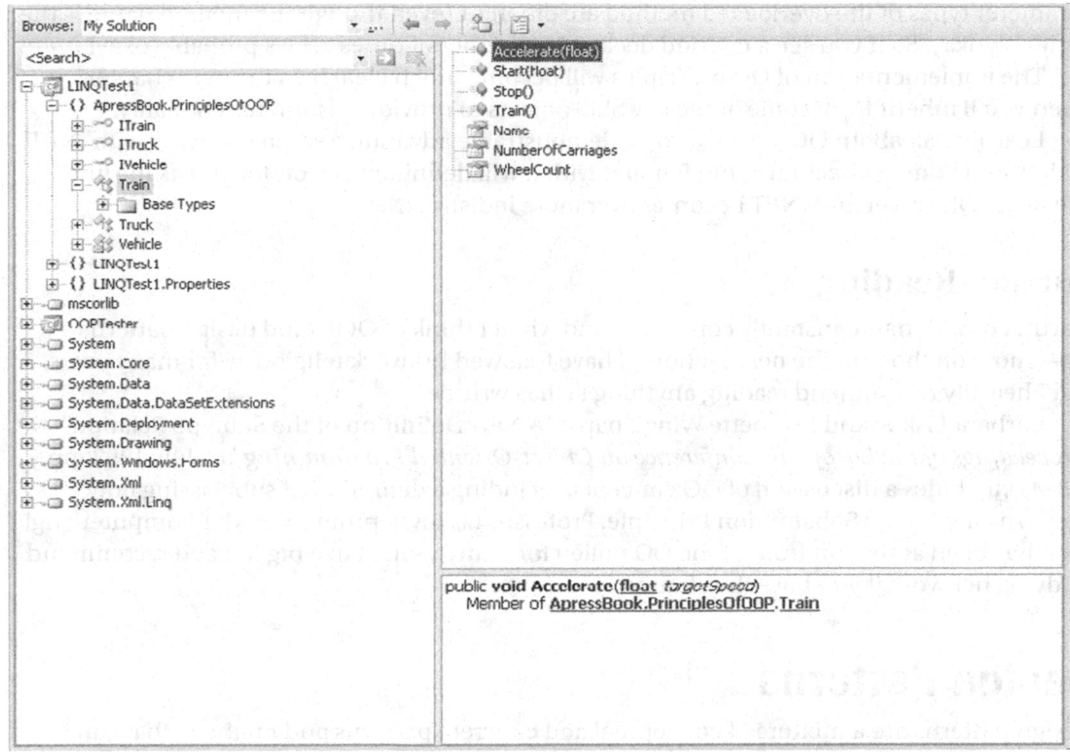

Figure 14-6. *The Train class exposes its properties and methods and those of its parent class.*

Having looked briefly at inheritance, I'll give you a view of some of the other OO concepts. Once you have the idea of how objects in OO work together, the remaining concepts are easily assimilated.

Polymorphism, Encapsulation, and Overloading

Polymorphism is the next concept to address. Taking the earlier example with the train and the truck, you can see quite easily how polymorphism works.

Imagine that the base interface's `Stop()` method means something different to the truck than it does for the train. For example, a stop command for the train could mean "emergency stop," whereas for a truck it could mean "slow down safely and come to a complete halt."

If the train and truck objects inherit from the `IVehicle` interface (and therefore are already provided with a base implementation of `Stop()`), you would therefore need to override the base interface method for `Stop()` in each object and provide individual implementations.

Encapsulation is a concept that can mean different things to different people. My take on it is that only the properties and methods of an object that need to be exposed should be exposed. This allows the implementation to work behind the scenes, and it can change as necessary without affecting other objects relying on it.

Overloading is the polymorphic practice of creating multiple methods with the same name but that take different parameters or different types of parameters. A method has a signature (the *method signature*) that identifies a method as being unique. The signature is created from the parameters and parameter types and thus, as long as the parameters and parameter types of the overloaded method are different (even though the method name is the same) it's okay. So if you see a method declared a number of times . . . it's probably okay!

The implementation of OO principles will become much clearer in the next chapter, when you'll inherit from some of the key SSIS objects to provide custom functionality.

Learning all about OO will give you a demonstrable advantage when you work with .NET. Taking some time to become more familiar with it will definitely pay off for you as the line between SQL Server and .NET becomes ever more indistinct.

Further Reading

Martin Fowler's name instantly comes to mind when I think of OOP (and design patterns too—more on those in the next section). I have followed his work religiously for many years, and I heartily recommend reading anything he has written.

Barbara Liskov and Jeannette Wing's paper "A New Definition of the Subtype Relation" (*Proceedings of the European Conference on Object-Oriented Programming '93*, July 1993, pp. 118–41) includes a discussion of OO concepts, including a definition of subclassing now known as the Liskov Substitution Principle. Professor Liskov, a prominent MIT computer engineer, has been at the forefront of the OO milieu for many years. I'm a big fan and recommend studying her work if you have the chance.

Design Patterns

Design patterns are a mixture of conceptual and concrete patterns and methods that can be implemented to solve common (and oft-encountered) programming problems. Each pattern provides a conceptual blueprint that has been proven to provide a satisfactory (most often OO) solution when implemented in code.

To attribute credit where it's due, design patterns were first discussed in 1977 by Christopher Alexander. Those design patterns were not software related, but they did provide the spark for the application of similar concepts in computer science years later.

The most basic design pattern of all is probably the Singleton. As the name suggests, this pattern is based on the principle that only a single instance of a class (or other object) is allowed—and that subsequent requests to instantiate the object return a reference to the original, single instance rather than a new instance. This pattern is used when a single-instance object is required to coordinate global operations of some kind.

I have heard of situations where the requirement to have a only single running instance of an application is said to follow the Singleton pattern . . . and I guess to a degree that's accurate. I personally think it's too simplistic an interpretation of the pattern, but the topic is always a good way to start a heated debate in meetings.

Design patterns are great and can be helpful. They really are for the more hardcore developer, however, and are pretty much a take-it-or-leave-it subject. Design patterns aren't required reading or essential knowledge for developing with SSIS, but I recommend learning more about them as your programming skills progress.

Further Reading

Design Patterns: Elements of Reusable Object-Oriented Software by Erich Gamma, Richard Helm, Ralph Johnson, and John Vlissides (Addison-Wesley, 1994) is on the bookshelf of every developer I know. It is an investment well worth making.

Each of the patterns the authors (known as the Gang of Four) describe in the book are squarely aimed toward OO programming. SQL-centric design patterns *are* slowly emerging from within the darkest recesses of the smartest brains around the world. You will probably be surprised, as are many developers, that you've been implementing these design patterns all along and didn't know they had an "official" name.

.NET Concepts

The big question for this section is how much you actually need to know about .NET architecture when you use .NET with SSIS (in whatever form that use may take).

I have a tendency to err on the side of the argument that says knowing too much is better than knowing too little. Still, some topics need only the briefest of mentions before I move on to the more important ones:

CLR: With the introduction of the CLR, Microsoft has provided an easy-to-use and feature-rich framework that exists symbiotically with the operating system. It takes care of pretty much everything to do with getting your code into an executable format and looking after it as it runs. Gone are the days where programmers need to look after memory allocation and deallocation. (You can still do that if you really want to, but it isn't really an issue when you code for SSIS.) Code running under the CLR is referred to as *managed* because the CLR environment regulates and manages all the important (but tedious) low-level resource management on your behalf.

CTS: The CTS describes how types—referring to the type of an object—are declared and used in the CLR.

CLS: The CLS describes a base subset of language features that must be included in a language for it to be used with the CLR.

MSIL: .NET code is compiled into an intermediate language ready for execution within the .NET Framework. MSIL is the Microsoft standard defined for this language.

Garbage collection: As I said in the CLR description, .NET looks after memory usage natively. This includes cleaning up references to objects that are no longer used or that have gone out of scope. If you are familiar with VB 6 you probably remember using the `set myObject = Nothing` statement to release references and return memory back to the operating system. .NET's garbage collector handles this transparently.

At this point you really don't need to know about the internals of .NET and how everything hangs together. A passing familiarity with some of the buzzwords should prove sufficient to at least start you on the path to becoming a .NET expert—if that is what you want to become. (And if you do, I can assure you it is an exciting and worthwhile endeavor that will reap many rewards.)

Everything You Need to Know About .NET but Were Afraid to Ask

Now I'll get down to the bare bones of what you need to know to start programming in a .NET language such as VB.NET or C#.

When it comes to the areas of SSIS for which writing code is relevant and necessary, Microsoft has provided a helping hand. Not only has it made VB.NET the language of choice (in my opinion, an easier language to learn than C# although no less powerful), but in areas such as the `Script Component`, behind-the-scenes code templates guide and assist the developer.

You'll find that I mix together information about C# and VB.NET in the remainder of this section. I've done this for two reasons. First, most enterprise-level applications of SSIS probably require custom components of some description. Since custom controls can be written in any CLR language, some developers might have more experience of C# than VB.NET (or C++ or Cobol.NET . . .). Second, some of you might know enough basic VB.NET to get by with the `Script Component` but want to learn the magnificent C# language in full. I hope some of my comments will help tip the scales in the direction of learning C#, because it is a better-designed language and also a gateway to other fantastic languages such as C++.

Let's dive in and take a look at some of the principles of .NET programming.

Scope and Access Modifiers

Scope in the SSIS Designer refers only to variables. In .NET, scope can be applied to classes, methods, variables, and all sorts of other objects. Table 14-1 lists the access modifiers used in both C# and VB.NET.

Table 14-1. *Access Modifiers for C# and VB.NET*

C# Scope Syntax	VB.NET Scope Syntax	Description
`public`	`Public`	Accessible anywhere from within the same project, other projects that reference the project, or from any assembly built from the project
`protected`	`Protected`	Accessible only from within the same class, or a derived class
`internal`	`Friend`	Accessible from within the same assembly, not from an outside assembly
`protected internal`	`Protected Friend`	Accessible from derived classes, from the same assembly, or both
`private`	`Private`	Accessible only from within the same class, structure, or module

In VB.NET, anything declared without an access modifier is `Public` by default, whereas in C#, it is `private` by default.

Types

Although the CTS defines a common set of types that allow interoperability between .NET languages, they are named and implemented in a subtly different way in each language. Table 14-2 compares the implementations.

Table 14-2. *Types for C#, VB.NET, and the Runtime*

C# Type	VB.NET Type	Runtime Type	Size
`bool`	`Boolean`	`System.Boolean`	4 bytes
`byte`	`Byte`	`System.Byte`	1 byte
`char`	`Char`	`System.Char`	2 bytes
`DateTime`	`Date`	`System.DateTime`	8 bytes
`double`	`Double`	`System.Double`	8 bytes
`decimal`	`Decimal`	`System.Decimal`	12 bytes
`int`	`Integer`	`System.Int32`	4 bytes
`long`	`Long`	`System.Int64`	8 bytes
`object`	`Object`	`System.Object` (class)	4 bytes
`short`	`Short`	`System.Int16`	2 bytes
`single`	`Single`	`System.Single`	4 bytes
`string`	`String`	`System.String` (class)	10 bytes + (2 * string length)

This covers the basics, certainly in terms of what you need to work on the `Script Component` and with custom components in Chapter 15. A few extra concepts will show their face at some point in this chapter and the next, but I'll look at them as they come up. Meanwhile, if you become familiar with the topics I've covered in this section, you shouldn't have too many problems moving forward.

Classes in the Script Component

The `Script Component` automatically generates a bunch of code to support the particular configuration you specify before you click Design Script....

A number of classes are generated for use and separated into three distinct logical blocks that, behind the scenes, are actually `.vb` class files. If you look in the Project Explorer in the code IDE, you can see this logical separation of `BufferWrapper`, `ComponentWrapper`, and `ScriptMain`. You can right-click the entries in the Project Explorer and select `Export [name of class file]` to save the `.vb` file to a file location.

The classes contained within `BufferWrapper` and `ComponentWrapper` are locked as read-only in the editor because they are generated depending on component configuration. If configuration of the component changes, the contents of these two class files is regenerated, and so anything added would be lost anyway—which is why they are set as read-only.

The `BufferWrapper` class file contains a generated class for each of the inputs and outputs configured in the component. Each class representing a buffer derives from `Microsoft.SqlServer.Dts.Pipeline.ScriptBuffer`, which is a part of the `Microsoft.SqlServer.TxScript.dll` assembly. The properties and methods generated in these classes provide access to the buffers; you can think of them as helper classes.

Figure 14-7 shows the class hierarchy of the individual buffer classes.

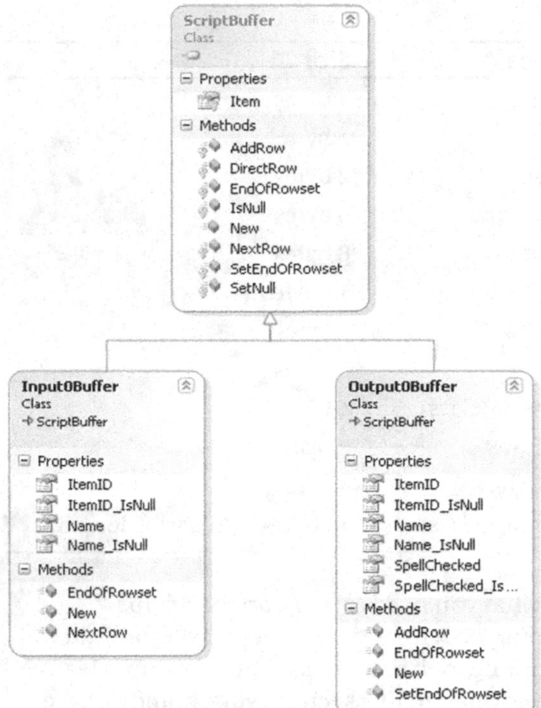

Figure 14-7. *Input and output buffers and their shared base class*

ComponentWrapper is the next class file to look at. It too is pregenerated, and also regenerated when configuration of the component changes. Classes are generated for connections and variables configured in the component and are made accessible through the third generated class, UserComponent. This class is derived from the Microsoft.SqlServer.Dts.Pipeline.ScriptComponent class in the Microsoft.SqlServer.TxScript.dll assembly and can be seen as another helper class that provides access to and manipulation of input and output buffers held in the BufferWrapper.

Finally, the ScriptMain class file contains a single generated class, ScriptMain, which doesn't get regenerated depending upon changes made to the configuration. This is the class that holds and executes any code you want to use for processing. The ScriptMain class derives from UserComponent, which means it has access to the input and output buffers and also methods and properties to manipulate them. Variables and connections can also be accessed because of the class's derivation from UserComponent.

Figure 14-8 shows the class hierarchy from ScriptMain through to the ComponentWrapper.

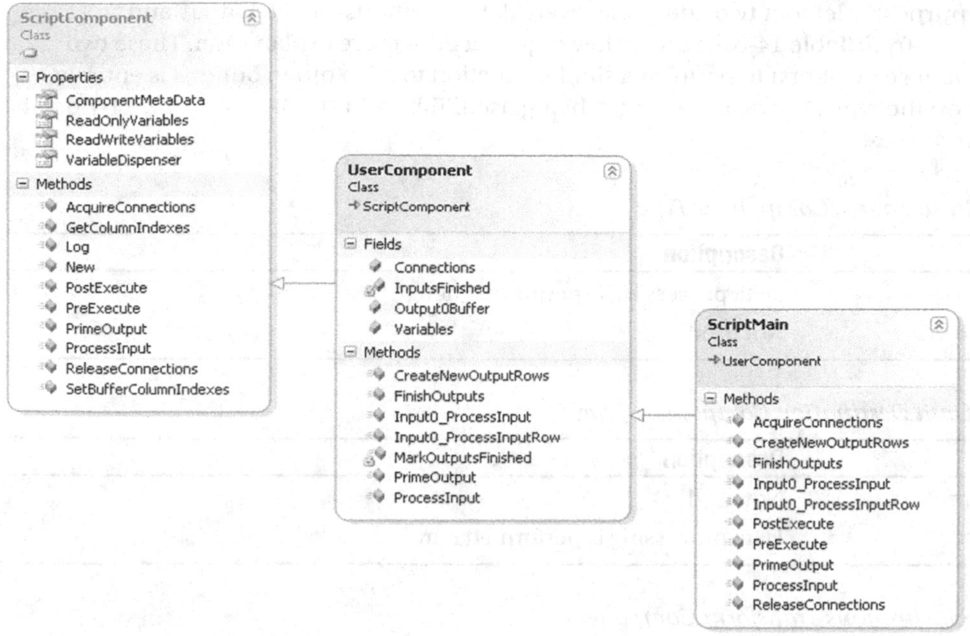

Figure 14-8. *Class hierarchy for the Script Component*

Thanks to OO, you have the flexibility to override any of the methods or properties from the `UserComponent` class and the `ScriptComponent` class in the derived `ScriptMain` class. This lets you implement your own functionality to replace that already held in the other classes.

The methods available for overriding in the `ScriptMain` class, along with their potential usage, are shown as Table 14-3.

Table 14-3. *Overridable Methods in ScriptMain*

Method	Description
`AcquireConnections`	Used to establish a connection to a connection manager
`CreateNewOutputRows`	Primarily used when creating a source-type `Script Component` to create new output rows
`FinishOutputs`	Used if you need to perform some operation against the outputs before the connection to them is closed
`[InputName(s)]_ProcessInput`	Can be used to control the processing of each row (using calls to `ProcessInputRow`) in cases where additional processing is required
`[InputName(s)]_ProcessInputRow`	Used for transformation-type `Script Components` to implement code to perform transform on a per-row basis
`PostExecute`	Can contain code to be executed before execution begins
`PreExecute`	Can contain code to be executed after execution finishes
`ReleaseConnections`	Used to disconnect from an external data source

I have purposely left out two additional overridable methods—`PrimeOutput` and `ProcessInput`—from Table 14-3, because they require a little more explanation. These two methods might seem at first to perform a similar function to each other, but this is entirely dependent on the type of `Script Component` being used. Tables 14-4, 14-5, 14-6 and 14-7 detail these different uses.

Table 14-4. *Data Source Component Type*

Method	Description
`PrimeOutput`	Data processing is performed here.
`ProcessInput`	Not used.

Table 14-5. *Data Destination Component Type*

Method	Description
`PrimeOutput`	Not used.
`ProcessInput`	Data processing is performed here.

Table 14-6. *Synchronous Transform Component Type*

Method	Description
`PrimeOutput`	Both data input and output are handled in this method.
`ProcessInput`	Not used.

Table 14-7. *Asynchronous Transform Component Type*

Method	Description
`PrimeOutput`	Handles the parsing of data from the input to the output buffers.
`ProcessInput`	This method handles the outputting of data.

This section serves as the first step in learning the intricacies of the `Script Component`. As I stated at the start, however, SSIS does lend a hand where possible and create code outlines for you inside the `ScriptMain` class where appropriate.

DEBUGGING THE SCRIPT COMPONENT

Breakpoints don't work in the `Script Component`. Instead, make use of some of the .NET base classes for features such as logging to the Event Log or leveraging `System.Diagnostics.Debug` and using DebugView (which is a great Sysinternals tool for viewing debug statements).

You can download DebugView from `http://www.microsoft.com/technet/sysinternals/utilities/debugview.mspx`.

Script Component Crash Course

My aim is to look at leveraging the SQLCLR to produce a `Script Component` that is actually of some use in real life, then in the next chapter to show how to produce similar functionality using Visual Studio to create a custom component (and subsequently a UI to round everything out nicely).

So what will this useful task do, exactly?

It would be nice to have a `Script Component` that performs a spellcheck on a column in every row of the Data Flow as it passes through the component. Obviously, this `Script Component` will be a transformation type.

Let's break it down and look at what you're going to need to do in terms of processing inside the script. The place to start is to look at the input requirements. To keep things simple, you'll allow in a single input—though of course you could create as many as you want or not have any at all.

In terms of any parameters you might want to pass into the component, perhaps taking in a string value that signifies the column to perform the operation on is a good idea—just to make the transform a little more dynamic. You also need a boolean variable to indicate whether you want the script to add a new column to the output collection to show whether the value has been changed because of the script operation. You can take these variables in via the `ReadOnlyVariables` property of the script configuration.

Preparation

You need a database table to work from, so I've included a script, as Listing 14-1, that will create one in your database for use in this example. As you can see, it a pretty simple two-column affair. The important thing to remember is that your `Script Component` will work against any data in the Data Flow.

Listing 14-1. *The Table-Creation Script*

```
CREATE TABLE [dbo].[ScriptExample]
(
        [ItemID] [int] NOT NULL,
        [Name] [nvarchar](50) NULL
)
GO
```

Now that you've got a source table you need some data to populate it. I suggest keeping the amount of data low for now just to enable simpler and more-rapid testing. Listing 14-2 is a script to populate the table with five rows of data.

Listing 14-2. *Adding Some Data to the New Table*

```
INSERT INTO [dbo].[ScriptExample] ([ItemID],[Name]) VALUES (1,'Jamess')
INSERT INTO [dbo].[ScriptExample] ([ItemID],[Name]) VALUES (2,'Diggital')
INSERT INTO [dbo].[ScriptExample] ([ItemID],[Name]) VALUES (3,'Management')
INSERT INTO [dbo].[ScriptExample] ([ItemID],[Name]) VALUES (4,'Misspelt')
INSERT INTO [dbo].[ScriptExample] ([ItemID],[Name]) VALUES (5,'Server')
GO
```

You need Microsoft Word installed on the same server as the SQL Server instance and also, if you don't already have them, the MS Word Primary Interop Assemblies. You can download them from the Microsoft web site by searching for "Office 2003 Update Redistributable Primary Interop Assemblies."

Once you have installed them, you need to go to the installation location on your hard disk—mine, for example, is `C:\Program Files\Microsoft Visual Studio 9.0\Visual Studio Tools for Office\PIA\Office11`. Once there, copy the `Microsoft.Office.Interop.Word.dll` file into the latest 1.x .NET Framework directory (mine is `c:\windows\Microsoft.Net\Framework\version 1.1.4322.573`).

With that done you now need to configure the .NET Framework and add the Word Interop Assembly into the GAC. From the Start menu, go to the Control Panel and then into Administrative Tools.

You should see a window that looks very much like Figure 14-9. Open up the .NET Framework 1.1 Configuration tool that is highlighted.

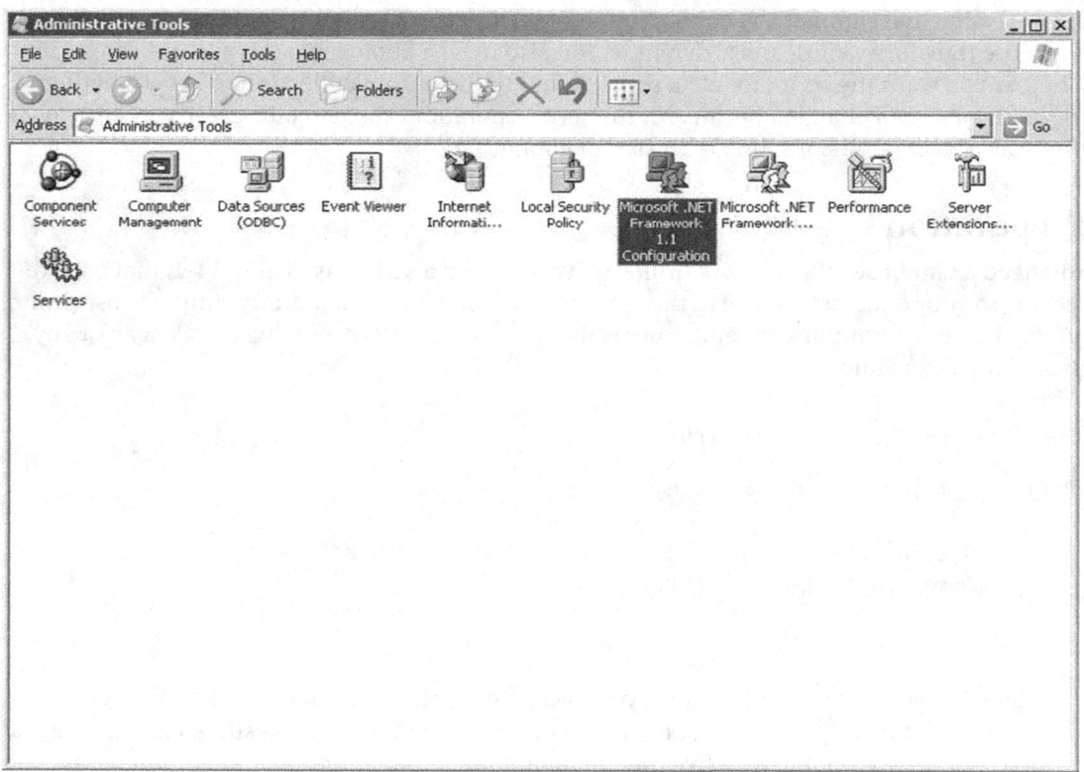

Figure 14-9. *Opening the .NET Framework 1.1 Configuration*

Once you're inside the configuration tool, you need to add the Interop file into the GAC. Figure 14-10 shows the view once the tool has opened.

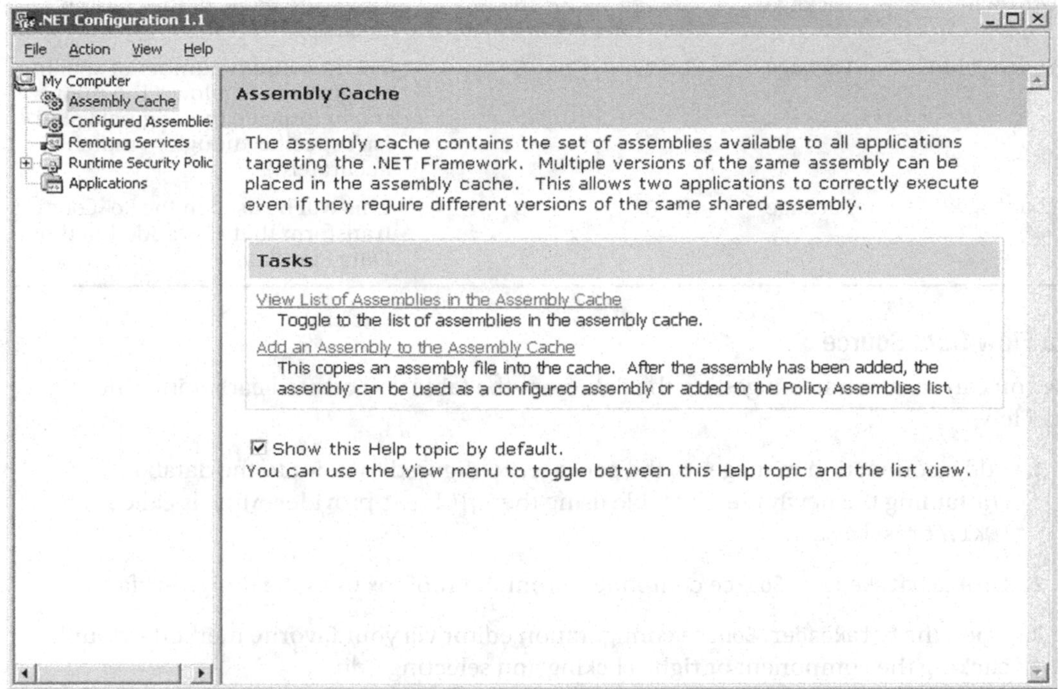

Figure 14-10. *.NET configuration*

Click on Add an Assembly to the Assembly Cache and select the `Microsoft.Office.Interop.Word.dll` file from the file browser that appears. Select Open to close the file dialog and add the file to the GAC.

Finally, as with all other examples in this book, you need to open BIDS/Visual Studio and create a new SSIS project. On the Control Flow design surface, drop a `Data Flow Task` and switch over onto the Data Flow design surface.

You are now done with preparation and can move on to the example.

Building the Data Flow

There are two parts to constructing the example. The first part is to deploy and configure the components in the Data Flow, and the second is to configure the script.

Let's kick off by creating the variables you'll need for this example. You should add the variables listed in Table 14-8. Ensure they are added at package level (which of course means you should not have any components selected on the design surface when you add the variables).

Table 14-8. *Variables and Their Properties*

Variable Name	Scope	Data Type	Value	Description
`columnToCheck`	Package	`String`	`Name`	Holds the name of the column to check.
`maxSuggestions`	Package	`Int32`	`5`	The maximum number of spelling suggestions to allow. (Too many might indicate the original value isn't specific enough to match accurately.)
`rowCount`	Package	`Int32`	`0`	This will be used in the `RowCount` transform that gets added to the Data Flow later.

Data Flow Data Source

Now you can concentrate on getting the data from the table you created earlier into the Data Flow:

1. Add a connection manager to the package, configured to point to the database containing the newly created table using the `SqlClient` provider. Mine is called `LOKI.Apressbook`.

2. Drop a `DataReader Source` component from the Toolbox onto the design surface.

3. Open the `DataReader Source` configuration editor via your favorite method—double-clicking the component or right-clicking and selecting Edit...

4. On the Connection Managers configuration tab (Figure 14-11), set the Connection Manager property to be the name of the connection manager specified in Step 1.

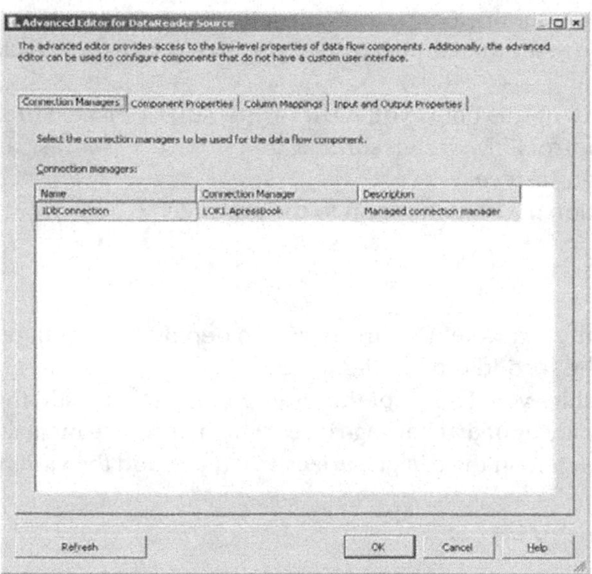

Figure 14-11. *The Connection Managers tab*

5. Move on to the Component Properties tab (Figure 14-12) and update the `SqlCommand` property so the value reads `SELECT * FROM ScriptExample`.

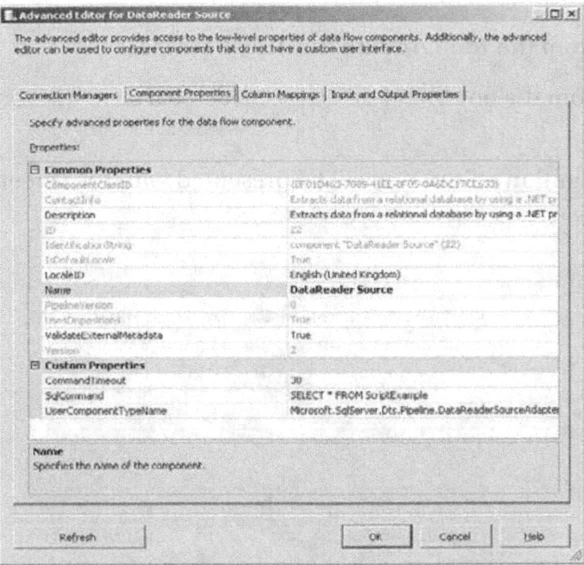

Figure 14-12. *The Component Properties tab*

6. Switch over to the Column Mappings tab (Figure 14-13) just to ensure everything looks as expected.

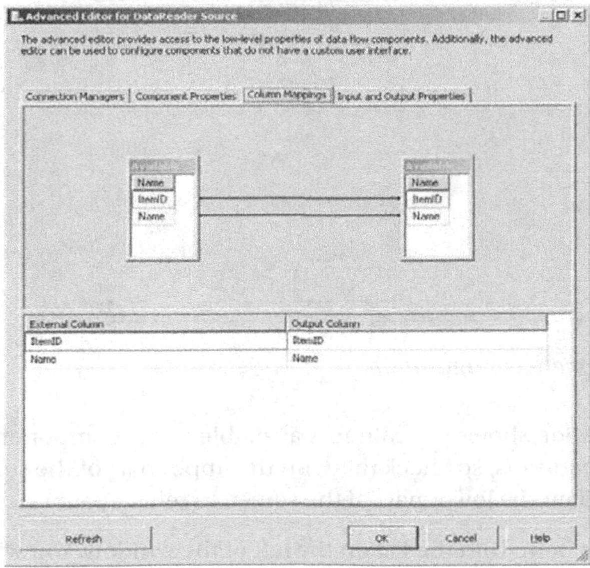

Figure 14-13. *Column Mappings as expected*

7. Click OK. You have finished configuring the `DataReader Source`.

Script Component

With data now primed and waiting in the Data Flow, you can start to work on the transform—the `Script Component`:

1. Drop the `Script Component` from the Toolbox onto the design surface.
2. Connect the success arrow from the bottom of the `DataReader Source` to the `Script Component`.
3. Open the component configuration editor. You will be presented with the screen shown in Figure 14-14.

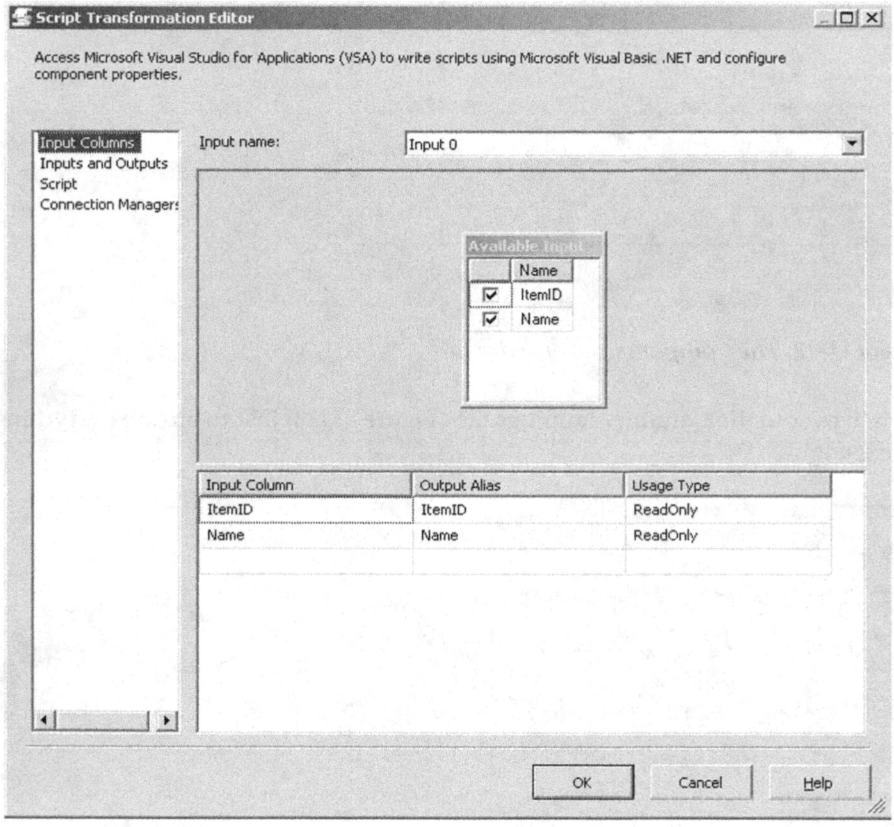

Figure 14-14. *The initial component configuration*

4. The Input Columns configuration shows the columns available to the component. For this example you'll use both columns, so check them on the upper part of the screen. This action populates the grid on the lower part of the screen to reflect your selections.
5. Select the Inputs and Outputs item from the list on the left of the window. You will see a screen similar to Figure 14-15. Before moving on to defining the individual columns, you need to tell the component to work asynchronously rather than synchronously. Although the transform you'll be performing lends itself nicely to synchronous

processing, configuring the component to be asynchronous will help give you a better understanding of the steps the script performs. (For the sake of completeness, however, you'll find a synchronous version of the same Script Component for download from `iFoo.org`.) For now, click on the `Output 0` item in the tree and change the `SynchronousInputID` property to `None`.

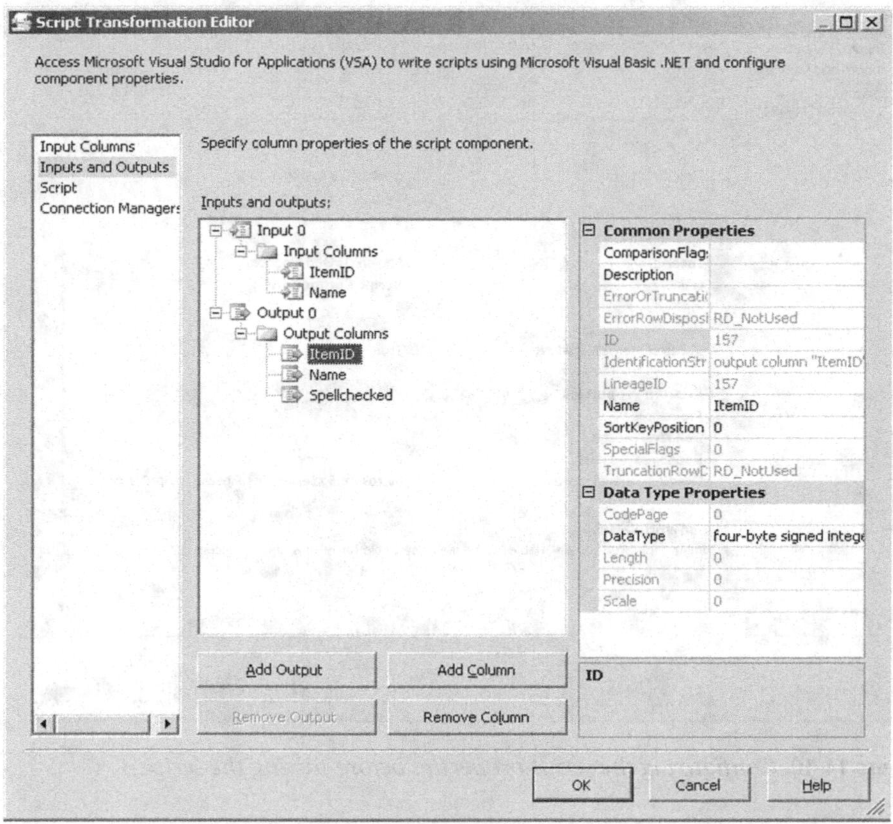

Figure 14-15. *Configuring inputs and outputs*

6. Now you need to add three new columns to `Output 0` to provide suitable output. Click the `Output Columns` folder under `Output 0` and, using the Add Column button, configure each of the new columns shown in Table 14-9.

Table 14-9. *Output-Column Configuration*

ColumnName	Data Type	Length
`ItemID`	four-byte signed integer [DT_I4]	
`Name`	Unicode string [DT_WSTR]	50
`SpellChecked`	Boolean [DT_BOOL]	

7. Move on to the script configuration by selecting the Script item in the list on the left side of the window. You will be presented by a screen like the one shown in Figure 14-16.

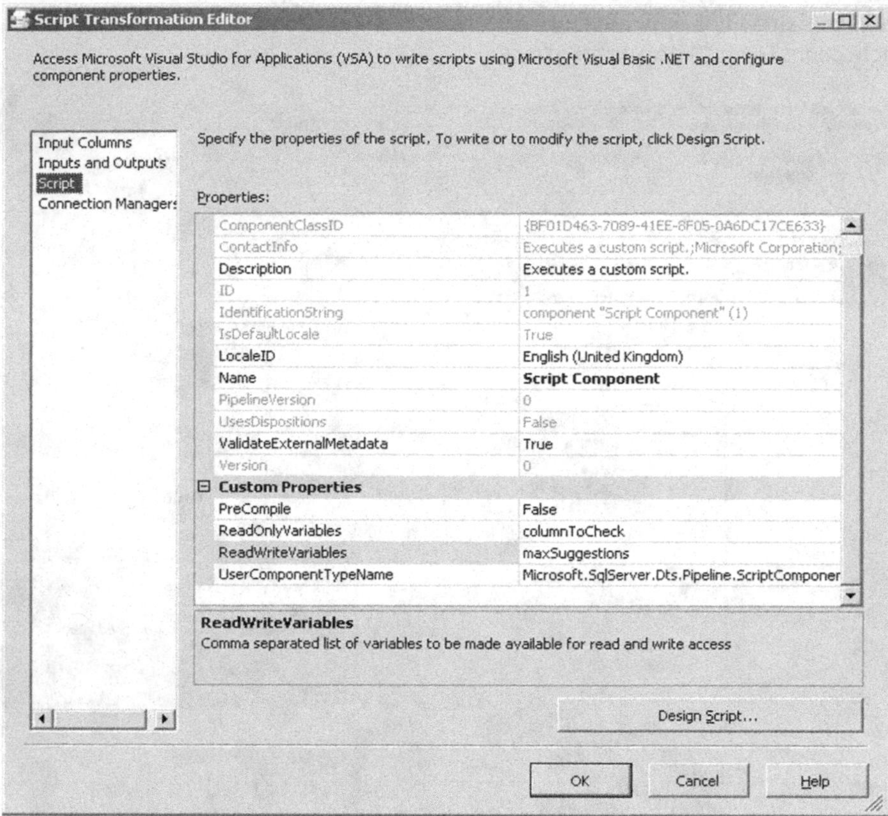

Figure 14-16. *Configuring the script properties before editing the script*

8. Configure the `ReadOnlyVariables` property with a value of `columnToCheck,maxSuggestions`.

■ **Warning** Do not use spaces in the comma-separated list of variables. This will cause an error because the space is counted as part of the variable name.

---

9. It's time to configure the script itself. Click on Design Script... to load up the script editor.

10. A reference to the Word Interop Assembly needs adding before you begin writing code. Go to the Project menu at the top of the screen and select Add Reference.... On the screen that appears, scroll down until you find the entry for `Microsoft.Office.Interop.Word`, select it, and then click Add. Click OK to add the reference and close the screen.

11. From now on you'll be exclusively editing the contents of the code window. Figure 14-17 shows my code window with new code already in place.

```
' Microsoft SQL Server Integration Services user script component
' This is your new script component in Microsoft Visual Basic .NET
' ScriptMain is the entrypoint class for script components

Imports System
Imports System.Data
Imports System.Math
Imports Microsoft.SqlServer.Dts.Pipeline.Wrapper
Imports Microsoft.SqlServer.Dts.Runtime.Wrapper

Imports System.Reflection
Imports Microsoft.Office.Interop.Word

Public Class ScriptMain
    Inherits UserComponent

    Dim _wordSpellChecker As Microsoft.Office.Interop.Word.Application

    Dim maxSuggestionsCount As Integer = 5

public overrides

    Public Overrides Sub PreExecute()

        MyBase.PreExecute()
```

Figure 14-17. *The code window with the new code already in place*

12. You'll add the new code a section at a time to avoid confusion and errors. First, just below the existing `Imports` lines at the top of the code, add the code shown in Listing 14-3. These `Imports` statements inform the IDE that you are using objects from the `System.Reflection` and `Microsoft.Office.Interop.Word` assemblies, letting you use shortened statements when you reference their methods and properties.

Listing 14-3. *The Imports for the Script*

```
Imports System.Reflection
Imports Microsoft.Office.Interop.Word
```

13. You need to add some *member-level* variables next. Member-level variables are accessible from within all methods within the script. Add the code from Listing 14-4 into the code just below the class declaration (`Public Class ScriptMain Inherits UserComponent`). The first line in Listing 14-4 declares a variable of type `Word.Application` object but does not create an instance of Word. The second line of code creates the `_maxSuggestionsCount` variable and initializes it with the value `5`. I've decided to give it a default value in case the SSIS variable `maxSuggestions` isn't passed into the script with a value.

Listing 14-4. *New Code for the Declaration of Member-Level Variables*

```
Private _wordSpellChecker As Microsoft.Office.Interop.Word.Application
Private _maxSuggestionsCount As Integer = 5
```

14. You need to override two methods—`PreProcess` and `PostProcess`. `PreProcess` contains the code to create an instance of the Word application and assign script variable values, and `PostProcess` has code to close down the Word instance. Listing 14-5 shows the code to use.

Listing 14-5. *PreProcess and PostProcess Methods*

```
Public Overrides Sub PreExecute()

        MyBase.PreExecute()

        ' create an instance of the application
        _wordSpellChecker = New Microsoft.Office.Interop.Word.Application()
        _maxSuggestionsCount = Me.Variables.maxSuggestions

    End Sub

    Public Overrides Sub PostExecute()

        MyBase.PostExecute()

        ' we can now quit
        _wordSpellChecker.Application.Quit()

    End Sub
```

15. You can now move on to adding the code that performs the processing on each row of data fed into the `Script Component`. Alter the `Input0_ProcessInputRow` method so that its contents match Listing 14-6.

Listing 14-6. *Contents of the Input0_ProcessInputRow Method*

```
Public Overrides Sub Input0_ProcessInputRow(ByVal Row As Input0Buffer)

        Dim isChanged As Boolean = False
        Dim targetValue As String = Row.Name
        Dim optionalParam As Object = Missing.Value

        ' perform the check - this is where we should be able to specify a dynamic
        ' column name as passed by the columnToCheck variable. There is no easy way
        ' to do this in the script component, however.
        ' This serves as a good example as to why using Custom Components might be a
        ' good idea if this kind of transform is used with any regularity.
        Dim suggestedValue As String = Execute(Row.Name)

        If (suggestedValue.Length > 0) Then
                ' flag that a change has happened
                isChanged = True
```

```
                ' set the value to pass out of the method to the suggested value
                targetValue = suggestedValue
        End If

        ' populate the output buffer and columns
        With Output0Buffer
                .AddRow()
                .ItemID = Row.ItemID
                .Name = targetValue
                .SpellChecked = isChanged
        End With

End Sub
```

16. **The final block of code to add is for a new method—`Execute`—that gets called from within the `Input0_ProcessInputRow` entry-point method. Add the code in Listing 14-7 below the `End Sub` statement of the `Input0_ProcessInputRow` method but before the `End Class` statement that is the last statement in the script code.**

Listing 14-7. *The Private Execute Method*

```
Private Function Execute(ByVal checkValue As String) As String

        Dim optionalParam As Object = Missing.Value
        Dim suggestedValue As String = String.Empty

        _wordSpellChecker.Application.Documents.Add(optionalParam,
optionalParam, optionalParam, optionalParam)

        If (checkValue.Length > 0) Then

                Dim theSuggestions As SpellingSuggestions =
_wordSpellChecker.GetSpellingSuggestions(checkValue, optionalParam, _
optionalParam, optionalParam, optionalParam,
optionalParam, optionalParam, optionalParam, optionalParam, _
optionalParam, optionalParam, optionalParam, optionalParam, _
optionalParam)

                ' if we get more than (parameter specified) suggestions, don't make
                ' the change.
                If (theSuggestions.Count > 0 And
theSuggestions.Count <= _maxSuggestionsCount) Then

                        ' pick the first value
                        Dim theSuggestion As SpellingSuggestion = theSuggestions(1)

                        suggestedValue = theSuggestion.Name
```

```
                End If

                _wordSpellChecker.Application.Documents.Close()

                Return suggestedValue

        End If

End Function
```

17. With the entry of all VB.NET code complete, click File ➤ Close and Return on the menu bar.

18. You should be returned to the `Script Component` configuration screen. Click OK to return to the Data Flow design surface.

Let's take a look in more detail at what the code in Listings 14-6 and 14-7 does.

In Listing 14-6, the `Input0_ProcessInputRow` method gets called for every row in the input collection. The first few variable-declaration lines set the method up with some initial values. The Boolean `isChanged` variable starts out being `false`, and `targetValue` is assigned the value of the column you're going to check. This allows you to update these variables depending on whether the spellcheck returns a changed value. Whether the values have changed or not, the same variables can be assigned to the output row.

After the comment block, a call is made to the `Execute` method (Listing 14-7), which performs the actual spellcheck. The single parameter that gets passed to the `Execute` method can be changed to check a different text column if necessary.

The next block of code in Listing 14-6 is a conditional block that performs a check to see if the length of the value returned from the `Execute` method call is more than `0`. If the length *is* greater than `0`, this indicates that the spellcheck has returned a value, so you must update the variables you declared earlier to reflect this. The `isChanged` variable gets set to `True`, and the `targetValue` variable gets updated to be the returned, corrected value from the method call.

The final code block adds a row—`Output0Buffer`—to the output-rows collection and populates the column values with either the original values (if the spellcheck has returned no rows) or the corrected values (if it has).

Note that you don't need to reset the values of `isChanged` or `targetValue`, because once execution has finished in this method, all variables go out of scope and are destroyed. They're re-created when the method is called again, to process the next row of data.

Now let's take a look at what happens inside the new `Execute` method in Listing 14-7.

First, the `Execute` method is declared as taking in a single string parameter and returning a string result. The `optionalParam` variable is declared here as type `Object` and is used to support the call to the Word Interop Assembly. Although it is initialized with the value `Missing.Value`, it does not get updated again because it serves only as a placeholder that enables the call to Word.

The Word object requires a document to be open to hold, temporarily, the text that will be spellchecked. This is what the `_wordSpellChecker.Application.Documents.Add` line does. You remove this temporary document before leaving the method.

The next step is a large conditional block that is executed only if the length of the checkValue parameter passed into the method is greater than 0. This makes sense, because there's no point performing any processing if no value has been passed in.

Inside the conditional block you declare a new variable of type SpellingSuggestions, which is a Word-defined collection of suggestions that get returned from the Word reference. The variable is initialized with the result of the call to the GetSpellingSuggestions method. Notice that only the first parameter of the call contains anything useful, which is the variable containing the value to check.

The final conditional block checks to see if the Word spellchecker has made any suggestions, and also if the number of suggestions is less than the number specified in the _maxSuggestionsCount member variable (which is populated from the read-only maxSuggestions variable passed into the Script Component). I include this because, as I mentioned elsewhere, having a greater number of spelling suggestions might indicate that the value being checked is too common or too badly spelled to be a good candidate for correction. The last act of this conditional block is to assign the first suggested value's .Name property from the spellcheck to the suggestedValue variable.

The Word document is closed, and the suggestedValue variable is returned out of the method to the caller (which in this case is the Input0_ProcessInputRow method).

You should have entered all the code listed above by this point. For the sake of clarity, however, I have included the full contents of the VB.NET script again as Listing 14-8. In case of problems you can refer to this code listing to double-check that your configuration is as expected.

Listing 14-8. *The Whole Script*

```
Public Overrides Sub PreExecute()

        MyBase.PreExecute()

        ' create an instance of the application
        _wordSpellChecker = New Microsoft.Office.Interop.Word.Application()
        _maxSuggestionsCount = Me.Variables.maxSuggestions

End Sub

Public Overrides Sub PostExecute()

        MyBase.PostExecute()

        ' we can now quit
        _wordSpellChecker.Application.Quit()

End Sub

Public Overrides Sub Input0_ProcessInputRow(ByVal Row As Input0Buffer)

        Dim isChanged As Boolean = False
        Dim targetValue As String = Row.Name
```

```
        Dim optionalParam As Object = Missing.Value

        ' perform the check - this is where we should be able to specify a dynamic
        ' column name as passed by the columnToCheck variable. There is no easy way
        ' to do this in the script component, however.
        ' This serves as a good example as to why using Custom Components might be a
        ' good idea if this kind of transform is used with any regularity.
        Dim suggestedValue As String = Execute(Row.Name)

        If (suggestedValue.Length > 0) Then
                ' flag that a change has happened
                isChanged = True
                ' set the value to pass out of the method to the suggested value
                targetValue = suggestedValue
        End If

        ' populate the output buffer and columns
        With Output0Buffer
                .AddRow()
                .ItemID = Row.ItemID
                .Name = targetValue
                .Spellchecked = isChanged
        End With

End Sub

Private Function Execute(ByVal checkValue As String) As String

        Dim optionalParam As Object = Missing.Value
        Dim visibleParam As Object = False

        Dim suggestedValue As String = String.Empty

        _wordSpellChecker.Application.Documents.Add(optionalParam,
optionalParam, optionalParam, optionalParam)

        If (checkValue.Length > 0) Then

                Dim suggestionMode As Object = Missing.Value

                Dim theSuggestions As SpellingSuggestions =
_wordSpellChecker.GetSpellingSuggestions(checkValue, optionalParam, _
optionalParam, optionalParam, optionalParam, _
optionalParam, optionalParam, optionalParam, optionalParam, _
optionalParam, optionalParam, optionalParam, optionalParam, _
optionalParam)
```

```
            ' if we get more than (parameter specified) suggestions, don't make
            ' the change.
            If (theSuggestions.Count > 0 And
theSuggestions.Count <= _maxSuggestionsCount) Then

                ' pick the first value
                Dim theSuggestion As SpellingSuggestion = theSuggestions(1)

                suggestedValue = theSuggestion.Name

            End If

            _wordSpellChecker.Application.Documents.Close()

            Return suggestedValue

        End If

End Function
```

With the Script Component fully configured, you should have a Data Flow design surface that looks very much like mine, shown in Figure 14-18. No warnings or errors should appear against either component.

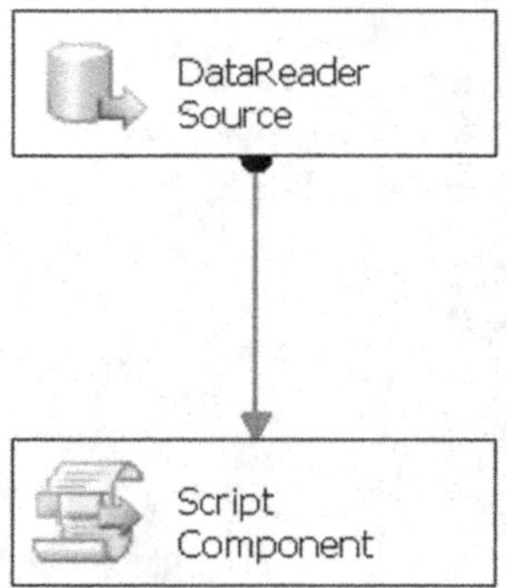

Figure 14-18. *Error-free Data Flow created from the example*

You can execute this package at this point if you like. You should see the individual components turn green to signify success. You could of course run into problems too. If you do, you should go through the example again and make sure you followed the steps accurately.

At this point the transformation that performs inside the Script Component has no visibility. You'll address that right now and take a look at the results.

Viewing the Results

The aim here is to add a `Row Count` component into the Data Flow and to use a Data Viewer to look inside the Data Flow at the results of the `Script Component` transform. Make sure you are still viewing the Data Flow design surface before following these steps:

1. Drop a `Row Count` component from the Toolbox onto the design surface.
2. Connect the green success arrow from the bottom of the `Script Component` to the `Row Count` component.
3. Open the `Row Count` configuration editor.
4. On the configuration screen presented, update the `VariableName` property to read `User::rowCount`. (This variable is defined in Table 14-1.)
5. Click OK to save settings and be returned to the Data Flow design surface.
6. Double-click the green success arrow you connected in Step 2. You're presented with the Data Flow Path Editor screen, shown in Figure 14-19.

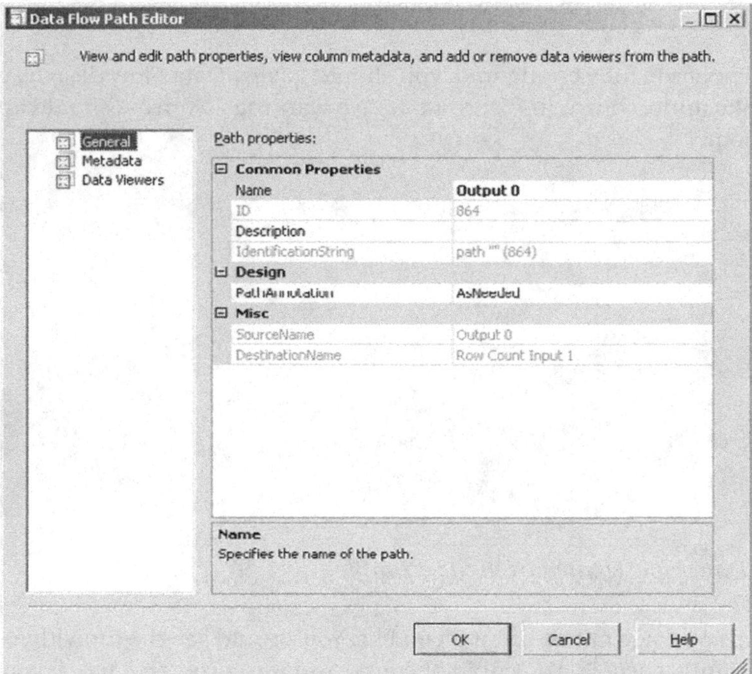

Figure 14-19. *The Data Flow Path Editor*

7. Click the Data Viewers list item to the left of the screen.
8. Click the Add... button. On the Configure Data Viewer screen that appears, the newly added Data Viewer should be visible in the grid. Click OK.
9. Click OK to close the Data Viewer configuration and return to the design surface.

When you test the execution of your package this time, you should see the Data Viewer you just configured appear when data hits that point in the flow. Figure 14-20 shows what you should expect.

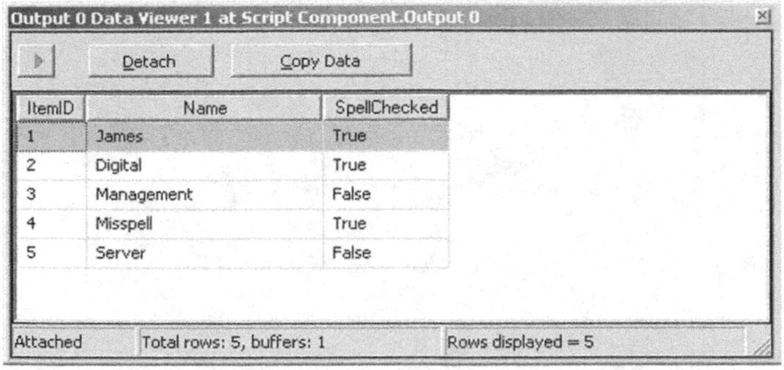

Output 0 Data Viewer 1 at Script Component.Output 0

Detach | Copy Data

ItemID	Name	SpellChecked
1	James	True
2	Digital	True
3	Management	False
4	Misspell	True
5	Server	False

Attached | Total rows: 5, buffers: 1 | Rows displayed = 5

Figure 14-20. *Expected results*

This is exactly the output we were looking for when starting the example: you can easily perform a spellcheck against whichever input column you specify inside the `Input0_ProcessInputRow` method.

Summary

This chapter shows that you don't need to be an expert programmer in VB.NET or any other language to produce relatively complex results from the `Script Component`. The most important thing is to have a good head for problem solving, which is the key skill for developers of any flavor.

Clearly defining the problem—what you are trying to achieve with the `Script Component`—is the first and most critical step. From there on, leveraging the facilities provided within the component to break the problem down further and create a solution should be much easier.

The more-observant reader will notice that the `Script Component` example uses no scope for pointing the transform dynamically at a user-specified column, even though this is a requirement I specified right at the start of the example. In fact, I have left comments in the `Input0_ProcessInputRow` method in Listings 14-6 and 14-8 that say it can be done, but it isn't as simple as it should be.

I have done this for a reason. It would be bad practice to create a `Script Component` that is *too* configurable. The problem is that a block of functionality would need to be copied and pasted into the code of the different `Script Components` to enable reuse. Not only does this go against the principles of code reuse, but it also gravely affects maintainability.

It's easy to say "don't do it like that," but fortunately I do have an alternative in mind. Since I need to address the requirement that the component should be configurable—which suggests that the component will be used more than once—creation of a custom component is justified in this case. Chapter 15 discusses this in depth, with particular reference to re-creating this example as a custom component but in an OO fashion—which means the functionality can be leveraged from within the `Script Component` too.

Summary

CHAPTER 15

Custom Components

Custom components are perhaps my favorite part of SSIS. The robust and scaleable architecture on which all SSIS components are constructed can fulfill even your most demanding business need. Custom components are the elixir of eternal life for SSIS, allowing the product to be extended far beyond original specification. Perhaps their most compelling aspect is how easy it is to produce them. This chapter is all about the design and creation of robust and professional custom components, concentrating on the Control Flow task and the Data Flow component.

To focus on the features of custom components that are most desired and required in the IT industry, I'll cover some other features only briefly. MSDN can provide you with minutiae on the order in which breakpoints or events are fired, and any number of other internal details.

The custom-component examples I include in this chapter are based, at least in part, on development I have performed for clients. The same ideas can be reused to provide the basis for a wide variety of components.

The development-tool requirements for creating a custom component, whatever its flavor, are surprisingly and gratifyingly simple:

- **SQL Server 2005**: You've got a copy of SQL Server, right?
- **Visual Studio 2005**: Use it to develop the custom component. You can get away with using C# 2005 Express or Visual Basic Express instead.
- **Your brain**: A clear idea of what you are trying to do is always helpful!

Building custom components can be a trying experience at first because so many collections, buffers, and overridable methods are available that it isn't immediately clear what needs doing and what can be left alone.

When I work on an SSIS package, I don't want to be held up by the implementation of tasks or components. (I've got the `Pivot` transform in mind as I write this.) Generally, I'll create custom components only if, by creating them, I can increase the efficiency or simplicity of a particular process or make it easier for a developer to implement encapsulated functionality quickly.

Custom components should offer as much assistance and ease of configuration as possible. It's much easier to create a custom component that puts the onus on the SSIS user in terms of adding and configuring output columns, setting `LineageIDs`, and all the other tasks that can make components less user friendly. I don't subscribe to this approach. I would much rather put a little more effort into building the component with a little more intelligence to ease the experience for the end user.

Taking a more intelligent approach, however, requires a more intimate understanding of the components and classes involved. This chapter provides this more complete examination.

What Flavor Would You Like?

The term *custom component* can be applied to a variety of SSIS objects. Each type needs to leverage different classes and interfaces within the SSIS object model.

Five types of custom components can be created. Three out of the five are pretty well catered for within SSIS already, so the need for creating custom versions rarely arises. That leaves you with custom Control Flow tasks and custom Data Flow components. Here I'll briefly describe the available types of custom components you might want to create. I'll supply more detail and examples as the chapter progresses.

Connection Managers

Custom connection managers must derive from the `Microsoft.SqlServer.Dts.Runtime.ConnectionManagerBase` abstract class. The most important methods to provide concrete implementation for are `AcquireConnection` and `ReleaseConnection`.

Figure 15-1 gives a visual account of the `ConnectionManagerBase` class.

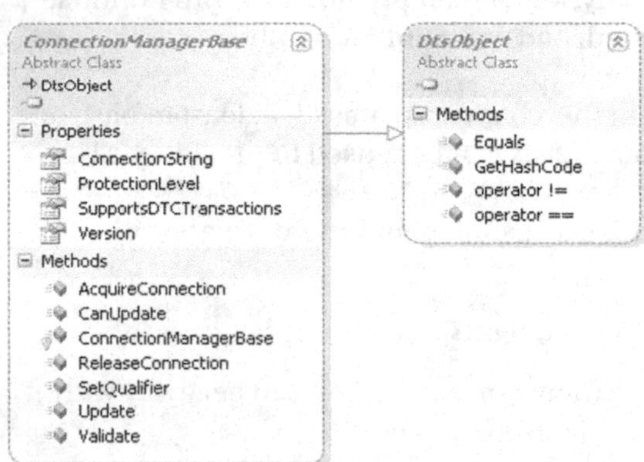

Figure 15-1. *A visualization of the ConnectionManagerBase abstract class*

Data Flow Components (Source, Transform, or Destination)

Irrespective of its type—source, transform, or destination—a custom Data Flow component must derive from the `Microsoft.SqlServer.Dts.Pipeline.PipelineComponent` abstract class. The minimum methods to provide concrete implementations for are `ProvideComponentProperties`, `PrimeOutput`, and `ProcessInput`.

Foreach Enumerators

Custom `Foreach` enumerators must derive from the `Microsoft.SqlServer.Dts.Runtime.ForeachEnumerator` abstract class and implement the `Microsoft.SqlServer.Dts.Runtime.IDTSComponentPersist` interface. is The most important method to provide a concrete implementation for is `GetEnumerator`.

Control Flow Tasks

Custom Control Flow tasks must derive from the `Microsoft.SqlServer.Dts.Runtime.Task` abstract class and implement the `Microsoft.SqlServer.Dts.Runtime.IDTSComponentPersist` and `Microsoft.SqlServer.Dts.Runtime.IDTSBreakpointSite` interfaces. The most important method to create an implementation for is `Execute`.

Log Providers

Custom log providers must inherit from `Microsoft.SqlServer.Dts.Runtime.LogProviderBase`. At a minimum you should create a concrete implementation of the `OpenLog`, `Log`, and `CloseLog` methods.

What Makes a Custom Component?

The *class library*—generally used to provide functionality separated by some logical boundary—is one of the staples of programming in its various forms. Class libraries are used to some degree in almost all theoretical and commercial programming. Everything from the operating system to the smallest of bedroom-coded applications use them. Class libraries are used extensively in the world of .NET, so Visual Studio includes support for creating them with minimal effort.

Class libraries compile to .NET assemblies (with the `.dll` file extension) in the filesystem; you can see hundreds of them by taking a look in the `Windows\Assembly` directory of your hard disk.

Take a look inside the SQL Server directory that contains the stock SSIS Data Flow components (and is the target directory for any custom Data Flow component). Figure 15-2 shows the directory, which in my case is `C:\Program Files\Microsoft SQL Server\90\DTS\PipelineComponents`.

Name	Size	Type
CommandDest.dll	156 KB	Application Extension
ConfigureUnDouble.dll	24 KB	Application Extension
exceldest.dll	164 KB	Application Extension
excelsrc.dll	174 KB	Application Extension
FlatFileDest.dll	250 KB	Application Extension
FlatFileSrc.dll	259 KB	Application Extension
LizardKingStudios.Services.SpellCheck.dll	16 KB	Application Extension
LizardKingStudios.SSIS.DataFlowTransforms.Spellingcheck.dll	28 KB	Application Extension
Microsoft.SqlServer.ADONETSrc.dll	58 KB	Application Extension
Microsoft.SqlServer.DataReaderDest.dll	50 KB	Application Extension
Microsoft.SqlServer.SqlCEDest.dll	50 KB	Application Extension
Microsoft.SqlServer.TxScript.dll	210 KB	Application Extension
Microsoft.SqlServer.XMLSrc.dll	106 KB	Application Extension
msmdlocal.dll	15,554 KB	Application Extension
msmdpp.dll	3,830 KB	Application Extension
OleDbDest.dll	164 KB	Application Extension
OleDbSrc.dll		
RawDest.dll		
RawSource.dll		
RecordSetDest.dll		
SqlDest.dll		
TxAgg.dll	200 KB	Application Extension
TxBestMatch.dll	427 KB	Application Extension
TxCharMap.dll	176 KB	Application Extension
TxCopyMap.dll	107 KB	Application Extension
TxDataConvert.dll	107 KB	Application Extension
TxDerived.dll	378 KB	Application Extension

Description: DTS - Data Transformation Services OLE DB Destinati
Company: Microsoft Corporation
File Version: 2005.90.3042.0
Date Created: 10/02/2007 05:23
Size: 163 KB

Figure 15-2. *Data Flow components are DLLs too.*

As you can see in Figure 15-2, the Data Flow components are DLLs too—class libraries—in this case, mostly created by Microsoft developers using C# to provide Data Flow functionality.

To make a long story short, custom components are simply class libraries with exposed public methods and properties and certain defined attributes that identify them as usable components to SSIS.

Irrespective of the type of component being created, every one of the different kinds of custom components requires the use of one or more of a select group of SSIS-specific interfaces. Leveraging these SSIS objects is the key to providing custom functionality.

In Chapter 14 I suggested that the developers of SSIS have provided a helping hand whenever possible by creating template code inside the `Script Component`. This is also true of the way the class hierarchy works. Clever stuff. In many ways the same is true of how the whole of SSIS is designed, in terms of the way the classes and interfaces work together and in the way they offer extensibility.

The number of variations, in terms of which classes and interfaces must be employed in a custom component to provide required functionality, is limitless. Although it's hard to provide specifics for every variation, I'll spend the remainder of this chapter looking at some of them and the methods the SSIS object model provides to support custom-component development.

SSIS Assemblies Supporting Components

All of the assemblies used to support the objects in SSIS are suitably impressive in their depth of complexity and scope of functionality. More impressive is the fact that only four assemblies (described in Table 5-1) need to be referenced in your components to provide custom functionality (though of course many more assemblies are in use behind the scenes).

Table 15-1. *SSIS Assemblies Used in Creating Custom Components*

Assembly	Description
`Microsoft.SqlServer.ManagedDTS.dll`	The managed runtime engine
`Microsoft.SqlServer.DTSRuntimeWrap.dll`	The wrapper for the native runtime engine
`Microsoft.SqlServer.PipelineHost.dll`	The managed Data Flow engine
`Microsoft.SqlServer.DTSPipelineWrap.dll`	The wrapper for the native Data Flow engine

Class Attributes

You use *class attributes* to identify your custom component to SSIS. Attributes are a method by which declarative information can be associated with constructs within your code. They are used with custom components so that the SSIS runtime can query them to discover the component's usage type and other necessary information.

Listing 15-1 shows an example of a class attribute that provides SSIS with information that indicates a custom Control Flow task has been created.

Listing 15-1. *The DTSTask Attribute in Action*

```
[DtsTask(TaskType = "DTS90", DisplayName="SampleTask",
 IconResource="LizardKingStudios.SSIS.ControlFlowTask.Sample.Icon.ico",
Description="Just a simple sample component.")]
    public class Sample : Task
```

Notice also that the `Sample` class is derived from `Task` (or, to give its fully qualified name, `Microsoft.SqlServer.Dts.Runtime.Task`)—but more on that shortly.

The information contained in the attributes is different for each of the custom components available. Table 15-2 details the minimum required attributes.

Table 15-2. *Component Types and Related Attributes*

Component Type	Attribute
Connection manager	`[DtsConnection(ConnectionType = "", DisplayName = "", Description = "", UITypeName = "")]`
Data Flow source	`[DtsPipelineComponent(DisplayName = "",ComponentType = ComponentType.SourceAdapter,IconResource = "")]`
Data Flow transform	`[DtsPipelineComponent(DisplayName="", Description="", IconResource="", ComponentType=ComponentType.Transform)]`
Data Flow destination	`[DtsPipelineComponent(DisplayName="", Description="", IconResource="", ComponentType=ComponentType.DestinationAdapter)]`
`Foreach` enumerator	`[DtsForEachEnumerator(DisplayName="", Description = "", UITypeName = "")]`
Control Flow task	`[DtsTask(DisplayName="", Description = "", UITypeName="")]`
Log provider	`[DtsLogProvider(DisplayName="", Description="", LogProviderType = "Custom")]`

Many more attribute parameters are available that SSIS can use. The complete list is presented across Tables 15-3 and 15-4. Table 15-3 shows the parameters that are common for all attributes.

Table 15-3. *Parameters Common to All Attributes*

Parameter	Description
`DisplayName`	The name for the component used in the designer.
`IconResource`	The task icon. Usually this points to a class-library icon resource.
`LocalizationType`	The class type that provides values for `DtsLocalizableAttribute`.
`UITypeName`	The fully qualified name of the UI assembly, including the class name. (This is covered in the later section on component UI.)

Table 15-4. *Additional Attribute Parameters*

Attribute	Parameter	Parameter Description
DtsConnection	ConnectionType	The type of connection manager
	ConnectionContact	Contact information for the component
DtsForEachEnumerator	ForEachEnumeratorContact	Contact information for the component
DtsLogProvider	LogProviderContact	Contact information for the component
	LogProviderType	The version of SSIS used to create the component
DtsPipelineComponent	ComponentType	The type of component—source, transform, or destination
	CurrentVersion	The version of the component
	NoEditor	Specifies whether the component supports the advanced editor
	RequiredProductLevel	Specifies the version of SQL Server that must be in use to use this component
DtsTask	RequiredProductLevel	Specifies the version of SQL Server that must be in use to leverage the custom component
	TaskContact	Contact information for the component
	TaskType	A text value providing a short description of the component (e.g., `Spellcheck`)

Deriving from and Overriding SSIS Classes

It's time to put some flesh on the bones by looking at the classes and interfaces offered by SSIS that support tasks in the Control Flow and components in the Data Flow. These same classes contain methods that can be overridden to provide custom functionality as necessary.

This section looks at both the Control Flow and the Data Flow and examines these methods, what they are used for, and the objects that are made available during execution.

Custom Control Flow Tasks

When it comes to custom functionality in SSIS, there is nothing easier than creating a Control Flow task. By referencing a handful of SSIS assemblies, specifying a class attribute, and deriving from `Microsoft.SqlServer.Dts.Runtime.Task`, you are immediately in a position to override the `Execute` method and provide custom functionality. Listing 15-2 shows the basic framework required for creating a custom Control Flow task.

Listing 15-2. *The Basic Control Flow Framework (C#)*

```
using System;
using Microsoft.SqlServer.Dts;
using Microsoft.SqlServer.Dts.Runtime;
```

```
using Microsoft.SqlServer.Dts.Pipeline;
using Microsoft.SqlServer.Dts.Pipeline.Wrapper;
using Microsoft.SqlServer.Dts.Runtime.Wrapper;

namespace LizardKingStudios.SSIS.ControlFlowTask
{
    [DtsTask(TaskType = "DTS90", DisplayName="SampleTask",
 IconResource="LizardKingStudios.SSIS.ControlFlowTask.Sample.Icon.ico",
Description="Just a simple sample component.")]
    public class Sample : Task
    {
        public override Microsoft.SqlServer.Dts.Runtime.DTSExecResult Execute(
Connections connections, Microsoft.SqlServer.Dts.Runtime.
VariableDispenser variableDispenser, IDTSComponentEvents componentEvents,
IDTSLogging log, object transaction)
        {
            return base.Execute(connections, variableDispenser, componentEvents,
log, transaction);
        }
    }
}
```

Tables 15-5, 15-6, and 15-7 provide details on the overridable methods and properties on offer. Remember that you don't need to override all of these methods or properties, and that in most cases you won't need to. If you don't provide overrides, the code in the base-class version of the method/property is executed instead.

Table 15-5. *Microsoft.SqlServer.Dts.Runtime.Task Methods and Properties*

Base-Class Object	Method or Property?	Description
`Execute`	Method	The business end of the task. This is where you write the code to fulfill the task-design goals. The method is called once only unless it is involved in a loop.
`InitializeTask`	Method	Any form of initialization can take place in this method, whether setting the initial value of a variable, or performing auditing, or anything else you can think of.
`Validate`	Method	This is a useful method to override because you can use it to provide validation operations that are particular to your custom task. This might take the form of checking to see if a set of files exists before execution . . . or anything else that might need validating. This method is called at least once but more likely multiple times during design and execution.

The methods shown in Table 15-5 are pretty fundamental in providing custom functionality; the next three methods, shown in Table 15-6, are less vital but still important, especially when you override them.

Table 15-6. *Microsoft.SqlServer.Dts.Runtime.Task Methods and Properties, Part II*

Base-Class Object	Method or Property?	Description
`CanUpdate`	Property	Indicates whether this task supports upgrading other tasks
`GetConnectionID`	Method	Returns the connection-manager ID if relevant
`GetConnectionName`	Method	Returns the connection name, if relevant
`ExecutionValue`	Property	A value returned as a consequence of execution
`WaitForMe`	Property	Indicates whether this is an event-driven task that reacts to events in the Control Flow
`Update`	Method	Informs the task it should begin the process of updating another task
`Version`	Property	Gives version information for the task

Now I'll give you a closer look at the methods that require more explanation, starting with the methods in Table 15-5.

The `InitializeTask` method is called by SSIS when a task is dropped onto the Control Flow design surface, as you might expect. The method has some interesting parameters that will prove useful to the budding custom-component developer. These properties are described briefly in Table 15-7.

Table 15-7. *InitializeTask Method Parameters*

Parameter	Description
`Connections`	A reference to package defined connections.
`variableDispenser`	A construct to dispense package variables. Accessors are available to get and set values in the variable dispenser.
`events`	Used to raise events from the task.
`log`	A reference to the package-logging object.
`eventInfos`	Describes events.
`logEntryInfos`	Describe log entries.
`refTracker`	Unused property.

The SSIS object model is expertly designed to provide almost intuitive support for the developer. This is evident once again in the `Validate` and `Execute` methods. Essentially they take in parameters that are very similar to those used with the `InitializeTask` method—so objects such as `Connections`, `VariableDispenser`, events, and logging are already familiar.

Custom Data Flow components

The Data Flow is a much more hostile environment in terms of complexity than the Control Flow. With a little patience and investigation, however, the mysteries of the Data Flow can be revealed.

You know by now that there are three different types of Data Flow component: source, transform, and destination. Irrespective of the type of Data Flow component being created, the custom code needs to derive from the `Microsoft.SqlServer.Dts.Pipeline.PipelineComponent` class. Custom functionality comes from overriding some of the exposed methods in the class, depending on the component type, the desired result, and the necessary level of complexity.

Let's take a look at the overridable methods available—design-time methods first, followed by the runtime methods. As you read on, don't forget that there is no reason to feel obliged to override each and every method in your custom component. You only need to override where the method will provide custom functionality.

Design-Time Methods

These methods are primarily called at Design Time—but as you will see in the case of `Validate`, for example, this doesn't preclude them from being called at runtime also.

ProvideComponentProperties

The `ProvideComponentProperties` method is called once when the component gets dropped onto the Data Flow. It's generally used for initializing the component, which might include setting the `SynchronousInputID` property on the component output collection to specify synchronicity, or creating a custom properties collection (`IDTSCustomPropertyCollection90`) and adding individual custom properties (`IDTSCustomProperty90`) that get exposed in the component configuration. In addition, outputs and inputs can be configured, and connections can be added and configured, via `RuntimeConnectionCollection`.

Validate

The `Validate` method is not only important but also incredibly useful, when configured correctly, in providing valuable feedback about configuration issues. `Validate` gets called a number of times during design time to ensure component configuration is viable and again at runtime as a final check. It's interesting to attach the Visual Studio debugger when creating a custom component and observe the execution of `Validate` by placing a breakpoint on the method. In fact, I'll come back to this point later on in the chapter when I get to the example.

The `Validate` method is another example of the great object model designed by Microsoft. The base method performs general component validation, which leaves the developer to add implementation-specific validation to the overridden method. This might include checking that columns are defined as `ReadOnly` instead of `ReadWrite`, or that important properties are populated. Problems can then be reported back either by raising of exceptions or issuing warning messages.

ReinitializeMetaData

The `ReinitializeMetaData` method is called when the `Validate` method returns `VS_NEEDSNEWMETADATA`, or when the user clicks the Refresh button. It can be used to provide setup for any column-level configuration required by the component or to provide reconfiguration if problems have been detected.

MapInputColumn and MapOutputColumn

`MapInputColumn` and `MapOutputColumn` can be used to create a mapping relationship between input/output columns and external metadata columns. But what are external metadata columns?

To support working offline, external metadata columns can provide a representation of real output columns that can, at points, be inaccessible. Use of external metadata columns is a "nice-to-have" feature rather than a concrete requirement. I rarely use offline mode in SSIS, though I appreciate there are times when it is necessary.

InsertInput, DeleteInput, SetInputProperty, InsertOutput, DeleteOutput, and SetOutputProperty

A number of methods support the manipulation of inputs and outputs in terms of their creation and deletion. Requirements might stipulate the desire to disallow either add or delete operations, or the setting of custom properties.

`InsertInput`, `DeleteInput`, and `SetInputProperty` are the methods to override to provide custom input handling. `InsertOutput`, `DeleteOutput`, and `SetOutputProperty` perform the same operations for outputs.

The example presented later in the chapter contains overrides of these methods that demonstrate how to use them in more detail.

SetOutputColumnDataTypeProperties and SetExternalMetadataColumnDataTypeProperties

Because input-column data types are set upstream, no methods are available for changing them. As you can imagine, however, you might need to update output-column data types, which are defined within the custom component.

For this reason, the object model provides two overridable methods. `SetOutputColumnDataTypeProperties` is used to update output-column data types, and `SetExternalMetadataColumnDataTypeProperties` is used for external metadata columns. More realistically, since it's rare to want to change a column data type arbitrarily, these methods can be overridden to prevent data types from being changed by the component consumer in the designer.

PerformUpgrade

The `PerformUpgrade` method can be used to update an existing version of a component.

RegisterEvents

If you have created a custom event, the `RegisterEvents` method can be overridden to register it for use.

RegisterLogEntries

Use the `RegisterLogEntries` method to register which custom events will be selectable in the package log.

SetComponentProperty

Once you have created a custom property that gets exposed to the design-time component configuration, the practice of setting the property's value is handled through the overridable `SetComponentProperty` method. This means that you can write code for the method that prevents updating the column property and displays a warning—or performs some kind of function based on the fact the value has changed.

SetInputColumnProperty, SetOutputColumnProperty, and SetExternalMetadataColumnProperty

Very much in the same vein as `SetComponentProperty`, the `SetInputColumnProperty`, `SetOutputColumnProperty`, and `SetExternalMetadataColumnProperty` methods can be overridden to contain code that, for example, allows or disallows the update of all columns or individual columns, depending on requirements.

SetUsageType

Use the `SetUsageType` method to indicate column usage. Depending on requirements, an input column might not be required and so its usage type can be set to `UT_IGNORED`. Columns being used can be read-only (`UT_READONLY`) or read/write (`UT_READWRITE`).

This method is generally overridden for the purpose of ensuring that the column usage has been correctly set (as component requirements dictate) by the designer and to raise warnings or errors if problems exist. Obviously, in-place updates to input-column values require the column to be of usage type `UT_READWRITE`; this is a good place to identify any issues.

OnInputPathAttached and OnOutputPathAttached

The `OnInputPathAttached` and `OnOutputPathAttached` methods are useful in manipulating and querying inputs and outputs at the time an upstream or downstream component is attached to the custom component. They also present an opportunity to provide validation of the columns being used for input—perhaps your custom component can only operate on text-based columns, for example—and warnings or errors can be raised.

Runtime Methods

The following methods are executed at runtime, usually only once. At this point in the component life cycle, all configuration has already taken place and been validated, and inputs and outputs are ready for use. This means no user-configuration changes take place from this point on, and so execution can run based on an stable and unchanging platform. I'll present these methods in execution order.

PrepareForExecute

The `PrepareForExecute` method rarely gets overridden. It's a kind of pre-`PreExecute` without any of the access to objects such as the buffer manager—so it's impossible to identify or query the contents of the input or output collections.

PreExecute

The `PreExecute` method represents the sweet spot in custom-component execution. Executed only once, it is the first point at runtime where all objects are available for examination—including the buffer manager—and serves as the ideal point for gathering everything required by the `PrimeOutput` or `ProcessInput` methods, which execute next.

I use this method all the time to gather the indexes of the input and output columns so I can precisely identify—using only an integer array (rather than accessing the collections directly)—the individual input and output columns being used in processing.

PrimeOutput

When you create a custom source component or an asynchronous transform component, `PrimeOutput` is used for performing processing against data held in the Data Flow. Generally this is used if the number of output columns doesn't match the number of input columns, and all rows are read into the buffer before component processing begins.

ProcessInput

When you create a destination component or either an asynchronous or synchronous transform component, `ProcessInput` is used for performing processing against data held in the Data Flow.

PostExecute

Use the `PostExecute` method to restore objects to how they were before execution. Alternatively, you might want to use this method to prepare a component-usage report or anything else that needs addressing after execution has completed.

Cleanup

The `Cleanup` method is similar to `PostExecute` in that it can be used to restore objects to preexecution state or provide any other postexecution processing, because it is executed immediately after processing has completed.

DescribeRedirectedErrorCode

`DescribeRedirectedErrorCode` is used to flesh out the information held against error rows (if any have been defined) and is called whenever a row of data is redirected to error output.

AcquireConnections

`AcquireConnections` is used to validate and cache connections. It is called at design time and runtime. At runtime the base-class processing makes all component connections available.

ReleaseConnections

`ReleaseConnections` is used to release any open connections that have been previously acquired. When you override it, you should call the necessary method on the connection to close it explicitly.

Putting It All Together

At this point you've looked at many of the principles involved in creating custom components of whatever type you fancy. Although I've given you a relatively brief rundown of the overridable methods presented for use to the `PipelineComponent`, it does serve as a suitable entrée for the rest of this chapter, in which I'll concentrate on applying the principles discussed. I think you'll find that everything becomes much clearer when you look at the application of all this theory.

It's time to put everything together and look at an example.

The Spellcheck Example, Part II

The example presented in Chapter 14 performed spellchecking functionality against values in the Data Flow by using the `Script Component`. As you discovered, the `Script Component` leaves a lot to be desired in terms of flexibility, code reuse, and code maintenance.

This section looks at an alternate way of providing the same functionality within the Data Flow, but in a more configurable and OO-friendly way.

Since one of the goals of any piece of development work is the Holy Grail of code reuse and easy maintenance, you should maximize the use of OO principles and architecture to produce the best possible results. I therefore suggest that you proceed to work according to the conceptual diagram in Figure 15-3.

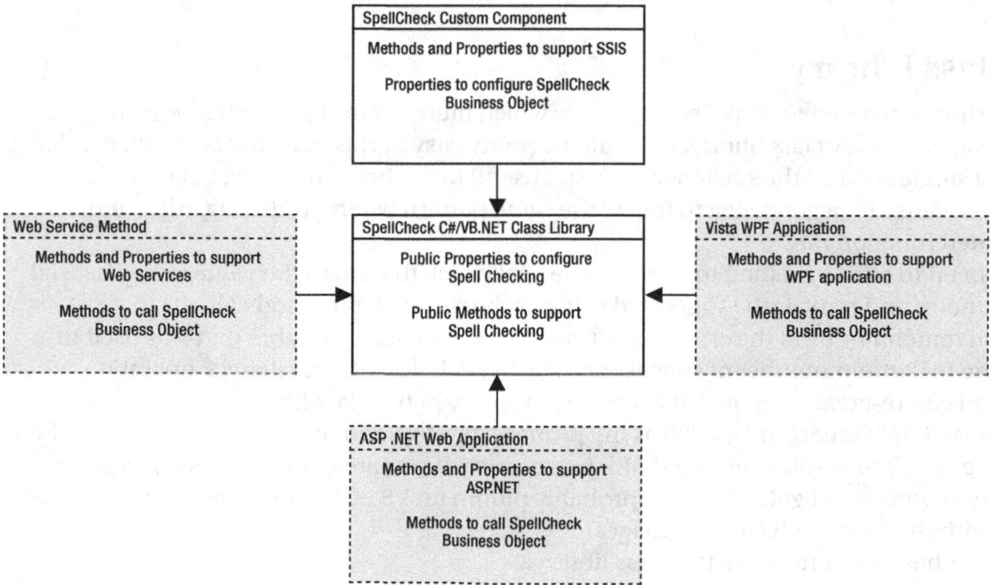

Figure 15-3. *Conceptual diagram for the spellcheck example*

Obviously, you'll work on the first object in this diagram, `SpellCheck Custom Component`; that's the whole point of the example. What do the other objects in the diagram represent?

The object in the center of the diagram represents a C# or VB.NET class library that you will create and use to perform the spellcheck on each value as it gets passed from the `SpellCheck Custom Component`. This raises the question of why you would want to split out the functionality rather than keep it all inside the custom component.

The answer to this question also explains the other grayed-out objects in Figure 15-3. You will not be creating any of these objects, but I've included them to illustrate the reason why you are creating the class library.

It makes sense to abstract out the spellcheck functionality into a class library because this makes it entirely reusable and readily maintainable. Imagine if, as in the diagram (back to those grayed-out objects again), you need to access the spellcheck service provided by the class library elsewhere in your IT infrastructure. The way this example is architected to have a centrally accessible class library will be perfect. In addition, .NET and Windows can more readily scale up the object's performance if usage increases at any point. A web service, a Windows Presentation Foundation (WPF) application, and an ASP.NET site all can concurrently leverage the service provided by this central class library.

Perhaps the more ".NET 3.0" way of doing all this would involve leveraging the Windows Communication Foundation (WCF) or exposing and consuming the spellcheck functionality via a web service. But that's for another time and another book. Instead, you'll concentrate only on those objects that aren't in gray—the custom component itself and the class library that supports it. For now you will make do with accessing the properties of the task through the Properties Explorer and the advanced editor in SSIS rather than producing a custom UI.

This example, therefore, is split into three sections. The first section concentrates on the creation of the class library, the second section on the new custom component, and the third and final section on using the new component inside the Data Flow.

Now that you have a clear plan of attack, let's go ahead and start re-creating the spellcheck example in this, our brave new world.

The Class Library

The first thing you need to do is decide exactly which methods and properties you are going to expose from your new class library. It should be pretty easy in this case, because you're offering only a single service, the spellcheck. It's still useful to go through the design process, however, because it's a good idea to follow the same pattern when producing other, more-complicated functionality.

You need to offer a method to perform the spellcheck that takes the value to be checked as a parameter and returns the suggested value as the result of a method call.

If you remember from the example in Chapter 14, you had a variable that was used to specify the maximum number of suggestions allowable before the spellcheck operation aborts. You can re-create this by using a public property in the class library.

Because I use Visual Studio 2005 as my primary development environment, I'll describe everything in this example from that IDE's perspective. If you are going to develop custom components with any regularity, you'll probably plump for VS 2005 too. Also, I will present all code in both the C# and VB.NET languages.

Follow these steps to create the class library:

1. Fire up Visual Studio 2005.

2. Select New ➤ Project from the menu, and select [Language] ➤ Windows ➤ Class Library from the Project Template dialog. [Language] means your language of choice in this instance.

   You can give your new project whatever name you choose—I'm going for `LizardKingStudios.Services.Spellcheck`. The first two parts of the name (`LizardKingStudios.Services`) refer to the namespace of the project, and the last part, `Spellcheck`, refers to the purpose of the project. This way, additional services can be collected under the same namespace. Figure 15-4 shows the New Project dialog, and Table 15-8 lists the settings I've used to set up the creation of the class library.

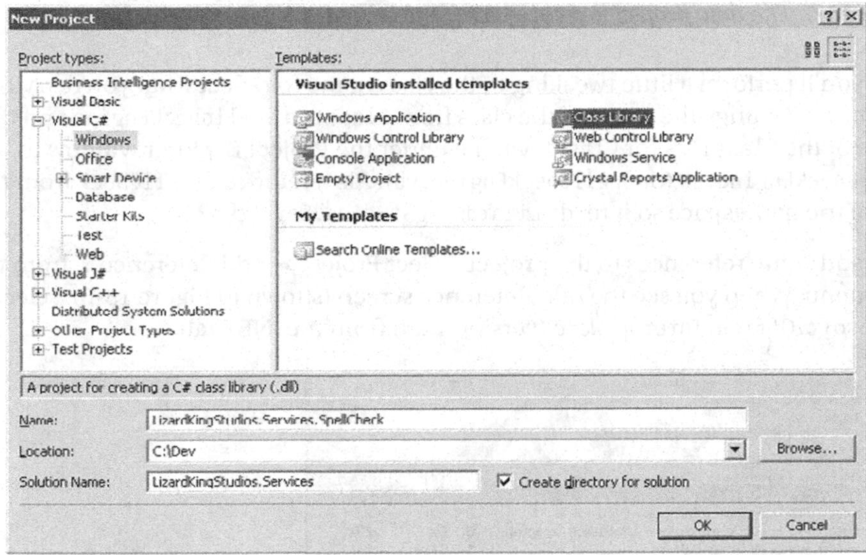

Figure 15-4. *Setting up the class-library project properties*

Table 15-8. *New Project Properties in Detail*

Property	Value	Description
Project type	Visual C# ➤ Windows	You can select VB.NET (or any other CLR language) instead.
Template	Class Library	The type of project you're creating.
Name	`LizardKingStudios.Services.SpellCheck`	The name of the project to create.
Location	`C:\Dev` (or other location)	The base location for the solution.
Solution Name	`LizardKingStudios.Services`	The name of the Visual Studio Solution to create what will be used to contain the services projects.
Create directory for solution	Checked	Creating a directory for the solution will keep things tidy and organized.

3. You should find yourself looking at the code template for a class library in the IDE, very much like Figure 15-5.

```
using System;
using System.Collections.Generic;
using System.Text;

namespace LizardKingStudios.Services.SpellCheck
{
    public class Class1
    {
    }
}
```

Figure 15-5. *The new project is created with the basic class-library template.*

Now you'll perform a little tweaking to the class name to reflect what you're trying to achieve. Change the name of the class from `Class1` to `SpellcheckEngine` and the name of the `Class1.cs` (or `Class1.vb`) file under the Project Explorer window to `SpellcheckEngine.cs` (or `SpellcheckEngine.vb`). Also, remove `.Spellcheck` from the end of the namespace so it reads `LizardKingStudios.Services`.

4. Now add some references to the project. Select Project ➤ Add Reference... from the IDE menu. When you see the Add Reference screen (shown in Figure 15-6), select `Microsoft.Office.Interop.Word` (version 12.0) from the .NET tab.

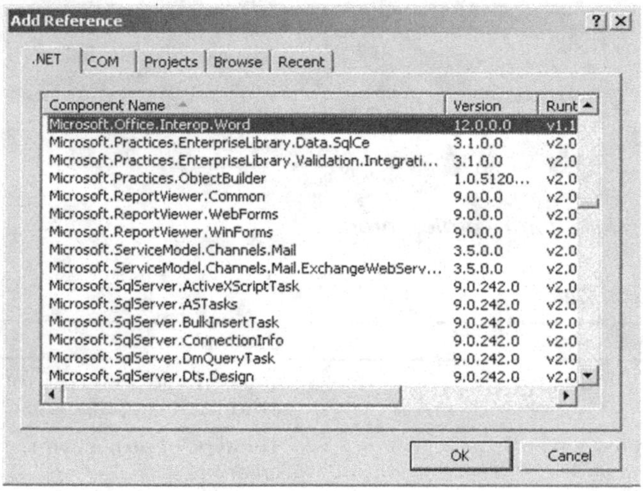

Add Reference

.NET | COM | Projects | Browse | Recent

Component Name	Version	Runt
Microsoft.Office.Interop.Word	12.0.0.0	v1.1
Microsoft.Practices.EnterpriseLibrary.Data.SqlCe	3.1.0.0	v2.0
Microsoft.Practices.EnterpriseLibrary.Validation.Integrati...	3.1.0.0	v2.0
Microsoft.Practices.ObjectBuilder	1.0.5120...	v2.0
Microsoft.ReportViewer.Common	9.0.0.0	v2.0
Microsoft.ReportViewer.WebForms	9.0.0.0	v2.0
Microsoft.ReportViewer.WinForms	9.0.0.0	v2.0
Microsoft.ServiceModel.Channels.Mail	3.5.0.0	v2.0
Microsoft.ServiceModel.Channels.Mail.ExchangeWebServ...	3.5.0.0	v2.0
Microsoft.SqlServer.ActiveXScriptTask	9.0.242.0	v2.0
Microsoft.SqlServer.ASTasks	9.0.242.0	v2.0
Microsoft.SqlServer.BulkInsertTask	9.0.242.0	v2.0
Microsoft.SqlServer.ConnectionInfo	9.0.242.0	v2.0
Microsoft.SqlServer.DmQueryTask	9.0.242.0	v2.0
Microsoft.SqlServer.Dts.Design	9.0.242.0	v2.0

OK | Cancel

Figure 15-6. *Adding the reference to the Word Primary Interop object*

If the `Microsoft.Office.Interop.Word` list item isn't showing, in all probability you didn't follow the example in Chapter 14 and therefore need, at the very least, to follow the steps presented in that example to download and install the Word Interop Assembly and register it in the GAC.

5. Click OK to close the dialog and add the reference.

6. At the very top of the code where the `using/imports` statements are listed, replace the statements to reflect those in Listing 15-3 (C#) or Listing 15-4 (VB.NET).

Listing 15-3. *Using Statements (C#)*

```
using System;
using System.Reflection;
using Microsoft.Office.Interop.Word;
```

Listing 15-4. *Imports Statements (VB.NET)*

```
Imports System
Imports System.Reflection
Imports Microsoft.Office.Interop.Word
```

7. Next you need to add some private member–level variables. Add the code from Listing 15-5 (C#) or Listing 15-6 (VB.NET) to the area after the class declaration but before the constructor code.

Listing 15-5. *Private-Member Variables to Add (C#)*

```
        private readonly Application _wordSpellChecker = new Application();
        private int _maxSuggestionsCount = 5;
```

Listing 15-6. *Private-Member Variables to Add (VB.NET)*

```
        Private _wordSpellChecker As Application = New Application()
        Private _maxSuggestionsCount As Integer = 5
```

8. Add the code from Listing 15-7 (for C#) or Listing 15-8 (for VB.NET) to the `SpellcheckEngine` constructor.

Listing 15-7. *Constructor Code (C#)*

```
        public Spellcheck()
        {
            object optional = Missing.Value;

            _wordSpellChecker.Application.Documents.Add(ref optional,
ref optional, ref optional, ref optional);
        }
```

Listing 15-8. *Constructor Code (VB.NET)*

```
    Public Sub New()

        Dim optionalValue As Object = Missing.Value

        _wordSpellChecker.Application.Documents.Add(optionalValue,
optionalValue, optionalValue, optionalValue)

    End Sub
```

9. Next you'll add a public property to handle the `MaxSuggestionsCount` value. Add the code shown in Figure 15-9 (for C#) or Figure 15-10 (for VB.NET) to provide the property.

Listing 15-9. *The MaxSuggestionsCount Property Accessor (C#)*

```
public int MaxSuggestionsCount
{
    get
    {
        return _maxSuggestionsCount;
    }
    set
    {
        _maxSuggestionsCount = value;

    }
}
```

Listing 15-10. *The MaxSuggestionsCount Property Accessor (VB.NET)*

```
Public Property MaxSuggestionsCount() As Integer
        Get
            Return _maxSuggestionsCount
        End Get
        Set(ByVal value As Integer)
            _maxSuggestionsCount = value
        End Set
    End Property
```

10. The final piece of code—the public `Execute` method—performs the spellcheck using the Word Interop Assembly. Add the code in Listing 15-11 (for C#) or Listing 15-12 (for VB.NET) after the property accessor described in Step 9.

Listing 15-11. *The Execute Method (C#)*

```
public string Execute(string checkValue)
{
    string suggestedValue = String.Empty;
    object optional = Missing.Value;

    if (checkValue.Length != 0)
    {
        SpellingSuggestions theSuggestions =
_wordSpellChecker.GetSpellingSuggestions(checkValue, ref optional,
                ref optional, ref optional, ref optional,
                ref optional, ref optional, ref optional, ref optional,
                ref optional, ref optional, ref optional, ref optional,
                ref optional);
```

```
                // if you get more than (parameter specified) suggestions, don't
                // make the change.
                if (theSuggestions.Count > 0 && theSuggestions.Count <=
_maxSuggestionsCount)
                {
                    try
                    {
                        // pick the first value
                        SpellingSuggestion theSuggestion = theSuggestions[1];

                        suggestedValue = theSuggestion.Name;
                    }
                    catch
                    {
                        // lets swallow it - implement error handling here!
                    }
                }
            }

            _wordSpellChecker.Application.Documents.Close(ref optional,
ref optional, ref optional);

            _wordSpellChecker.Application.Quit(ref optional,
ref optional, ref optional);

            return suggestedValue;
        }
    }
}
```

Listing 15-12. *The Public Execute Method (VB.NET)*

```
    Public Function Execute(ByVal checkValue As String) As String

        Dim suggestedValue As String = String.Empty

        If (checkValue.Length <> 0) Then

            Dim optionalValue As Object = Missing.Value
            Dim ignoreUppercase As Object = True
            Dim suggestionMode As Object = Missing.Value

            Dim theSuggestions As SpellingSuggestions =
_wordSpellChecker.GetSpellingSuggestions(checkValue, optionalValue,
                optionalValue, optionalValue, optionalValue, _
                optionalValue, optionalValue, optionalValue, optionalValue, _
                optionalValue, optionalValue, optionalValue, optionalValue, _
```

```
            optionalValue)

        ' if you get more than (parameter specified) suggestions, don't make
        ' the change.
        If (theSuggestions.Count > 0 And theSuggestions.Count <=
_maxSuggestionsCount) Then

            Try

                ' pick1 the first value
                Dim theSuggestion As SpellingSuggestion = theSuggestions(1)

                suggestedValue = theSuggestion.Name
            Catch
                ' lets swallow it - implement error handling here!
            End Try

        End If

    End If

    Return suggestedValue

End Function
```

You should notice certain similarities between the code you used inside the Script Component in Chapter 14 and what you're using here. This should come as no surprise, since you're producing a class library to perform the same task. It's worth stopping at this point to look at some of the differences, which are few but interesting.

The first thing to note is that there is no mention of SSIS or Pipeline or any other SSIS object in the code. This is because you aren't producing the class library to be used solely by SSIS and therefore you shouldn't—and won't—include reference to a particular use. Also, you won't be leveraging any of the SSIS objects to help out in any way with the class library, for the same reasons. Because you are not referencing these SSIS objects, you have no access to a PreExecute or PostExecute method to initialize the Word object you'll be using.

That's fine, though, because by creating a class library you have a constructor, which is the first method to be called when a class library is instantiated. This constructor takes the form of a void declaration, generally as the first block of content in any class. You can use the constructor to initialize the Word object so it is available for use during the class-library instance's lifetime.

For completeness and accuracy, Listings 15-13 and 15-14 contain all the code for the class library in both C# and VB.NET. These listings represent the code that you should be seeing in the Visual Studio code editor window at this point of the example.

Listing 15-13. *Complete Code for the Class Library (C#)*

```
using System;
using System.Reflection;
using Microsoft.Office.Interop.Word;

namespace LizardKingStudios.Services
{
    public class SpellcheckEngine
    {
        private Microsoft.Office.Interop.Word.Application
_wordSpellChecker = new Application();
        private _Document _theDocument;
        private int _maxSuggestionsCount = 5;

        public transformSpellCheck()
        {
            object optional = Missing.Value;

            _wordSpellChecker.Application.Documents.Add(
ref optional, ref optional, ref optional, ref optional);
        }

        public int MaxSuggestionsCount
        {
            get
            {
                return _maxSuggestionsCount;
            }
            set
            {
                _maxSuggestionsCount = value;

            }
        }

        public string Execute(string checkValue)
        {
            string suggestedValue = String.Empty;

            if (checkValue.Length!=0)
            {
                object optional = Missing.Value;
                object ignoreUppercase = true;
                object suggestionMode = Missing.Value;

                SpellingSuggestions theSuggestions =
_wordSpellChecker.GetSpellingSuggestions(checkValue, ref optional,
```

```
                    ref optional, ref optional, ref optional,
                    ref optional, ref optional, ref optional, ref optional,
                    ref optional, ref optional, ref optional, ref optional,
                    ref optional);

                // if you get more than (parameter specified) suggestions, don't
                // make the change.
                if (theSuggestions.Count > 0 && theSuggestions.Count <=
_maxSuggestionsCount)
                {
                    try
                    {
                        // pick1 the first value
                        SpellingSuggestion theSuggestion = theSuggestions[1];

                        suggestedValue = theSuggestion.Name;
                    }
                    catch
                    {
                        // lets swallow it - implement error handling here!
                    }
                }
            }

            return suggestedValue;

        }
    }
}
```

Listing 15-14. *Complete Code for the Class Library (VB.NET)*

```
Imports System
Imports System.Reflection
Imports Microsoft.Office.Interop.Word

Public Class SpellcheckEngine

    Private _wordSpellChecker As Application = New Application()
    Private _maxSuggestionsCount As Integer = 5

    Public Sub New()

        Dim optionalValue As Object = Missing.Value

        _wordSpellChecker.Application.Documents.Add(optionalValue, optionalValue,
optionalValue, optionalValue)
```

```
    End Sub

    Public Property MaxSuggestionsCount() As Integer
        Get
            Return _maxSuggestionsCount
        End Get
        Set(ByVal value As Integer)
            _maxSuggestionsCount = value
        End Set
    End Property

    Public Function Execute(ByVal checkValue As String) As String

        Dim suggestedValue As String = String.Empty

        If (checkValue.Length <> 0) Then

            Dim optionalValue As Object = Missing.Value
            Dim ignoreUppercase As Object = True
            Dim suggestionMode As Object = Missing.Value

            Dim theSuggestions As SpellingSuggestions =
_wordSpellChecker.GetSpellingSuggestions(checkValue, optionalValue, _
                optionalValue, optionalValue, optionalValue, _
                optionalValue, optionalValue, optionalValue, optionalValue, _
                optionalValue, optionalValue, optionalValue, optionalValue, _
                optionalValue)

            ' if you get more than (parameter specified) suggestions, don't make
            ' the change.
            If (theSuggestions.Count > 0 And theSuggestions.Count <=
_maxSuggestionsCount) Then

                Try

                    ' pick1 the first value
                    Dim theSuggestion As SpellingSuggestion = theSuggestions(1)

                    suggestedValue = theSuggestion.Name
                Catch
                    ' lets swallow it - implement error handling here!
                End Try

            End If

        End If
```

```
        Return suggestedValue

    End Function

End Class
```

11. Now that the class-library code is complete, you can sign the compiled assembly and build and deploy it to the GAC.

    You need to perform some tasks in Visual Studio's project-properties area. From the IDE menu, select Project ➤ `LizardKingStudios.Services.Spellcheck Properties` to be presented with a similar screen to the one shown in Figure 15-7.

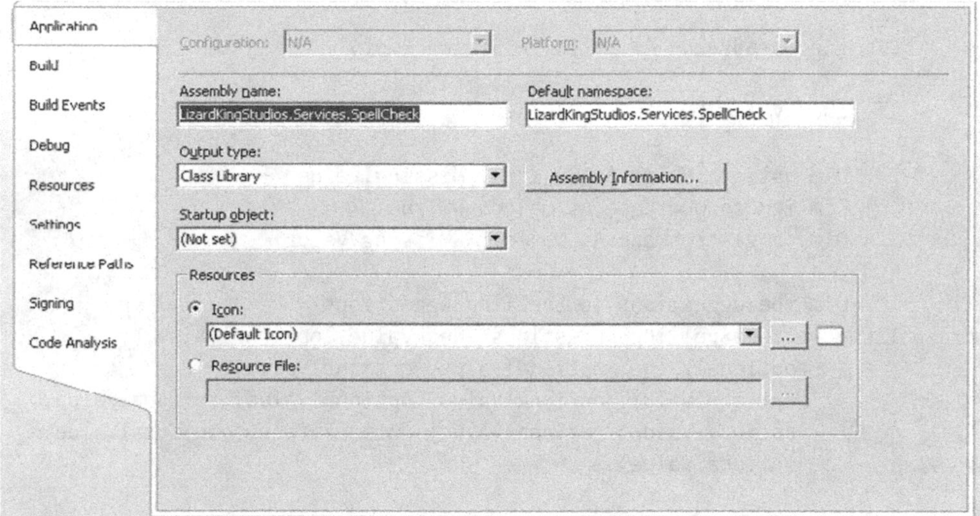

Figure 15-7. *Project-properties configuration*

12. Select the Signing tab and create a new key to sign the assembly.

13. Select the Build Events tab and, in the Post-Build event property, enter the value shown in Listing 15-15. This copies the assembly to the proper .NET assembly location each time it is compiled and uses `gacutil.exe` to register the assembly into the GAC to make it available to SSIS.

Listing 15-15. *The Post-Build Event Value*

```
"$(DevEnvDir)..\..\SDK\v2.0\Bin\gacutil.exe" /if "$(TargetPath)"
xcopy /Y "$(TargetPath)" "C:\WINDOWS\Microsoft.NET\Framework\v2.0.50727"
```

14. Close the project-properties window and, from the IDE menu, select Build ➤ Build `LizardKingStudios.Services.Spellcheck`.

15. The project should compile and report no errors or warnings of any kind. This means a successful compilation has taken place and that the generated assembly has been copied to the proper assemblies directory without error.

You're finished with the first part of this example. You now have a compiled and working class library to perform the spellcheck, and it is available for use from any other .NET-compliant source such those shown in Figure 15-3.

Your next task is to create a Data Flow transform component with which to call the spellcheck class library, provide it with data, and return from it the result.

The Custom Data Flow Transform Component

Now we're getting somewhere. Let's keep things nice and slow and create a custom transform component for the Data Flow by applying the principles discussed earlier in the chapter.

When developing multitier projects such as this one, I keep the previous instance of Visual Studio open and open up another so that I have easy access to the code for editing or fixing bugs. So you'll continue this example by doing the same:

1. Open up a new Visual Studio 2005 instance.

2. Select New ➤ Project from the menu, and select [Language] ➤ Windows ➤ Class Library from the Project Template dialog. [Language] means your language of choice.

   You can give your new project whatever name you choose—I'm going for `LizardKingStudios.SSIS.DataFlowTransforms.SpellCheck`. Again, the first parts of the name (`LizardKingStudios.SSIS.DataFlowTransforms`) refer to the namespace of the project, and the last part, `Spellcheck`, refers to the purpose of the project. This way, additional SSIS Data Flow components can be collected under the same namespace. Figure 15-8 shows the New Project dialog, and Table 15-9 lists the settings I've used to set up the creation of the class library.

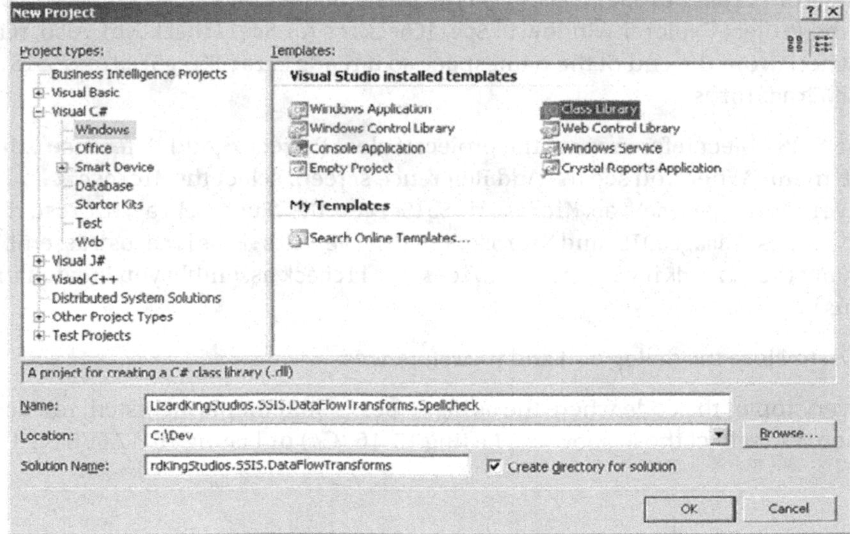

Figure 15-8. *Setting up the class-library project properties*

Table 15-9. *New Project Properties in Detail*

Property	Value	Description
Project type	Visual C# ➤ Windows	You can select VB.NET (or any other CLR language) instead.
Template	Class Library	The type of project you're creating.
Name	`LizardKingStudios.SSIS.DataFlowTransforms.SpellCheck`	The name of the project to create.
Location	C:\Dev (or other location)	The base location for the solution.
Solution Name	`LizardKingStudios.SSIS.DataFlowTransforms`	The name of the Visual Studio solution to create that will be used to contain `DataFlowTransforms` projects.
Create directory for solution	Checked	Creating a directory for the solution will keep things tidy and organized.

3. You should find yourself looking at the code template for a class library in the IDE, very much like Figure 15-9.

```
using System;
using System.Collections.Generic;
using System.Text;

namespace LizardKingStudios.SSIS.DataFlowTransforms.Spellcheck
{
    public class Class1
    {
    }
}
```

Figure 15-9. *The new project is created with the basic class-library template.*

Tweaking the class name to reflect what you're trying to achieve. Change the name of the class from `Class1` to `SpellCheck` and the name of the `Class1.cs` (or `Class1.vb`) file under the Project Explorer window to `SpellCheck.cs` (or `Spellcheck.vb`). Also, remove `.SpellCheck` from the end of the namespace so it reads `LizardKingStudios.SSIS.DataFlowTransforms`.

4. Add the SSIS object references to the project. Select Project ➤ Add Reference… from the IDE menu. When you see the Add Reference screen, select the `Microsoft.SqlServer.Dts.PipelineWrap`, `Microsoft.SqlServer.Dts.RuntimeWrap`, `Microsoft.SqlServer.Dts.ManagedDTS`, and `Microsoft.SqlServer.Dts.PipelineHost` assemblies and finally the `LizardKingStudios.Services.Spellcheck` assembly you created in the previous section.

5. Click OK to close the dialog and add the references.

6. At the very top of the code where the `using/imports` statements are listed, replace the statements to reflect those shown as Listing 15-16 (C#) or Listing 15-17 (VB.NET).

Listing 15-16. *Using Statements (C#)*

```
using System;
using Microsoft.SqlServer.Dts;
using Microsoft.SqlServer.Dts.Pipeline;
using Microsoft.SqlServer.Dts.Pipeline.Wrapper;
using Microsoft.SqlServer.Dts.Runtime.Wrapper;
using LizardKingStudios.Services.SpellCheck;
```

Listing 15-17. *Imports Statements (VB.NET)*

```
Imports System
Imports Microsoft.SqlServer.Dts
Imports Microsoft.SqlServer.Dts.Pipeline
Imports Microsoft.SqlServer.Dts.Pipeline.Wrapper
Imports Microsoft.SqlServer.Dts.Runtime.Wrapper
Imports LizardKingStudios.Services.SpellCheck
```

7. You need to add a class attribute now so that the compiled assembly will be recognized by SSIS as a Data Flow transform component. It needs to be added on the line above the class declaration. While you are here you can also specify the class from which the `SpellCheck` class should derive—`PipelineComponent`. Listing 15-18 (C#) shows the attribute that should be added and the code after the class declaration line that specifies the base class to derive from. Listing 15-19 shows the same code in VB.NET.

Listing 15-18. *Namespace and Class Declaration, Including Attribute (C#)*

```
namespace LizardKingStudios.SSIS.DataFlowTransforms
{
    [DtsPipelineComponent(DisplayName = "LizardKing Spellchecker",
Description = "Sample Data Flow Component from the Apress book Pro SSIS",
IconResource = "LizardKingStudios.SSIS.DataFlowTranforms.Icon.ico",
ComponentType = ComponentType.Transform)]
    public class SpellCheck : PipelineComponent
    {
```

Listing 15-19. *Namespace and Class Declaration, Including Attribute (VB.NET)*

```
Namespace LizardKingStudios.SSIS.DataflowTransformsVB

    <DtsPipelineComponent(ComponentType:=ComponentType.Transform,
Description:="Sample Data Flow Component from the Apress book Pro SSIS",
DisplayName:="Lizard King Spellchecker",
IconResource:="LizardKingStudios.SSIS.DataFlowTranforms.Icon.ico")> _
    Public Class SpellCheck
        Inherits PipelineComponent
```

Now that your new class derives from `PipelineComponent`, you have access to all the objects in the object model with which to support the transformation of data (in this case, spellchecking) contained in the Data Flow data pipeline.

8. Now add three member variables. Listings 15-20 (C#) and 15-21 (VB.NET) show the code to use.

Listing 15-20. *Member-Variable Declarations (C#)*

```
        private PipelineBuffer outputBuffer;
        private int[] inputColumnBufferIndexes;
        private int[] outputColumnBufferIndexes;
```

Listing 15-21. *Member-Variable Declarations (VB.NET)*

```
Private outputBuffer As PipelineBuffer
        Private inputColumnBufferIndexes() As Integer
        Private outputColumnBufferIndexes() As Integer
```

The outputBuffer variable is used as a single reference to the output pipeline buffer for all methods in the class. The two integer array variables are used to store column buffer indexes for each column defined in the input and output buffers—but I'll get to that in more detail shortly.

9. The code in Listing 15-22 (C#) or Listing 15-23 (VB.NET) should be added next. This is a simple helper method that, when called, raises a FireError event containing a message that describes any problem encountered. You will see it referred to repeatedly in subsequent code.

Listing 15-22. *Reusable Validation Helper Method (C#)*

```
        private void PostError(string message)
        {
            bool cancel = false;
            this.ComponentMetaData.FireError(0, this.ComponentMetaData.Name,
message, "", 0, out cancel);
        }
```

Listing 15-23. *Reusable Validation-Support Methods (VB.NET)*

```
        Private Sub PostError(ByVal message As String)

            Dim cancel As Boolean = False
            Me.ComponentMetaData.FireError(0, Me.ComponentMetaData.Name,
message, "", 0, cancel)

        End Sub
```

10. It's time to start implementing custom functionality, so you need to begin overriding methods to contain the custom code. First up is the Validate method. Enter the code shown in Listing 15-24 (C#) or Listing 15-25 (VB.NET).

Listing 15-24. *Overriden Validate Method (C#)*

```
        public override DTSValidationStatus Validate()
        {
            DTSValidationStatus status = base.Validate();
            if (status == DTSValidationStatus.VS_ISCORRUPT)
            {
                return status;
            }

            IDTSComponentMetaData90 metadata = this.ComponentMetaData;
            IDTSCustomPropertyCollection90 componentCustomProperties =
metadata.CustomPropertyCollection;
            try
            {
                IDTSCustomProperty90 customProperty =
componentCustomProperties["InputColumnToCheck"];
                string s = (string)customProperty.Value;
                if (s.Length == 0)
                {
                    PostError("InputColumnToCheck must be populated");
                    return DTSValidationStatus.VS_ISCORRUPT;
                }
            }
            catch (System.Runtime.InteropServices.COMException e)
            {
                if (e.ErrorCode == HResults.DTS_E_ELEMENTNOTFOUND)
                {
                    PostError("Custom property 'InputColumnToCheck' not found in
component custom property collection");
                    return DTSValidationStatus.VS_ISCORRUPT;
                }
                else
                {
                    throw e;
                }
            }
            if (metadata.InputCollection.Count != 1)
            {
                PostError("Component requires exactly one input.");
                return DTSValidationStatus.VS_ISCORRUPT;
            }

            IDTSInput90 input = metadata.InputCollection[0];
            IDTSInputColumnCollection90 inputColumns = input.InputColumnCollection;

            for (int j = 0; j < inputColumns.Count; j++)
            {
```

```
                IDTSInputColumn90 column = inputColumns[j];
                if (column.IsValid)
                {
                    // validation code can go in here for allowing only string types
                }
            }
            return status;
        }
```

Listing 15-25. *Overriden Validation Method (VB.NET)*

```
        Public Overrides Function Validate() As DTSValidationStatus

            Dim status As DTSValidationStatus = MyBase.Validate()
            If (status = DTSValidationStatus.VS_ISCORRUPT) Then
                Return status
            End If

            Dim metadata As IDTSComponentMetaData90 = Me.ComponentMetaData
            Dim componentCustomProperties As IDTSCustomPropertyCollection90 =
metadata.CustomPropertyCollection
            Try
                Dim customProperty As IDTSCustomProperty90 =
componentCustomProperties("InputColumnToCheck")
                Dim s As String = CType(customProperty.Value, String)
                If (s.Length = 0) Then
                    PostError("InputColumnToCheck must be populated")
                    Return DTSValidationStatus.VS_ISCORRUPT
                End If
            Catch e As System.Runtime.InteropServices.COMException
                If (e.ErrorCode = HResults.DTS_E_ELEMENTNOTFOUND) Then
                    PostError("Custom property 'InputColumnToCheck' not found in
component custom property collection")
                    Return DTSValidationStatus.VS_ISCORRUPT
                Else

                    Throw e
                End If
            End Try
            If (metadata.InputCollection.Count <> 1) Then

                PostError("Component requires exactly one input.")
                Return DTSValidationStatus.VS_ISCORRUPT
            End If

            Dim input As IDTSInput90 = metadata.InputCollection(0)
            Dim inputColumns As IDTSInputColumnCollection90 =
input.InputColumnCollection
```

```
        Dim j As Integer
        For j = 0 To inputColumns.Count - 1 Step j + 1
            Dim column As IDTSInputColumn90 = inputColumns(j)
            If (column.IsValid) Then

                ' validation code can go in here for allowing only string types
            End If
        Next
        Return status
    End Function
```

As you can see, the first thing the overridden method does is make a call to the base class's `Validate` method to execute parent code (`DTSValidationStatus status = base.Validate();`). Once this is complete, custom code is introduced to make validity checks for problems you are particularly concerned with or interested in trapping. The checks are made against the `DTSValidationStatus` type variable, `status`.

Notice how the code references a custom property called `InputColumnToCheck`. A number of different validation checks are performed for this custom property, including that it exists and that it is populated. This is important to check because the component cannot run successfully without knowing which input column is being spellchecked.

11. Listing 15-26 (C#) and Listing 15-27 (VB.NET) contain overridden methods concerning the addition and removal of inputs and outputs. The opportunity to add inputs or outputs is made available in the general component-configuration editor on the Inputs and Outputs tab. Because you want to limit the user's ability to add or remove inputs and outputs using this configuration screen, you must override the base methods and provide a suitable rebuke to the user (via the `PostError` method created earlier in the example) and not fulfill the user request.

Listing 15-26. *Overriden Methods for Adding and Removing Inputs and Outputs (C#)*

```
        public override IDTSInput90 InsertInput(DTSInsertPlacement insertPlacement,
int inputID)
        {
            PostError("Component requires exactly one input. New input is
forbidden.");
            throw new
PipelineComponentHResultException(HResults.DTS_E_CANTADDINPUT);
        }

        public override void DeleteInput(int inputID)
        {
            PostError("Component requires exactly one input. Deleted input
is forbidden.");
            throw new PipelineComponentHResultException(
HResults.DTS_E_CANTDELETEINPUT);
        }
```

```
        public override IDTSOutput90 InsertOutput(DTSInsertPlacement
insertPlacement, int outputID)
        {

            PostError("Component requires exactly one output. New output
is forbidden.");
            throw new PipelineComponentHResultException(
HResults.DTS_E_CANTADDOUTPUT);
        }

        public override void DeleteOutput(int outputID)
        {
            PostError("Component requires exactly one output. Deleted output
is forbidden.");
            throw new PipelineComponentHResultException(
HResults.DTS_E_CANTDELETEOUTPUT);
        }

        public override IDTSOutputColumn90 InsertOutputColumnAt(int outputID,
int outputColumnIndex, string name, string description)
        {
            PostError("Component does not allow addition of output columns.");
            throw new PipelineComponentHResultException(
HResults.DTS_E_CANTADDCOLUMN);
        }
```

Listing 15-27. *Overriden Methods for Adding and Removing Inputs and Outputs (VB.NET)*

```
        Public Overrides Function InsertInput(

ByVal insertPlacement As DTSInsertPlacement,

ByVal inputID As Integer) As IDTSInput90

            PostError("Component requires exactly one input. New input
is forbidden.")
            Throw New PipelineComponentHResultException(
HResults.DTS_E_CANTADDINPUT)

        End Function

        Public Overrides Sub DeleteInput(ByVal inputID As Integer)

            PostError("Component requires exactly one input. Deleted input
is forbidden.")
            Throw New PipelineComponentHResultException(
HResults.DTS_E_CANTDELETEINPUT)

        End Sub
```

```
        Public Overrides Function InsertOutput(
ByVal insertPlacement As DTSInsertPlacement,
ByVal outputID As Integer) As IDTSOutput90

            PostError("Component requires exactly one output. New output
is forbidden.")
            Throw New PipelineComponentHResultException(
HResults.DTS_E_CANTADDOUTPUT)

        End Function

        Public Overrides Sub DeleteOutput(ByVal outputID As Integer)

            PostError("Component requires exactly one output. Deleted output
is forbidden.")
            Throw New PipelineComponentHResultException(
HResults.DTS_E_CANTDELETEOUTPUT)

        End Sub

        Public Overrides Function InsertOutputColumnAt(ByVal outputID As Integer,
ByVal outputColumnIndex As Integer,
ByVal name As String,
ByVal description As String) As IDTSOutputColumn90

            PostError("Component does not allow addition of output columns.")
            Throw New PipelineComponentHResultException(
HResults.DTS_E_CANTADDCOLUMN)

        End Function
```

12. The next code to add, found in Listing 15-28 (C#) and Listing 15-29 (VB.NET), overrides the `OnInputPathAttached` method. Based on the new input-columns collection (new because a new upstream input has just been attached to the component), a new output column of the same name and data type is created for each of the new input columns.

    Two additional columns are also added. The first, `isSuggested`, holds a boolean value denoting whether a spelling change has occurred for the specified input-column value. The second, `suggestedValue`, holds the updated value suggested by the spellcheck operation.

Listing 15-28. *Overriding OnInputPathAttached (C#)*

```
        public override void OnInputPathAttached(int inputID)
        {
            base.OnInputPathAttached(inputID);
```

```
            IDTSInput90 input = ComponentMetaData.InputCollection.GetObjectByID(
inputID);
            IDTSOutput90 output = ComponentMetaData.OutputCollection[0];
            IDTSVirtualInput90 vInput = input.GetVirtualInput();

            foreach (IDTSVirtualInputColumn90 vCol in
vInput.VirtualInputColumnCollection)
            {
                IDTSOutputColumn90 outCol = output.OutputColumnCollection.New();
                outCol.Name = vCol.Name;
                outCol.SetDataTypeProperties(vCol.DataType, vCol.Length,
vCol.Precision, vCol.Scale, vCol.CodePage);
            }

            IDTSOutputColumn90 outputColumn = output.OutputColumnCollection.New();

            outputColumn.Name = "isSuggested";
            outputColumn.SetDataTypeProperties(DataType.DT_BOOL, 0, 0, 0, 0);
            outputColumn =
this.ComponentMetaData.OutputCollection[0].OutputColumnCollection.New();
            outputColumn.Name = "suggestedValue";
            outputColumn.SetDataTypeProperties(DataType.DT_STR, 50, 0, 0, 1252);

        }
```

Listing 15-29. *Overriding OnInputPathAttached (VB.NET)*

```
        Public Overrides Sub OnInputPathAttached(ByVal inputID As Integer)

            MyBase.OnInputPathAttached(inputID)

            Dim input As IDTSInput90 =
ComponentMetaData.InputCollection.GetObjectByID(inputID)
            Dim output As IDTSOutput90 = ComponentMetaData.OutputCollection(0)
            Dim vInput As IDTSVirtualInput90 = input.GetVirtualInput()

            Dim vCol As IDTSVirtualInputColumn90
            For Each vCol In vInput.VirtualInputColumnCollection
                Dim outCol As IDTSOutputColumn90 =
output.OutputColumnCollection.New()
                outCol.Name = vCol.Name
                outCol.SetDataTypeProperties(
vCol.DataType, vCol.Length, vCol.Precision, vCol.Scale, vCol.CodePage)
            Next

            Dim outputColumn As IDTSOutputColumn90 =
output.OutputColumnCollection.New()
```

```
            outputColumn.Name = "isSuggested"
            outputColumn.SetDataTypeProperties(DataType.DT_BOOL, 0, 0, 0, 0)
            outputColumn =
Me.ComponentMetaData.OutputCollection(0).OutputColumnCollection.New()
            outputColumn.Name = "suggestedValue"
            outputColumn.SetDataTypeProperties(DataType.DT_STR, 50, 0, 0, 1252)

        End Sub
```

13. Listing 15-30 (C#) and Listing 15-31 (VB.NET) provide the code to override the `ProvideComponentProperties` method. This method is used to provide some component initialization and to add two custom properties. These properties are exposed to the configuration editor on the Data Flow design surface to be updated by the user as applicable.

Listing 15-30. *ProvideComponentProperties (C#)*

```
        public override void ProvideComponentProperties()
        {
            base.ProvideComponentProperties();

            ComponentMetaData.OutputCollection[0].SynchronousInputID = 0;

            IDTSCustomPropertyCollection90 customProperties =
this.ComponentMetaData.CustomPropertyCollection;
            IDTSCustomProperty90 customProperty = customProperties.New();

            customProperty.Name = "InputColumnToCheck";
            customProperty.Value = "";
            customProperty = customProperties.New();
            customProperty.Name = "MaxSuggestionsCount";
            customProperty.Value = "5";

        }
```

Listing 15-31. *ProvidingComponentProperties (VB.NET)*

```
        Public Overrides Sub ProvideComponentProperties()

            MyBase.ProvideComponentProperties()

            ComponentMetaData.OutputCollection(0).SynchronousInputID = 0

            Dim customProperties As IDTSCustomPropertyCollection90 =
 Me.ComponentMetaData.CustomPropertyCollection
            Dim customProperty As IDTSCustomProperty90 = customProperties.New()

            customProperty.Name = "InputColumnToCheck"
```

```
        customProperty.Value = ""
        customProperty = customProperties.New()
        customProperty.Name = "MaxSuggestionsCount"
        customProperty.Value = "5"

    End Sub
```

Figure 15-10 shows the custom properties as they appear in the component-configuration editor.

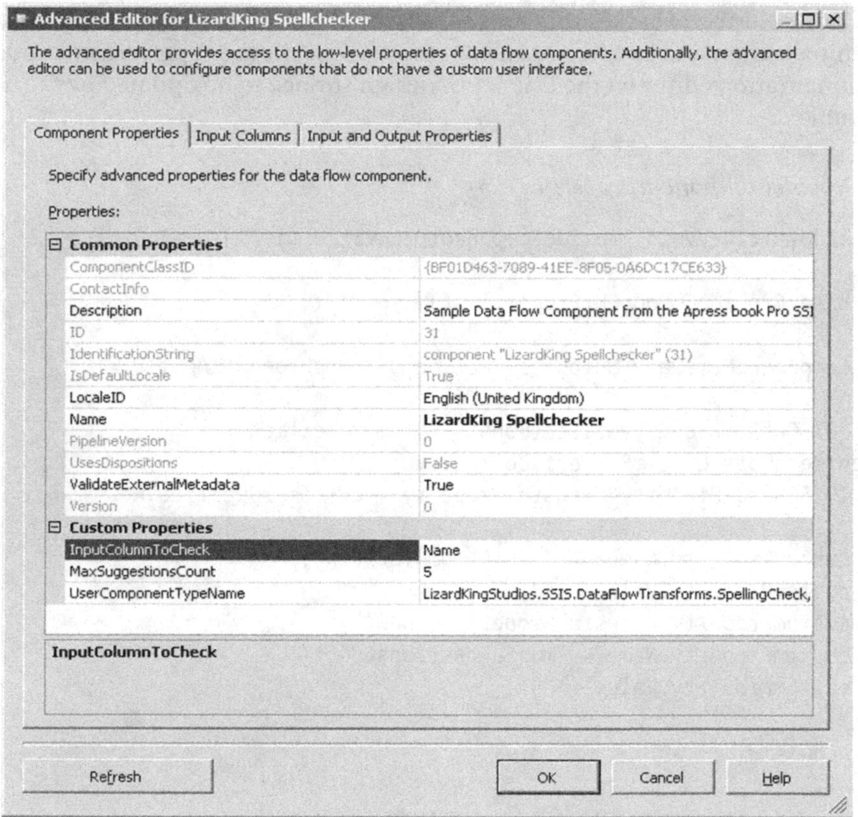

Figure 15-10. *The newly added properties appear under Custom Properties.*

14. The next piece of code (Listing 15-32 for C# or Listing 15-33 for VB.NET) is where you override the `SetComponentProperty` method. As I stated earlier in the chapter, this method can be used to validate the property value—whether it contains an acceptable value or, as is the case with your code, that the value is populated at all.

Listing 15-32. *SetComponentProperty (C#)*

```
        public override IDTSCustomProperty90 SetComponentProperty(
string propertyName, object propertyValue)
```

```
        {
            if (propertyName == "InputColumnToCheck")
            {
                string value = (string)propertyValue;
                if (value.Length == 0)
                {
                    PostError("InputColumnToCheck must be populated.");
                    throw new PipelineComponentHResultException(
HResults.DTS_E_FAILEDTOSETPROPERTY);
                }
                else
                {
                    return base.SetComponentProperty(propertyName, propertyValue);
                }
            }
            else
            {
                PostError("Specified property name [" + propertyName + "]
not expected.");
                throw new PipelineComponentHResultException(
HResults.DTS_E_FAILEDTOSETPROPERTY);
            }
        }
```

Listing 15-33. *SetComponentProperty (VB.NET)*

```
        Public Overrides Function SetComponentProperty(
ByVal propertyName As String,
ByVal propertyValue As Object) As IDTSCustomProperty90

            If (propertyName = "InputColumnToCheck") Then

                Dim value As String = CType(propertyValue, String)
                If (value.Length = 0) Then

                    PostError("InputColumnToCheck must be populated.")
                    Throw New PipelineComponentHResultException(
HResults.DTS_E_FAILEDTOSETPROPERTY)

                Else

                    Return MyBase.SetComponentProperty(propertyName, propertyValue)
                End If

            Else
```

```
                PostError("Specified property name [" + propertyName + "]
not expected.")
                Throw New PipelineComponentHResultException(
HResults.DTS_E_FAILEDTOSETPROPERTY)
            End If
        End Function
```

15. Now things are getting exciting—you're moving on to runtime methods. Listing 15-34 (C#) and Listing 15-35 (VB.NET) show the next method override you need to implement. This time you're concerned with `PreExecute`. Remember that the `PreExecute` method is used to provide final runtime configuration before the processing of data from the input buffer takes place.

    In your code this method is used as an opportunity to populate the two integer array member variables declared earlier in the example. You loop through the input and output collections to retrieve and store each column's ID.

Listing 15-34. *PreExecute (C#)*

```
        public override void PreExecute()
        {
            IDTSInput90 input = ComponentMetaData.InputCollection[0];
            IDTSOutput90 output = ComponentMetaData.OutputCollection[0];

            inputColumnBufferIndexes = new int[input.InputColumnCollection.Count];
            outputColumnBufferIndexes =
new int[output.OutputColumnCollection.Count];

            for (int col = 0; col < input.InputColumnCollection.Count; col++)
               inputColumnBufferIndexes[col] =
BufferManager.FindColumnByLineageID(input.Buffer,
input.InputColumnCollection[col].LineageID);

            for (int col = 0; col < output.OutputColumnCollection.Count; col++)
               outputColumnBufferIndexes[col] =
BufferManager.FindColumnByLineageID(output.Buffer,
output.OutputColumnCollection[col].LineageID);
        }
```

Listing 15-35. *PreExecute (VB.NET)*

```
        Public Overrides Sub PreExecute()

            Dim input As IDTSInput90 = ComponentMetaData.InputCollection(0)
            Dim output As IDTSOutput90 = ComponentMetaData.OutputCollection(0)

            inputColumnBufferIndexes =
```

```
New Integer(input.InputColumnCollection.Count) {}
            outputColumnBufferIndexes =
New Integer(output.OutputColumnCollection.Count) {}

            Dim col As Integer
            For col = 0 To input.InputColumnCollection.Count - 1 Step col + 1
                inputColumnBufferIndexes(col) =
BufferManager.FindColumnByLineageID(input.Buffer,
input.InputColumnCollection(col).LineageID)
            Next

            For col = 0 To output.OutputColumnCollection.Count - 1 Step col + 1
                outputColumnBufferIndexes(col) =
BufferManager.FindColumnByLineageID(output.Buffer,
output.OutputColumnCollection(col).LineageID)
            Next
        End Sub
```

16. Now you get to `PrimeOutput`, which is a nice simple override in this instance. `PrimeOutput` gets called once because of the nature of the component you are creating. This is an opportunity to assign the first buffer from the `PipelineBuffer` array to the `outputBuffer` member variable. Listing 15-36 (C#) and Listing 15-37 (VB.NET) show the code required.

Listing 15-36. *PrimeOutput (C#)*

```
       public override void PrimeOutput(int outputs, int[] outputIDs,

PipelineBuffer[] buffers)
        {
            if (buffers.Length != 0)
                outputBuffer = buffers[0];
        }
```

Listing 15-37. *PrimeOutput (VB.NET)*

```
       Public Overrides Sub PrimeOutput(ByVal outputs As Integer,

ByVal outputIDs As Integer(), ByVal buffers As PipelineBuffer())

            If (buffers.Length <> 0) Then
                outputBuffer = buffers(0)
            End If

        End Sub
```

17. The code in Listing 15-38 (C#) and Listing 15-39 (VB.NET) is the override method for `ProcessInput`. This method gets called once for each row of data in the input buffer.

Listing 15-38. *ProcessInput (C#)*

```
        public override void ProcessInput(int inputID, PipelineBuffer buffer)
        {
            string suggestedValue = String.Empty;
            string checkValue;
            SpellcheckEngine spellEngine = new SpellcheckEngine();
            int colId = -1;
            // set maxsuggestionscount property in our spellcheck class library
            spellEngine.MaxSuggestionsCount = Convert.ToInt32(
ComponentMetaData.CustomPropertyCollection["MaxSuggestionsCount"].Value.ToString()
);
            IDTSInput90 input =
ComponentMetaData.InputCollection.GetObjectByID(inputID);

            // loop through each item in the input.InputColumnCollection collection
            // and compare the value to the supplied InputColumnToCheck property
            // value. This identifies the lineage id of the column you will be
            // performing the spellcheck operation on.
            for (int colIndex = 0; colIndex < input.InputColumnCollection.Count;
colIndex++ )
            {
                if (input.InputColumnCollection[colIndex].Name.ToUpper() ==
 ComponentMetaData.CustomPropertyCollection[
"InputColumnToCheck"].Value.ToString().ToUpper())
                {

                    colId = input.InputColumnCollection[colIndex].LineageID;
                    break;
                }
            }

            int theColIndex = BufferManager.FindColumnByLineageID(
input.Buffer, colId);

            if (!buffer.EndOfRowset)
            {
                while (buffer.NextRow())
                {
                    // perform the spellcheck for the specified column
                    checkValue = buffer[theColIndex].ToString();
                    suggestedValue = spellEngine.Execute(checkValue);
```

```
                    outputBuffer.AddRow();

                    // loop through each of the input columns and pass their values
                    // to their mapped output columns
                    for (int x = 0; x < inputColumnBufferIndexes.Length; x++)
                    {
                        outputBuffer[outputColumnBufferIndexes[x]] =
buffer[inputColumnBufferIndexes[x]];
                    }

                    // update the two new columns with the spellchecked value
                    // (and the indicator of whether a suggestion has been made or
                    // not).
                    if (suggestedValue.Length == 0)
                        outputBuffer[outputColumnBufferIndexes[
outputColumnBufferIndexes.Length - 2]] = "false";
                    else
                        outputBuffer[outputColumnBufferIndexes[
outputColumnBufferIndexes.Length - 2]] = "true";

                    outputBuffer[outputColumnBufferIndexes[
outputColumnBufferIndexes.Length-1]] = suggestedValue;

                }
            }
            else
            {
               // inform SSIS that you have finished processing the rows because you
               // are at the end of the rowset.
                outputBuffer.SetEndOfRowset();
            }
        }
    }
```

Listing 15-39. *ProcessInput (VB.NET)*

```
        Public Overrides Sub ProcessInput(ByVal inputID As Integer,

ByVal buffer As PipelineBuffer)

            Dim suggestedValue As String = String.Empty
            Dim checkValue As String
            Dim spellEngine As SpellcheckEngine = New SpellcheckEngine()
            Dim colId As Integer = -1
            ' set maxsuggestionscount property in our spellcheck class library
            spellEngine.MaxSuggestionsCount = Convert.ToInt32(ComponentMetaData.
```

```
CustomPropertyCollection("MaxSuggestionsCount").Value.ToString())
            Dim input As IDTSInput90 = ComponentMetaData.InputCollection.
GetObjectByID(inputID)

            ' loop through each item in the input.InputColumnCollection collection
            ' and compare the value to the supplied InputColumnToCheck property
            ' value. This identifies the lineage id of the column you will be
            ' performing the spellcheck operation on.
            Dim colIndex As Integer
            For colIndex = 0 To input.InputColumnCollection.Count - 1 Step colIndex➥
        + 1
                If (input.InputColumnCollection(colIndex).Name.ToUpper() =
ComponentMetaData.CustomPropertyCollection("InputColumnToCheck").
Value.ToString().ToUpper()) Then

                    colId = input.InputColumnCollection(colIndex).LineageID
                    Exit For
                End If
            Next

            Dim theColIndex As Integer = BufferManager.FindColumnByLineageID(
input.Buffer, colId)

            If (Not buffer.EndOfRowset) Then
                While buffer.NextRow()
                    ' perform the spellcheck for the specified column
                    checkValue = buffer(theColIndex).ToString()
                    suggestedValue = spellEngine.Execute(checkValue)

                    ' loop through each of the input columns and pass their values
                    ' to their mapped output columns
                    outputBuffer.AddRow()

                    Dim x As Integer
                    For x = 0 To inputColumnBufferIndexes.Length - 1 Step x + 1
                        outputBuffer(outputColumnBufferIndexes(x)) =
buffer(inputColumnBufferIndexes(x))
                    Next

                    ' update the two new columns with the spellchecked value (and
                    ' the indicator of whether a suggestion has been made or not).

                    If (suggestedValue.Length = 0) Then
                        outputBuffer(outputColumnBufferIndexes(
outputColumnBufferIndexes.Length - 2)) = "false"
                    Else
                        outputBuffer(outputColumnBufferIndexes(
```

```
outputColumnBufferIndexes.Length - 2)) = "true"

                        outputBuffer(outputColumnBufferIndexes(
outputColumnBufferIndexes.Length - 1)) = suggestedValue
                    End If
                End While
            Else
                ' inform SSIS that you have finished processing the rows
                ' because you are at the end of the rowset.
                outputBuffer.SetEndOfRowset()
            End If
        End Sub
```

The code for `ProcessInput` is fairly simple, though one or two important principles are hidden away that warrant closer examination. The first thing to note is that the line of code that adds a new row to the output buffer—`outputBuffer.AddRow()`—is vital, because the output buffer is empty until rows are added. Once a row is added, that row can have its column values updated by the remainder of the code. Another important point is to ensure that when `buffer.EndOfRowset` evaluates to `true`, `outputBuffer.SetEndOfRowset()` is called to inform SSIS that processing has completed.

For the sake of accuracy and troubleshooting, I'm including the complete code listing for this custom component as Listing 15-40 (C#) and Listing 15-41 (VB.NET). If you encounter any problems following the approach above, the complete listings should help identify the issue.

Listing 15-40. *The Complete Custom-Component Code (C#)*

```
using System;
using Microsoft.SqlServer.Dts;
using Microsoft.SqlServer.Dts.Pipeline;
using Microsoft.SqlServer.Dts.Pipeline.Wrapper;
using Microsoft.SqlServer.Dts.Runtime.Wrapper;
using LizardKingStudios.Services.SpellCheck;

namespace LizardKingStudios.SSIS.DataFlowTransforms
{
    [DtsPipelineComponent(DisplayName = "LizardKing Spellchecker",
Description = "Sample Data Flow Component from the Apress book Pro SSIS",
IconResource = "LizardKingStudios.SSIS.DataFlowTranforms.Icon.ico",
ComponentType = ComponentType.Transform)]
    public class SpellCheck : PipelineComponent
    {
        PipelineBuffer outputBuffer;
        private int[] inputColumnBufferIndexes;
        private int[] outputColumnBufferIndexes;

        private void PostError(string message)
```

```
        {
            bool cancel = false;
            this.ComponentMetaData.FireError(0, this.ComponentMetaData.Name,
message, "", 0, out cancel);
        }

        public override DTSValidationStatus Validate()
        {
            DTSValidationStatus status = base.Validate();
            if (status == DTSValidationStatus.VS_ISCORRUPT)
            {
                return status;
            }

            IDTSComponentMetaData90 metadata = this.ComponentMetaData;
            IDTSCustomPropertyCollection90 componentCustomProperties =
metadata.CustomPropertyCollection;
            try
            {
                IDTSCustomProperty90 customProperty =
componentCustomProperties["InputColumnToCheck"];
                string s = (string)customProperty.Value;
                if (s.Length == 0)
                {
                    PostError("InputColumnToCheck must be populated");
                    return DTSValidationStatus.VS_ISCORRUPT;
                }
            }
            catch (System.Runtime.InteropServices.COMException e)
            {
                if (e.ErrorCode == HResults.DTS_E_ELEMENTNOTFOUND)
                {
                    PostError("Custom property 'InputColumnToCheck' not found in
component custom property collection");
                    return DTSValidationStatus.VS_ISCORRUPT;
                }
                else
                {
                    throw e;
                }
            }
            if (metadata.InputCollection.Count != 1)
            {
                PostError("Component requires exactly one input.");
                return DTSValidationStatus.VS_ISCORRUPT;
            }

            IDTSInput90 input = metadata.InputCollection[0];
```

```
            IDTSInputColumnCollection90 inputColumns = input.InputColumnCollection;

            for (int j = 0; j < inputColumns.Count; j++)
            {
                IDTSInputColumn90 column = inputColumns[j];
                if (column.IsValid)
                {
                    // validation code can go in here for allowing only string types
                }
            }
            return status;
        }

        public override IDTSInput90 InsertInput(
DTSInsertPlacement insertPlacement, int inputID)
        {
            PostError("Component requires exactly one input.
New input is forbidden.");
            throw new PipelineComponentHResultException(
HResults.DTS_E_CANTADDINPUT);
        }

        public override void DeleteInput(int inputID)
        {
            PostError("Component requires exactly one input.
Deleted input is forbidden.");
            throw new PipelineComponentHResultException(
HResults.DTS_E_CANTDELETEINPUT);
        }

        public override IDTSOutput90 InsertOutput(
DTSInsertPlacement insertPlacement, int outputID)
        {

            PostError("Component requires exactly one output.
New output is forbidden.");
            throw new PipelineComponentHResultException(
HResults.DTS_E_CANTADDOUTPUT);
        }

        public override void DeleteOutput(int outputID)
        {
            PostError("Component requires exactly one output.
Deleted output is forbidden.");
            throw new PipelineComponentHResultException(
HResults.DTS_E_CANTDELETEOUTPUT);
        }
```

```
        public override IDTSOutputColumn90 InsertOutputColumnAt(int outputID,
int outputColumnIndex, string name, string description)
        {
            PostError("Component does not allow addition of output columns.");
            throw new PipelineComponentHResultException(
HResults.DTS_E_CANTADDCOLUMN);
        }

        public override IDTSInputColumn90 SetUsageType(int inputID,
IDTSVirtualInput90 virtualInput, int lineageID, DTSUsageType usageType)
        {
            IDTSInputColumn90 inputColumn = null;
            switch (usageType)
            {
                case DTSUsageType.UT_READWRITE:

                case DTSUsageType.UT_READONLY:

                case DTSUsageType.UT_IGNORED:
                    inputColumn = base.SetUsageType(inputID, virtualInput,
lineageID, usageType);
                    return inputColumn;
                default:
                    throw new PipelineComponentHResultException(
HResults.DTS_E_CANTSETUSAGETYPE);
            }
        }

        public override void OnInputPathAttached(int inputID)
        {
            base.OnInputPathAttached(inputID);

            IDTSInput90 input = ComponentMetaData.InputCollection.
GetObjectByID(inputID);
            IDTSOutput90 output = ComponentMetaData.OutputCollection[0];
            IDTSVirtualInput90 vInput = input.GetVirtualInput();

            foreach (IDTSVirtualInputColumn90 vCol in
vInput.VirtualInputColumnCollection)
            {
                IDTSOutputColumn90 outCol = output.OutputColumnCollection.New();
                outCol.Name = vCol.Name;
                outCol.SetDataTypeProperties(vCol.DataType, vCol.Length,
vCol.Precision, vCol.Scale, vCol.CodePage);
            }

            IDTSOutputColumn90 outputColumn = output.OutputColumnCollection.New();
```

```
            outputColumn.Name = "isSuggested";
            outputColumn.SetDataTypeProperties(DataType.DT_BOOL, 0, 0, 0, 0);
            outputColumn = this.ComponentMetaData.OutputCollection[0].
OutputColumnCollection.New();
            outputColumn.Name = "suggestedValue";
            outputColumn.SetDataTypeProperties(DataType.DT_STR, 50, 0, 0, 1252);

        }

        public override void ProvideComponentProperties()
        {
            base.ProvideComponentProperties();

            ComponentMetaData.OutputCollection[0].SynchronousInputID = 0;

            IDTSCustomPropertyCollection90 customProperties =
this.ComponentMetaData.CustomPropertyCollection;
            IDTSCustomProperty90 customProperty = customProperties.New();

            customProperty.Name = "InputColumnToCheck";
            customProperty.Value = "";
            customProperty = customProperties.New();
            customProperty.Name = "MaxSuggestionsCount";
            customProperty.Value = "5";

        }

        public override IDTSCustomProperty90 SetComponentProperty(
string propertyName, object propertyValue)
        {
            if (propertyName == "InputColumnToCheck")
            {
                string value = (string)propertyValue;
                if (value.Length == 0)
                {
                    PostError("InputColumnToCheck must be populated.");
                    throw new PipelineComponentHResultException(
HResults.DTS_E_FAILEDTOSETPROPERTY);
                }
                else
                {
                    return base.SetComponentProperty(propertyName, propertyValue);
                }
            }
            else
            {
                PostError("Specified property name [" + propertyName + "]
```

```
not expected.");
                throw new PipelineComponentHResultException(
HResults.DTS_E_FAILEDTOSETPROPERTY);
            }
        }

        public override void PreExecute()
        {
             IDTSInput90 input = ComponentMetaData.InputCollection[0];
             IDTSOutput90 output = ComponentMetaData.OutputCollection[0];

             inputColumnBufferIndexes = new int[input.InputColumnCollection.Count];
             outputColumnBufferIndexes =
new int[output.OutputColumnCollection.Count];

             for (int col = 0; col < input.InputColumnCollection.Count; col++)
                inputColumnBufferIndexes[col] = BufferManager.FindColumnByLineageID(
input.Buffer, input.InputColumnCollection[col].LineageID);

             for (int col = 0; col < output.OutputColumnCollection.Count; col++)
                outputColumnBufferIndexes[col] =
BufferManager.FindColumnByLineageID(
output.Buffer, output.OutputColumnCollection[col].LineageID);
        }

        public override void PrimeOutput(int outputs, int[] outputIDs,
PipelineBuffer[] buffers)
        {
            if (buffers.Length != 0)
                outputBuffer = buffers[0];
        }

        public override void ProcessInput(int inputID, PipelineBuffer buffer)
        {
            string suggestedValue = String.Empty;
            string checkValue;
            SpellcheckEngine spellEngine = new SpellcheckEngine();
            int colId = -1;

            spellEngine.MaxSuggestionsCount = Convert.ToInt32(
 ComponentMetaData.CustomPropertyCollection["MaxSuggestionsCount"].
Value.ToString() );
            IDTSInput90 input = ComponentMetaData.InputCollection.
GetObjectByID(inputID);

            for (int colIndex = 0; colIndex < input.InputColumnCollection.Count;
colIndex++ )
```

```
            {
                if (input.InputColumnCollection[colIndex].Name.ToUpper() ==
 ComponentMetaData.CustomPropertyCollection["InputColumnToCheck"].
Value.ToString().ToUpper())
                {

                    colId = input.InputColumnCollection[colIndex].LineageID;
                    break;
                }
            }

            int theColIndex = BufferManager.FindColumnByLineageID(
input.Buffer, colId);

            if (!buffer.EndOfRowset)
            {
                while (buffer.NextRow())
                {
                    // perform the spellcheck for the specified column
                    checkValue = buffer[theColIndex].ToString();
                    suggestedValue = spellEngine.Execute(checkValue);

                    outputBuffer.AddRow();

                    for (int x = 0; x < inputColumnBufferIndexes.Length; x++)
                    {
                        outputBuffer[outputColumnBufferIndexes[x]] =
buffer[inputColumnBufferIndexes[x]];
                    }

                    if (suggestedValue.Length == 0)
                        outputBuffer[outputColumnBufferIndexes[outputColumn
BufferIndexes.Length - 2]] = "false";
                    else
                        outputBuffer[outputColumnBufferIndexes[outputColumn
BufferIndexes.Length - 2]] = "true";

                    outputBuffer[outputColumnBufferIndexes[outputColumn
BufferIndexes.Length-1]] = suggestedValue;

                }
            }
            else
            {
                outputBuffer.SetEndOfRowset();
```

```
            }
        }
    }
}
```

Listing 15-41. *The Complete Custom-Component Code (VB.NET)*

```
Imports System
Imports Microsoft.SqlServer.Dts
Imports Microsoft.SqlServer.Dts.Pipeline
Imports Microsoft.SqlServer.Dts.Pipeline.Wrapper
Imports Microsoft.SqlServer.Dts.Runtime.Wrapper
Imports LizardKingStudios.Services.SpellCheck

Namespace LizardKingStudios.SSIS.DataflowTransformsVB

<DtsPipelineComponent(ComponentType:=ComponentType.Transform,
Description:="Sample Data Flow Component from the Apress book Pro SSIS",
DisplayName:="Lizard King Spellchecker",
IconResource:="LizardKingStudios.SSIS.DataFlowTranforms.Icon.ico")> _
    Public Class SpellCheck
        Inherits PipelineComponent

        Dim outputBuffer As PipelineBuffer
        Private inputColumnBufferIndexes() As Integer
        Private outputColumnBufferIndexes() As Integer

        Private Sub PostError(ByVal message As String)

            Dim cancel As Boolean = False
            Me.ComponentMetaData.FireError(0, Me.ComponentMetaData.Name,
message, "", 0, cancel)

        End Sub

        Private Function promoteStatus(ByVal currentStatus As DTSValidationStatus,
ByVal NewStatus As DTSValidationStatus) As DTSValidationStatus
            Select Case currentStatus
                Case DTSValidationStatus.VS_ISVALID

                    Select Case NewStatus
                        Case DTSValidationStatus.VS_ISBROKEN

                        Case DTSValidationStatus.VS_ISCORRUPT

                        Case DTSValidationStatus.VS_NEEDSNEWMETADATA
                            currentStatus = NewStatus
```

```
                Case DTSValidationStatus.VS_ISVALID

                Case Else

                    Throw New System.ApplicationException("Internal Error:
A value outside the scope of the status enumeration was found.")
            End Select

        Case DTSValidationStatus.VS_ISBROKEN

            Select Case NewStatus
                Case DTSValidationStatus.VS_ISCORRUPT

                Case DTSValidationStatus.VS_NEEDSNEWMETADATA

                    currentStatus = NewStatus
                Case DTSValidationStatus.VS_ISVALID

                Case DTSValidationStatus.VS_ISBROKEN

                Case Else

                    Throw New System.ApplicationException("Internal Error:
 A value outside the scope of the status enumeration was found.")
            End Select
        Case DTSValidationStatus.VS_NEEDSNEWMETADATA

            Select Case NewStatus
                Case DTSValidationStatus.VS_ISCORRUPT

                    currentStatus = NewStatus
                Case DTSValidationStatus.VS_ISVALID

                Case DTSValidationStatus.VS_ISBROKEN

                Case DTSValidationStatus.VS_NEEDSNEWMETADATA

                Case Else

                    Throw New System.ApplicationException("Internal Error:
A value outside the scope of the status enumeration was found.")
            End Select

        Case DTSValidationStatus.VS_ISCORRUPT

            Select Case NewStatus
                Case DTSValidationStatus.VS_ISCORRUPT
```

```
                        Case DTSValidationStatus.VS_ISVALID

                        Case DTSValidationStatus.VS_ISBROKEN

                        Case DTSValidationStatus.VS_NEEDSNEWMETADATA

                        Case Else

                            Throw New System.ApplicationException("Internal Error:
A value outside the scope of the status enumeration was found.")
                    End Select
                Case Else

                    Throw New System.ApplicationException("Internal Error:
A value outside the scope of the status enumeration was found.")
            End Select
            Return currentStatus

        End Function

        Public Overrides Function Validate() As DTSValidationStatus

            Dim status As DTSValidationStatus = MyBase.Validate()
            If (status = DTSValidationStatus.VS_ISCORRUPT) Then
                Return status
            End If

            Dim metadata As IDTSComponentMetaData90 = Me.ComponentMetaData
            Dim componentCustomProperties As IDTSCustomPropertyCollection90 =
 metadata.CustomPropertyCollection
            Try
                Dim customProperty As IDTSCustomProperty90 =
componentCustomProperties("InputColumnToCheck")
                Dim s As String = CType(customProperty.Value, String)
                If (s.Length = 0) Then
                    PostError("InputColumnToCheck must be populated")
                    Return DTSValidationStatus.VS_ISCORRUPT
                End If
            Catch e As System.Runtime.InteropServices.COMException
                If (e.ErrorCode = HResults.DTS_E_ELEMENTNOTFOUND) Then
                    PostError("Custom property 'InputColumnToCheck' not found in
component custom property collection")
                    Return DTSValidationStatus.VS_ISCORRUPT
                Else

                    Throw e
                End If
            End Try
```

```
            If (metadata.InputCollection.Count <> 1) Then

                PostError("Component requires exactly one input.")
                Return DTSValidationStatus.VS_ISCORRUPT
            End If

            Dim input As IDTSInput90 = metadata.InputCollection(0)
            Dim inputColumns As IDTSInputColumnCollection90 =
input.InputColumnCollection

            Dim j As Integer
            For j = 0 To inputColumns.Count - 1 Step j + 1
                Dim column As IDTSInputColumn90 = inputColumns(j)
                If (column.IsValid) Then

                    ' validation code can go in here for allowing only string types
                End If
            Next
            Return status
        End Function

        Public Overrides Function InsertInput(ByVal insertPlacement As
DTSInsertPlacement, ByVal inputID As Integer) As IDTSInput90

            PostError("Component requires exactly one input.
New input is forbidden.")
            Throw New PipelineComponentHResultException(
HResults.DTS_E_CANTADDINPUT)

        End Function

        Public Overrides Sub DeleteInput(ByVal inputID As Integer)

            PostError("Component requires exactly one input.
Deleted input is forbidden.")
            Throw New PipelineComponentHResultException(
HResults.DTS_E_CANTDELETEINPUT)

        End Sub

        Public Overrides Function InsertOutput(ByVal insertPlacement As
DTSInsertPlacement, ByVal outputID As Integer) As IDTSOutput90

            PostError("Component requires exactly one output.
New output is forbidden.")
            Throw New PipelineComponentHResultException(
HResults.DTS_E_CANTADDOUTPUT)
```

```
        End Function

        Public Overrides Sub DeleteOutput(ByVal outputID As Integer)

            PostError("Component requires exactly one output.
Deleted output is forbidden.")
            Throw New PipelineComponentHResultException(
HResults.DTS_E_CANTDELETEOUTPUT)

        End Sub

        Public Overrides Function InsertOutputColumnAt(ByVal outputID As Integer,
ByVal outputColumnIndex As Integer, ByVal name As String,
ByVal description As String) As IDTSOutputColumn90

            PostError("Component does not allow addition of output columns.")
            Throw New PipelineComponentHResultException(
HResults.DTS_E_CANTADDCOLUMN)

        End Function

        Public Overrides Function SetUsageType(ByVal inputID As Integer,
ByVal virtualInput As IDTSVirtualInput90, ByVal lineageID As Integer,
ByVal usageType As DTSUsageType) As IDTSInputColumn90

            Dim inputColumn As IDTSInputColumn90 = Nothing
            Select Case usageType
                Case DTSUsageType.UT_READWRITE


                Case DTSUsageType.UT_READONLY


                Case DTSUsageType.UT_IGNORED

                    inputColumn = MyBase.SetUsageType(inputID, virtualInput,
lineageID, usageType)
                    Return inputColumn
                Case Else

                    Throw New PipelineComponentHResultException(
HResults.DTS_E_CANTSETUSAGETYPE)
            End Select

        End Function
```

```
        Public Overrides Sub OnInputPathAttached(ByVal inputID As Integer)

            MyBase.OnInputPathAttached(inputID)

            Dim input As IDTSInput90 = ComponentMetaData.InputCollection.
GetObjectByID(inputID)
            Dim output As IDTSOutput90 = ComponentMetaData.OutputCollection(0)
            Dim vInput As IDTSVirtualInput90 = input.GetVirtualInput()

            Dim vCol As IDTSVirtualInputColumn90
            For Each vCol In vInput.VirtualInputColumnCollection
                Dim outCol As IDTSOutputColumn90 =
output.OutputColumnCollection.New()
                outCol.Name = vCol.Name
                outCol.SetDataTypeProperties(vCol.DataType, vCol.Length,
vCol.Precision, vCol.Scale, vCol.CodePage)
            Next

            Dim outputColumn As IDTSOutputColumn90 =
output.OutputColumnCollection.New()

            outputColumn.Name = "isSuggested"
            outputColumn.SetDataTypeProperties(DataType.DT_BOOL, 0, 0, 0, 0)
            outputColumn = Me.ComponentMetaData.OutputCollection(0).
OutputColumnCollection.New()
            outputColumn.Name = "suggestedValue"
            outputColumn.SetDataTypeProperties(DataType.DT_STR, 50, 0, 0, 1252)

        End Sub

        Public Overrides Sub ProvideComponentProperties()

            MyBase.ProvideComponentProperties()

            ComponentMetaData.OutputCollection(0).SynchronousInputID = 0

            Dim customProperties As IDTSCustomPropertyCollection90 =
 Me.ComponentMetaData.CustomPropertyCollection
            Dim customProperty As IDTSCustomProperty90 = customProperties.New()

            customProperty.Name = "InputColumnToCheck"
            customProperty.Value = ""
            customProperty = customProperties.New()
            customProperty.Name = "MaxSuggestionsCount"
            customProperty.Value = "5"

        End Sub
```

```
        Public Overrides Function SetComponentProperty(
ByVal propertyName As String, ByVal propertyValue As Object)
As IDTSCustomProperty90

            If (propertyName = "InputColumnToCheck") Then

                Dim value As String = CType(propertyValue, String)
                If (value.Length = 0) Then

                    PostError("InputColumnToCheck must be populated.")
                    Throw New PipelineComponentHResultException(
HResults.DTS_E_FAILEDTOSETPROPERTY)

                Else

                    Return MyBase.SetComponentProperty(propertyName, propertyValue)
                End If

            Else

                PostError("Specified property name [" + propertyName + "]
not expected.")
                Throw New PipelineComponentHResultException(
HResults.DTS_E_FAILEDTOSETPROPERTY)
            End If
        End Function

        Public Overrides Sub PreExecute()

            Dim input As IDTSInput90 = ComponentMetaData.InputCollection(0)
            Dim output As IDTSOutput90 = ComponentMetaData.OutputCollection(0)

            inputColumnBufferIndexes = New Integer(
input.InputColumnCollection.Count) {}
            outputColumnBufferIndexes = New Integer(
output.OutputColumnCollection.Count) {}

            Dim col As Integer
            For col = 0 To input.InputColumnCollection.Count - 1 Step col + 1
                inputColumnBufferIndexes(col) =
BufferManager.FindColumnByLineageID(input.Buffer,
input.InputColumnCollection(col).LineageID)
            Next

            For col = 0 To output.OutputColumnCollection.Count - 1 Step col + 1
                outputColumnBufferIndexes(col) =
BufferManager.FindColumnByLineageID(output.Buffer,
```

```
output.OutputColumnCollection(col).LineageID)
            Next
        End Sub

        Public Overrides Sub PrimeOutput(ByVal outputs As Integer,
ByVal outputIDs As Integer(), ByVal buffers As PipelineBuffer())

            If (buffers.Length <> 0) Then
                outputBuffer = buffers(0)
            End If

        End Sub

        Public Overrides Sub ProcessInput(ByVal inputID As Integer,
ByVal buffer As PipelineBuffer)

            Dim suggestedValue As String = String.Empty
            Dim checkValue As String
            Dim spellEngine As SpellcheckEngine = New SpellcheckEngine()
            Dim colId As Integer = -1

            spellEngine.MaxSuggestionsCount =
 Convert.ToInt32(ComponentMetaData.
CustomPropertyCollection("MaxSuggestionsCount").Value.ToString())
            Dim input As IDTSInput90 = ComponentMetaData.InputCollection.
GetObjectByID(inputID)

            Dim colIndex As Integer
            For colIndex = 0 To input.InputColumnCollection.Count - 1 Step
colIndex + 1
                If (input.InputColumnCollection(colIndex).Name.ToUpper() =
 ComponentMetaData.CustomPropertyCollection("InputColumnToCheck").
Value.ToString().ToUpper()) Then

                    colId = input.InputColumnCollection(colIndex).LineageID
                    Exit For
                End If
            Next

            Dim theColIndex As Integer = BufferManager.FindColumnByLineageID(
input.Buffer, colId)

            If (Not buffer.EndOfRowset) Then
                While buffer.NextRow()
                    ' perform the spellcheck for the specified column
                    checkValue = buffer(theColIndex).ToString()
                    suggestedValue = spellEngine.Execute(checkValue)
```

```
                    outputBuffer.AddRow()

                    Dim x As Integer
                    For x = 0 To inputColumnBufferIndexes.Length - 1 Step x + 1
                        outputBuffer(outputColumnBufferIndexes(x)) = buffer(
inputColumnBufferIndexes(x))
                    Next

                    If (suggestedValue.Length = 0) Then
                        outputBuffer(outputColumnBufferIndexes(
outputColumnBufferIndexes.Length - 2)) = "false"
                    Else
                        outputBuffer(outputColumnBufferIndexes(
outputColumnBufferIndexes.Length - 2)) = "true"

                        outputBuffer(outputColumnBufferIndexes(
outputColumnBufferIndexes.Length - 1)) = suggestedValue
                    End If
                End While
            Else
                outputBuffer.SetEndOfRowset()
            End If
        End Sub
    End Class
End Namespace
```

18. Now that the code is complete, you can build and deploy the compiled custom component to the GAC. You need to perform some tasks in Visual Studio's project-properties area, so select Project ➤ `LizardKingStudios.Services.Spellcheck Properties` from the IDE menu. You'll be presented with the familiar properties-configuration screen.

19. Select the Signing tab and create a new key to sign the assembly.

20. Select the Build Events tab and enter the value shown in Listing 15-42 as the value for Pre-Build event. This removes previous versions from the GAC and deletes the component file from the custom-components directory.

Listing 15-42. *The Pre-Build Event Value*

```
"$(DevEnvDir)..\..\SDK\v2.0\Bin\gacutil.exe" /f /u "$(TargetPath)"
del "c:\Program Files\Microsoft SQL Server\90\DTS\PipelineComponents\$(
TargetFileName)"
```

21. Enter the value shown in Listing 15-43 as the value for the Post-Build event. This copies the assembly to the proper .NET assembly location each time it is compiled to make it available to SSIS.

Listing 15-43. *The Post-Build Event Value*

```
"$(DevEnvDir)..\..\SDK\v2.0\Bin\gacutil.exe" /if "$(TargetPath)"
xcopy "$(TargetPath)" "c:\Program Files\Microsoft SQL Server\90\DTS\
PipelineComponents"
```

22. Close the project-properties window and, from the IDE menu, select Build ➤ Build `LizardKingStudios.SSIS.DataFlowTransforms.SpellCheck`.
23. The project should compile and report no errors or warnings of any kind. This means a successful compilation has taken place and that the generated assembly has been copied to the proper SSIS directory without error!

You're now finished with the second part of this example. You have a compiled and working class library and a working custom component. Now all that is required is an SSIS package to test it.

Optionally Adding an Icon

When you create an icon for use in SSIS, a 16 × 16 256-color image is required for use in the Toolbox, and a 32 × 32 256-color image is required for use on the design surface. Both icons should be part of the same icon file. The icon file should be part of the compiled project as a resource. The attribute specified in Step 7 in the preceding set of steps already has the icon parameter of the attribute defined—`IconResource = "LizardKingStudios.SSIS.DataFlowTranforms.Icon.ico"`—so for this example if you want to add an icon, create one and add it to the project as `LizardKingStudios.SSIS.DataFlowTransforms.Icon.ico`. You will see it shortly in the SSIS designer.

The SSIS Data Flow

You can now finish the example by creating a new package and dropping the new custom component onto the design surface with a source component, just as you did in Chapter 14.

In fact, the only difference between the new package you need to create to test the component and the example presented in Chapter 14 is that instead of using the `Script Component`, you'll be using your new custom component.

Since this is the final chapter of this book, I am fully confident that you are more than capable of putting together the package without quite so much detail as I've given previously. Nonetheless, you should follow the steps below to get to the point where your new custom component can strut its stuff!

As with all other examples in this book, you need to open up BIDS/Visual Studio and create a new SSIS project. Drop a Data Flow Task onto the Control Flow design surface and switch to the Data Flow design surface.

Data Flow Data Source

Follow these steps to configure the Data Flow source for the package:

1. Right-click the Toolbox and select Choose Items... After your hard disk chugs away for a few minutes you will see the screen shown in Figure 15-11.

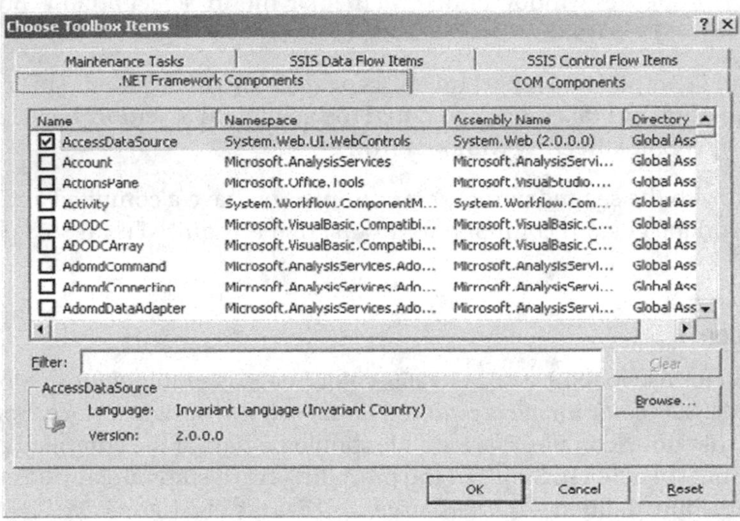

Figure 15-11. *The Choose Toolbox Items dialog*

2. Click the SSIS Data Flow Items tab. After some further chugging you should see a screen like Figure 15-12. If you scroll down a little you should see the `LizardKing Spellchecker` list item. Tick the checkbox next to it and click OK. The Toolbox now has your shiny new custom component nestled between the existing stock components.

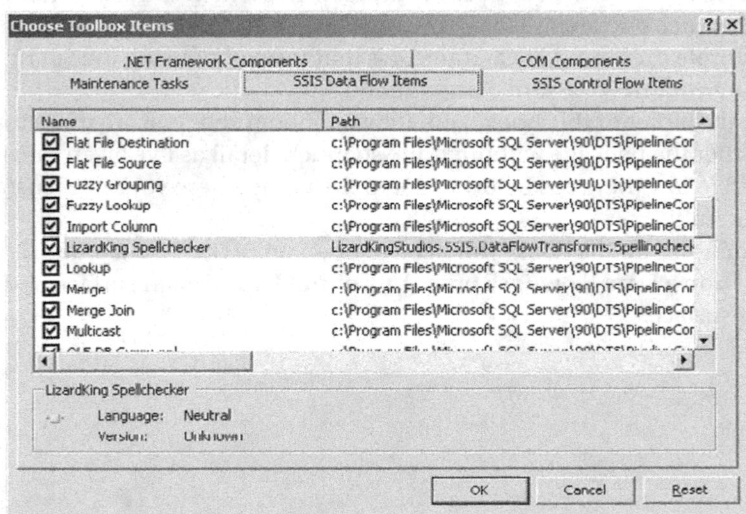

Figure 15-12. *There's the new custom component!*

3. Back on the design surface, use an `ADO.NET` connection manager with the `SqlClient` provider to add a connection manager to the package, configured to point to the database containing the newly created table. Mine is called `LOKI.Apressbook`.
4. Drop a `DataReader Source` component from the Toolbox onto the design surface.
5. Open the `DataReader Source` configuration editor via your favorite method—double-clicking on the component or right-clicking and selecting Edit....
6. On the Connection Managers configuration tab (Figure 15-13), set the Connection Manager property to be the name of the connection manager you specified in Step 1.

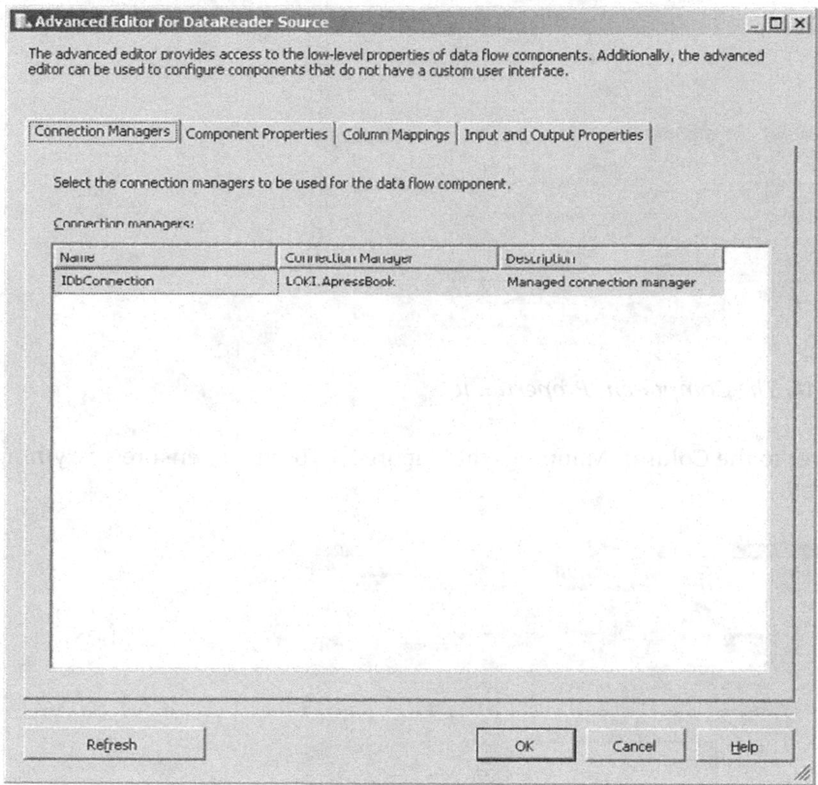

Figure 15-13. *The Connection Manager tab*

7. Move on to the Component Properties tab (Figure 15-14) and update the `SqlCommand` property so the value reads `SELECT * FROM ScriptExample`.

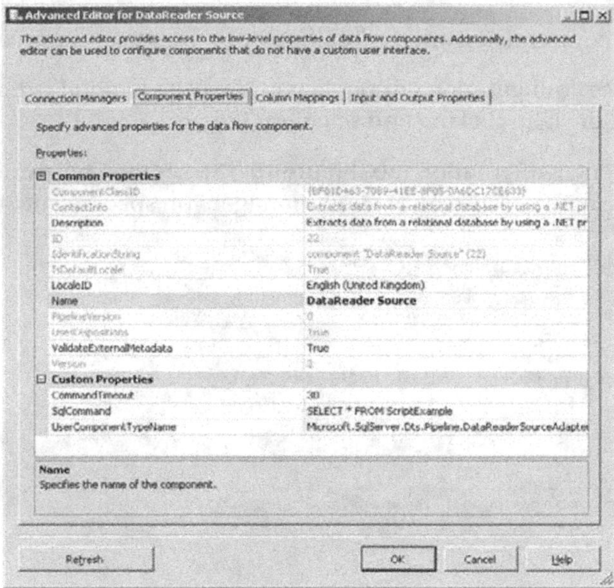

Figure 15-14. *The Component Properties tab*

8. Switch over to the Column Mappings tab (Figure 15-15) just to ensure everything looks as expected.

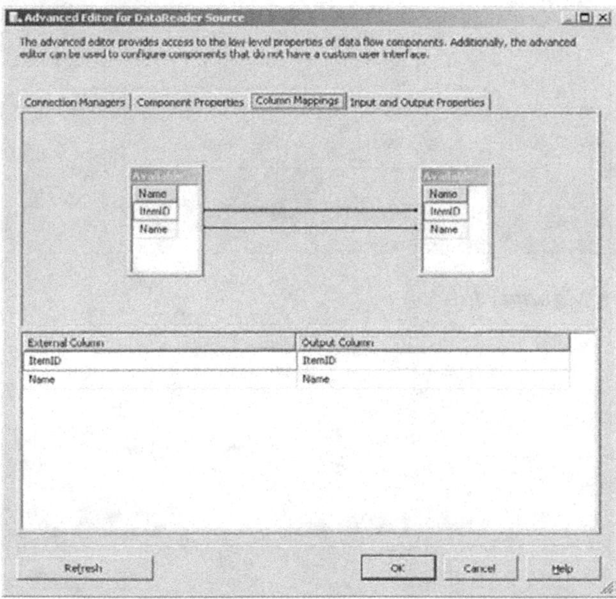

Figure 15-15. *Column Mappings are as expected.*

9. Click OK. You have finished configuring the `DataReader Source`.

Data Flow Transformation

With data now waiting in the Data Flow you can start to work on the transform—your new `LizardKing Spellchecker` custom component:

1. Drop the new `LizardKing Spellchecker` component from the Toolbox onto the design surface. Connect the green arrow dangling off the `DataReader Source` to the `LizardKing Spellchecker` custom component.

2. Double-click the `LizardKing Spellchecker` component to get to the configuration editor. You will see the screen presented as Figure 15-16.

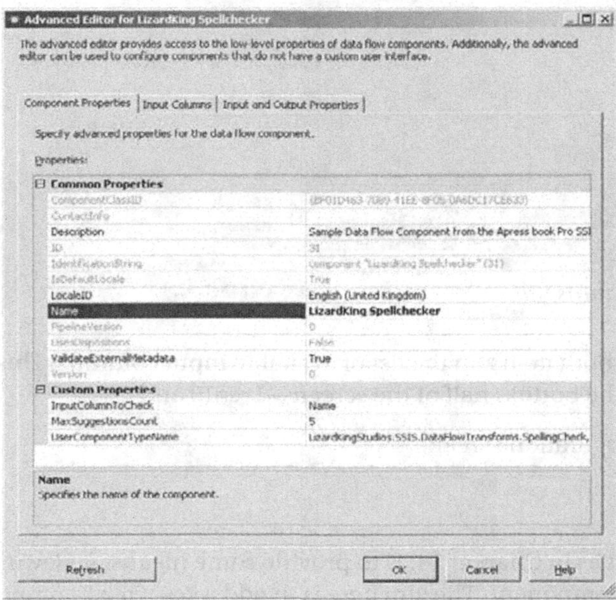

Figure 15-16. *The first tab of the configuration editor for our custom component*

3. Configure the two custom properties: set the `InputColumnToCheck` property value to `Name` and, for now, leave the `MaxSuggestionsCount` property value at `5`.

4. Click on the Input Columns tab. You will see a screen just like Figure 15-17.

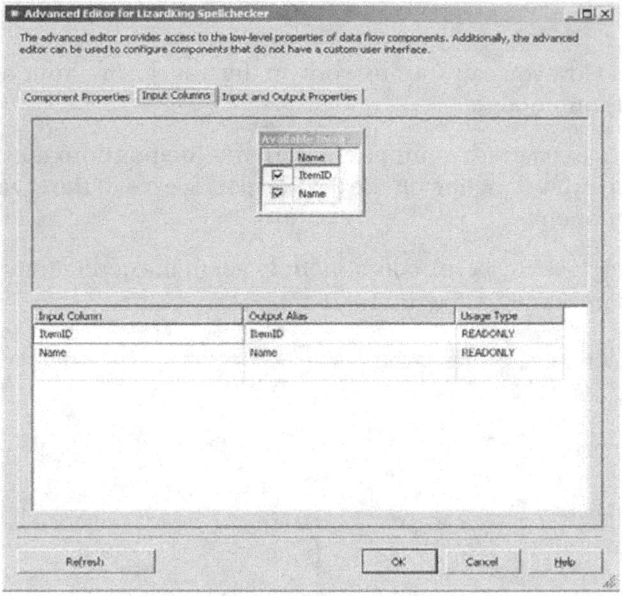

Figure 15-17. *The Input Columns tab*

5. Place a checkmark next to both items on the list of available input columns. This adds two items into the grid in the bottom half of the screen—`ItemID` and `Name`.
6. Select OK to close the configuration screen.

Viewing the Results

The final work you need to do, just as in Chapter 14, is to provide some means of viewing the data as it flows past your custom component. The aim here is to add a `Row Count` component into the Data Flow and to use a Data Viewer to look inside the Data Flow at the results of the new custom transform component.

Make sure you are still viewing the Data Flow design surface before following these steps:

1. Add a Data Flow scoped variable, `rowCount` (data type `Int32`).
2. Drop a Row Count component from the Toolbox onto the design surface.
3. Connect the green success arrow from the bottom of the `LizardKing Spellchecker` component to the Row Count component.
4. Open the `Row Count` configuration editor.
5. On the configuration screen presented, update the `VariableName` property to read `User::rowCount`. (This variable was defined in Step 1.)
6. Select OK to save settings and be returned to the Data Flow design surface.

7. Double-click the green success arrow you connected in Step 2. You're presented with the screen shown in Figure 15-18, the Data Flow Path Editor.

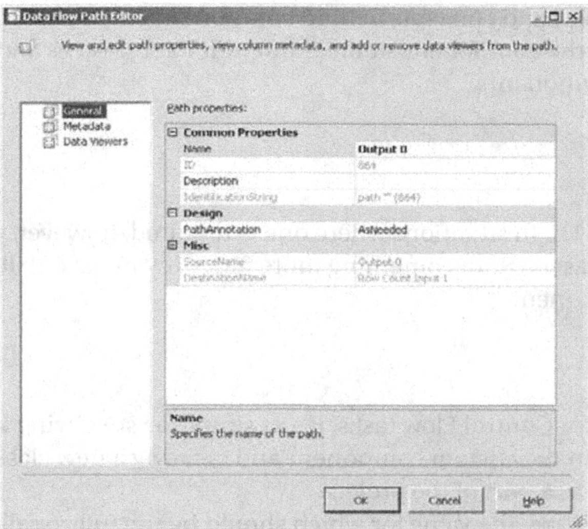

Figure 15-18. *The Data Flow Path Editor*

8. Click on the Data Viewers list item to the left of the screen.

9. Click the Add... button. On the Configure Data Viewer screen that appears, just click OK. The newly added Data Viewer should have appeared in the grid.

10. Select OK to close the Configure Data Viewer screen and return to the design surface.

When you test the execution of your package, you should see some results in the form of the Data Viewer you just configured appearing when data hits that point in the flow. Figure 15-19 shows what you should expect. It should look at least slightly familiar!

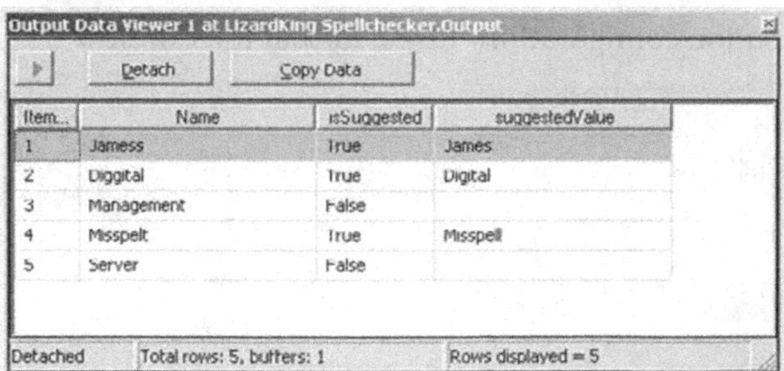

Figure 15-19. *Expected results*

Give yourself a big pat on the back—you've created a pretty useful custom component from first principles all the way through to full implementation. Not only that, but you also have a class library that can be reused in many different ways and from an assortment of technologies.

In the spirit of keeping things as simple as possible I have left plenty of scope within the custom component for improvement. Areas such as error handling and more-robust validation are missing, and I've purposely made things a little . . . clunkier . . . than necessary to demonstrate more clearly the principles and concepts behind component creation.

My advice is to play around with the component, adding different data sources and using it in conjunction with other stock components.

Designers

Not every task or component needs a UI. In situations where one is required, however, you can easily create a Windows Forms–based UI (or something more fancy if you have skills elsewhere) and integrate it with the component.

Control Flow UIs

When it comes to creating designers for Control Flow tasks, it's as simple as specifying an additional class-attribute parameter in the custom component and creating a new class library that features a Windows Form as a part of the project.

The additional attribute is `UITypeName`, the value for which should be the fully qualified name of the new class library that contains the Windows Form UI.

The class library—which should reference the `Microsoft.SqlServer.Dts.Design.dll` assembly, and to which the `UITypeName` attribute points—should implement `IDtsComponentUI` and override methods, including `IDtsComponentUI.Delete`, `IDtsComponentUI.Help`, `IDtsComponentUI.New` or `IDtsComponentUI.Initialize` depending on requirements.

I am not going to go any further looking at Control Flow designers for two reasons. The first reason is that they aren't particularly complex and can be added very easily using the information I've just given you. The second reason is that experience tells me that, on balance, custom Control Flow tasks aren't all that prevalent anyway, so you could spend more time looking at something more interesting, such as runtime UIs.

Data Flow Component UIs

Employment of UIs isn't limited to preexecution configuration. Take a look at the Confirm Suggestion screen in Figure 15-20.

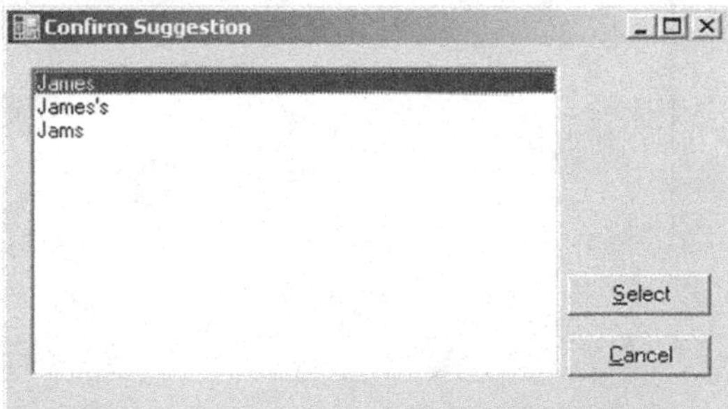

Figure 15-20. *What's this?! It's an execution-time UI!*

Yes, we're back to the spellcheck example, but with something new to add. If you followed the example closely you will have observed that whenever the Word spellcheck functionality makes more than a single spelling suggestion, the component chooses the first suggestion in the list.

I have fulfilled requirements for clients in the past where part of the ETL process is monitored and managed with direct human interaction. This might be for data-cleansing reasons in situations not dissimilar to our spellcheck example.

The preferable solution, as far as I am concerned, is to provide more-intelligent processing that performs (for example) recursive feedback to provide more-accurate data cleansing. The customer is always right, of course, so implementing some kind of UI when rogue data is identified was the requirement I was given.

To create the UI in Figure 15-20, follow these steps:

1. Open up the class-library project you created as the first example in this chapter (`LizardKingStudios.Services.Spellcheck`).
2. Add a new item—a Windows Form—to the project, and rename the new file to `userConfirm.cs` (or `userConfirm.vb`).
3. Completely replace the code in `userConfirm.cs` (or `userConfirm.vb`) with the code in Listing 15-44 (for C#) or Listing 15-45 (for VB.NET).
4. On the form designer, add a list box named `Suggestions`, a command button named `selectSuggestion`, and a command button named `cancelForm`.
5. Arrange the controls in a pleasing manner; then compile the project.

Listing 15-44. *The UI Code (C#)*

```
using System;
using System.Windows.Forms;
using Microsoft.Office.Interop.Word;

namespace LizardKingStudios.Services.SpellCheck
{
    public partial class userConfirm : Form
    {
        private SpellingSuggestions _suggestionsList = null;
        private string _selectedValue = String.Empty;

        public userConfirm()
        {
            InitializeComponent();
        }

        public SpellingSuggestions suggestionsList
        {
            set
            {
                _suggestionsList = value;
```

```
                loadSuggestionsList();
            }
        }

        public string selectedValue
        {
            get
            {
                return _selectedValue;
            }
        }

        private void loadSuggestionsList()
        {
            if (_suggestionsList!=null)
            {
                foreach (SpellingSuggestion theSuggestion in _suggestionsList)
                {
                    Suggestions.Items.Add(theSuggestion.Name);
                }

                Suggestions.SelectedIndex = 0;
            }
        }

        private void selectSuggestion_Click(object sender, EventArgs e)
        {
            if (Suggestions.SelectedIndex==-1)
            {
                MessageBox.Show("You must select a suggestion first!");
            }
            else
            {
                _selectedValue = Suggestions.SelectedItem.ToString();

                MessageBox.Show("selected: " + _selectedValue);
                this.Close();
            }
        }

        private void cancelForm_Click(object sender, EventArgs e)
        {
            this.Close();
        }
    }
}
```

Listing 15-45. *The UI Code (VB.NET)*

```
Imports System
Imports System.Windows.Forms
Imports Microsoft.Office.Interop.Word

Namespace LizardKingStudios.Services.Spellcheck
    Partial Public Class userConfirm
        Inherits Form

        Private _suggestionsList As SpellingSuggestions = Nothing
        Private _selectedValue As String = String.Empty

        Public Sub New()

            InitializeComponent()

        End Sub

        Public WriteOnly Property suggestionsList() As SpellingSuggestions
            Set(ByVal Value As SpellingSuggestions)

                _suggestionsList = Value

                loadSuggestionsList()
            End Set
        End Property

        Public ReadOnly Property selectedValue() As String
            Get
                Return _selectedValue
            End Get
        End Property

        Private Sub loadSuggestionsList()

            If (Not _suggestionsList Is Nothing) Then

                Dim theSuggestion As SpellingSuggestion
                For Each theSuggestion In _suggestionsList
                    Suggestions.Items.Add(theSuggestion.Name)
                Next

                Suggestions.SelectedIndex = 0

            End If
        End Sub
```

```
        Private Sub selectSuggestion_Click(ByVal sender As Object, ByVal e As
EventArgs)

            If (Suggestions.SelectedIndex = -1) Then

                MessageBox.Show("You must select a suggestion first!")

            Else

                _selectedValue = Suggestions.SelectedItem.ToString()

                MessageBox.Show("selected: " + _selectedValue)
                Me.Close()
            End If
        End Sub

        Private Sub cancelForm_Click(ByVal sender As Object, ByVal e As EventArgs)
            Me.Close()
        End Sub

        Private Sub userConfirm_Load(ByVal sender As System.Object,
ByVal e As System.EventArgs) Handles MyBase.Load

        End Sub
    End Class
End Namespace
```

6. Run the package to test the custom component. You'll see a custom UI appear if the Word spellchecker provides more than one suggestion. A list is provided in the UI for selection purposes, and any corrections chosen are propagated back to the class library (and in this case, in turn back to the Data Flow).

Thanks to the OOP approach of creating a class library containing your actual business logic (the spellcheck), you can make alterations to the UI without needing to recompile any assemblies (or custom components!).

Summary

This chapter does not contain absolutely everything you need to know about creating and using custom components in SSIS. What it does contain, however, is a focus on the most pertinent parts.

The reality is that most custom components will be within the Data Flow, because that's where the data lies. My experiences certainly back that up.

The examples in this chapter and the information presented give you the confidence to move your skills forward and take on the previously daunting task of creating reusable, flexible, and properly useful custom components.

Finally, for those of you interested in getting more involved with SSIS development, I have created a SourceForge project (`http://sourceforge.net/projects/ssisextender`) for extending SSIS way beyond original specification. Although plenty of custom components are floating around out there in Internet land, and there's something to learn from all of them, it would be great if they could all reside in a single, not-for-profit repository.

APPENDIX A

Interview with Donald Farmer

This appendix contains the full text of my interview with Donald Farmer, SSIS *Übermensch* at Microsoft. He has moved on to work with the SSAS data-mining team, but his involvement in and influence over SSIS should not be underestimated. Plus he's a Scotsman, so we have a certain amount of shared heritage, which grants him even more respect from me!

James Wightman (JW): *If you were a vegetable, which one would you be and why (neeps and tatties excluded!)?*

Donald Farmer (DF): A Jerusalem artichoke. They're not from Jerusalem and they're not artichokes—that kind of contrariness appeals to me. FYI, the name comes from Girasol—which is Spanish for sunflower, because they also turn towards the sun.

JW: *Microsoft doesn't seem to be publicly pushing the SSIS side of SQL Server 2005 just now as much as I would have expected. Do you think it is waiting for the 2005 product to settle into the enterprise first?*

It's important to remember that SSIS is not a stand-alone product, and so is promoted along with SQL Server. In that context, SSIS does feature heavily in most SQL Server presentations—we were the first application shown in the launch keynote, for example, and we have been on stage doing demos in many, if not most, major SQL Server events.

JW: *I'd be interested to know about the perspective from which you approached the implementation and feature set of SSIS. In terms of function, did you start by examining DTS with a look to reimagining it? Or did you (as I suspect) take a clean slate and work from there? Obviously from a technology viewpoint you had considerations like integrating .NET Framework support and the design decisions around that, but was the feature set (both internal and external) provided by the new SQL Server engine tailored in particular ways so as to better integrate (and give a more rich feature set to) SSIS? I ask this because SSIS certainly feels like a more integrated and natural product than DTS, which by comparison (using it now) almost feels like a third-party add-on.*

DF: The team approached the implementation of SSIS from two perspectives: what capabilities were needed to enable SQL Server to succeed in the data warehousing market, and what architecture best enabled those capabilities. There was a balancing act required as to what extent we would take dependencies on SQL Server features, and to what extent we would build a fully stand-alone product. Like all balancing acts there was a lot of hand-waving until we felt comfortable with where we were! This required us to work closely with the relational-engine team—on bulk-load interfaces for example. However, there is also deep integration with the Analysis Services and Data Mining engines, and with the management toolset, all of which provides a more organic data-management experience for SQL Server users.

JW: *In the brief for creating SSIS for SQL Server 2005, I would identify the components and abilities as being one part DTS, one part "common" ETL tools, and one part the application of tools and features included from insight and experience. Would you say that's an accurate description? In these terms, what were the design goals for SSIS? Were there issues around balancing support for existing DTS function (and user base expectation) vs. design brief?*

DF: Previously I mentioned two perspectives from which we approached SSIS implementation—what data-warehousing capabilities were needed, and the architecture that best enabled those capabilities. We did not allow DTS-compatibility considerations to constrain us from achieving the best in these areas. So, for example, the Data Flow behavior in SSIS is simply totally different from the data-pump behavior in DTS. In other areas, we did not need to be so radical—so Control Flow in SSIS is outwardly more familiar to DTS users who are used to working with tasks, although under the hood the redesign is also radical.

One big advantage over existing ETL tools is how SSIS enables developers to create their own custom components. I can imagine this presented a particular set of challenges and obstacles both during design and implementation. Was including this feature a major part of the SSIS project? Was the ability to create custom components developed first, then the components included with SSIS built using this ability (I imagine not)? What particular problems were there to overcome in offering custom-component support?

Microsoft, and especially the SQL Server BI teams, have a great reputation for working with ISV [independent software vendor] partners—so, enabling an awesome ISV integration story was very important from the beginning. However, it is worth pointing out that the supported interfaces for extending SSIS with custom components are managed code, while most of the components we wrote ourselves are in native code. There are a number of reasons for this, perhaps the most important being the ease with which we can support managed-code APIs, samples, etc., and the growing popularity of managed-code languages. As for problems, the most interesting have been simply explaining to third parties just how radical the capability is. ISVs used to integrating with DTS or with other ETL tools often do not quite realize how much better it is to be able to work directly against the SSIS memory buffers. When they do, they often discover that their components perform many times faster in SSIS than when integrated with other ETL applications.

JW: *In terms of function, SSIS surpasses commercially available ETL tools such as SAS and Datastage. In terms of flexibility, SSIS goes way beyond these products. Would you say that SSIS is also aimed at a different type of user than these other tools? Perhaps both a more technically savvy but not necessarily BI-focused developer as well as the more traditional BI/MI specialist? In the IT industry we are already seeing the "SQL Server developer" skills in demand: do you think you have created a completely new career type by introducing such a powerful tool as a standard part of a widely accepted database technology?*

DF: I tend to agree with you on our flexibility—which is partly a result of a great architecture and partly a requirement that drives, as our user base is so broad. DTS in its day was a handy utility for DBAs, a low-end ETL tool for the data warehouse architect, and an interesting environment for developers to extend. SSIS still needs to be a utility, is still a favorite with developers and covers a much wider range of data integration scenarios. I often talk about a particular kind of SSIS (and SQL Server) user that I call the "data artisan." They are database-centric developers who use tools when they can, write code when they need to, and also have a responsibility for architecture and administration. They do about four jobs—and SSIS is a major component in their toolkit. So yes, SSIS has created or extended a new role. Even more interestingly, in a few years time where are you going to find ETL skills? In SQL Server shops, where every DBA and developer will likely have had at least some hands-on experience with a very capable ETL application. You really won't be able to say that of Oracle Warehouse Builder, or IBM Datastage.

JW: *I know that Valve Software (creators of Half-Life and fellow Seattleites) uses a proprietary database technology for its Steam product, though it does have an ETL mechanism to get the data into SQL Server for offline querying. I talked with the lead developer at length about SQL Server vs. their proprietary database and the perceived performance advantages they get by using it; extreme performance was the driving factor. A comparable product—but on an infinitely larger scale—would be Xbox Live. Is SQL Server used in the back end of Xbox Live to support the service? And if it isn't, what are the reasons behind that? If it is, what has been done to provide the necessary performance in serving so many simultaneous requests? Is it more than a profusion of high-end hardware (in conjunction with superior database design)?*

DF: At Microsoft, we're famous for eating our own dog food, and yes SQL Server is used throughout the business for its high-end operations, including Live services, Xbox, and AdCenter. In some cases, these teams extend the application themselves with custom components into areas where there is not yet enough commercial demand for us to put those features into the retail product. Without giving away too many secrets of the internal teams, some things they have done to squeeze extra from the engines include writing highly specialized schedulers tuned for their precise needs, or data-source components that can parse their specific file types at near-optimal speeds. There is a great synergy between our internal users and the product teams, and many of their innovations and ideas have helped to improve the product and greatly influence our designs.

JW: *What advantages do you think offering CTP (Community Technology Preview) software is to today's developers? Has it been a good thing for SQL Server 2005?*

DF: CTPs are great for the product team—and appear to be great for our customers. So far feedback has been very positive. My only concern is when I see customers going too near production levels on early CTPs. Through a release cycle you may see three or four CTPs—without a guaranteed upgrade or compatibility path between them. So moving from one to the next three times may be a lot of work, and is not risk free. Now we could, of course, put work in to ensure an upgrade path—but that work uses up cycles we could be spending on the final product. I see users adapting to this pattern more easily now: they expect CTPs to be "closer to the metal" than a traditional beta cycle. More cautious customers will perhaps wait until later CTPs with supported upgrade paths. But I can tell you, it's a great feeling to get a feature into the hands of committed and excited customers early in the cycle. The feedback to the team enables us to meet those customers' needs far better than we can just by consulting in the abstract.

JW: *Given the time, if you could have included one more feature into SSIS, what would it have been?*

Having written a book on scripting, I am hopelessly biased. I would love to have seen C# scripting in SSIS 2005. More objectively, I would have liked to enable even more flexible options for caching in the `Lookup` component. Keep your eyes open for these features in future versions!

JW: *Could you please sum up what you think SSIS offers over other tools meant for the same purpose?*

DF: Value for money, for one thing! If that is not a critical factor, I love the interactivity of the visual debugger. I was recently visiting with a customer who uses another very capable data-integration tool. As I helped them with some warehousing problems, I wanted to tweak their ETL processes. In SSIS I could have dived in there, made some changes, run through the debugger with visualizers and breakpoints, and validated what I was doing using a row counter as a dummy destination. Instead I had to create temporary tables, reconfigure the server and the metadata repository, run the modified jobs, and then trawl through logs and reports. Coming back to SSIS, I hugely appreciated the ability to roll up my sleeves and get on with the work. I guess I'm a "data artisan" at heart myself!

APPENDIX B

The Package Object

For reference purposes, this appendix lists all properties exposed by the SSIS package at object level—not only those accessible through the Properties pane in Visual Studio. Many of the properties are used to support the SSIS infrastructure and, in reality, you will probably never touch them. Still, they might be useful for whatever customization work you have in mind. Keep this appendix handy so you can refer to it when needed.

You will notice I've used C#-like syntax to describe each property, with the data type of the property first, followed by the name, followed by the default value should one exist. I have also listed all package methods in a similar format. Again, be aware that not all of these properties and methods are exposed through the IDE.

Package Properties

`System.Int64` Certificate Context

Read/write property representing the certificate context.

`System.Object` Certificate Object

Read/write property that represents the actual package certificate, expressed as a `System.Object` type.

`System.String` CheckpointFileName

Read/write property that is the filename for the file used to store checkpoint information for restarting packages.

`DTSRuntimeWrap.DTSCheckpointUsage` CheckpointUsage

Read/write property for specifying package restart criteria. Possible values are

```
Never
IfExists
Always
```

`System.Bool` CheckSignatureOnLoad

Read/write property for whether the digital signature is checked when a package stored as XML is loaded.

`DTSRuntimeWrap.IDTSConfigurations90` Configurations

Read-only collection of configurations for your package. As the name suggests, it is possible to have multiple configurations for each package.

`DTSRuntimeWrap.IDTSConnections90` Connections

Read-only collection of connection managers for the package.

`System.DateTime` CreationDate

Read/write property holding the package creation date/time.

`System.String` CreationName

Read-only property representing the string value needed to instantiate the `DtsContainer` object.

`System.String` CreatorComputerName

Read/write property for the hostname of the computer used to create the package.

`System.String` CreatorName

Read/write property for the package-creator name.

`System.Bool` DebugMode

Read/write property to set whether the `DtsContainer` is running in debug mode. Internally, as a consequence, this setting also determines whether the `OnBreakpointHit` event is fired.

`System.Bool` DelayValidation

Read/write property indicating whether validation of the task is delayed by performing validation at runtime.

`System.String` Description

Read/write property for the description of this `DtsContainer` object.

`DTSRuntimeWrap.IDTSEvents` DesignEvents

Read/write property that is meant to show if the Designer or other UI is to receive design-time events.

`System.Bool` Disable

Read/write property for whether this executable is disabled at runtime.

`System.Bool` DisableEventHandlers

Read/write property for whether event handlers on the package are disabled.

`System.Bool` EnableConfigurations

Read/write property for whether this package is to use configurations.

`System.Bool` EncryptCheckpoints

Read/write property for whether to use encryption with checkpoint files.

`DTSRuntimeWrap.IDTSErrors90` Errors

Read-only property that returns the package errors collection.

`DTSRuntimeWrap.IDTSEventHandlers90` EventHandlers

Read-only property that returns a `System.Collections.IEnumerable`-implemented collection of event handlers.

`DTSRuntimeWrap.IDTSEventInfos90` EventInfos

Read-only property that returns a `System.Collections.IEnumerable`-implemented collection of `EventInfos`.

`DTSRuntimeWrap.IDTSExecutables90` Executables

Read-only property that returns a `System.Collections.IEnumerable`-implemented collection of executables held within the package.

`System.Int32` ExecutionDuration

Read-only property that returns the number of milliseconds for which this container executed.

`DTSRuntimeWrap.DTSExecResult` ExecutionResult

Read-only property that returns a representation of the execution result of this `DtsContainer`:

`Canceled`

Processing for this task was cancelled.

`Completion`

The task processing finished to completion.

`Failure`

The task failed processing.

`Success`

The task processing finished to completion and set a `Success` status.

`DTSRuntimeWrap.DTSExecStatus` ExecutionStatus

Read-only property that returns a representation of the execution status of this `DtsContainer`:

`Abend`

An internal error has been experienced. Execution terminated abnormally.

`Completed`

Processing has completed. The `ExecutionResult` is updated.

`Executing`

Processing is taking place.

`None` (default)

Task is idle.

`Suspended`

Processing has been suspending by hitting a breakpoint.

`Validating`

The task is being validated.

Expressions

This is a special case of expression usage. When considered at package level, expressions can be used to set the value of properties, on an individual property-by-property basis. As such the expressions you enter are stored as part of the `packageClass` subclass and are accessed using `System.String` properties.

`DTSRuntimeWrap.IDTSExtendedProperties90` ExtendedProperties

Read-only property that returns a `System.Collections.IEnumerable`-implemented collection of extended properties.

`System.Bool` FailPackageOnFailure

Although this property is advertised as being an available package property, it isn't. Instead, it applies only to objects at a level within the package. An attempt to set this property to anything other than `False` will throw an exception.

`System.Bool` FailParentOnFailure

Read/write property that signifies whether to fail the parent container of a child container if processing fails.

`System.Object` ForcedExecutionValue

Read/write property that signifies the desired return value of the package. `0` is the default value of this property.

`DTSRuntimeWrap.DTSForcedExecResult` ForceExecutionResult

Read/write property that enables the ability to force the result value of the package after processing. Possible values are

`None`

`Success`

`Failure`

`Completion`

`System.Bool` ForceExecutionValue

Read/write property that relates to whether the container execution value should be forced to return the value held in `ForcedExecutionValue`.

`System.String` ID

Read-only property that returns a representation of the `DtsContainer`'s Globally Unique Identifier (GUID).

`System.Bool` InteractiveMode

Read/write property that specifies whether tasks should display UI objects while under execution.

System.Bool IsDefaultLocaleID

Read-only property for discovering whether this container uses the default locale.

System.Int32 IsolationLevel

Read/write property for specifying or retrieving the transaction isolation level. The enumeration is `System.Transactions.IsolationLevel`. Possible values are

`Unspecified`

A different isolation level than the one specified is being used, but the level cannot be determined. An exception is thrown if this value is set.

`Chaos`

Changes from more highly isolated transactions will not be overwritten.

`ReadCommitted`

Volatile data cannot be read but can be modified.

`ReadUncommitted`

Volatile data can be read and modified.

`RepeatableRead`

Volatile data can be read but not modified. New data can be added.

`Serializable`

Volatile data can be read but not modified, and no new data can be added during the transaction.

`Snapshot`

Volatile data can be read. Before a transaction modifies data, it verifies if another transaction has changed the data after it was initially read. If the data has been updated, an error is raised. This allows a transaction to get to the previously committed value of the data.

System.Int32 LocaleID

Read/write property indicating the locale ID to use with this `DtsContainer`.

DTSRuntimeWrap.IDTSLogEntryInfos90 LogEntryInfos

Read-only property that returns an `System.Collections.IEnumerable`-implementing `LogEntryInfos` collection.

DTSRuntimeWrap.DTSLoggingMode LoggingMode

Read/write property indicating the logging mode of the package. The enumeration is

```
Disabled

Enabled

UseParentSetting
```

DTSRuntimeWrap.IDTSLoggingOptions90 LoggingOptions

Read-only property that returns `IDTSLoggingOptions90`, which holds filtering and logging resources.

DTSRuntimeWrap.IDTSLogProviders90 LogProviders

Read-only property that returns an `System.Collections.IEnumerable` implementing `IDTSLogProviders90` collection of log providers for this package.

System.Int32 MaxConcurrentExecutables

Read/write property specifying the maximum number of threads that can be created by this package.

System.Int32 MaximumErrorCount

Read/write property for the maximum number of allowable errors in a package before processing is halted.

System.String Name

Read/write property pertaining to the given name of the `DtsContainer`.

System.Bool OfflineMode

Read/write property that relates to whether the packages is working in offline mode.

System.String PackagePassword

Write-only property that sets the package password.

DTSRuntimeWrap.DTSPriorityClass PackagePriorityClass

Read/write property for the thread priority of this package. In order of priority, these are

```
Default

AboveNormal

Normal

BelowNormal

Idle
```

`DTSRuntimeWrap.DTSPackageType` PackageType

Read/write property that refers to the tool that created the package. It is an enumeration consisting of

`Default`

Undefined.

`DTSDesigner`

The package was created in SQL Server 2000.

`DTSDesigner90`

The package was created in the SSIS Designer in SSIS.

`DTSWizard`

The package was created by the SQL Server Import and Export Wizard.

`SQLDBMaint`

DBMaint created the package.

`SQLReplication`

The package was generated to support transformable subscriptions in replication.

`DTSRuntimeWrap.IDTSContainer90` Parent

Read-only property that returns the container that is the parent of this container—if it exists.

`DTSRuntimeWrap.IDTSPrecedenceConstraints90` PrecedenceConstraints

Read-only property that returns an `System.Collections.IEnumerable`-implementing object containing precedence-constraint objects.

`DTSRuntimeWrap.IDTSProperties90` Properties

Read-only property that returns an `System.Collections.IEnumerable`-implementing object containing `Properties` objects.

`DTSRuntimeWrap.DTSProtectionLevel` ProtectionLevel

Read/write property supporting the use of the `DTSProtectionLevel` enumeration.

If you use a configuration file to store sensitive information you'll want to secure it somehow. Two different methods are used for encryption. The MS Data Protection API (DPAPI) is used for key-based encryption, while the `TripleDES` class is used for encryption that is password-based. Possible values are

`DontSaveSensitive`

Sensitive information in the package is replaced with blanks before saving.

`EncryptAllWithPassword`

Using `TripleDES`, this setting encrypts the package with a simple password.

`EncryptAllWithUserKey`

Using DPAPI, this setting encrypts the package using keys based on the user profile. Only the same user using the same profile can load the package.

`EncryptSensitiveWithPassword`

Using TripleDES, this setting encrypts only sensitive information contained in the package by using a password.

`EncryptSensitiveWithUserKey`

Using DPAPI, this setting encrypts the entire package by using keys based on the current user. Only the same user using the same profile can load the package. If a different user opens the package, the sensitive information is replaced with blanks.

`ServerStorage`

Encrypts the package within a SQL Server `msdb` database. Database roles are used for security.

`System.Bool` SaveCheckpoints

Read/write property for specifying whether checkpoints should be saved.

`System.ComponentModel.ISite` Site

A *site* is, essentially, a structure that holds information relating to this specific container instance. Containers use the site construct to manage and communicate their child components. In this case, the use of sites in SSIS is very much internal, and I would be surprised if you ever have to lay hands on the concept.

`System.DateTime` StartTime

Read-only property specifying the time that package execution began.

`System.DateTime` StopTime

Read-only property specifying the time that package execution ended.

`System.Bool` SuppressConfigurationWarnings

Read-only property indicating whether warnings generated by configurations are suppressed.

`System.Bool` SuspendRequired

Read/write property indicating whether a task should suspend upon encountering a breakpoint. The runtime engine sets this property internally for tasks and containers when a breakpoint is reached.

Dts.Runtime.DTSTransactionOption TransactionOption

Read/write property supported by the DTSTransactionOption enumeration detailing the transactional participation level of the package. Remember that transactions can propagate down the package hierarchy and are accessible to any subcontainer or executable that is set to support them.

NotSupported

Starts transaction: No

Participates in transactions: No

Required

Starts Transaction: Yes, if no transaction exists.

Participates in transactions: Yes, if a transaction already exists.

Supported (Default setting)

Starts transaction: No

Participates in transactions: Yes, if a transaction already exists.

System.Bool UpdateObjects

Read/write property supporting the dynamic updating of extensible objects (such as containers and executables) when the package is loaded. This means that if this property is set to True, the SSIS runtime engine will attempt to find updated versions of your referenced objects when it loads the package into memory.

At runtime level, CanUpdate is called on any updated versions of objects that are found, with the old object GUID being passed as a parameter. Should an updated version be available, the new object's Update method is used to pass in the old object XML by reference and update it to the new XML. In most cases CanUpdate is implemented to return false and the Update set to return the same XML as is input.

DTSRuntimeWrap.IDTSVariableDispenser90 VariableDispenser

Read-only property that gives an entry point into dealing with the access, locking, and unlocking of variables.

DTSRuntimeWrap.IDTSVariables90 Variables

Read-only property that returns an IEnumerable-implementing object representing a collection of package-level variables.

System.Int32 VersionBuild

Read/write property for the version build number.

`System.String` VersionComments

Read/write property to hold comments against the package.

`System.String` VersionGUID

Read-only property that returns the package GUID. This GUID is set when the package is first created.

`System.Int32` VersionMajor

Read/write property for the major version build number.

`System.Int32` VersionMinor

Read/write property for the minor version build number.

`DTSRuntimeWrap.IDTSWarnings90` Warnings

Read-only property that returns an `IEnumerable`-implementing object representing a collection of warnings that are set on the package.

Package Methods

Void AcceptBreakpointManager (inherited from DtsContainer)

This method is called by the runtime engine when a task or container is created, and passes it a `BreakpointManager` manager to allow the task to create, remove, and check the status of breakpoints. This method is called by the runtime and is not used in code.

`DTSRuntimeWrap.DTSSignatureStatus` CheckSignature

Returns a `DTSSignatureStatus` enumeration that shows if the package has been flagged to have a digital signature. If so, the enumeration indicates the signature validity:

```
DTSSS_GOOD

DTSSS_INVALID

DTSSS_NOTPRESENT

DTSSS_UNTRUSTED
```

Void Dispose (Inherited from DtsContainer)

Performs application-defined tasks associated with freeing, releasing, or resetting unmanaged resources.

`System.Bool` Equals (Inherited from DtsObject)

Overloaded. Determines whether two object instances are equal.

ManagedDTS.DTSExecResult Execute

Overloaded. Returns a `DTSExecResult` enumeration that contains information about the success or failure of the package execution.

`Cancelled`

The task was cancelled.

`Completion`

The task ran to completion.

`Failure`

The task failed.

`Success`

The task ran successfully.

Void ExportConfigurationFile

Creates an XML file that contains all deployable variables in the package.

DTSRuntimeWrap.IDTSEnumReferencedObjects90 FindReferencedObjects

Returns a reference object enumeration.

DTSRuntimeWrap.IDTSBreakpointTargets90 GetBreakpointTargets

Returns a `BreakpointTargets` collection. Depending on the setting of the `onlyEnabled` parameter, the collection contains all breakpoint targets in the package, or only enabled breakpoint targets.

System.String GetExpression

Returns a string that contains the expression for the specified property. Null means no expression is assigned.

System.Int32 GetHashCode (Inherited from DtsObject)

Returns the hash code for this instance.

System.Object GetObjectFromPackagePath

Returns a package property and the object from the specified package path.

System.String GetPackagePath

Returns a string that contains the relative path to the package location.

Void ImportConfigurationFile

Loads a configuration file associated with the package.

Void LoadFromXML

Overloaded. Loads a package and all its objects that have been saved in memory in XML format. Use the `Application` class to load packages that have been saved to the filesystem.

Void LoadUserCertificateByHash

Loads the certificate for the package according to the certificate hash.

Void LoadUserCertificateByName

Loads the certificate for the package according to the certificate name.

System.Bool op_Equality (Inherited from DtsObject)

Determines whether the two specified objects have the same value.

System.Bool op_Inequality (Inherited from DtsObject)

Determines whether the two specified objects do not have the same value.

Void ProcessConfiguration

Allows you to set configuration information for a package and its objects.

Void RegenerateID

Creates a new GUID for the package and updates the package ID property.

Void ResumeExecution (Inherited from DtsContainer)

Resumes execution of the task after pausing. The task or container is resumed by the runtime engine.

Void SaveToXML

Overloaded. Saves the package in an XML format.

Void SetExpression

Assigns the specified expression to the property. Specify `null` to remove an existing expression from the property.

Void SuspendExecution (Inherited from DtsContainer)

Called when the executable needs to suspend. This method is called by the runtime engine.

`System.String` ToString

`ManagedDTS.DTSExecResult` Validate

Overloaded. Returns a `DTSExecResult` enumeration that contains information about the success or failure of the package validation:

`Cancelled`

The task was cancelled.

`Completion`

The task ran to completion.

`Failure`

The task failed.

`Success`

The task ran successfully.

APPENDIX C

The Control Flow Object

This appendix is a reference guide to the properties exposed in the individual Control Flow tasks at object level, starting with properties common to all tasks. It lists all properties exposed at object level—not only those accessible through the Properties window in Visual Studio. Many of the properties are used to support the SSIS infrastructure and, in reality, you will probably never touch them.

C#-like syntax is used to describe each property, with the data type of the property first, followed by the name, followed by the default value if one exists. Be aware, however, that not all of these properties and methods are exposed through the IDE.

Control Flow Common Properties

The properties listed and described in this section are common to all Control Flow tasks and are included here to avoid repetition.

`System.Bool` Disable

Read/write property for whether this executable is disabled at runtime.

`System.Bool` DelayValidation

Read/write property indicating whether validation of the task is delayed by performing validation at runtime.

`System.String` Description

Read/write property for the description of this Control Flow object.

`System.Bool` DisableEventHandlers

Read/write property for whether event handlers for a Control Flow item are disabled.

`System.String` ExecValueVariable

Read/write property specifying the name of the custom variable that should be used to store the output from the task execution. Effectively a return status.

Expressions

This is a special case of expression usage. The value of individual properties, as defined by the evaluation of an expression, can be specified by this property.

`System.Bool` FailPackageOnFailure

Read/write property specifying whether to fail the entire package if this Control Flow item fails.

`System.Bool` FailParentOnFailure

Read/write property that signifies whether to fail the parent container of the Control Flow item if processing fails.

`System.Object` ForcedExecutionValue

Read/write property that signifies the desired return value of the package. 0 is the default value of this property.

ForcedExecutionValueType

Read/write property that is an enumeration of the possible data types for the `ForcedExecutionValue`.

`DTSRuntimeWrap.DTSForcedExecResult` ForceExecutionResult

Read/write property that enables the ability to force the result value of the package after processing. Possible values are

`None`

`Success`

`Failure`

`Completion`

`System.Bool` ForceExecutionValue

Read/write property that relates to whether the container execution value should be forced to return the value held in `ForcedExecutionValue`.

`System.String` ID

Read-only property that returns a representation of the object's Globally Unique Identifier (GUID).

`System.Int32` IsolationLevel

Read/write property for specifying or retrieving the transaction isolation level. The enumeration is `System.Transactions.IsolationLevel`. Possible values are

`Unspecified`

A different isolation level than the one specified is being used, but the level cannot be determined. An exception is thrown if this value is set.

`Chaos`

Changes from more highly isolated transactions will not be overwritten.

`ReadCommitted`

Volatile data cannot be read but can be modified.

`ReadUncommitted`

Volatile data can be read and modified.

`RepeatableRead`

Volatile data can be read but not modified. New data can be added.

`Serializable`

Volatile data can be read but not modified, and no new data can be added during the transaction.

`Snapshot`

Volatile data can be read. Before a transaction modifies data, it verifies if another transaction has changed the data after it was initially read. If the data has been updated, an error is raised. This allows a transaction to get to the previously committed value of the data.

`System.Int32` LocaleID

Read/write property indicating the locale to use.

`DTSRuntimeWrap.DTSLoggingMode` LoggingMode

Read/write property indicating the logging mode of the package. The enumeration is

`Disabled`

`Enabled`

`UseParentSetting`

`System.Int32` MaximumErrorCount

Read/write property for the maximum number of allowable errors in a package before processing is halted.

`System.String` Name

Read/write property pertaining to the given name of the item.

`Dts.Runtime.DTSTransactionOption` TransactionOption

Read/write property supported by the `DTSTransactionOption` enumeration detailing the transactional participation level of the package. Remember that transactions can propagate down the package hierarchy and are accessible to any subcontainer or executable that is set to support them:

`NotSupported`

Starts transaction: No

Participates in transactions: No

`Required`

Starts Transaction: Yes, if no transaction exists.

Participates in transactions: Yes, if a transaction already exists.

`Supported` (Default setting)

Starts transaction: No

Participates in transactions: Yes, if a transaction already exists.

Control Flow Task Properties

This section looks at the custom properties exposed by each of the different stock Control Flow tasks.

Analysis Services Processing Task

Connection

Read/write property setting the name of the SSAS connection manager to use.

Object List

Read/write property collection of the SSAS objects to process. Can be a single object or many objects in a batch.

Processing Order

A property specifying parallel or sequential processing:

`Parallel`

- `Maximum parallel tasks`
- `Let the server decide`
- `1, 2, 4, 8, 16, 32, 64,` or `128`

`Sequential`

- `Transaction mode`
- `One transaction`
- `Separate Transactions`

`Writeback Table Option`

- `Create`
- `Create Always`
- `Use existing`

Process Affected Objects

Read/write property specifying whether to process related/affected objects.

Key error action

`Convert to unknown`

`Discard record`

Stop on error

`Number of errors`

`On error action`

- `Stop Processing`
- `Stop Logging`

Key not found

`Ignore error`

`Report and Continue`

`Report and Stop`

Duplicate key

`Ignore error`

`Report and Continue`

`Report and Stop`

Null key converted to unknown

`Ignore error`

`Report and Continue`

`Report and Stop`

Null key not allowed

`Ignore error`

`Report and Continue`

`Report and Stop`

Error log path

The location to store the error log.

Bulk Insert Task

Long BatchSize

Read/write property for the batch size of the insert task. This `long` integer specifies the row count of each batch. Setting this value to `0` means all of the data is loaded as a single batch.

`bool` CheckConstraints

Read/write property indicating whether to enforce table and column check constraints.

`string` CodePage

Read/write property for the code page of the data stored in the source data file.

`DTSBulkInsert_DataFileType` DataFileType

Read/write property indicating the data type to use during the load operation. Potential values are

`DTSBulkInsert_DataFileType_Char`

`DTSBulkInsert_DataFileType_Native`

Native (database) data types. Create the native data file by bulk copying data from SQL Server using the `bcp` utility.

`DTSBulkInsert_DataFileType_WideChar`

For use with Unicode characters.

`DTSBulkInsert_DataFileType_WideNative`

Native (database) data types—except in `char`, `varchar`, and text columns—that store data as Unicode. Create the `widenative` data file by bulk copying data from SQL Server using the `bcp` utility.

The `widenative` type offers better performance than `widechar`. If the data file contains ANSI extended characters, specify `widenative`.

`string` DestinationConnection

Read/write property supplying the name of the destination connection object.

`string` DestinationTableName

Read/write property supplying the name of the destination table name.

`string` FieldTerminator

Read/write property specifying the field terminator in `char` and `widechar` data types.

`bool` FireTriggers

Read/write property indicating whether insert triggers should fire during `Bulk Insert`.

Long FirstRow

Read/write property specifying the first row in the input file from which copying should start.

`string` FormatFile

Read/write property supplying the name and location of a format file.

`bool` KeepIdentity

Read/write property indicating whether identity values should be used within the `Bulk Insert` operation.

`bool` KeepNulls

Read/write property indicating whether empty values should use a `Null` value or if default values should be used instead as part of the `Bulk Insert`.

Long LastRow

Read/write property specifying the number of the last row to copy.

Long MaximumErrors

Read/write property that specifies the maximum number of errors allowed before the operation fails.

`string` RowTerminator

Read/write property specifying the row terminator in `char` and `widechar` datafiles.

`string` SortedData

Read/write property supplying the `ORDER BY` clause for the data.

`string` SourceConnection

Read/write property supplying the name of the source connection.

`bool` TableLock

Read/write property to specify whether the destination table should be locked during the operation.

`bool` UseFormatFile

Read/write property to indicate whether the format file specified in `FormatFile` should be used.

Data Mining Query Task

`string` InputConnection

Read/write property identifying an SSAS project or database.

`List` InputParameters

Read/write property specifying a collection of variables for use with a parameterized DMX query.

`string` ModelName

Read/write property identifying the mining model upon which this query is based.

`string` ModelStructureName

Read/write property identifying the mining structure upon which this query is based.

`string` OutputConnection

Read/write property identifying an OLE DB connection string for where the operation result will go.

`string` OutputTableName

Read/write property for the name of the table that will hold the query results.

`bool` OverwriteOutputTable

Read/write property specifying whether the output of the query should overwrite existing results.

`string` QueryString

Read/write property containing the transformation used to create the query.

`List` ResultParameters

Read/write property containing a collection of variables used to store DMX query results.

Execute Package Task

`bool` ExecuteOutOfProcess

Read/write property to specify whether the child package executes in a new process of its own or within the parent process.

Execute Process Task

`string` Arguments

Read/write property containing space-separated arguments that are passed to the executable as command-line arguments.

`string` Executable

Read/write property specifying the filename of the executable file to run.

`bool` FailTaskIfReturnCodeIsNotSuccess

Read/write property indicating whether the task should fail if the return code differs from the value in `SuccessValue`.

`bool` RequireFullFileName

Read/write property indicating whether the full name of the executable is required.

`string` StandardErrorVariable

Read/write property specifying the name of the variable used to store the executable error output.

`string` StandardInputVariable

Read/write property specifying the name of the variable used as an input to the executable.

`string` StandardOutputVariable

Read/write property specifying the name of the variable used to store output from the executable.

`Int` SuccessValue

Read/write property specifying the value that should be returned from the process upon successful completion.

`bool` TerminateProcessAfterTimeOut

Read/write property indicating whether the process should be terminated after the time held in the `Timeout` property.

`Long` TimeOut

Read/write property specifying the length of time in Seconds a Process can run before being considered timed out.

`ProcessWindowStyle` WindowStyle

Read/write property specifying the window style for the executable process.

`string` WorkingDirectory

Read/write property supplying the working directory for the process.

Execute SQL Task

`bool` BypassPrepare

Read/write property indicating whether the task should skip SQL statement preparation.

`string` Connection

Read/write property specifying the name of the connection manager.

`bool` IsStoredProcedure

Read/write property indicating whether the SQL statement specified refers to a stored procedure.

`ResultSetType` ResultSetType

Read/write property indicating the type of result set returned by the task:

`ResultSetType_None`

The SQL statement does not return a result set.

`ResultSetType_Rowset`

The result set has multiple rows.

`ResultSetType_SingleRow`

The result set is a single row.

`ResultSetType_XML`

The result set is an XML result set.

`string` SqlStatementSource

Read/write property specifying the name of the source containing the SQL statement.

`SqlStatementSourceType` SqlStatementSourceType

Read/write property indicating the type of SQL statement source from the `SqlStatementSource` property:

`DirectInput`

The SQL statement is stored directly in the `SqlStatementSource`.

`FileConnection`

The SQL statement is stored in a file. The `SqlStatementSource` property identifies the name of a `File` connection manager.

`Variable`

The SQL statement is stored in a variable, named in the `SqlStatementSource` property.

`UInt` TimeOut

Read/write property setting the maximum number of seconds before `TimeOut` occurs.

File System Task

`DTSFileSystemAttributes` Attributes

Read/write property specifying the attributes to apply to destination file/directory:

`Archive`

`Hidden`

`Normal`

`ReadOnly`

`System`

string Destination

Read/write property identifying the destination file or folder.

bool IsDestinationPathVariable

Read/write property specifying whether the `Destination` property refers to a variable.

bool IsSourcePathVariable

Read/write property specifying whether the `Source` property refers to a variable.

DTSFileSystemOperation Operation

```
CopyDirectory
CopyFile
CreateDirectory
DeleteDirectory
DeleteDirectoryContent
DeleteFile
MoveDirectory
MoveFile
RenameFile
SetAttributes
```

string OperationName

Read/write property specifying the name of the operation.

bool OverwriteDestinationFile

Read/write property specifying whether to overwrite the destination file or folder.

string Source

Read/write property identifying the source file or folder.

FTP Task

string Connection

Read/write property specifying the name of the connection manager.

bool IsLocalPathVariable

Read/write property specifying whether the `LocalPath` property refers to a variable.

bool IsRemotePathVariable

Read/write property specifying whether the `RemotePath` property refers to a variable.

bool IsTransferTypeASCII

Read/write property specifying whether the transfer type is ASCII.

string LocalPath

Read/write property identifying the local file or folder.

DTSFTPOp Operation

```
DeleteLocal
DeleteRemote
MakeDirLocal
MakeDirRemote
Receive
RemoveDirLocal
RemoveDirRemote
Send
```

string OperationName

Read/write property specifying the name of the operation.

bool OverwriteDestination

Read/write property specifying whether to overwrite the destination file or folder.

string RemotePath

Read/write property identifying the remote file or folder.

bool StopOnOperationFailure

Read/write property specifying whether the task should stop on failure.

Message Queue Task

`string` CurrentExecutingPackageID

Read/write property specifying the executing package ID.

`bool` DataFileOverWritable

Read/write property specifying whether the data-file message can overwrite an existing file.

`string` DTSMessageLineageID

Read/write property specifying the message lineage ID.

`string` DTSMessagePackageID

Read/write property specifying the message package ID.

`string` DTSMessageVersionID

Read/write property specifying the message version ID.

`bool` ErrorIfMessageTimeOut

Read/write property specifying whether the task should fail on timeout.

`string` MessageDataFile

Read/write property specifying the data file name when the `MessageType` property is `DataFile`.

`string` MessageString

Read/write property specifying the message content.

`MQMessageType` MessageType

Read/write property specifying the message type.

`string` MessageVariables

Read/write property listing the variables used when the `MessageType` property is `Variables`.

`string` MsmqConnection

Read/write property identifying the connection for the MSQQ server.

`string` OperationDescription

Read/write property supplying the operation description.

Long ReceiveMessageTimeOut

Read/write property specifying the number of seconds before a message times out.

MQMessageType ReceiveMessageType

Read/write property specifying the receive message type.

string ReceiveVariableMessage

Read/write property identifying the variable to use to store the received message.

bool RemoveFromQueue

Read/write property specifying whether a message should be removed from the message queue.

string SaveDataFileName

Read/write property specifying the filename to which data should be saved.

MQStringMessageCompare StringCompareType

Read/write property specifying the comparison method for a string message when the `MQMessageType` is `Receiver`.

string StringCompareValue

Read/write property supplying a value to that a received message should be compared when the `MQMessageType` is `Receiver`.

string StringMessageToVariableName

Read/write property specifying the name of the variable to which the message contents are saved.

MQType TaskType

Read/write property identifying whether the message is being sent or received.

bool Use2000Format

Read/write property specifying whether to use SQL Server 2000 message format.

bool UseEncryption

Read/write property identifying whether the message uses encryption.

Script Task

string EntryPoint

Read/write property identifying the class name of the entry point in the code.

bool PreCompile

Read/write property specifying whether to compile the script on saving the package.

IDTSVariables90 ReadOnlyVariables

Read/write property for the `ReadOnlyVariables` collection.

string ReadWriteVariables

Read/write property specifying a list of read/write variables, separated by commas.

string ScriptLanguage

Read/write property specifying the language the script is written in. Currently only VB.NET is supported.

Send Mail Task

string BCCLine

Read/write property specifying a semicolon-delimited list of BCC recipients.

string CCLine

Read/write property specifying a semicolon delimited list of CC recipients.

string FileAttachments

Read/write property specifying a list of files to be attached to the e-mail. The pipe character is used to delimit the list.

string FromLine

Read/write property supplying the From e-mail address.

string MessageSource

Read/write property specifying the e-mail message body.

SendMailMessageSourceType MessageSourceType

Read/write property specifying the source type of the `MessageSource`:

`DirectInput`

The message source is contained as text in the `MessageSource` property.

`FileConnection`

The message source is contained in the file named in the `MessageSource` property.

`Variable`

The message source is contained in the variable named in the `MessageSource` property.

MailPriority Priority

Read/write property for the message priority.

string SmtpConnection

Read/write property specifying the connection details of the SMTP server.

string Subject

Read/write property specifying the e-mail Subject.

string ToLine

Read/write property supplying a semicolon-separated list of the To e-mail addresses.

Transfer Database Task

TransferAction Action

Read/write property indicating the `TranferAction` type:

`Copy`

Copy the database between the source and destination Servers, leaving the source database intact.

`Move`

Copy the database between the source and destination Servers, removing the source database as per a normal move operation.

string DestinationConnection

Read/write property specifying the SMO connection manager.

string DestinationDatabaseFiles

Read/write property containing the Universal Naming Convention (UNC) location of the destination database files. This property is only used when the `Method` property is `Offline` since SMO is not used.

string DestinationDatabaseName

Read/write property supplying the name of the destination database name.

bool DestinationOverwrite

Read/write property specifying whether to overwrite the destination database if it already exists.

TransferMethod Method

Read/write property identifying whether to use Online or Offline transfer method:

Online

The database transfer is performed without taking the source database offline. SMO is used to transfer the objects. The user running the package must be a member of the sysadmin role.

Offline

The database transfer is performed by taking the source database offline, detaching it from the source server, copying/moving it, then reattaching it on the target server. If the Action property is set to Copy, the source database is also reattached at the end of this process. The user running the package must be a member of the sysadmin role or be the database owner.

bool ReattachSourceDatabase

Read/write property specifying whether to reattach the source database after the transfer operation when the Action property is Copy.

string SourceConnection

Read/write property specifying the name of the source connection.

string SourceDatabaseFiles

Read/write property containing the UNC path of the source database files. This property only used when the Method property is Offline since SMO is not used.

string SourceDatabaseName

Read/write property supplying the name of the source database.

Transfer Error Messages

string DestinationConnection

Read/write property identifying the name of the destination connection.

StringCollection ErrorMessageLanguageList

Read/write property containing the error messages to transfer.

StringCollection ErrorMessageList

Read/write property containing the language IDs to transfer.

`IfObjectExists` IfObjectExists

Read/write property specifying what should happen if an identical error object exists on the destination.

`string` SourceConnection

Read/write property identifying the name of the source connection.

`bool` TransferAllErrorMessages

Read/write property specifying whether to transfer all error messages or only those specified.

Transfer Jobs Task

`string` DestinationConnection

Read/write property identifying the name of the destination connection.

`bool` EnableJobsAtDestination

Read/write property specifying whether transferred jobs should be enabled at the destination.

`IfObjectExists` IfObjectExists

Read/write property specifying what should happen if an identical job exists on the destination:

`FailTask`

If the job already exists on the destination server, fail the task.

`Overwrite`

If the job already exists on the destination server, overwrite it.

`Skip`

If the job already exists on the destination server, skip the copy operation for that job.

`StringCollection` JobsList

Read/write property containing a list of the jobs to transfer.

`string` SourceConnection

Read/write property identifying the name of the source connection.

`bool` TransferAllJobs

Read/write property specifying whether to transfer all jobs or only those specified.

Transfer Logins Task

bool CopySids

Read/write property specifying whether to copy `Login Security Identifiers`. For the login to be recognized at the destination, SIDs must be copied if this task is used in conjunction with the `Transfer Database` task.

StringCollection DatabasesList

Read/write property containing the source databases from which to transfer logins.

string DestinationConnection

Read/write property identifying the name of the destination connection.

IfObjectExists IfObjectExists

Read/write property specifying what should happen if an identical job exists on the destination:

`FailTask`

`Overwrite`

`Skip`

StringCollection LoginsList

Read/write property containing a comma-separated list of logins to transfer.

LoginsToTransfer LoginsToTransfer

Read/write property containing which logins should be transferred:

`AllLogins`

`AllLoginsFromSelectedDatabases`

Transfer only logins in the `LoginsList` property that have access to the databases in the `DatabasesList` property.

`SelectedLogins`

Transfer only logins contained in `DatabasesList` property collection.

string SourceConnection

Read/write property identifying the name of the source connection.

Transfer Master Stored Procedures Task

string DestinationConnection

Read/write property identifying the name of the destination connection.

IfObjectExists IfObjectExists

Read/write property specifying what should happen if an identical job exists on the destination:

```
FailTask
Overwrite
Skip
```

string SourceConnection

Read/write property identifying the name of the source connection.

StringCollection StoredProceduresList

Read/write property containing a comma-delimited list of stored procedures to transfer.

bool TransferAllStoredProcedures

Read/write property specifying whether to transfer all stored procedures or only those specified.

Transfer SQL Server Objects Task

bool CopyAllDefaults = false

bool CopyAllLogins = false

bool CopyAllObjects = false

bool CopyAllPartitionFunctions = false

bool CopyAllPartitionSchemes = false

bool CopyAllRules = false

bool CopyAllSchemas = false

bool CopyAllSqlAssemblies = false

bool CopyAllStoredProcedures = false

bool CopyAllTables = false

bool CopyAllUSerDefinedAggregates = false

bool CopyAllUserDefinedDataTypes = false

bool CopyAllUserDefinedFunctions = false

bool CopyAllUserDefinedTypes = false

bool CopyAllUsers = false

bool CopyAllViews = false

bool CopyAllXmlSchemaCollections = false

bool CopyData = false

bool CopyDatabaseRoles = false

bool CopyDatabaseUsers = false

bool CopyForeignKeys = false

bool CopyFullTextIndexes = false

bool CopyIndexes = false

bool CopyObjectLevelPermissions = false

bool CopyPrimaryKeys = false

bool CopySchema = false

bool CopySqlServerLogins = false

bool CopyTriggers = false

StringCollection DefaultsList

Read/write property collection of `Defaults` to transfer if the `CopyAllDefaults` property is `false`.

string DestinationConnection

Read/write property specifying the name of the destination SMO connection manager.

string DestinationDatabase

Read/write property specifying the name of the destination database to use in the operation.

bool DestinationTranslateChar

Read/write property specifying the value of the `AutoTranslate` property in the destination connection string.

bool DropObjectsFirst

Read/write property indicating whether to drop destination objects if they exist during the transfer operation.

ExistingData ExistingData

Read/write property specifying whether data being transferred should append to or replace existing data:

```
Append
Replace
```

bool GenerateScriptsInUnicode

Read/write property indicating whether object-generation scripts should be generated using Unicode.

bool IncludeDependentObjects

Read/write property indicating whether dependent objects relating to selected source objects should be transferred as part of the operation.

bool IncludeExtendedProperties

Read/write property indicating whether to transfer the `Extended Properties` of source objects as part of the operation.

StringCollection LoginsList

Read/write property collection of `Logins` to transfer if the `CopyAllLogins` property is `false`.

StringCollection PartitionFunctionsList

Read/write property collection of `PartitionFunctions` to transfer if the `CopyAllPartitionFunctions` property is `false`.

StringCollection PartitionSchemesList

Read/write property collection of `PartitionSchemes` to transfer if the `CopyAllPartitionSchemes` property is `false`.

StringCollection RulesList

Read/write property collection of `Rules` to transfer if the `CopyAllRules` property is `false`.

StringCollection SchemasList

Read/write property collection of Schemas to transfer if the `CopyAllSchemas` property is `false`.

string SourceConnection

Read/write property specifying the name of the source SMO connection manager.

string SourceDatabase

Read/write property supplying the name of the source database to use in the operation.

bool SourceTranslateChar

Read/write property specifying the source `AutoTranslate` property in the connection string.

StringCollection SqlAssembliesList

Read/write property collection of CLR `SqlAssemblies` to transfer if the `CopyAllSqlAssemblies` property is `false`.

StringCollection StoredProceduresList

Read/write property collection of `Stored Procedures` to transfer if the `CopyAllStoredProcedures` property is `false`.

StringCollection TablesList

Read/write property collection of `Tables` to transfer if the `CopyAllTables` property is `false`.

bool UseCollation

Read/write property indicating whether `Collation` should be used.

StringCollection UserDefinedAggregatesList

Read/write property collection of `UserDefinedAggregates` to transfer if the `CopyAllUserDefinedAggregates` property is `false`.

StringCollection UserDefinedDataTypesList

Read/write property collection of `UserDefinedDataTypes` to transfer if the `CopyAllUserDefinedDataTypes` property is `false`.

StringCollection UserDefinedFunctionsList

Read/write property collection of `UserDefinedFunctions` to transfer if the `CopyAllUserDefinedFunctions` property is false.

StringCollection UserDefinedTypesList

Read/write property collection of `UserDefinedTypes` to transfer if the `CopyAllUserDefinedTypes` property is `false`.

StringCollection UsersList

Read/write property collection of `Users` to transfer if the `CopyAllUsers` property is false.

StringCollection ViewsList

Read/write property collection of `Views` to transfer if the `CopyAllViews` property is `false`.

StringCollection XmlSchemaCollectionsList

Read/write property collection of `XmlSchemaCollections` to transfer if the `CopyAllXmlSchemaCollections` property is `false`.

Web Service Task

string Connection

Read/write property specifying the name of the HTTP connection.

string OutputLocation

Read/write property specifying the location to output the results from the `WebMethod` call. This could be a variable name or a folder and filename.

DTSOutputType OutputType

Read/write property specifying the output type:

`File`

`Variable`

`bool` OverwriteWsdlFile

Read/write property indicating whether the stored WSDL file should be overwritten.

`string` ServiceName

Read/write property specifying the name of the web service.

`string` WsdlFile

Read/write property specifying the name and location of the WSDL file.

WMI Data Reader Task

`string` Destination

Read/write property specifying the name of the destination for this operation.

`DestinationType` DestinationType

Read/write property specifying the type of destination for the operation:

`FileConnection`

`Variable`

`Object` Output

Read/write property specifying the object used to hold the results of the operation.

`OutputType` OutputType

Read/write property specifying the type of output required:

`DataTable`

`PropertyNameAndValue`

Return a string containing name/value of the property specified in the `Output` property.

`PropertyValue`

Return a string containing value of the property specified in the `Output` property.

`OverwriteDestination` OverwriteDestination

Read/write property specifying what to do should there be existing data at the destination:

`AppendToDestination`

`KeepOriginal`

`OverwriteDestination`

`string` WmiConnection

Read/write property specifying the name of the `WMIConn`.

`string` WqlQuerySource

Read/write property specifying the source of the WQL query.

`QuerySourceType` WqlQuerySourceType

Read/write property specifying the WQL query source type to use.

WMI Event Watcher Task

`ActionAtEvent` ActionAtEvent

Read/write property specifying how the task should behave when it receives a WMI event:

`LogTheEvent`

`LogTheEventAndFireDTSEvent`

`ActionAtTimeout` ActionAtTimeout

Read/write property specifying how the task should behave when the `Timeout` threshold is reached without receiving a WMI event:

`LogTheEvent`

`LogTheEventAndFireDTSEvent`

`AfterEvent` AfterEvent

Read/write property specifying how the task should behave when the specified event is received:

`ReturnWithFailure`

`ReturnWithSuccess`

`WatchForTheEventAgain`

`AfterTimeout` AfterTimeout

Read/write property specifying how the task should behave after the `Timeout` threshold is reached:

`ReturnWithFailure`

`ReturnWithSuccess`

`WatchForTheEventAgain`

`Int` NumberOfEvents

Read/write property specifying how many WMI events the task should watch for.

`Int` Timeout

Read/write property specifying how many seconds the task should wait before timing out.

`string` WmiConnection

Read/write property specifying the name of the `WMIConn` to use.

`string` WqlQuerySource

Read/write property specifying the source of the WQL query to execute.

`QuerySourceType` WqlQuerySourceType

Read/write property specifying the type of source to be used as held by the `WqlQuerySource` property:

`DirectInput`

`FileConnection`

`Variable`

XML Task

`string` Destination

Read/write property specifying the connection or variable name to which the task saves results.

`DTSXMLSaveResultTo` DestinationType

Read/write property specifying the destination type.

`DTSXMLDiffAlgorithm` DiffAlgorithm

Read/write property specifying the comparison algorithm to use when the `OperationType` property is `Diff`:

`Auto`

The algorithm to use for the comparison operation is chosen automatically by the component. This choice is based upon the size and estimated number of changes anticipated.

`Fast`

The comparison is performed on a node-by-node basis. Although this method might be fast, it can be less accurate because, for example, in situations where a move operation has been performed, an add and remove operation might be detected.

`Precise`

Use the Zhang-Shasha algorithm to perform the comparison. This algorithm is used to find the editing distance between trees and is very accurate—though XML documents with many changes will take much longer to analyze.

`string` DiffGramDestination

Read/write property specifying the connection or variable name to that the diffgram document is saved.

`DTSXMLSaveResultsTo` DiffGramDestinationType

Read/write property specifying the `DiffGramDestination` type.

`DTSXMLDiffOptions` DiffOptions

Read/write property specifying comparison options used by the operation while comparing documents when the `OperationType` property is `Diff`:

`IgnoreChildOrder`

The order of child nodes of each element is ignored.

`IgnoreComments`

Comment nodes are not compared.

`IgnoreDtd`

The document type declaration (DTD) is not compared.

`IgnoreNamespaces`

The namespace Uniform Resource Identifiers (URIs) of the element and attribute names are not compared. Name prefixes are also ignored.

`IgnorePI`

The namespace URIs of the element and attribute names are not compared. Name prefixes are also ignored.

`IgnorePrefixes`

The prefixes of element and attribute names are not compared.

`IgnoreWhitespace`

Significant white spaces are not compared and all text nodes are normalized by discarding leading and trailing white space characters. Sequences of white space characters are replaced with a single space.

`IgnoreXmlDecl`

The XML declaration is not compared.

`None`

None of the enumeration options is used.

`bool` FailOnDifference

Read/write property specifying whether the task fails if validation fails.

`bool` FailOnValidationFail

Read/write property specifying whether the operation fails if validation fails.

`ArrayList` NodeList

Read-only property collection containing the results of the XPath operation.

`DTSXMLOperation` OperationType

Read/write property specifying the type of operation to perform:

`Diff`

Compares two XML documents. By using the source XML document as a base document, the `Diff` operation compares it to another XML document, detects the differences, and then writes the differences to an XML diffgram document. This operation includes properties for customizing the comparison.

`Merge`

Merges two XML documents. By using the source XML document as a base document, it merges a second document into the base document. The operation can specify a merge location in the document.

`Patch`

Applies the output from the Diff operation (a diffgram document) to an XML document to create a new parent document that can include content from the diffgram document.

`Validate`

Validates the XML document against a DTD or XML Schema definition (XSD).

`XPATH`

Performs XPath queries and evaluations.

`XSLT`

Performs XSL transformations on XML documents.

`bool` OverwriteDestination

Read/write property specifying whether to overwrite existing destination files.

`bool` PutResultInOneNode

Read/write property indicating whether the results of the operation should be placed in a single node.

`bool` SaveDiffGram

Read/write property indicating whether diffgram comparison results should be saved.

`bool` SaveOperationResult

Read/write property indicating whether to save `Diff` output.

`string` SecondOperand

Read/write property that, with operations of the type that uses two operands, specifies either the connection name, variable name, or text value.

`DTSXMLSourceType` SecondOperandType

Read/write property specifying the type contained in the `SecondOperand` property:

`DirectInput`

`FileConnection`

`Variable`

`string` Source

Read/write property specifying the connection name, variable, or text to use in the operation.

`DTSXMLSourceType` SourceType

Read/write property specifying the type contained in the `Source` property:

`DirectInput`

`FileConnection`

`Variable`

`DTSXMLValidationType` ValidationType

Read/write property specifying the type of validation to use in the task:

`DTD`

`XSD`

DTSXMLXPathOperation XPathOperation

Read/write property specifying the `XPathOperation` type to use in the task:

`Evaluation`

Used when an evaluation is required.

`NodeList`

Used when XML fragment is required.

`Values`

Used when a concatenated inner text value is required.

string XPathStringSource

Read/write property specifying the source of the XPath used.

DTSXMLSourceType XPathStringSourceType

Read/write property specifying the type of the source contained in the `XPathStringSource` property:

`DirectInput`

`FileConnection`

`Variable`

APPENDIX D

Maintenance Plans Reference

Maintenance-plan tasks offer a slight departure from the usual Control Flow tasks that are used on the Control Flow design surface. In code, maintenance tasks have the `DtsTask` attribute specified as you might expect for a Control Flow task, but the `TaskType` parameter is set to `DBMAINT90`. This appendix is a reference to the assemblies, classes, and properties of the maintenance-plan tasks in SSIS.

All maintenance-plan tasks are expressed as individual classes within a single assembly—`Microsoft.SqlServer.MaintenancePlanTasks.dll`. In turn, each of these classes derives from the `DatabaseMaintenanceBaseTask` and implements an interface that represents the additional properties and methods required for each maintenance task.

Maintenance-Plan Tasks Common Properties

The common properties for maintenance tasks are inherited from the `DatabaseMaintenanceBaseTask` and `ExecuteSQLTask` classes. Maintenance tasks must also implement the `IContextSelection` interface and the `ITaskDescriptionInterface` interface.

Properties That Inherit from DatabaseMaintenanceBaseTask

DatabaseSelection DatabaseSelectionType

Read/write property. In tasks where a database selection is required, this property is used to specify a particular grouping of databases or that a specific one should be used (in the `SelectedDatabases` property). Possible values are

```
None
All
System
User
Specific
```

`bool` ExtendedLogging

Read/write property. Indicates that extended logging should be used.

string LocalConnectionForLogging

Read/write property. Indicates that a local connection should be used to connect to the logging destination.

ObjectType ObjectTypeSelection

Read/write property. The type of object to perform an operation on can be indicated using this property—only in tasks that require this level of information. Possible values are

```
Invalid = -1

Table = 0

TableView = 2

View = 1
```

string RunId

Read/write property.The RunId of the particular maintenance plan task.

ArrayList SelectedDatabases

Read/write property. A list of databases selected, where appropriate.

ArrayList SelectedTables

Read/write property. A list of selected tables, where appropriate.

int ServerVersion

Read/write property. Relates to the server version required to use the component.

StringCollection SqlBatchCommands

Protected read-only property. A list of SQL commands to execute, where appropriate.

TableSelection TableSelectionType

Read/write property. Indicates the tables that are selected, where appropriate. If set to `specific`, the `SelectedTables` property holds a list of the tables on which to perform operations:

```
None

All

Specific
```

string TaskConnectionName

Read/write property. Holds the connection name for the task.

string TaskName

Read/write property. Holds the name for the task.

bool TaskNameWasModified

Read/write property. Indicates whether the task name has been modified.

Properties That Inherit from ExecuteSQLTask

As a consequence of the object model, the following common properties are also exposed to any maintenance task inherited from ExecuteSQLTask. Because maintenance tasks are, as I said in Chapter 7, just wrappers to T-SQL statements, it makes sense that the maintenance operation to be performed is generated inside the maintenance-task code as SQL and passed on to ExecuteSQLTask for execution.

bool BypassPrepare

Read/write property. Specifies whether the generated SQL statement should be prepared before execution.

uint CodePage

Read/write property. Specifies the CodePage to use.

string Connection

Read/write property. Specifies the name of the connection to use for the operation.

object ExecutionValue

Read only. This is the execution value returned as a consequence of execution.

bool IsStoredProcedure

Read/write property. Specifies whether the SQL statement is a stored procedure.

IDTSParameterBindings ParameterBindings

Read only. Returns an ITDSParameterBindings object representing the parameter bindings of the class.

IDTSResultBindings ResultSetBindings

Read only. Returns an IDTSResultBindings object representing the result set bindings of the class.

ResultSetType ResultSetType

Read/write property. Specifies the type of result set being returned:

```
ResultSetType_None
ResultSetType_Rowset
ResultSetType_SingleRow
ResultSetType_XML
```

`string` SqlStatementSource

Read/write property. Contains the SQL statement to execute or the name of a variable that contains the SQL statement, depending upon the value in the `SqlStatementSourceType` property.

SqlStatementSourceType SqlStatementSourceType

Read/write property. Indicates the location of the SQL statement to use:

```
DirectInput = 1
FileConnection = 2
Variable = 3
```

`uint` TimeOut

Read/write property. Stores the timeout value for the SQL operation in seconds.

Properties Whose Implementations Are Enforced by the IContextSelection Interface

`bool` TaskAllowesDatabaseSelection [sic]

Read/write property indicating whether the task should allow the selection of specific databases.

`bool` TaskAllowesTableSelection [sic]

Read/write property indicating whether the task should allow the selection of specific tables in the database. The `ITaskDescription` interface enforces the implementation of the `Description` property.

Maintenance-Plan Tasks

Backup Database

BackupActionType BackupAction

Read/write property specifying the type of backup operation to perform:

`Database`

Back up data files.

`Files`

Back up specified files.

`Log`

Back up transaction log.

DeviceType BackupDeviceType

Read/write property specifying the type of backup media/device.

`File`

`LogicalDevice`

`Pipe`

`Tape`

`VirtualDevice`

string BackupFileExtension

Read/write property specifying the file extension of the backup file.

bool BackupIsIncremental

Read/write property indicating whether to make an incremental backup.

DeviceType BackupPhisycalDestinationType [sic]

`File`

`LogicalDevice`

`Pipe`

`Tape`

`VirtualDevice`

`string` Connection

Read/write property specifying the name of the connection to the server upon which the database(s) reside.

`bool` CreateSubFolder

Read/write property specifying whether to create a subfolder for each database specified for the operation.

`DatabaseSelection` DatabaseSelectionType

Read/write property specifying which databases are selected for the operation:

`None`

`All`

`System`

`User`

`Specific`

`string` DestinationAutoFolderPath

Read/write property specifying the base folder for the backup operation.

`DestinationType` DestinationCreationType

Read/write property specifying the `DestinationCreationType`:

`Auto`

`Manual`

`ArrayList` DestinationManualList

Read/write property collection of destination folders for the backup.

`ActionForExistingBackups` ExistingBackupsAction

Read/write property specifying how the task should handle existing backup files:

`Append`

`Overwrite`

`Date` ExpireDate

Read/write property specifying the expiration date of the backup.

string FileGroupsFiles

Read/write property collection specifying the FileGroups to back up when the BackupAction property is Files.

bool InDays

Read/write property indicating whether the backup expires in the number of days held in the RetainDays property (true), or if it expires on the date in the ExpireDate property (false).

Int32 RetainDays

Read/write property specifying how many days the backup set is valid for.

bool UseExpiration

Read/write property specifying which expiration settings should be used.

bool VerifyIntegrity

Read/write property specifying whether to verify the integrity of the backup set.

Check Database Integrity

bool IncludeIndexes

Read/write property specifying whether to include indexes in the integrity check.

Execute SQL Server Agent Job

string AgentJobId

Read/write property specifying the name of the SQL Server Agent job to execute.

History Cleanup Task

Int32 OlderThanTimeUnits

Read/write property specifying the number of time units the task should use to remove records before.

TimeUnitType OlderThanTimeUnitType

Read/write property indicating the time unit for the value held in the OlderThanTimeUnits property:

```
Day
Hour
Month
Week
Year
```

`bool` RemoveBackupRestorHistory [sic]

Read/write property specifying whether to remove backup/restore history.

`bool` RemoveDbMaintHistory

Read/write property specifying whether to remove database-maintenance history.

`bool` RemoveSqlAgentHistory

Read/write property specifying whether to remove SQL Agent history.

Maintenance Cleanup Task

`bool` AgeBased

Read/write property indicating whether the task should operate based upon records before a specified time period.

`bool` CleanSubFolders

Read/write property indicating whether the first-level subfolder should be traversed to.

`bool` DeleteSpecificFile

Read/write property indicating whether a specific file should be deleted.

`string` FileExtension

Read/write property specifying the file extension of the files to delete (d.g., *.sql).

`string` FilePath

Read/write property supplying the path and filename of the specific file to delete—if the `DeleteSpecificFile` property is `true`.

`FileType` FileTypeSpecified

`FileBackup`

Delete backup files.

`FileReport`

Delete reports files.

`string` FolderPath

Read/write property specifying the folder path within which files with the specified `FileExtension` property will be deleted.

int OlderThanTimeUnits

Read/write property specifying which records will be removed that are older than the age (in time units) specified by this property.

TimeUnitType OlderThanTimeUnitType

Read/write property indicating the time unit for the value held in the `OlderThanTimeUnits` property:

```
Day

Hour

Month

Week

Year
```

Notify Operator Task

string Message

Read/write property supplying the message to send to the user.

StringCollection OperatorNotify

Read/write property collection specifying the users to whom notifications should be sent.

string Profile

Read/write property specifying the profile to use.

Rebuild Index Task

bool AdvKeepOnline

Read/write property indicating whether to keep the database online while executing the task.

bool AdvSortInTempdb

Read/write property indicating whether to perform the index sort in TempDb.

int ReindexPercentage

Read/write property specifying the desired reindex percentage.

bool ReindexWithOriginalAmount

Read/write property indicating that the reindexing operation should perform reindexing to the original value.

Reorganize Index Task

`bool` CompactLargeObjects

Read/write property indicating whether to compact large objects.

Shrink Database Task

`int` DatabaseSizeLimit

Read/write property specifying the maximum size the database should grow to before shrinking.

`int` PercentLimit

Read/write property specifying the amount of free space to remain after shrink operation.

`bool` ReturnFreedSpace

Read/write property indicating whether freed space should be returned to the database (`False`) or the operating system (`True`).

Execute T-SQL Task

All properties for this task are derived from parent classes.

Update Statistics Task

`int` UpdateSampleValue

Read/write property specifying the sample value to use in the operation.

`ScanType` UpdateScanType

Read/write property specifying the scan type of the operation to use in conjunction with the `UpdateSampleValue` property:

- `Percent`
- `Rows`
- `Fullscan`
- `Resample`
- `Default`

UpdateType

Read/write property specifying the object statistics to update:

- `Index`
- `Column`
- `All`

APPENDIX E

Data Flow Object Reference

This appendix gives a list of the common properties of the Data Flow object. All components created to work with the Data Flow will have these properties at a minimum.

`string` BLOBTempStoragePath

Read/write property specifying a folder location to use for temporary BLOB storage.

`string` BufferTempStoragePath

Read/write property specifying a folder location to use for temporary buffer storage.

`int` DefaultBufferMaxRows

Read/write property specifying the maximum number of allowed rows in an `IDTSBuffer90` buffer.

`int` DefaultBufferSize

Read/write property specifying the default size used to create an `IDTSBuffer90` buffer.

`bool` DelayValidation

Read/write property identifying whether validation is delayed until execution. This is useful when you work with connections and components that might be unavailable while the package is being designed.

`string` Description

Read/write property containing the Data Flow container description.

`bool` Disable

Read/write property identifying whether the Data Flow container is disabled.

`bool` DisableEventHandlers

Read/write property identifying whether the Data Flow container's event handlers are disabled.

Long EngineThreads

Read/write property specifying the number of threads the Data Flow uses.

`System.String` ExecValueVariable

Read/write property specifying the name of the custom variable that should be used to store the output from the task execution. Effectively a return status.

Expressions

This is a special case of expression usage. The value of individual properties, as defined by the evaluation of an expression, can be specified by this property.

`System.Bool` FailPackageOnFailure

Read/write property specifying whether to fail the entire package if a Data Flow component fails.

`System.Bool` FailParentOnFailure

Read/write property that signifies whether to fail the parent container of the Control Flow item if processing fails.

`System.Object` ForcedExecutionValue

Read/write property that signifies the desired return value of the Package. `0` is the default value of this property.

ForcedExecutionValueType

Read/write property that is an enumeration of the possible data types for `ForcedExecutionValue`.

`DTSRuntimeWrap.DTSForcedExecResult` ForceExecutionResult

Read/write property that enables the ability to force the result value of the package after processing. Possible values are

```
None

Success

Failure
```

CompletionSystem.Bool

ForceExecutionValue

Read/write property that relates to whether the container execution value should be forced to return the value held in `ForcedExecutionValue`.

GUID ID

Read-only property specifying the unique ID of the Data Flow task.

`System.Int32` IsolationLevel

Read/write property for specifying or retrieving the transaction isolation level. The enumeration is `System.Transactions.IsolationLevel`. Possible values are

`Unspecified`

A different isolation level than the one specified is being used, but the level cannot be determined. An exception is thrown if this value is set.

`Chaos`

Changes from more highly isolated transactions will not be overwritten.

`ReadCommitted`

Volatile data cannot be read but can be modified.

`ReadUncommitted`

Volatile data can be read and modified.

`RepeatableRead`

Volatile data can be read but not modified. New data can be added.

`Serializable`

Volatile data can be read but not modified, and no new data can be added during the transaction.

`Snapshot`

Volatile data can be read. Before a transaction modifies data, it verifies if another transaction has changed the data after it was initially read. If the data has been updated, an error is raised. This allows a transaction to get to the previously committed value of the data.

`System.Int32` LocaleID

Read/write property indicating the `LocaleID` to use.

`DTSRuntimeWrap.DTSLoggingMode` LoggingMode

Read/write property indicating the logging mode of the package. The enumeration is

`Disabled`

`Enabled`

`UseParentSetting`

`System.Int32` MaximumErrorCount

Read/write property for the maximum number of allowable errors in a package before processing is halted.

`System.String` Name

Read/write property pertaining to the given name of the item.

`bool` RunInOptimizedMode

Read/write property specifying whether the task should run in *optimized mode*. Essentially, optimized mode cleans up the Data Flow by removing unused items such as columns and components in the execution plan. It's like a fail-safe option for overlooked issues that, although they don't cause errors, do cause performance degradation.

`Dts.Runtime.DTSTransactionOption` TransactionOption

Read/write property supported by the `DTSTransactionOption` enumeration detailing the transactional participation level of the Data Flow:

`NotSupported`

Starts transaction: No

Participates in transactions: No

`Required`

Starts transaction: Yes, if no transaction exists.

Participates in transactions: Yes, if a transaction already exists.

`Supported` (Default setting)

Starts transaction: No

Participates in transactions: Yes, if a transaction already exists.

Index

D

E

F

W

X